McGraw-Hill Reading

 Education

Bothell, WA • Chicago, IL • Columbus, OH • New York, NY

 TextEvaluator™

ETS and the ETS logo are registered trademarks of Educational Testing Service (ETS).
TextEvaluator is a trademark of Educational Testing Service.

Cover and Title Pages: Nathan Love

www.mheonline.com/readingwonders

C

The McGraw·Hill Companies

Mc Graw Hill **Education**

Send all inquiries to:
McGraw-Hill Education
Two Penn Plaza
New York, New York 10121

Printed in China

7 8 9 DSS 17 16 15 14

CCSS Reading/Language Arts Program

Program Authors

Dr. Diane August
Managing Director,
American Institutes for Research
Washington, D.C.

Dr. Donald Bear
Iowa State University
Ames, Iowa

Dr. Janice A. Dole
University of Utah
Salt Lake City, Utah

Dr. Jana Echevarria
California State University, Long Beach
Long Beach, California

Dr. Douglas Fisher
San Diego State University
San Diego, California

Dr. David J. Francis
University of Houston
Houston, Texas

Dr. Vicki Gibson
Educational Consultant
Gibson Hasbrouck and Associates
Wellesley, Massachusetts

Dr. Jan Hasbrouck
Educational Consultant
and Researcher
J.H. Consulting
Vancouver, Washington
Gibson Hasbrouck and Associates
Wellesley, Massachusetts

Margaret Kilgo
Educational Consultant
Kilgo Consulting, Inc.
Austin, Texas

Dr. Jay McTighe
Educational Consultant
Jay McTighe and Associates
Columbia, Maryland

Dr. Scott G. Paris
Vice President, Research
Educational Testing Service
Princeton, New Jersey

Dr. Timothy Shanahan
University of Illinois at Chicago
Chicago, Illinois

Dr. Josefina V. Tinajero
University of Texas at El Paso
El Paso, Texas

Education

Bothell, WA • Chicago, IL • Columbus, OH • New York, NY

PROGRAM AUTHORS

Dr. Diane August

American Institutes for Research, Washington, D.C.

Managing Director focused on literacy and science for ELLs for the Education, Human Development and the Workforce Division

Dr. Donald R. Bear

Iowa State University

Professor, Iowa State University

Author of *Words Their Way, Words Their Way with English Learners, Vocabulary Their Way,* and *Words Their Way with Struggling Readers, 4–12*

Dr. Janice A. Dole

University of Utah

Professor, University of Utah

Director, Utah Center for Reading and Literacy

Content Facilitator, National Assessment of Educational Progress (NAEP)

CCSS Consultant to Literacy Coaches, Salt Lake City School District, Utah

Dr. Jana Echevarria

California State University, Long Beach

Professor Emerita of Education, California State University

Author of *Making Content Comprehensible for English Learners: The SIOP Model*

Dr. Douglas Fisher

San Diego State University

Co-Director, Center for the Advancement of Reading, California State University

Author of *Language Arts Workshop: Purposeful Reading and Writing Instruction* and *Reading for Information in Elementary School*

Dr. David J. Francis

University of Houston

Director of the Center for Research on Educational Achievement and Teaching of English Language Learners (CREATE)

Dr. Vicki Gibson

Educational Consultant
Gibson Hasbrouck and Associates

Author of *Differentiated Instruction: Grouping for Success, Differentiated Instruction: Guidelines for Implementation,* and *Managing Behaviors to Support Differentiated Instruction*

Dr. Jan Hasbrouck

J.H. Consulting
Gibson Hasbrouck and Associates

Developed Oral Reading Fluency Norms for Grades 1–8

Author of *The Reading Coach: A How-to Manual for Success* and *Educators as Physicians: Using RTI Assessments for Effective Decision-Making*

Margaret Kilgo

Educational Consultant
Kilgo Consulting, Inc., Austin, TX

Developed Data-Driven Decisions process for evaluating student performance by standard

Member of Common Core State Standards Anchor Standards Committee for Reading and Writing

Dr. Scott G. Paris

Educational Testing Service,
Vice President, Research

Professor, Nanyang Technological
University, Singapore, 2008–2011

Professor of Education and Psychology,
University of Michigan, 1978–2008

Dr. Timothy Shanahan

University of Illinois at Chicago

Distinguished Professor, Urban Education

Director, UIC Center for Literacy

Chair, Department of Curriculum &
Instruction

Member, English Language Arts Work
Team and Writer of the Common Core
State Standards

President, International Reading
Association, 2006

Dr. Josefina V. Tinajero

University of Texas at El Paso

Dean of College of Education

President of TABE

Board of Directors for the American
Association of Colleges for Teacher
Education (AACTE)

Governing Board of the National Network
for Educational Renewal (NNER)

Consulting Authors

Kathy R. Bumgardner

National Literacy Consultant

Strategies Unlimited, Inc.
Gastonia, NC

Jay McTighe

Jay McTighe and Associates

Author of *The Understanding by Design
Guide to Creating High Quality Units* with
G. Wiggins; *Schooling by Design: Mission,
Action, Achievement* with G. Wiggins;
and *Differentiated Instruction and
Understanding By Design* with C. Tomlinson

Dr. Doris Walker-Dalhouse

Marquette University

Associate Professor, Department
of Educational Policy & Leadership

Author of articles on multicultural
literature, struggling readers, and
reading instruction in urban schools

Dinah Zike

Educational Consultant

Dinah-Might Activities, Inc.
San Antonio, TX

Program Reviewers

Kelly Aeppli-Campbell
Escambia County School District
Pensacola, FL

Marjorie J. Archer
Broward County Public Schools
Davie, FL

Whitney Augustine
Brevard Public Schools
Melbourne, FL

Antonio C. Campbell
Washington County School District
Saint George, UT

Helen Dunne
Gilbert Public School District
Gilbert, AZ

David P. Frydman
Clark County School District
Las Vegas, NV

Fran Gregory
Metropolitan Nashville Public Schools
Nashville, TN

Veronica Allen Hunt
Clark County School District
Las Vegas, NV

Michele Jacobs
Dee-Mack CUSD #701
Mackinaw, IL

LaVita Johnson Spears
Broward County Public Schools
Pembroke Pines, FL

Randall B. Kincaid
Sevier County Schools
Sevierville, TN

Matt Melamed
Community Consolidated School
  District 46
Grayslake, IL

Angela L. Reese,
Bay District Schools
Panama City, FL

Eddie Thompson
Fairfield City School District
Fairfield Township, OH

Patricia Vasseur Sosa
Miami-Dade County Public Schools
Miami, FL

Dr. Elizabeth Watson
Hazelwood School District
Hazelwood, MO

TEACHING WITH

McGraw-Hill Reading
Wonders

INTRODUCE

Weekly Concept
Grade Appropriate
Topics, including Science
and Social Studies

- **Videos**
- **Photographs**
- **Interactive Graphic Organizers**

Reading/Writing Workshop

TEACH

Close Reading
Short Complex Texts

Minilessons
Comprehension
Strategies and Skills
Genre
Vocabulary Strategies
Writing Traits

Grammar Handbook

- **Visual Glossary**
- **Interactive Minilessons**
- **Interactive Graphic Organizers**

Reading/Writing Workshop

APPLY

Close Reading
Anchor Texts
Extended Complex Texts
Application of
Strategies and Skills

- **e Books**
- **Interactive Texts**
- **Listening Library**
- **English/Spanish Summaries**

Literature Anthology

Master the Common Core State Standards!

DIFFERENTIATE

- e Books
- Interactive Texts
- Leveled Reader Search
- Listening Library
- Interactive Activities

Leveled Readers

Leveled Readers
Small Group Instruction
with Differentiated Texts

INTEGRATE

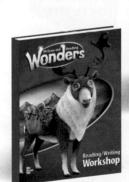

- Online Research
- Writer's Workspace
- Interactive Group Projects

Collection of Texts

Research and Inquiry
Short and Sustained Research Projects

Text Connections
Reading Across Texts

Write About Reading
Analytical Writing

ASSESS

- Online Assessment
- Test Generator
- Reports

**Weekly
Assessment**

**Unit
Assessment**

**Benchmark
Assessment**

Weekly Assessment

Unit Assessment

Benchmark Assessment

TEACHING WITH READING WONDERS **vii**

PROGRAM COMPONENTS

Reading/Writing Workshop

Literature Anthology

Teacher Editions

Leveled Readers

Classroom Library Tradebooks

Your Turn Practice Book

Visual Vocabulary Cards

Leveled Workstation Activity Cards

CCSS Assessing the Common Core State Standards

Sound-Spelling Cards

High-Frequency Word Cards

Response Board

Weekly Assessment

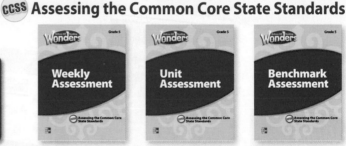
Unit Assessment

Benchmark Assessment

👉 **Go Digital**

 For the Teacher

 For the Students

For the Teacher

 Plan
Customizable Lesson Plans

 Assess
Online Assessments Reports and Scoring

 Professional Development
Lesson and CCSS Videos

 Teach
Classroom Presentation Tools Instructional Lessons

 Collaborate
Online Class Conversations Interactive Group Projects

Additional Online Resources
Leveled Practice
Grammar Practice
Phonics/Spelling
ELL Activities
Genre Study
Reader's Theater
Tier 2 Intervention

 Manage and Assign
Student Grouping and Assignments

 School to Home
Digital Open House Activities and Messages

For the Students

 My To Do List
Assignments Assessment

 Words to Know
Build Vocabulary

 Read
e Books Interactive Texts

 Play
Interactive Games

Write
Interactive Writing

 School to Home
Activities for Home
Messages from the Teacher
Class Wall of Student Work

www.connected.mcgraw-hill.com

UNIT 5 CONTENTS

Unit Planning

Weekly Lessons

Writing Process

Genre Writing: Informative

Model Lesson

Extended Complex Text

Program Information

(t to b) Alan Schein Photography/Corbis; UniversalImagesGroup/Hulton Archive/Getty Images; Richard Ellis/
The Image Bank/Getty Images; Richard Herrmann/Minden Pictures; Adrian Dennis/AFP/Getty Images

UNIT OVERVIEW

Text Complexity Range for Grades 4–5

Lexile
740 ——————————————— 1010
TextEvaluator™
23 ——————————————— 51

Week 1	Week 2	Week 3

READING

Week 1 — NEW PERSPECTIVES

ESSENTIAL QUESTION
What experiences can change the way you see yourself and the world around you?

Build Background

CCSS **Vocabulary**
L.5.6
disdain, focused, genius, perspective, prospect, stunned, superb, transition
Context Clues

CCSS **Comprehension**
RL.5.1
Strategy: Make Predictions
Skill: Character, Setting, Plot: Compare and Contrast
Genre: Realistic Fiction
Analytical Writing Write About Reading

CCSS **Word Study**
RF.5.3a
Suffixes

CCSS **Fluency**
RF.5.4b
Expression

Week 2 — BETTER TOGETHER

ESSENTIAL QUESTION
How do shared experiences help people adapt to change?

Build Background

CCSS **Vocabulary**
L.5.6
assume, guarantee, nominate, obviously, rely, supportive, sympathy, weakling
Idioms

CCSS **Comprehension**
RL.5.1
Strategy: Make Predictions
Skill: Character, Setting, Plot: Compare and Contrast
Genre: Historical Fiction
Analytical Writing Write About Reading

CCSS **Word Study**
RF.5.3a
Homophones

CCSS **Fluency**
RF.5.4b
Expression and Phrasing

Week 3 — OUR CHANGING EARTH

ESSENTIAL QUESTION
What changes in the environment affect living things?

Build Background

CCSS **Vocabulary**
L.5.6
atmosphere, decays, gradual, impact, noticeably, receding, stability, variations
Context Clues

CCSS **Comprehension**
RI.5.3
Strategy: Ask and Answer Questions
Skill: Text Structure: Compare and Contrast
Genre: Expository Text
Analytical Writing Write About Reading

CCSS **Word Study**
RF.5.3a
Prefixes

CCSS **Fluency**
RF.5.4b
Rate

LANGUAGE ARTS

Week 1

CCSS **Writing**
W.5.10
Trait: Organization

CCSS **Grammar**
L.3.1i
Clauses

CCSS **Spelling**
L.5.2e
Suffixes

CCSS **Vocabulary**
L.5.4a
Build Vocabulary

Week 2

CCSS **Writing**
W.5.10
Trait: Sentence Fluency

CCSS **Grammar**
L.3.1i
Complex Sentences

CCSS **Spelling**
L.5.2e
Homophones

CCSS **Vocabulary**
L.5.5b
Build Vocabulary

Week 3

CCSS **Writing**
W.5.10
Trait: Ideas

CCSS **Grammar**
L.5.2d
Adjectives

CCSS **Spelling**
L.5.2e
Prefixes

CCSS **Vocabulary**
L.5.4a
Build Vocabulary

 Writing Process **Genre Writing: Informative** Informational Article T344–T349

UNIT 5

Review and Assess

Week 4	Week 5	Week 6
NOW WE KNOW	**SCIENTIFIC VIEWPOINTS**	

Week 4 — NOW WE KNOW

ESSENTIAL QUESTION
How can scientific knowledge change over time?

Build Background

CCSS Vocabulary
L.5.6
approximately, astronomical, calculation, criteria, diameter, evaluate, orbit, spheres
Greek Roots

CCSS Comprehension
RI.5.5
Strategy: Ask and Answer Questions
Skill: Text Structure: Cause and Effect
Genre: Expository Text

Analytical Writing Write About Reading

CCSS Word Study
RF.5.3a
Suffixes *-less* and *-ness*

CCSS Fluency
RF.5.4c
Accuracy

Week 5 — SCIENTIFIC VIEWPOINTS

ESSENTIAL QUESTION
How do natural events and human activities affect the environment?

Build Background

CCSS Vocabulary
L.5.6
agricultural, declined, disorder, identify, probable, thrive, unexpected, widespread
Root Words

CCSS Comprehension
RI.6.6
Strategy: Ask and Answer Questions
Skill: Author's Point of View
Genre: Persuasive Article

Analytical Writing Write About Reading

CCSS Word Study
RF.5.3a
Suffix *-ion*

CCSS Fluency
RF.5.4b
Expression and Phrasing

Week 6

CCSS Reader's Theater
RF.5.4b
Focus on Vocabulary
Fluency: Intonation, Phrasing, Accuracy

CCSS Reading Digitally
RI.5.7
Notetaking
Navigating Links

CCSS Research and Inquiry
W.5.7
Interviewing
Unit Projects
Presentation of Ideas

Unit 5 Assessment

Unit Assessment Book
pages 108–136

Fluency Assessment
pages 282–291

CCSS Writing
W.5.10
Trait: Organization

CCSS Grammar
L.3.1g
Adjectives That Compare

CCSS Spelling
L.5.2e
Suffixes *-less* and *-ness*

CCSS Vocabulary
L.5.4b
Build Vocabulary

CCSS Writing
W.5.1d
Trait: Organization

CCSS Grammar
L.3.1g
Comparing with *Good* and *Bad*

CCSS Spelling
L.5.2e
Suffix *-ion*

CCSS Vocabulary
L.5.4b
Build Vocabulary

CCSS Writing
SL.5.4
Share Your Writing
Portfolio Choice

Genre Writing: Informative Research Report T350–T355

UNIT OPENER

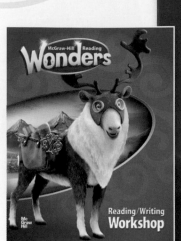

Reading/Writing Workshop

Unit 5

What's Next?

The BIG Idea
In what ways can things change?

304

surprising sunlight—
yesterday a maple tree
where my father stands

metamorphosis—
look, caterpillar, how much
we will learn today

the longer you look
at the meadow, the more birds
you will hear singing

—Jean LeBlanc

305

READING/WRITING WORKSHOP, pp. 304–305

The Big Idea *In what ways can things change?*

Talk About It

Have students read the Big Idea aloud. Ask them to identify changes that have happened in their lives. Students may list changes such as moving, switching schools, or joining a new team or club. Encourage students to discuss why those changes took place and how they felt about them.

Ask: *How can change have both positive and negative impacts?* Have students discuss in partners or in groups and then share their ideas.

Music Links Introduce a song at the start of the unit. Go to www.connected.mcgraw-hill.com, Resources Media: Music to find audio recordings, song lyrics, and activities.

Read the Poems: Haiku

Read aloud the three haiku. Ask students questions to explore the theme.

→ In the first haiku, what causes the "surprising sunlight"?

→ What does a caterpillar's experience teach us?

→ How might looking longer at a meadow make a person hear more birds singing?

Form Remind students that haiku are three-line poems with a set number of syllables in each line. Have students count the syllables (5–7–5).

Imagery Have students draw a picture that represents the image that formed in their minds as they read. Ask pairs to compare and contrast their drawings. Discuss how the poet uses sensory language to help readers envision each event.

RESEARCH AND INQUIRY

Weekly Projects Each week students will produce a project related to the Essential Question. They will then develop one of these projects more fully for the Week 6 Unit Project. Through their research, students will focus their attention on:

→ conducting an interview.

→ organizing information.

Shared Research Board You may wish to develop a Shared Research Board. Students can post ideas and information about the unit theme as well as summaries, notes, graphic organizers, or facts they gather as they do their research. They can also post notes with questions they have as they conduct their research.

WEEKLY PROJECTS

Students work in pairs or small groups.

Week 1 Cause-and-Effect Chart, T28

Week 2 Presentation, T92

Week 3 Web Site Entry or Podcast, T156

Week 4 Summary, T220

Week 5 Bibliography, T284

WEEK 6 UNIT PROJECT

Students work in small groups to complete and present one of the following projects.

→ Multimedia Presentation

→ Formal Presentation

→ Slide Show

→ Mock Interview

→ Persuasive Speech

WRITING

Analytical Writing Write About Reading As students read and reread each week for close reading of text, students will take notes, cite evidence to support their ideas and opinions, write summaries of text, or develop character sketches.

Writing Every Day: Focus on Writing Traits

Each week, students will focus on a writing trait. After analyzing an expert and student model, students will draft and revise shorter writing entries in their writer's notebook, applying the trait to their writing.

Writing Process: Focus on Informative Writing

Over the course of the unit, students will develop one to two longer informative texts. They will work through the various stages of the writing process, allowing them time to continue revising their writing and conferencing with peers and teacher.

WEEKLY WRITING TRAITS

Week 1 Organization, T30

Week 2 Sentence Fluency, T94

Week 3 Ideas, T158

Week 4 Organization, T222

Week 5 Organization, T286

GENRE WRITING: INFORMATIVE TEXT

Choose one or complete both 2–3 week writing process lessons over the course of the unit.

Informational Article, T344–T349

Research Report, T350–T355

Go Digital

COLLABORATE
Post student questions and monitor student online discussions. Create a Shared Research Board.

Go Digital

WRITER'S WORKSPACE
Ask students to work through their genre writing using the online tools.

Text Complexity Range for Grades 4–5

Lexile
740 — 1010
TextEvaluator™
23 — 51

Wonders
McGraw-Hill Reading

Reading/Writing Workshop

McGraw Hill

TEACH AND MODEL

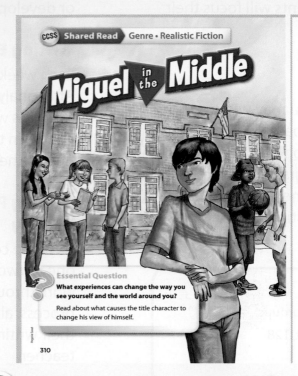

CCSS **Shared Read** Genre • Realistic Fiction

Miguel in the Middle

For as long as I can remember, I've always been in the middle. I'm the middle child in my family. I've always sat in the middle of the classroom in school. Even my first and last names, Miguel Martinez, start with an M—the middle letter of the alphabet.

Luckily, I'm also in the middle of a large circle of friends. Most of them are classmates in school—well, at least they were until now. You see, I started middle school in September, and the **transition** from elementary school caused some painful changes for me. All of my closest friends go to a different middle school in the area, because of the way our school district is mapped out. The only classmate I know from my old school is Jake, who's a **genius** in math, but since it's not my favorite subject, we never became friends.

Another big change is that I'm no longer situated in the middle of the classroom. My seat is now in the front row. Also, my new teachers shovel tons more homework at us (especially in math) than we used to get. So you can imagine why my heart wasn't exactly dancing when middle school began.

 Essential Question
What experiences can change the way you see yourself and the world around you?
Read about what causes the title character to change his view of himself.

310

311

✔ Vocabulary

disdain
focused
genius
perspective
prospect
stunned
superb
transition

🔍 Close Reading of Complex Text

Shared Read "Miguel in the Middle," 310–317

Genre Realistic Fiction

Lexile 890L

ⒺⓉⓈ *TextEvaluator*™ 49

Minilessons

✔ **Comprehension Strategy** .... Make Predictions, T18–T19

✔ **Comprehension Skill** .... Character, Setting, Plot: Compare and Contrast, T20–T21

✔ **Genre** .... Realistic Fiction, T22–T23

✔ **Vocabulary Strategy** .... Context Clues, T24–T25

✔ **Writing Traits** .... Organization, T30–T31

Grammar Handbook .... Clauses, T34–T35

✔ Tested Skills CCSS

☞ **Go** Digital

www.connected.mcgraw-hill.com

NEW PERSPECTIVES

Essential Question

What experiences can change the way you see yourself and the world around you?

WEEK 1 →

APPLY WITH CLOSE READING

Complex Text

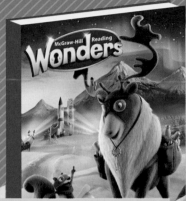

Literature Anthology

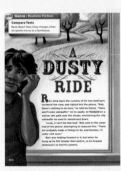

PAIRED READ

Ida B … and Her Plans to Maximize Fun, Avoid Disaster, and (Possibly) Save the World, 346–357

Genre Realistic Fiction

Lexile 970L

ETS *TextEvaluator*™ 49

"A Dusty Ride," 360–363

Genre Realistic Fiction

Lexile 890L

ETS *TextEvaluator*™ 42

Differentiated Text

Leveled Readers *Include Paired Reads*

APPROACHING

Lexile 740L

ETS *TextEvaluator*™ 55

ON LEVEL

Lexile 810L

ETS *TextEvaluator*™ 54

BEYOND

Lexile 900L

ETS *TextEvaluator*™ 54

ELL

Lexile 550L

ETS *TextEvaluator*™ 35

Extended Complex Text

The Penderwicks: A Summer Tale of Four Sisters, Two Rabbits, and a Very Interesting Boy

Genre Realistic Fiction

Lexile 800L

ETS *TextEvaluator*™ 42

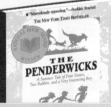

Classroom Library

Ida B … and Her Plans to Maximize Fun, Avoid Disaster, and (Possibly) Save the World

Genre Realistic Fiction

Lexile 970L

ETS *TextEvaluator*™ 49

Classroom Library lessons available online.

TEACH AND MANAGE

How You Teach

INTRODUCE

Weekly Concept
New Perspectives

Reading/Writing Workshop
306–307

TEACH

Close Reading
"Miguel in the Middle"

Minilessons
Make Predictions, Compare and
Contrast Settings, Realistic Fiction,
Context Clues, Writing Traits

**Reading/Writing
Workshop
310–319**

APPLY

Close Reading
Ida B ...
"A Dusty Ride"

**Literature
Anthology
346–363**

☞ **Go Digital**

| Interactive Whiteboard | Interactive Whiteboard | Mobile |

How Students Practice

WEEKLY CONTRACT

PDF Online

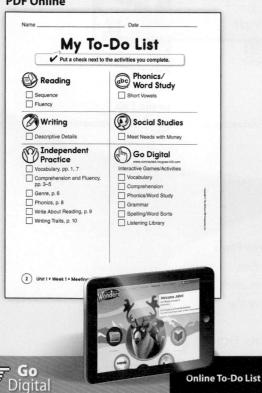

LEVELED PRACTICE AND ONLINE ACTIVITIES

Your Turn Practice Book
201–210

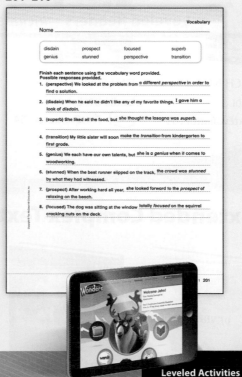

Leveled Readers

☞ **Go Digital**

| Online To-Do List | Leveled Activities | Writer's Workspace |

DIFFERENTIATE

SMALL GROUP INSTRUCTION

Leveled Readers

Mobile

INTEGRATE

Research and Inquiry
Cause-and-Effect Chart, T28

Text Connections
Compare Experiences, T29

Write About Reading
Analytical Writing Write an Analysis, T29

Online Research and Writing

ASSESS

Wonders
Weekly Assessment
Grade 5

Assessing the Common Core State Standards

Weekly Assessment
241–252

Online Assessment

LEVELED WORKSTATION CARDS

More Activities on back

21

Plants, Animals, and You

All plants and animals, including humans, are alike in some ways. They have some of the same needs. All plants and animals also have differences. These differences make each living thing special.

• Draw a picture of a plant or an animal on an index card. Label it. On a second index card, write one thing that all plants and animals have in common. Below that, write one thing that is only true about the plant

SCIENCE

8

Organization: Strong Openings

Read Min's opening paragraph for a report about the phases of the moon.

Have you ever wondered why the moon changes? It has to do with the earth, the moon, and the sun. You will read about how the sun lights the moon and the earth, moon, and sun. Then I will explain of the moon a

• Does Min's opening grab your attention? Tell your partner why or why not. Use examples to explain.

WRITING

3

Context Clues

Sometimes you can use **comparisons** to figure out the meaning of unfamiliar words.

A baby elephant is much smaller than its mom. The mom is gargantuan.

miniscule

massive

• On word cards, write size words such as *miniscule, miniature, microscopic, infinitesimal, Lilliputian, immense, massive, gargantuan, colossal, humongous.* Mix the cards up and place them face down.

• Choose three cards, and ask your partner to choose three. Look up the meanings of your words.

• Write sentences that use comparisons to show the meanings of your words.

You need
> paper and pen or pencil
> index cards
> dictionary

20 Minutes

PHONICS/WORD STUDY

5

Compare and Contrast Settings

Compare and contrast the effects of different settings on the characters in a story.

• Choose a story you have read that has more than one setting.

• Make a Venn diagram. Write the name of the main character above the center section. Label the left oval as one setting, and label the right oval as the second setting.

• In the center section, write how the character is the same in both settings. In the outer sections, tell how the character is different in each setting.

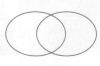

You need
> paper and pen or pencil
> graphic organizers

30 Minutes

READING

Go Digital! www.connected.mcgraw-hill.com • Interactive Games and Activities • Grade 5

DEVELOPING READERS AND WRITERS

Write to Sources and Research

Character, Setting, Plot: Compare and Contrast, T20–T21

Note Taking, T25B, T25P

Summarize, T25N

Compare and Contrast, T25N

Make Connections: Essential Question, T25N, T25R, T29

Key Details, T25P, T25Q

Research and Inquiry, T28

Analyze Main Idea and Details, T29

Comparing Texts, T41, T49, T53, T59

Predictive Writing, T25B

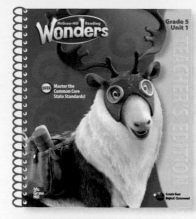

Teacher's Edition

Summarize, p. 359
Compare and Contrast, p. 359

Literature Anthology

Interactive Whiteboard

Leveled Readers
Comparing Texts
Compare and Contrast

Compare and Contrast, pp. 203–205
Genre, p. 206
Analyze Main Idea and Details, p. 209

Your Turn Practice Book

Informative Text
Informational Article, T344–T349

Conferencing Routines
Teacher Conferences, T346
Peer Conferences, T347

Interactive Whiteboard

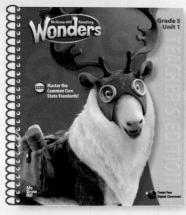

Teacher's Edition

Leveled Workstation Card
Informational Article, Card 29

Writer's Workspace
Informative Text:
Informational Article
Writing Process
Multimedia Presentations

Writing Traits • Write Every Day

Writing Trait: Organization
Strong Openings, T30–T31

Conferencing Routines
Teacher Conferences, T32
Peer Conferences, T33

Teacher's Edition

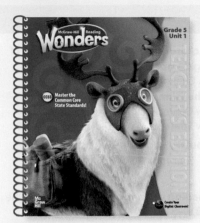

Organization:
Strong Openings,
pp. 318–319

Reading/Writing Workshop

Organization:
Strong
Openings, 8

Leveled Workstation Card

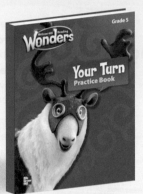

Organization: Strong
Openings, p. 210

Your Turn Practice Book

Interactive Whiteboard

Grammar and Spelling

Grammar
Clauses, T34–T35

Spelling
Suffixes, T36–T37

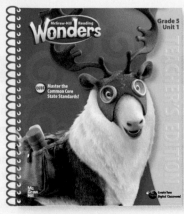

Teacher's Edition

Interactive Whiteboard

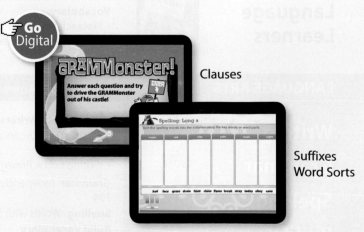

Clauses

Suffixes
Word Sorts

Online Spelling and Grammar Games

SUGGESTED LESSON PLAN

	DAY 1	DAY 2

READING

Whole Group

Teach, Model and Apply

Reading/Writing Workshop

Build Background New Perspectives, T10–T11
Listening Comprehension Interactive Read Aloud: "A Change of Heart," T12–T13
Comprehension
• Preview Genre: Realistic Fiction, T22–T23
• Preview Strategy: Make Predictions, T18–T19
✔ **Vocabulary** Words in Context, T14–T15
Practice *Your Turn* 201

Close Reading of Complex Text "Miguel in the Middle," 310–313

✔ **Comprehension**
• Strategy: Make Predictions, T18–T19
• Skill: Character, Setting, Plot: Compare and Contrast Settings, T20–T21
• Write About Reading *Analytical Writing*
• Genre: Realistic Fiction, T22–T23
✔ **Vocabulary** Strategy: Context Clues: Comparison, T24–T25
Practice *Your Turn* 203–207

DIFFERENTIATED INSTRUCTION Choose across the week to meet your students' needs.

Small Group

Approaching Level

Leveled Reader *King of the Board,* T40–T41
Word Study/Decoding Review Words with Suffixes, T42 **TIER 2**
Vocabulary
• Review High-Frequency Words, T44 **TIER 2**
• Identify Related Words, T45

Leveled Reader *King of the Board,* T40–T41
Vocabulary Review Vocabulary Words, T44 **TIER 2**
Comprehension
• Contrast Characters T46 **TIER 2**
• Review Compare and Contrast Settings, T47

On Level

Leveled Reader *Snap Happy,* T48–T49
Vocabulary Review Vocabulary Words, T50

Leveled Reader *Snap Happy,* T48–T49
Comprehension Review Compare and Contrast Settings, T51

Beyond Level

Leveled Reader *No Place Like Home,* T52–T53
Vocabulary Review Domain-Specific Words, T54

Leveled Reader *No Place Like Home,* T52–T53
Comprehension Review Compare and Contrast Settings, T55

English Language Learners

Shared Read "Miguel in the Middle," T56–T57
Word Study/Decoding Review Words with Suffixes, T42
Vocabulary
• Preteach Vocabulary, T60
• Review High-Frequency Words, T44

Leveled Reader *Snap Happy,* T58–T59
Vocabulary Review Vocabulary, T60
Writing Writing Trait: Organization, T62
Grammar Independent and Dependent Clauses, T63

LANGUAGE ARTS Writing Process: Informational Article T344–T349 Use with Weeks 1–3

Whole Group

Writing
Grammar
Spelling
Build Vocabulary

✔ **Readers to Writers**
• Writing Trait: Organization/Strong Openings, T30–T31
• Writing Entry: Prewrite and Draft, T32
Grammar Independent and Dependent Clauses, T34
Spelling Words with Suffixes, T36
Build Vocabulary
• Connect to Words, T38
• Academic Vocabulary, T38

Readers to Writers
• Writing Entry: Revise, T32
Grammar Independent and Dependent Clauses, T34
Spelling Words with Suffixes, T36
Build Vocabulary
• Expand Vocabulary, T38
• Review Synonyms and Antonyms, T38

DAY 3	**DAY 4**	**DAY 5** Review and Assess

READING

Word Study/Decoding Suffixes, T26–T27 **Practice** *Your Turn* 208	**Fluency** Expression, T27 **Integrate Ideas** *Analytical Writing* • Research and Inquiry, T28 **Practice** *Your Turn* 203–205	**Integrate Ideas** *Analytical Writing* • Research and Inquiry, T28 • Text Connections, T29 • Write About Reading, T29 **Practice** *Your Turn* 209
Close Reading *Ida B ...*, 346–359 *Analytical Writing* Literature Anthology	**Close Reading** "A Dusty Ride," 360–363 *Analytical Writing*	

DIFFERENTIATED INSTRUCTION

Leveled Reader *King of the Board,* T40–T41 **Word Study/Decoding** Build Words with Suffixes, T42 ② **Fluency** Expression, T46 ② **Vocabulary** Context Clues, T45	**Leveled Reader** Paired Read: "All on Her Own," T41 *Analytical Writing* **Word Study/Decoding** Practice Words with Suffixes, T43	**Leveled Reader** Literature Circle, T41 **Comprehension** Self-Selected Reading, T47
Leveled Reader *Snap Happy,* T48–T49 **Vocabulary** Context Clues, T50	**Leveled Reader** Paired Read: "Drum Roll for Justin," T49 *Analytical Writing*	**Leveled Reader** Literature Circle, T49 **Comprehension** Self-Selected Reading, T51
Leveled Reader *No Place Like Home,* T52–T53 **Vocabulary** • Context Clues, T54 • Independent Study, T54 *Gifted and Talented*	**Leveled Reader** Paired Read: "Mealtime Mystery," T53 *Analytical Writing*	**Leveled Reader** Literature Circle, T53 **Comprehension** • Self-Selected Reading, T55 • Independent Study: Perspectives, T55 *Gifted and Talented*
Leveled Reader *Snap Happy,* T58–T59 **Word Study/Decoding** Build Words with Suffixes, T42 **Vocabulary** Context Clues, T61 **Spelling** Words with Suffixes, T62	**Leveled Reader** Paired Read: "Drum Roll for Justin," T59 *Analytical Writing* **Vocabulary** Additional Vocabulary, T61 **Word Study/Decoding** Practice Words with Suffixes, T43	**Leveled Reader** Literature Circle, T59

LANGUAGE ARTS

Readers to Writers • Writing Entry: Prewrite and Draft, T33 **Grammar** Mechanics and Usage, T35 **Spelling** Words with Suffixes, T37 **Build Vocabulary** • Reinforce the Words, T39 • Context Clues, T39	**Readers to Writers** • Writing Entry: Revise, T33 **Grammar** Independent and Dependent Clauses, T35 **Spelling** Words with Suffixes, T37 **Build Vocabulary** • Connect to Writing, T39 • Shades of Meaning, T39	**Readers to Writers** • Writing Entry: Share and Reflect, T33 **Grammar** Independent and Dependent Clauses, T35 **Spelling** Words with Suffixes, T37 **Build Vocabulary** • Word Squares, T39 • Morphology, T39

DIFFERENTIATE TO ACCELERATE

A C T Scaffold to **A**ccess **C**omplex **T**ext

Qualitative   Quantitative

Reader and Task

TEXT COMPLEXITY

IF ➤ the text complexity of a particular selection is too difficult for students

THEN ➤ see the references noted in the chart below for scaffolded instruction to help students Access Complex Text.

	Reading/Writing Workshop	**Literature Anthology**	**Leveled Readers**		**Classroom Library**

Approaching · On Level · Beyond · ELL

Quantitative	"Miguel in the Middle" **Lexile** 890 *TextEvaluator* 49	*Ida B...and Her Plans to Maximize Fun, Avoid Disaster, and (Possibly) Save the World* **Lexile** 970 *TextEvaluator* 49 "A Dusty Ride" **Lexile** 890 *TextEvaluator* 42	**Approaching Level** **Lexile** 740 *TextEvaluator* 55 **Beyond Level** **Lexile** 900 *TextEvaluator* 54	**On Level** **Lexile** 810 *TextEvaluator* 54 **ELL** **Lexile** 550 *TextEvaluator* 35	*The Penderwicks* **Lexile** 800 *TextEvaluator* 42 *Ida B...and Her Plans to Maximize Fun, Avoid Disaster, and (Possibly) Save the World* **Lexile** 970 *TextEvaluator* 49
Qualitative	**What Makes the Text Complex?** • **Connection of Ideas** Theme T17 • **Compare and Contrast** T21 **A C T** *See Scaffolded Instruction in Teacher's Edition T17 and T21.*	**What Makes the Text Complex?** • **Organization** Novel T25A, T25I; Background Information T25G • **Sentence Structure** T25C, T25K • **Connection of Ideas** References T25E, T25Q • **Prior Knowledge** Introduction T25K • **Specific Vocabulary** Context Clues T25O **A C T** *See Scaffolded Instruction in Teacher's Edition T25A–T25R.*	**What Makes the Text Complex?** • **Specific Vocabulary** • **Sentence Structure** • **Connection of Ideas** • **Genre** **A C T** *See Level Up lessons online for Leveled Readers.*		**What Makes the Text Complex?** • **Genre** • **Specific Vocabulary** • **Prior Knowledge** • **Sentence Structure** • **Organization** • **Purpose** • **Connection of Ideas** **A C T** *See Scaffolded Instruction in Teacher's Edition T360-T361.*
Reader and Task	The Introduce the Concept lesson on pages T10-T11 will help determine the reader's knowledge and engagement in the weekly concept. See pages T16-T25 and T28-T29 for questions and tasks for this text.	The Introduce the Concept lesson on pages T10-T11 will help determine the reader's knowledge and engagement in the weekly concept. See pages T25A-T25R and T28-T29 for questions and tasks for this text.	The Introduce the Concept lesson on pages T10-T11 will help determine the reader's knowledge and engagement in the weekly concept. See pages T40-T41, T48-T49, T52-T53, T58-T59, and T28-T29 for questions and tasks for this text.		The Introduce the Concept lesson on pages T10-T11 will help determine the reader's knowledge and engagement in the weekly concept. See pages T360-T361 for questions and tasks for this text.

Monitor and *Differentiate*

IF → you need to differentiate instruction

THEN → use the Quick Checks to assess students' needs and select the appropriate small group instruction focus.

 Quick Check

Comprehension Strategy Make Predictions T19
Comprehension Skill Character, Setting, Plot: Compare and Contrast T21
Genre Realistic Fiction T23
Vocabulary Strategy Context Clues T25
Word Study/Fluency Suffixes, Expression T27

If No →
| Approaching Level | Reteach T40–T47 |
| ELL | Develop T56–T63 |

If Yes →
| On Level | Review T48–T51 |
| Beyond Level | Extend T52–T55 |

Level Up with Leveled Readers

IF → students can read their leveled text fluently and answer comprehension questions

THEN → work with the next level up to accelerate students' reading with more complex text.

Beyond — *No Place Like Home* — T49

On Level — *Snap Happy* — T59

Approaching — *King of the Board* — T41

ELL — *Snap Happy*

ENGLISH LANGUAGE LEARNERS
SCAFFOLD

IF ELL students need additional support **THEN** → scaffold instruction using the small group suggestions.

Reading/Writing Workshop "Miguel in the Middle" T56–T57	Leveled Reader *Snap Happy* T58–T59 "Drum Roll for Justin" T59	Additional Vocabulary T61 activity disdain district especially imagine suggestions	Context Clues T61	Writing Trait: Organization T62	Spelling Words with Suffixes T62	Grammar Independent and Dependent Clauses T63

Note: Include ELL Students in all small groups based on their needs.

→ Introduce the Concept

Reading/Writing Workshop

OBJECTIVES

CCSS Engage effectively in a range of collaborative discussions (one-on-one, in groups, and teacher-led) with diverse partners on *grade 5 topics and texts*, building on others' ideas and expressing their own clearly. Pose and respond to specific questions by making comments that contribute to the discussion and elaborate on the remarks of others. **SL.5.1c**

ACADEMIC LANGUAGE

• *perspective, transition*
• Cognate: *perspectiva*

 MINILESSON 10 Mins

Build Background

ESSENTIAL QUESTION

What experiences can change the way you see yourself and the world around you?

Have students read the Essential Question on page 306 of the **Reading/Writing Workshop**. Tell them that new experiences can change their **perspective**, or point of view.

Discuss the aerial view of the city. Then focus on how a new perspective can help a person make a **transition**, or change, in life.

→ When you walk down a city street, it may be hard to realize how big and busy the city is.

→ A view from the top of a skyscraper can make you realize the vastness of the city. This new **perspective** helps you to see and learn things about the city that could not be seen from a ground view.

Talk About It

 COLLABORATE

Ask: *What is an experience that changed your **perspective**? How did this experience help you make a **transition** in your life?* Have partners discuss.

→ Model adding words about changing your perspective to the graphic organizer. Then brainstorm words and phrases with students and add their contributions.

→ Have partners discuss what they have learned about changing their perspective. They can add to the organizer by generating additional words and phrases related to changing their perspective.

Collaborative Conversations

Ask and Answer Questions As students engage in partner, small-group, and whole-class discussions, encourage them to ask and answer questions. Remind students to

→ ask questions to clarify ideas or comments.

→ give others a chance to think before responding.

→ answer questions thoughtfully with complete ideas.

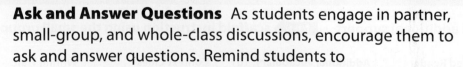

Go Digital

Discuss the Concept

Watch Video

Use Graphic Organizer

Weekly Concept New Perspectives

? Essential Question

What experiences can change the way you see yourself and the world around you?

📖 *Go Digital!*

The View from Here

When you walk down the street, a city like this appears one way. When you go high up, your perspective of the same city changes.

► From the top of this skyscraper in New York City, a visitor can see how tall, vast, and bustling with people this big city is!

► In the transition back to the ground, you may see the city streets in a whole new way, too!

Talk About It 👥 COLLABORATE

Write words you have learned about how you can change your perspective. Then talk about one experience that made you see the world in a new way.

New Perspectives ◯◯◯

306   307

READING/WRITING WORKSHOP, pp. 306–307

ELL ENGLISH LANGUAGE LEARNERS SCAFFOLD

Beginning	Intermediate	Advanced/High
Use Visuals Point to the photograph and say: *The word* perspective *means "view." This perspective, or view, is from a tall building.* Have students repeat. Ask: *What can you see from this perspective?* Repeat correct responses slowly and clearly for the class to hear.	**Describe** Have students describe the photograph. Say: *Let's think about a new perspective, or new view.* Ask: *How would your perspective of the city change if the photo was taken by a person standing on the sidewalk? What do you think we would see then?* Elicit details to support responses.	**Discuss** Have students discuss the photograph. Ask: *From this perspective, what do you notice about the city? Why is it helpful to look at things from a new or different perspective?* Elicit details to support students' responses.

GRAPHIC ORGANIZER 140

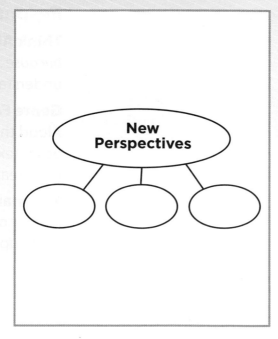

New Perspectives

→ # Listening Comprehension

MINILESSON

10 Mins

Interactive Read Aloud

Connect to Concept: New Perspectives

Remind students that having new experiences, such as making a new friend or moving to a new city, can change the way we think about ourselves and the world around us. Let students know that you will be reading aloud a story about a boy who discovers a new interest and a new way of seeing himself.

Preview Genre: Realistic Fiction

Explain that the text you will read aloud is realistic fiction. Discuss features of realistic fiction:

→ is set in a place that could really exist

→ includes characters like those found in real life

→ includes events and problems that could really happen

Preview Comprehension Strategy: Make Predictions

Point out that making predictions before and during reading gives readers a purpose. Good readers use the details in a story to predict what will happen next. As they continue reading, they check their predictions against the text and revise them if needed.

Use the Think Alouds on page T13 to model the strategy.

Respond to Reading

Think Aloud Clouds Display Think Aloud Master 3: *I predicted _____ because …* to reinforce how you used the make predictions strategy to understand content.

Genre Features With students, discuss the elements of the Read Aloud that let them know it is realistic fiction. Ask them to think about other texts that you have read or they have read independently that were realistic fiction.

Summarize Invite students to retell the story of "A Change of Heart" in their own words. Encourage them to focus on the main events that make up the plot.

OBJECTIVES

CCSS Summarize a written text read aloud or information presented in diverse media and formats, including visually, quantitatively, and orally. **SL.5.2**

• Listen for a purpose

• Identify characteristics of realistic fiction

ACADEMIC LANGUAGE

• *realistic fiction, make predictions*

• Cognates: *ficción realista, predicciones*

View Illustrations

I predicted _____ because…

Model Think Alouds

Genre	Features

Genre Chart

A Change of Heart

Narin prepared to kick the ball to one of the forward players when Max, the opposing team's most powerful defender, blocked the pass with the inside of his foot and took possession of the ball. Narin lost his balance and crash-landed on his side. The coach called time out.

"My shoulder really hurts," Narin said as the coach helped him to his feet. It was only a practice game, but for Narin, it was a chance to prove he could handle playing midfield. He hoped his shoulder would heal in time for next week's big game. **1**

The next day his father took Narin to see the family doctor. After examining Narin's shoulder, the doctor delivered his verdict: "You'll have to avoid contact sports for the next few months." Narin was devastated. He loved playing sports and couldn't imagine doing anything else with his free time.

Narin's parents, who had come from Cambodia, knew how challenging it is to give up something you love. "Maybe it's time to try something new," they advised. Narin said he'd think about it. **2**

At lunch a few days later, Narin's friend Tony sat beside him. "Hector quit the cast," Tony said. "Our drama group needs someone to take his place. You should try out! You'd be perfect."

"I don't know, Tony. I'm no actor. I've never been in a play, and besides, acting isn't my thing."

Tony refused to give up. By the end of the week, he persuaded Narin to try out for Hector's part. The director was impressed with Narin's performance and offered him the role, which he accepted, though half-heartedly. **3**

But after his first rehearsal, Narin couldn't believe how much fun he was having. Once again he was part of a team, only this time the other players were actors, and like the guys on his soccer team, they were all working together toward the same goal.

"Hey, Narin, what do you think about acting now?" Tony asked as they put away the props.

"It's not what I expected," Narin answered. "When our director gave me a 'thumbs up,' it felt like I had just kicked the ball right into the net!"

1 **Think Aloud** Next week's game is really important to Narin. I **predict** his shoulder will heal in time for him to play.

2 **Think Aloud** I have to revise my prediction. Narin can't play in the big game. His parents encouraged him to try something new. I **predict** he will find something else to do.

3 **Think Aloud** I can confirm my earlier prediction. Narin is trying something new. Based on the title, I **predict** that he will have a change of heart and enjoy being in the play.

Andersen Ross/Blend Images/Getty Images

→ Vocabulary

Reading/Writing Workshop

OBJECTIVES

CCSS Acquire and use accurately grade-appropriate general academic and domain-specific words and phrases, including those that signal contrast, addition, and other logical relationships (e.g., *however, although, nevertheless, similarly, moreover, in addition*). **L.5.6**

ACADEMIC LANGUAGE

• *perspective, transition*
• Cognate: *perspectiva*

10 Mins MINILESSON

Words in Context

Model the Routine

Introduce each vocabulary word using the Vocabulary Routine found on the **Visual Vocabulary Cards**.

Visual Vocabulary Cards

Vocabu...
Define:
Example:
Ask:

Vocabulary Routine

Define: **Disdain** is a feeling of dislike for someone or something you think is unworthy.

Example: Rebecca likes to eat many vegetables, but she always shows disdain for broccoli.

Ask: What is a synonym for *disdain*?

disdain

Use Visual Glossary

Definitions

→ **focused**   A **focused** person is able to concentrate on one thing.

→ **genius**   A **genius** is an extremely intelligent or talented person.
   Cognate: *genio*

→ **perspective**   Your **perspective** is your point of view, or the way you see things.
   Cognate: *perspectiva*

→ **prospect**   A **prospect** is something you look forward to or expect.

→ **stunned**   If you are **stunned**, you are shocked and confused.

→ **superb**   Something that is **superb** is excellent.

→ **transition**   A **transition** is a change from one form, condition, or activity to another.

Talk About It

COLLABORATE

Have students work with partners and discuss the photograph and definition for each word. Ask them to talk about how the sentence relates to the definition. Then ask students to choose three words and write questions for their partner to answer.

Go Digital

CCSS Words to Know

Vocabulary

Use the picture and the sentences to talk with a partner about each word.

disdain
Rebecca likes to eat many vegetables, but she always shows **disdain** for broccoli.

What is a synonym for disdain?

focused
Ellie pays attention and stays **focused** during class discussions.

What is an antonym for focused?

genius
My sister is a **genius** when it comes to fixing computer problems.

How might a mechanical genius help other people?

perspective
Binoculars gave Kyle a closer **perspective** of the boat in the harbor.

How does a telescope affect your perspective of the moon?

prospect
Gillian was happy at the **prospect** of traveling to Paris next year.

Why might the prospect of moving be both exciting and scary?

stunned
Luis was **stunned** by the unexpected test grade.

What kinds of events have stunned you?

superb
The cooking teacher praised his student for the **superb** dish.

What is a synonym for superb?

transition
Max was afraid to make the **transition** from walking to riding a bus to school.

How might you prepare a young child for this transition?

Your Turn COLLABORATE

Pick three words. Write three questions for your partner to answer.

Go Digital! *Use the online visual glossary*

308   309

READING/WRITING WORKSHOP, pp. 308–309

ELL ENGLISH LANGUAGE LEARNERS SCAFFOLD

Beginning

Use Visuals Say: *Let's look at the photograph for* disdain. Point to the girl. Say: Disdain *means "dislike."* Have students repeat. Use facial expressions to reinforce the meaning of the word. Ask: *If you feel disdain for a video game, do you like it?* Give students ample time to answer. Say: Disdain *in Spanish is* desdén.

Intermediate

Describe Have students describe the photograph for *disdain*. Help them with pronunciation. Say: *I feel disdain for loud music early in the morning.* Provide this sentence frame and help students complete it appropriately: *I feel disdain for _____.* Correct responses for grammar and pronunciation.

Advanced/High

Discuss Ask students to read the sample sentence and discuss the photograph for *disdain* with partners. They should then discuss what they feel disdain for and how they show their disdain. Have students share what they discussed with the class. Elicit details to support students' responses.

ON-LEVEL PRACTICE BOOK p. 201

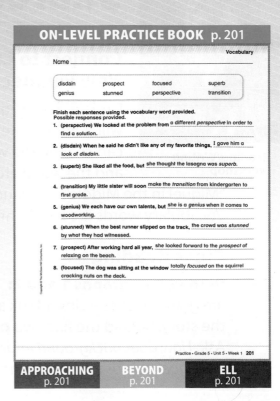

| APPROACHING | BEYOND | ELL |
| p. 201 | p. 201 | p. 201 |

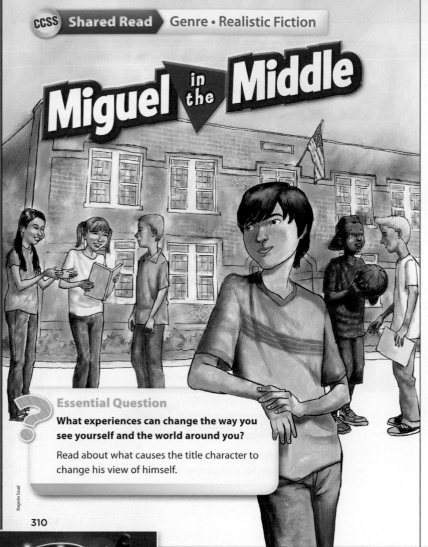

CCSS Shared Read — Genre • Realistic Fiction

Miguel in the Middle

Essential Question

What experiences can change the way you see yourself and the world around you?

Read about what causes the title character to change his view of himself.

310

For as long as I can remember, I've always been in the middle. I'm the middle child in my family. I've always sat in the middle of the classroom in school. Even my first and last names, Miguel Martinez, start with an M—the middle letter of the alphabet.

Luckily, I'm also in the middle of a large circle of friends. Most of them are classmates in school—well, at least they were until now. You see, I started middle school in September, and the **transition** from elementary school caused some painful changes for me. All of my closest friends go to a different middle school in the area, because of the way our school district is mapped out. The only classmate I know from my old school is Jake, who's a **genius** in math, but since it's not my favorite subject, we never became friends.

Another big change is that I'm no longer situated in the middle of the classroom. My seat is now in the front row. Also, my new teachers shovel tons more homework at us (especially in math) than we used to get. So you can imagine why my heart wasn't exactly dancing when middle school began.

TONIGHT'S MATH HOMEWORK

311

READING/WRITING WORKSHOP, pp. 310–311

Reading/Writing Workshop

Shared Read

Lexile 890   *TextEvaluator* 49

Connect to Concept: New Perspectives

Explain that "Miguel in the Middle" will demonstrate how experiences can change the way you see yourself and the world around you. Read "Miguel in the Middle" with students. Note that Vocabulary words are highlighted in the text.

Close Reading

Reread Paragraphs 1 and 2: Explain that you are going to take a closer look at the beginning of the story. Reread the first two paragraphs together. Ask: *How does background information provided by Miguel help us understand how he sees himself?*

Model how to cite details to answer the question.

I learn that Miguel is used to being in the middle. He is the middle child in his family, he sits in the middle of his classrooms, and he is in the middle of a group of friends. Going to a new school has caused some painful changes for Miguel, mainly because he is no longer with his close friends.

Reread Paragraph 3: Model how to use information in the third paragraph to compare and contrast the settings of Miguel's old elementary school and his new middle school.

In elementary school, Miguel sat in the middle of the classroom. In his new middle school, he sits in the front row. The school also assigns a lot more homework than he is used to, especially in math.

By the end of October, Jake and I had become good friends. It happened because I was so hopeless trying to do my math homework. I have a **disdain** for math—especially fractions. To me, fractions are a foreign language—I may as well be trying to learn Greek or Latin. So one day, I approached Jake after school.

"Hey, Jake," I began, "I was wondering if you could—"

"Help you with the math homework, right?" he said, completing my sentence. "Sure, I'd be happy to help you, Miguel."

I was **stunned** because, to be truthful, I wasn't sure until that moment if Jake even knew my name. And yet here he was, happy to save me from drowning in my sea of math problems.

That night, Jake and I had a study session, and it was time well spent. I must admit that Jake's a **superb** math teacher. He used slices of a pizza pie to explain the idea of eighths and sixteenths, and by the end of the night, I finally understood why eight-sixteenths is the same as one-half!

The next day in class, I was even able to answer one of the math problems our teacher put on the chalkboard. She was surprised when I raised my hand, and guess what—so was I!

They say time flies when you're having fun, and I guess it's really true. I can't believe winter vacation is almost here! The school days have been flying by like a jet plane. I suppose it's because I'm a much more **focused** student—especially in math—than I ever was before. Until this year, I always looked forward to the **prospect** of a school break. Now, I actually feel sad that I'll be away from middle school for two weeks.

The other day, the most amazing thing happened when our teacher gave us a math brainteaser. She asked, "If you wrote all the numbers from one to one hundred, how many times would you write a nine?" The question was harder than it seemed.

Most of the students said ten, although some clever kids said eleven, because they realized that ninety-nine has two nines, not just one. But Jake and I were the only students with the correct answer—twenty! Everyone else forgot to count all the nineties.

Jake and I plan to hang out together during winter break. He promised to show me the Math Museum downtown. It won't just be us, however, since all my new friends from middle school will come, too. You see, even though I now have a completely different **perspective** on math, some things haven't changed. I'm still in the middle of a large circle of friends!

Make Connections

Discuss the ways that Miguel changed after entering middle school. What caused him to change? **ESSENTIAL QUESTION**

When has a new place changed the way you see yourself or the world around you? **TEXT TO SELF**

312

313

READING/WRITING WORKSHOP, pp. 312–313

Make Connections

ESSENTIAL QUESTION

Encourage students to use text evidence as they discuss how and why Miguel changes in middle school. Have students explain, using the text, how our experiences can change our perspectives.

Continue Close Reading

Use the following lessons for focused rereadings.

→ Make Predictions, pp. T18–T19

→ Character, Setting, Plot: Compare and Contrast, pp. T20–T21

→ Realistic Fiction, pp. T22–T23

→ Context Clues, pp. T24–T25

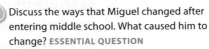

A C T Access Complex Text

▶ **Connection of Ideas**

Guide students to connect Miguel's success in math to success in middle school.

→ *How does Miguel feel about math at the beginning?* (It is his least favorite subject.)

→ *How does he feel about math at the end?* (He is much more focused. He volunteers, and he correctly answers a brainteaser.)

→ *How did learning math help Miguel?* (Miguel was challenged by math at his new school. Jake helped him, and this gave Miguel more confidence and a new friend.)

→ Comprehension Strategy

Reading/Writing Workshop

 MINILESSON 10 Mins

Make Predictions

Go Digital

Present the Lesson

OBJECTIVES

CCSS Quote accurately from a text when explaining what the text says explicitly and when drawing inferences from the text. **RL.5.1**

ACADEMIC LANGUAGE

• *make predictions, realistic fiction*

• Cognates: *predicciones, ficción realistsa*

1 Explain

Explain to students that when they read a realistic fiction text, they can make predictions about upcoming events.

→ Remind students to pause periodically during their reading and think about what might happen next in the story or how a certain character might behave.

→ Explain that students should use details in the story to make predictions. These details may describe the characters, the setting, or the plot—such as problems that the characters face.

→ As students continue reading, they can confirm if their predictions were accurate and, if necessary, revise them based on new details and information in the text.

Point out that making, confirming, and revising predictions is a good way to maintain focus while reading and to understand more clearly what is happening in a story.

2 Model Close Reading: Text Evidence

Using details in the second paragraph on page 311, model making a prediction about how Miguel will feel in his new school. When you read that Miguel's friends are going to another school, you might predict that Miguel will be unhappy. When you read that Jake is the only classmate Miguel knows, you might revise your prediction to reflect that Jake will become a friend.

3 Guided Practice of Close Reading

COLLABORATE

Have students work in pairs to make predictions about events in the story after the first page. Ask them to point out the text evidence that supported their predictions. Then have partners identify details in subsequent pages of the story that help them confirm or revise their predictions.

CCSS Comprehension Strategy

Make Predictions

When you **make predictions** as you read text, you use text details to help you think about what might happen next. You can confirm your predictions if they are correct. If they are not correct, you can revise them.

 ## Find Text Evidence

When you read the second paragraph of "Miguel in the Middle" on page 311, you might make a prediction about how Miguel will feel in his new school.

page 311

For as long as I can remember, I've always been in the middle. I'm the middle child in my family. I've always sat in the middle of the classroom in school. Even my first and last names, Miguel Martinez, start with an M—the middle letter of the alphabet.

Luckily, I'm also in the middle of a large circle of friends. Most of them are classmates in school—well, at least they were until now. You see, I started middle school in September, and the **transition** from elementary school caused some painful changes for me. All of my closest friends go to a different middle school in the area, because of the way our school district is mapped out. The only classmate I know from my old school is Jake, who's a **genius** in math, but since it's not my favorite subject, we never became friends.

When I read that all of Miguel's friends had gone to a different school, I predicted that Miguel will be unhappy in his new school. When Miguel mentioned Jake, I revised this by predicting that Jake may become a friend.

Your Turn

What did you predict would happen after the first page? Point to the text evidence that supported your prediction. As you read, use the strategy Make Predictions.

314

READING/WRITING WORKSHOP, p. 314

Beginning

Determine Read aloud the second paragraph with students. Identify and explain the meaning of phrases such as *painful changes* and *mapped out.* Ask: *Does Miguel need a friend in his new school?* (yes) *Who might become Miguel's friend?* (Jake)

Intermediate

Describe Read the second paragraph with students. Help them describe why going from elementary to middle school has been hard for Miguel. Ask: *Based on details in the text, how might Jake learn to deal with the changes in his new school?*

Advanced/High

Identify Have students read aloud the second paragraph and make a prediction based on details in the text. Have partners share their predictions and identify details in the text they used to make them.

Monitor and *Differentiate*

✓ Quick Check

Do students make predictions about the story? Can they identify details in the text that support their predictions?

Small Group Instruction

If No → | **Approaching Level** | Reteach p. T40
| **ELL** | Develop p. T57
If Yes → | **On Level** | Review p. T48
| **Beyond Level** | Extend p. T52

ON-LEVEL PRACTICE BOOK pp. 203–204

Comprehension and Fluency

Name _____

Read the passage. Use the make predictions strategy to help you understand what you are reading.

Bringing Home Laddie

    "Papa, let's go!" Sofia was dressed and waiting on the shabby wooden
12 porch. Her father couldn't hear her. He was in the neighbor's garden,
24 digging up an ancient tree stump. Sofia shifted her feet and picked at the
38 peeling paint on the railing. The sun hammered down on the porch, so
51 that it was not merely hot, but sweltering. It would serve Papa right if she
66 melted away like the Wicked Witch of the West. Why should Sofia have to
80 wait? Why couldn't their neighbor, Mrs. Stone, wait instead? Then Papa
91 could drive Sofia to the animal shelter now to adopt her new dog.
104   Sofia peered into the shadows of the house. "Mom," she yelled, "Papa
116 promised we could go early. Do I have to walk?" She could imagine how
130 unhappy she'd look—just another stray dog trudging dejectedly down
140 the road.
156   Her mother came to the door, a damp dish towel in her hand. "Sofia,
169 come help me." Sofia stayed where she was, as rooted as the neighbor's
181 tree stump. "Standing here won't make your father finish any sooner. If
191 you help me, he'll be here before you know it."
202   Sofia gave a sigh of profound suffering and followed her mother
213 through the cool house into the spotless, lemony kitchen. She leaned
225 against the counter and dried the dishes her mother handed her—along
240 with a reminder of the promise she'd made to take care of the dog herself.
254 "I know, Mom, I know," Sofia whined. To her surprise, by the time the
268 dishes were dry, Papa was back. The time really had passed quickly, just as
273 Mom had said it would.
285   When Sofia and her parents arrived at the shelter, an attendant escorted
297 them to the dogs' quarters, a glaring concrete courtyard lined with tiny
310 cages on all four sides. Its smell was revolting—a mixture of mouthwash
    and Papa's old fishing bucket.

Practice · Grade 5 · Unit 5 · Week 1   **203**

| **APPROACHING** pp. 203–204 | **BEYOND** pp. 203–204 | **ELL** pp. 203–204 |

→ Comprehension Skill

MINILESSON
10 Mins

Character, Setting, Plot: Compare and Contrast

Reading/Writing Workshop

OBJECTIVES

CCSS Quote accurately from a text when explaining what the text says explicitly and when drawing inferences from the text. **RL.5.1**

CCSS Compare and contrast two or more characters, settings, or events in a story or drama, drawing on specific details in the text. **RL.5.3**

ACADEMIC LANGUAGE

• compare, contrast, setting, character

• Cognates: comparar, contrastar

SKILLS TRACE

CHARACTER, SETTING, PLOT

Introduce U1W1

Review U1W2, U1W6, U2W2, U2W6, U3W6, U4W6, U5W1, U5W2, U6W6

Assess U1, U2, U5

1 Explain

Explain to students that when they compare and contrast, they analyze how people, places, or things are alike and different.

→ Remind students that a story's **setting** is when and where it takes place. As a story progresses, the setting often changes.

→ To compare and contrast settings in a story, students must first note details that the author presents about place and time. Then they must decide how these places and times are alike and different.

→ Explain that different settings often affect a character in different ways. Students should review details about how a character responds to different settings in the story.

2 Model Close Reading: Text Evidence

Identify the two settings introduced in the second and third paragraphs on page 311: Miguel's old elementary school and his new middle school. Model identifying important details related to the two settings and describing Miguel's response to each.

 Write About Reading: Compare and Contrast Model how to use details listed on the organizer to compare and contrast Miguel's feelings about his old elementary school and his new middle school.

3 Guided Practice of Close Reading

 Have pairs complete a graphic organizer for the rest of "Miguel in the Middle." Encourage students to reread the story for key details about the settings and their effects on Miguel.

 Write About Reading: Compare and Contrast Have partners compare and contrast the effects that the two settings have on Miguel. *How has Miguel both changed and stayed the same as a result of changes in his school setting?* Ask volunteers to share their work with the class.

Go Digital

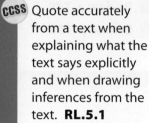

Present the Lesson

Compare and Contrast

When you **compare and contrast settings** in a story, you figure out how the places and times are alike and different. In a story with more than one setting, you can compare and contrast the effects of the different settings on the characters.

Find Text Evidence

By contrasting the settings in "Miguel in the Middle" on page 311, I find that Miguel was happy in his old school and unhappy in the new one. However, he wants to have friends no matter where he is.

Old School	Miguel	New School
"I'm in the middle of a large circle of friends."	He wants to have friends, no matter where he is.	"The only classmate I know is Jake."

Your Turn

COLLABORATE

Reread the rest of "Miguel in the Middle." Record details about Miguel's old school and new school in the graphic organizer. In the center, describe how Miguel remains the same in both places.

Go Digital! *Use the interactive graphic organizer*

315

READING/WRITING WORKSHOP, p. 315

A C T **A**ccess **C**omplex **T**ext

▶ Connection of Ideas

Help students compare Miguel's feelings at the story's beginning to his feelings at the end.

→ *At the beginning, how does Miguel feel about his new school?* (He feels alone because none of his friends go there.)

→ *At the end, how have Miguel's feelings changed?* (He enjoys his new school so much that he is sad to be on break.)

→ *How did the change come about?* (Miguel tried a new subject and made a new friend.)

Monitor and *Differentiate*

✔ Quick Check

Are students able to identify ways in which the two schools are alike and different? Do they describe the effects of the settings on Miguel?

Small Group Instruction

If No →	Approaching Level	Reteach p. T47
	ELL	Develop p. T57
If Yes →	On Level	Review p. T51
	Beyond Level	Extend p. T55

ON-LEVEL PRACTICE BOOK pp. 203–205

Comprehension: **Compare and Contrast and Fluency**

Name _____

A. Reread the passage and answer the questions. Possible responses provided.

1. Contrast the first dog and Laddie. How are they different?
The first dog is small, gaunt, forlorn, and frightened. Laddie is large, active, healthy, and friendly.

2. How does Sofia change from the beginning of the story to the end?
At the beginning of the story, she is anxious and impatient. By the end of the story, she is relieved and cheerful.

3. What causes the change in Sofia?
She is nervous and impatient about going to the animal shelter. Once she adopts Laddie, she is relieved and cheerful about her choice.

4. How are the settings of the animal shelter and Sofia's kitchen different?
The kitchen is spotless and smells like lemon. The shelter is concrete, has tiny cages full of dogs, and has a terrible smell.

B. Work with a partner. Read the passage aloud. Pay attention to expression. Stop after one minute. Fill out the chart.

	Words Read	–	Number of Errors	=	Words Correct Score
First Read		–		=	
Second Read		–		=	

Practice • Grade 5 • Unit 5 • Week 1 **205**

APPROACHING pp. 203–205	BEYOND pp. 203–205	ELL pp. 203–205

→ Genre: Literature

Reading/Writing Workshop

OBJECTIVES

CCSS Determine the meaning of words and phrases as they are used in a text, including figurative language such as metaphors and similes. **RL.5.4**

CCSS Describe how a narrator's or speaker's point of view influences how events are described. **RL.5.6**

ACADEMIC LANGUAGE

• *realistic fiction, narrator, figurative language*
• Cognates: *ficción realista, narrador(a)*

MINILESSON 10 Mins

Realistic Fiction

1 Explain

Share with students the following characteristics of **realistic fiction**:

→ Realistic fiction is set in places that could be found in real life and contains characters that are like real people.

→ The events and conflicts that characters face in realistic fiction are very similar to those faced by people in real life.

→ As in other types of fiction, events in realistic fiction stories are related by a narrator. Sometimes this narrator describes events from a first-person point of view.

→ Realistic fiction stories may also contain figurative language such as hyperbole, metaphors, similes, and personification.

Explain to students that identifying these characteristics while they read can make their experience with realistic fiction more interesting and enjoyable.

2 Model Close Reading: Text Evidence

Model identifying characteristics of realistic fiction on page 311 of "Miguel in the Middle," such as the fact that it takes place in a realistic setting: a middle school.

Narrator Point out the pronoun *I* in the first paragraph. Explain that words such as *I* and *me* indicate that story events are being narrated from a first-person point of view. In other words, Miguel is telling his own story.

Figurative Language Point out that Miguel's teachers are not really using a shovel to give tons of homework. Miguel uses a metaphor to compare the way teachers assign homework to shoveling, or piling on. He also uses hyperbole (*tons*) to exaggerate how much homework they assign, showing that he thinks it is excessive.

3 Guided Practice of Close Reading

Have partners describe how the narrator's point of view affects "Miguel in the Middle" and identify examples of figurative language. Have pairs share their findings with the class.

Go Digital

Present the Lesson

 **Genre** Literature

Realistic Fiction

The selection "Miguel in the Middle" is realistic fiction.

Realistic fiction:
- Has characters and settings that could actually exist
- May have a first-person narrator
- May include figurative language, such as hyperbole and metaphor

 Find Text Evidence

I see that "Miguel in the Middle" is realistic fiction. Miguel attends middle school. When Miguel says that teachers shovel tons more homework, he is using hyperbole, as people do. Shovel is used as a metaphor to show how the homework seems to be assigned.

page 311

Narrator The narrator is the person who tells the story.

Figurative Language Figurative language paints a word picture. Hyperbole exaggerates, and metaphors compare unlike things.

Your Turn COLLABORATE

How does the narrator's point of view affect "Miguel in the Middle"? Point out any figurative language.

316

READING/WRITING WORKSHOP, p. 316

Monitor and *Differentiate*

 Quick Check

Can students describe how the narrator's point of view affects the story and identify examples of figurative language?

Small Group Instruction

If No → | Approaching Level | Reteach p. T41
| ELL | Develop p. T59
If Yes → | On Level | Review p. T49
| Beyond Level | Extend p. T53

ON-LEVEL PRACTICE BOOK p. 206

Genre/Literary Element

Name _____

The Spelling Bee

Gabe stood in the wings of the high school auditorium. The stage was huge, with chairs for 45 students. There were 3,000 people in the audience. "This is very different from our school's auditorium," he thought. "Ours holds only 300 people, and our stage isn't big enough to hold a fly." Gabe had won his school's spelling bee, but he doubted he would do well here. "I'll do the best I can," Gabe said to himself as he stepped onto the stage and focused on the spelling bee. By the end of the day, Gabe had made it to the state finals, and he felt a lot better about himself.

Answer the questions about the text.

1. How do you know this text is realistic fiction? What makes the characters, events, and dialogue realistic?
The characters are like real people, and the events are ones that happen in real life. The dialogue sounds the way real people speak.

2. Write an example of figurative language found in the text. Explain why it is figurative language.
"our stage isn't big enough to hold a fly." This is a hyperbole. Gabe's exaggerating the smallness of his stage; it isn't possible for a stage to be this small.

3. Who is the narrator of the story? Explain how you know.
The narrator is someone outside the story. I know because the narrator uses third-person pronouns to describe Gabe.

4. Write a descriptive detail from the text that tells how Gabe felt after the spelling bee. How does this detail help you experience the text as realistic?
"Gabe had made it to the state finals, and he felt a lot better about himself."
It helps me see and hear how Gabe felt. His feelings seem real.

206 Practice • Grade 5 • Unit 5 • Week 1

| APPROACHING p. 206 | BEYOND p. 206 | ELL p. 206 |

ELL ENGLISH LANGUAGE LEARNERS SCAFFOLD

Beginning	**Intermediate**	**Advanced/High**
Understand Read aloud the third paragraph on page 311. Point to the word *my.* Ask: *Is Miguel telling the story?* (yes) *Is he in middle school?* (yes) *Does he think he has too much homework?* (yes) *Does he sound like a realistic character in a realistic setting?* (yes)	**Describe** Reread the third paragraph with students. Ask: *Who is the narrator in this story?* (Miguel) *How does Miguel describe how the teachers assign homework in middle school?* (They shovel tons of it.) Have partners explain why this description is an example of figurative language.	**Distinguish** Have students reread page 311. Ask them to identify the narrator's point of view and any realistic details about the setting and characters. Then have partners identify examples of figurative language on the page.

Vocabulary Strategy

Reading/Writing Workshop

OBJECTIVES

ccss Use context (e.g., cause/effect relationships and comparisons in text) as a clue to the meaning of a word or phrase. **L.5.4a**

ACADEMIC LANGUAGE

• *context clues, comparison*

• Cognate: *comparación*

 MINILESSON
10 Mins

Context Clues

1 Explain

Remind students that they can use context clues within a sentence or a paragraph to figure out the meaning of an unknown or multiple-meaning word.

→ One kind of context clue students can often use is a **comparison**. This is a word or phrase within the same sentence or in a nearby sentence that has a similar meaning or is used in a similar way as the unfamiliar word.

→ Students should also look for nearby words and phrases that give examples or provide a further description of the unfamiliar word.

2 Model Close Reading: Text Evidence

Model using the comparison in the second paragraph on page 311 to determine the meaning of *district* in *school district*. Describe how you use the earlier phrase *a different middle school in the area* to determine that *district* has a similar meaning as *area*.

3 Guided Practice of Close Reading

Have pairs figure out the meanings of *situated, session,* and *brainteaser.* Encourage students to go back to the text and use context clues in the form of comparisons to help them determine each word's meaning.

Go Digital

Present the Lesson

SKILLS TRACE

CONTEXT CLUES: COMPARISON

Introduce U3W2

Review U3W2, U3W3, U5W1, U5W4

Assess U3, U5

Vocabulary Strategy CCSS

Context Clues

When you find an unfamiliar or multiple meaning word in a sentence, you can look for sentence clues such as **comparisons** to help you figure out the meaning.

 Find Text Evidence

When I read the second paragraph of "Miguel in the Middle," I can use the comparison a different middle school in the area *to figure out the meaning of* district *in school district. District* must *mean the same as "area."*

> All of my closest friends go to **a different middle school in the area,** because of the way our school **district** is mapped out.

Your Turn

Use context clues to figure out the meanings of the following words in "Miguel in the Middle."
   situated, *page 311*
   session, *page 312*
   brainteaser, *page 313*

317

READING/WRITING WORKSHOP, p. 317

Monitor and *Differentiate*

✓ **Quick Check**

Can students use comparisons and other context clues to figure out the meanings of unfamiliar words?

⬇

Small Group Instruction

If No →	**Approaching Level**	Reteach p. T45
	ELL	Develop p. T61
If Yes →	**On Level**	Review p. T50
	Beyond Level	Extend p. T54

 ENGLISH LANGUAGE LEARNERS SCAFFOLD

Beginning	Intermediate	Advanced/High
Understand Point out and define *situated, session,* and *brainteaser.* Help students replace them with comparison words in the text: *seat, time, question.* Provide sentence frames: *Being seated means being ____ somewhere. If you had a good time working out, you had a good workout ____. A difficult question is a ____.*	**Identify** Point out the words *situated, session,* and *brainteaser* in the text and define them for students. Then have partners identify context clues in the form of comparisons that help them identify each word's meaning. Elicit from students how cognates helped them understand the text.	**Derive Meaning** Point out the words *situated, session,* and *brainteaser* in the text and ask students to determine their meanings by using context clues in the form of comparisons. Ask students to find cognates and share them with partners.

ON-LEVEL PRACTICE BOOK p. 207

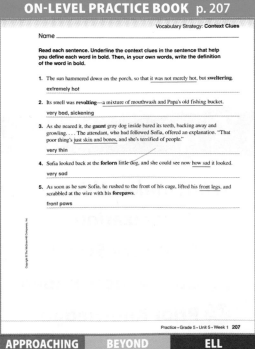

| APPROACHING p. 207 | BEYOND p. 207 | ELL p. 207 |

Develop Comprehension

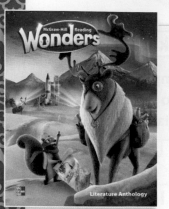

Ida B ...

Literature Anthology

Text Complexity Range

Lexile

740 — 970 — 1010

TextEvaluator™

23 — 49 — 51

Options for Close Reading

→ Whole Class

→ Small Group

→ Independent

CCSS Genre · Realistic Fiction

Ida B

...and Her Plans to Maximize Fun, Avoid Disaster, and (Possibly) Save the World

by Katherine Hannigan
illustrated by Steven Mach

Essential Question
What experiences can change the way you see yourself and the world around you?

Read about how Ida B's experience at school gives her a new perspective.

Go Digital!

346

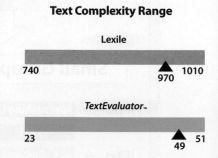

Access Complex Text

What makes this text complex?

▶ **Organization**

▶ **Sentence Structure**

▶ **Connection of Ideas**

▶ **Prior Knowledge**

▶ Organization

Explain that this selection is an excerpt, or a part, of a full-length novel. The text in italics on page 347 is an introduction that summarizes key information about what has happened so far in the story.

→ *What problems does Ida B have?* (Her mother has cancer, her family has to sell part of their orchard, and Ida B has to start attending public school.)

Ida B is an independent girl who loves spending time in her family's apple orchard. Unfortunately, Ida B's world turns upside down when her mother is diagnosed with cancer. Her parents are forced to sell part of the orchard to pay medical bills, which means that many of Ida B's beloved trees will be cut down to make room for houses. But that's just the beginning. Ida B finds out that her days of being home-schooled are coming to an end and that she must attend public school.

Upset by her mother's illness and her parents' decisions, Ida B stubbornly decides to distance herself from her parents and new classmates. Instead she chooses to spend time with her dog, Rufus, and cat, Lulu. But through the persistence and encouragement of her teacher, Ms. W., Ida B's iron will begins to dissolve.

1

347

Ida B and Her Plans to Maximize Fun, Avoid Disaster, and (Possibly) Save the World Copyright © 2004 by Katherine Hannigan. Used with permission of HarperCollins Children's Books.

LITERATURE ANTHOLOGY, pp. 346–347

Predictive Writing

Have students read the title, preview the illustrations, and write their predictions about what this selection will be about.

ESSENTIAL QUESTION

Ask a student to read aloud the Essential Question. Have students discuss how the story might help them answer the question.

Note Taking: Use the Graphic Organizer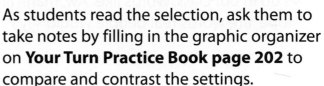

As students read the selection, ask them to take notes by filling in the graphic organizer on **Your Turn Practice Book page 202** to compare and contrast the settings.

1 **Skill: Character, Setting, Plot: Compare and Contrast Settings**

What was Ida B's home like before her mother got cancer? (Ida enjoyed the apple orchard and was home-schooled.) What was it like after? (The trees were cut down and she had to go to public school.) Record this information in your organizer.

→ *Why is this information about Ida B important?* (It will help readers understand Ida B's feelings and behavior during the story.)

Develop Comprehension

2 Genre: Realistic Fiction

Realistic fiction has characters and settings that could really exist. In what ways are the characters and setting realistic on page 348? (The teacher, Ms. W., says things a real teacher would say, such as "use your inside voice." The students are chattering and doing worksheets, which is something we do in our class. Words like "Aw, man!" and "Nope" are words real people would say.)

One day after lunch Ms. W. told the class, "I know it's time to read, but I don't think I can do it today. My voice is too tired."

She put her hand on her throat and scrunched up her face like something was paining her. It was the same face she'd make when Simone Martini was just about yelling across the room to Patrice Polinski, and Ms. W. would say, "Simone, use your inside voice. You are hurting my ears."

Everybody looked up from their chattering or worksheets at just about the same time, in exactly the same direction, with the same expression on their faces: a mix of thirty percent shock, twenty percent disbelief, and fifty percent plain old sad.

"Aw, man!" Matthew Dribble said right out loud.

I felt like the bottom had just dropped out of my stomach and everything I ate for lunch was tumbling around in my gut.

2 "Nope, my voice is just too tired," Ms. W. said, and, sure enough, it was sounding weak and raspy. "And we were going to read *Alexandra Potemkin and the Space Shuttle to Planet Z*, too. Well, that's disappointing."

348

A C T Access Complex Text

▶ Sentence Structure

Point out that this story has a first person narrator, Ida B. The sentences are written in a way that Ida B. might speak them, so the construction may be unusual. Have students reread paragraph three on page 348.

→ *How many sentences are in this paragraph?* (one)

→ *What is Ida describing?* (the responses of her classmates to Mrs. W.'s announcement)

→ *What does the sentence show about Ida B.?* (It shows how much detail she notices about a single moment, from the way classmates move, to the expressions on their faces.)

Ms. W. sat down, put her head in her hand, and her body wilted. Like not only was her voice tired, but every bone in her body needed a rest.

"Please?" begged Alice Mae Grunderman.

"Please, Ms. Washington?" asked Patrice and Simone at the same time, with the same moon-eyed face.

And then everybody got the idea, and it became a sort of song with a verse of "Please, Ms. Washington" and a chorus of "Please, please, please."

But Ms. W.'s voice was deteriorating at an alarming speed, because now she could only speak in a hoarse whisper, and everybody had to stop with their "please"ing just to hear her.

"I'm sorry, but I can't."

She paused, and we could all tell by the look on her face that she was thinking hard. So we stayed quiet to give her some room.

"Maybe," she said, looking up and forcing a weak smile, "we could have a guest reader, just for today?"

Well, it was hard to imagine anybody but Ms. W. reading, and we all just sat there for a minute. Then one by one, people started nodding their heads and looking at each other and nodding more and smiling, because nobody wanted to miss story time, not even Tina Poleetie, who usually slept through it.

And after a couple of minutes of that, people started looking at Ms. W., nodding their heads real hard, sticking out their chests, and saying out loud, "I think that's a great idea" and "Yes, let's have a guest reader today," because they were realizing that maybe they could be the Guest Reader and Star Student of the Afternoon. They wanted to remind Ms. Washington that not only were they **superb** readers, but wonderful human beings, too.

349

LITERATURE ANTHOLOGY, pp. 348–349

❸ Vocabulary: Context Clues

You can use sentence clues, such as comparisons, to figure out the meaning of *deteriorating*. How does Ms. W.'s voice sound at the bottom of page 348? (weak and raspy) Compare this to the way the author describes her voice in paragraph five on page 349. ("Now she could only speak in a hoarse whisper.") Use the comparison to define *deteriorating*. (getting worse)

❹ Strategy: Make Predictions

Teacher Think Aloud When I read, I use details in the story to predict what might happen next. I read that Ms. W.'s voice is too tired to read and she suggests a guest reader. I predict that many of the students will volunteer to read, but I don't think Ida will volunteer because I read on page 347 that she "distances herself" from her classmates. As I continue reading, I will look for details that help me confirm or revise this prediction.

ELL Restate long sentences as shorter, simpler sentences, replacing complex vocabulary with more common words. For example, restate paragraph three on page 348:

→ *Everybody stopped what they were doing. They looked up. They all looked at Ms. W. They were surprised. They didn't believe her. They were sad that she wouldn't read.*

→ *How does the class feel about Ms. W.'s decision?* (They are sad.)

Develop Comprehension

5 Literary Elements: Narrator

The narrator is the person who tells the story. Who is the narrator in *Ida B*? How can you tell? (Ida is the narrator. Ms. W. addresses the narrator as "Ida," so we know the pronouns *me* and *I* refer to Ida.)

6 Author's Craft: Word Choice

Authors choose words that bring a story to life. Reread the second paragraph on page 350. Why does the author use the phrase *like it was her last request* instead of simply saying Ms. W. spoke weakly? (Adding the phrase makes the narrator's style more colorful, humorous, and interesting.)

STOP AND CHECK

Make Predictions How will Ida B respond to Ms. W.'s request? (I think Ida will agree to read. She says that she is "hypnotized" by Ms. W. and compares herself to" a dog that would go fetch Ms. W.'s stick," so I think Ida will do whatever Ms. W. asks her to do.)

Especially Calvin "Big-Headed" Faribault, who actually raised his hand, and I just knew it was to volunteer out of the kindness of his big, fat, big-headed heart.

5 But Ms. W. didn't even look in Calvin's direction. "Ida, since I know you've read the book," she said to me weakly, like it was 6 her last request, "could you please read the first chapter today?"

Well, I was so shocked and embarrassed, sitting there with my mouth wide open, that I almost couldn't tell that all the other kids were staring at me with their mouths wide open, too. Making words into story music like Ms. W. did was the one thing I wanted to do more than just about anything in the world. But telling a story out loud in front of my class at Ernest B. Lawson Elementary School was nearly the last thing I'd want to do in my entire life. I was so confused about whether I should be happy or scared, I just sat there.

Ms. W. got up, walked over to me, put her face next to my **stunned** and frozen one, and whispered, "Ida, I need your help."

And there I was, hypnotized by that woman again. I was like a dog that would go fetch Ms. W.'s stick, even if it was in a snake's hole under a thorn bush that had just been sprayed by a skunk.

STOP AND CHECK

Make Predictions
How will Ida B respond to Ms. W.'s request? Look for details in the story to Make a Prediction.

350

A C T Access Complex Text

► Connection of Ideas

To understand Ida's references on page 351, students will need to connect with the information they read in the introduction on page 347.

→ *What is the Terrify the People Who Bought Our Land Project?* (This project is probably her plan to upset the people who bought part of their orchard.)

→ *Who is Rufus?* (Rufus is Ida's dog.)

Point out that when authors use a simile, or a comparison, they may continue it later in the story. Reread the last paragraph on page 350 with students.

→ *What simile does the author use?* (She compares Ida to a dog that would fetch a stick for Ms. W.)

→ *How does the author continue the simile on page 351?* (Ida is "trotting off, looking for that stick.")

I looked at Ms. W., just scared now, because I knew I was going to do it but I didn't know how.

"I know you'll be great," she croaked.

And in my head I was already trotting off, looking for that stick, even though I could smell the stink and the thorns were pricking me.

"Do you want to sit there, or in my chair?" Ms. W. asked.

"I'll sit here," I mumbled.

She set the book down on my desk, brought her chair over, sat down next to me, put her head back, and closed her eyes.

"Whenever you're ready, Ida," she rasped.

Ms. W. had given me quite a few books to read already because it only took me one or two days at the most to read them, unless I was working on my Terrify the People Who Bought Our Land Project. *Alexandra Potemkin and the Space Shuttle to Planet Z* was my favorite so far. It was Rufus's favorite, too.

I got tingly in my fingers thinking about opening up the book and reading those words out loud, making my voice go high and low, rough and smooth, like I did in my room. But my legs were shivering like they were out in a blizzard, and my stomach was flipping forward, then backward, forward, then backward, thinking about all of those people looking at me and hearing my voice.

I closed my eyes, put my right hand on top of the book, and passed it lightly across the cover. It was cool and smooth like a stone from the bottom of the brook, and it stilled me. A whole other world is inside there, I thought to myself, and that's where I want to be.

I opened the book and got ready to read the title, but I could feel everybody's eyes on me, crowding me so there was hardly any air. The only sounds that came out of me were little peeps, like a baby bird chirping *"Alexandra Potemkin and the Space Shuttle to Planet Z."*

(7)

351

LITERATURE ANTHOLOGY, pp. 350–351

(7) Skill: Character, Setting, Plot: Compare and Contrast Setting

How does Ida feel about reading? (She is excited about reading and enjoys it.) How are Ida's feelings about reading out loud different at home and at school? Paraphrase what she says. (At home, she feels confident and loves changing her voice as she reads. At school, she feels nervous about other people hearing her read aloud.) Add these details to your organizer.

At School
feels nervous about reading aloud

Ida B
likes reading

At Home
loves reading aloud in her room

ELL Students may need support understanding the simile on page 350 and other figurative language the author uses. Use restatement and pantomime to clarify "I was like a dog …," "My legs were shivering like they were out in a blizzard," and "It was cool and smooth like a stone."

→ *Does Ida B like Ms. W. or dislike her?* (She likes her.)

→ *Does Ida B feel calm or nervous about reading in class?* (nervous)

→ *How does touching the book make Ida B feel?* (calm)

Develop Comprehension

8 Skill: Make Inferences

How do you think Ida feels once she starts reading? What evidence supports your inference? Share your inference with a partner. (At first, Ida is nervous, but her nervousness disappears once she starts reading. The text says that "after a few minutes, I left that classroom and went into the story." This makes me think she has forgotten to be nervous.)

Ms. Washington, with her eyes still closed, leaned over and whispered, "You'll have to read louder, honey, so everyone can hear."

"Yes, ma'am," I whispered back. I took a deep breath, filled my stomach up with air, and then made my muscles squeeze it out, so it pushed a big gust of wind over my voice box and out my mouth.

"Chapter One," I bellowed. My voice was so loud it surprised me, and I jumped back a little in my chair.

But nobody laughed. They were listening.

The book is about Alexandra, and her parents think she is quite difficult, but actually she is a **genius** who is assisting the also-genius scientist Professor Zelinski in her quest to explore the lost planet Z. Alexandra gets into some trouble, but really she is just a very **focused** person.

8 At first, I was worrying about all of those people watching and listening. But after a few minutes, I left that classroom and went into the story. I was in Alexandra's laboratory instead of at school, and I was just saying out loud everything I saw her do or felt her feel. I let my voice tell the way she did it and saw it and felt it.

352

A C T Access Complex Text

▶ Organization

Explain that the author interrupts the sequence of events to give readers background information. Reread paragraph five on page 352.

→ *What is the purpose of this paragraph?* (It summarizes the plot of the story Ida reads to the class.)

→ *Does Ida actually leave the classroom in the next paragraph? Why does the author phrase it this way?* (No. It shows how she gets so involved in the story that she visualizes the setting and imagines the character's actions and feelings.)

And I was so looking forward to seeing what happened next, I forgot that I was reading. All of a sudden it was the end of the chapter and it was like I was snatched out of a dream and couldn't quite recall where I was. I looked around and saw I was sitting at a desk, there was a book in front of me, kids were staring at me, and slowly I remembered. **(9)**

I glanced over at Ms. W., and she smiled and whispered, "Thank you very much, Ida. That was lovely."

I handed Ms. W. the book, and we got back to work and everything was just like always, except that Ms. W. had to write all the instructions on the board instead of talking them.

At study time when I went to Ronnie's desk, he looked right in my eyes and said, "You read real good, Ida." And this time it was me staring down at my shoes like they might disappear if I didn't keep watching them.

My throat got stopped up so I could hardly say, "Thank you."

Nothing was different except the warm glow that was in my belly and my arms and my legs and my head and wouldn't go away. Even on the long, cruddy bus ride home.

STOP AND CHECK

Confirm or Revise Predictions How does Ida B respond to the challenge of reading in front of the class? What does this tell about her? Use the strategy Confirm or Revise Predictions.

353

LITERATURE ANTHOLOGY, pp. 352–353

---

9 Ask and Answer Questions

Generate a question of your own about the text and share it with a partner. For example, you might ask, "Why does Ida forget where she is?" To find the answer, paraphrase the first paragraph on page 353. (Ida gets so interested in what happens next that she forgets where she is.)

STOP AND CHECK

Confirm or Revise Predictions How does Ida B respond to the challenge of reading in front of the class? What does this tell you about her?

Teacher Think Aloud I predicted that although Ida would not volunteer, she would agree to read. Did what I read since confirm that prediction? Do I need to revise it?

Prompt students to apply the strategy in a Think Aloud and paraphrase the text that helped them confirm or revise this prediction.

Student Think Aloud Ida does read in front of the class, and she reads very well even though she is nervous at first.

ELL Read aloud paragraphs five and six on page 352. Restate the summary of the book in simpler language: *Alexandra and Professor Zelinksi explore planet Z. Alexandra gets into some trouble.* Point to the illustration of Ida reading and the space shuttle.

Ask:
→ *Do the students imagine the space shuttle, or is it real?* (They imagine it.)
→ *Is Ida enjoying the story, or does she dislike it?* (Ida enjoys it.)

Develop Comprehension

10 Skill: Character, Setting, Plot: Compare and Contrast Setting

What does Ida do after school? (She goes home and tells her parents about her day.) On an ordinary day, what does Ida feel like? (She feels unhappy. There is no joy floating inside her.) How does Ida feel today? (She is happy. There is a warmth and brightness inside of her.) Add these similarities and differences to your organizer.

Ordinary Day
feels unhappy

goes home after school

Today
feels happy, warm, and bright

"How was school today, Ida B?" Mama and Daddy would ask me every day after I first went back to Ernest B. Lawson Elementary School.

And every day I'd say, "It was O.K.," which now also stood for Overwhelming Kalamity.

"Well, what did you do?"

And I would just tell them the facts, hard and cold like my heart. "We had English, then we had science, then we went to the gym..." with no ups or downs or any part of the real me in there.

It was the same thing every day, and it was so boring and old and dry like stale bread I couldn't believe they kept trying for as long as they did.

After a while, though, they gave up. They'd just say, "How are you doing, Ida B?"

"O.K.," I'd mumble.

And that would be it. I didn't think they needed any more words than that to let them know that there was nothing close to joy floating around inside me.

10 But this day was different. The good feeling I had from reading that story out loud had been growing bit by bit all afternoon, till it ended up being a full-blown happiness by the time I got home. I'd keep thinking about what I did, and how it felt, and the warm brightness in me would get bigger and stronger and shinier every time.

354

A C T Access Complex Text

▶ **Organization**

Explain that authors often divide their writing into chapters at the natural breaks in a story. Point out that the shift in the setting from page 353 to page 354 is a natural break that the author could have used to start a new chapter.

→ *How does the setting change from page 353 to 354?* (The story moves from school to Ida's home.)

Explain that sometimes stories may flash back in time to give details about previous events. Read aloud the first paragraph on page 354.

→ *Which part of the first sentence helps you recognize that Ida is describing an earlier time?* (the phrase "would ask me every day after I first went back") *What is the purpose of going back?* (It helps readers understand how this day is different.)

My legs wanted to skip down the drive instead of walk. My mouth wanted to smile instead of scowl. My arms wanted to hug somebody instead of holding my backpack to my chest like a shield. My heart was horrified.

That happiness would not be satisfied staying inside me, either. It wanted to be shared. And it didn't mind who it shared itself with, including Mama and Daddy. **⑪**

I could just imagine having dinner with the two of them and all kinds of good feelings spilling out of me. There I'd be, grinning and gabbing, and the next thing you'd know Mama and Daddy would be thinking that I had transformed into my old perky self, that school was the best thing that ever happened to me, and maybe everything had worked out just fine after all.

And that would not be acceptable.

I was not going to let that happiness compromise my stand that, even though good things might happen in the world from time to time, nothing was right in my family or in my valley.

So I tried to get rid of some of it before dinnertime by **⑫** telling Rufus and Lulu about my Out Loud Reading Adventure. I sat them both on my bed, and while Lulu glared at Rufus with the deadliest **disdain**, I told them my story. Two thumps of Rufus's tail and a bored yawn from Lulu, though, didn't quiet that feeling down at all.

355

LITERATURE ANTHOLOGY, pp. 354–355

⑪ Author's Craft: Personification

Personification gives nonhuman things human characteristics. What human characteristic does the author give to happiness? What does Ida's reaction to her feeling of happiness tell you about Ida? (Happiness wouldn't be satisfied staying inside Ida, and it wanted to be shared, even with her parents. Ida's reaction tells me that Ida does not want to show her parents that she's happy.)

⑫ Strategy: Make Predictions

What do you think will happen at dinner time? Turn to a partner and make a prediction. Paraphrase details from the text that you used to help you make your prediction. Confirm or revise your prediction when you read on.

Student Think Aloud I think Ida won't be able to hide her happiness at dinner time because even though she tries to get rid of her happiness by talking to her pets, the feeling doesn't quiet down at all.

ELL Read aloud the first sentence on page 354, emphasizing the phrase *Daddy would ask me every day.* Explain that the word *would* is used to tell about an on-going action in the past.

→ Read aloud the second sentence, and point to *I'd.* Say: *This contraction stands for* I would.

→ *When did Ida tell her parents "It was O.K."?* (every day)

→ *How did Ida usually feel about school?* (She did not like it very much.) *How does she feel today?* (She feels good about it.)

Develop Comprehension

13 Skill: Character, Setting, Plot: Compare and Contrast Setting

What is Ida doing that she does every night? (She is eating dinner.) How does Ida usually act at dinner? (She doesn't talk.) How does she act tonight? (She's so happy that she has to talk about her day.) Add these details to your organizer.

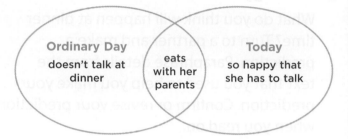

Ordinary Day
doesn't talk at dinner

eats with her parents

Today
so happy that she has to talk

By the time I sat down to dinner, that happiness was doing somersaults of excitement in my stomach. It was jiggling with delight at the **prospect** of telling Mama and Daddy about my day. It was itching to talk about how pleased I was with Ms. W. and the stories she gave me, and reading *Alexandra Potemkin and the Space Shuttle to Planet Z* most of all. It even wanted to start chatting about Ronnie.

I tried to get away before any of the pleasure leaked out of me.

"I'm not hungry. Can I be excused?" I asked.

Daddy, however, was prepared to spoil my plan. "You need to eat your dinner, Ida B," he said.

"Eat a little bit, honey," Mama added.

Well, by that point my heart was beating extra hard trying to keep that happiness down and quiet, and it was losing ground fast. I realized I'd have to let some of it out so I could rein the rest of it in and get control of my insides again.

I focused on my carrots, lining them up with my fork vertically, then horizontally, then zigzag. And I released one tiny tidbit of cheer.

"I read a book out loud to my class today," I said, struggling to keep my voice low and even.

Daddy looked up and stared, like he didn't quite know what to do with a bit of conversation from me.

"Oh, Ida B, did you like it?" Mama asked, smiling at me.

I just nodded my head.

"What did you read?" Mama kept on.

"Just a book about a girl," I told those carrots.

"Did you know the book, or was that the first time you read it?"

"I read it before."

"Were you scared reading in front of all of those people, Ida B?"

 I shrugged, like it was such a not-big-deal I could hardly recall. "Not really."

356

A C T Access Complex Text

▶ Prior Knowledge

Explain the description of Mama's "bald head" and "pale skin" in the last paragraph. Remind students that they learned in the introduction that Ida B's mother was diagnosed with cancer. Explain that one of the side effects of the treatment for cancer, chemotherapy, is that patients often lose their hair.

▶ Sentence Structure

Help students understand Ida B's struggle by breaking down complex sentences in paragraph six on page 356.

→ *What is Ida B's heart trying to do?* (It's trying to keep the happiness hidden.) *Is it working?* (No, it's losing ground.)

"Was it wonderful, baby?" Mama asked.

And as soon as Mama said it, I felt every drop of the goodness from reading that story. It flooded my insides, and I couldn't stop the happiness from pouring out of me.

"Yes," I said.

Then I looked right at Mama, for the first time in what seemed like forever, and she wasn't looking at me, but into me. She was pulling me to her with her eyes, like she used to do. All of a sudden I could see the light that was Mama's shining out of her eyes. I couldn't help smiling at it.

"Be careful," my heart warned me.

But I was having a hard time remembering that there was anything to be careful about. Because if I just looked at Mama's eyes, and not her bald head or her pale skin, I could tell that the part of her I thought had gone away forever was still there and glowing, only from deep down inside her.

> **STOP AND CHECK**
>
> Visualize How does Ida B's behavior toward her parents change? Visualizing her actions may help you.

357

LITERATURE ANTHOLOGY, pp. 356–357

STOP AND CHECK

Visualize How does Ida B's behavior toward her parents change? (At first, Ida refuses to talk to them and share any kind of happiness with them. However, reading aloud at school changes her, and she begins opening up to them again.)

Return to Predictions

Review students' predictions and purposes for reading. Ask them to answer the Essential Question. (Going to new places, meeting new people, and trying new things can all change the way we see ourselves and the world around us.)

→ *What does she realize?* (She would have to let out a little bit of happiness so she could hold in the rest and get control of herself again.)*What can you infer about Ida B. from this paragraph?* (Ida is stubbornly trying to feel the way she planned to feel, rather than how she actually feels.)

Explain "losing ground" and "rein it in" on page 356.

→ *"Losing ground" means "losing a battle or fight." What is Ida B fighting?* (expressing her happiness)

→ *"Rein it in" means "get control." Is it easy or hard for Ida B to rein in her happiness?* (hard)

Help students understand how Ida B tries to hide her feelings from her parents.

About the Author

Meet the Author

Katherine Hannigan

Have students read the biography of the author. Ask:

→ How does Katherine Hannigan incorporate elements of her own life into her stories?

→ What does Hannigan think about the character, Ida B?

Author's Purpose

To Entertain

Review that when authors write to entertain, they want readers to relate to their characters. Students may say that the author chose to write from Ida B's point of view so readers could know her thoughts and feelings throughout the story. By writing in the first person, the author helps readers connect to Ida B's experiences.

Author's Craft

Figurative Language

Explain that figurative language helps us think about familiar ideas in new ways. Discuss what figurative language adds to the writing.

→ Personification gives human qualities to nonhuman things. Example: *happiness was doing somersaults of excitement in my stomach.* (p. 356)

→ Have students find other examples of personification, such as *happiness would not be satisfied staying inside me* (p. 355) and *It was jiggling with delight at the prospect of telling Mom and Dad about my day.* (p. 356)

About the Author

Katherine Hannigan

spent her childhood in western New York, where she used her imagination to create stories with the dolls in her closet or paper characters cut from valentines. Years later, after earning a college degree in painting, she moved to Iowa to teach. Her new surroundings, which included several apple trees, inspired her to write *Ida B*.

Like Ida B, Katherine is an animal lover who owns a pet cat. However, the author doesn't see herself as being exactly like her storybook heroine. She says, "Hers is the life I would have chosen, if I could have. And I think I try to live up to her example—brave and true, full of fun, and fiercely loving."

Author's Purpose

Why do you think the author chose to write *Ida B* from Ida B's point of view? How did this help you understand the character?

358

LITERATURE ANTHOLOGY, pp. 358–359

Respond to Reading

Summarize

Summarize the events in the story that cause a change in Ida B. Details from your Venn Diagram may help you.

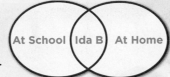

At School | Ida B | At Home

Text Evidence

1. How is Ida B a realistic character? Give examples of what she says and does that show she is a realistic character. **GENRE**

2. How does each setting affect Ida B's behavior? Explain how her behavior is similar and different in each place. **COMPARE AND CONTRAST**

3. What is the meaning of the word *hypnotized* in the last paragraph of page 350? Use the comparison in the surrounding sentences to help you figure out the word's meaning. **CONTEXT CLUES: COMPARISON**

4. Write about how Ida B interacts with characters in each setting. Explain how she responds to Ms. W. at school and her mother at home. **WRITE ABOUT READING**

Make Connections

Talk about how Ida B's experience of reading in class gave her a new perspective of herself and others. **ESSENTIAL QUESTION**

What other kinds of experiences in school might help students see themselves or the world around them differently? **TEXT TO WORLD**

359

Make Connections

Essential Question Have partners work together to write about and discuss how Ida B's experience of reading aloud in class changes her.

Text to World After students discuss other experiences in school that might help them see themselves or the world differently, have volunteers share specific examples of school experiences that changed them.

Respond to Reading

Summarize

Review with students the information from their organizers. Model how to use the information to summarize *Ida B . . . .*

Write About Reading: Compare and Contrast Ask students to write a paragraph telling how each setting affected Ida B throughout the story. Remind them to start with a sentence that names the title and genre. Have them share with a partner.

Text Evidence

1. **Genre** <u>Answer</u> Ida B is realistic because she responds to events in a way a real person would. <u>Evidence</u> When Ms. W. asks Ida to read in front of the class, she is "shocked and embarrassed." She is confused about whether she "should be happy or scared."

2. **Compare and Contrast** <u>Answer</u> Ida B is quiet and distant at school and at home. In each place, she does something she didn't want to do, but then doing it makes her happy. <u>Evidence</u> At first, Ida "distances herself from her parents and classmates." Later, "the good feeling [she] had from reading that story out loud has been growing."

3. **Context Clues** <u>Answer</u> *Hypnotized* means "controlled by suggestions." <u>Evidence</u> Ms. W. whispers to Ida, who compares herself to a dog that fetches a stick even if it's in a dangerous place.

4. **Write About Reading: Compare and Contrast** When Ida B is called on to read aloud, she is reluctant, but she does what Ms. W. asks. When her mother asks Ida about her day, Ida reluctantly tells her what she does but not how she feels.

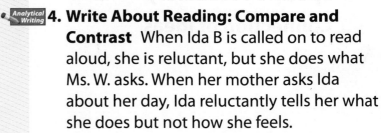

Develop Comprehension

Literature Anthology

"A Dusty Ride"

Text Complexity Range

Lexile

740 ▲ 1010
890

TextEvaluator™

23 ▲ 51
42

Options for Close Reading

→ Whole Class
→ Small Group
→ Independent

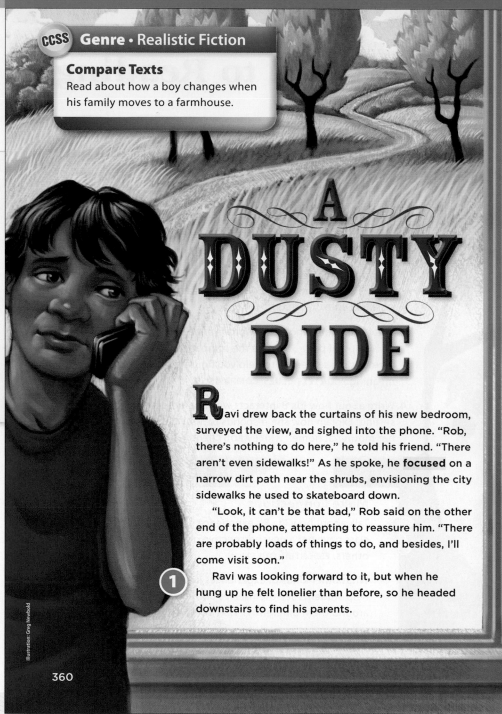

CCSS **Genre · Realistic Fiction**

Compare Texts
Read about how a boy changes when his family moves to a farmhouse.

A DUSTY RIDE

Ravi drew back the curtains of his new bedroom, surveyed the view, and sighed into the phone. "Rob, there's nothing to do here," he told his friend. "There aren't even sidewalks!" As he spoke, he **focused** on a narrow dirt path near the shrubs, envisioning the city sidewalks he used to skateboard down.

"Look, it can't be that bad," Rob said on the other end of the phone, attempting to reassure him. "There are probably loads of things to do, and besides, I'll come visit soon."

(1) Ravi was looking forward to it, but when he hung up he felt lonelier than before, so he headed downstairs to find his parents.

Illustration: Greg Newbold

360

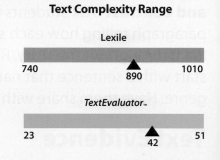

A C T Access Complex Text

What makes this text complex?

▶ **Specific Vocabulary**
▶ **Connection of Ideas**

▶ Specific Vocabulary

Review strategies for finding the meaning of unfamiliar words, such as using context clues, word parts, or a dictionary. Point out the word *enthusiasm* in the third paragraph on page 361.

→ *Reread the paragraph. Use the context to figure out the meaning of* enthusiasm. (excitement, interest)

"How's it going?" Ravi's mother asked, unpacking files in the office.

His dad adjusted a desk near the window, stood back to admire the room, and exclaimed, "What a change! To have fresh air right at my desk! Isn't it great, Ravi?"

Even though Ravi didn't agree, he didn't say so because it was his dad who had jumped at his company's offer to work outside the city. His mother, sharing his father's enthusiasm for a change, had decided to work from home, too, and before Ravi knew it, they had found a farmhouse to call home. Everyone, it seemed, had adjusted to the **transition** except Ravi.

He muttered a half-hearted reply, "Yeah, great," and then asked, "Can I go out for a little while?"

"Sure! Yes," his dad encouraged, "go explore!"

Outside, Ravi wondered, *Explore what?* Although he'd been there several weeks, he hadn't seen anything worth exploring. Then he remembered the dirt path he saw earlier and headed toward the side of the house.

Ravi had not gotten far down the path when he heard the hedgerow nearby rustle. As the shrubs began to shake, he detected heavy breathing and what sounded like a snort. Picturing a gigantic beast on the other side, Ravi retreated but then paused at the sound of a voice. He turned to see a woman on horseback emerge from the shrubs.

Seeing Ravi, the woman pulled the reins, stopping the horse in its tracks. He'd never seen a horse up close, and from his **perspective**, it was a towering giant.

361

LITERATURE ANTHOLOGY, pp. 360–361

Compare Texts *Analytical Writing*

Students will read another realistic fiction story about a new experience that changes a character. Ask students to do a close reading of the text to understand the content. Encourage students to **make predictions** or use other strategies they know that will help them. Then have students reread and take notes. Students will then use the text evidence that they gathered to compare this text with *Ida B....*

1 Ask and Answer Questions

What change is Ravi facing? How does he feel about it? Why?

Analytical Writing **Write About Reading** Discuss the questions with a partner. Write your response, and support it with evidence. (Ravi has moved to a new home outside the city. He is bored and lonely because he can't do the things he enjoyed in the city. For example, he misses having sidewalks for skateboarding. He says, "there's nothing to do here." He also misses his friends. After he speaks to Rob, he feels lonelier than ever.)

→ *What clues did you use?* (Ravi's dad "jumped at" the offer, and the words of Ravi's mother show that she is excited.)

→ Continue with *perceived, maneuvering,* and *retreated.* Have students verify the meanings in a dictionary.

 Explain these idiomatic expressions on page 361:

→ *To "jump at" an offer or a chance means "to take it with enthusiasm." Tell me a chance you would jump at.* (a chance to go to the beach)

→ *"Before I knew it" means "suddenly or quickly." Use it to tell someone that the bus arrived quickly.* (The bus arrived before I knew it.)

Develop Comprehension

2 Ask and Answer Questions

When Lila first asks Ravi if he'd like to ride Dusty, how does Ravi feel about the offer? Turn to a partner and paraphrase Ravi's reaction. (Ravi is not sure if he wants to accept. He is interested but also scared, because Dusty is so tall.)

3 Ask and Answer Questions

By the end of the story, how does Ravi feel about Dusty?

Analytical Writing **Write About Reading** Take notes about Ravi's feelings. (By the end of the story, Ravi loves Dusty and is not afraid of him. When he is riding Dusty, he forgets he is far from his friends. Ravi pets Dusty, and when Lila asks if he would like to learn horseback riding, he says that would be great.)

Illustration: Greg Newbold

"Hi!" the woman said, dismounting. "I hope we didn't scare you. I'm Lila, this is Dusty, and we live at the farm down the road. I was just coming by to welcome you!"

Sensing Ravi's hesitation, Lila explained, "No need to be scared of this old guy. In fact, Dusty is rather unique because he seems to sense your feelings: If you're scared, he gets nervous, but if you're calm, he's as cool as a cucumber." She gave him a wink, and added, "But Dusty has a way of calming people."

Ravi's parents came outside upon hearing Lila's voice, and, as the three introduced themselves, Ravi eyed the horse uneasily and noticed that the horse seemed to eye him, too.

Before Lila left, she said to them, "You should come on by! Maybe you'd even like to take a ride, Ravi? Dusty is a great tour guide."

"Yeah, maybe. Thanks," Ravi replied, but as he watched Lila ride away, the thought of being so high up on such an animal quickly turned his interest into doubt.

The next week, when he and his parents visited the farm, Lila and Dusty greeted them at the gate, eager for a ride. Ravi hadn't come up with a good excuse, and even if he had, Lila was hard to say no to. "C'mon up!" Lila said. "Grab my hand, set your left foot in that stirrup there, and then swing your leg over." Remembering what Lila had said the week before, Ravi took a deep breath to calm him, looked Dusty squarely in the eyes, and then climbed on.

As the horse settled under the added weight, Lila adjusted the reins and they took off at a measured trot.

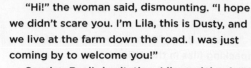

A C T Access Complex Text

▶ Connection of Ideas

Remind students that if a story refers to an earlier event that they don't remember, they can go back and reread. Read aloud the sentence, *Remembering what Lila had said the week before, Ravi took a deep breath to calm him, looked Dusty squarely in the eyes, and climbed on.*

→ *What did Lila tell Ravi the week before?* (She said that Dusty senses and responds to people's feelings. If they are scared, he gets nervous; if they are calm, he stays calm.)

→ *How does Ravi use what Lila said to help himself and Dusty?* (He breathes to calm himself then looks Dusty in the eyes to show he's not afraid.)

Lila toured Ravi around the farm, telling him about raising chickens, pigs, and cows, and every now and then asking, "Right Dusty?" as if he would reply. Dusty seemed to nod knowingly.

When they passed the horse stables, Ravi was surprised, and asked, "You have more horses?"

"Oh, yes, I have many," Lila replied. "But Dusty's my favorite."

I'm beginning to see why, thought Ravi. Riding with Dusty made him forget he was so far away from his friends.

As they trotted back to Ravi's waiting parents, Ravi petted Dusty, looking forward to his next visit.

"So what do you think? Would you like to learn horseback riding?" Lila asked. "Eventually you could ride Dusty yourself."

"Wow, that would be great!" Ravi replied, then turned to his parents and asked, "May I?" At that, Dusty jerked his head up as if asking, too. They all burst into laughter.

"Who could say no to that?" his Dad answered. **3**

Make Connections

How does Ravi's experience with Lila and Dusty change his view of his new home? **ESSENTIAL QUESTION**

Think of a character from another story who also adjusts to a change. How does each character's perspective change? **TEXT TO TEXT**

363

LITERATURE ANTHOLOGY, pp. 362–363

Make Connections ⟵ *Analytical Writing*

Essential Question

Suggest that students begin by listing what Ravi does not like about living in the country. Then have students explain how his experience changes his mind.

Text to Text Have partners compare their responses to the Ask and Answer Questions prompts with what they read in *Ida B....* Then have partners report to the class the similarities between the characters and their experiences in each story. (Both Ida B and Ravi face changes in their lives. Ida B is forced to go to a school she doesn't like, and Ravi has moved to the country, where he doesn't want to live. The perspectives of both characters change when they do something scary that turns out well. Ida B does a great job of reading a story to her class, and she starts to like school. Ravi rides a horse for the first time with a neighbor, and he enjoys it, so he now has something to look forward to doing in his new home.)

ELL In the second paragraph on page 362, point to the sentence that begins, "If you're scared ...." Point out the cognate nervous/*nervioso.*

→ Discuss the idiom "cool as a cucumber." Ask students to use the context, "if you're calm, he's as cool as a cucumber" to understand the meaning of the phrase. (calm)

→ *If you are nervous, are you as cool as a cucumber?* (no)

→ Word Study/Fluency

MINILESSON 20 Mins

Suffixes

OBJECTIVES

CCSS Know and apply grade-level phonics and word analysis skills in decoding words. Use combined knowledge of all letter-sound correspondences, syllabication patterns, and morphology (e.g., roots and affixes) to read accurately unfamiliar multisyllabic words in context and out of context. **RF.5.3a**

CCSS Read on-level prose and poetry orally with accuracy, appropriate rate, and expression on successive readings. **RF.5.4b**

Rate: 129–149 WCPM

ACADEMIC LANGUAGE
• *expression*
• Cognate: *expresión*

1 Explain

Explain that a suffix is a letter or group of letters added to a base word or root. The addition of a suffix changes the word's meaning and can also change the its part of speech. Review with students that the most common suffixes are *-s, -es* (plurals), *-ing* (present tense), and *-ed* (past tense).

2 Model

Write the following suffixes and sample words on the board. Model using the meaning of the suffix to determine the meaning of the sample word.

→ *-ful,* means "full of"; forms an adjective
The *joyful* children played in the snow.

→ *-ion, -tion, -ation, -ition,* mean "act or process of"; forms a noun
This book explains the *formation* of the mountain range.

→ *-less,* means "without"; forms an adjective
The *careless* skater tripped and fell.

→ *-ist,* means "person who"; forms a noun
The *artist* used clay to make her sculpture.

3 Guided Practice

Write the following words on the board. Using the first word, model underlining the suffix and then reading the word. Have students underline the suffixes in the remaining words. Then have them read the words chorally.

inspection	expression	chemist	discussion
helpful	violinist	description	fearful
creation	narration	healthful	biologist
admiration	stylist	fearless	thoughtful
wonderful	weightless	dentist	thankful

Refer to the sound transfers chart in the **Language Transfers Handbook** to identify sounds that do not transfer in Spanish, Cantonese, Vietnamese, Hmong, and Korean.

View "Miguel in the Middle"

Read Multisyllabic Words

Transition to Longer Words Write the following word pairs on the board. Have students read the first word in each pair. Then model how to read the multisyllabic words with suffixes. Point out each suffix as you read the words to help students gain awareness of these common word parts.

educate, education	penny, penniless
prepare, preparation	science, scientist
beauty, beautiful	breath, breathless
humor, humorless	purpose, purposeful
add, addition	piano, pianist
indent, indentation	resent, resentful

When finished, have students chorally read the words as you point to them in random order and at varying speeds.

Expression

Explain/Model Review with students how reading with expression can help them better understand and enjoy what they read. Turn to "Miguel in the Middle," **Reading/Writing Workshop** pages 310–313. Read page 312 aloud, using expression to illustrate how Miguel feels about math, his problems with trying to learn it, and his relief when he gains some understanding.

Remind students that you will be listening for their use of expression as you monitor their reading during the week.

Practice/Apply Have partners alternate reading paragraphs in the passage, modeling the expression you used.

Daily Fluency Practice

Students can practice fluency using **Your Turn Practice Book** passages.

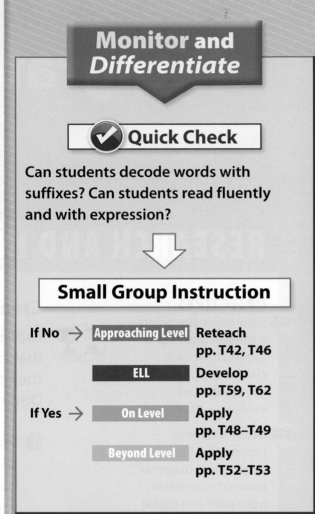

Monitor and *Differentiate*

✓ Quick Check

Can students decode words with suffixes? Can students read fluently and with expression?

Small Group Instruction

If No →	Approaching Level	Reteach pp. T42, T46
	ELL	Develop pp. T59, T62
If Yes →	On Level	Apply pp. T48–T49
	Beyond Level	Apply pp. T52–T53

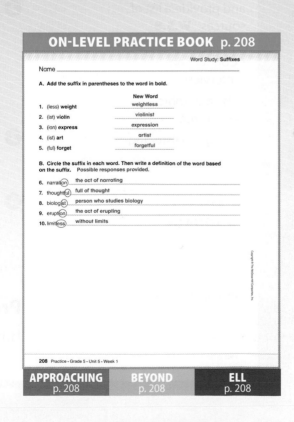

ON-LEVEL PRACTICE BOOK p. 208

APPROACHING p. 208	BEYOND p. 208	ELL p. 208

→ **Wrap Up the Week**
Integrate Ideas

👈 **Go** Digital

www.connected.mcgraw-hill.com
RESOURCES
Research and Inquiry

RESEARCH AND INQUIRY

New Perspectives

OBJECTIVES

 Summarize the points a speaker makes and explain how each claim is supported by reasons and evidence. **SL.5.3**

 Recall relevant information from experiences or gather relevant information from print and digital sources; summarize or paraphrase information in notes and finished work, and provide a list of sources. **W.5.8**

- Conduct an interview.
- Use a graphic organizer.
- Use good listening skills.

ACADEMIC LANGUAGE
- *cause, effect, interview*
- Cognates: *causa, efecto, entrevista*

Create a Cause-and-Effect Chart

COLLABORATE

Explain that each student will interview a partner about past experiences that changed the way that person sees herself or himself. Students will then create a cause-and-effect organizer for three different experiences. Discuss the following steps:

1 **Plan Interview Questions** Before they begin their interviews, students should plan questions they want to ask their partners. For example, they might ask, *What is one experience from your past that changed how you see yourself? What happened because of that experience?* Have students post their questions on the Shared Research Board. Caution students to be sensitive and not ask embarrassing or overly personal questions.

2 **Conduct the Interview** Have students ask their partners the interview questions. Encourage them to use good listening skills and to take notes about their partners' answers. Use the online Listening Checklist to evaluate their listening skills. Have them note any new questions and answers that arise during the interview.

3 **Guided Practice** Give partners a copy of Graphic Organizer 85. Model completing the graphic organizer using a cause-and-effect sequence.

4 **Create a Cause-and-Effect Chart** Have students use their notes to list three cause-and-effect sequences on the graphic organizer. Then have them draw a conclusion from the results of their interviews and summarize what they demonstrate about new perspectives.

Present the Cause-and-Effect Chart

Have partners share their cause-and-effect charts with another pair.

TEXT CONNECTIONS Analytical Writing

OBJECTIVES

CCSS Integrate information from several texts on the same topic in order to write or speak about the subject knowledgeably. **RI.5.9**

CCSS Review the key ideas expressed and draw conclusions in light of information and knowledge gained from the discussions. **SL.5.1d**

Text to Text

Cite Evidence Tell students they will work in groups to compare the experiences of the characters from the week's readings and how those experiences led to changes in perspective. Model how to make comparisons using examples from "Miguel in the Middle," **Reading/Writing Workshop** pages 310–313 and the **Leveled Readers**. Have students review the week's selections and their notes and graphic organizers. Help them set up an Accordion Foldable® to organize their findings. Students should record a brief summary of each main character's experience and how it changed his or her perspective. They should then draw some conclusions related to the week's Essential Question.

How Experiences Change Our Perspectives | Experiences at School | Experiences at Home | Changes in Perspectives | Conclusions

Dinah Zike's **FOLDABLES**®

Present Information Have groups meet to present their summaries and conclusions. Prompt discussion about the differences in students' interpretations of how and why the characters changed and in students' overall conclusions.

WRITE ABOUT READING Analytical Writing

OBJECTIVES

CCSS Draw evidence from literary or informational texts to support analysis, reflection, and research. **W.5.9**

Write an Analysis

Cite Evidence Explain that students will write about one of the stories they read this week. Using text evidence, students will analyze a story and give their opinion as to how well an author uses details to show setting.

Discuss how to analyze a story by asking *how* or *why* questions.

→ How does the author use details to make the setting clear?

→ Why is a setting easy to imagine?

Read and discuss the student model on **Your Turn Practice Book** page 209. Then have students choose a realistic fiction story they have read and review their notes about the setting. Have them write a paragraph to show how well the author used details to show setting. Remind students that good opinion writers present their reasons in a logical order and include complex sentences.

Present Your Ideas Ask partners to share their paragraphs and discuss how the evidence they cited from the text supports their opinions.

Readers to Writers

Reading/Writing Workshop

MINILESSON
10 Mins

Writing Traits: Organization

Strong Openings

Expert Model Explain that good writers create strong openings that make readers want to keep reading. The first sentence, or lead, grabs the readers' attention. In narrative writing, the opening often includes descriptive details that introduce the setting, the central person or character, and the problem he or she faces. It helps set the story in motion.

In informative writing, the opening introduces the topic and makes the writer's purpose clear. Writers may begin with a question, a short anecdote, or an interesting fact. They will state their main idea clearly so that readers know what they will learn from the writing.

In all writing, a strong opening is one that makes readers want to continue reading beyond the introduction.

COLLABORATE

Read aloud the expert model from "Miguel in the Middle." Ask students to think about how the first sentence includes an interesting phrase ("always been in the middle") to pique their curiosity. Have students talk with partners to discuss how the opening gives details about the main character and the problem he will face.

Student Model Remind students that a strong opening introduces the story in a way that captures the readers' interest. Read aloud the student model "My Trip to Ride Park." As students follow along, have them focus on how the writer's changes add interest.

COLLABORATE

Invite partners to talk about the model and the changes the writer made to improve the opening. Ask them to suggest other changes Laura could make to create a strong opening.

Go Digital

Expert Model

Student Model

OBJECTIVES

CCSS Introduce a topic clearly, provide a general observation and focus, and group related information logically; include formatting (e.g., headings), illustrations, and multimedia when useful to aiding comprehension. **W.5.2a**

CCSS Write routinely over extended time frames (time for research, reflection, and revision) and shorter time frames (a single sitting or a day or two) for a range of discipline-specific tasks, purposes, and audiences. **W.5.10**

ACADEMIC LANGUAGE

• *organization, opening, details*
• Cognates: *organización, detalles*

Genre Writing

Informational Text

For full writing process lessons and rubrics, see:
→ Informational Article, pp. T344–T349
→ Research Report, pp. T350–T355

 CCSS **Writing Traits** Organization

Readers to...

When writers organize their stories, they start with a **strong opening** to make readers want to continue reading. Descriptive details that give the writing a sense of style, character, and place can help make an opening strong. Reread the opening lines from "Miguel in the Middle" to see how the writer grabs the reader's interest.

Strong Openings

How does the opening sentence grab your attention? Identify three details in the paragraph that help explain the opening sentence.

Expert Model

For as long as I can remember, I've always been in the middle. I'm the middle child in my family. I've always sat in the middle of the classroom in school. Even my first and last names, Miguel Martinez, start with an M—the middle letter of the alphabet.

318

Writers

Laura wrote a narrative about her first visit to an amusement park. Read her revised opening.

Student Model

My Trip to Ride Park

It was ~~lots of fun~~. the most exciting day of my life My family and I visited Ride Park for the first time. Friends had told me ~~about the~~ rides. how great the rides were Yet "great" does not begin to describe them. how I felt on When you soar 40 stories high, get tossed like a salad, and dive 30 feet under water, it doesn't just feel great. It feels amazing!!!

319

Editing Marks

∧ Add
∧ Add a comma.
✐ Take out.
SP Check spelling.
≡ Make a capital letter.

Grammar Handbook

Independent and Dependent Clauses
See page 453.

Your Turn

✓ Identify details that Laura included to show that her story is realistic fiction.
✓ Look at independent and dependent clauses Laura used.
✓ Tell how Laura's changes created a stronger opening.

Go Digital!
Write online in Writer's Workspace

READING/WRITING WORKSHOP, pp. 318–319

ELL ENGLISH LANGUAGE LEARNERS SCAFFOLD

Provide support to help English Language Learners understand the writing trait.

Beginning	Intermediate	Advanced/High
Respond Orally Have students complete the sentence frames about the Expert Model. *The narrator says that he is always in the middle. He is the _____ child in his family. He sits in the _____ of the classroom. His names start in the _____ of the alphabet.*	**Practice** Ask students to complete the sentence frames. *The narrator repeats the word _____. He is the middle _____. He sits in the middle of the _____. Both of his names start with _____. This makes me wonder how the narrator feels about always being _____.*	**Understand** Check for understanding. Ask: *How does the repetition of the word* middle *help create a strong opening? What other ways could the writer have created a strong opening?*

Writing Every Day: Organization

 DAY **1**

DAY **2**

Writing Entry: Strong Openings

Prewrite Provide students with the prompt below.

Describe a place you have visited. Include a strong opening.

Have partners list different places they have visited. Ask them to jot down details about each place and their visit to it that they might include in their drafts.

Draft Have each student select a place to write about. Remind students to include a strong opening in their drafts.

Focus on Strong Openings

Use **Your Turn Practice Book** page 210 to model writing a strong opening.

I had waited a long time for a trip to the water park. The biggest slide was really high, but it was supposed to be fun.

Model revising the last sentence to add interest.

I craned my neck to find the top of the tallest slide and shuddered.

Discuss how adding details grabs the readers' attention. Guide students to revise the first sentence to add interest.

Writing Entry: Strong Openings

Revise Have students revise their writing from Day 1 to make the opening stronger. Encourage them to include engaging details to grab readers' interest.

Use the **Conferencing Routines**. Circulate among students and stop briefly to talk with individuals. Provide time for peer review.

Edit Have students use Grammar Handbook page 453 in the **Reading/Writing Workshop** to edit for errors in independent and dependent clauses.

Conferencing Routines

Teacher Conferences

STEP 1

Talk about the strengths of the writing.

The opening drew me in. The details you included make the place sound exciting.

STEP 2

Focus on how the writer uses the target trait for the week.

The details about _____ showed your feelings about the place. Try adding a sentence that hints at what you will tell about in the body paragraphs. That will make me want to keep reading.

STEP 3

Make concrete suggestions for revisions. Have students work on a specific assignment, such as those to the right, and then meet with you to review progress.

DAY 3

Writing Entry: Strong Openings

Prewrite Ask students to search their Writer's Notebooks for another topic they might like to write about. Or, provide a prompt, such as the following:

Tell about an activity you do with your friends. Include a strong opening.

Draft Once students have chosen their topics, ask them to create a chart with details they might include in their writing. Students can use their charts to begin their drafts.

DAY 4

Writing Entry: Strong Openings

Revise Have students revise the draft writing from Day 3 by adding descriptive details that make their opening clearer and more interesting. As students revise, hold teacher conferences with individual students. You may also wish to have students work with partners to peer conference.

Edit Invite students to review the rules for dependent and independent clauses on Grammar Handbook page 453 in the **Reading/Writing Workshop** and then check their drafts for errors.

DAY 5

Share and Reflect

Discuss with students what they learned about strong openings. Invite volunteers to read and compare draft text with text that has been revised. Have students discuss the writing by focusing on the importance of a strong opening. Allow time for individuals to reflect on their own writing progress and record observations in their Writer's Notebooks.

Suggested Revisions

Provide specific direction to help focus young writers.

Focus on a Sentence

Read the draft and target one sentence for revision. *Rewrite the lead sentence so that it better grabs the readers' attention.*

Focus on a Section

Underline a section that needs to be revised. Provide specific suggestions. *The opening draws me in, but it could include more descriptive details to make your topic clearer.*

Focus on a Revision Strategy

Underline a section. Have students use a specific revision strategy, such as rearranging. *The sentences in the opening are out of order. Rearrange them so that the details about _____ come first.*

Peer Conferences

Focus peer response groups on creating a strong opening.

- ☑ Does the writing include an interesting first sentence?
- ☑ Does the opening introduce the topic clearly?
- ☑ Are the sentences in a logical order?
- ☑ What can be added to the opening to make the reader want to keep reading?

→ Grammar: Clauses

Reading/Writing Workshop

OBJECTIVES

CCSS Demonstrate command of the conventions of standard English grammar and usage when writing or speaking. Produce simple, compound, and complex sentences. **L.3.1i**

CCSS Explain the function of conjunctions, prepositions, and interjections in general and their function in particular sentences. **L.5.1a**

Proofread sentences.

Go Digital

Clauses

Grammar Activities

DAY 1

DAILY LANGUAGE ACTIVITY

The oakville daily told about the festival. There will be games rides and music. (1: Oakville Daily; 2: games, rides,)

Introduce Independent and Dependent Clauses

→ A **clause** is a group of words that has a subject and a predicate.

→ An **independent clause** has one complete subject and one complete predicate and can stand alone as a sentence. *Max plays the guitar.*

→ A **dependent clause** cannot stand alone as a sentence. It is introduced by a **subordinating conjunction** such as *if* or *because*. *I will sing if Max plays the guitar.*

Have partners discuss clauses using page 453 of the Grammar Handbook in **Reading/Writing Workshop**.

DAY 2

DAILY LANGUAGE ACTIVITY

I couldv'e gone to the movies. Carla went to the movies, Sharon went with her. (1: could've; 2: movies, and)

Review Independent and Dependent Clauses

Remind students that an independent clause can stand alone as a sentence and a dependent clause cannot.

Introduce Complex Sentences

→ A **complex sentence** contains an independent clause and a dependent clause. *I asked Sam for help because he has fixed many computers.*

→ A comma is used after an introductory dependent clause. *Whenever my cousins visit, we play football.*

TALK ABOUT IT

COLLABORATE

USE BOTH KINDS OF CLAUSES

Have partners take turns using an independent clause to tell about a change that affected a friendship. The listening partner should repeat the sentence, adding a dependent clause.

ADD A CLAUSE

Have partners write three dependent clauses and trade them with another pair. One partner should read the clause aloud; the other should add an independent clause to make a full sentence.

DAY **3**

We fed the puppys at the animal shelter. I took some treats and put it in there bowls. (1: puppies; 2: them; 3: their)

Mechanics and Usage: Appositives

→ An appositive is a noun or noun phrase that explains or describes a noun or pronoun next to it.

→ An appositive may come before or after a noun or a pronoun.

→ Commas are used to set off many appositives. *Mrs. Kane, an archeologist, studies artifacts.*

As students write, refer them to Grammar Handbook page 479.

DAY **4**

DAILY LANGUAGE ACTIVITY

Sylvia a friend from school came to my party. Her and me have been friends a long time. (1: Sylvia,; 2: school,; 3: She and I)

Proofread

Have students correct errors in these sentences:

1. I read a book, while I was waiting for dance class. (book while)

2. If you go outside now you will be cold. (now,)

3. We missed the movie. Because we were late. (movie because)

4. When the competition was over Mrs. Sanders the principal announced the winner. (1: over,; 2: Sanders,; 3: principal,)

Have students check their work using Grammar Handbook pages 453 and 479.

DAY **5**

DAILY LANGUAGE ACTIVITY

We meet at the Park on sundays. After we play soccer we have lunch. (1: park; 2: Sundays; 3: soccer,)

Assess

Use the Daily Language Activity and Grammar Practice Reproducibles page 105 for assessment.

Reteach

Use Grammar Practice Reproducibles pages 101–104 and selected pages from the Grammar Handbook for additional reteaching. Remind students that it is important to use independent and dependent clauses correctly as they speak and write.

Check students' writing for use of the skill and listen for it in their speaking. Assign Grammar Revision Assignments in their Writer's Notebooks as needed.

See Grammar Practice Reproducibles pp. 101–105.

PASS IT ON

Have one group begin a story with a complex sentence, then pass the story to the next group. Continue until all groups have added a complex sentence. Then read aloud the story.

STORY SUMMARY

Have partners take turns summarizing a story the class has read, using at least one complex sentence. Ask the listening partner to identify the complex sentence and the subordinating conjunction.

PLAY AN APPOSITIVE QUIZ

Have students write down three independent clauses about three famous people and place them in a pile. Students will take turns selecting a paper and adding an appositive.

Spelling: Suffixes

OBJECTIVES

CCSS Spell grade-appropriate words correctly, consulting references as needed.
L.5.2e

Spelling Words

serious	comfortable	microscopic
furious	finally	allergic
eruption	destruction	scientific
usually	apparently	safety
direction	completely	activity
position	eventually	sickness
forgetful	carefully	

Review distance, ambulance, substance
Challenge aquatic, mathematics

Differentiated Spelling

Approaching Level

serious	comfortable	electric
furious	finally	allergic
eruption	usually	pacific
happily	destruction	safety
direction	sadly	activity
position	eventually	sickness
forgetful	carefully	

Beyond Level

seriously	comfortably	allergic
furiously	subconscious	scientific
aquatic	destruction	enjoyable
eruption	unforgettable	charitable
sensible	questionable	microscopic
eventually	mathematics	argument
forgetful	improvement	

DAY 1

Assess Prior Knowledge

Read the spelling words aloud, emphasizing the suffix in each word.

Point out the suffixes in *erup**tion***, *aller**gic***, and *final**ly***. Draw a line under the suffix as you say the word. Explain that a suffix is one or more letters added to the end of a word. A suffix changes the meaning and part of speech of the base word.

Demonstrate sorting spelling words according to the part of speech determined by the suffix. Sort a few words with the same part of speech. Ask students to name other everyday words with these suffixes.

Use the Dictation Sentences from Day 5 to give the pretest. Say the underlined word, read the sentence, and repeat the word. Have students write the words. Then have students check their papers.

DAY 2

Spiral Review

Review words with the suffixes *-ance* and *-ence*. Read each sentence below, repeat the review word, and have students write the word.

1. The <u>distance</u> is not far.
2. An <u>ambulance</u> arrived at the scene.
3. An unknown <u>substance</u> was leaking from the car.

Have students trade papers and check their spellings.

Challenge Words. Review this week's suffixes. Read each sentence below, repeat the challenge word, and have students write the word.

1. The whale is an <u>aquatic</u> mammal.
2. Ryan loves <u>mathematics</u> because he enjoys working with numbers.

Have students check and correct their spellings and write the words in their word study notebooks.

 # WORD SORTS

COLLABORATE

OPEN SORT

Have students cut apart the **Spelling Word Cards** in the Online Resource Book and initial the back of each card. Have them read the words aloud with partners. Then have partners do an **open sort**. Have them record their sorts in their word study notebooks.

PATTERN SORT

Complete the **pattern sort** from Day 1 by using the Spelling Word Cards. Point out the different suffixes and each word's part of speech. Partners should compare and check their sorts. Have them record their sorts in their word study notebooks.

DAY 3

Word Meanings

Have students copy the definitions below into their word study notebooks. Say the definitions aloud. Then ask students to write the spelling word that matches each definition.

1. an illness or disease (sickness)
2. an explosion (eruption)
3. totally; entirely (completely)

Challenge students to create definitions for their other spelling, review, or challenge words. Have partners share their definitions and match words to the correct definitions.

See Phonics/Spelling Reproducibles pp. 121–126.

SPEED SORT

Have partners do a **speed sort** to see who is fastest. Then have them do a word hunt in this week's readings to find words with the suffixes found in this week's words. Have them record the words in their word study notebooks.

DAY 4

Proofread and Write

Write these sentences on the board. Have students circle and correct each misspelled word. Ask them to use a print or a digital dictionary to check and correct their spellings.

1. Micrascopic creatures are studied in sientific labs. (Microscopic, scientific)
2. Gene finaly found an aktivity he enjoys. (finally, activity)
3. It is important to think about the safetey of people who are alergic to peanuts. (safety, allergic)
4. Dad usally has a great sense of direcshun. (usually, direction)

Error Correction Remind students that the suffix is often a separate syllable added to the base word. Some suffixes, such as -ic, affect the spelling of the base word.

BLIND SORT

Have partners do a **blind sort:** one reads a Spelling Word Card; the other tells under which part of speech it belongs. Have partners compare and discuss their sorts. Then have partners play Go Fish with the cards, using parts of speech as the "fish."

DAY 5

Assess

Use the Dictation Sentences for the posttest. Have students list the misspelled words in their word study notebooks. Look for students' use of these words in their writings.

Dictation Sentences

1. He had a <u>serious</u> look on his face.
2. Mom was <u>furious</u> when the cat broke the vase.
3. The volcanic <u>eruption</u> happened 20 years ago.
4. Kevin <u>usually</u> eats lunch at noon.
5. We went in the wrong <u>direction</u>.
6. The switch was in the "on" <u>position</u>.
7. My sister is very <u>forgetful</u>.
8. My bed is very <u>comfortable</u>.
9. I <u>finally</u> finished the essay.
10. The fire caused a lot of <u>destruction</u>.
11. She <u>apparently</u> left the building.
12. I <u>completely</u> lost track of time.
13. He will <u>eventually</u> finish his work.
14. I packed the box very <u>carefully</u>.
15. The <u>microscopic</u> ants were hard to see.
16. Dad is <u>allergic</u> to cats.
17. It was a <u>scientific</u> study.
18. <u>Safety</u> is my number one concern.
19. My favorite <u>activity</u> is running.
20. Molly's <u>sickness</u> lasted for days.

Have students self-correct their tests.

SPELLING **T37**

Build Vocabulary

DAY 1

DAY 2

OBJECTIVES

 CCSS Use context (e.g., cause/effect relationships and comparisons in text) as a clue to the meaning of a word or phrase. **L.5.4a**

 CCSS Demonstrate understanding of figurative language, word relationships, and nuances in word meanings. Use the relationship between particular words (e.g., synonyms, antonyms, homographs) to better understand each of the words. **L.5.5c**

Vocabulary Words

disdain	prospect
focused	stunned
genius	superb
perspective	transition

Go Digital

Vocabulary

Vocabulary Activities

Connect to Words

Practice this week's vocabulary.

1. Tell about a time you felt **disdain** for something.
2. At what time of day are you most **focused**?
3. Whom do you feel is a musical **genius** and why?
4. Describe an event that changed your **perspective**.
5. How would you feel about the **prospect** of taking a trip to Alaska?
6. In what situations might a person be **stunned**?
7. Describe a **superb** meal.
8. What **transition** might be difficult for someone?

Expand Vocabulary

Help students generate different forms of this week's words by adding, changing, or removing inflectional endings.

→ Draw a T-chart on the board. Write *prospect* in the first column. Then write *prospects* in the second column. Read aloud the words with students.

→ Have students share sentences using each form of *prospect*.

→ Students should add to the chart for *genius* and *transition*, and then share sentences using the different forms of the words.

→ Have students copy the chart in their word study notebooks.

BUILD MORE VOCABULARY

COLLABORATE

ACADEMIC VOCABULARY

→ Display *approached, transformed,* and *persistence*.

→ Define the words and discuss their meanings with students.

→ Write *approachable* under *approached*. Have partners write other words with the same root and define them. Then have partners ask and answer questions using the words.

→ Repeat with *transformed* and *persistence*.

SYNONYMS AND ANTONYMS

Remind students that synonyms are words with similar meanings and antonyms are words with opposite meanings.

→ Have partners choose a vocabulary word and use a thesaurus to look up its synonyms and antonyms.

→ Have students write the vocabulary word they chose and its synonyms and antonyms in their word study notebooks.

DAY 3

Reinforce the Words

Review vocabulary words from this week and last week. Have students orally complete each sentence stem.

1. Lisa felt <u>disdain</u> for the task because ____.
2. One famous <u>genius</u> is ____.
3. I was so <u>focused</u> that ____.
4. I am excited by the <u>prospect</u> of a <u>superb</u> ____.
5. I was <u>stunned</u> that ____.
6. The music was <u>meaningful</u> to ____.
7. The <u>plumes</u> on the ostrich costume were ____.
8. The <u>barren</u> land was ____.
9. His <u>expression</u> when he won showed ____.

DAY 4

Connect to Writing

→ Have students write sentences in their word study notebooks using this week's vocabulary.

→ Tell them to write sentences that provide word information they learned from this week's readings.

→ Provide the Day 3 sentence stems 1–5 for students needing extra support.

Write About Vocabulary Have students write something they learned from this week's words in their word study notebooks. For example, they might write about the contributions a *genius* has made to society or about a change in their own *perspective*.

DAY 5

Word Squares

Ask students to create Word Squares for each vocabulary word.

→ In the first square, students write the word (e.g, *stunned*).

→ In the second square, students write their own definition of the word and any related words, such as synonyms (e.g., *shocked, astonished*).

→ In the third square, students draw a simple illustration that will help them remember the word (e.g., a person with a surprised face).

→ In the fourth square, students write nonexamples, including antonyms for the word (e.g., *unsurprised, indifferent*).

Have partners discuss their squares.

CONTEXT CLUES

Remind students to look for comparisons to help figure out the meanings of unfamiliar words.

→ Display **Your Turn Practice Book pages 203–204.** Model how to compare and contrast nearby text to figure out the meaning of *sweltering* in the first paragraph on page 203.

→ Have students complete page 207.

→ Partners can confirm meanings in a print or an online dictionary.

SHADES OF MEANING

Help students generate words related to the concept of *perspective*. Draw a word web and write *perspective* in the center.

→ Have partners generate related words to add to the web.

→ Add words and phrases not included such as *first person, third person, eyewitness, angle, painting,* and *editorial*.

→ Ask students to copy the word web in their word study notebooks.

MORPHOLOGY

Use *transition* as a springboard for students to learn more words.

→ Have students research the origin of *transition* using a dictionary.

→ Elicit from students that the word comes from the Latin *transire*, meaning "to go across," or "to pass over or by."

→ Ask partners to do a search for other words with the same origin and record them in their word study notebooks (e.g., *transit, transitory, transient*).

Approaching Level

Leveled Reader:
King of the Board

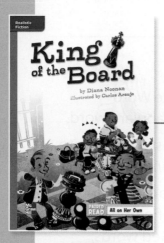

Lexile 740
TextEvaluator™ 55

OBJECTIVES

CCSS Quote accurately from a text when explaining what the text says explicitly and when drawing inferences from the text. **RL.5.1**

CCSS Compare and contrast two or more characters, settings, or events in a story or drama, drawing on specific details in the text (e.g., how characters interact). **RL.5.3**

CCSS Read on-level prose and poetry orally with accuracy, appropriate rate, and expression on successive readings. **RF.5.4b**

ACADEMIC LANGUAGE

• *realistic fiction, make predictions, compare, contrast, characters*

• Cognates: *ficción realista, predicciones, comparar, contrastar*

Before Reading

Preview and Predict

→ Read the Essential Question with students.

→ Have students preview the title, table of contents, and first page of *King of the Board*. Students should use the text and illustrations to predict what they think the selection will be about. They can confirm or revise their predictions as they read on.

Review Genre: Realistic Fiction

Tell students that this text is realistic fiction. In realistic fiction, the setting is a place or places that could be found in real life. The characters are like real people. The events and problems the characters experience are similar to those experienced by real people. Have students identify features of realistic fiction in *King of the Board*.

During Reading

Close Reading

Note Taking: Ask students to use their graphic organizer as they read.

Pages 2–4 *Turn to a partner and explain how Clinton is different from the other members of his family.* (They all enjoy playing sports, but he does not.) *What context clues on page 3 help you identify the meaning of* disdain? (*scorn* and *wouldn't want to be around me*)

Pages 5–6 *What interests Clinton at the new games area?* (a giant checkerboard with large chess pieces) *Turn to a partner and make a prediction about what Clinton might do next, based on details in the text.* (He may ask to play chess on the giant board or he might decide to join a chess club.)

Pages 7–11 *Turn to a partner and tell if your prediction matched the text or how you revised it.* (It matched the text. Clinton decides to follow the players' advice and join a chess club.) *Explain how Clinton's obsession with chess affects his actions.* (He uses the Internet and library books to learn about chess. He watches two women playing and gives them some suggestions.)

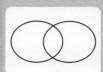

Use Graphic Organizer

Pages 12–13 *How does Clinton begin to resemble the rest of his family?* (He scrambles to get out of the house to get involved in his sport.) *Turn to a partner and make a prediction about who will watch the tournament and if Clinton will win.* (Clinton's parents and brother Adam will go to the tournament, and Clinton will win the trophy.)

Page 14 *Turn to a partner and tell if your prediction matched the text or how you revised it.* (It did not match the text. I revised it after I read that Clinton's entire family attends, and he does not win the trophy.) *What award does Clinton win?* (Most Promising New Player)

Page 15 *What is in the box?* (a chess set) *How does Clinton's experience change the way he thinks of himself?* (He realizes that, like his family members, he has found his sport. He feels very happy and proud.)

After Reading

Respond to Reading Revisit the Essential Question and ask students to complete the Text Evidence Questions on page 16.

Analytical Writing **Write About Reading** Check that students have correctly compared and contrasted the settings on pages 2 and 12.

Fluency: Expression

Model Model reading page 3 with appropriate expression. Next, read the passage aloud and have students read along with you.

Apply Have students practice reading the passage with partners.

PAIRED READ

"All on Her Own"

Make Connections:
Write About It **Analytical Writing**

Before reading, ask students to note that the genre of this text is also realistic fiction. Then discuss the Essential Question. After reading, ask students to write connections between *King of the Board* and "All on Her Own."

Leveled Reader

FOCUS ON LITERARY ELEMENTS

Students can extend their knowledge of literary elements by completing the figurative language activity on page 20.

Literature Circles

Ask students to conduct a literature circle using the Thinkmark questions to guide the discussion. You may wish to have a whole-class discussion, using both selections in the Leveled Reader, about how our experiences can change the way we see ourselves and our world.

Level Up

Level-up lessons available online.

IF students read the **Approaching Level** fluently and answered the questions

THEN pair them with students who have proficiently read the **On Level** and have students

• echo-read the **On Level** main selection.

• identify two characteristics that help them know that the story is realistic fiction.

A C T Access Complex Text

The **On Level** challenges students by including more **figurative language** and **complex sentence structures**.

Approaching Level

Word Study/Decoding

REVIEW WORDS WITH SUFFIXES

 TIER **2**

OBJECTIVES

 Know and apply grade-level phonics and word analysis skills in decoding words. Use combined knowledge of all letter-sound correspondences, syllabication patterns, and morphology (e.g., roots and affixes) to read accurately unfamiliar multisyllabic words in context and out of context. **RF.5.3a**

Decode words with suffixes.

 I Do Review with students that a suffix is a group of letters added to the end of a base word or root that changes that word's meaning and often its part of speech. Write the word *hope* on the board and read it aloud. Remind students that *hope* is a noun. Then explain that the suffix *-ful* means "full of." Add *-ful* to the end of *hope*. Read the word *hopeful* aloud and explain that it is an adjective meaning "full of hope."

 We Do Write the suffix *-less* on the board. Review that this suffix means "without." Then write the word *hopeless*. Read the word aloud and model using the meaning of the suffix to determine that *hopeless* means "without hope." Write the words *careful* and *careless* on the board. Guide students to use the meaning of the suffix to define each word.

 You Do Add the following examples to the board: *joyful, joyless*. Have students identify each suffix, tell its meaning, and give the meaning of the word in which it appears.

BUILD WORDS WITH SUFFIXES

TIER **2**

OBJECTIVES

 Use combined knowledge of all letter-sound correspondences, syllabication patterns, and morphology (e.g., roots and affixes) to read accurately unfamiliar multisyllabic words in context and out of context. **RF.5.3a**

Build words with suffixes.

 I Do Tell students that they will build new words using suffixes. Write the suffixes *-ful, -less, -ion,* and *-ist* and the words *violin, discuss, clue,* and *play* on the board. Model reading each suffix or word aloud.

 We Do Work with students to combine the words and suffixes to form new words. Have them chorally read the words *playful, clueless, discussion,* and *violinist*.

 You Do Write other words on the board, such as *aim, help, inspect,* and *art*. Ask partners to add the suffixes to form new words. Then have them determine their meanings. Finally, have students share with the class the words they built.

PRACTICE WORDS WITH SUFFIXES

OBJECTIVES
Know and apply grade-level phonics and word analysis skills in decoding words. Use combined knowledge of all letter-sound correspondences, syllabication patterns, and morphology (e.g., roots and affixes) to read accurately unfamiliar multisyllabic words in context and out of context. **RF.5.3a**

Practice words with suffixes.

 I Do Write these words on the board: *cheerful, tireless, soloist, preparation.* Read each word aloud, identify each suffix and its meaning, and then give the meaning of each word.

 We Do Write the words *celebration, harmless, tasteful, reaction, exhibition,* and *scientist* on the board. Model how to decode and figure out the meaning of the first word. Then have students decode and give the meaning of each of the remaining words. As necessary, help students identify and define the suffix in each word.

You Do To provide additional practice, write the following words on the board. Read aloud the first word, identify the suffix and its meaning, and give the word's meaning.

faithful	cloudless	painful	competition
airless	addition	nameless	animation
pianist	flavorful	collection	humorless

Then have students read the remaining words aloud. Ask them to identify each suffix and its meaning and then give the meaning of each word.

Afterward, point to the words in the list in random order for students to read chorally.

ENGLISH LANGUAGE LEARNERS

For the **ELLs** who need **phonics, decoding,** and **fluency** practice, use scaffolding methods as necessary to ensure students understand the meaning of the words. Refer to the **Language Transfers Handbook** for phonics elements that may not transfer in students' native languages.

Approaching Level

Vocabulary

TIER 2

REVIEW HIGH-FREQUENCY WORDS

 OBJECTIVES
Acquire and use accurately grade-appropriate general academic and domain-specific words and phrases, including those that signal contrast, addition, and other logical relationships (e.g., *however, although, nevertheless, similarly, moreover, in addition*).
L.5.6

 I Do
Use **High-Frequency Word Cards** 161–170. Display one word at a time, following the routine:

Display the word. Read the word. Then spell the word.

 We Do
Ask students to state the word and spell the word with you. Model using the word in a sentence and have students repeat after you.

 You Do
Display the word. Ask students to say the word then spell it. When completed, quickly flip through the word card set as students chorally read the words. Provide opportunities for students to use the words in speaking and writing. For example, provide sentence starters such as *At the zoo, I saw _____.* Ask students to write each word in their Writer's Notebook.

TIER 2

REVIEW VOCABULARY WORDS

 OBJECTIVES
Acquire and use accurately grade-appropriate general academic and domain-specific words and phrases, including those that signal contrast, addition, and other logical relationships (e.g., *however, although, nevertheless, similarly, moreover, in addition*).
L.5.6

I Do
Display each **Visual Vocabulary Card** and state the word. Explain how the photograph illustrates the word. State the example sentence and repeat the word.

 We Do
Point to the word on the card and read the word with students. Ask them to repeat the word. Engage students in structured partner talk about the image as prompted on the back of the vocabulary card.

 You Do
Display each visual in random order, hiding the word. Have students match the definitions and context sentences of the words to the visuals displayed.

IDENTIFY RELATED WORDS

OBJECTIVES

 CCSS Demonstrate understanding of figurative language, word relationships, and nuances in word meanings. Use the relationship between particular words (e.g., synonyms, antonyms, homographs) to better understand each of the words. **L.5.5c**

 I Do Display the *disdain* **Visual Vocabulary Card** and say aloud the word set *disdain, scorn, discover*. Point out that the word *scorn* means almost the same thing as *disdain*.

 We Do Display the vocabulary card for *focused*. Say aloud the word set *focused, fuzzy, intent*. With students, identify that *intent* has almost the same meaning as *focused*.

You Do Using the word sets below, display the remaining cards one at a time, saying aloud the word set. Ask students to identify the word that has almost the same meaning as the first word in the set.

genius, intellectual, failure

prospect, possibility, disrespect

superb, serious, excellent

stunned, surprised, relaxed

transition, change, start

perspective, spectacle, viewpoint

CONTEXT CLUES

OBJECTIVES

 CCSS Determine or clarify the meaning of unknown and multiple-meaning words and phrases based on *grade 5 reading and content*, choosing flexibly from a range of strategies. Use context (e.g., cause/effect relationships and comparisons in text) as a clue to the meaning of a word or phrase. **L.5.4a**

 I Do Display the Comprehension and Fluency passage on **Approaching Reproducibles** pages 203–204. Read aloud paragraph 1. Point to the word *sweltering*. Tell students that they can look for context clues within the paragraph or in a nearby paragraph to figure out the meaning of the word.

Think Aloud Before the word sweltering, I see the phrase *not only hot, but*. This context clue in the form of a comparison makes me think that *hot* and *sweltering* have similar meanings.

 We Do Have students point to the word *dejectedly* in the second paragraph on page 203. Discuss how to use the comparison word *unhappy*, which appears earlier in the sentence, to figure out the meaning of *dejectedly*.

 You Do Have students find comparison words in context on page 204 that help them determine the meaning of *gaunt* (paragraph 1), *forlorn* (paragraph 2), and *forepaws* (paragraph 3).

→ Approaching Level

Comprehension

FLUENCY

 OBJECTIVES
Read on-level prose and poetry orally with accuracy, appropriate rate, and expression on successive readings. **RF.5.4b**

Read fluently with good expression.

 I Do Explain that reading a selection out loud is not just about reading the words correctly. Readers should change the sound of their voice to help show the meaning of what they read. Read the first paragraph of the Comprehension and Fluency passage on **Approaching Reproducibles** pages 203–204. Tell students to listen to your expression.

 We Do Read the rest of the page aloud and have students read after you, using the same expression. Explain that you used punctuation cues and your knowledge of word meanings to guide how you changed the sound of your voice.

 You Do Have partners take turns reading sentences from the Comprehension and Fluency passage. Remind them to focus on their expression. Listen in and provide corrective feedback as needed by modeling proper fluency.

CONTRAST CHARACTERS

 OBJECTIVES
Compare and contrast two or more characters, settings, or events in a story or drama, drawing on specific details in the text (e.g., how characters interact). **RL.5.3**

 I Do Explain that when you contrast characters, you tell how they are different. You might contrast two characters' personalities or reactions to situations. Read aloud the first paragraph of "Bringing Home Laddie" on **Approaching Reproducibles** pages 203–204. Then write: *Sofia is in a hurry. Papa is not.* Explain that this is one way the characters are different.

 We Do Continue reading the first page of the Comprehension and Fluency passage in the **Approaching Reproducibles** selection. Ask: *How are Mom and Sofia different?* Help students answer the question by pointing out that Mom is patient and calm and Sofia is stubborn and anxious.

 You Do Have students read the rest of the passage. Have partners identify another difference between two characters, such as between the two dogs Sofia meets. Review with students the differences they identify. Discuss how they used specific details to contrast the characters.

REVIEW COMPARE AND CONTRAST SETTINGS

OBJECTIVES

 Compare and contrast two or more characters, settings, or events in a story or drama, drawing on specific details in the text (e.g., how characters interact). **RL.5.3**

 I Do Explain to students that they can also compare and contrast the settings in a story. In order to compare and contrast settings, they should identify ways the settings are alike and different and how they affect the characters.

 We Do Choral-read the first and fourth paragraphs of the Comprehension and Fluency passage on **Approaching Reproducibles** pages 203–204. Guide students to compare and contrast outside with the kitchen. Discuss how Sofia feels in each place.

You Do Have students read the remainder of the passage and find similarities and differences in the settings—for example, between the shelter and Sofia's home. Ask them to discuss how the settings affect Sofia's feelings and actions.

SELF-SELECTED READING

OBJECTIVES

 Compare and contrast two or more characters, settings, or events in a story or drama, drawing on specific details in the text (e.g., how characters interact). **RL.5.3**

Make, confirm, and revise predictions based on details in the text.

Read Independently

Have students choose a realistic fiction book for sustained silent reading. Remind students that:

→ when they compare and contrast, they discover how things are alike and different.

→ making, confirming, and revising predictions by using details in the text will help them stay focused on and engaged with the story.

Read Purposefully

Have students record comparisons and contrasts on Graphic Organizer 66 as they read independently. After they finish, students can conduct a Book Talk about what they read.

→ Students should share their organizers and their favorite part of the story.

→ They should tell the group if they confirmed a prediction after reading on or if they revised it based on new details in the text.

→ On Level

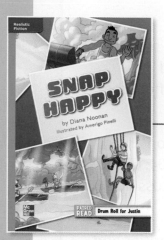

Lexile 810
TextEvaluator™ 54

CCSS **OBJECTIVES**
Quote accurately from a text when explaining what the text says explicitly and when drawing inferences from the text. **RL.5.1**

CCSS Compare and contrast two or more characters, settings, or events in a story or drama, drawing on specific details in the text (e.g., how characters interact). **RL.5.3**

CCSS Read on-level prose and poetry orally with accuracy, appropriate rate, and expression on successive readings. **RF.5.4b**

ACADEMIC LANGUAGE

• *realistic fiction, make predictions, compare, contrast, characters*

• Cognates: *ficción realista, predicciones, comparar, contrastar*

Leveled Reader:
Snap Happy

Leveled Readers

Before Reading

Preview and Predict

→ Read the Essential Question with students.

→ Have students preview the title, table of contents, and first page of *Snap Happy*. Students should use details in the text to predict what they think the selection will be about. Tell them that as they read, they should try to confirm or revise their predictions as necessary.

Review Genre: Realistic Fiction

Tell students that this text is realistic fiction. In realistic fiction, the setting is a place or places that could be found in real life. The characters are like real people. The events and problems the characters experience are similar to those experienced by real people. Have students identify features of realistic fiction in *Snap Happy*.

During Reading

Close Reading

Note Taking: Ask students to use their graphic organizer as they read.

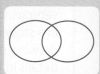

Use Graphic Organizer

Pages 2–3 *Compare and contrast where the children are with where they want to be.* (They are at their grandparents' cabin by the lake, which they have visited many times. They wish they were back in town or somewhere more exciting.) *What does* disdain *on page 2 mean? What context clues help you answer?* (*Disdain* means "intense dislike." The context clues show that it means the opposite of the word *interested.*)

Pages 4–5 *How do Tim and Madison feel about entering the contest?* (They believe that there is nothing exciting or new to do at Cave Lake, so they don't feel enthusiastic about entering.) *Turn to a partner and predict what they will do about the contest.* (They will not enter it.)

Pages 7–10 *Identify different activities the children photograph.* (a family looking at the lake through clear plastic bucket bottoms, an art class, bird watchers, a man cooking, rock climbers, a karate class) *How does their attitude about Cave Lake change?* (They see how exciting life is at the lake and how many different activities there are to enjoy.)

Tell a partner if your prediction matched the text or how you revised it. (It did not match the text, because Tim and Madison enter the contest.)

Pages 11–13 *What discovery do Tim and Madison make?* (Bert's shed is like a museum about the lake.) *Turn to a partner and predict the contest results.* (The children will win with their photographs of Bert's shed.)

Pages 14–15 *Turn to a partner and tell if your prediction matched the text or how you revised it.* (It matched the text; the children win the prize.) *How does the prize compare with the rest of the children's summer?* (The helicopter ride is awesome, but the children enjoy helping Bert even more.) *How does Tim's experience change the way he sees himself and the world around him?* (He learns to appreciate life at the lake.)

After Reading

Respond to Reading Revisit the Essential Question and ask students to complete the Text Evidence Questions on page 16.

Analytical Writing **Write About Reading** Check that students correctly compared and contrasted Bert's shed with the natural setting of Cave Lake.

Fluency: Expression

Model Model reading page 2 with appropriate expression. Next, read the passage aloud and have students read along with you.

Apply Have students practice reading the passage with partners.

PAIRED READ

"Drum Roll for Justin"

Make Connections: Write About It **Analytical Writing**

Before reading, ask students to note that the genre of this text is also realistic fiction. Then discuss the Essential Question. After reading, ask students to write connections between what they learned from *Snap Happy* and "Drum Roll for Justin."

Leveled Reader

FOCUS ON LITERARY ELEMENTS

Students can extend their knowledge of literary elements by completing the figurative language activity on page 20.

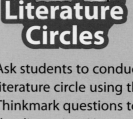

Literature Circles

Ask students to conduct a literature circle using the Thinkmark questions to guide the discussion. You may wish to have a whole-class discussion, using both selections in the Leveled Reader, about how our experiences can change the way we see ourselves and our world.

Level Up

Level-up lessons available online.

IF students read the On Level fluently and answered the questions

THEN pair them with students who have proficiently read the Beyond Level and have students

• partner-read the Beyond Level main selection.

• compare and contrast settings in the text.

A C T Access Complex Text

The Beyond Level challenges students by including more **figurative language** and **complex sentence structures.**

On Level

Vocabulary

REVIEW VOCABULARY WORDS

 OBJECTIVES
Acquire and use accurately grade-appropriate general academic and domain-specific words and phrases, including those that signal contrast, addition, and other logical relationships (e.g., *however, although, nevertheless, similarly, moreover, in addition*).
L.5.6

 Use the **Visual Vocabulary Cards** to review the key selection words *disdain, focused, genius, prospect, stunned,* and *superb*. Point to each, read it aloud, and have students repeat.

 Ask these questions. Help students explain their answers.

→ What might cause you to look at someone with *disdain*?

→ What is something that is easy for you to stay *focused* on?

→ Who is someone you think is a *genius*?

 Have students work in pairs to respond to these questions and explain their answers.

→ What is a *prospect* you have for your future?

→ What would make you feel *stunned*?

→ How would you describe a *superb* meal?

CONTEXT CLUES

 OBJECTIVES
Determine or clarify the meaning of unknown and multiple-meaning words and phrases based on *grade 5 reading and content,* choosing flexibly from a range of strategies. Use context (e.g., cause/effect relationships and comparisons in text) as a clue to the meaning of a word or phrase. **L.5.4a**

 Remind students they can use context clues within the paragraph or in a nearby paragraph to determine the meaning of an unknown word. One type of context clue is a comparison. Use paragraph 1 of the Comprehension and Fluency passage on **Your Turn Practice Book** pages 203–204 to model.

Think Aloud I want to know what the word *sweltering* means. When I reread the sentence, I see the phrase *not merely hot, but*. This context clue helps me understand that *hot* and *sweltering* have similar meanings.

 Have students read paragraph 2 on page 203, where they encounter *dejectedly*. Help students determine its meaning by using the comparison word *unhappy*.

 Have partners use comparisons in context on page 204 to determine the meaning of the words *gaunt* (paragraph 1), *forlorn* (paragraph 2), and *forepaws* (paragraph 3).

Comprehension

REVIEW COMPARE AND CONTRAST SETTINGS

OBJECTIVES
Compare and contrast two or more characters, settings, or events in a story or drama, drawing on specific details in the text (e.g., how characters interact). **RL.5.3**

 I Do

Review with students that they can compare and contrast the settings in two or more stories, or they can compare and contrast two or more settings in the same story. In order to compare and contrast settings, they should identify ways the settings are alike and different and how they affect the characters.

 We Do

Have volunteers take turns reading the first four paragraphs of the Comprehension and Fluency passage on **Your Turn Practice Book** pages 203–204. Work with students to identify similarities and differences between the outside and the kitchen.

 You Do

Have partners read the rest of the passage and identify similarities and differences in the settings, such as those between the shelter and Sofia's home. Then have them discuss how the different settings affect Sofia and her dog.

SELF-SELECTED READING

OBJECTIVES
Compare and contrast two or more characters, settings, or events in a story or drama, drawing on specific details in the text (e.g., how characters interact). **RL.5.3**

Make, confirm, and revise predictions based on details in the text.

Read Independently

Have students choose a realistic fiction book for sustained silent reading.

→ Before they read, have students preview the book.

→ As students read, remind them to make, confirm, and revise predictions.

Read Purposefully

Encourage students to select books that interest them.

→ As students read, have them fill in Graphic Organizer 66 to compare and contrast settings.

→ They can use the organizer to help them write a summary of the book.

→ Ask students to share their reactions to the book.

→ Beyond Level

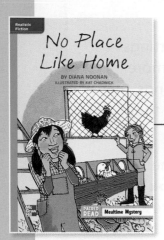

Realistic Fiction

No Place Like Home
BY DIANA NOONAN
ILLUSTRATED BY KAT CHADWICK

PAIRED READ Mealtime Mystery

Lexile 900
TextEvaluator™ 54

OBJECTIVES

 Quote accurately from a text when explaining what the text says explicitly and when drawing inferences from the text. **RL.5.1**

 Compare and contrast two or more characters, settings, or events in a story or drama, drawing on specific details in the text (e.g., how characters interact). **RL.5.3**

Read on-level prose and poetry orally with accuracy, appropriate rate, and expression on successive readings. **RF.5.4b**

ACADEMIC LANGUAGE

- *realistic fiction, make predictions, compare, contrast, characters*
- Cognates: *ficción realista, predicciones, comparar, contrastar*

Leveled Reader:
No Place Like Home

Go Digital

Leveled Readers

Before Reading

Preview and Predict

→ Have students read the Essential Question.

→ Have students preview the title, table of contents, and first page of *No Place Like Home*. Students should predict what they think the selection will be about. Tell them that as they read, they should try to confirm or revise their predictions based on new details in the text.

Review Genre: Realistic Fiction

Tell students that this text is realistic fiction. In realistic fiction, the setting is a place or places that could be found in real life. The characters are like real people. The events and problems experienced by the characters are similar to those experienced by people in real life. Have students identify features of realistic fiction in *No Place Like Home*.

During Reading

Close Reading

Note Taking: Ask students to use their graphic organizer as they read.

Pages 2–4 *How do comparison words and other context clues in the surrounding sentences help you understand the meaning of* exasperated *on page 2?* (*Exasperated* must have a similar meaning as *annoyed,* which appears in the next sentence. Mom is exasperated, or annoyed, because she has been trying unsuccessfully to get Jo's attention.) *How does Jo imagine Ryoko will feel about staying on a farm, based on differences between Oakden and Tokyo?* (Jo thinks that Ryoko will not like the quiet and chores of farm life because she prefers the malls and excitement of a big city like Tokyo.) *Turn to a partner and predict how Ryoko will respond to life on the farm.* (She will be homesick and not enjoy farm life.)

Pages 5–8 *Turn to a partner and tell if your prediction matched the text.* (So far, it seems to match. Ryoko spends most of her time in her room.) *What clues in this chapter show that Ryoko will become more involved in life on the farm?* (Mom makes a plan to give Ryoko a farm experience. Ryoko nods and accepts the idea of playing cards with Jo after dinner.)

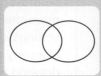

Use Graphic Organizer

Pages 9–12 *Identify the different chores that Jo shows Ryoko how to do.* (feed the pigs and chickens, hold the pet bantam, gather eggs) *How is Ryoko's response different than what Jo expects?* (Jo expects that Ryoko will not like the chores, but she seems fascinated by them.) *Did you need to revise your prediction after learning new details?* (Yes. Ryoko now seems to be enjoying herself, so I predict that she will like farm life.)

Pages 13–15 *How has Ryoko's behavior changed?* (At first she was very quiet and shy, but now she is eager to participate in life on the farm.) *Turn to a partner and explain how having Ryoko visit changes the way Jo sees herself and the farm.* (Jo realizes that she has a lot to share and that living on a farm is special. She sees the farm from a new perspective.)

After Reading

Respond to Reading Revisit the Essential Question and ask students to complete the Text Evidence Questions on page 16.

Analytical Writing **Write About Reading** Check that students have correctly described how the farm setting affects Ryoko.

Fluency: Expression

Model Model reading page 3 with appropriate expression. Next, read the passage aloud and have students read along with you.

Apply Have students practice reading the passage with partners.

PAIRED READ

Leveled Reader

"Mealtime Mystery"

Make Connections: Write About It **Analytical Writing**

Before reading, ask students to note that the genre of this text is also realistic fiction. Then discuss the Essential Question. After reading, ask students to write connections between *No Place Like Home* and "Mealtime Mystery."

FOCUS ON LITERARY ELEMENTS

Students can extend their knowledge of literary elements by completing the figurative language activity on page 20.

Literature Circles

Ask students to conduct a literature circle using the Thinkmark questions to guide the discussion. You may wish to have a whole-class discussion, using both selections in the Leveled Reader, about how new experiences can change the way we see ourselves and the world around us.

Gifted and Talented

Synthesize Challenge students to think of what might happen if Jo were to go to Tokyo to visit Ryoko. Students should consider Jo's likely reaction and then describe the visit in detail. Since Jo has seen how Ryoko adjusted to farm life in the United States, how could she use that information to help her adjust to life in Tokyo? How could the visit change the way Jo sees herself and her world? Have students use information from the story as a guide to completing the activity.

→ Beyond Level

Vocabulary

REVIEW DOMAIN-SPECIFIC WORDS

OBJECTIVES
Acquire and use accurately grade-appropriate general academic and domain-specific words and phrases, including those that signal contrast, addition, and other logical relationships. **L.5.6**

 Model

Use the **Visual Vocabulary Cards** to review the meaning of the words *perspective* and *transition*. Use each word in a context sentence.

Write the words *adjustment* and *maturity* on the board and discuss the meanings with students. Help students write a context sentence for each word.

 Apply

Have students work in pairs to review the meanings of the words *profound* and *responsibility* and how they relate to the story. Then have partners write sentences using the words.

CONTEXT CLUES

OBJECTIVES
Determine or clarify the meaning of unknown and multiple-meaning words and phrases based on *grade 5 reading and content,* choosing flexibly from a range of strategies. Use context (e.g., cause/effect relationships and comparisons in text) as a clue to the meaning of a word or phrase. **L.5.4a**

 Model

Read aloud the first paragraph of the Comprehension and Fluency passage on **Beyond Reproducibles** pages 203–204. Model how to use a comparison in context to determine the meaning of the word *sweltering*.

Think Aloud When I reread the sentence, I see the phrase *not merely hot, but*. This comparison context clue makes me think that *hot* and *sweltering* have similar meanings.

With students, continue reading the first page. Help them determine the meaning of *dejectedly* using the comparison word *unhappy*.

 Apply

Have pairs of students read the rest of the passage. On page 204, ask them to use comparison context clues to determine the meanings of *gaunt* (paragraph 1), *forlorn* (paragraph 2), and *forepaws* (paragraph 3).

 Gifted and Talented

Independent Study Challenge students to write three adjectives, exchange them with a partner, and then write a sentence for each of their partners' adjectives that contains a comparison word or phrase.

Comprehension

REVIEW COMPARE AND CONTRAST SETTINGS

OBJECTIVES
Compare and contrast two or more characters, settings, or events in a story or drama, drawing on specific details in the text (e.g., how characters interact). **RL.5.3**

Model Review with students that they can compare and contrast the settings in two or more stories, or they can compare and contrast two or more settings in the same story. In order to compare and contrast settings, they should identify ways the settings are alike and different and how they affect the characters.

Have students read the first page of the Comprehension and Fluency passage on **Beyond Reproducibles** pages 203–204. Ask open-ended questions to facilitate discussion, such as *How are two settings described in the story similar? How are they different?* Students should support their responses with details from the passage.

Apply Have students read the rest of the passage and compare and contrast the settings as they fill in Graphic Organizer 66 independently. Then have partners use their work to describe how the different settings affect the main character.

SELF-SELECTED READING

OBJECTIVES
Compare and contrast two or more characters, settings, or events in a story or drama, drawing on specific details in the text (e.g., how characters interact). **RL.5.3**

Make, confirm, and revise predictions based on details in the text.

Read Independently

Have students choose a realistic fiction book for sustained silent reading.

→ Ask them to use Graphic Organizer 66 to compare and contrast settings.

→ Remind them to make, confirm, and revise predictions as they read.

Read Purposefully

Encourage students to keep a reading journal. Suggest that they select books with characters and plots that interest them.

→ Students can write summaries of the books in their journals.

→ Ask students to share their feelings about the books with classmates.

Independent Study Challenge students to discuss how their books relate to the weekly theme of new perspectives. Have students use all of their reading materials to compare the different ways that experiences can change the way we see the world.

→ English Language Learners

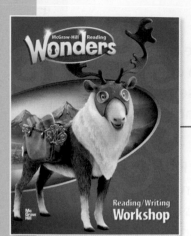

Reading/Writing Workshop

OBJECTIVES

 Quote accurately from a text when explaining what the text says explicitly and when drawing inferences from the text. **RL.5.1**

CCSS Compare and contrast two or more characters, settings, or events in a story or drama, drawing on specific details in the text (e.g., how characters interact). **RL.5.3**

LANGUAGE OBJECTIVE

Compare and contrast two or more settings in a story.

ACADEMIC LANGUAGE

• *compare, contrast, setting, context clues, make predictions*

• Cognates: *comparar, contrastar, predicciones*

Shared Read
Miguel in the Middle

Before Reading

Build Background

Read the Essential Question: *What experiences can change the way you see yourself and the world around you?*

→ Explain the meaning of the Essential Question, including the vocabulary in the question: *Experiences are things that happen to you. The way you see yourself and the world is how you think and feel about yourself and the people and places you know.*

→ **Model an answer:** *Seeing a familiar place from a new perspective can change the way you think about it. After I looking down on the city streets from the top of a tall building, I thought differently about my city.*

→ Ask students a question that ties the Essential Question to their own background knowledge: *Turn to a partner and think of an experience you have had and how it changed the way you see yourself and the world. Discuss how your knowledge helped you.* Call on several pairs.

During Reading

Interactive Question-Response

→ Ask questions that help students understand the meaning of the text after each paragraph.

→ Reinforce the meanings of key vocabulary.

→ Ask students questions that require them to use key vocabulary.

→ Reinforce strategies and skills of the week by modeling.

Go Digital

View "Miguel in the Middle"

Page 311

Paragraph 1
This story is about a boy who is always in the middle. Draw a circle and point to the center: *This is the middle.* Draw a line and point to the mid-point. *This is the middle. The middle is not the beginning. It is not the end. It is not first. It is not last. The middle is in between.* Choral-read the paragraph.

Paragraph 2
Explain and Model Compare and Contrast
Explain that when you compare, you look at how people, places, and things are alike. When you contrast, you look at differences. Read aloud the second paragraph. *There are two different settings, or places, mentioned in this paragraph. What are they?* (Miguel's old elementary school and his new middle school)

Explain and Model Context Clues Reread the paragraph to help students understand how using context clues can help them figure out the meaning of the vocabulary word *transition* in the third sentence. Help them locate the word *changes* in the same sentence. *I know that the word* changes *means that something is different. I read that Miguel changed from elementary to middle school, so I can figure out that* transition *means "a change."*

Paragraph 3
What other big changes does Miguel have in his classroom? (He is sitting in the front row, instead of in the middle of the classroom. He has more homework now.)

Page 312

Paragraph 1
Choral-read the paragraph. Have students tell a partner what Miguel means when he says, "To me, fractions are a foreign language." (He doesn't understand all the words and concepts used in math problems.)

Explain and Model the Strategy *As I read, I can make predictions about what will happen in the story. I read that Miguel and Jake become friends because Miguel is hopeless at math. I predict that Jake will help Miguel with his math homework.*

Paragraph 5
Use a circle of paper to demonstrate how Jake used pizza to explain fractions to Miguel. Then remind students of the prediction you made earlier. *Can I confirm my prediction?* (Yes, Jake helps Miguel understand his math homework.)

Page 313

Paragraph 1
How does Miguel describe himself as a student? (he's more focused) *Is Miguel happy or sad to be away from middle school for two weeks?* (sad)

Paragraphs 2–3
Guide students to use context clues to figure out the meaning of *brainteaser*. *Which students got the correct answer to the brainteaser?* (Jake and Miguel)

Paragraph 4
Read the paragraph aloud with a partner. How is Miguel still the same? How is he different? (He likes math more than he used to, but he is still in the middle of a group of friends.)

After Reading

Make Connections
→ Review the Essential Question: *What experiences can change the way you see yourself and the world around you?*

→ Make text connections.

→ Have students complete **ELL Reproducibles** pages 203–205.

English Language Learners

Leveled Reader:
Snap Happy

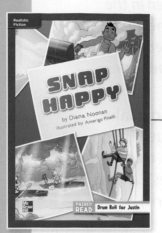

Lexile 550
TextEvaluator™ 35

Go Digital

Leveled Readers

OBJECTIVES

CCSS Quote accurately from a text when explaining what the text says explicitly and when drawing inferences from the text. **RL.5.1**

CCSS Compare and contrast two or more characters, settings, or events in a story or drama, drawing on specific details in the text (e.g., how characters interact). **RL.5.3**

CCSS Read on-level prose and poetry orally with accuracy, appropriate rate, and expression on successive readings. **RF.5.4b**

ACADEMIC LANGUAGE

• *make predictions, realistic fiction, compare, contrast, characters*

• Cognates: *predicción, ficción realista, comparar, contrastar*

Before Reading

Preview and Predict

→ Read the Essential Question: *What experiences can change the way you see yourself and the world around you?*

→ Refer to The View from Here: *How can a new perspective change the way we see familiar things?*

→ Preview *Snap Happy* and "Drum Roll for Justin": *Our purpose for reading is to learn about how different experiences can change us.*

Vocabulary

Use the **Visual Vocabulary Cards** to pre-teach the ELL vocabulary: *treat, guilty, counts, arranged.* Use the routine found on the cards.

During Reading

Interactive Question-Response

Note Taking: Ask students to use the graphic organizer on **ELL Reproducibles** page 202. Use the questions below after each page is read with students. As you read, define vocabulary in context and use visuals to help students understand key vocabulary.

Pages 2–3 *Are the main character and his sister excited to be at Cave Lake?* (no) *Why not?* (They go there every year.)

Pages 4–5 Have students complete the sentence frame: *The main character, Tim, and his sister, Madison, need a ____ to enter the contest.* (camera) *How will they get a camera?* (They will borrow it from a friend.)

Pages 6–9 *What do the kids photograph?* Use the illustrations to guide students in their response. (a family looking at the water, an art class, a tour group, a man cooking, rock climbers, a karate class) *Does their attitude about the contest change?* (yes)

Page 10 *Does Tim think that they will win the contest?* (no) *Reread the last line on the page. Then turn to a partner and make a prediction about what will happen next.* (I predict Bert will help Tim and Madison.)

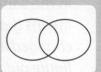

Use Graphic Organizer

Pages 11–13 *Bert's shed is full of old photographs and cameras. Tim thinks it is like _____.* (a museum) *What is Tim's idea?* (He wants to take pictures of Bert's shed to enter in the competition.)

Pages 14–15 Remind students of the prediction they made earlier. *Turn to a partner and tell if what happened in the story matched your prediction.* Choral read the last paragraph on page 14. *In Tim's opinion, what was the best part about winning the contest?* (People found out about Bert's collection.)

After Reading

Respond to Reading Revisit the Essential Question and ask students to complete the Text Evidence Questions on page 16.

Analytical Writing **Write About Reading** Check that students correctly compared and contrasted Tim and Madison with the other kids in the competition.

Fluency: Expression

Model Model reading page 2 with appropriate expression and phrasing. Then have students echo read along with you.

Apply Have students practice reading with partners.

PAIRED READ

Leveled Reader

"Drum Roll for Justin"

Make Connections:
Write About It *Analytical Writing*

Before reading, point out that the genre of this text is also realistic fiction and discuss the Essential Question. After reading, ask students to list connections between *Snap Happy* and "Drum Roll for Justin."

FOCUS ON LITERARY ELEMENTS

Students can extend their knowledge of figurative language by completing the activity on page 20.

Literature Circles

Ask students to conduct a literature circle using the Thinkmark questions to guide the discussion. You may wish to have a whole-class discussion, using both selections in the Leveled Reader, on the topic of changes due to new experiences.

Level Up

Level-up lessons available online.

IF students read the **ELL Level** fluently and answered the questions,

THEN pair them with students who have proficiently read **On Level** and have ELL students

• echo-read the **On Level** main selection.

• list words with which they have difficulty and discuss them with a partner.

A C T Access Complex Text

The **On Level** challenges students by including more **domain-specific words** and **complex sentence structures**.

→ English Language Learners
Vocabulary

PRETEACH VOCABULARY

 OBJECTIVES
Acquire and use accurately grade-appropriate general academic and domain-specific words and phrases, including those that signal contrast, addition, and other logical relationships. **L.5.6**

LANGUAGE OBJECTIVE
Use vocabulary words.

 I Do
Preteach vocabulary from "Miguel in the Middle" following the Vocabulary Routine found on the **Visual Vocabulary Cards** for the words *disdain, focused, genius, perspective, prospect, stunned, superb,* and *transition*.

 We Do
After completing the Vocabulary Routine for each word, point to the word on the card and read the word with students. Ask them to repeat the word.

 You Do
Have students work with a partner to use two or more words in sentences or questions. Then have each pair read the sentences aloud.

Beginning	Intermediate	Advanced/High
Help students write the sentences correctly and read them aloud.	Ask students to write one sentence and one question.	Challenge students to write a sentence or a question for each word.

REVIEW VOCABULARY

 OBJECTIVES
Acquire and use accurately grade-appropriate general academic and domain-specific words and phrases, including those that signal contrast, addition, and other logical relationships. **L.5.6**

LANGUAGE OBJECTIVE
Use vocabulary words.

 I Do
Review the previous week's vocabulary words over a few days. Read each word aloud, pointing to the word on the **Visual Vocabulary Card**. Have students repeat. Then follow the Vocabulary Routine on the back of each card.

 We Do
Review the words. Read the definition for a word and have students name the word that matches the definition. Ask them to use the word in a sentence.

 You Do
In pairs, have students write definitions for two or more words. Ask them to read their definitions aloud and have the class guess the word they are defining.

Beginning	Intermediate	Advanced/High
Help students write definitions and read them aloud.	Ask students to write their definitions as complete sentences.	Have students write a definition for each word.

CONTEXT CLUES

OBJECTIVES

CCSS Determine or clarify the meaning of unknown and multiple-meaning words and phrases based on grade 5 reading and content, choosing flexibly from a range of strategies. Use context (e.g., cause/effect relationships and comparisons in text) as a clue to the meaning of a word or phrase. **L.5.4a**

LANGUAGE OBJECTIVE

Identify and use context clues.

I Do Read aloud the first paragraph of the Comprehension and Fluency passage on **ELL Reproducibles** pages 203–204, while students follow along. Summarize the paragraph. Point to the word *sweltering*. Explain to students that context clues can help them determine the meaning.

Think Aloud I am not sure what *sweltering* means, but I see context clues that help me. The weather is described as not just hot, but sweltering. So *sweltering* must mean "very hot."

We Do Have students point to the word *gaunt* in the second paragraph on page 204. Guide students to look for the context clue "just skin and bones." Write the definition of the word on the board.

You Do In pairs, have students write a definition for *forlorn* (page 204, paragraph 2) and *forepaws* (page 204, paragraph 3) using context clues.

Beginning	Intermediate	Advanced/High
Help students locate the words and context clues.	Ask students to locate and read aloud the context clues.	Have students use the word in a sentence.

ADDITIONAL VOCABULARY

OBJECTIVES

CCSS Acquire and use accurately grade-appropriate general academic and domain-specific words and phrases, including those that signal contrast, addition, and other logical relationships. **L.5.6**

LANGUAGE OBJECTIVE

Use academic language and high-frequency words.

I Do List some academic language and high-frequency words from "Miguel in the Middle": *district, especially, imagine*; and *Snap Happy*: *disdain, suggestions, activity*. Define each word for students: Especially *means "in particular."*

We Do Model using the words for students in a sentence: *He liked the puppies, especially the one in the window. The teacher assigned more homework, especially in math.* Then provide sentence frames and complete them with students: *I especially like _____.*

You Do Have pairs make up their own sentences and share them with the class to complete them.

Beginning	Intermediate	Advanced/High
Provide sentence frames and have students complete them.	Provide sentence starters for students, if necessary.	Have students write a definition for each word they used.

English Language Learners
Writing/Spelling

WRITING TRAIT: ORGANIZATION

 OBJECTIVES
Write routinely over extended time frames (time for research, reflection, and revision) and shorter time frames (a single sitting or a day or two) for a range of discipline-specific tasks, purposes, and audiences. **W.5.10**

LANGUAGE OBJECTIVE
Write a strong opening.

 I Do Explain that when writers organize their stories, they start with a strong opening. The opening should get the reader's attention and make the reader want to continue reading. Read the Expert Model aloud as students follow along.

We Do Discuss what makes the Expert Model a strong opening. Point out that the first sentence makes you want to keep reading to find out why the narrator is always in the middle. Brainstorm other ways a writer might get a reader's attention.

You Do Have students write their own introductory paragraph, using the first sentence of "Miguel in the Middle" as a model: *For as long as I can remember, _____.* Edit students' writing and have them revise.

Beginning	Intermediate	Advanced/High
Have students copy the edited sentences.	Have students add more details to engage the reader.	Have students add details and explain why they engage the reader.

SPELL WORDS WITH SUFFIXES

 OBJECTIVES
Spell grade-appropriate words correctly, consulting references as needed. **L.5.2e**

LANGUAGE OBJECTIVE
Spell words with suffixes.

 I Do Read aloud the Spelling Words on page T36, segmenting them into syllables, and attaching a spelling to each sound. Point out the suffix in each word. Have students repeat the words.

 We Do Read the Dictation Sentences on page T37 aloud for students. With each sentence, read the underlined word slowly, segmenting it into syllables. Have students repeat after you and write the word.

 You Do Display the words. Have students exchange their list with a partner to check the spelling and write the words correctly.

Beginning	Intermediate	Advanced/High
Help students copy the words with correct spelling and say the words aloud.	After students have corrected their words, have pairs quiz each other.	After students have corrected their words, have them discuss challenging words.

Grammar

INDEPENDENT AND DEPENDENT CLAUSES

OBJECTIVES

CCSS Demonstrate command of the conventions of standard English grammar and usage when writing or speaking. Explain the function of conjunctions, prepositions, and interjections in general and their function in particular sentences. **L.5.1a**

LANGUAGE OBJECTIVE

Identify and use independent and dependent clauses.

Language Transfers Handbook

Speakers of Cantonese may have difficulties with clauses that include prepositions. Speakers of this language may need additional support with the use of prepositions in clauses that include prepositional phrases.

I Do

Remind students that a clause is a group of words that has a subject and a predicate. An independent clause is a complete thought and can stand alone as a sentence. A dependent clause does not form a complete thought and cannot stand alone as a sentence. Write on the board: *I cannot play soccer.* Explain that it is an independent clause. Then write: *because I have to study.* Explain that it is a dependent clause. Model joining the clauses to form a sentence.

We Do

Write the clauses below on the board. Help students identify whether each is a dependent or an independent clause. Work with them to make the dependent clauses into complete sentences.

if it doesn't rain

We will go on a picnic.

because it is fun

You Do

Have students work in pairs to write two sentences. One should have only an independent clause. The other should have a dependent and an independent clause.

Beginning	Intermediate	Advanced/High
Help students form sentences with both independent and dependent clauses and then copy the sentences. Read the sentences aloud and have students repeat.	Ask students to underline the independent clauses and circle the dependent clauses in their sentences.	Have students circle the dependent clause and explain why they needed to join it to an independent clause.

For extra support, have students complete the activities in the **Grammar Practice Reproducibles** during the week, using the routine below:

→ Explain the grammar skill.

→ Model the first activity in the Grammar Practice Reproducibles.

→ Have the whole group complete the next couple of activities, then do the rest with a partner.

→ Review the activities with correct answers.

PROGRESS MONITORING

Weekly Assessment

CCSS **TESTED SKILLS**

✔ **COMPREHENSION:**	✔ **VOCABULARY:**	✔ **WRITING:**
Character, Setting, Plot: Compare and Contrast Settings **RL.5.1, RL.5.3**	Context Clues: Comparison **L.5.4a**	Writing About Text **RL.5.1, RL.5.3, W.5.9a**

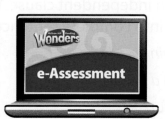

Assessment Includes

→ Performance Tasks

→ Approaching-Level Assessment online PDFs

Fluency Goal 129 to 149 words correct per minute (WCPM)

Accuracy Rate Goal 95% or higher

Administer oral reading fluency assessments using the following schedule:

→ **Weeks 1, 3, 5** Provide Approaching-Level students at least three oral reading fluency assessments during the unit.

→ **Weeks 2 and 4** Provide On-Level students at least two oral reading fluency assessments during the unit.

→ **Week 6** If necessary, provide Beyond-Level students an oral reading fluency assessment at this time.

Also Available: Selection Tests online PDFs

Go Digital! www.connected.mcgraw-hill.com

Using Assessment Results

TESTED SKILLS	If ...	Then ...
COMPREHENSION	Students answer 0–6 multiple-choice items correctly ...	... assign Lessons 43–45 on Compare and Contrast from the ***Tier 2 Comprehension Intervention online PDFs.***
VOCABULARY	Students answer 0–6 multiple-choice items correctly ...	... assign Lesson 141 on Using Comparison Clues from the ***Tier 2 Vocabulary Intervention online PDFs.***
WRITING	Students score less than "3" on the constructed responses ...	... assign Lessons 43–45 on Compare and Contrast and/or Write About Reading Lesson 194 from the ***Tier 2 Comprehension Intervention online PDFs.***
FLUENCY	Students have a WCPM score of 120–128 ...	... assign a lesson from Section 1, 7, 8, 9, or 10 of the ***Tier 2 Fluency Intervention online PDFs.***
	Students have a WCPM score of 0–119 ...	... assign a lesson from Section 2, 3, 4, 5, or 6 of the ***Tier 2 Fluency Intervention online PDFs.***

Response to Intervention

Use the appropriate sections of the ***Placement and Dignostic Assessment*** as well as students' assessment results to designate students requiring:

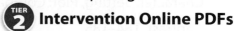 **Intervention Online PDFs**

 **WonderWorks Intervention Program**

Text Complexity Range for Grades 4–5

Lexile	
740	1010

TextEvaluator™	
23	51

Reading/Writing Workshop

McGraw-Hill Reading

Wonders

Mc Graw Hill

TEACH AND MODEL

CCSS **Shared Read**   Genre · Historical Fiction

The Day the Rollets
Got Their Moxie Back

Essential Question
How do shared experiences help people adapt to change?

Read about how a family comes together during a period of great hardship in the United States.

324

Sometimes, the thing that gets you through hard times comes like a bolt from the blue. That's what my older brother's letter was like, traveling across the country from a work camp in Wyoming. It was 1937, and Ricky was helping to build facilities for a new state park as part of President Roosevelt's employment program. Though the program created jobs for young men like Ricky, it hadn't helped our dad find work yet.

I imagined Ricky looking up at snow-capped mountains and sparkling skies, breathing in the smell of evergreens as his work crew turned trees into lumber and lumber into buildings. It almost made an 11-year-old **weakling** like me want to become a lumberjack.

Back in our New York City apartment, the air smelled like meatloaf and cabbage. Dad sat slant-wise in his chair by the window, **obviously** trying to catch the last rays of sunlight rather than turn on a light. My older sister Ruth and I lay on the floor comparing the letters Ricky had sent us. "Shirley, Ricky says they had a talent show, and he wore a grass skirt and did a hula dance while playing the ukulele!" Ruth reported with delight. "I'll bet he was the cat's pajamas!"

"It'd be swell to have our own talent show!" I replied.

"Should I start sewing grass skirts?" Mom asked from the kitchen, which was just the corner where someone had plopped down a stove next to a sink and an icebox. "Now come set the table. Dinner's almost ready."

325

✔ Vocabulary

assume

guarantee

nominate

obviously

rely

supportive

sympathy

weakling

🔍 Close Reading of Complex Text

Shared Read "The Day the Rollets Got Their Moxie Back," 324–331

Genre Historical Fiction

Lexile 900L

ETS *TextEvaluator*™ 48

Minilessons

✔ **Comprehension Strategy** .... Make Predictions, T82–T83

✔ **Comprehension Skill** .... Character, Setting, Plot: Compare and Contrast, T84–T85

✔ **Genre** .... Historical Fiction, T86–T87

✔ **Vocabulary Strategy** .... Idioms, T88–T89

✔ **Writing Traits** .... Sentence Fluency, T94–T95

Grammar Handbook .... Complex Sentences, T98–T99

✔ Tested Skills CCSS

 👉 **Go Digital**

www.connected.mcgraw-hill.com

BETTER TOGETHER

Essential Question

How do shared experiences help people adapt to change?

WEEK 2

APPLY WITH CLOSE READING

Literature Anthology

Complex Text

Bud, Not Buddy, 364–377
Genre Historical Fiction
Lexile 950L
ETS *TextEvaluator* 44

PAIRED READ

"Musical Impressions of the Great Depression," 380–383
Genre Expository Text
Lexile 990L
ETS *TextEvaluator* 49

Differentiated Text

Leveled Readers *Include Paired Reads*

APPROACHING
Lexile 710L
ETS *TextEvaluator* 41

ON LEVEL
Lexile 830L
ETS *TextEvaluator* 51

BEYOND
Lexile 900L
ETS *TextEvaluator* 53

ELL
Lexile 520L
ETS *TextEvaluator* 34

Extended Complex Text

The Penderwicks: A Summer Tale of Four Sisters, Two Rabbits, and a Very Interesting Boy
Genre Realistic Fiction
Lexile 800L
ETS *TextEvaluator* 42

Classroom Library

Ida B ... and Her Plans to Maximize Fun, Avoid Disaster, and (Possibly) Save the World
Genre Realistic Fiction
Lexile 970L
ETS *TextEvaluator* 49

Classroom Library lessons available online.

⟩ TEACH AND MANAGE

How You Teach

INTRODUCE

Weekly Concept
Better Together

Reading/Writing Workshop
320–321

TEACH

Close Reading
"The Day the Rollets Got Their Moxie Back"

Minilessons
Make Predictions, Compare and Contrast Characters, Historical Fiction, Idioms, Writing Traits

Reading/Writing Workshop
324–333

APPLY

Close Reading
Bud, Not Buddy

"Musical Impressions of the Great Depression"

Literature Anthology
364–383

👉 **Go Digital**

 Interactive Whiteboard

 Interactive Whiteboard

 Mobile

How Students Practice

WEEKLY CONTRACT

PDF Online

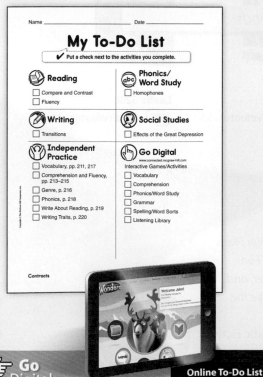

LEVELED PRACTICE AND ONLINE ACTIVITIES

Your Turn Practice Book
211–220

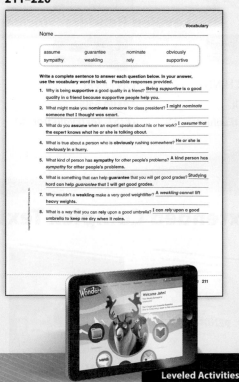

Leveled Readers

👉 **Go Digital**

Online To-Do List

 Leveled Activities

Writer's Workspace

DIFFERENTIATE

SMALL GROUP INSTRUCTION

Leveled Readers

INTEGRATE

Research and Inquiry
Presentation, T92

Text Connections
Compare Shared Experiences, T93

Write About Reading
Analytical Writing Write an Analysis, T93

ASSESS

Weekly Assessment
253–264

Mobile

Online Research and Writing

Online Assessment

LEVELED WORKSTATION CARDS

 **More Activities on back**

22
Great Depression Stories

Artists, writers, and musicians helped tell stories from the Great Depression.

- Find information and photographs about the Great Depression and its effect on people.

- Choose one photograph. Write

The Great Depression began in 1929. It was caused by ...

SOCIAL ST

13
Sentence Fluency: Transitions

Read Patti's paragraph about the three states of water.

Water is found in three states. It can be a liquid. Water from a faucet is liquid. Water can be a solid. Ice in the freezer is water. Water can be vapor in the air is gaseous state.

- Identify places in Patti's writing where she could add transitions, such as *for example*, *next*, *as a result*, or *finally*.

- Revise Patti's writing to include transitions.

WRITING

12
Idioms, Adages, and Proverbs

Idioms are expressions that cannot be understood from the words in them. Adages and proverbs are sayings that have been used and shared over time.

Stubborn as a...

Activity 1: Idioms
- Research and find five idioms such as It's raining cats and dogs.

- Draw a picture of one idiom and have a partner figure out what it is.

Activity 2: Adages and Proverbs
- Research one adage and one proverb.

- Draw a picture or each one and label it with the saying.

You need
› paper and pencil
› reference books or Internet
› crayons or markers

PHONICS/WORD STUDY

4
Compare and Contrast Characters

Compare and contrast characters to understand how their personalities and traits affect the events.

- Choose two characters from a story that you and your partner have read.

- Make a Three-Pocket Foldable®. Label the first pocket for one character, the middle pocket for "Both," and the third pocket for the second character.

- On index cards, write traits of each character. Place them into the correct pockets of the Foldable®. Discuss how you sorted them. How do the characters affect the events?

You need
› story
› Three-Pocket Foldable®
› index cards, pen

READING

DEVELOPING READERS AND WRITERS

Write About Reading • Analytical Writing

Write to Sources and Research

Character, Setting, Plot: Compare and Contrast, T84–T85

Note Taking, T89B, T89R

Summarize, T89P

Compare and Contrast, T89P

Make Connections: Essential Question, T89P, T89T, T93

Key Details, T89R, T89S

Research and Inquiry, T92

Analyze to Share an Opinion, T93

Comparing Texts, T105, T113, T117, T123

Predictive Writing, T89B

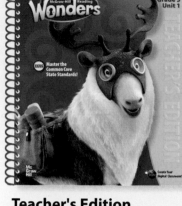

Teacher's Edition

Literature Anthology

Summarize, p. 379
Compare and Contrast, p. 379

Interactive Whiteboard

Leveled Readers
Comparing Texts
Compare and Contrast

Your Turn Practice Book

Compare and Contrast, pp. 213–215
Genre, p. 216
Analyze to Share an Opinion, p. 219

Writing Process • Genre Writing

Informative Text
Informational Article, T344–T349

Conferencing Routines
Teacher Conferences, T346
Peer Conferences, T347

Interactive Whiteboard

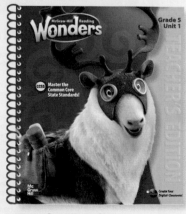

Teacher's Edition

Leveled Workstation Card
Informational Article, Card 29

Writer's Workspace
Informative Text:
Informational Article
Writing Process
Multimedia Presentations

Writing Traits • Write Every Day

Writing Trait: Sentence Fluency
Transitions, T94–T95

Conferencing Routines
Teacher Conferences, T96
Peer Conferences, T97

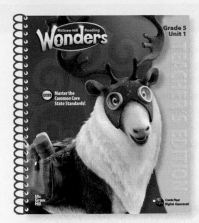

Teacher's Edition

Sentence Fluency:
Transitions,
pp. 332–333

Reading/Writing Workshop

Interactive Whiteboard

Sentence
Fluency:
Transitions, 13

Leveled Workstation Card

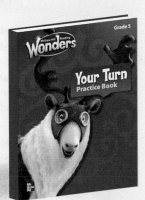

Sentence Fluency:
Transitions, p. 220

Your Turn Practice Book

Grammar and Spelling

Grammar
Complex Sentences,
T98–T99

Spelling
Homophones, T100–T101

Interactive Whiteboard

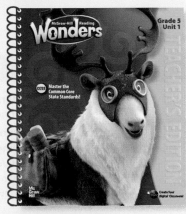

Teacher's Edition

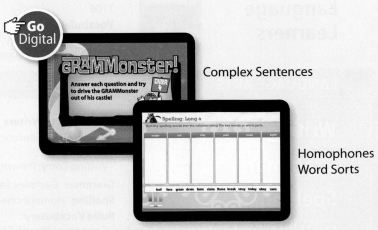

Complex Sentences

Homophones
Word Sorts

Online Spelling and Grammar Games

SUGGESTED LESSON PLAN

✓ TESTED SKILLS (CCSS)

		DAY 1	DAY 2

READING

Whole Group

Teach, Model and Apply

Reading/Writing Workshop

DAY 1

Build Background Better Together, T74–T75
Listening Comprehension Interactive Read Aloud: "Starting Over," T76–T77
Comprehension
• Preview Genre: Historical Fiction, T86–T87
• Preview Strategy: Make Predictions, T82–T83
✓ **Vocabulary** Words in Context, T78–T79
Practice Your Turn 211

Close Reading of Complex Text "The Day the Rollets Got Their Moxie Back," 324–327

DAY 2

✓ **Comprehension**
• Strategy: Make Predictions, T82–T83
• Skill: Character, Setting, Plot: Compare and Contrast Characters, T84–T85
• Write About Reading • Analytical Writing
• Genre: Historical Fiction, T86–T87
✓ **Vocabulary** Strategy: Idioms, T88–T89
Practice Your Turn 212–217

DIFFERENTIATED INSTRUCTION   Choose across the week to meet your students' needs.

Small Group

Approaching Level

DAY 1

Leveled Reader The Picture Palace, T104–T105
Word Study/Decoding Review Homophones, T106 (TIER 2)
Vocabulary
• Review High-Frequency Words, T108 (TIER 2)
• Understand Vocabulary Words, T109

DAY 2

Leveled Reader The Picture Palace, T104–T105
Vocabulary Review Vocabulary Words, T108 (TIER 2)
Comprehension
• Identify Important Details About Characters, T110 (TIER 2)
• Review Compare and Contrast Characters, T111

On Level

DAY 1

Leveled Reader Hard Times, T112–T113
Vocabulary Review Vocabulary Words, T114

DAY 2

Leveled Reader Hard Times, T112–T113
Comprehension Review Compare and Contrast Characters, T115

Beyond Level

DAY 1

Leveled Reader Woodpecker Warriors, T116–T117
Vocabulary Review Domain-Specific Words, T118

DAY 2

Leveled Reader Woodpecker Warriors, T116–T117
Comprehension Review Compare and Contrast Characters, T119

English Language Learners

DAY 1

Shared Read "The Day the Rollets Got Their Moxie Back," T120–T121
Word Study/Decoding Review Homophones, T106
Vocabulary
• Preteach Vocabulary, T124
• Review High-Frequency Words, T108

DAY 2

Leveled Reader Hard Times, T122–T123
Vocabulary Review Vocabulary, T124
Writing Writing Trait: Sentence Fluency, T126
Grammar Complex Sentences, T127

LANGUAGE ARTS   Writing Process: Informational Article T344–T349 Use with Weeks 1–3

Whole Group

Writing
Grammar
Spelling
Build Vocabulary

DAY 1

✓ **Readers to Writers**
• Writing Trait: Sentence Fluency/Transitions, T94–T95
• Writing Entry: Prewrite and Draft, T96
Grammar Complex Sentences, T98
Spelling Homophones, T100
Build Vocabulary
• Connect to Words, T102
• Academic Vocabulary, T102

DAY 2

Readers to Writers
• Writing Entry: Revise, T96
Grammar Complex Sentences, T98
Spelling Homophones, T100
Build Vocabulary
• Expand Vocabulary, T102
• Review Simile and Metaphor, T102

DAY 3	DAY 4	DAY 5 Review and Assess

READING

Word Study/Decoding Homophones, T90–T91
Practice *Your Turn* 218

Close Reading *Bud, Not Buddy,* 364–379 • *Analytical Writing*

Literature Anthology

Fluency Expression and Phrasing, T91
Integrate Ideas • *Analytical Writing*
• Research and Inquiry, T92

Practice *Your Turn* 213–215

Close Reading "Musical Impressions of the Great Depression," 380–383 • *Analytical Writing*

Integrate Ideas • *Analytical Writing*
• Research and Inquiry, T92
• Text Connections, T93
• Write About Reading, T93

Practice *Your Turn* 219

DIFFERENTIATED INSTRUCTION

Leveled Reader *The Picture Palace,* T104–T105
Word Study/Decoding Build Homophones, T106 **TIER 2**
Fluency Expression and Phrasing, T110 **TIER 2**
Vocabulary Idioms, T109

Leveled Reader "The Golden Age of Hollywood," T105 • *Analytical Writing*
Word Study/Decoding Practice Homophones, T107

Leveled Reader Literature Circle, T105
Comprehension Self-Selected Reading, T111

Leveled Reader *Hard Times,* T112–T113
Vocabulary Idioms, T114

Leveled Reader "Chicago: Jazz Central," T113 • *Analytical Writing*

Leveled Reader Literature Circle, T113
Comprehension Self-Selected Reading, T115

Leveled Reader *Woodpecker Warriors,* T116–T117
Vocabulary
• Idioms, T118
• Independent Study, T118 *Gifted and Talented*

Leveled Reader "A Chance to Work," T117 • *Analytical Writing*

Leveled Reader Literature Circle, T117
Comprehension *Gifted and Talented*
• Self-Selected Reading, T119
• Independent Study: Shared Experiences, T119

Leveled Reader *Hard Times,* T122–T123
Word Study/Decoding Build Homophones, T106
Vocabulary Idioms, T125
Spelling Homophones, T126

Leveled Reader "Chicago: Jazz Central," T123 • *Analytical Writing*
Vocabulary Additional Vocabulary, T125
Word Study/Decoding Practice Homophones, T107

Leveled Reader Literature Circle, T123

LANGUAGE ARTS

Readers to Writers
• Writing Entry: Prewrite and Draft, T97

Grammar Mechanics and Usage, T99
Spelling Homophones, T101
Build Vocabulary
• Reinforce the Words, T103
• Idioms, T103

Readers to Writers
• Writing Entry: Revise, T97

Grammar Complex Sentences, T99
Spelling Homophones, T101
Build Vocabulary
• Connect to Writing, T103
• Shades of Meaning, T103

Readers to Writers
• Writing Entry: Share and Reflect, T97

Grammar Complex Sentences, T99
Spelling Homophones, T101
Build Vocabulary
• Word Squares, T103
• Morphology, T103

DIFFERENTIATE TO ACCELERATE

A C T Scaffold to Access Complex Text

Qualitative **Quantitative**

Reader and Task

TEXT COMPLEXITY

IF ▶ the text complexity of a particular selection is too difficult for students

THEN ▶ see the references noted in the chart below for scaffolded instruction to help students Access Complex Text.

	Reading/Writing Workshop	**Literature Anthology**	**Leveled Readers**	**Classroom Library**

Quantitative	"The Day the Rollets Got Their Moxie Back" **Lexile** 900 *TextEvaluator*™ 48	*Bud, Not Buddy* **Lexile** 950 *TextEvaluator*™ 44 "Musical Impressions of the Great Depression" **Lexile** 990 *TextEvaluator*™ 49	**Approaching Level** **Lexile** 710 *TextEvaluator*™ 42 **Beyond Level** **Lexile** 900 *TextEvaluator*™ 53 **On Level** **Lexile** 830 *TextEvaluator*™ 51 **ELL** **Lexile** 520 *TextEvaluator*™ 34	*The Penderwicks* **Lexile** 800 *TextEvaluator*™ 42 *Ida B...and Her Plans to Maximize Fun, Avoid Disaster, and (Possibly) Save the World* **Lexile** 970 *TextEvaluator*™ 49
Qualitative	**What Makes the Text Complex?** • **Prior Knowledge** 1930s T81 • **Connection of Ideas** Inferences T83 **ACT** *See Scaffolded Instruction in Teacher's Edition T81 and T83.*	**What Makes the Text Complex?** • **Prior Knowledge** Great Depression T89A • **Connection of Ideas** Introduction T89C; Actions T89E, T89G • **Specific Vocabulary** Slang T89I; Music T89K; Investing T89Q; Government T89S • **Genre** Historical Fiction T89M **ACT** *See Scaffolded Instruction in Teacher's Edition T89A–T89R.*	**What Makes the Text Complex?** • **Specific Vocabulary** • **Sentence Structure** • **Connection of Ideas** • **Genre** **ACT** *See Level Up lessons online for Leveled Readers.*	**What Makes the Text Complex?** • Genre • Specific Vocabulary • Prior Knowledge • Sentence Structure • Organization • Purpose • Connection of Ideas **ACT** *See Scaffolded Instruction in Teacher's Edition T360-T361.*
Reader and Task	The Introduce the Concept lesson on pages T74–T75 will help determine the reader's knowledge and engagement in the weekly concept. See pages T80–T89 and T92–T93 for questions and tasks for this text.	The Introduce the Concept lesson on pages T74–T75 will help determine the reader's knowledge and engagement in the weekly concept. See pages T89A–T89R and T92–T93 for questions and tasks for this text.	The Introduce the Concept lesson on pages T74–T75 will help determine the reader's knowledge and engagement in the weekly concept. See pages T104–T105, T112–T113, T116–T117, T122–T123, and T92–T93 for questions and tasks for this text.	The Introduce the Concept lesson on pages T74–T75 will help determine the reader's knowledge and engagement in the weekly concept. See pages T360-T361 for questions and tasks for this text.

Monitor and *Differentiate*

IF you need to differentiate instruction

THEN use the Quick Checks to assess students' needs and select the appropriate small group instruction focus.

 Quick Check

Comprehension Strategy Make Predictions T83

Comprehension Skill Character, Setting, Plot: Compare and Contrast T85

Genre Historical Fiction T87

Vocabulary Strategy Idioms T89

Word Study/Fluency Homophones, Expression and Phrasing T91

If No →

Approaching Level	Reteach T104–T111
ELL	Develop T120–T127

If Yes →

On Level	Review T112–T115
Beyond Level	Extend T116–T119

Level Up with Leveled Readers

IF students can read their leveled text fluently and answer comprehension questions

THEN work with the next level up to accelerate students' reading with more complex text.

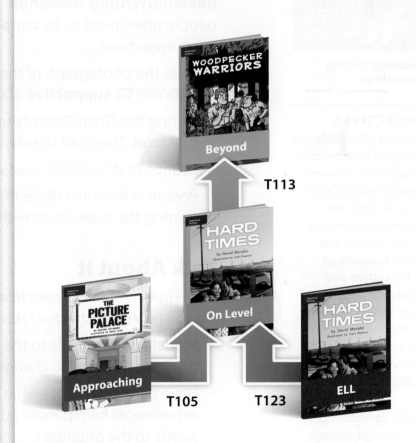

T113

T105   T123

ENGLISH LANGUAGE LEARNERS
SCAFFOLD

IF ELL students need additional support **THEN** scaffold instruction using the small group suggestions.

Reading/Writing Workshop "The Day the Rollets Got Their Moxie Back" T120–T121	Leveled Reader *Hard Times* T122–T123 "Chicago: Jazz Central" T123	Additional Vocabulary T125 chaos parade employment rumors facilities twins	Idioms T125	Writing Trait: Sentence Fluency T126	Spelling Homophones T126	Grammar Complex Sentences T127

Note: Include ELL Students in all small groups based on their needs.

→ Introduce the Concept

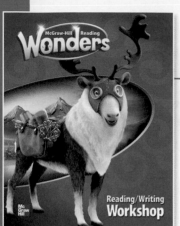

Reading/Writing Workshop

OBJECTIVES

CCSS Engage effectively in a range of collaborative discussions (one-on-one, in groups, and teacher-led) with diverse partners on *grade 5 topics and texts*, building on others' ideas and expressing their own clearly. Follow agreed-upon rules for discussions and carry out assigned roles. **SL.5.1b**

Build background knowledge about how people adapt to change.

ACADEMIC LANGUAGE
supportive, rely

  MINILESSON 10 Mins

Build Background

ESSENTIAL QUESTION
How do shared experiences help people adapt to change?

Have students read the Essential Question on page 320 of the **Reading/Writing Workshop**. Tell them that during difficult times, people often need to be **supportive** of each other, providing help or encouragement.

Discuss the photograph of the soup kitchen line. Focus on ways that people can be **supportive** of others who are in difficult circumstances.

→ During the Great Depression, many people did not have money to buy food. They had to **rely**, or depend, on the generosity of others.

→ Groups that supplied food were **supportive** of the unemployed.

→ People in lines like these may have felt lonely and afraid. Perhaps sharing the experience with others made it easier to handle.

Talk About It

COLLABORATE

Ask: *How were you **supportive** of others during a time of change? How did you **rely** on each other?* Have students discuss in pairs or groups.

→ Model adding words to the graphic organizer about working together to adapt to changes. Add students' contributions.

→ Have partners discuss what they have learned about how shared experiences help people adapt to change. They can add related words to the organizer.

Collaborative Conversations

Take On Discussion Roles As students engage in partner, small-group, and whole-class discussions, encourage them to take on roles to help keep the discussion on track that include

→ a questioner who asks questions in order to keep everyone involved and keep the discussion moving.

→ a recorder who takes notes and later reports to the class.

→ a discussion monitor who keeps the group on topic and makes sure everyone gets a turn to talk.

Go Digital

Discuss the Concept

Watch Video

View Photos

Use Graphic Organizer

Weekly Concept Better Together

? Essential Question
How do shared experiences help people adapt to change?

Go Digital!

Through Thick and Thin

When times get tough, people have to rely on each other to help them adapt to changing situations. Even small gestures can help.

During the Great Depression, many businesses closed, causing widespread unemployment.

In cities like this one, supportive groups gave unemployed people free soup, coffee, and doughnuts as they waited for work. The shared meal helped them not feel so alone.

Talk About It

Write words you have learned about how people help each other adapt to change. Then talk about a time that other people helped you adapt to a change.

Adapting to Change Together

READING/WRITING WORKSHOP, pp. 320–321

ENGLISH LANGUAGE LEARNERS SCAFFOLD

Beginning

Use Visuals Point to the photograph of people in line. Say: *These people in line needed food during difficult times. Special groups helped by giving them food. These groups were supportive.* Elicit that another word for *supportive* is *helpful*. Ask: *Why are these people standing in line?* Elaborate or clarify as needed.

Intermediate

Describe Help students describe the photograph. Ask: *What do you think the people in the picture need?* Wait for students to respond. Then ask: *How were others supportive of these people?* Repeat correct answers, correcting grammar and pronunciation if needed.

Advanced/High

Discuss Have students discuss the photograph. Ask: *What experience do these people share? How does this experience help them adapt to change?* Elicit reasons that people needed to rely on others and be supportive during the Great Depression.

GRAPHIC ORGANIZER 140

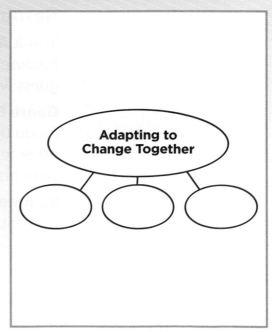

Adapting to Change Together

→ Listening Comprehension

MINILESSON
10 Mins

Interactive Read Aloud

OBJECTIVES

CCSS Summarize a written text read aloud or information presented in diverse media and formats, including visually, quantitatively, and orally. **SL.5.2**

• Listen for a purpose.
• Identify characteristics of historical fiction.

ACADEMIC LANGUAGE

• *historical fiction, make predictions*
• Cognates: *ficción histórica, predicciones*

Connect to Concept: Better Together

Tell students that people that share an experience can often help each other adapt to change. Let students know that you will be reading aloud a passage about a boy who has to adjust to living in a new place.

Preview Genre: Historical Fiction

Explain that the text you will read aloud is historical fiction. Discuss the features of historical fiction:

→ includes events and settings typical of the period in which the story is set

→ includes characters who speak and act like people from a particular time and place in the past

→ often includes real as well as made-up people and events

Preview Comprehension Strategy: Make Predictions

Explain that readers use information in a story to make predictions about what might happen. Point out that making predictions provides readers with a purpose. They can read on to check their predictions against what happens in the text and revise them if necessary.

Use the Think Alouds on page T77 to model the strategy.

Respond to Reading

Think Aloud Clouds Display Think Aloud Master 3: *I predicted ____ because…* to reinforce how you used the make predictions strategy to guess what would happen.

Genre Features With students, discuss the elements of the Read Aloud that let them know it is historical fiction. Ask them to think about other texts that you have read or they have read independently that were historical fiction.

Summarize Have students restate the most important information from "Starting Over" in their own words.

Go Digital

View Ilustrations

Model Think Alouds

Genre Chart

Starting Over

Tomasso looked out over the ship's railing, trying to catch a glimpse of the city that would be his new home. After two weeks at sea, he and his parents had finally reached America. During the voyage, everyone was talking about what happened last month—the Titanic, which was supposed to be an unsinkable ship, had hit an iceberg and gone down. Luckily, the ship Tomasso and his family were traveling on had made the voyage successfully.

Tomasso and his parents were coming to America in search of opportunity. His aunt and uncle had immigrated to America from Italy two years earlier and opened a successful market. Soon, Tomasso and his parents would join them in New York City.

Tomasso was excited about his new home, especially because he would see his cousin, Paulo, but he was scared, too. He didn't speak English, he was already homesick for his village, and he missed the field where he and Paulo used to play "You Can't Catch Me," a game they had invented. Tomasso wondered about Paulo. Did he speak English? Where—and what—did he play now? **1**

As his family made their way through the city, Tomasso marveled at how busy and loud New York was! Noisy motorcars rattled up and down every block, horse-drawn carriages clattered and bounced over the cobblestoned streets, and men called out as they peddled food from large carts. It was like nothing he had ever experienced.

Finally, they arrived at their new home. Paulo and his family were waiting for them. "Hello," Paulo greeted him, and Tomasso's jaw dropped—Paulo was speaking English!

"Come with me," Paulo laughed, switching to Italian. He led Tomasso down the street to a park.

"I know how you feel," said Paulo, "because I felt the same way when I first arrived. You think you'll never fit in here, but you will. When I feel homesick, I come to this park. Later, I'll start teaching you English, but right now, You Can't Catch Me!" **2**

Tomasso grinned and began chasing Paulo. America was already starting to feel like home! **3**

1 Think Aloud Tomasso is scared, but he is looking forward to seeing Paulo. I **predict** that Paulo will be able help Tomasso adjust to life in America.

2 Think Aloud I **predicted** that Paulo would help Tomasso. I think I'm right, because Paulo is going to teach him English. He also shows him where they can play their old game.

3 Think Aloud I can confirm my **prediction** that Paulo would help Tomasso adjust to life in America. With Paulo's help, Tomasso is already starting to feel at home.

→ Vocabulary

Reading/Writing Workshop

OBJECTIVES
Acquire and use accurately grade-appropriate general academic and domain-specific words and phrases, inluding those that signal contrast, addition, and other logical relationships (e.g., *however, although, nevertheless, similarly, moreover, in addition*). **L.5.6**

ACADEMIC LANGUAGE
rely, supportive

MINILESSON 10 Mins — Words in Context

Model the Routine

Introduce each vocabulary word using the Vocabulary Routine found on the **Visual Vocabulary Cards**.

Visual Vocabulary Cards

Vocabu...
Define:
Example:
Ask:

Vocabulary Routine

Define: When you **assume** something, you take it for granted, or suppose it is so.

Example: Caitlyn could only assume the cat broke the flower pot.

Ask: What might you assume if you awaken to snow on a school day?

Definitions

→ **guarantee** — To **guarantee** is to make sure or certain of something. **Cognate:** *garantizar*

→ **nominate** — If you **nominate** someone, you suggest or propose that the person be chosen, such as a candidate for an office. **Cognate:** *nominar*

→ **obviously** — If something is done **obviously**, it is easily seen or understood. **Cognate:** *obviamente*

→ **rely** — To **rely** is to trust or depend on someone or something.

→ **supportive** — When you are **supportive**, you provide approval, aid, or encouragement to others.

→ **sympathy** — If you feel **sympathy** toward someone, you feel and understand their troubles.

→ **weakling** — A **weakling** is a person who lacks physical strength.

Talk About It

Have students work with a partner and talk about the photograph and definition for each word. Ask them to discuss how the sentence relates to the definition. Then ask students to choose three words and write questions for their partner to answer.

Go Digital

assume

Use Visual Glossary

CCSS Words to Know

Vocabulary

Use the picture and the sentences to talk with a partner about each word.

assume
Caitlyn could only **assume** the cat broke the flower pot.

What might you *assume* if you awaken to snow on a school day?

guarantee
With such dark clouds approaching, Henrik can **guarantee** that it will rain soon.

When else might you *guarantee* something?

nominate
The team will **nominate** the best candidates to run for class president.

Why might you *nominate* a particular person for a task or position?

obviously
The hand-knitted scarf was **obviously** too long for Marta's little brother.

What kinds of clothes are *obviously* wrong for a cold day?

rely
To make a basket, Calvin must **rely** on the skills his coaches taught him.

When have you had to *rely* on someone else?

supportive
The audience's **supportive** applause boosted Clare's energy.

In what other ways can you be *supportive* of a performer on stage?

sympathy
Erik's dad offered **sympathy** when his team lost the game.

When else might you express *sympathy* to someone?

weakling
Being tired and ill in bed made Emily feel like a **weakling**.

At what other times might you feel like a *weakling*?

Your Turn
COLLABORATE

Pick three vocabulary words. Then write three questions for your partner to answer.

Go Digital! *Use the online visual glossary*

322

323

READING/WRITING WORKSHOP, pp. 322–323

ELL ENGLISH LANGUAGE LEARNERS SCAFFOLD

Beginning	Intermediate	Advanced/High
Use Visuals Say: *The word* assume *means to think something is true.* Elicit that another word for *assume* is *believe.* Have students look at the photograph for *assume* and name things they see in the picture. Ask: *What do you assume will happen next? Why?* Clarify responses as needed.	**Describe** Have students describe the photograph for *assume.* Review its meaning. Then say: *When I see dark clouds, I assume it will rain.* Have students complete this frame: *When I see _____, I assume _____.* Correct responses for grammar and pronunciation.	**Discuss** Ask students to talk about the photograph for *assume* with a partner. Ask: *What might you assume if you saw a long line at the movie theater?* Circulate as partners discuss and elicit details to support students' responses.

VOCABULARY T79

CCSS **Shared Read** Genre • Historical Fiction

The Day the Rollets
Got Their Moxie Back

Essential Question

How do shared experiences help people adapt to change?

Read about how a family comes together during a period of great hardship in the United States.

324

Sometimes, the thing that gets you through hard times comes like a bolt from the blue. That's what my older brother's letter was like, traveling across the country from a work camp in Wyoming. It was 1937, and Ricky was helping to build facilities for a new state park as part of President Roosevelt's employment program. Though the program created jobs for young men like Ricky, it hadn't helped our dad find work yet.

I imagined Ricky looking up at snow-capped mountains and sparkling skies, breathing in the smell of evergreens as his work crew turned trees into lumber and lumber into buildings. It almost made an 11-year-old **weakling** like me want to become a lumberjack.

Back in our New York City apartment, the air smelled like meatloaf and cabbage. Dad sat slant-wise in his chair by the window, **obviously** trying to catch the last rays of sunlight rather than turn on a light. My older sister Ruth and I lay on the floor comparing the letters Ricky had sent us. "Shirley, Ricky says they had a talent show, and he wore a grass skirt and did a hula dance while playing the ukulele!" Ruth reported with delight. "I'll bet he was the cat's pajamas!"

"It'd be swell to have our own talent show!" I replied.

"Should I start sewing grass skirts?" Mom asked from the kitchen, which was just the corner where someone had plopped down a stove next to a sink and an icebox. "Now come set the table. Dinner's almost ready."

325

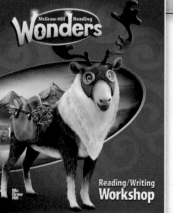

Reading/Writing Workshop

READING/WRITING WORKSHOP, pp. 324–325

Shared Read

Lexile 900   *TextEvaluator*™ 48

Connect to Concept: Better Together

Explain that "The Day the Rollets Got Their Moxie Back" will demonstrate how shared experiences can help people adapt to change. Read the story with students. Note that previously taught vocabulary words are highlighted in the text.

Close Reading

Reread Paragraph 1: Tell students that you are going to take a closer look at the beginning of the story. Reread the first paragraph together. Ask: *What details in the story help us identify its genre?* Model how to cite evidence to answer.

The narrator uses the phrase *hard times* and mentions that the year is 1937 and that her brother is working in President Roosevelt's employment program. These details and my prior knowledge help me understand that the story takes place during the Great Depression, an actual period of tough economic times in U.S. history. I think this story is an example of historical fiction.

Reread Paragraphs 2 and 3: Model how to compare and contrast the two settings described.

The narrator describes Wyoming as being full of snow-capped mountains and sparkling skies and smelling of evergreens. In contrast, the narrator describes the apartment in New York City as being dimly lit and smelling of meatloaf and cabbage.

Dad stayed where he was, sullen and spent. "Any jobs in the paper?" Mom asked, her voice rich with **sympathy**. Dad shook his head no. He had worked as an artist in the theater for years, but most productions were still strapped for cash. Dad sketched posters for shows that did get the green light, just to keep his skills sharp. He even designed posters for "Rollet's Follies," with Ruth and me depicted in watercolor costumes.

For dinner, Mom served a baked loaf of whatever ingredients she had that worked well together. From the reddish color, I could **assume** that she had snuck in beets. "I **guarantee** you'll like these beets," she said, reading my frown. "It's beet loaf, the meatless meat loaf," she sang as she served up slices.

Ruth fidgeted in her seat, still excited about the talent show. Though calm on the outside, inside I was all atwitter, too.

Over the next week, Ruth and I practiced our Hawaiian dance routine. Our parents worried about heating bills as cold weather settled in. One Saturday, my father decided to grin and bear it, and grab some hot coffee at the local soup kitchen, where he hoped to hear about available jobs. Ruth and I begged to go along. Since the kitchen offered doughnuts and hot chocolate on weekends, he agreed.

Ron Mazellan

326

Most everyone in line was bundled up against the cold. Many of us had to **rely** on two or three threadbare layers. Like many other men, Dad bowed his head as if in shame.

The line moved slowly. Bored, Ruth began practicing her dance steps. I sang an upbeat tune to give her some music. Around us, downturned hats lifted to reveal frowns becoming smiles. Soon, folks began clapping along. Egged on by the **supportive** response, Ruth twirled and swayed like there was no tomorrow.

"Those girls sure have moxie!" someone shouted.

"They've got heart, all right!" offered another. "Why, they oughta be in pictures!"

"With performances like that, I'd **nominate** them for an Academy Award!" a woman called out.

"Those are my girls!" Dad declared, his head held high.

Everyone burst into applause. For those short moments, the past didn't matter, and the future blossomed ahead of us like a beautiful flower. I couldn't wait to write Ricky and tell him the news.

Make Connections

Talk about ways that Ricky, Ruth, and Shirley helped each other adapt to the times. **ESSENTIAL QUESTION**

Think about a time when others helped you adapt to a new situation. How did your experience compare with the Rollet family's? **TEXT TO SELF**

327

READING/WRITING WORKSHOP, pp. 326–327

Make Connections

ESSENTIAL QUESTION

Remind students to use text evidence as they discuss how the characters helped one other adapt to hard times. Ask students to explain how shared experiences help people adapt to change.

Continue Close Reading

Use the following lessons for focused rereadings.

→ Make Predictions, pp. T82–T83

→ Character, Setting, Plot: Compare and Contrast, pp. T84–T85

→ Historical Fiction, pp. T86–T87

→ Idioms, pp. T88–T89

ACT Access Complex Text

▶ **Prior Knowledge**

Historical fiction may use unfamiliar language and describe unfamiliar events.

→ Tell students that the word *moxie* means "courage or determination, particularly in times of difficulty." The first known use of the word *moxie* was in 1930.

→ During the 1930s, many countries in the world experienced tough economic times and high unemployment rates. This period in history is known as the Great Depression.

→ Comprehension Strategy

Reading/Writing Workshop

OBJECTIVES

CCSS Quote accurately from a text when explaining what the text says explicitly and when drawing inferences from the text. **RL.5.1**

Make, confirm, and revise predictions based on details in the text.

ACADEMIC LANGUAGE

- *make predictions, historical fiction*
- Cognates: *predicciones, ficción histórica*

MINILESSON 10 Mins

Make Predictions

1 Explain

Remind students that when they read historical fiction, they should make predictions about what might happen next.

→ Students should use details in the text, such as what characters do, say, and think, to help them predict what might happen later in the story.

→ As they continue reading, they should confirm their predictions or revise them as necessary based on additional information in the text.

Tell students that making predictions gives readers a purpose and helps keep them actively engaged in a story.

2 Model Close Reading: Text Evidence

Model using details in the title to make predictions about who the main characters are (the Rollets) and what kind of ending the story will have (positive, because they get something back).

3 Guided Practice of Close Reading

COLLABORATE

Have partners use the girls' reactions to a letter from their older brother Ricky to predict what will happen next. Encourage students to reread page 325 for details about how the sisters react to their brother's letter. Have partners identify details in subsequent pages of the story that help them confirm or revise their predictions.

Go Digital

Present the Lesson

COMPREHENSION STRATEGY

 CCSS Comprehension Strategy

Make Predictions

As you read a story, clues in the text can help you predict what will happen next. Making predictions helps you read with purpose. As you continue to read, you can find out if your predictions are correct. If they are not correct, you can revise them.

Find Text Evidence

You can make predictions about the story "The Day the Rollets Got Their Moxie Back," beginning with the title on page 324.

page 324

CCSS Shared Read · Genre · Historical Fiction
The Day the Rollets
Got Their Moxie Back

From the title, I predict that the main characters in the story will be the Rollets. I don't know what Moxie means, but the story will probably have a positive ending since the Rollets will get back something that they have been missing.

Your Turn

Based on the girls' reactions to the letters from their older brother, Ricky, what did you predict might happen next? As you read, use the strategy Make Predictions.

328

READING/WRITING WORKSHOP, p. 328

 A C T **A**ccess **C**omplex **T**ext

▶ **Connection of Ideas**

Have students connect details in the story to make predictions. Point out Ricky's letters on page 325.

→ *What event does Ricky mention?* (being in a talent show)

→ *How do Ruth and Shirley respond?* (Ruth says Ricky must have been "the cat's pajamas," and Shirley says it would be "swell" to have their own talent show.)

→ *What might you predict from these details?* (The idea of a talent show will come back in the story.)

Monitor and *Differentiate*

✓ **Quick Check**

Can students identify and use details from the story to make, confirm, and revise predictions?

⬇

Small Group Instruction

If No → | Approaching Level | Reteach p. T104 |
| ELL | Develop p. T121 |

If Yes → | On Level | Review p. T112 |
| Beyond Level | Extend p. T116 |

ON-LEVEL PRACTICE BOOK pp. 213–214

Comprehension and Fluency

Name _____

Read the passage. Use the make predictions strategy to check your understanding.

Nancy's First Interview

    Nancy poured herself a bowl of cornflakes as her father finished a
12 telephone call. "You're really putting me on the spot," he said to the
25 person at the other end of the line. "I already have a commitment today,
39 Jim." After a few moments, Mr. Jenson sighed and hung up the telephone.
52 Nancy looked up from her breakfast, preparing for bad news.
62   Her father gave her a sad smile. "I'm really sorry, Nance, but I have
76 to work today. We'll have to reschedule our fishing trip." Mr. Jenson was
89 a reporter for the city newspaper. After the stock market crash of 1929,
102 his newspaper had laid off most of the reporters. Four years later, they
115 still had only a skeleton crew. He was glad to have a job, but he was
131 overworked and underpaid.
134   Nancy shrugged, trying not to look too upset. She wished she could do
147 something to comfort her dad. The last thing she wanted was to make him
161 feel guilty. "It's okay, Dad," she said, forcing a cheerful smile.
172   "The worst part is that our photographers are on other assignments,"
183 he grumbled, shaking his head. He paused for a moment, lost in thought.
196 "Nancy," he said, "do you remember when I showed you how to use
209 my camera?" She nodded. "Do you think you could help me today? I
222 can't carry all of the equipment by myself, and we'd get to spend some
236 time together."
238   Nancy jumped up from her chair and ran to her bedroom to change out
252 of her fishing clothes. "Make tracks," her dad called down the hallway.
264 "We're in a hurry!"

Practice · Grade 5 · Unit 5 · Week 2 **213**

| APPROACHING pp.213–214 | BEYOND pp.213–214 | ELL pp.213–214 |

→ Comprehension Skill

Reading/Writing Workshop

Character, Setting, Plot: Compare and Contrast

1 Explain

Explain to students that when they compare and contrast, they analyze how two people, places, or things are alike and different.

→ To **compare and contrast characters** in a story, students must review details in the text that reveal how the various characters are both similar and different. These details may include the characters' thoughts, feelings, words, actions, traits, and responses to events.

→ Explain that the characters' personalities and actions affect the events in a story but can also be changed by these events.

→ By comparing and contrasting different characters, students can better understand both the characters and the plot in a story.

2 Model Close Reading: Text Evidence

Model identifying important details that tell about the characters during the dinner scene on page 326. Then model using the details on the graphic organizer to compare and contrast the behavior of the mother, father, and two sisters.

 Write About Reading: Compare and Contrast Model for students how to use details from the organizer to write a summary that compares and contrasts how the different family members respond to their family's situation and why.

3 Guided Practice of Close Reading

 Have pairs use the graphic organizer to record details about the characters' feelings outside the soup kitchen at the start of the scene. Then have them record details about how the characters' feelings change as the scene progresses. Discuss each character as students complete the organizer.

 Write About Reading: Compare and Contrast Have pairs write a summary that compares and contrasts the characters' feelings and responses at the beginning and at the end of the scene on page 327. Ask them to share their summaries with the class.

Go Digital

Present the Lesson

OBJECTIVES

 CCSS Compare and contrast two or more characters, settings, or events in a story or drama, drawing on specific details in the text (e.g., how characters interact). **RL.5.3**

CCSS Quote accurately from a text when explaining what the text says explicitly and when drawing inferences from the text. **RL.5.1**

ACADEMIC LANGUAGE

• *compare, contrast, characters*

• Cognates: *comparar, contrastar*

SKILLS TRACE

CHARACTER, SETTING, PLOT

Introduce U1W1

Review U1W2, U1W6, U2W2, U2W6, U3W6, U4W6, U5W1, U5W2, U6W6

Assess U1, U2, U5

Comprehension Skill CCSS

Compare and Contrast

The characters in a story may be similar to or different from one another in their traits, actions, and responses to events. You **compare and contrast characters** to help you better understand how their personalities and actions affect events, or are changed by events.

 Find Text Evidence

When I reread the dinner scene on page 326 of "The Day the Rollets Got Their Moxie Back," I can use text details to compare each family member's different responses to their difficult situation.

Mother
sings, tries to make the best of things

Father
sullen, shakes head, tired

Event
Dinner at the Rollets'

Ruth
excited and fidgety, dreaming of show

Shirley
quiet yet excited, dreaming of show

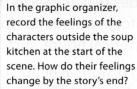 **Your Turn** COLLABORATE

In the graphic organizer, record the feelings of the characters outside the soup kitchen at the start of the scene. How do their feelings change by the story's end?

Go Digital!
Use the interactive graphic organizer

329

READING/WRITING WORKSHOP, p. 329

 **ENGLISH LANGUAGE LEARNERS SCAFFOLD**

Beginning	Intermediate	Advanced/High
Use Visuals Read aloud the dinner scene on page 326. Use facial expressions to convey *sullen* and *spent*. Have students pantomime shaking their heads for "no" and the action of fidgeting. Help students compare and contrast: *Dad is _____, but Ruth is _____.*	**Identify** Reread page 326 with students. Use facial expressions to convey *sullen* and *spent*. Ask: *How does Dad act during dinner? Why? How does Mom try to keep their spirits up? What does Ruth do and feel?* Help students use these details to compare and contrast: *Dad is _____, so Mom _____. Meanwhile, Ruth is _____.*	**Describe** Have students compare and contrast the behavior of the family members during the dinner scene on page 326. Then have partners identify details in the text that help them make inferences about why the characters behave in these ways.

Monitor and *Differentiate*

✓ Quick Check

Are students able to use details from the graphic organizer to compare and contrast the characters' behavior accurately and effectively?

⬇

Small Group Instruction

If No →	**Approaching Level**	Reteach p. T111
	ELL	Develop p. T121
If Yes →	**On Level**	Review p. T115
	Beyond Level	Extend p. T119

ON-LEVEL PRACTICE BOOK pp. 213–215

Comprehension: **Compare and Contrast and Fluency**

Name _____

A. Reread the passage and answer the questions. Possible responses provided.

1. Why does Nancy go with Mr. Jenson on his newspaper assignment?
   The newspaper's photographers are all busy and he needs her to take pictures.

2. How does the Carters' home contrast with the Jensons' house?
   The Carters' home is smaller, less clean, and has old broken furniture.

3. What similarities does Nancy see when she compares her own family with the Carters?
   Both families stick together and help each other through tough times.

4. When Mr. Jenson says that Nancy is a "chip off the old block," is he comparing or contrasting the two of them? Explain.
   He is comparing Nancy and himself and saying that she is a lot like him.

B. Work with a partner. Read the passage aloud. Pay attention to expression and phrasing. Stop after one minute. Fill out the chart.

	Words Read	–	Number of Errors	=	Words Correct Score
First Read		–		=	
Second Read		–		=	

Practice · Grade 5 · Unit 5 · Week 2 215

APPROACHING pp. 213–215	BEYOND pp. 213–215	ELL pp. 213–215

→ Genre: Literature

Reading/Writing Workshop

MINILESSON
10 Mins

Historical Fiction

Go Digital

Present the Lesson

1 Explain

Share with students the following characteristics of **historical fiction**:

→ Historical fiction features events and settings that are typical of a particular period in history.

→ Characters in historical fiction speak and act like the people from a particular time and place in the past.

→ Historical fiction often includes real as well as made-up people and events. For example, a story with made-up main characters might mention an actual historical figure, such as a president.

Explain to students that reading historical fiction can sometimes require some prior knowledge about the time and place of the story.

2 Model Close Reading: Text Evidence

Model using details from the story (the year 1937, President Roosevelt) as well as dialect typical of a specific time and place in history (*swell, icebox*) to identify "The Day the Rollets Got Their Moxie Back" as historical fiction.

Dialect Remind students that characters sometimes use dialect, or speech typical of a time or place. This dialect may include words, phrases, and idioms that are no longer commonly used. On page 325, point out the words *swell* and *icebox*. Ask: *What words that mean the same things as* swell *and* icebox *do we use today? Why might the author of the story have included words like* swell *and* icebox?

3 Guided Practice of Close Reading

COLLABORATE

Have students work with partners to list two examples of dialect in "The Day the Rollets Got Their Moxie Back." Partners should discuss what the examples of dialect might mean and why the author might have included them. Have partners share and compare their findings with the class.

OBJECTIVES

CCSS Quote accurately from a text when explaining what the text says explicitly and when drawing inferences from the text. **RL.5.1**

CCSS Use knowledge of language and its conventions when writing, speaking, reading, or listening. Compare and contrast the varieties of English (e.g., dialects, registers) used in stories, dramas, or poems. **L.5.3b**

ACADEMIC LANGUAGE

• *historical fiction, characters, dialect*

• Cognates: *ficción histórica, dialecto*

 CCSS **Genre** Literature

Historical Fiction

The selection "The Day the Rollets Got Their Moxie Back" is historical fiction.

Historical fiction:
- Features events and settings typical of the time period in which the story is set
- Includes characters who act like and speak the dialect of people from a particular place in the past

 Find Text Evidence

I can tell that "The Day the Rollets Got Their Moxie Back" is historical fiction. The year is 1937, and President Roosevelt was real. Rollet family members are fictional but use dialect of the time.

page 325

Dialect Characters sometimes use dialect, which is speech typical of a place or time. Dialect may include words, phrases, and idioms that might sound unfamiliar.

Your Turn COLLABORATE

List two examples of dialect in "The Day the Rollets Got Their Moxie Back." Why might an author include dialect in historical fiction?

330

READING/WRITING WORKSHOP, p. 330

 **ENGLISH LANGUAGE LEARNERS SCAFFOLD**

Beginning	**Intermediate**	**Advanced/High**
Understand Point to the date 1937 and to President Roosevelt's name on page 325. Ask: *Does the story take place in 1937 when Franklin Roosevelt was President?* (yes) Help students point to the word *icebox* on page 325. Pantomime opening a refrigerator. Ask: *Was the word* icebox *used in the past to mean refrigerator?* (yes)	**Identify** Reread the first paragraph on page 325. Ask: *When does this story take place?* (1937) Reread the last two paragraphs on page 325. Ask: *What words do we use today that mean the same thing as* swell? (great, awesome) *What do we call an icebox today?* (a refrigerator) Help students identify reasons why the author uses words like these in the story.	**Explain** Have students reread the first paragraph and then the last two paragraphs on page 325. Ask: *When does this story take place?* Have partners discuss other words that mean the same things as *swell* and *icebox* and explain why the author uses these older terms in the story.

✓ **Quick Check**

Are students able to identify examples of dialect in the story? Are they able to explain why an author would include dialect in historical fiction?

⬇

Small Group Instruction

If No →	**Approaching Level**	Reteach p. T105
	ELL	Develop p. T123
If Yes →	**On Level**	Review p. T113
	Beyond Level	Extend p. T117

ON-LEVEL PRACTICE BOOK p. 216

Genre/Literary Element

Name _____

Afternoons Alone

Rusty moped around the empty house. Grandpa had been helping to build tanks at the factory since America declared war against Japan. Without him, there was nobody to fish with. There was no one to talk with in the afternoon.

Yesterday, his friend Corey had told Rusty, "Every day, after school, I clean house and do chores. Then, when Mom returns home from the tank factory, we can have some fun time together."

"How keen it will be when the war ends!" exclaimed Rusty.

"We'll have lots of family time then," Corey said excitedly.

Rusty eyed the dirty windows in his house and said to himself, "Maybe I can help with some chores, too."

Answer the questions about the text.

1. How do you know that this text is historical fiction?
It takes place in an earlier time. America declared war against Japan in 1941.

2. What events in the text are typical of the time period in which the text is set?
Men and women work in the tank factory.

3. Write an example of dialect in the text and tell what it means.
Answers will vary but should include: "moped around" (acted sad); "keen" (terrific); "eyed" (looked at).

216 Practice • Grade 5 • Unit 5 • Week 2

APPROACHING p. 216	**BEYOND** p. 216	**ELL** p. 216

→ Vocabulary Strategy

MINILESSON
10 Mins

Idioms

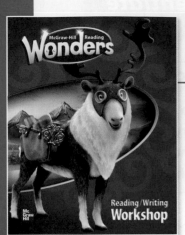

Reading/Writing Workshop

CCSS **OBJECTIVES**
Demonstrate understanding of figurative language, word relationships, and nuances in word meanings. Recognize and explain the meaning of common idioms, adages, and proverbs. **L.5.5b**

ACADEMIC LANGUAGE
idioms, context clues

1 Explain

Explain to students that an idiom is an expression that cannot be defined by the words in it. Just like people in real life, characters in stories commonly use idioms to convey their ideas.

→ Point out that idioms add color and expression to spoken and written language.

→ To determine the meaning of idioms, students can often use surrounding words and sentences as context clues.

Explain that authors may use idioms in historical fiction to make characters appear more realistic and to reflect the time period in which the story is set.

2 Model Close Reading: Text Evidence

Model using the surrounding context clues to infer the meaning of the idiom "a bolt from the blue" in the first sentence on page 325. Point out that Ricky's letter, like a bolt of lightning from a blue sky, came unexpectedly, seemingly from out of nowhere.

3 Guided Practice of Close Reading

COLLABORATE

Have partners figure out the meanings of the idioms "the cat's pajamas" (page 325), "get the green light" (page 326), "grin and bear it" (page 326), and "like there was no tomorrow" (page 327). Encourage students to use context clues in the surrounding sentences to help them determine each idiom's meaning.

Go Digital

Present the Lesson

SKILLS TRACE

IDIOMS

Introduce U1W2

Review U1W2, U1W5, U3W1, U5W2

Assess U1, U5

Vocabulary Strategy CCSS

Idioms

An **idiom** is an expression that cannot be defined by the words in it. Surrounding words and sentences can offer context clues to help you understand the meaning of an idiom.

 Find Text Evidence

I'm not sure what the idiom a bolt from the blue *means on page 325. When I think of a "bolt," I think of lightning and how quickly and unpredictably it can strike. Letters often come unexpectedly, as if out of nowhere. That must be the meaning.*

Sometimes, the thing that gets you through hard times comes like a bolt from the blue. That's what my older brother's letter was like, traveling across the country from a work camp in Wyoming.

Your Turn

 COLLABORATE

Use context clues to explain the meanings of the following idioms from "How the Rollets Got Their Moxie Back."

the cat's pajamas, *page 325*
get the green light, *page 326*
grin and bear it, *page 326*
like there was no tomorrow, *page 327*

Ron Mazellan

331

READING/WRITING WORKSHOP, p. 331

 ENGLISH LANGUAGE LEARNERS SCAFFOLD

Beginning	Intermediate	Advanced/High
Recognize Point to and read aloud the idiom "get the green light" on page 326. Show students a picture of a traffic stoplight. Ask them to tell what the green light means. Ask: *So if shows got the green light, were they allowed to move forward and be performed?* (yes)	**Identify** Read aloud and explain the meaning of the idiom "grin and bear it" on page 326. Have pairs work together to identify context clues, such as *grab some hot coffee* and *local soup kitchen,* that help them determine the meaning of the idiom. Repeat this process with other idioms in the text.	**Derive meaning** Point out the idiom "the cat's pajamas" on page 325. Have partners determine its meaning and discuss how context clues helped them. Point out the Spanish cognate *pijama.* Repeat the process with other idioms in the text.

Monitor and *Differentiate*

 Quick Check

Can students use context clues to determine the meanings of different idioms in the story?

⬇

Small Group Instruction

If No →	**Approaching Level**	Reteach p. T109
	ELL	Develop p. T125
If Yes →	**On Level**	Review p. T114
	Beyond Level	Extend p. T118

ON-LEVEL PRACTICE BOOK p. 217

Vocabulary Strategy: **Idioms**

Name _____

Read each passage. Underline the idiom in each one. Then, on the lines below the passage, restate the idiom in your own words. Possible responses provided.

1. "You're really <u>putting me on the spot</u>," he said to the person at the other end of the line. "I already have a commitment today, Jim."

   forcing me to make an unpleasant choice

2. After the stock market crash of 1929, his newspaper had laid off most of the reporters. Four years later, they still had only a <u>skeleton crew</u>. He was glad to have a job, but he was overworked and underpaid.

   very small number of workers

3. Nancy jumped up from her chair and ran to her bedroom to change out of her fishing clothes. "<u>Make tracks</u>," her dad called down the hallway. "We're in a hurry!"

   hurry up

4. He explained that they had owned a farm in Oklahoma, but lost it when costs rose. "Upkeep <u>cost an arm and a leg</u>, and the drought killed our chances of a good crop."

   cost a lot of money

5. Mr. Jenson grinned and ruffled Nancy's hair. "I taught her everything she knows," he said. "She's <u>a chip off the old block</u>."

   just like her father

Practice • Grade 5 • Unit 5 • Week 2   **217**

APPROACHING p. 217	BEYOND p. 217	ELL p. 217

Develop Comprehension

Literature Anthology

Bud, Not Buddy

Text Complexity Range

Lexile

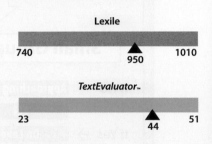

740   950   1010

TextEvaluator™

23   44   51

Options for Close Reading

→ Whole Class

→ Small Group

→ Independent

CCSS Genre · Historical Fiction

①

Essential Question

How do shared experiences help people adapt to change?

Read about how a band helps a boy adjust to a new home.

Go Digital!

364

A C T Access Complex Text

What makes this text complex?

▶ **Prior Knowledge**

▶ **Connection of Ideas**

▶ **Specific Vocabulary**

▶ **Genre**

▶ Prior Knowledge

Students may know little about the Great Depression, the historical period in which the story is set. Point out that the introduction on page 365 says that Bud grew up during the Great Depression. Elicit what students already know about this period in U.S. history. Supplement their prior knowledge with this information:

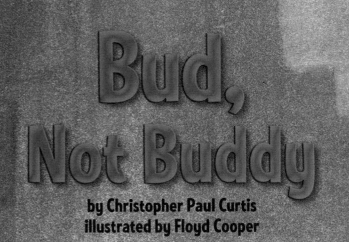

Bud, Not Buddy

by Christopher Paul Curtis
illustrated by Floyd Cooper

Bud is a motherless ten-year-old boy growing up in Flint, Michigan during the Great Depression, shuttling between orphanages and foster homes. Bud doesn't have much, but he has a few special things. One is a set of rules—"Bud Caldwell's Rules and Things for Having a Funner Life"—about everything he's learned so far about surviving. He also has a suitcase full of treasured possessions: photos, a blanket, some special stones, and flyers advertising a famous band. While these items are the only mementoes Bud has of his mother, they also provide clues that Bud thinks may help him find a special man he's never met—his father.

Bud tracks down Herman E. Calloway, the well-known band leader who Bud believes to be his father. Calloway turns out to be a gruff old man who claims not to know anything about the boy. Fortunately, Calloway's band members, Grace Thomas, "Steady Eddie" Patrick, Jimmy Wesley, Chug "Doo-Doo Bug" Cross, Roy "Dirty Deed" Breed, and Doug "the Thug" Tennant, take a liking to Bud. After Bud joins the band for a meal at the Sweet Pea restaurant, where he breaks down and cries out of exhaustion and relief, Bud is invited to spend the night in a spare room at "Grand Calloway Station," Herman Calloway's large and busy home. The next morning, a still-tired Bud doesn't remember getting in bed, and wonders if he was put there by Miss Thomas. As Bud shakes off sleep, he hears voices in the house and follows them downstairs.

365

LITERATURE ANTHOLOGY, pp. 364–365

Predictive Writing

Have students read the title, preview the illustrations, and write their predictions about what this selection will be about.

ESSENTIAL QUESTION

Ask a student to read the Essential Question. Have students discuss how the story might help them answer the question.

Note Taking:
Use the Graphic Organizer

As students read the selection, ask them to take notes by filling in the graphic organizer on **Your Turn Practice Book page 212** to compare and contrast characters.

❶ Text Feature: Illustrations

Look at the illustration on page 364. What items do you see that show this story is set during an earlier time in history? (The cars are antique models. The boy's clothes and suitcase aren't modern.)

The Great Depression began in 1929 and ended around 1940. During that time, many people lost their jobs and homes. Thousands of children had to live in orphanages, sometimes because their families could not afford to care for them, or because their parents left them to find work. When possible, the children were placed in foster homes.

ELL Help students understand the word *depression* in this story. Tell them that the root of the word is *press*, and the prefix *de-* means *down*. Use your hands to press down on something. During the Great Depression, the economy was depressed.

→ *Was the economy higher or lower during the Great Depression?* (lower)

Develop Comprehension

❷ Vocabulary: Idioms

What is the meaning of the idiom, "so that's how the cookie's going to crumble," on page 366? Use the surrounding words and sentences to give you a clue. (It means things will happen in a certain way. It refers to what Mr. Calloway plans to do about Bud.) What is another idiom on page 366? What does it mean? ("Making a break" means getting ready to leave suddenly.)

❸ Literary Element: Dialect

Dialect is a specific way of speaking. Different regions of the country often have their own dialects, as have different groups throughout history. What is a synonym for dialect? (slang) What examples of dialect can you find on page 366? ("I'ma"; "uh-oh") What does "I'ma" mean? (It means "I am going to.")

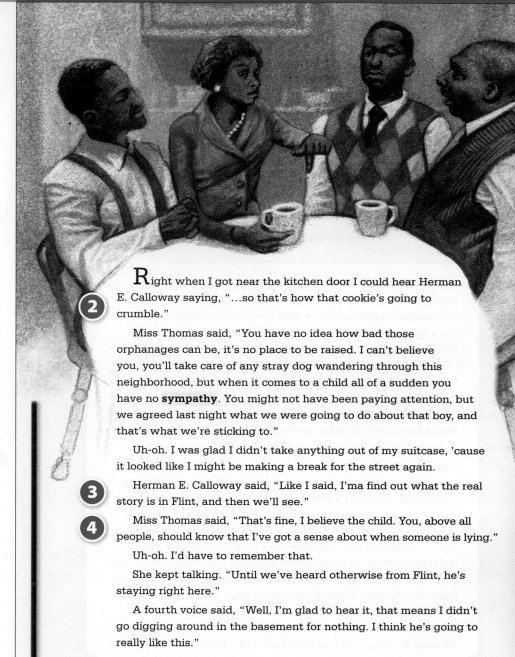

❷ Right when I got near the kitchen door I could hear Herman E. Calloway saying, "…so that's how that cookie's going to crumble."

Miss Thomas said, "You have no idea how bad those orphanages can be, it's no place to be raised. I can't believe you, you'll take care of any stray dog wandering through this neighborhood, but when it comes to a child all of a sudden you have no **sympathy**. You might not have been paying attention, but we agreed last night what we were going to do about that boy, and that's what we're sticking to."

Uh-oh. I was glad I didn't take anything out of my suitcase, 'cause it looked like I might be making a break for the street again.

❸ Herman E. Calloway said, "Like I said, I'ma find out what the real story is in Flint, and then we'll see."

❹ Miss Thomas said, "That's fine, I believe the child. You, above all people, should know that I've got a sense about when someone is lying."

Uh-oh. I'd have to remember that.

She kept talking. "Until we've heard otherwise from Flint, he's staying right here."

A fourth voice said, "Well, I'm glad to hear it, that means I didn't go digging around in the basement for nothing. I think he's going to really like this."

366

A C T Access Complex Text

▶ Connection of Ideas

Help students connect the introduction on page 365 with the beginning of the story on page 366.

→ *Why is the text on page 365 set in italics?* (It's a summary of what has happened before the story begins.)

→ *Where is Bud at the start of the first scene?* (He is in Herman Calloway's house.)

→ *Where was Bud before he met the band?* (in orphanages and foster homes in Flint, MI)

→ *What are the adults talking about?* (whether Bud can stay with them or not)

→ *Why does Bud think he might have to make a break for the street?* (If he can't stay with the band, he does not want to go back to the orphanage.)

It was Steady Eddie and it sounded like he had something for me!

I ran back up the steps on my tiptoes and down the hall to the little dead girl's room. I stood outside the room and closed the door loud enough that they could hear it downstairs. I *clump-clump-clump*ed down the hall to the door that Miss Thomas said was the bathroom.

When I was done I pulled on a chain that made the water come down. The loud noise made me jump back.

Man, these inside-the-house outhouses were hard to get used to. I washed my hands with running hot water and closed the bathroom door kind of loud.

I *clump-clump-clump*ed down the steps, stopping a couple of times to yawn real loud.

When I walked into the kitchen they all had looks on their faces like they hadn't been talking about me at all.

I said, "Good morning, Mr. Calloway," but I didn't really mean it, then said, "Good morning, Miss Thomas, good morning, Mr. Jimmy, good morning, Steady Eddie."

STOP AND CHECK

Make Predictions Why does Bud go back upstairs? What do you think Steady Eddie will give him? Look for details in the story to Make a Prediction.

367

LITERATURE ANTHOLOGY, pp. 366–367

---

④ Strategy: Make Predictions

Teacher Think Aloud As I read, I can use clues in the text to make predictions. I know that Bud has been in and out of orphanages and foster homes. I know there were a lot of orphans during the Depression. I predict that Herman will find out Bud is telling the truth and will let him stay with the band. As I continue to read, I will either confirm or revise my predictions.

⑤ Genre: Historical Fiction

What evidence do you see on this page that tells you this is historical fiction? Share your answer with a partner. (Bud pulls a chain to make water come down into the toilet. He talks about "inside-the-house outhouses.")

STOP AND CHECK

Make Predictions Why does Bud go back upstairs? (He wants to make sure the people downstairs know he is coming down.) What do you think Steady Eddie has for him? (It's probably a musical instrument. Steady Eddie is a musician, and musicians often have many instruments.)

ELL Read aloud the first sentence of the introduction on page 365. Explain that Bud has been living in an orphanage, a home for children without parents to care for them. Point out the cognate: orphanage/*orfanato*. Read aloud what Miss Thomas says about orphanages on page 366.

→ Have students point to the word "orphanages" and pronounce it. Finger-trace the root *orphan* and define it: "a child without parents."

→ *Does Miss Thomas like or dislike orphanages? What word shows you?* (The word *bad* shows that she dislikes them.)

Develop Comprehension

6 **Vocabulary: Idioms**

What is the meaning of "what's the scoop?" ("How are you? What's going on?") What is the meaning of "cop a squat?" ("Have a seat.")

7 **Skill: Character, Setting, Plot: Compare and Contrast Characters**

Compare everybody's response to Bud's arrival in the kitchen. (Everyone but Herman E. Calloway is pleasant to Bud.) Add this information to your graphic organizer to compare and contrast characters' actions.

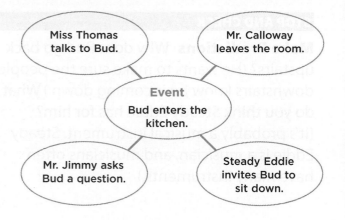

Miss Thomas talks to Bud.

Mr. Calloway leaves the room.

Event
Bud enters the kitchen.

Mr. Jimmy asks Bud a question.

Steady Eddie invites Bud to sit down.

I noticed right away that Miss Thomas didn't have all her diamond rings on, I guess it would've been hard sleeping with them flashing lights up at you, she must have to keep them closed up in a box that the sparkles can't get out of. I noticed too that even without the rings Miss Thomas still had to be the most beautiful woman in the world.

They smiled and said, "Good morning, Bud." All except Herman E. Calloway. He got up from the table and said, "I don't like the way Loudean is sounding, I'ma have a look at her plugs."

He went outside through a door at the back of the kitchen.

Miss Thomas said, "Bud, we'd just about given up on you. Do you usually sleep until after noon?"

After noon? Man, I couldn't believe it, I'd slept as long as those rich folks in the moving pictures!

"No, ma'am, that's the first time I ever did that."

She said, "I know you must be starving, but if you can hold out for another half hour or so Mr. Jimmy's going to make everyone's lunch. Think you can wait?"

"Yes, ma'am." A half hour wasn't nothing to wait, no matter how hungry you were.

Mr. Jimmy said, "So what's the scoop, little man?"

I didn't know what that meant so I said, "Nothing, sir."

Steady Eddie said, "How'd you sleep, kiddo?"

"Great, sir." Oops, I forgot I wasn't supposed to call the band men *sir*.

6 He said, "Cop a squat." He pointed at a chair. I guessed that meant "sit down," so I did.

7 Miss Thomas said, "Were your ears burning last night, Bud?"

Man, all these Grand Rapids people really do talk funny. I only came from the other side of the state and it was like they talked some strange language out here. I said, "What, ma'am?"

She said, "There's an old saying that when people talk about you behind your back your ears start to get real warm, kind of like they were burning."

368

A C T Access Complex Text

▶ Connection of Ideas

Tell students that when they read fiction, they should try to connect the characters' actions to the characters' wants and needs. Have students recall what the adults said on pages 366–367 and connect it with their actions when Bud appears.

→ *When Bud enters, Calloway says he needs to check the plugs on the car. Is this true? How do you know?*

(Probably not; he's making an excuse to leave. Earlier, he made it clear he was not in favor of Bud staying.)

→ *How do Miss Thomas and the band members treat Bud?* (They are kind and friendly. Earlier, Steady Eddie approved of Miss Thomas's suggestion that Bud stay with the band.)

I said, "No, ma'am, my ears felt just fine."

She said, "Well, they should've been burning, you were the subject of a very long conversation last night. But as sound asleep as you were, I'm really not all that surprised you didn't notice. I had to check your pulse to make sure you were still alive!"

Shucks! I knew it. She did come in when I was conked out and took my doggone pants and shirt off and put me there. Man, this was real embarrassing.

Miss Thomas said, "Mr. Calloway and the band and I talked about you for a long time. We've come up with something we want to discuss with you, but we need your help in deciding what to do."

Uh-oh. That was Rules and Things Number 36, or something, that meant I was going to have to get ready to go fetch something for her.

I said, "Yes, ma'am?" **8**

369

8 Strategy: Make Predictions

Teacher Think Aloud Miss Thomas says the adults need Bud's help in deciding what to do. Bud thinks he is going to have to fetch something. The clues I see don't lead me to make that prediction. I know that Miss Thomas wants to take care of him. I don't think she will put Bud to work. Do you think Bud is right? What help do you predict Miss Thomas wants from Bud?

Prompt students to apply the strategy in a Think Aloud. Have them turn to a partner and paraphrase Miss Thomas's dialogue and Bud's thoughts. Then have them predict what is going to happen next. Remind them to check their predictions as they continue reading, and either confirm or revise them.

Student Think Aloud I think Miss Thomas is going to ask if Bud wants to stay with the band. She said earlier, "he's staying right here." As I read more of the story, I will look for evidence to help me either confirm or revise my prediction.

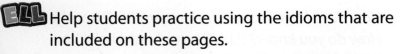 Help students practice using the idioms that are included on these pages.

→ Have students repeat the idiom, "What's the scoop?" Then ask: *How might I answer this question if you asked me?* (Possible response: You might say, "I'm teaching class right now!")

→ Ask students to show you how to "cop a squat." (sit down) If they have difficulty, show them what to do and ask them again.

→ Pantomime or ask a volunteer to demonstrate "conked out." (sleeping deeply)

LITERATURE ANTHOLOGY **T89F**

Develop Comprehension

9 Vocabulary: Idioms

What is the meaning of "split my face in half?" (His smile noticeably spread across his face.) What context clues did you use to help you figure it out? ("I'm going to assume that smile…"; "Before that grin gets stuck on your face…")

10 Ask and Answer Questions

What question do you have about the text? Share your question with a partner. For example, you might ask, "What does Miss Thomas mean when she says Mr. Calloway is going to give Bud's spirit a test?" To find the answer, try rereading and paraphrasing the text. Ask your partner for help. (Mr. Calloway is too stubborn, but he does not want to admit it. He may not be pleasant or cooperative with Bud. Bud will have to learn how to deal with Mr. Calloway to help change Mr. Calloway's mind.)

She said, "We've got to talk to some people in Flint first, but if they say it's all right, we were hoping that you'd stay here at Grand Calloway Station for a while."

9 A gigantic smile split my face in half.

Miss Thomas said, "I'm going to **assume** that that smile means yes."

I said, "Yes, ma'am! Thank you, ma'am!"

Miss Thomas said, "Before that grin gets stuck on your face, let me tell you you're going to have lots of chores and things to take care of around here, Bud, you'll be expected to pull your own weight the best you can. We all like a very clean house and none of us are too used to having children around, so we're all going to have to learn to be patient with each other. There's one person in particular that you're going to have to be very patient with. Do you know who I mean?"

I sure did. "Yes, ma'am, it's Mr. Calloway."

She said, "Good boy, give him some time. He really needs help with a lot of different things, he swears someone's adding weight onto that bass fiddle of his every year, but he's just getting older. He can use some young, wiry hands to help him around. Think you can handle that?"

Now I knew for sure she'd looked at my legs, she must've thought I was a real **weakling**.

I said, "Yes, ma'am, my legs are a lot stronger than they look, most folks are surprised by that."

10 Miss Thomas said, "I don't doubt that at all, Bud. I'm not worried about your body being strong, I'm more concerned about your spirit. Lord knows Mr. Calloway is going to give it a test."

I said, "Yes, ma'am, my spirit's a lot stronger than it looks too, most folks are really surprised by that."

She smiled and said, "Very good, but you know what, Bud?"

"What, ma'am?"

"I knew you were an old toughie the minute I saw you."

I smiled again.

370

A C T Access Complex Text

▶ Connection of Ideas

Ask students to pay attention to the relationship between Miss Thomas and Bud. In particular, ask them to notice how they interact.

→ *In what manner is Miss Thomas speaking to Bud on pages 370–371? How do you know?* (Miss Thomas is speaking to Bud very honestly and directly. She stares him right in the face and holds his arms.)

→ *How does Miss Thomas feel toward Bud?* (motherly) *How do you know?* (She "looked right hard" in Bud's face, "just like Momma used to.")

→ *Why do you think Miss Thomas feels this way about Bud?* (She knows that Bud is an orphan, and that it's difficult to grow up without a mother, so she wants to offer him as much support as she can.)

She said, "Our schedule's pretty heavy for the next couple of months, and then come September we'll have to see about school for you, but we'll be doing a lot of traveling right around Michigan, so I hope you don't mind long car trips."

"No, ma'am."

She said, "That's great, Bud. Something tells me you were a godsend to us, you keep that in mind all of the time, OK?"

"Yes, ma'am."

Then she did something that made me feel strange. She stood up, grabbed both my arms and looked right hard in my face, just like Momma used to, she said, "Really, Bud, I want you to always keep that in mind, this might get hard for you some of the time and I don't always travel with the band, so I don't want you to forget what I'm telling you."

I said, "No, ma'am, I won't." **12**

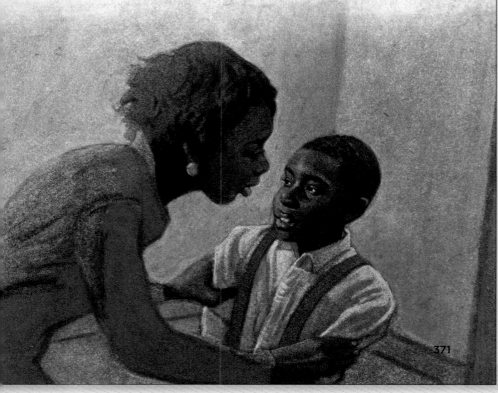

371

LITERATURE ANTHOLOGY, pp. 370–371

⑪ Author's Craft: Figurative Language

Read the third paragraph on page 371. What two things are being compared? (Miss Thomas compares Bud to a godsend.) Is this a simile or a metaphor? How do you know? (It is a metaphor because it compares two things without the words *like* or *as*.)

⑫ Skill: Make Inferences

Why does Miss Thomas hold onto Bud's arms and tell him not to forget their conversation? (She knows he is happy to be with them, but he might not realize how hard it is to work with a band.) What does she think Bud might do if things get hard? (She might think that he will run away from them.) What information about Miss Thomas and Bud help you make these inferences? Use text evidence to help you. (Miss Thomas says to Bud, "this might get hard for you some of the time and I don't always travel with the band, so I don't want you to forget what I'm telling you." She says this because Bud has a history of running away.)

ELL To help students understand the relationships in this story, help them follow the dialogue more closely by clarifying the use of pronouns.

→ Read the first paragraph on page 370 aloud. *Does the pronoun* they *refer to the band or to the people in Flint?* (the people in Flint)

→ *Who do the pronouns* him *and* he *refer to on page 370?* (Mr. Calloway)

Develop Comprehension

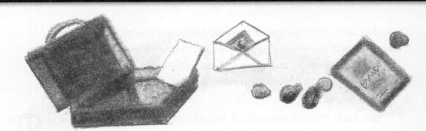

13 **Literary Element: Dialect**

What examples of dialect can you find on page 372? (In the first paragraph, Steady Eddie says "your'n." In the middle of the page, Eddie talks about something not being "copacetic.")

14 **Skill: Character, Setting, Plot: Compare and Contrast Characters**

Bud says he wasn't sure if he liked the way the talk with Steady Eddie was going. What might he think Steady Eddie wanted to do? (Bud might have thought that Steady Eddie wanted to take away his things and his suitcase.) How does Bud feel about Steady Eddie after seeing the gift? (He is thankful and appreciative.) How does the way Steady Eddie treats Bud compare to the way Miss Thomas treats him? (Both Steady Eddie and Miss Thomas are kind to Bud. Miss Thomas offers to take care of Bud, and Steady Eddie gives him a new suitcase.)

Steady Eddie said, "Since you're going to be part of the family there's some things we've got to talk about. Now I've noticed the tight grip you keep on that old suitcase of your'n. I need to know how attached to it you are."

"I carry it with me everywhere I go 'cause all my things are in there." I wasn't sure if I liked the way this talk was going.

Steady Eddie said, "That's what I need to know, are you attached to the suitcase, or is it the things inside that are important?"

I'd never thought about that before, I'd always thought of the suitcase and the things inside together.

I said, "The things I got from my mother are the most important."

He said, "Good, 'cause if you're going to be traveling with us it just wouldn't look too copacetic for you to be carrying that ratty old bag."

He reached under the kitchen table and pulled out one of those funny-looking suitcases that the band kept all their instruments in. This one looked like a baby one to his.

He put it on the table, opened it and said, "Since you're going to be traveling with Herman E. Calloway and the Worthy Swarthys, which is known far and wide as a very classy band, it's only fitting that you quit carrying your things in that cardboard suitcase.

"This is my old alto saxophone case, I've been hanging on to it for three years now, ever since the horn got stole right off the stage in Saginaw, but it doesn't look like I'm ever gonna get it back, so I figured you might as well keep your momma's things in it."

14 Wow! "Thank you, Steady Eddie!"

372

A C T Access Complex Text

▶ **Specific Vocabulary**

Read aloud the sixth paragraph on page 372. Explain that the word *copacetic* is an American slang word that was mostly used during the early- to mid-1900s meaning "fine, excellent, or highly satisfactory." The author's use of *copacetic* in the story adds to the historical accuracy and authenticity of the text.

→ *What modern slang word could the author use in place of the word* copacetic*?* (Possible responses: cool, awesome)

→ *Why is the word* copacetic *a better choice than the word* good*?* (It is a more interesting word, and it is specific to the character because it shows that Steady Eddie does not talk down to Bud.)

I pulled my new case over to me. The inside of it had a great big dent where Steady Eddie's saxophone used to go, now there wasn't anything in it but a little raggedy pink towel. The case had some soft smooth black stuff all over the inside of it, it covered everything, even the dent. There was a real old smell that came out of it too, like dried-up slobber and something dead. It smelled great! **15**

The back kitchen door opened and I thought Herman E. Calloway was coming back in to ruin everybody's fun, but it was the rest of the band.

Everybody said hello, poured themselves some coffee, then sat down at the table.

Doo-Doo Bug said, "I see Mr. C's got Loudean's carburetor tore down again, anything wrong?"

Miss Thomas said, "There's lots wrong, but not with that car." **16**

They all laughed so I joined in too.

I patted my new case and said, "This here's my case now, I'm going to be going around with you."

They smiled and Dirty Deed said, "So we hear. Glad to have you on board, partner."

373

LITERATURE ANTHOLOGY, pp. 372–373

---

15 Author's Craft: Figurative Language

Reread the first paragraph on page 373. What two things are being compared? (The smell from the saxophone case is being compared to "dried-up slobber" and "something dead.") Is this a simile or a metaphor? How do you know? (It is a simile because it uses the word *like* in the comparison.)

16 Skill: Make Inferences

Miss Thomas says, "There's lots wrong, but not with that car." What do you think she means? What evidence helps you make this inference? (She means that the car isn't the problem. The problem is that Mr. Calloway isn't getting along well with the rest of the band, and he and Miss Thomas disagree about having Bud stay with the band. The band members seem to be in favor of having Bud stay with them. Bud mentions that Mr. Calloway will "ruin everybody's fun.")

ELL Say the word *copacetic* and have students repeat it. Give examples of the meaning: "*I got an* A *on the test. That's copacetic." "My best friend is coming to my house this weekend. How copacetic!*"

→ Brainstorm with students things that could be copacetic. Have them appropriately use the word *copacetic* in a sentence.

→ Clarify other unfamiliar words or phrases, such as "have you on board," meaning "have you joining us."

Develop Comprehension

17 Skill: Character, Setting, Plot: Compare and Contrast Characters

Compare the characters' reactions after Steady Eddie gives Bud a gift. (Bud is excited and grateful. Steady Eddie says he'll have to practice. The Thug wants to give Bud a nickname. Miss Thomas isn't interested.) Add the information to your organizer.

Bud is excited and grateful.

Steady Eddy tells Bud about practice.

Event
Bud gets a recorder.

The Thug wants to give Bud a name.

Miss Thomas is not interested.

STOP AND CHECK

Confirm or Revise Predictions What does Steady Eddie give Bud? (a recorder) How does this make Bud feel? (Bud feels grateful and excited to learn music. The illustration is a clue that shows he is happy.)

Steady Eddie said, "I was just about to tell him some of the things Herman E. Calloway requires of anybody in his band."

The Thug said, "Otherwise known as Herman E. Calloway's Rules to **Guarantee** You Have No Female Companionship, No Alcohol, and No Fun at All."

"Rule number one, practice two hours a day."

Mr. Jimmy said, "That's a good one."

Steady Eddie said, "So I got you this, Bud."

Steady Eddie had another present for me! This was a long, brown, skinny wooden flute. I was going to have to learn music!

He said, "It's called a recorder. Once you've developed a little wind, and some tone and a embouchure we'll move on to something a little more complicated."

Those must've been more of those Grand Rapids words 'cause they sure weren't like any American talk I ever heard before.

I said, "Thank you!"

STOP AND CHECK

Confirm or Revise Predictions What does Steady Eddie give Bud? How does this make Bud feel? Confirming or Revising your Prediction may help you.

374

A C T Access Complex Text

▶ Specific Vocabulary

Point out that the author uses musical terms that give the story a more authentic feel. Explain the meaning of each musical term.

→ *A recorder is a wind instrument, similar to a flute, usually made of wood or plastic. The player blows into the mouthpiece and opens or closes the finger holes to make music.*

→ Point to the recorder in the illustration on page 374. Say: *Show me how you would play a recorder.*

→ Tone *is the sound of an instrument or voice.*

→ Embouchure *is the position and use of the lips, tongue, and teeth in playing a wind instrument.*

Steady Eddie said, "Don't thank me until you've been through a couple of hours of blowing scales. We'll see if you're still grateful then."

The Thug said, "Now all that's left is to give little stuff here a name."

Miss Thomas said, "You know, I don't like the way Loudean's been sounding, I think I'm gonna go check the air in the trunk." She picked her coffee up and started to leave the kitchen. **17**

Doo-Doo Bug said, "You don't have to leave, Miss Thomas."

"Darling, I know that, it's just that this is one of those man things that you all think is so mysterious and special that I have absolutely no interest in. The only thing I can hope is that the process has improved since you four were given your names." Then she left the room. **18**

As soon as she was gone Steady Eddie told me, "Hand me your ax and stand up, Bud." I was starting to catch on to this Grand Rapids talk, I remember that a ax was a instrument. I handed Steady my recorder and stood up in front of him.

He said, "Uh-uh, she was right, this is mysterious and special, so that grin's got to go, brother."

I tried to tie down my smile.

Steady said, "Mr. Jimmy, you're the senior musician here, would you proceed?"

Mr. Jimmy said, "Gentlemen, the floor's open for names for the newest member of the band, Bud-not-Buddy."

They started acting like they were in school. The Thug raised his hand and Mr. Jimmy pointed at him.

Thug said, "Mr. Chairman, in light of the boy's performance last night at the Sweet Pea, I **nominate** the name Waterworks Willie."

Shucks, I was hoping they'd forgot about that.

Mr. Jimmy said, "You're out of order, Douglas."

Steady raised his hand. "Mr. Chairman, this boy's **obviously** going to be a musician, he slept until twelve-thirty today, so I propose that we call him Sleepy."

Mr. Jimmy said, "The name Sleepy is before the board, any comments?" **19**

375

18 **Author's Craft: Humor**

How does the author show humor when the band debates a band name for Bud? Paraphrase the text in your response. (Miss Thomas jokes with the band members and says the process is a "man thing," so she leaves. She says she hopes Bud gets a better name than the others.)

19 **Strategy: Make Predictions**

Reread the last four paragraphs on page 375. Turn to a partner and say a name you predict the band might give Bud. Look for details in the story that may help you.

Student Think Aloud Mr. Jimmy said that Thug was out of order in referring to the time when Bud cried, so I'm sure they want to use a name that highlights something positive and strong about Bud. He was brave to travel alone and resourceful in finding the band, like a detective, so I think it will have something to do with that. As I read ahead, I'll look for the name they give him and confirm or revise my prediction.

→ Scales *are a series of notes in ascending or descending order. Why do musicians practice playing scales?* (to get better and faster)

→ Invite students who play an instrument to share additional information with the class.

 Share with students these cognates: tone/*tono,* flute/*flauta,* embouchure/*embocadura.* Ask:

→ *Do you hear or see the tone of an instrument?* (hear)

→ *What parts of the body do you use to develop an embouchure?* (lips, tongue, teeth)

→ *Are recorders and flutes large or small instruments?* (small)

Develop Comprehension

20 Skill: Character, Setting, Plot: Compare and Contrast Characters

What name does each band member suggest? (Mr. Jimmy strikes down "Waterworks Willie." Doo-Doo Bug says "the Bone." Thug says "LaBone." Steady Eddie says "Sleepy," and then suggests they compromise by using both names, "Sleepy LaBone.") Add the information to your organizer to compare and contrast the characters' responses to giving Bud a stage name.

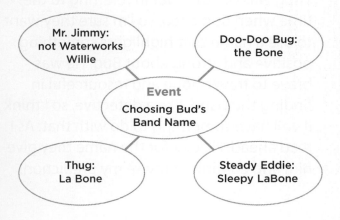

Mr. Jimmy: not Waterworks Willie

Doo-Doo Bug: the Bone

Event
Choosing Bud's Band Name

Thug: La Bone

Steady Eddie: Sleepy LaBone

Dirty Deed said, "Too simple. I think we need something that lets folks know about how slim the boy is."

Doo-Doo Bug said, "How about the Bone?"

Steady said, "Not enough class, he needs something so people will know right off that the boy's got class."

Mr. Jimmy said, "How do you say *bone* in French? French always makes things sound a lot classier."

The Thug said, "That's easy, *bone* in French is *la bone*."

Doo-Doo Bug said, "*La bone*, nah, it don't have a ring to it."

Steady Eddie said, "I got it, we'll compromise. How about Sleepy LaBone?"

I couldn't tie the smile down anymore, that was about the best name I'd ever heard in my life!

Mr. Jimmy said, "Let me try it out. Ladies and gentlemen, thank you very much for coming out on this cold November night, this night that will live in history, this night that for the first time on any stage anywhere, you have listened to the smooth saxophonical musings of that prodigy of the reed, Mr. Sleepy LaBone!"

The whole crowd broke out clapping.

The Thug said, "What can I say but *bang*!"

Dirty Deed said, "You nailed him!"

Doo-Doo Bug said, "That is definitely smooth."

Steady said, "My man!"

Mr. Jimmy said, "Kneel down, young man."

I got down on one knee.

Mr. Jimmy tapped me on the head three times with my recorder and said, "Arise and welcome to the band, Mr. Sleepy LaBone."

I got off my knee and looked at my bandmates.

Sleepy LaBone. Shucks, that was the kind of name that was enough to make you forget folks had ever called you Buddy, or even Clarence. That was the kind of name that was enough to make you practice *four* hours every day, just so you could live up to it!

376

A C T Access Complex Text

▶ **Genre**

Reread page 376 aloud with students. Point out the author's use of slang in the dialogue. Note that after the band gives Bud his name, they slip into slang that was typical of the period. This is a literary device authors often use in historical fiction. Ask students to rephrase each man's comment in standard modern English.

→ Thug: "What can I say but bang!" (I think that's great!)

→ Dirty Deed: "You nailed him!" (You got his name exactly right!)

→ Doo-Doo Bug: "That is definitely smooth." (That name sounds good.)

→ Steady Eddie: "My man!" (You're all right with me!)

STOP AND CHECK

Summarize How do the band members decide Bud's new name? How does Bud feel about becoming a part of the band? Summarizing the events may help you.

377

LITERATURE ANTHOLOGY, pp. 376–377

Return to Predictions

Review students' predictions and purposes for reading. Ask them to answer the Essential Question. (The experiences Bud has with the band help him adapt to his move. The experiences the band members have with Bud help them adjust to having a young boy with them.)

STOP AND CHECK

Summarize How do the band members decide Bud's new name? (They think of words to describe Bud's characteristics and qualities, and then compromise and combine two words into a name.) **How does Bud feel about the new name?** (He likes the name. He says it will make him want to practice every day to live up to it.)

ELL Say: *Band members often gave each other names that characterize them.* Ask questions about Bud's new name and help students find text clues to answer them.

→ *Who thinks of the name* Sleepy? Why? (Steady Eddie thought of the name because Bud slept until 12:30.)

→ *What part of the name shows that Bud is slim?* (Bone)

→ *Why is* La *added?* (The French word sounds classy, or special.)

About the Author

Meet the Author and the Illustrator

Christopher Paul Curtis

Have students read the biography of the author. Ask:

→ How might Christopher Curtis's experiences with his own grandfather helped him write this story?

→ How do Floyd Cooper's illustrations help you visualize the story?

Author's Purpose

To Entertain

Review that the author's purpose is to entertain, but he may have had more reasons. Students may say that he wrote to inform readers about life during the Great Depression or to write about his family's history. He names the jazz band leader in *Bud, Not Buddy*, after his grandfather.

Author's Craft

Sensory Details and Images

Point out that Christopher says writers need to have "really good ears and really good eyes." He uses descriptions that include sights and sounds that show what life was like in a certain time and place. Discuss what these descriptions add to the story.

→ The words *clump-clump-clumped* on page 367 tell the reader how loud Bud's feet sound as he walks.

→ Have students find other examples of sights and sounds, like "flashing lights up at you …" on page 368.

About the Author and Illustrator

Christopher Paul Curtis says that good writers need to have "really good ears and really good eyes." He fills his books with sights and sounds to give readers a feel for what life was really like for the characters in a given place and time. Christopher's own grandparents lived through the Great Depression and became models for characters. His grandfather was the lead musician of Herman Curtis and the Dusky Devastators of the Depression.

Christopher won a Newbery medal award and a Coretta Scott King award for *Bud, Not Buddy*.

Floyd Cooper was born and raised in Tulsa, Oklahoma but moved to New York as an adult to work as an illustrator. Floyd creates his award-winning illustrations using oil paint—and an eraser! Once the paint dries, Floyd erases some of the paint, leaving behind warm colors that illuminate the story. Floyd's illustrations have won him many honors, including the Coretta Scott King award for illustrators.

Author's Purpose

The author's main purpose for writing *Bud, Not Buddy* is to entertain. What other reasons do you think the author had in writing this story?

378

LITERATURE ANTHOLOGY, pp. 378–379

Respond to Reading

Summarize

Use key events and details to summarize Bud's experience with the band in *Bud, Not Buddy*. Information from your Character Web may help you.

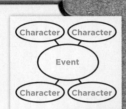

Text Evidence

1. How do you know that *Bud, Not Buddy* is historical fiction? Give details about the setting and characters. **GENRE**

2. How does each character react to the news that Bud is joining the band? Use details from the story. **COMPARE AND CONTRAST**

3. What is the meaning of the expression *pull your own weight* on page 370? Use context clues and your knowledge of idioms to help you figure out the meaning. **IDIOMS**

4. Write about how Miss Thomas and Steady Eddie interact with Bud. Use details to explain how each character treats Bud. **WRITE ABOUT READING**

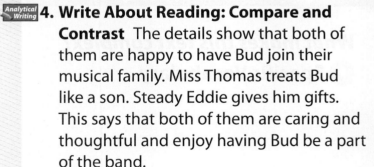

Make Connections

? Talk about how becoming a member of the band helps Bud adapt to life at "Grand Calloway Station." **ESSENTIAL QUESTION**

How will the band members' lives change once Bud joins them? Give an example of another kind of change that a group of people might face together. What benefit would come from sharing the experience? **TEXT TO WORLD**

379

Make Connections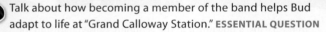

Essential Question Have partners discuss and list examples from the story that show how Bud adapts when the band members make him one of the group. Have pairs discuss their ideas with the class.

Text to World After students describe the changes the band will face when Bud joins, guide them to think of an example from their own life when they faced a change with a group of people, such as a family move.

Respond to Reading

Summarize

Review with students the information from their organizers. Model how to use the information to summarize *Bud, Not Buddy*.

Analytical Writing **Write About Reading: Compare and Contrast** Remind students that a summary retells the most important events or ideas. Ask students to use the information in their organizers to write a summary of the selection. Have them share their summaries with a partner.

Text Evidence

1. **Genre** <u>Answer</u> The story is set during the Great Depression and in a real city. <u>Evidence</u> "Bud is a motherless ten-year-old boy growing up in Flint, Michigan, during the Great Depression."

2. **Compare and Contrast** <u>Answer</u> Bud trusts Miss Thomas and most of the band. He is curious about Herman Calloway, but senses tension. <u>Evidence</u> Mr. Calloway argues with Miss Thomas about Bud staying with the band.

3. **Idioms** <u>Answer</u> It means to do an equal amount of work as the band. <u>Evidence</u> Just before the expression is used, Miss Thomas mentions "lots of chores" and "things to take care of around here."

4. **Analytical Writing** **Write About Reading: Compare and Contrast** The details show that both of them are happy to have Bud join their musical family. Miss Thomas treats Bud like a son. Steady Eddie gives him gifts. This says that both of them are caring and thoughtful and enjoy having Bud be a part of the band.

Develop Comprehension

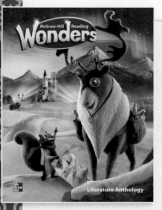

Literature Anthology

"Musical Impressions of the Great Depression"

Text Complexity Range

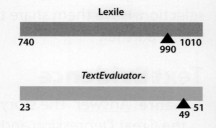

Lexile

740 ——————————— ▲ 1010
990

TextEvaluator™

23 ——————————— ▲ 51
49

Options for Close Reading

→ Whole Class
→ Small Group
→ Independent

CCSS **Genre · Expository Text**

Compare Texts
Read about how music provided hope for people during the Great Depression.

MUSICAL IMPRESSIONS of the Great Depression

In the 1930s, a downturn in the economy caused hardship for millions of people that lasted for years. This period became known as the Great Depression. To some, it seemed the difficult times might never end. Others remained hopeful that good times were just around the corner. The music of this era reflected both perspectives.

380

ACT Access Complex Text

What makes this text complex?
▶ **Specific Vocabulary**

▶ Specific Vocabulary

Point out that a *stock market* is a system that allows people to put money into, or invest in, companies by buying stock. If a company does well, the stock price rises. If it fails, the value of the stock plummets. In 1929, the stock market collapsed and many people lost a lot of money. This collapse triggered a decade of widespread poverty—the Great Depression.

The Great Depression

After a decade of prosperity called the Roaring Twenties, economic progress in the United States changed abruptly. In October of 1929, the stock market collapsed and left thousands of investors broke. In turn, many companies laid off workers that they could no longer afford to pay. Around the same time, a massive drought destroyed crops and also left many farmers penniless. With so few resources, people across the country struggled to get by.

Sympathy through Song

Many songs of the 1930s, particularly in folk and country music, recounted people's stories of loss and hardship. The songwriter Woody Guthrie followed farm workers who traveled west to California hoping to find work. He saw that they often encountered new and tougher challenges. Guthrie expressed **sympathy** for them through songs like "Dust Bowl Blues" and "Goin' Down the Road Feeling Bad." He hoped to restore people's sense of dignity.

Meanwhile, across the country, The Carter Family performed similar songs, such as "Worried Man Blues," describing life in the Appalachian Mountains where resources were scarce. Listeners found comfort in the knowledge that they were not alone in their struggles. **1**

During the 1930s, bands like this one (left) lifted people's spirits. Woody Guthrie (right) toured the country and composed songs about the challenges people faced.

Eric Schaal/Time & Life Pictures/Getty Images

381

LITERATURE ANTHOLOGY, pp. 380–381

Compare Texts

Students will read another selection about the value of shared experience, this time an expository text. Ask students to do a close reading of the text to understand the content. Encourage students to use the **reread** strategy or other strategies they know that will help them. They will also take notes as they read. Students will then use the text evidence that they gathered to compare this text with *Bud, Not Buddy.*

1 Ask and Answer Questions

How did folk music help people struggling with the Great Depression?

Analytical Writing **Write About Reading** Paraphrase the ideas in the section "Sympathy through Song." (By recounting their stories of hardship, the music helped people keep their dignity. It also comforted them in knowing that others shared their struggles.)

Read aloud the first two sentences on page 381.

→ Point out that *prosperity* comes from the word *prosper,* which means "to do very well." *What happens to many businesses in a time of prosperity?* (They make a lot of money.)

→ *"The Roaring Twenties" refers to a decade, a period of ten years. Which decade does it refer to?* (1920s)

ELL Point out the cognates: prosperity/*prosperidad,* company/*compañía.*

→ *In the 1930s, companies, or businesses, could not make money. Farms also could not make money because of a terrible drought.*

→ *Was there prosperity?* (no) *Many people could not get jobs, so they had no ____.* (money)

Develop Comprehension

A popular style of music called swing inspired people to dance.

2 Ask and Answer Questions

What do you think the author means by saying "people left their problems behind them and escaped on the dance floor?"

Analytical Writing **Write About Reading** Use clues from the text to write your answer. (Swing music had "upbeat" and "positive rhythms" that people could dance to, and people used this music to lift their spirits.)

3 Ask and Answer Questions

Music is not a necessity, unlike food and shelter, which are. With little money available, do you think President Roosevelt was wise to spend government money on free concerts for the public? Turn to a partner and discuss your opinion, giving examples from the text to support it. (Possible response: Yes, music made people happier. Happiness can help people get through hard times. The Federal Music Project provided concerts that also helped musicians in a practical way by giving them jobs.)

On the Up-Swing

Times were certainly hard in the country. In the nation's cities, the situation was equally difficult. In some African-American communities, unemployment soared above fifty percent. These challenges reminded some of earlier times of slavery, and many found comfort in the musical styles of that era: gospel and blues.

Jazz, a newer form of music with upbeat rhythms, lifted people's spirits. Band leaders like Duke Ellington and Count Basie created a new, high-energy style of jazz called swing. Around the country, people of all races responded to these positive rhythms. People left their problems behind them and escaped onto the dance floor.

In New York, Broadway musicals delighted theatergoers. Many musicals offered light entertainment, while others addressed the current hardships through songs, such as "Brother, Can You Spare a Dime?" Radio helped spread these songs beyond the city, connecting people across the country and creating nationwide hits.

Bettmann/Corbis

382

A C T Access Complex Text

▶ Specific Vocabulary

Help students understand terms from the section "Reaction from the Government."

→ Legislation *means "law" or "lawmaking." What part of the word can help you remember this?* (The first part of the word is the same as in *legal*.)

→ Explain that a federal project is one that is run by the national government. In the United States, each city and state has its own government, but the federal government is for the whole country.

→ *What does the author mean by "federally supported concerts"?* (The term refers to concerts paid for by the U.S. government.)

Reaction from the Government

While some blamed the government for hard times, President Franklin Delano Roosevelt (FDR) created programs the public could **rely** on for assistance and new opportunities. This legislation became known as the New Deal. As part of a program called the Works Progress Administration, FDR initiated the Federal Music Project in 1935. His wife, Eleanor, promoted its main goals. These were to help musicians find work and to **guarantee** all people access to the arts, regardless of their financial situation. ③

Eleanor Roosevelt (standing, center) supported the work of musicians.

Before long, federally supported concerts and shows played on the radio and in music halls across the country. Throughout the nation, teachers provided free voice and instrument lessons to help promote participation and music appreciation. The government's **supportive** programs also paid musicians to travel and record styles of folk music from different regions. These recordings were preserved in our country's Library of Congress.

By the end of the 1930s, the hardest days of the Great Depression had passed. Times had been tough, but music had offered a way for people to share their fears and keep up their hopes. The music remains a legacy of this era that has inspired musicians to this day.

Make Connections

How did the shared experience of music help people adapt to the changes caused by the Great Depression? **ESSENTIAL QUESTION**

How have characters in a story helped each other adapt to a change? How are their actions similar to the way people helped each other get through the Great Depression? **TEXT TO TEXT**

W.P.A. FEDERAL THEATRE PRESENTS

SING FOR YOUR SUPPER
A Topical Musical Revue
ADELPHI THEATRE
54ᵗʰ STREET EAST OF 7ᵗʰ AVE

A poster for a government-funded performance

383

LITERATURE ANTHOLOGY, pp. 382–383

Make Connections • *Analytical Writing*

Essential Question Discuss the changes that drought brought to farmers and that sudden poverty brought to many others during the Great Depression. Then have students review the selection to recall how different kinds of music—folk, jazz, and musicals—helped people cope with these changes.

Text to Text Have students work with a partner use their responses to the Ask and Answer Questions prompts and what they read in *Bud, Not Buddy* to discuss the ways people helped each other adapt. Have partners share their responses with the class. (Possible response: During the Great Depression, listening to music helped people in several ways. It gave them a sense of dignity, it made them feel less alone, and it let them have fun. Being part of a performing group helped people in similar ways. For example, in *Bud, Not Buddy*, the band members took pride in their music, and they always had each other for company. They also had a lot of fun joking around together.)

ELL As you discuss the section, "Reaction from the Government," help students understand the New Deal as it relates to music.

→ Point out the cognates: musician/*músico*, concert/*concierto*.

→ *During the Great Depression, President Roosevelt started programs to help the poor. Some of these programs brought concerts to people free of charge. This helped the musicians too. How?* (The musicians could make money performing.)

Word Study/Fluency

Homophones

MINILESSON 20 Mins

OBJECTIVES

CCSS Know and apply grade-level phonics and word analysis skills in decoding words. Use combined knowledge of all letter-sound correspondences, syllabication patterns, and morphology (e.g., roots and affixes) to read accurately unfamiliar multisyllabic words in context and out of context. **RF.5.3a**

CCSS Read on-level prose and poetry orally with accuracy, appropriate rate, and expression on successive readings. **RF.5.4b**

Rate: 129–149 WCPM

ACADEMIC LANGUAGE

• *expression, phrasing*
• Cognates: *expresión, fraseo*

Refer to the sound transfers chart in the **Language Transfers Handbook** to identify sounds that do not transfer in Spanish, Cantonese, Vietnamese, Hmong, and Korean.

1 Explain

Tell students that homophones are words that sound alike but are spelled differently and have different meanings, such as *ate* and *eight*. Explain that readers use context clues from words surrounding the homophone to determine its meaning.

2 Model

Write the following homophones on the board. Pronounce the homophones, and give possible definitions for each word in the pair. Then read the sentences, modeling how to use context clues to determine the meaning of the word.

→ *pear, pair*
I pulled a **pear** from the tree and bit into the juicy fruit.
I chose a **pair** of brown shoes to wear to school.

→ *hole, whole*
I fell down and tore a **hole** in my jeans.
This pie is so good, I could eat the **whole** thing!

→ *way, weigh*
We took a wrong turn on the **way** to the soccer game.
The judges at the fair will **weigh** my biggest pumpkin.

3 Guided Practice

Write the following homophones on the board. Guide students to come up with a definition and a sentence for each word.

seen	scene	right	write
cent	sent	buy	by
deer	dear	guest	guessed
you	ewe	sell	cell
break	brake	mail	male

Go Digital

Homophones

Present the Lesson

View "The Day the Rollets Got Their Moxie Back"

Read Multisyllabic Words

Transition to Longer Words Write the following homophones on the board. Have students read each word and use their knowledge of phonics patterns to decode each homophone.

Model how to determine the meaning of each word. Point to the word, read it aloud, and use it in a sentence that has context clues to the word's meaning. Then have students identify the context clues and provide a definition for the word.

weather	whether	principal	principle
cereal	serial	minor	miner
presents	presence	seller	cellar
friar	fryer	capitol	capital
ceiling	sealing	attendants	attendance
assistants	assistance	aloud	allowed

After you complete the activity, have students write their own sentences that include homophones from the list.

 **FLUENCY** ←

Expression and Phrasing

Explain/Model Review with students how punctuation marks such as commas, periods, and question marks can help them break text into meaningful phrases. Turn to "The Day the Rollets Got Their Moxie Back," **Reading/Writing Workshop** pages 324–327. Read page 326 aloud, emphasizing the use of expression and phrasing as you read.

Remind students that you will be listening for their use of expression and phrasing as you monitor their reading during the week.

Practice/Apply Have partners alternate reading paragraphs in the passage, modeling the expression you used.

Daily Fluency Practice

Students can practice fluency using **Your Turn Practice Book** passages.

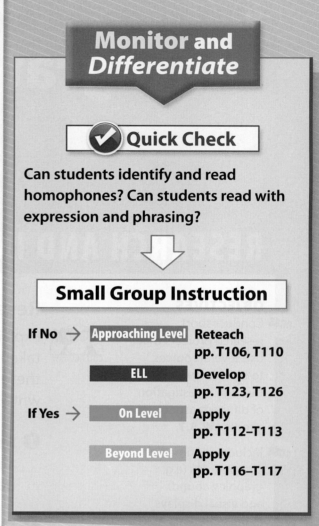

Monitor and *Differentiate*

✓ **Quick Check**

Can students identify and read homophones? Can students read with expression and phrasing?

⬇

Small Group Instruction

If No → **Approaching Level** Reteach pp. T106, T110

ELL Develop pp. T123, T126

If Yes → **On Level** Apply pp. T112–T113

Beyond Level Apply pp. T116–T117

ON-LEVEL PRACTICE BOOK p. 218

Word Study: Homophones

Name _____

| stationery | presents | pray | colonel | manner |
| pier | council | presence | waist | suite |

A. Read each pair of words below. Circle the word that is a homophone of a word from the box above. Then write a word from the box to form a homophone pair.

1. (weel) sweat _____ suite
2. stationing (stationary) _____ stationery
3. count (counsel) _____ council
4. (manor) mansion _____ manner
5. (kernel) color _____ colonel

B. Choose three homophone pairs from above. Write a sentence using each pair of words. Possible responses provided.

6. We saw the famous *colonel* eating a *kernel* of corn. _____

7. She stood in a *stationary* position as she wrote the letter on her *stationery*. _____

8. He went to the town *council* to seek *counsel* for his problem. _____

218 Practice • Grade 5 • Unit 5 • Week 2

| APPROACHING p. 218 | BEYOND p. 218 | ELL p. 218 |

☞ **Go** Digital

www.connected.mcgraw-hill.com
RESOURCES
Research and Inquiry

→ **Wrap Up the Week**
Integrate Ideas

RESEARCH AND INQUIRY 🌐 SOCIAL STUDIES

Better Together

OBJECTIVES

CCSS Conduct short research projects that use several sources to build knowledge through investigation of different aspects of a topic. **W.5.7**

CCSS Include multimedia components (e.g. graphics, sound) and visual displays in presentations when appropriate to enhance the development of main ideas or themes. **SL.5.5**

• Evaluate media.
• Use technology to present information.

ACADEMIC LANGUAGE

• *Great Depression, presentation*
• Cognates: *Gran Depresión, presentacíon*

Research Photographs from the Great Depression

COLLABORATE

Explain that students will work in small groups to research photographs taken during the Great Depression. Specifically, they will research how these photographs depicted people working together in hard times and write captions that explain this. Discuss the following steps:

❶ **Research the Great Depression** Have groups gather information about the Great Depression, such as dates, examples of hardships people endured, and ways people overcame these hardships.

❷ **Choose Photographs** Help students brainstorm search terms that will lead them to photographs taken during the Great Depression. Ask them to record who is in the photos, where and when it was taken, and by whom if they can. Have students post four or five chosen photos to the Shared Research Board.

❸ **Guided Practice** Model for students how to use available information to write a photo caption. Remind them to note the subject, date, location, photographer, and main idea for each photograph if known.

❹ **Create a Presentation** Have groups use their photos to create a slide show. They may also choose short video clips and music from the period to accompany their presentations. Encourage groups to assign roles, such as first speaker, second speaker, and slide show operator.

Present Your Findings

Have each group give its presentation to another group. Suggest that students use online Presenting Checklist 1.

UniversalImagesGroup/Hulton Archive/Getty Images

TEXT CONNECTIONS

OBJECTIVES

CCSS Integrate information from several texts on the same topic in order to write or speak about the subject knowledgeably. **RI.5.9**

CCSS Review the key ideas expressed and draw conclusions in light of information and knowledge gained from the discussions. **SL.5.1d**

Text to Text

Cite Evidence Tell students that they will work in groups to compare the effects of shared experiences in this week's reading and draw conclusions about the Essential Question: *How do shared experiences help people adapt to change?* Model how to make comparisons using examples from the week's **Leveled Readers** and from "The Day the Rollets Got Their Moxie Back," **Reading/ Writing Workshop** pages 324–327.

Have students review the week's reading and their notes and graphic organizers. Help each group set up a Layered Book Foldable® to organize information about shared experiences from the week's texts. Have them use the information to draw conclusions about how experiences like these can help people adapt to change.

Present Information Have groups present their findings to the class. Prompt discussion of differences in their examples or conclusions.

Shared Experiences

What are the changes?

What are the shared experiences?

How did the characters adapt?

Conclusions

Dinah Zike's
FOLDABLES

WRITE ABOUT READING

OBJECTIVES

CCSS Draw evidence from literary or informational texts to support analysis, reflection, and research. **W.5.9**

Write an Analysis

Cite Evidence Explain that students will write about a historical fiction story they read this week. Using text evidence, students will analyze how an author used details to develop the setting.

Discuss how to analyze setting by asking *how* and *why* questions.

→ How does the author show that the story takes place during a specific time in history?

→ Why are details about the setting important to the story?

Use **Your Turn Practice Book** page 219 to read and discuss the student model. Have students choose a historical fiction story they have read and review their notes on the characters, settings, and events. Have them write to explain how an author uses details to show that the story takes place during a specific time in history. Remind students that good explanatory writing presents ideas in a logical order and uses complex sentences.

Present Your Ideas Ask partners to share their paragraphs and discuss how the evidence they cited from the text supports their ideas.

→ # Readers to Writers

Reading/Writing Workshop

OBJECTIVES

CCSS Link ideas within and across categories of information using words, phrases, and clauses (e.g., *in contrast*, *especially*). **W.5.2c**

CCSS Write routinely over extended time frames (time for research, reflection, and revision) and shorter time frames (a single sitting or a day or two) for a range of discipline-specific tasks, purposes, and audiences. **W.5.10**

Analyze models to understand sentence fluency.

ACADEMIC LANGUAGE
- *fluency, transitions, phrases, clauses*
- Cognates: *transiciones, cláusulas*

 MINILESSON 10 Mins

Writing Traits: Sentence Fluency

Transitions

Expert Model Explain that good writers use transitional words, phrases, and clauses to make their sentences flow more smoothly and to connect ideas. Transitions such as *in addition* or *especially* connect two related ideas, while *in contrast* and *however* connect two different ideas. The phrases *for example* and *specifically* introduce examples, while *consequently* and *as a result* show cause-and-effect relationships. Words such as *after* and *soon* show the order of events and actions.

 COLLABORATE

Read aloud the expert model from "The Day the Rollets Got Their Moxie Back." Ask students to listen for transitional language that helps guide the reader through the story. Have students talk with partners to identify words, phrases, and clauses that clarify time and place in the story, as well as other transitions the writer used.

Student Model Remind students that transitional words, phrases, and clauses connect ideas and sentences. Read aloud the student model "The Hazens' House." As students follow along, have them focus on how the writer's changes help connect ideas.

 COLLABORATE

Invite partners to talk about the model and the transitions Angela added to improve sentence fluency. Ask them to suggest other transitions Angela could use to connect ideas and sentences in the story.

Go Digital

Expert Model

Student Model

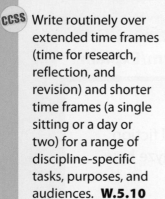 **Genre Writing**

Informational Text

For full writing process lessons and rubrics see:
→ Informational Article, pp. T344–T349
→ Research Report, pp. T350–T355

CCSS Writing Traits | Sentence Fluency

Readers to...

Writers often include **transitions** that will help guide the reader through a text. Reread this passage from "The Day the Rollets Got Their Moxie Back" to see how the author uses transitional words and phrases to link events and ideas in the story.

Transitions

Identify the transitions the author used to clarify time and place. What other kinds of transitions did the author use to connect ideas and events?

_____

Expert Model

The line moved slowly. Bored, Ruth began practicing her dance steps. I sang an upbeat tune to give her some music. Around us, downturned hats lifted to reveal frowns becoming smiles. Soon, folks began clapping along. Egged on by the supportive response, Ruth twirled and swayed like there was no tomorrow.

Ron Mazellan

332

Writers

Angela wrote a narrative about a volunteer experience she shared with her family. Read Angela's revision of this section.

Student Model

The Hazens' House

The Hazens' old house burned down in a fire last summer. *Over the past months,* People donated money to help them. ~~They~~ *The Hazens* had enough to buy materials for a new house. *but* They could not *afford* (sp) workers. All of us in town pitched in. *While* My parents sawed boards. My brother and I nailed them to wooden frames. *After a day of hard work,* Then the walls went up. Everyone was so proud to help out, they cheered!

333

Editing Marks

∧ Add
∧ Add a comma.
∽ Take out.
(SP) Check spelling.
≡ Make a capital letter.

Grammar Handbook

Complex Sentences
See page 453.

Your Turn   COLLABORATE

☑ Identify the transitions Angela used in her narrative. What is their purpose?

☑ What complex sentences did Angela use?

☑ Tell how Angela's revisions improved her writing.

Go Digital!
Write online in Writer's Workspace

READING/WRITING WORKSHOP, pp. 332–333

ELL ENGLISH LANGUAGE LEARNERS SCAFFOLD

Provide support to help English Language Learners understand the writing trait.

Beginning	**Intermediate**	**Advanced/High**
Respond Orally Draw students' attention to the Student Model. Help students choose the right word in each sentence frame: *They had enough to buy materials, [and/ but] they could not afford workers. [Before/After] a day of hard work, the walls went up.*	**Practice** Help students complete the sentence frames. *The Hazens had enough money to buy materials, _____ they could not afford workers. Angela nailed boards with her brother, _____ their parents sawed them. _____ a day of hard work, the walls went up.*	**Understand** Check for understanding. Ask: *Which transitional words, phrases, and clauses does Angela use? What relationships between ideas do these transitions show? What other transitions could Angela have included instead?*

Writing Every Day: Sentence Fluency

DAY **1**

DAY **2**

Writing Entry: Transitions

Prewrite Provide students with the prompt below.

Explain something that you and your family work together to do. Use transitions to connect ideas.

Have partners list different projects they do with their families. For each, have them jot down what they do and where and when they do it.

Draft Have each student select one activity from the list. As they draft, remind students to use transitions to connect ideas.

Focus on Transitions

Use **Your Turn Practice Book** page 220 to model adding transitions.

We help clean up the local park. I pick up trash. My mom gathers items for recycling. We take everything to the waste collection site. We head home.

Model adding transitions to connect sentences.

While I pick up trash, my mom gathers items for recycling.

Discuss how adding transitions connects ideas. Guide students to add more transitions to the model.

Writing Entry: Transitions

Revise Have students revise their writing from Day 1 by adding two or three transitions.

Use the **Conferencing Routines**. Circulate among students and stop briefly to talk with individuals. Provide time for peer review.

Edit Have students use Grammar Handbook page 453 in the **Reading/Writing Workshop** to edit for errors in complex sentences.

Conferencing Routines

Teacher Conferences

STEP 1

Talk about the strengths of the writing.

You have included clear details that help me visualize the activity you do together.

STEP 2

Focus on how the writer used the target trait for the week.

You used the transition words ____ and ____ to make connections between ideas. It would help me if you used transition words to connect the ideas in these sentences, as well.

STEP 3

Make concrete suggestions for revisions. Have students work on a specific assignment, such as those to the right, and then meet with you to review progress.

DAY 3

Writing Entry: Transitions

Prewrite Ask students to search their Writer's Notebooks for topics for a new draft. Or, provide a prompt such as the following:

Explain ways people work together to help someone else. Use transitions to connect ideas.

Draft Once students have chosen their topics, ask them to create a concept web to plan their writing. Have them think about the information that they might include in their writing. Students can use their charts to begin their drafts.

DAY 4

Writing Entry: Transitions

Revise Have students revise the draft writing from Day 3 by adding transitions to connect ideas. As students revise, hold teacher conferences with individual students. You may also wish to have students work with partners to peer conference.

Edit Invite students to review the rules for complex sentences on Grammar Handbook page 453 in the **Reading/Writing Workshop** and then check their drafts for errors.

DAY 5

Share and Reflect

Discuss with students what they learned about transitions. Invite volunteers to read and compare draft text with text that has been revised. Have students discuss the writing by focusing on the importance of using transitions to connect ideas and sentences. Allow time for individuals to reflect on their own writing progress and record observations in their Writer's Notebooks.

Suggested Revisions

Provide specific direction to help focus young writers.

Focus on a Sentence
Read the draft and target one sentence for revision. *Rewrite this sentence by adding a transition that connects it to the next sentence.*

Focus on a Section
Underline a section that needs to be revised. Provide specific suggestions. *I'm not clear on how the ideas in this section are related. What transition can you add to make it clear?*

Focus on a Revision Strategy
Underline a section. Have students use a specific revision strategy, such as rearranging. *Check that your ideas are in a logical order, and rearrange sentences or clauses to make them clearer.*

Peer Conferences

Focus peer response groups on adding transitions to connect ideas.

- ☑ Does the writing include transition words, phrases, or clauses?
- ☑ Do ideas flow logically from one to the next?
- ☑ Are any parts of the writing confusing?
- ☑ What other transition words, phrases, or clauses can be added to connect the ideas?

Grammar: Complex Sentences

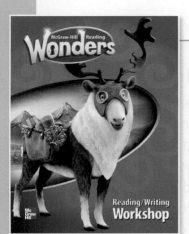

Reading/Writing Workshop

OBJECTIVES

CCSS Demonstrate command of the conventions of standard English grammar and usage when writing or speaking. Produce simple, compound, and complex sentences. **L.3.1i**

CCSS Explain the function of conjunctions, prepositions, and interjections in general and their function in particular sentences. **L.5.1a**

Proofread sentences.

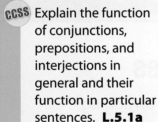

Go Digital

Complex Sentences

Grammar Activities

DAY 1

DAILY LANGUAGE ACTIVITY

Juan and him wear bike helmets. They usually goes from school to the Library. (1: he; 2: go; 3: library)

Introduce Complex Sentences

→ A **complex sentence** contains an independent clause and a dependent clause.

→ Dependent clauses are introduced by **subordinating conjunctions** such as *while, because, if,* and *although*. <u>*While I read*</u>*, I took notes.*

→ Dependent clauses can also be introduced by **relative pronouns** such as *who, whose, which, whom,* and *that,* and **relative adverbs** such as *where, when,* and *why. I'll meet you* <u>*where*</u> *we play ball. The shirt* <u>*that*</u> *is blue is mine.*

Have partners discuss using page 453 of the Grammar Handbook.

DAY 2

DAILY LANGUAGE ACTIVITY

Its almost time for there race. The coarse looks difficult. (1: It's; 2: their; 3: course)

Review Complex Sentences

Remind students that an independent clause can stand on its own while a dependent clause cannot.

Introduce More Complex Sentences

→ A dependent clause in a complex sentence can come after an independent clause. *I read the biography* <u>*because it looked interesting*</u>.

→ A dependent clause in a complex sentence can also come before an independent clause, separated by a comma. <u>*When we were out,*</u> *our dog chewed the table.*

 # TALK ABOUT IT

COLLABORATE

USE COMPLEX SENTENCES

Ask partners to use complex sentences to describe a change they have experienced. As they talk, students should listen to be sure they use at least one complex sentence.

BEAT THE TIMER

Set a timer. Have groups write as many complex sentences as they can in five minutes. When the timer rings, groups stop writing. Groups review their sentences to make sure they are punctuated correctly.

DAY

DAY

DAY

DAILY LANGUAGE ACTIVITY

We road our bikes to pike park. We swam hiked fished and camped. (1: rode; 2: Pike Park; 3: swam, hiked, fished,)

DAILY LANGUAGE ACTIVITY

My youngest sister who is nine years old plays soccer. She wears shoes, that have cleats. (1: sister,; 2: old,; 3: shoes that)

DAILY LANGUAGE ACTIVITY

Your right about Mr. Ko the librarian. He helped me find "Webster's dictionary." (1: You're; 2: Ko,; 3: *Webster's Dictionary*.)

Mechanics and Usage: Commas with Clauses

→ An **essential clause** is necessary to identify a person or thing that is being described. It is not separated by commas. *The dog that was barking scared me.*

→ A **nonessential clause** is not necessary to the meaning of the sentence. Commas are needed to set apart the clause. *My grandmother, who is ninety years old, swims three laps every day.*

As students write, refer them to Grammar Handbook page 479 for commas.

Proofread

Have students correct errors in these sentences:

1. Because I was thirsty. I drank water. (thirsty, I)

2. I couldn't practice. Because I had homework. (practice because)

3. The runner, who won the race, was thrilled. (1: runner who; 2: race was)

4. Alice Green, who loves to bake made our snacks. (bake,)

Have students check their work using Grammar Handbook pages 453 and 479.

Assess

Use the Daily Language Activity and Grammar Practice Reproducibles page 110 for assessment.

Reteach

Use Grammar Practice Reproducibles pages 106–109 and selected pages from the Grammar Handbook for additional reteaching. Remind students that it is important to use complex sentences correctly as they speak and write.

Check students' writing for use of the skill and listen for it in their speaking. Assign Grammar Revision Assignments in their Writer's Notebooks as needed.

See Grammar Practice Reproducibles pp. 106–110.

WRITE A SKIT

Have groups write a brief skit. Each character must have one line that is a complex sentence. Have audience members raise hands when they hear a complex sentence.

QUIZ A FRIEND

Have students write five complex sentences. Three of the sentences should have a dependent clause before an independent clause that purposely leaves out a comma. Partners exchange sentences and add the punctuation.

NAME THAT CLAUSE

Have groups write five sentences with essential clauses and five sentences with nonessential clauses. Groups read their sentences aloud to the class. The audience calls out "essential" or "nonessential."

Spelling: Homophones

DAY 1

Spelling Words

sweet	waist	presence
suite	manor	presents
pray	manner	council
prey	pier	counsel
poll	peer	stationery
pole	currant	stationary
waste	current	

Review eruption, forgetful, allergic
Challenge kernel, colonel

Differentiated Spelling

Approaching Level

sweet	waist	presents
suite	manner	presence
peel	manor	choose
peal	pier	chews
poll	peer	flower
pole	you're	flour
waste	your	

Beyond Level

sweet	aloud	presents
suite	manner	presence
principal	manor	council
principle	current	counsel
bazaar	currant	stationery
bizarre	pier	stationary
allowed	peer	

Assess Prior Knowledge

Read the spelling words aloud.

Explain that homophones are words that have the same pronunciation but different spellings and meanings. Point out the spellings and meanings for *sweet* ("pleasant tasting") and *suite* ("set of rooms").

Demonstrate sorting the spelling words by part of speech. Some spelling words may have more than one part of speech. For example, *current* can be both a noun and an adjective. Ask students to name some other everyday words that are homophones.

Use the Dictation Sentences from Day 5 to give the pretest. Say the underlined word, read the sentence, and repeat the word. Have students write the words. Then have students check their papers.

DAY 2

Spiral Review

Review the suffixes in *eruption*, *forgetful*, and *allergic*. Read each sentence below, repeat the review word, and have students write the word.

1. The <u>eruption</u> only lasted for a few minutes.
2. James makes "to do" lists because he is <u>forgetful</u>.
3. People who have hay fever are <u>allergic</u> to certain plants.

Have students trade papers and check their spellings.

Challenge Words Review homophones. Read each sentence below, repeat the challenge word, and have students write the word.

1. Every <u>kernel</u> of the popcorn popped.
2. The <u>colonel</u> gave strict orders.

Have students check and correct their spellings and write the words in their word study notebooks.

WORD SORTS

COLLABORATE

OPEN SORT

Have students cut apart the **Spelling Word Cards** in the Online Resource Book and initial the back of each card. Have them read the words aloud with partners. Then have partners do an **open sort**. Have them record their sorts in their word study notebooks.

PATTERN SORT

Complete the **pattern sort** from Day 1 by using the Spelling Word Cards. Point out the different spellings in the homophones and their parts of speech. Partners should compare and check their sorts. Have them record their sorts in their word study notebooks.

DAY 3

Word Meanings

Write *peer* and *pier* on the board and model how to create a word association list with each word. For example: *peer—friend, pal, buddy; pier—dock, fishing, wooden.*

1. Ask students to choose a pair of homophones and make similar lists for each word.

2. Have students share their lists with the class.

3. Challenge students to use the pair of homophones in the same sentence so that the meaning of each word is clear. For example: *I fished from the pier with my peer from school.*

Have students write their word groups and example sentences in their word study notebooks.

See Phonics/Spelling Reproducibles pp. 127–132.

SPEED SORT

Have partners do a **speed sort** to see who is fastest. Then have them do a word hunt in this week's readings to find homophones. Have them record the words in their word study notebooks.

DAY 4

Proofread and Write

Write these sentences on the board. Have students circle and correct each misspelled word. Have students use a print or a digital dictionary to check and correct their spellings.

1. Lita's manor is both suite and kind. (manner, sweet)

2. Last night the city counsel met to discuss topics of currant interest. (council, current)

3. Pat listed the presence he wanted for his birthday on a sheet of stationary. (presents, stationery)

4. John dropped his fishing poll from the peer. (pole, pier)

Error Correction Remind students that they should use context clues to determine which homophone should be used.

BLIND SORT

Have partners do a **blind sort**: one reads a Spelling Word Card and uses the word in a sentence; the other spells the homophone and sorts it by its part of speech. Have partners take turns until both have sorted all their words.

DAY 5

Assess

Use the Dictation Sentences for the posttest. Have students list the misspelled words in their word study notebooks. Look for students' use of these words in their writings.

> **Dictation Sentences**
>
> 1. The orange tasted <u>sweet</u>.
> 2. Our hotel room was a <u>suite</u>.
> 3. We decided to <u>pray</u> for rain.
> 4. The badger let his <u>prey</u> escape.
> 5. I took a <u>poll</u> of student opinions.
> 6. The flag hung on a <u>pole</u>.
> 7. Let's not <u>waste</u> any time.
> 8. These slacks are too tight around the <u>waist</u>.
> 9. The <u>manor</u> house was grand.
> 10. Jay's <u>manner</u> of speaking is formal.
> 11. The boat docked at the <u>pier</u>.
> 12. Hector is my <u>peer</u>.
> 13. A <u>currant</u> is a kind of berry.
> 14. The <u>current</u> carried the boat.
> 15. The <u>presence</u> of friends is comforting.
> 16. Aunt Beth sends us <u>presents.</u>
> 17. The town <u>council</u> meets today.
> 18. Her <u>counsel</u> is fair and wise.
> 19. Mom writes letters on colorful <u>stationery</u>.
> 20. The guard was <u>stationary</u>.
>
> Have students self-correct their tests.

Build Vocabulary

OBJECTIVES

 CCSS Demonstrate understanding of figurative language, word relationships, and nuances in word meanings. Recognize and explain the meaning of common idioms, adages, and proverbs. **L.5.5b**

CCSS Use the relationship between particular words (e.g., synonyms, antonyms, homographs) to better understand each of the words. **L.5.5c**

Expand vocabulary by adding inflectional endings and suffixes.

Vocabulary Words

assume	rely
guarantee	supportive
nominate	sympathy
obviously	weakling

 Go Digital

Vocabulary

Vocabulary Activities

Connect to Words

Practice this week's vocabulary.

1. What do you **assume** will happen this week?
2. Why do stores **guarantee** their products?
3. Whom would you **nominate** as the nicest person you know?
4. Describe a time when you were **obviously** wrong.
5. Whom do you **rely** on?
6. Who is **supportive** of you?
7. When do people usually feel **sympathy**?
8. When might someone feel like a **weakling**?

Expand Vocabulary

Help students generate different forms of this week's words by adding, changing, or removing inflectional endings.

→ Draw a four-column chart on the board. Write *assume* in the first column. Then write *assumes, assumed,* and *assuming* in the other columns. Read aloud the words with students.

→ Have students share sentences using each form of *assume.*

→ Students should add to the chart for *guarantee, nominate,* and *rely,* then share sentences using the different forms of the words.

→ Have students copy the chart in their word study notebooks.

BUILD MORE VOCABULARY

COLLABORATE

ACADEMIC VOCABULARY

→ Display *employment, productions,* and *economic.*

→ Define the words and discuss their meanings with students.

→ Write *employ* under *employment.* Have partners write other words with the same root and define them. Then have partners ask and answer questions using the words.

→ Repeat with *productions* and *economic.*

SIMILE AND METAPHOR

Remind students that similes and metaphors create word pictures by comparing two unlike subjects. Similes use *like* or *as.*

→ Write: *Dan is a real bear sometimes. He can be as prickly as a porcupine.* Discuss the effects of the metaphor and the simile.

→ Have partners brainstorm other animal metaphors and similes.

→ Have students write the examples in their word study notebooks.

DAY 3

Reinforce the Words

Review this week's and last week's vocabulary words. Have students orally complete each sentence stem.

1. Don't <u>assume</u> someone is a <u>weakling</u> because ____.
2. I <u>guarantee</u> that we will finish the ____.
3. The class will <u>nominate</u> Carlos for ____.
4. He <u>obviously</u> felt <u>sympathy</u> for Lisa because ____.
5. He is a <u>genius</u> at ____.
6. I was <u>stunned</u> that ____.
7. Molly felt cheered by the <u>prospect</u> of ____.
8. Her <u>focused</u> research resulted in a <u>superb</u> ____.
9. He has <u>disdain</u> for ____.

DAY 4

Connect to Writing

→ Have students write sentences in their word study notebooks using this week's vocabulary.

→ Tell them to write sentences that provide word information they learned from this week's readings.

→ Provide the Day 3 sentence stems 1–4 for students needing extra support.

Write About Vocabulary Have students write something they learned from this week's words in their word study notebooks. For example, they might write about how people need to be *supportive* of each other and to rely on one another when going through a difficult time.

DAY 5

Word Squares

Ask students to create Word Squares for each vocabulary word.

→ In the first square, students write the word (e.g., *guarantee*).

→ In the second square, students write their own definition of the word and any related words, such as synonyms (e.g., *promise, assure, pledge*).

→ In the third square, students draw a simple illustration that will help them remember the word (e.g., drawing of two people shaking hands).

→ In the fourth square, students write nonexamples, including antonyms for the word (e.g., *disregard, undermine*).

Have partners discuss their squares.

IDIOMS

Elicit from students that idioms are phrases that cannot be understood from a literal interpretation.

→ Display **Your Turn Practice Book pages 213–214.** Model how to figure out the meaning of the idiom "putting me on the spot" in the first paragraph on page 213.

→ Have students complete page 217.

→ Partners can confirm meanings in a print or an online dictionary.

SHADES OF MEANING

Help students generate synonyms for *rely*. Draw a word web. Write *rely* in the center circle.

→ Have partners generate words to add to the word web. Ask students to use a thesaurus.

→ Add words and phrases not included such as *depend, trust in, count on, be sure of*.

→ Ask students to copy the words in their word study notebooks.

MORPHOLOGY

Use *nominate* as a springboard for students to learn more words. Draw a T-chart. Write *nominate* in the left column.

→ In the right column of the T-chart, write *-ion* and *-or*. Discuss how the suffixes change the meaning and part of speech.

→ Have students add the suffixes to *nominate*. Review the meanings of the new words.

→ Ask partners to do a search for other words with these suffixes.

→ Approaching Level

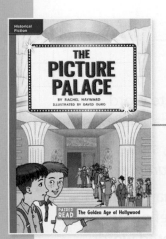

Lexile 710
TextEvaluator™ 41

OBJECTIVES

CCSS Quote accurately from a text when explaining what the text says explicitly and when drawing inferences from the text. **RL.5.1**

CCSS Compare and contrast two or more characters, settings, or events in a story or drama, drawing on specific details in the text (e.g., how characters interact). **RL.5.3**

CCSS Read on-level prose and poetry orally with accuracy, appropriate rate, and expression on successive readings. **RF.5.4b**

ACADEMIC LANGUAGE

- historical fiction, make predictions, compare, contrast, characters, idiom

- Cognates: ficción histórica, predicciones, comparar, contrastar

Leveled Reader:
The Picture Palace

Before Reading

Preview and Predict

→ Read the Essential Question with students.

→ Have students preview the title, table of contents, and first page of *The Picture Palace*. Students should use the text and illustrations to predict what they think the selection will be about. Tell them that they should try to confirm or revise their predictions as they read on.

Review Genre: Historical Fiction

Tell students that this text is historical fiction. Historical fiction features settings that could have existed and events that could have taken place during a particular period in history. The characters act and talk like people from that particular time and place. Historical fiction often contains both real and made-up events and characters. As they read, have students identify features of historical fiction in *The Picture Palace*.

During Reading

Close Reading

Note Taking: Ask students to use their graphic organizer as they read.

Pages 2–4 *Compare and contrast the impact the stock market crash had on Frank's family and Joey's family.* (Frank's father lost his job and had to get a lower-paying one, and the family had to sell their house. Still, they have an apartment and enough food, while Joey's family have sometimes been evicted because they were unable to make rent.) *What does the idiom "cute as a bug's ear" mean?* (It must mean "very cute or sweet." Mrs. Fisher thinks that Joey is a nice boy.)

Pages 5–7 *Compare and contrast the ways Frank and Joey respond to Marie.* (Frank says he is too busy, but Joey stops to play with her.) *Turn to a partner and make a prediction about how the window washing will turn out.* (The boys will make enough money to go to the movies.)

Pages 8–10 *Turn to a partner and tell if your prediction matched the text or how you revised it.* (It did not match the text, because no one wanted their help. I think they will now win the money at Bank Night.)

Go Digital

Leveled Readers

Use Graphic Organizer

Paraphrase how the boys respond to problems. (They try to wash windows in another, wealthier part of town. When the man's papers scatter, Joey quickly collects them.) *What does the idiom "you shred it, wheat" mean?* (Joey agrees with Frank, so it must mean "you're right.")

Pages 11–13 *Why does Frank tell Joey to "go low"?* (It will make it easier to get through the crowd.) *Turn to a partner and make a prediction about Joey's success.* (Joey will win the money.)

Pages 14–15 *Did your prediction match the text, or did you need to revise it?* (It matched; Joey wins the money.) *What happens afterwards?* (He gets a job delivering papers.) *How does the boys' shared experience help them adapt to change?* (They find success by helping each other.)

After Reading

Respond to Reading Revisit the Essential Question and ask students to complete the Text Evidence Questions on page 16.

Analytical Writing **Write About Reading** Check that students have described a change Joey might have to make to start work early every day.

Fluency: Expression and Phrasing

Model Model reading page 4 with appropriate expression and phrasing. Next, read the passage aloud and have students read along.

Apply Have students practice reading the passage with partners.

PAIRED READ

"The Golden Age of Hollywood"

Make Connections: Write About It *Analytical Writing*

Before reading, ask students to note that the genre of this text is expository text. Then discuss the Essential Question. After reading, ask students to write connections between *The Picture Palace* and "The Golden Age of Hollywood."

Leveled Reader

Analytical Writing

COMPARE TEXTS

→ Have students use text evidence to compare how a shared experience helps people adapt in a historical fiction story and an expository text.

Literature Circles

Ask students to conduct a literature circle using the Thinkmark questions to guide the discussion. You may wish to have a whole-class discussion, using both selections in the Leveled Reader, about how shared experiences help people adapt to change.

Level Up

Level-up lessons available online.

IF students read the **Approaching Level** fluently and answered the questions,

THEN pair them with students who have proficiently read the **On Level** and have students

• echo-read the **On Level** main selection.

• identify two traits that help them know that the story is historical fiction.

A C T ccess omplex ext

The **On Level** challenges students by including more **idioms** and **complex sentence structures**.

Approaching Level

Word Study/Decoding

REVIEW HOMOPHONES

OBJECTIVES

 Know and apply grade-level phonics and word analysis skills in decoding words. **RF.5.3**

Decode homophones.

 I Do Write *tale* and *tail* on the board. Explain that *tale* and *tail* are homophones, or words that sound alike but are spelled differently and have different meanings. Tell students that readers use context clues from the surrounding words to determine the meaning of a homophone. Use *tail* and *tale* in sentences that provide context clues about their meanings.

We Do Write this sentence on the board: *I write with my right hand, but Tia uses her left*. Guide students to identify *write* and *right* as homophones. Discuss how to use context clues from the sentence to figure out the meaning of each word.

 You Do Add the following sentences to the board: *I see a boat sailing on the sea. We guessed what time our guest would arrive at our home*. Have students identify the homophone pair in each sentence. Then have them use context clues to determine the meanings of each word in the pair.

BUILD HOMOPHONES

OBJECTIVES

 Know and apply grade-level phonics and word analysis skills in decoding words. Use combined knowledge of all letter-sound correspondences, syllabication patterns, and morphology (e.g., roots and affixes) to read accurately unfamiliar multisyllabic words in context and out of context. **RF.5.3a**

Build homophones.

 I Do Display the **Word-Building Cards** *ple* and *ry* and write the word parts *princi, pal, mer,* and *mar* on the board. Model reading each card and word part.

 We Do Work with students to combine the Word-Building Cards and word parts to form homophones. Have them chorally read the homophone pairs *principal, principle* and *merry, marry*. Work with students to use each word correctly in a sentence.

 You Do Write on the board other word parts, such as *sell, cell, er,* and *ar*. Have students combine the word parts to create a pair of homophones. Review with students the meaning of each word in the pair and then have partners use each word in a sentence. Ask students to share their sentences with the class.

PRACTICE HOMOPHONES

OBJECTIVES

CCSS Know and apply grade-level phonics and word analysis skills in decoding words. Use combined knowledge of all letter-sound correspondences, syllabication patterns, and morphology (e.g., roots and affixes) to read accurately unfamiliar multisyllabic words in context and out of context. **RF.5.3a**

Practice homophones.

 I Do Write this homophone pair on the board: *overdo, overdue.* Read the words aloud, and use each in a sentence. Then discuss the meaning of each word.

 We Do Write these sentences on the board: *Your concern about the test should lessen after you review the lesson. I would like to open the presents in your warm presence.* Model how to identify the homophones in the first sentence and how to use context clues to determine the meaning of each one. Then have students identify and give the meaning of each homophone in the second sentence.

 You Do To provide additional practice, write these homophone pairs on the board. Read aloud the first pair and give the meaning of each word.

weight, wait	forth, fourth	you, ewe
freeze, frees	flower, flour	patience, patients
knew, new	symbol, cymbal	weather, whether

Then have students read aloud the remaining homophone pairs. Ask them to use a dictionary to find the meaning of each word. Afterward, point to the word pairs in the list in random order for students to read chorally.

ELL ENGLISH LANGUAGE LEARNERS

For the **ELLs** who need **phonics, decoding,** and **fluency** practice, use scaffolding methods as necessary to ensure students understand the meaning of the words. Refer to the **Language Transfers Handbook** for phonics elements that may not transfer in students' native languages.

Approaching Level

Vocabulary

REVIEW HIGH-FREQUENCY WORDS

TIER 2

 OBJECTIVES
Acquire and use accurately grade-appropriate general academic and domain-specific words and phrases, including those that signal contrast, addition, and other logical relationships (e.g., *however, although, nevertheless, similarly, moreover, in addition*).
L.5.6

I Do Use **High-Frequency Word Cards** 171–180. Display one word at a time, following the routine:
Display the word. Read the word. Then spell the word.

We Do Ask students to state the word and spell the word with you. Model using the word in a sentence and have students repeat after you.

You Do Display the word. Ask students to say the word then spell it. When completed, quickly flip through the word card set as students chorally read the words. Provide opportunities for students to use the words in speaking and writing. For example, provide sentence starters such as *I want some _____*. Ask students to write each word in their Writer's Notebook.

REVIEW VOCABULARY WORDS

TIER 2

 OBJECTIVES
Acquire and use accurately grade-appropriate general academic and domain-specific words and phrases, including those that signal contrast, addition, and other logical relationships (e.g., *however, although, nevertheless, similarly, moreover, in addition*).
L.5.6

I Do Display each **Visual Vocabulary Card** and state the word. Explain how the photograph illustrates the word. State the example sentence and repeat the word.

We Do Point to the word on the card and read the word with students. Ask them to repeat the word. Engage students in structured partner talk about the image as prompted on the back of the vocabulary card.

You Do Display each visual in random order, hiding the word. Have students match the definitions and context sentences of the words to the visuals displayed.

UNDERSTAND VOCABULARY WORDS

OBJECTIVES

Acquire and use accurately grade-appropriate general academic and domain-specific words and phrases, including those that signal contrast, addition, and other logical relationships (e.g., *however, although, nevertheless, similarly, moreover, in addition*). **L.5.6**

 I Do

Display the *assume* **Visual Vocabulary Card**. Ask: *What would you* assume *if someone was crying?* Explain that you would assume, or suppose, that the person was upset.

 We Do

Ask these questions and help students respond and explain their answers.

→ What is something you might *guarantee* your parents?

→ Who would you *nominate* for class president?

→ Why should exit signs be *obviously* marked?

You Do

Have pairs respond to these questions and explain their answers.

→ When have you felt *sympathy* for a friend?

→ What might you tell a friend who feels like a *weakling*?

→ Who is someone you *rely* on?

→ What might a *supportive* coach say to you?

IDIOMS

OBJECTIVES

Demonstrate understanding of figurative language, word relationships, and nuances in word meanings. Recognize and explain the meaning of common idioms, adages, and proverbs. **L.5.5b**

 I Do

Display the Comprehension and Fluency passage on **Approaching Reproducibles** pages 213–214. Read aloud the first and second paragraphs. Point to the idiom *skeleton crew*. Tell students that they can look for context clues to figure out the meaning of the idiom.

Think Aloud I'm not sure what *skeleton crew* means. In the sentence before, I learn that Mr. Jenson's newspaper laid off most of its reporters. Later in this sentence, I learn that Mr. Jenson is overworked. I think *skeleton crew* means "just enough workers to keep a business running."

 We Do

Have students read the fifth paragraph, where they encounter the idiom *Make tracks*. Have students figure out the idiom's meaning by looking for context clues. Point out the context clue *"We're in a hurry!"*

 You Do

Have students use clues to find the meaning of other idioms in the selection using clues from the passage.

Approaching Level

Comprehension

FLUENCY

 OBJECTIVES
Read with sufficient accuracy and fluency to support comprehension. Read on-level prose and poetry orally with accuracy, appropriate rate, and expression on successive readings. **RF.5.4b**

Read fluently with good expression and phrasing.

 I Do Explain that good readers group words together into meaningful chunks. They also change their volume, tone, and emphasis to show the meaning of the text. Read the first two paragraphs of the Comprehension and Fluency passage on **Approaching Reproducibles** pages 213–214. Tell students to listen for your phrasing and the way you change your volume, tone, and emphasis to show the meaning of what you read.

 We Do Read the rest of the page aloud and have students repeat each sentence after you, matching your phrasing and expression. Point out that you pause at punctuation marks and at the end of phrases, rather than running all your words together.

 You Do Have partners take turns reading sentences from the Comprehension and Fluency passage. Remind them to focus on their phrasing and expression. Provide corrective feedback as needed by modeling proper fluency.

IDENTIFY IMPORTANT DETAILS ABOUT CHARACTERS

 OBJECTIVES
Quote accurately from a text when explaining what the text says explicitly and when drawing inferences from the text. **RL.5.1**

 I Do Remind students to pay attention to what characters do and say and how they respond to story events. Read aloud the first three paragraphs of the Comprehension and Fluency passage on **Approaching Reproducibles** pages 213–214. Identify important details about the main characters. Although Mr. Jenson is unhappy, he agrees to work when he gets the call. Although Nancy is sad that her father has to work, she understands and tries not to make him feel guilty.

 We Do Have students read the fourth and fifth paragraphs of the passage. Ask: *What details do we learn about how the characters respond to events?* Guide students to identify that Mr. Jenson thinks of a way to turn a negative situation into a positive one, and that Nancy is quick to follow his lead.

 You Do Have students read the rest of the passage and identify important details about the characters. Review the details students identify and help them explain why they are important.

REVIEW COMPARE AND CONTRAST CHARACTERS

OBJECTIVES

CCSS Compare and contrast two or more characters, settings, or events in a story or drama, drawing on specific details in the text (e.g., how characters interact). **RL.5.3**

CCSS Quote accurately from a text when explaining what the text says explicitly and when drawing inferences from the text. **RL.5.1**

I Do Review with students that story characters can be similar to or different from each other. Comparing and contrasting characters helps readers understand how characters affect events in a story but can also be changed by them.

We Do Read the first three paragraphs of the Comprehension and Fluency passage on **Approaching Reproducibles** pages 213–214 together. Model how to compare and contrast the ways that Nancy and her father respond to the change of plans. Point out that while both characters are unhappy that they can't go fishing, they try to do what they think is right.

You Do Have students read the rest of the passage and identify similarities and differences between the characters. Ask them to discuss how the characters' feelings and actions affect story events and how story events affect them in turn.

SELF-SELECTED READING

OBJECTIVES

CCSS Compare and contrast two or more characters, settings, or events in a story or drama, drawing on specific details in the text (e.g., how characters interact). **RL.5.3**

CCSS Quote accurately from a text when explaining what the text says explicitly and when drawing inferences from the text. **RL.5.1**

Make, confirm, and revise predictions based on details in the text.

Read Independently

Have students choose a historical fiction book for sustained silent reading. Remind students that:

→ comparing and contrasting characters can help them better understand the characters and plot in a story.

→ they can use clues in the story to make predictions about what will happen next.

Read Purposefully

Using Graphic Organizer 62, have students record how each character responds to an important event. After they finish, they can conduct a Book Talk about the books they read.

→ Students should share their organizers and the most interesting historical detail they learned from reading the texts.

→ They should also tell the group about any predictions they revised after reading on and learning new details.

→ On Level

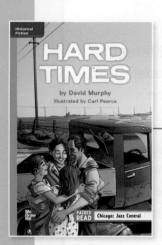

Lexile 830
TextEvaluator™ 51

OBJECTIVES

 Quote accurately from a text when explaining what the text says explicitly and when drawing inferences from the text. **RL.5.1**

 Compare and contrast two or more characters, settings, or events in a story or drama, drawing on specific details in the text (e.g., how characters interact). **RL.5.3**

 Read on-level prose and poetry orally with accuracy, appropriate rate, and expression on successive readings. **RF.5.4b**

ACADEMIC LANGUAGE

• *historical fiction, make predictions, compare, contrast, characters, idiom*

• Cognates: *ficción histórica, predicciones, comparar, contrastar*

Leveled Reader: *Hard Times*

Before Reading

Preview and Predict

→ Read the Essential Question with students.

→ Have students preview the title, table of contents, and first page of *Hard Times*. Students should use the text and illustrations to predict what they think the selection will be about. Tell them to try to confirm or revise their predictions as they continue reading.

Review Genre: Historical Fiction

Tell students that this text is historical fiction. Historical fiction features settings that could have existed and events that could have taken place during a particular period in history. The characters act and talk like people from that particular time and place. Historical fiction often contains both real and made-up events and characters. As they read, have students identify features of historical fiction in *Hard Times*.

During Reading

Close Reading

Note Taking: Ask students to use their graphic organizer as they read.

Pages 2–3 *How is this birthday different for the twins than their birthday four years ago?* (Now, four years after the Great Depression began, their family is having a hard time making payments on their farm.)

Pages 4–6 *How does John think of each of his twin children?* (Ruth is fiery and impulsive. Ritchie is serious and responsible.) *Paraphrase the family's discussion.* (They discuss ways to earn money to keep the farm. They eventually agree with Ruth's suggestion that John go to Chicago and find work sketching portraits.) *Turn to a partner and predict if this plan will be a success.* (Yes, John's portraits will earn enough money to make the payments on the farm.) *What does the idiom "spit it out" mean?* (Since Ruth says she has an idea, "spit it out" must mean "say it.")

Pages 7–9 *Compare and contrast Ruth and Ritchie's behavior and personalities.* (Ritchie eats slowly and carefully and is calm. Ruth eats quickly and messily and has a jealous temper.)

Go Digital

Leveled Readers

Use Graphic Organizer

Pages 10–11 *What prediction did you make when you read about the rattlesnake?* (Ritchie will help Ruth escape.) *Did your prediction match the text?* (Yes. Ritchie tells her to back away slowly.) *How does Ritchie know what to do?* (He read about rattlesnakes in his father's almanac.)

Pages 12–15 *Turn to a partner and describe how Ruth reacts to their parents' decision to move to Chicago.* (Ruth says she loves the farm and doesn't want to move. When John explains that they can move back eventually, she calls attention to Ritchie's idea for making money.) *Do you think the family will be successful in Chicago? Why or why not?* (They will be successful because John will make portraits and Ritchie will sell his cookbook.) *How does the family's shared experience help them adapt to change?* (They all work together so they can stay together.)

After Reading

Respond to Reading Revisit the Essential Question and ask students to complete the Text Evidence Questions on page 16.

Analytical Writing **Write About Reading** Check that students have correctly compared and contrasted Ruth and Ritchie's reactions to the rattlesnake and described what these reactions reveal about their personalities.

Fluency: Expression and Phrasing

Model Model reading page 4 with appropriate expression and phrasing. Next, read the passage aloud and have students read along.

Apply Have students practice reading the passage with partners.

PAIRED READ

"Chicago: Jazz Central"

Make Connections:
Write About It **Analytical Writing**

Before reading, ask students to note that the genre of this text is expository text. Then discuss the Essential Question. After reading, ask students to make connections between *Hard Times* and "Chicago: Jazz Central."

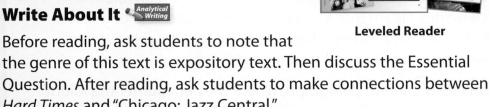

Leveled Reader

Analytical Writing

COMPARE TEXTS

→ Have students use text evidence to compare how a shared experience helps people adapt in a historical fiction story and an expository text.

Literature Circles

Ask students to conduct a literature circle using the Thinkmark questions to guide the discussion. You may wish to have a whole-class discussion, using both selections in the Leveled Reader, about how shared experiences help people adapt to change.

Level Up

Level-up lessons available online.

IF students read the On Level fluently and answered the questions,

THEN pair them with students who have proficiently read the Beyond Level and have students

- partner-read the Beyond Level main selection.

- describe techniques the author uses to convey a specific time and place in history.

A C T Access Complex Text

The Beyond Level challenges students by including more **idioms** and **complex sentence structures**.

On Level

Vocabulary

REVIEW VOCABULARY WORDS

 OBJECTIVES
Acquire and use accurately grade-appropriate general academic and domain-specific words and phrases, including those that signal contrast, addition, and other logical relationships (e.g., *however, although, nevertheless, similarly, moreover, in addition*). **L.5.6**

 I Do

Use the **Visual Vocabulary Cards** to review the key selection words *assume, guarantee, nominate, obviously, sympathy,* and *weakling*. Point to each word, read it aloud, and have students repeat it.

 We Do

Ask these questions. Help students explain their answers.

→ If you *assume* something is true, do you know for certain or do you suppose it is true?

→ What is something you might *guarantee* your teacher?

→ Would you *nominate* a dishonest or an honest person?

 You Do

Have students work in pairs to respond to these questions and explain their answers.

→ How would you *obviously* show your excitement?

→ Would you feel *sympathy* for a team that lost a soccer match?

→ Would a *weakling* struggle to carry a heavy object?

IDIOMS

 OBJECTIVES
Demonstrate understanding of figurative language, word relationships, and nuances in word meanings. Recognize and explain the meaning of common idioms, adages, and proverbs. **L.5.5b**

 I Do

Remind students that context clues can help them figure out the meaning of idioms. Use the Comprehension and Fluency passage on **Your Turn Practice Book** pages 213–214 to model.

Think Aloud I know that *skeleton crew* in paragraph 2 is an idiom. In the sentence before, I learn that Mr. Jenson's newspaper laid off most of its reporters. In the next sentence, I learn that he is overworked. I think *skeleton crew* means "just enough workers to keep a business running."

 We Do

Have students read the fifth paragraph, where they encounter the idiom *make tracks*. Help students figure out the definition by using the context clue *"We're in a hurry!"*

You Do

Have students work in pairs to determine the meanings of the idioms *cost an arm and a leg* (page 214, paragraph 6) and *a chip off the old block* (page 214, last paragraph) as they read the rest of the selection.

Comprehension

REVIEW COMPARE AND CONTRAST CHARACTERS

OBJECTIVES

 Compare and contrast two or more characters, settings, or events in a story or drama, drawing on specific details in the text (e.g., how characters interact). **RL.5.3**

 Quote accurately from a text when explaining what the text says explicitly and when drawing inferences from the text. **RL.5.1**

I Do Review with students that characters in a story may be similar or different from one another. Comparing and contrasting characters helps you understand how characters affect events in a story and how characters are changed by these events.

We Do Have a volunteer read the first three paragraphs of the Comprehension and Fluency passage on **Your Turn Practice Book** pages 213–214. Model identifying how Mr. Jenson responds to the change in plans. Then work with students to compare and contrast Nancy's response with Mr. Jenson's.

You Do Have partners compare and contrast how different characters respond to events in the rest of the passage. Ask pairs to explain how the characters' feelings and actions influence story events and are also changed by them.

SELF-SELECTED READING

OBJECTIVES

 Compare and contrast two or more characters, settings, or events in a story or drama, drawing on specific details in the text (e.g., how characters interact). **RL.5.3**

 Quote accurately from a text when explaining what the text says explicitly and when drawing inferences from the text. **RL.5.1**

Make, confirm, and revise predictions based on details in the text.

Read Independently

Have students choose a historical fiction book for sustained silent reading.

→ Before they read, have students preview the book, reading the title and viewing the front and back cover.

→ As students read, remind them to use clues in the text to make, confirm, and revise predictions.

Read Purposefully

Encourage students to select books about historical periods that interest them.

→ As students read, have them record comparisons and contrasts in the text on Graphic Organizer 62.

→ They can use the organizer to help them write a summary of the book.

→ Ask students to share their reactions about the book with classmates.

Beyond Level

Lexile 900
TextEvaluator 54

OBJECTIVES

CCSS Quote accurately from a text when explaining what the text says explicitly and when drawing inferences from the text. **RL.5.1**

CCSS Compare and contrast two or more characters, settings, or events in a story or drama, drawing on specific details in the text (e.g., how characters interact). **RL.5.3**

CCSS Read on-level prose and poetry orally with accuracy, appropriate rate, and expression on successive readings. **RF.5.4b**

ACADEMIC LANGUAGE

• *historical fiction, make predictions, compare, contrast, characters, idiom*

• Cognates: *ficción histórica, predicciones, comparar, contrastar*

Leveled Reader: *Woodpecker Warriors*

Go Digital

Leveled Readers

Before Reading

Preview and Predict

→ Have students read the Essential Question.

→ Have students preview the title, table of contents, and first page of *Woodpecker Warriors*. Students should predict what they think the selection will be about. Tell them to try to confirm or revise their predictions as they continue reading.

Review Genre: Historical Fiction

Tell students that this text is historical fiction. Historical fiction features settings that could have existed and events that could have taken place during a particular period in history. The characters act and talk like people from that particular time and place. Historical fiction often contains both real and made-up events and characters. Have students identify features of historical fiction in *Woodpecker Warriors*.

During Reading

Close Reading

Note Taking: Ask students to use their graphic organizer as they read.

Use Graphic Organizer

Pages 2–5 *What does the idiom "make tracks" mean? Use context clues to help you answer.* (Since Jim and June need to make grocery deliveries, it must mean "move quickly.") *How do June and Uncle Dan differ in the way they greet Archie and Bob? Why?* (June is polite, but Uncle Dan is rude. Uncle Dan thinks they are taking jobs from local men.) *Turn to a partner and predict if Uncle Dan's attitude will change.* (Yes, something will happen to change his mind about the CCC workers.)

Pages 6–9 *Turn to a partner and tell if your prediction matched the text.* (Not yet. Uncle Dan is still unfriendly. I will keep reading to see if I need to revise my prediction.) *Compare and contrast Archie's and Bob's personalities and feelings about the CCC.* (Bob is outgoing and complains about the hard work. Archie is quiet and enjoys life in the camp.)

Pages 10–11 *Compare how Mr. Taylor and Uncle Dan treat Archie.* (Mr. Taylor is friendly, but Uncle Dan is still rude.)

What suggestion does Archie make to Uncle Dan? How does he respond? (Archie suggests that Uncle Dan should work with the CCC. Uncle Dan scoffs at the idea.) *Do you want to revise your prediction about Uncle Dan's feelings? Explain.* (Not yet. Something may still change his mind.)

Pages 12–15 *Turn to a partner and summarize the events related to the fire.* (The workers and the townsmen work together to put out the fire. Uncle Dan and Archie cut down a dangerous tree. Uncle Dan changes his mind about the CCC workers after their speedy response to the fire.) *Turn to a partner and explain how the shared experience helped Uncle Dan adapt to change.* (Uncle Dan learned to overcome his prejudices about the CCC and appreciate the chance to work with Archie.)

After Reading

Respond to Reading Revisit the Essential Question and ask students to complete the Text Evidence Questions on page 16.

Analytical Writing **Write About Reading** Check that students have correctly compared and contrasted the characters of June and Jim. Make sure they include details that support their descriptions of the characters.

Fluency: Expression and Phrasing

Model Model reading page 4 with appropriate expression and phrasing. Next, read the passage aloud and have students read along.

Apply Have students practice reading the passage with partners.

PAIRED READ

Leveled Reader

"A Chance to Work"

Make Connections: Write About It 🔖 *Analytical Writing*

Before reading, ask students to note that the genre of this text is expository text. Then discuss the Essential Question. After reading, ask students to write connections between what they learned from *Woodpecker Warriors* and "A Chance to Work."

✏️ Analytical Writing

COMPARE TEXTS

→ Have students use text evidence to compare how a shared experience helps people adapt in a historical fiction story and an expository text.

Literature Circles

Ask students to conduct a literature circle using the Thinkmark questions to guide the discussion. You may wish to have a whole-class discussion, using both selections in the Leveled Reader, about how shared experiences help people adapt to change.

Gifted and Talented

Synthesize Have students write a dialogue between Uncle Dan and Archie that takes place six months later. The dialogue should focus on how their shared experience at the fire helped each of them adapt to the changes taking place in the town and in the country as a whole. The dialogue should also include details about their experiences since the time of the fire. Encourage students to research the time period to ensure authenticity in their dialogues.

→ Beyond Level

Vocabulary

REVIEW DOMAIN-SPECIFIC WORDS

OBJECTIVES
Acquire and use accurately grade-appropriate general academic and domain-specific words and phrases, including those that signal contrast, addition, and other logical relationships.
L.5.6

 Model

Use the **Visual Vocabulary Cards** to review the meanings of the words *rely* and *supportive*. Use each word in a context sentence.

Write the words *enroll* and *foremen* on the board and discuss the meanings with students. Then help students write a context sentence for each word.

 Apply

Have students work in pairs to find the meanings of the words *obligation* and *remorse*. Then have partners write sentences using the words.

IDIOMS

OBJECTIVES
Demonstrate understanding of figurative language, word relationships, and nuances in word meanings. Recognize and explain the meaning of common idioms, adages, and proverbs. **L.5.5b**

 Model

Read aloud the first two paragraphs of the Comprehension and Fluency passage on **Beyond Reproducibles** pages 213–214.

Think Aloud When I read the second paragraph, I am unsure of the meaning of the idiom *skeleton crew*. In the previous sentence, I learn that Nancy's father is overworked. I think *skeleton crew* means "just enough workers to keep a business running."

With students, read aloud the fifth paragraph. Help them figure out the meaning of *make tracks*.

 Apply

Have pairs of students read the rest of the passage. Ask them to use context clues to determine the meanings of the following idioms: *cost an arm and a leg* (page 214, paragraph 6), and *a chip off the old block* (page 214, last paragraph).

Gifted and Talented

Independent Study Challenge students to identify three additional examples of idioms they know of or have encountered in other books. Have them draw a picture of the literal meaning of the expression and the figurative meaning. Then have them use each idiom in an original sentence that shows its meaning.

Comprehension

REVIEW COMPARE AND CONTRAST CHARACTERS

OBJECTIVES

Compare and contrast two or more characters, settings, or events in a story or drama, drawing on specific details in the text (e.g., how characters interact) **RL.5.3**

Quote accurately from a text when explaining what the text says explicitly and when drawing inferences from the text. **RL.5.1**

Model Review with students that characters in a story may be similar or different. Comparing and contrasting characters helps readers understand how characters affect events and how characters are changed by events.

Have students read the first and second paragraphs of the Comprehension and Fluency passage on **Beyond Reproducibles** pages 213–214. Ask open-ended questions to facilitate discussion such as *How do the characters respond to events? How are responses similar or different?* Students should support their responses with details from the selection.

Apply As they independently fill in Graphic Organizer 62, have students identify similarities and differences in the way the characters respond to events in the rest of the passage. Then have partners use their work to explain how the characters' actions and feelings both affect story events and are changed by them.

SELF-SELECTED READING

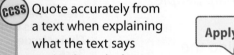

OBJECTIVES

Compare and contrast two or more characters, settings, or events in a story or drama, drawing on specific details in the text (e.g., how characters interact). **RL.5.3**

Quote accurately from a text when explaining what the text says explicitly and when drawing inferences from the text. **RL.5.1**

Make, confirm, and revise predictions based on details in the text.

Read Independently

Have students choose a historical fiction book for sustained silent reading.

→ As students read, have them record comparisons and contrasts on Graphic Organizer 62.

→ Remind them to make, confirm, and revise predictions as they read.

Read Purposefully

Encourage students to keep a reading journal. Suggest that they select books about historical periods that interest them.

→ Students can write summaries of the books in their journals.

→ Ask students to share their reactions to the books with classmates.

Independent Study Challenge students to discuss how their books relate to the weekly theme of people being better together. Have students use all of their reading materials to compare ways that shared experiences help people adapt to change.

→ English Language Learners

Shared Read

The Day the Rollets Got Their Moxie Back

Reading/Writing Workshop

Go Digital

Before Reading

Build Background

Read the Essential Question: *How do shared experiences help people adapt to change?*

→ Explain the meaning of the Essential Question, including the vocabulary in the question: *Shared experiences are things that happen to both you and other people at the same time.* Adapt *means "to change because your situation changes."*

→ **Model an answer:** *When several people are going through the same situation, each person understands how the others feel. They probably know what to do or say to help one another.*

→ Ask students a question that ties the Essential Question to their own background knowledge: *Turn to a partner and think of an experience you shared with friends or family members that led to changes. Discuss how the shared experience helped all of you adapt to the changes. Call on several pairs.*

During Reading

Interactive Question-Response

→ Ask questions that help students understand the meaning of the text after each paragraph.

→ Reinforce the meanings of key vocabulary.

→ Ask students questions that require them to use key vocabulary.

→ Reinforce strategies and skills of the week by modeling.

 OBJECTIVES

CCSS Quote accurately from a text when explaining what the text says explicitly and when drawing inferences from the text. **RL.5.1**

CCSS Compare and contrast two or more characters, settings, or events in a story or drama, drawing on specific details in the text (e.g., how characters interact). **RL.5.3**

LANGUAGE OBJECTIVE
Compare and contrast two or more characters in a story.

ACADEMIC LANGUAGE
• *make predictions, idiom, compare, contrast, character*
• Cognates: *predicciones, comparar, contrastar*

Page 324

Read aloud the title. Tell students that the word *moxie* means "determination and courage."

Explain and Model the Strategy *Using the title, I can predict what the story will be about. I think the Rollet family is having a difficult time, but they will find a way to regain their courage and determination.*

Page 325

Paragraph 1
Explain and Model Idioms Read the paragraph and have students repeat the idiom "a bolt from the blue." Explain that the idiom means something unexpected. *What is described as a bolt from the blue?* (Ricky's letter)

When does the story take place? (1937) Explain that this time period is called the Great Depression and many people were out of work. *Does the narrator's father have a job?* (no)

Paragraphs 3–4
What did Ricky write about in his letter? (a talent show) *Ricky's letter gives Shirley an idea. What is it?* (She thinks they should have their own talent show.)

Page 326

Paragraphs 1–2
Explain and Model Compare and Contrast
Explain that when you compare characters, you look at how they are alike. When you contrast characters, you look at how they are different. Point out the words used to describe Dad, *sullen* and *spent*, and define them for students. *Why does he feel this way?* (because he is out of work) Compare and contrast his character with the character of Mom. *How does Mom try to lighten everyone's spirits?* (She jokes about the meatless meat loaf and sings a little song about it.)

Which context clues help you figure out the meaning of the idiom get the green light? (A green traffic light means cars can go, so it must mean that the shows are approved and can go forward.)

Paragraph 3
Choral-read the paragraph. Point to the word *fidgeted*. Have students show what it looks like to fidget in their seats.

Paragraph 4
Complete the sentence: On Saturday Dad and the girls go to _____. (the soup kitchen) *Why do they go there?* (Dad hopes to hear about available jobs.)

Page 327

Paragraph 1
How are Dad's actions like those of the other men? (They all bow their heads.) Demonstrate bowing your head.

Paragraphs 2–7
How do the people in line change after the girls begin singing and dancing? (They go from frowning with their heads down to smiling with their heads up and clapping.) Have students pantomime how the people look before and after the girls perform.

Remind students of the prediction you made before reading. *Did our prediction match what happened in the story?* (yes) *How did the Rollets get their moxie back?* (When people applaud for their singing and dancing, they feel like anything is possible.)

After Reading

Make Connections

→ Review the Essential Question: *How do shared experiences help people adapt to change?*

→ Make text connections and have students complete **ELL Reproducibles** pages 213–215.

English Language Learners

Lexile 520
TextEvaluator™ 34

OBJECTIVES

CCSS Quote accurately from a text when explaining what the text says explicitly and when drawing inferences from the text. **RL.5.1**

CCSS Compare and contrast two or more characters, settings, or events in a story or drama, drawing on specific details in the text (e.g., how characters interact). **RL.5.3**

CCSS Read on-level prose and poetry orally with accuracy, appropriate rate, and expression on successive readings. **RF.5.4b**

ACADEMIC LANGUAGE

• *make predictions, historical fiction, compare, contrast*

• Cognates: *predicciones, ficción histórica, comparar, contrastar*

Leveled Reader:
Hard Times

Go Digital

Leveled Readers

Before Reading

Preview and Predict

→ Read the Essential Question: *How do shared experiences help people adapt to change?*

→ Refer to Through Thick and Thin: *How can people be supportive of others during difficult times?*

→ Preview *Hard Times* and "Chicago: Jazz Central": *Our purpose for reading is to learn about how changes cause people to make big decisions.*

Vocabulary

Use the **Visual Vocabulary Cards** to pre-teach the ELL vocabulary: *chaos, stubborn, afford, assembled*. Use the routine found on the cards. Point out the cognate: *caos.*

During Reading

Interactive Question-Response

Note Taking: Ask students to use the graphic organizer on **ELL Reproducibles** page 212. Use the questions below after each page is read with students. As you read, define vocabulary in context and use visuals to help students understand key vocabulary.

Pages 2–3 Choral read the second paragraph on page 2. *During what time period does this story take place?* (the Great Depression) *What problem does the Tillerman family face?* (They are struggling to make a living on the farm.)

Pages 4–6 Point to the word *sketching* and explain that it means *drawing*. Model making a sketch. *Turn to a partner and retell Ruth's idea for how her dad can make money.* (She thinks he should make sketches of people and sell them.) *Where is Mr. Tillerman going to go to try selling his sketches?* (Chicago)

Pages 7–9 *Ruth and Ritchie do many chores on the farm.* Have students pantomime flipping pancakes, milking a cow, and sawing wood. Have them describe each action: *I am _____.*

Use Graphic Organizer

Pages 10–11 Have students pause after reading the second paragraph on page 10. *Make a prediction about what will happen next.* (Ritchie will help Ruth.) Have students read on to confirm or revise their predictions.

Pages 12–15 Point to the illustration on page 14. *What gifts does Mr. Tillerman bring from Chicago?* (a mute, a book, material for a dress) Explain how a mute is used with a trumpet. Then choral read the last paragraph on page 14. *What does Mr. Tillerman want the family to do?* (move to Chicago)

After Reading

Respond to Reading Revisit the Essential Question and ask students to complete the Text Evidence Questions on page 16.

Analytical Writing **Write About Reading** Check that students have correctly compared and contrasted Ruth and Ritchie's reactions to the rattlesnake and described what these reactions reveal about their personalities.

Fluency: Expression and Phrasing

Model Model reading page 4 with appropriate expression and phrasing. Then have students echo read along with you.

Apply Have students practice reading with partners.

PAIRED READ

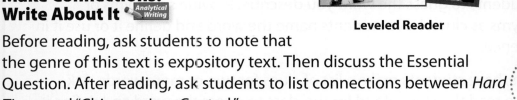

Leveled Reader

"Chicago: Jazz Central"

**Make Connections:
Write About It** *Analytical Writing*

Before reading, ask students to note that the genre of this text is expository text. Then discuss the Essential Question. After reading, ask students to list connections between *Hard Times* and "Chicago: Jazz Central."

Analytical Writing

COMPARE TEXTS

→ Have students use text evidence to compare how a shared experience helps people adapt in a historical fiction story and an expository text.

Literature Circles

Ask students to conduct a literature circle using the Thinkmark questions to guide the discussion. You may wish to use both selections in the Leveled Reader to have a whole-class discussion about how shared experiences help people adapt to change.

Level Up

Level-up lessons available online.

IF students read the **ELL Level** fluently and answered the questions,

THEN pair them with students who have proficiently read **On Level** and have ELL students

• echo-read the **On Level** main selection.

• list words with which they have difficulty and discuss them with a partner.

A C T Access Complex Text

The **On Level** challenges students by including more **domain-specific words** and **complex sentence structures**.

English Language Learners
Vocabulary

PRETEACH VOCABULARY

OBJECTIVES
 Acquire and use accurately grade-appropriate general academic and domain-specific words and phrases, including those that signal contrast, addition, and other logical relationships. **L.5.6**

LANGUAGE OBJECTIVE
Use vocabulary words.

 Preteach vocabulary from "The Day the Rollets Got Their Moxie Back," following the Vocabulary Routine found on the **Visual Vocabulary Cards** for the words *assume, guarantee, nominate, obviously, rely, supportive, sympathy,* and *weakling.*

 After completing the Vocabulary Routine for each word, point to the word on the card and read the word with students. Ask them to repeat the word.

You Do Have students write a definition for a word of their choosing. Ask them to read the definition to a partner, and have the partner name the word that matches the definition.

Beginning	Intermediate	Advanced/High
Help students write the definition correctly and read it aloud.	Ask students to write the definition as a complete sentence.	Challenge students to write a definition for each word.

REVIEW VOCABULARY

OBJECTIVES
 Acquire and use accurately grade-appropriate general academic and domain-specific words and phrases, including those that signal contrast, addition, and other logical relationships. **L.5.6**

LANGUAGE OBJECTIVE
Use vocabulary words.

I Do Review the previous week's vocabulary words. The words can be reviewed over a few days. Read each word aloud, pointing to the word on the **Visual Vocabulary Card**. Have students repeat after you. Then follow the Vocabulary Routine on the back of each card.

 Ask students to guess the word you describe. Provide synonyms or antonyms as clues. Have students name the word and define it or use it in a sentence.

 In pairs, have students make a list of clues for two or more words. Ask them to read the clues aloud for the class to guess the word and define it or use it in a sentence.

Beginning	Intermediate	Advanced/High
Help students list clue words and read them aloud.	Have students write clues as sentences.	Ask students to use synonyms or antonyms in their clues.

IDIOMS

OBJECTIVES
(CCSS) Demonstrate understanding of figurative language, word relationships, and nuances in word meanings. Recognize and explain the meaning of common idioms, adages, and proverbs. **L.5.5b**

LANGUAGE OBJECTIVES
Interpret idioms.

I Do Read aloud the first two paragraphs of the Comprehension and Fluency passage on **ELL Reproducibles** pages 213–214, while students follow along. Summarize the paragraphs. Point to the idiom "skeleton crew." Tell students that context clues can help them figure out the meaning of the idiom.

Think Aloud I'm not sure what "skeleton crew" means. In the previous sentence, I see that most of the reporters at Mr. Jenson's job have been laid off. Working on a skeleton crew must mean "working with few people."

We Do Have students point to the idiom "make tracks" in the last paragraph on page 213. Find context clues with students, guiding them to see that Nancy and her dad are in a hurry. Write the definition of the idiom on the board.

You Do In pairs, have students write a definition for the idioms "cost an arm and a leg" and "a chip off the old block" on page 214 using context clues.

Beginning	Intermediate	Advanced/High
Help students locate the idioms and context clues.	Ask students to locate and read aloud the context clues for each idiom.	Have students use an idiom in a sentence.

ADDITIONAL VOCABULARY

OBJECTIVES
(CCSS) Acquire and use accurately grade-appropriate general academic and domain-specific words and phrases, including those that signal contrast, addition, and other logical relationships. **L.5.6**

LANGUAGE OBJECTIVE
Use academic vocabulary and high-frequency words.

I Do List some academic vocabulary and high-frequency words from "The Day the Rollets Got Their Moxie Back": *employment, facilities, lumber*; and *Hard Times*: *twins, parade, chaos, rumors*. Define each word for students: *Employment is work you are paid to do.*

We Do Model using the words for students in a sentence: *She has had steady employment since she moved here. Dad has been looking for employment as an artist.* Then provide sentence frames and complete them with students: *I hope to find employment as a _____.*

You Do Have pairs make up their own sentences and share them with the class to complete them.

Beginning	Intermediate	Advanced/High
Provide sentence frames and help students complete them.	Provide sentence starters for students.	Have students write definitions for the words they used.

English Language Learners
Writing/Spelling

WRITING TRAIT: SENTENCE FLUENCY

 OBJECTIVES
Link ideas within and across categories of information using words, phrases, and causes (e.g., *in contrast, especially*). **W.5.2c**

LANGUAGE OBJECTIVE
Use transitions in writing.

 I Do Explain that good writers include transitional words, phrases, and clauses to guide the reader through a text. Provide examples such as *however, for example, after,* and *soon.* Read the Expert Model aloud as students follow along. Identify the transitions.

 We Do Read aloud the first three paragraphs of "The Day the Rollets Got Their Moxie Back." Identify the transitions "It was 1937," "Though," and "Back in our New York City apartment." Discuss how they help to orient the reader. List other examples of transitions on the board and model sentences.

 You Do Have students write their own paragraph, using at least two of the transitions you discussed. Edit each pair's writing.

Beginning	Intermediate	Advanced/High
Have students copy the edited sentences.	Have students add more transitional words, phrases, or clauses.	Have students identify their transitions and explain how they connect ideas.

SPELL HOMOPHONES

 OBJECTIVES
Demonstrate command of the conventions of standard English capitalization, punctuation, and spelling when writing. Spell grade-appropriate words correctly consulting references as needed. **L.5.2e**

LANGUAGE OBJECTIVE
Spell homophones.

 I Do Read aloud the Spelling Words on page T100, segmenting them into syllables and attaching a spelling to each sound. Point out that homophones are words that sound alike but have different spellings and meanings. Have students repeat the words.

 We Do Read the Dictation Sentences on page T101 aloud for students. With each sentence, read the underlined word slowly, segmenting it into syllables. Have students repeat after you and write the word.

 You Do Display the words. Have students exchange their list with a partner to check the spelling and write the words correctly.

Beginning	Intermediate	Advanced/High
Help students copy the words with correct spelling and say the words aloud.	After students have corrected their words, have pairs quiz each other.	After students have corrected their words, have them identify words that were challenging for them and use them in sentences.

Grammar

COMPLEX SENTENCES

OBJECTIVES

 CCSS Demonstrate command of the conventions of standard English grammar and usage when writing or speaking. Explain the function of conjunctions, prepositions, and interjections in general and their function in particular sentences. **L.5.1a**

LANGUAGE OBJECTIVE

Write complex sentences.

Language Transfers Handbook

Speakers of Cantonese and Vietnamese may omit pronouns in clauses. Reinforce the use of pronouns in dependent clauses.

 I Do

Review independent and dependent clauses. Explain that complex sentences have an independent clause and a dependent clause. Write: *Because I was tired, I went to bed.* Underline the dependent clause, pointing out the conjunction and the comma. Explain that when a dependent clause comes at the beginning of a sentence, it is followed by a comma.

 We Do

Write the sentences below on the board. Have students underline the independent clause once and the dependent clause twice. Read each sentence aloud, modeling the pause at the comma. Then have students repeat.

> *When my dog barks, I take him outside.*
>
> *After I do my homework, I make a snack.*
>
> *Because I woke up late, I was late to school.*

 You Do

Brainstorm a list of dependent clauses with students. Have students work in pairs to choose two dependent clauses and add an independent clause to each. Have them read their completed sentences aloud.

Beginning	Intermediate	Advanced/High
Help students copy their sentences and underline the independent clause once and the dependent clause twice. Read the sentences aloud. Have students repeat.	Ask students to underline the independent clause once and the dependent clause twice.	Have students underline the independent clause once and the dependent clause twice. Ask them to identify the conjunction and check their comma use.

For extra support, have students complete the activities in the **Grammar Practice Reproducibles** during the week, using the routine below:

→ Explain the grammar skill.

→ Model the first activity in the Grammar Practice Reproducibles.

→ Have the whole group complete the next couple of activities, then do the rest with a partner.

→ Review the activities with correct answers.

PROGRESS MONITORING

Weekly Assessment

✓ COMPREHENSION:	✓ VOCABULARY:	✓ WRITING:
Character, Setting, Plot: Compare and Contrast Characters **RL.5.3, RL.5.1**	Idioms **L.5.5b**	Writing About Text **RL.5.3, RL.5.1, W.5.9a**

Assessment Includes

→ Performance Tasks

→ Approaching-Level Assessment online PDFs

Fluency Goal 129 to 149 words correct per minute (WCPM)

Accuracy Rate Goal 95% or higher

Administer oral reading fluency assessments using the following schedule:

→ **Weeks 1, 3, 5** Provide Approaching-Level students at least three oral reading fluency assessments during the unit.

→ **Weeks 2 and 4** Provide On-Level students at least two oral reading fluency assessments during the unit.

→ **Week 6** If necessary, provide Beyond-Level students an oral reading fluency assessment at this time.

Also Available: Selection Tests online PDFs

Go Digital! www.connected.mcgraw-hill.com

Using Assessment Results

✓ TESTED SKILLS	If ...	Then ...
COMPREHENSION	Students answer 0–6 multiple-choice items correctly ...	... assign Lessons 43–45 on Compare and Contrast from the *Tier 2 Comprehension Intervention online PDFs*.
VOCABULARY	Students answer 0–6 multiple-choice items correctly ...	... assign Lesson 166 on Idioms, Proverbs, and Adages from the *Tier 2 Vocabulary Intervention online PDFs*.
WRITING	Students score less than "3" on the constructed responses ...	... assign Lessons 43–45 on Compare and Contrast and/or Write About Reading Lesson 194 from the *Tier 2 Comprehension Intervention online PDFs*.
FLUENCY	Students have a WCPM score of 120–128 ...	... assign a lesson from Section 1, 7, 8, 9, or 10 of the *Tier 2 Fluency Intervention online PDFs*.
	Students have a WCPM score of 0–119 ...	... assign a lesson from Section 2, 3, 4, 5, or 6 of the *Tier 2 Fluency Intervention online PDFs*.

Response to Intervention

Use the appropriate sections of the *Placement and Dignostic Assessment* as well as students' assessment results to designate students requiring:

TIER 2 Intervention Online PDFs

TIER 3 WonderWorks Intervention Program

WEEKLY OVERVIEW

Text Complexity Range for Grades 4–5

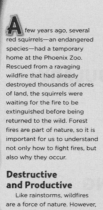

Lexile

740   *TextEvaluator*™   1010

23   51

Reading/Writing Workshop

TEACH AND MODEL

✔ Vocabulary

atmosphere

decays

gradual

impact

noticeably

receding

stability

variations

 **☞ Go** Digital

www.connected.mcgraw-hill.com

Close Reading of Complex Text

Shared Read "Forests on Fire," 338–345

Genre Expository Text

Lexile 960L

ETS *TextEvaluator*™ 53

Minilessons   ✔ Tested Skills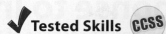

✔ **Comprehension Strategy** .... Ask and Answer Questions, T146–T147

✔ **Comprehension Skill** .... Text Structure: Compare and Contrast, T148–T149

✔ **Genre** .... Expository Text, T150–T151

✔ **Vocabulary Strategy** .... Context Clues, T152–T153

✔ **Writing Traits** .... Ideas, T158–T159

Grammar Handbook .... Adjectives, T162–T163

OUR CHANGING EARTH
Essential Question
What changes in the environment
affect living things?

WEEK 3 →

APPLY WITH CLOSE READING

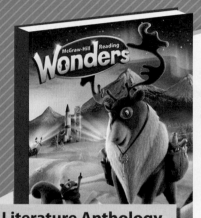

Literature Anthology

Literature Anthology

Complex Text

PAIRED READ

Global Warming, 384–397
Genre Expository Text
Lexile 980L
(ETS) *TextEvaluator* 46

"When Volcanoes Erupt," 400–403
Genre Expository Text
Lexile 1040L
(ETS) *TextEvaluator* 40

Differentiated Text

Leveled Readers *Include Paired Reads*

APPROACHING
Lexile 830L
(ETS) *TextEvaluator* 38

ON LEVEL
Lexile 950L
(ETS) *TextEvaluator* 48

BEYOND
Lexile 990L
(ETS) *TextEvaluator* 48

ELL
Lexile 870L
(ETS) *TextEvaluator* 36

Extended Complex Text

*Volcano: The Eruption
and Healing of Mount
St. Helens*
Genre Expository Text
Lexile 830L
(ETS) *TextEvaluator* 31

Classroom Library

*Arctic Lights,
Arctic Nights*
Genre Expository Text
Lexile 890L
(ETS) *TextEvaluator* 36

Classroom
Library
lessons available
online.

TEACH AND MANAGE

How You Teach

INTRODUCE

Weekly Concept
Our Changing Earth

Reading/Writing Workshop
334–335

TEACH

Close Reading
"Forests on Fire"

Minilessons
Ask and Answer Questions, Compare and Contrast, Expository Text, Context Clues: Paragraph Clues, Writing Traits

Reading/Writing Workshop
338–347

APPLY

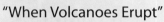

Close Reading
Global Warming

"When Volcanoes Erupt"

Literature Anthology
384–403

👉 **Go Digital**

 Interactive Whiteboard

 Interactive Whiteboard

 Mobile

How Students Practice

WEEKLY CONTRACT

PDF Online

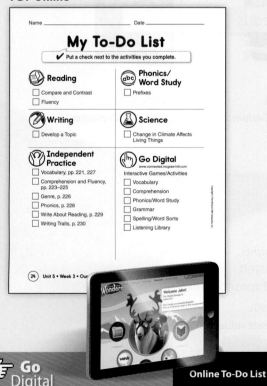

LEVELED PRACTICE AND ONLINE ACTIVITIES

Your Turn Practice Book
221–230

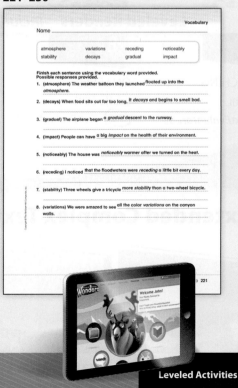

Leveled Readers

👉 **Go Digital**

Online To-Do List

Leveled Activities

Writer's Workspace

Go Digital! www.connected.mcgraw-hill.com

DIFFERENTIATE

SMALL GROUP INSTRUCTION

Leveled Readers

Mobile

INTEGRATE

Research and Inquiry
Web Site Entry or Podcast, T156

Text Connections
Compare Environmental Changes, T157

Write About Reading
Analytical Writing Write an Analysis, T157

Online Research and Writing

ASSESS

Weekly Assessment
265–276

Online Assessment

LEVELED WORKSTATION CARDS

More Activities on back

23
Climate in the News

SCIENCE

Many factors influence the climate. Changes in climate affect living things.

- Work with a partner. List several characteristics of a climate you know.

- Think about what would happen if that

6
Ideas: Develop a Topic

WRITING

Read what Jamal wrote about taking care of a pet.

Pet lizards can be a lot of work. You need to feed them twice a day. Their tanks need to be kept clean and at the right temperature. Watch the lizard in its tank.

- What information about the topic did you learn from Jamal's paragraph? What questions do you still have?

1
Context Clues

PHONICS/WORD STUDY

Clues to word meanings may appear in **sentences** and **paragraphs**, or as **definitions** or **restatements**.

Kaylie used *calligraphy*, or beautiful writing, when she wrote the letter.

- Find a selection you read this week that contains a word did not know. Write the word.

- Look for context clues to help you figure out the meaning. Use a dictionary to check the definition.

- Write a sentence for the word and provide a context clue for its meaning. Underline the word.

- Exchange sentences with a partner. Identify context clues to figure out the word's meaning.

You need
20 Minutes
> reading selection
> paper and pen or pencil
> dictionary

14
Text Structure: Compare and Contrast

READING

Some texts organize ideas by showing how things are alike and different.

- Choose an informational text you have read this week.

- Find two things that the author compares and contrasts.

- Make a Venn diagram. Where the circles overlap, write how the two things are the same. In the outer circles, write how they are different.

- Explain to your partner how you learned from the comparisons.

You need
30
> informational text that compares two things
> paper and pen or pencil

Go Digital! www.connected.mcgraw-hill.com • Interactive Games and Activities • Grade 5

DEVELOPING READERS AND WRITERS

Write About Reading • Analytical Writing

Write to Sources and Research

Text Structure: Compare and Contrast, T148–T149

Note Taking, T153B, T153R

Summarize, T153P

Compare and Contrast, T153P

Make Connections: Essential Question, T153P, T153T, T157

Key Details: T153R, T153S

Research and Inquiry, T156

Analyze to Inform/Explain, T157

Comparing Texts, T169, T177, T181, T187

Predictive Writing, T153B

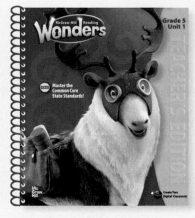

Teacher's Edition

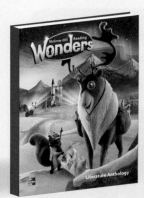

Literature Anthology

Summarize, p. 399
Compare and Contrast, p. 399

Leveled Readers
Comparing Texts
Compare and Contrast

Your Turn Practice Book

Compare and Contrast, pp. 223–225
Genre, p. 226
Analyze to Inform/Explain, p. 229

Go Digital

Interactive Whiteboard

Writing Process • Genre Writing

Informative Text
Informational Article, T344–T349

Conferencing Routines
Teacher Conferences, T346
Peer Conferences, T347

Go Digital

Interactive Whiteboard

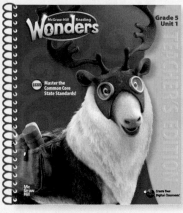

Teacher's Edition

Leveled Workstation Card
Informational Article, Card 29

Go Digital

Writer's Workspace
Informative Text:
Informational Article
Writing Process
Multimedia Presentations

Writing Traits • Write Every Day

Writing Trait: Ideas
Develop a Topic, T158–T159

Conferencing Routines
Teacher Conferences, T160
Peer Conferences, T161

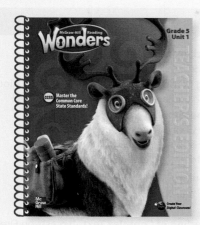

Teacher's Edition

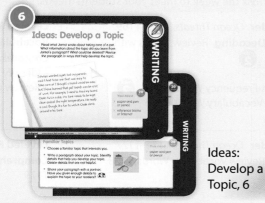

Ideas: Develop a Topic, pp. 346–347

Reading/Writing Workshop

Interactive Whiteboard

Ideas: Develop a Topic, 6

Leveled Workstation Card

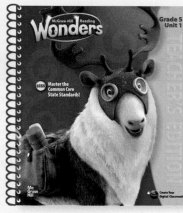

Ideas: Develop a Topic, p. 230

Your Turn Practice Book

Grammar and Spelling

Grammar
Adjectives, T162–T163

Spelling
Prefixes, T164–T165

Interactive Whiteboard

Teacher's Edition

Adjectives

Prefixes
Word Sorts

Online Spelling and Grammar Games

SUGGESTED LESSON PLAN

✓ **TESTED SKILLS** CCSS

	DAY 1	DAY 2

Whole Group

READING

Teach, Model and Apply

Reading/Writing Workshop

DAY 1

Build Background Our Changing Earth, T138–T139

Listening Comprehension Interactive Read Aloud: "Changing Climate, Changing Lives," T140–T141

Comprehension
• Preview Genre: Expository Text, T150–T151
• Preview Strategy: Ask and Answer Questions, T146–T147

✓ **Vocabulary** Words in Context, T142–T143

Practice *Your Turn* 221

Close Reading of Complex Text "Forests on Fire," 338–341

DAY 2

✓ **Comprehension**
• Strategy: Ask and Answer Questions, T146–T147
• Skill: Text Structure: Compare and Contrast, T148–T149
• Write About Reading *Analytical Writing*
• Genre: Expository Text, T150–T151

✓ **Vocabulary** Context Clues, T152–T153

Practice *Your Turn* 222–227

Small Group

DIFFERENTIATED INSTRUCTION   Choose across the week to meet your students' needs.

Approaching Level

DAY 1

Leveled Reader *Ocean Threats,* T168–T169

Word Study/Decoding Review Words with Prefixes, T170 **TIER 2**

Vocabulary
• Review High-Frequency Words, T172 **TIER 2**
• Understand Vocabulary Words, T173

DAY 2

Leveled Reader *Ocean Threats,* T168–T169

Vocabulary Review Vocabulary Words, T172 **TIER 2**

Comprehension
• Identify Differences, T174 **TIER 2**
• Review Compare and Contrast, T175

On Level

DAY 1

Leveled Reader *Ocean Threats,* T176–T177

Vocabulary Review Vocabulary Words, T178

DAY 2

Leveled Reader *Ocean Threats,* T176–T177

Comprehension Review Compare and Contrast, T179

Beyond Level

DAY 1

Leveled Reader *Ocean Threats,* T180–T181

Vocabulary Review Domain-Specific Words, T182

DAY 2

Leveled Reader *Ocean Threats,* T180–T181

Comprehension Review Compare and Contrast, T183

English Language Learners

DAY 1

Shared Read "Forests on Fire," T184–T185

Word Study/Decoding Review Words with Prefixes, T170

Vocabulary
• Preteach Vocabulary, T188
• Review High-Frequency Words, T172

DAY 2

Leveled Reader *Ocean Threats,* T186–T187

Vocabulary Review Vocabulary, T188

Writing Writing Trait: Ideas, T190

Grammar Adjectives, T191

Whole Group

LANGUAGE ARTS   Writing Process: Informational Article T344–T349 Use with Weeks 1–3

Writing
Grammar
Spelling
Build Vocabulary

DAY 1

✓ **Readers to Writers**
• Writing Trait: Ideas/Develop a Topic, T158–T159
• Writing Entry: Prewrite and Draft, T160

Grammar Adjectives, T162

Spelling Prefixes, T164

Build Vocabulary
• Connect to Words, T166
• Academic Vocabulary, T166

DAY 2

Readers to Writers
• Writing Entry: Revise, T160

Grammar Adjectives, T162

Spelling Prefixes, T164

Build Vocabulary
• Expand Vocabulary, T166
• Review Prefixes and Suffixes, T166

DAY 3	DAY 4	DAY 5 Review and Assess

READING

Word Study/Decoding Prefixes, T154–T155
Practice *Your Turn* 228

Close Reading *Global Warming,*
384–399 🎤 *Analytical Writing*

Literature Anthology

Fluency Rate, T155
Integrate Ideas 🎤 *Analytical Writing*
• Research and Inquiry, T156

Practice *Your Turn* 223–225

Close Reading "When Volcanoes Erupt," 400–403
🎤 *Analytical Writing*

Integrate Ideas 🎤 *Analytical Writing*
• Research and Inquiry, T156
• Text Connections, T157
• Write About Reading, T157

Practice *Your Turn* 229

DIFFERENTIATED INSTRUCTION

Leveled Reader *Ocean Threats,* T168–T169
Word Study/Decoding Build Words with Prefixes, T170 ⑂TIER 2
Fluency Rate, T174 ⑂TIER 2
Vocabulary Context Clues, T173

Leveled Reader Paired Read: "Floating Trash," T169
🎤 *Analytical Writing*
Word Study/Decoding Practice Words with Prefixes, T171

Leveled Reader Literature Circle, T169
Comprehension Self-Selected Reading, T175

Leveled Reader *Ocean Threats,* T176–T177
Vocabulary Context Clues, T178

Leveled Reader Paired Read: "Floating Trash," T177
🎤 *Analytical Writing*

Leveled Reader Literature Circle, T177
Comprehension Self-Selected Reading, T179

Leveled Reader *Ocean Threats,* T180–T181
Vocabulary
• Context Clues, T182
• Shades of Meaning, T182
⭐ *Gifted and Talented*

Leveled Reader Paired Read: "Floating Trash," T181
🎤 *Analytical Writing*

Leveled Reader Literature Circle, T181
Comprehension
• Self-Selected Reading, T183
• Independent Study: Environment, T183
⭐ *Gifted and Talented*

Leveled Reader *Ocean Threats,* T186–T187
Word Study/Decoding Build Words with Prefixes, T170
Vocabulary Context Clues, T189
Spelling Words with Prefixes, T190

Leveled Reader Paired Read: "Floating Trash," T187
🎤 *Analytical Writing*
Vocabulary Additional Vocabulary, T189
Word Study/Decoding Practice Words with Prefixes, T171

Leveled Reader Literature Circle, T187

LANGUAGE ARTS

Readers to Writers
• Writing Entry: Prewrite and Draft, T161
Grammar Mechanics and Usage, T163
Spelling Prefixes, T165
Build Vocabulary
• Reinforce the Words, T167
• Context Clues, T167

Readers to Writers
• Writing Entry: Revise, T161
Grammar Adjectives, T163
Spelling Prefixes, T165
Build Vocabulary
• Connect to Writing, T167
• Shades of Meaning, T167

Readers to Writers
• Writing Entry: Share and Reflect, T161
Grammar Adjectives, T163
Spelling Prefixes, T165
Build Vocabulary
• Word Squares, T167
• Morphology, T167

DIFFERENTIATE TO ACCELERATE

  Scaffold to Access Complex Text

IF the text complexity of a particular selection is too difficult for students

THEN see the references noted in the chart below for scaffolded instruction to help students Access Complex Text.

Qualitative / Quantitative
Reader and Task
TEXT COMPLEXITY

	Reading/Writing Workshop	Literature Anthology	Leveled Readers	Classroom Library

Quantitative	"Forests on Fire" **Lexile** 960 *TextEvaluator*™ 53	*Global Warming* **Lexile** 980 *TextEvaluator*™ 46 "When Volcanoes Erupt" **Lexile** 1040 *TextEvaluator*™ 40	**Approaching Level** **Lexile** 830 *TextEvaluator*™ 38 **Beyond Level** **Lexile** 990 *TextEvaluator*™ 48 **On Level** **Lexile** 950 *TextEvaluator*™ 48 **ELL** **Lexile** 870 *TextEvaluator*™ 36	*Volcano: The Eruption and Healing of Mount St. Helens* **Lexile** 830 *TextEvaluator*™ 31 *Arctic Lights, Arctic Nights* **Lexile** 890 *TextEvaluator*™ 36
Qualitative	**What Makes the Text Complex?** • **Organization** Compare and Contrast T145 • **Specific Vocabulary** Domain-Specific Words T153 **ACT** *See Scaffolded Instruction in Teacher's Edition T145 and T153.*	**What Makes the Text Complex?** • **Organization** Expository Text T153A • **Prior Knowledge** Science T153C • **Connection of Ideas** New Information T153E, T153S; Global Warming T153M • **Organization** Cause and Effect T153G • **Specific Vocabulary** Context Clues T153I, T153Q • **Purpose** Expository Text T153K **ACT** *See Scaffolded Instruction in Teacher's Edition T153A–T153T.*	**What Makes the Text Complex?** • **Specific Vocabulary** • **Sentence Structure** • **Connection of Ideas** • **Genre** **ACT** *See Level Up lessons online for Leveled Readers.*	**What Makes the Text Complex?** • **Genre** • **Specific Vocabulary** • **Prior Knowledge** • **Sentence Structure** • **Organization** • **Purpose** • **Connection of Ideas** **ACT** *See Scaffolded Instruction in Teacher's Edition T360-T361.*
Reader and Task	The Introduce the Concept lesson on pages T138–T139 will help determine the reader's knowledge and engagement in the weekly concept. See pages T144–T153 and T156–T157 for questions and tasks for this text.	The Introduce the Concept lesson on pages T138–T139 will help determine the reader's knowledge and engagement in the weekly concept. See pages T153A–T153T and T156–T157 for questions and tasks for this text.	The Introduce the Concept lesson on pages T138–T139 will help determine the reader's knowledge and engagement in the weekly concept. See pages T168–T169, T176–T177, T180–T181, T186–T187, and T156–T157 for questions and tasks for this text.	The Introduce the Concept lesson on pages T138–T139 will help determine the reader's knowledge and engagement in the weekly concept. See pages T360-T361 for questions and tasks for this text.

Go Digital! www.connected.mcgraw-hill.com

Monitor and *Differentiate*

IF → you need to differentiate instruction

THEN → use the Quick Checks to assess students' needs and select the appropriate small group instruction focus.

 Quick Check

Comprehension Strategy Ask and Answer Questions T147

Comprehension Skill Text Structure: Compare and Contrast T149

Genre Expository Text T151

Vocabulary Strategy Context Clues T153

Word Study/Fluency Prefixes, Rate T155

If No →
| Approaching Level | Reteach T168–T175 |
| ELL | Develop T184–T191 |

If Yes →
| On Level | Review T176–T179 |
| Beyond Level | Extend T180–T183 |

Level Up with Leveled Readers

IF → students can read their leveled text fluently and answer comprehension questions

THEN → work with the next level up to accelerate students' reading with more complex text.

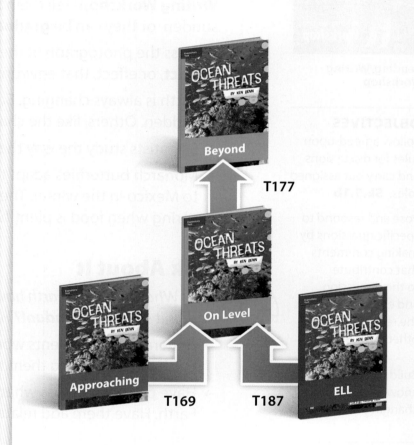

T177

T169   T187

ENGLISH LANGUAGE LEARNERS SCAFFOLD

IF ELL students need additional support   **THEN** scaffold instruction using the small group suggestions.

Reading/Writing Workshop "Forests on Fire" T184–T185	Leveled Reader *Ocean Threats* T186–T187 "Floating Trash" T187	Additional Vocabulary T189 algae · flames destroyed · force environment · nutrients	Context Clues T189	Writing Trait: Ideas T190	Spelling Words with Prefixes T190	Grammar Adjectives T191

Note: Include ELL Students in all small groups based on their needs.

Introduce the Concept

Reading/Writing Workshop

OBJECTIVES

 CCSS Follow agreed-upon rules for discussions and carry out assigned roles. **SL.5.1b**

CCSS Pose and respond to specific questions by making comments that contribute to the discussion and elaborate on the remarks of others. **SL.5.1c**

Build background knowledge on our changing Earth.

ACADEMIC LANGUAGE

• *gradual, impact*
• Cognate: *gradual*

MINILESSON 10 Mins

Build Background

ESSENTIAL QUESTION
What changes in the environment affect living things?

Have students read the Essential Question on page 334 of the **Reading/Writing Workshop**. Tell them that changes in the environment can be sudden, or they can be **gradual**, happening bit by bit over time.

Discuss the photograph of the monarch butterflies. Focus on the **impact**, or effect, that environmental changes have on living things.

→ Earth is always changing. Some changes, like a volcanic eruption, are sudden. Others, like the change of seasons, are more **gradual**.

→ Scientists study the way the change of seasons affects living things.

→ Monarch butterflies adapt to the change by migrating, or traveling, to Mexico in the winter. They return to their northern homes in the spring when food is plentiful again.

Talk About It

COLLABORATE

Ask: *What change in Earth have you thought about? What **impact** has it had? Is it sudden or **gradual**?* Have students discuss in pairs or groups.

→ Generate with students words and phrases related to the changing Earth. Model adding them to the graphic organizer.

→ Have partners discuss what they have learned about the changing Earth. Have them add related ideas to the graphic organizer.

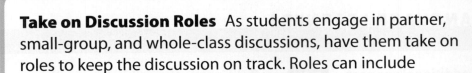

Collaborative Conversations

Take on Discussion Roles As students engage in partner, small-group, and whole-class discussions, have them take on roles to keep the discussion on track. Roles can include

→ a questioner who asks questions in order to keep everyone involved and keep the discussion moving.

→ a recorder who takes notes and later reports to the class.

→ a discussion monitor who keeps the group on topic and makes sure everyone gets a turn to talk.

Go Digital

Discuss the Concept

Watch Video

View Photos

Use Graphic Organizer

Essential Question
What changes in the environment affect living things?

Go Digital!

A Change in the Air

Earth is in a constant state of change. Some changes, such as a volcano erupting, may happen quickly. Other changes are gradual.

▶ One change scientists study is the impact of seasons on animals and plants.

▶ Each winter, for example, these Monarch butterflies migrate south to Mexico. They live in colonies like this one before heading north in the spring, when food is plentiful.

Talk About It

Write words you have learned about the changing Earth. Then talk about one change you have wondered about.

Changing Earth

334   335

READING/WRITING WORKSHOP, pp. 334–335

(David) Richard Ellis/The Image Bank/Getty Images; (in border) Ingram Publishing/Alamy

ELL ENGLISH LANGUAGE LEARNERS SCAFFOLD

Beginning

Use Visuals Point to the photograph. Say: *Monarch butterflies go to Mexico in the winter. Winter will change into spring in a gradual way.* Elicit that *gradual* means "slow." Ask: *Will the Monarchs return to their northern homes in the spring?* Point out that *gradual* in Spanish is *gradual*.

Intermediate

Describe Have students describe what they see in the photograph. Then ask: *Is the change of seasons fast or gradual? Why do you think Monarch butterflies fly south in the winter?* Correct pronunciation as needed.

Advanced/High

Discuss Ask students to discuss the photograph and talk about the change of seasons and Monarch butterflies. Ask questions to help them elaborate. *What happens in the winter? How does this change impact, or influence, Monarch butterflies?* Repeat correct responses slowly and clearly.

GRAPHIC ORGANIZER 140

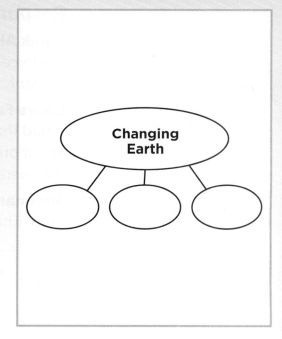

Changing Earth

→ Listening Comprehension

Interactive Read Aloud

OBJECTIVES

CCSS Summarize a written text read aloud or information presented in diverse media and formats, including visually, quantitatively, and orally. **SL.5.2**

• Listen for a purpose.
• Identify characteristics of expository text.

ACADEMIC LANGUAGE
• *expository text, ask and answer questions*
• Cognate: *texto expositivo*

Connect to Concept: Our Changing Earth

Tell students that Earth is an ever-changing environment, and that our planet's changes affect all living things. Let students know that you will be reading aloud a passage that shows how planting trees can help cities prepare for the possibility of climate change.

Preview Genre: Expository Text

Explain that the text you will read aloud is expository text. Discuss the features of expository text:

→ gives information about a topic

→ develops the topic with facts, examples, and explanations

→ presents information in a logical order

Preview Comprehension Strategy: Ask and Answer Questions

Point out that readers can check their understanding of a text by asking questions as they read. If they have trouble answering a question, they can reread that section of text. After reading, it's helpful to ask and answer the question *What is the main idea of this text?*

Use the Think Alouds on page T141 to model the strategy.

Respond to Reading

Think Aloud Clouds Display Think Aloud Master 1: *I wonder…* to reinforce how you used the ask and answer strategy to understand content.

Genre Features With students, discuss the elements of the Read Aloud that let them know that it is expository text. Ask them to think about other texts that you have read or they have read independently that were expository text.

Summarize Have students restate the most important information from "Changing Climate, Changing Lives" in their own words.

Go Digital

View Photos

Model Think Alouds

Genre Chart

Changing Climate, Changing Lives

Changes in the weather affect us all. When it rains, we try to stay dry. When it's cold, we try to stay warm. Weather in a region over a long period of time is known as climate. Climate affects us even more than one day's weather. We adapt to our climate. We dress differently in a hot climate than in a cold one. We build different types of homes. In a wet climate we behave differently than in a dry one. Different species of plants and animals flourish in different climates.

A Changing Climate

What happens, then, when the climate begins to change? Many scientists have suggested that the world's climate is growing warmer. Not everyone agrees with this idea. However, many experts believe it is wise to plan for a warmer future. One strategy recommended to help us cool off our cities is to plant more trees.

Planting Trees for the Future

Can planting more trees really make a difference? Some studies have shown that an abundance of shade trees can lower summertime temperatures in cities. It can also reduce air-conditioning costs and purify the air by absorbing harmful gases such as carbon dioxide. Cities such as New York, Minneapolis, Washington, Denver, and Baltimore have started tree-planting programs to help reduce temperatures and improve air quality. **1**

Chicago's Solutions

Forecasts predict that by the end of the 21st century, Chicago's summers could be as warm as Alabama's. To provide some relief, Chicago has begun planting several thousand trees a year. Chicago city planners chose trees that could best adapt to a warmer climate. Familiar trees on Chicago streets, such as the ash tree, were banned. They would not be able to survive the pests and diseases that might come with warmer temperatures. Instead, trees that can adapt better, such as the bald cypress, are finding a new home in Chicago. **2** Like people, trees will need to adapt to thrive if our climate changes. **3**

1 Think Aloud This section begins with a question. I'm going to **ask and answer** a similar question: "How can planting trees make a difference?" The text says trees can help lower temperatures and purify the air.

2 Think Aloud To be sure I understand this section, I'm going to **ask and answer** the question: "Why is Chicago planting new types of trees?" It's because some trees adapt better to warmer temperatures.

3 Think Aloud Now that I've finished reading this text, I'm going to **ask and answer** the question: "What is the main idea?" I think the main idea is that trees can help cities adapt to changes in climate.

Ariel Skelley/Blend Images/ Getty Images

→ Vocabulary

Reading/Writing Workshop

OBJECTIVES
Acquire and use accurately grade-appropriate general academic and domain-specific words and phrases, including those that signal contrast, addition, and other logical relationships (e.g., *however, although, nevertheless, similarly, moreover, in addition*). **L.5.6**

ACADEMIC LANGUAGE
- *gradual, impact*
- Cognate: *gradual*

MINILESSON 10 Mins

Words in Context

Model the Routine
Introduce each vocabulary word using the Vocabulary Routine found on the **Visual Vocabulary Cards**.

Visual Vocabulary Cards

Vocabu...
Define:
Example:
Ask:

Vocabulary Routine

Define: The **atmosphere** is the layer of gases around Earth.

Example: Clouds form in our atmosphere, the layer of gases around Earth.

Ask: Why is the Earth's atmosphere important?

Definitions

→ **decays**   If something **decays**, it rots.

→ **gradual**   When a change is **gradual**, it happens slowly.
Cognate: *gradual*

→ **impact**   Something that has an **impact** has a strong effect.

→ **noticeably**   If a plant has grown **noticeably**, it is easy to see that it has gotten bigger.

→ **receding**   When something is **receding**, it is moving back or away.

→ **stability**   If something has **stability**, it is solid, steady, and doesn't change much.
Cognate: *estabilidad*

→ **variations**   A **variation** is the amount that something changes, such as a variation in the temperature.
Cognate: *variaciones (variación)*

Talk About It

COLLABORATE

Have students work with a partner and talk about the photograph and definition for each word. Ask them to discuss how the sentence relates to the definition. Then ask students to choose three words and write questions for their partner to answer.

Vocabulary

CCSS Words to Know

Use the picture and the sentences to talk with a partner about each word.

atmosphere

Clouds form in our **atmosphere**, the layer of gases around Earth.

Why is the Earth's atmosphere important?

decays

When fruit **decays**, or rots, it is not very tasty and should not be eaten.

What does a banana look like as it decays?

gradual

The release of sand in an hourglass is **gradual**, so that it takes one hour.

What is a gradual event or change you have seen?

impact

A veterinarian has a big **impact** on the health of a pet.

Who has had an important impact on your life?

noticeably

José's hair was **noticeably** shorter after his haircut.

What is a synonym for noticeably?

receding

As I drove away, the mountain seemed to be **receding** in the distance.

If it was receding, was it getting close?

stability

While his sprained leg healed, Stephan used crutches for **stability** when walking.

If a thing has stability, is it shaky or steady?

variations

In the valley, there are many **variations** in the color green.

Where might you see variations in the color blue?

Your Turn   COLLABORATE

Pick three words. Write three questions for your partner to answer.

Go Digital! Use the online visual glossary

336

337

READING/WRITING WORKSHOP, pp. 336–337

ELL ENGLISH LANGUAGE LEARNERS SCAFFOLD

Beginning

Use Visuals Point to the photo for *atmosphere*. Say: *The atmosphere is a layer of gases around Earth.* Have students repeat. Ask: *Where is the atmosphere?* Elaborate on responses. Point out that in Spanish, the word for *atmosphere* is *atmósfera*.

Intermediate

Describe Have students describe the photo for *atmosphere* with a partner. Ask: *What is the atmosphere? Where is it?* Correct the meaning of responses as needed. Then have students draw a picture of the Earth and the atmosphere.

Advanced/High

Discuss Ask students to talk about the photo for *atmosphere* with a partner and work together to write a definition and sentence. Circulate to clarify meaning and correct responses as needed.

ON-LEVEL PRACTICE BOOK p. 221

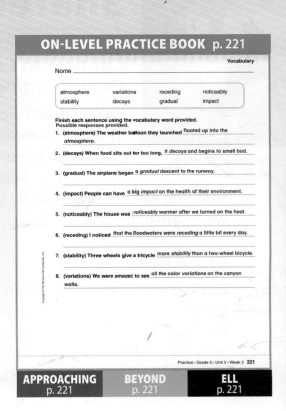

Name _____

| atmosphere | variations | receding | noticeably |
| stability | decays | gradual | impact |

Finish each sentence using the vocabulary word provided. Possible responses provided.

1. (atmosphere) The weather balloon they launched floated up into the atmosphere.

2. (decays) When food sits out for too long, it decays and begins to smell bad.

3. (gradual) The airplane began a gradual descent to the runway.

4. (impact) People can have a big impact on the health of their environment.

5. (noticeably) The house was noticeably warmer after we turned on the heat.

6. (receding) I noticed that the floodwaters were receding a little bit every day.

7. (stability) Three wheels give a tricycle more stability than a two-wheel bicycle.

8. (variations) We were amazed to see all the color variations on the canyon walls.

Practice · Grade 5 · Unit 5 · Week 3 221

| APPROACHING p. 221 | BEYOND p. 221 | ELL p. 221 |

Forests on Fire

Essential Question

What changes in the environment affect living things?

Read about the effects of forest fires on plants, animals, and people.

338

A few years ago, several red squirrels—an endangered species—had a temporary home at the Phoenix Zoo. Rescued from a ravaging wildfire that had already destroyed thousands of acres of land, the squirrels were waiting for the fire to be extinguished before being returned to the wild. Forest fires are part of nature, so it is important for us to understand not only how to fight fires, but also why they occur.

Destructive and Productive

Like rainstorms, wildfires are a force of nature. However, unlike rainstorms, wildfires are almost always destructive. They consume everything in their way, including plants, trees, and animals. Sometimes, they take human lives and homes as well.

Like a big storm, the destructive power of wildfires is terrifying. On the other hand, naturally occurring wildfires are also productive forces. Whether their flames race through a forest, a prairie, or acres of brush, these fires produce necessary changes in their environment. Like rain, they can allow new life to flourish.

Benefits of Naturally Occurring Wildfires

A naturally occurring wildfire, sometimes called a forest fire, happens without any human cause. Three factors must be present for one to burn. These include fuel, such as dry grasses; oxygen, which is in our **atmosphere**; and a heat source to ignite the fuel. A lightning strike usually sparks a naturally occurring wildfire. The danger of fire is highest during a drought, when an area has experienced little rain.

Wildfires have happened throughout history, and they help to regenerate Earth and its species. When vegetation **decays**, wildfires clear it away so that new plant life can grow.

339

Reading/Writing Workshop

Shared Read

READING/WRITING WORKSHOP, pp. 338–339

Lexile 960   *TextEvaluator*™ 53

Connect to Concept: Our Changing Earth

Explain that "Forests on Fire" will give more information about how changes in the environment affect living things. Read the text with students. Note that previously taught vocabulary words are highlighted.

Close Reading

Reread Paragraph 1: Explain that you are going to take a closer look at the beginning of "Forests on Fire." Reread the first paragraph together. Ask: *How does the author introduce the topic?* Model how to cite details to answer the question.

The author starts with an anecdote, or brief account, of how red squirrels found a temporary home in a zoo after being rescued from a wildfire. This anecdote leads me to think that I will probably read more about the effects of wildfires.

Reread Paragraphs 2 and 3: Model how to identify the way ideas in the text are organized.

I see that the author writes about ways that rainstorms and wildfires are both alike and different. For example, the author explains that both rainstorms and wildfires are forces of nature but that wildfires, unlike rainstorms, are almost always destructive. These details help me understand that the text has a compare-contrast text structure.

Open cone | New seedling | A young forest

The black spruce tree needs a fire's heat to cause its cones to open and scatter seeds. Eventually, seedlings sprout, and a new forest will grow.

Fire also releases nutrients back into the soil, making it more fertile. And by eliminating leafy canopies of mature trees, fire allows nourishing sunlight to reach a forest floor.

Often, this new plant life will be better adapted to fire than what existed before. Some species will have fire-resistant roots, leaves, or bark. Other species will actually depend on fire to reproduce and thrive.

Stability and Diversity

Among its benefits, fire promotes **stability**. By eliminating invasive species that can take over an area, fire encourages the healthy growth of a region's own vegetation.

At the same time, fire promotes diversity. It ensures that plant life will exist at different stages of development. For example, a forest recently struck by fire will have new seedlings. Not far away, in a forest struck by fire twenty years earlier, there may be small trees. And nearby, there may be a forest of mature trees, untouched by fire for years.

These **variations** in plant life provide food and habitats for different kinds of insects, birds, and mammals. Woodpeckers eat insects in burned-out trees. Sparrows depend on seeds for food. Predators such as foxes are drawn by small prey. Forests at different stages attract a diversity of animals to a region.

340

The Human Factor

Although wildfires have benefits, they also are feared and misunderstood. As a result, our government tried to suppress them completely throughout the 20th century. This policy had a negative **impact** on the environment. The **gradual** buildup of decayed vegetation provided more fuel to feed fires. Consequently, wildfires became **noticeably** fiercer.

More recently, the government has used two different strategies to manage wildfires. One is to try to limit fires before they burn out of control. The other is to set small "prescribed" fires to reduce the amount of fuel in the environment. Hopefully, the danger of catastrophic fires is now **receding**.

Unfortunately, human carelessness, such as a campfire left to smolder, also can start a fire. While a natural or prescribed wildfire can be beneficial, this is not true of fires that result from malice or mistakes. These happen at times and places that may cause irreparable damage to plant, animal, and human life. Fires cannot control themselves, so humans will always have to figure out how best to handle them.

Whether wildfires are small or large, firefighters are needed to help contain them.

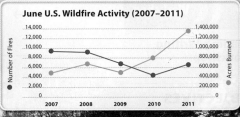

June U.S. Wildfire Activity (2007–2011)

Make Connections

Talk about how wildfires change the environment for plants. **ESSENTIAL QUESTION**

Why is it important for you to be careful around a fire of any kind, even in a home? **TEXT TO SELF**

341

READING/WRITING WORKSHOP, pp. 340–341

Make Connections

ESSENTIAL QUESTION

Encourage students to use text evidence as they discuss how wildfires change the environment for plants. Ask students to explain, using the text, how changes in the environment affect living things.

Continue Close Reading

Use the following lessons for focused rereadings.

→ Ask and Answer Questions, pp. T146–T147

→ Text Structure: Compare and Contrast, pp. T148–T149

→ Expository Text, pp. T150–T151

→ Context Clues, pp. T152–T153

ACT Access Complex Text

▶ Organization

In addition to comparing and contrasting two different things (such as rainstorms and wildfires), a text may compare and contrast different aspects of the same thing.

→ Reread paragraphs two and three on page 339. How can wildfires be both destructive and productive? (They consume plants, trees, animals, and homes, but they also allow new life to flourish.)

→ Reread paragraphs three and four on page 340. What opposite effects do wildfires have? (They promote stability and diversity.)

Comprehension Strategy

 MINILESSON **10** Mins

Ask and Answer Questions

Reading/Writing Workshop

OBJECTIVES

CCSS Quote accurately from a text when explaining what the text says explicitly and when drawing inferences from the text. **RI.5.1**

Ask and answer questions to increase understanding.

ACADEMIC LANGUAGE

• *ask and answer questions, expository text*

• Cognate: *texto expositivo*

1 Explain

Explain that when they read expository texts, students should stop occasionally to ask themselves questions. Asking and answering questions about the text will help them better understand it.

→ Remind students that if they are unable to answer a question they have asked themselves, they should go back and reread the section of text that caused confusion.

→ When reading expository texts, students should ask themselves what the main idea of the section or article is. Then they should review the text to find key details that help them identify it.

Remind students that asking and answering questions about a text keeps readers actively engaged in the process and helps them monitor their comprehension as they go.

2 Model Close Reading: Text Evidence

Model how to ask and answer questions about the section "Destructive and Productive" on page 339. Tell students you can look for details in the section to help you answer the question *What is the main idea?* Point out that details about how wildfires destroy plants, trees, and animals but also produce changes that allow new life to grow help you determine that the main idea of the section is that wildfires are destructive and productive.

3 Guided Practice of Close Reading

 COLLABORATE

Have pairs ask and answer a question about the section "Benefits of Naturally Occurring Wildfires" on pages 339 and 340. Encourage each partner to ask a question and point out details from the text that help them answer. Have partners discuss other sections of "Forests on Fire" about which they might want to ask and answer questions.

Go Digital

Present the Lesson

CCSS Comprehension Strategy

Ask and Answer Questions

To be sure you understand what you read, ask questions about the text. If you have trouble answering the question, reread the section. At the end of an expository text, ask: *What is the main idea?* Then find details to support your answer.

Find Text Evidence

To check your understanding of the section "Destructive and Productive" on page 339, you might ask yourself, *What is the main idea?*

page 339

Like a big storm, the destructive power of wildfires is terrifying. On the other hand, naturally occurring wildfires are also productive forces. Whether their flames race through a forest, a prairie, or acres of brush, these fires produce necessary changes in their environment. Like rain, they can allow new life to flourish.

[The main idea is that wildfires are both destructive and productive. Details such as how wildfires in a forest or prairie produce necessary changes help support the main idea.

Your Turn

COLLABORATE

Ask and answer a question about the information in the section "Benefits of Naturally Occurring Wildfires" on page 339. Use this strategy as you read.

342

READING/WRITING WORKSHOP, p. 342

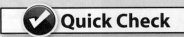
Monitor and *Differentiate*

✔ Quick Check

Are students able to ask questions about the text? Do they reread to find the answers?

Small Group Instruction

If No → | **Approaching Level** | Reteach p. T168
| **ELL** | Develop p. T185
If Yes → | **On Level** | Review p. T176
| **Beyond Level** | Extend p. T180

ELL ENGLISH LANGUAGE LEARNERS SCAFFOLD

Beginning	Intermediate	Advanced/High
Understand Read aloud "Destructive and Productive" on page 339. Point out difficult words: *destructive, consume, productive, flourish.* Define them. Help students replace them with words they know. Ask: *Do wildfires destroy life?* (yes) *Do they also allow new life to grow?* (yes)	**Identify** Reread the section "Destructive and Productive" on page 339 with students. Point out that it may be confusing because wildfires have two opposite effects. Ask: *How can wildfires be destructive? How can they also be productive?* Provide a sentence frame: *The main idea of the section is that wildfires ____.*	**Discuss** Have students reread the section "Destructive and Productive" and elicit why it may be confusing. Encourage partners to ask each other questions about the text and use details to answer. Then have them use their questions and answers to determine the main idea in the section.

ON-LEVEL PRACTICE BOOK pp. 223–224

Comprehension and Fluency

Name _____

Read the passage. Use the ask and answer questions strategy to help you understand what you read.

Of Floods and Fish

10	The Mississippi River flows more than two thousand miles from
24	Minnesota to the Gulf of Mexico. Every few years, it floods. In April and
37	May, 2011, a combination of melting snow and falling rain along the upper
52	part of the river caused the lower part of the river to overrun its banks.
59	Floods cause widespread destruction. Floodwaters damage and
68	sometimes knock down buildings. They destroy farmland and animal
79	habitats. With nowhere to live, the animals often move into populated
92	areas. What about the fish? Because they live in water, shouldn't a flood
107	be good for them? As it turns out, floods can hurt fish populations just as
	they harm many animals that live on the land.

116	**The Dead Zone**
119	The Mississippi floodwaters proved most detrimental to the fish and
129	other ocean life in the Gulf of Mexico. The Mississippi River is made
142	of fresh water. The Gulf is made of salt water. The extra river water
156	that flowed into the Gulf endangered the native saltwater fish. More
167	harmful, though, were the pollutants the river water carried with it. As the
180	swollen Mississippi washed over the land and crops, it picked up the fertilizer and
191	pesticides that farmers had used on the land and crops. These chemicals
203	are poisonous to ocean life. The river then dumped these poisons into
215	the Gulf. The extra river water and the farm runoff created a dead zone
229	along the coast. A dead zone is an area of water that does not have enough
245	oxygen to support life.

Practice • Grade 5 • Unit 5 • Week 3 **223**

APPROACHING pp. 223–224	BEYOND pp. 223–224	ELL pp. 223–224

COMPREHENSION STRATEGY **T147**

Comprehension Skill

Reading/Writing Workshop

OBJECTIVES

CCSS Explain the relationships or interactions between two or more individuals, events, ideas, or concepts in a historical, scientific, or technical text based on specific information in the text. **RI.5.3**

Identify the overall structure of a text.

ACADEMIC LANGUAGE

- *compare, contrast*
- Cognates: *comparar, contrastar*

Text Structure: Compare and Contrast

Go Digital

Present the Lesson

1 Explain

Explain to students that a text's structure is the way ideas within it are organized. Some texts organize ideas by comparing and contrasting, or showing how two things are alike and different.

→ Explain that students can better understand individual ideas in a text if they recognize how the author compares and contrasts them with other ideas.

→ Point out that authors often use signal words and phrases to help readers understand that they are comparing and contrasting two things or ideas. Examples include *like* and *just as* (to show similarities) and *unlike, however,* and *on the other hand* (to show differences).

2 Model Close Reading: Text Evidence

Identify the compare-and-contrast signal words *like* and *unlike* in the section "Destructive and Productive" on page 339. Then model using the details on the graphic organizer to identify how wildfires and rainstorms are both alike and different.

 Write About Reading: Paraphrase Model how to use the details from the organizer to paraphrase information about how wildfires and rainstorms are alike and different.

3 Guided Practice of Close Reading

 Have students work in pairs to complete a graphic organizer for the section "The Human Factor" on page 341 by comparing and contrasting the different ways humans impact fires.

 Write About Reading: Paraphrase Have pairs paraphrase information about how humans have helped and hindered understanding of wildfires. Remind students that to paraphrase is to summarize important facts from the selection in their own words. Have pairs share their paraphrases with the class.

SKILLS TRACE

TEXT STRUCTURE

Introduce U1W3

Review U1W4, U1W6, U2W1, U2W3, U4W6, U5W3, U5W4, U5W6, U6W3, U6W4

Assess U1, U2, U5, U6

Comprehension Skill

Compare and Contrast

Writers may organize a text to show how an idea is similar to or different from another idea. To figure out if a writer is using a compare-and-contrast structure, look for signal words and phrases such as *however*, *on the other hand*, and *just as*.

Find Text Evidence

The first section tells how wildfires are both like *storms and* unlike *storms. This comparison helps me understand that both forces of nature have uses. Wildfires may be mostly destructive, but, like storms, they can be useful, too.*

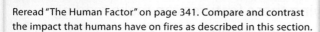

Rainstorms and Wildfires

Rainstorms   Wildfires

Both

Mostly help plant, animal, human life

Can be destructive

Are forces of nature

Mostly destroy plant, animal, and human life

Can be helpful

Your Turn

Reread "The Human Factor" on page 341. Compare and contrast the impact that humans have on fires as described in this section.

Go Digital! *Use the interactive graphic organizer*

343

READING/WRITING WORKSHOP, p. 343

ENGLISH LANGUAGE LEARNERS SCAFFOLD

ELL

Beginning	Intermediate	Advanced/High
Identify Reread the first paragraph of "Destructive and Productive" on page 339. Ask: *Are both rainstorms and wildfires forces of nature?* (yes) Point out that this is one way they are alike. *Are wildfires more destructive than rainstorms?* (yes) Point out that this is one way they are different.	**Understand** Reread the first paragraph of "Destructive and Productive" with students. Ask: *How are rainstorms and wildfires alike? How are they are different?* Then have students complete these sentence frames: *Both rainstorms and wildfires are ____. However, ____ are more destructive than ____.*	**Compare and Contrast** Have students reread the section "Destructive and Productive" on page 339. Have partners compare and contrast rainstorms and wildfires using details from the text. Elicit details to support students' responses.

Monitor and *Differentiate*

✓ Quick Check

As students complete the graphic organizer, do they compare and contrast the different ways that humans impact wildfires?

⬇

Small Group Instruction

If No →	Approaching Level	Reteach p. T175
	ELL	Develop p. T185
If Yes →	On Level	Review p. T179
	Beyond Level	Extend p. T183

ON-LEVEL PRACTICE BOOK pp. 223–225

Comprehension: **Compare and Contrast and Fluency**

Name ____

A. Reread the passage and answer the questions. Possible responses provided.

1. What comparison does the phrase *just as* indicate in the second paragraph?
The phrase compares the harm that flooding does to fish populations to the harm it does to animals that live on land.

2. In what way are the main ideas of the sections called "The Dead Zone" and "Threat of Invasion" alike?
Both sections describe how Mississippi floodwaters threaten wildlife.

3. Are the ideas in the section "Supporting Life" similar to or different from the ideas in the previous two sections? Explain.
The word *despite* indicates that the ideas in this section differ from the ideas in the previous sections. This section describes the benefits of floodwaters, while the previous sections describe problems created by floodwaters.

B. Work with a partner. Read the passage aloud. Pay attention to rate. Stop after one minute. Fill out the chart.

	Words Read	–	Number of Errors	=	Words Correct Score
First Read		–		=	
Second Read		–		=	

Practice · Grade 5 · Unit 5 · Week 3 **225**

APPROACHING pp. 223–225	BEYOND pp. 223–225	ELL pp. 223–225

→ Genre: Informational Text

MINILESSON
10 Mins

Expository Text

1 Explain

Share with students the following characteristics of **expository text**.

→ Expository text is a nonfiction text that gives readers factual information about a topic. This information is often organized into sections with headings.

→ The author of an expository text develops the topic by providing facts, details, examples, and explanations.

→ Expository text often includes text features such as photographs and graphs that help readers visualize information in the text or obtain additional information about the topic.

Explain to students that identifying these features can make reading an expository text easier and more interesting.

2 Model Close Reading: Text Evidence

Model identifying and using factual information and text features throughout "Forests on Fire" to identify it as expository text.

Photographs Point out that the photographs, labels, and captions throughout the selection help readers visualize information in the text and also give additional information about the topic.

Graph Explain that the line graph on page 341 shows the number of fires each year and the number of acres burned. Point out that this is additional information that is not found in the text. Ask: *How do the numbers in the graph connect to the information in "The Human Factor"?*

3 Guided Practice of Close Reading

COLLABORATE

Have pairs discuss the information they learn from the graph on page 341 and answer this question: *What may have caused so many acres to burn in 2011?* Remind them to examine the title, numbers, and lines on the graph and discuss what each indicates. Ask partners to share their work with the class.

Reading/Writing Workshop

OBJECTIVES

CCSS Interpret information presented visually, orally, or quantitatively (e.g., in charts, graphs, diagrams, time lines, animations, or interactive elements on Web pages) and explain how the information contributes to an understanding of the text in which it appears. **RI.4.7**

CCSS By the end of the year, read and comprehend informational texts, including history/social studies, science, and technical texts, at the high end of the grades 4–5 text complexity band independently and proficiently. **RI.5.10**

ACADEMIC LANGUAGE

• *expository text, graph*

• Cognates: *texto expositivo, gráfico*

Go Digital

Present the Lesson

CCSS **Genre** Informational Text

Expository Text

The selection "Forests on Fire" is expository text.

Expository text:
- Gives information about a topic
- Develops the topic with facts, examples, and explanations
- May include graphs and photographs

Find Text Evidence

I can tell that "Forests on Fire" is expository text. The selection gives facts about the causes of wildfires and explains more about them. Photographs, captions, and a graph add information.

 page 341

Photographs Photographs provide visual information. **Captions** also add information.

Graphs A graph is a diagram that shows numerical information, including changes over time. A title tells what the graph will show.

Your Turn

Discuss the graph on page 341. What may have caused so many acres to burn in 2011?

344

READING/WRITING WORKSHOP, p. 344

 **Monitor and *Differentiate***

✓ **Quick Check**

Are students able to discuss the graph on page 341 and explain what may have caused so many acres to burn in 2011?

Small Group Instruction

If No →	Approaching Level	Reteach p. T169
	ELL	Develop p. T187
If Yes →	On Level	Review p. T177
	Beyond Level	Extend p. T181

ENGLISH LANGUAGE LEARNERS SCAFFOLD

Beginning	Intermediate	Advanced/High
Use Visuals Have students point to the graph on page 341. Point out the Spanish cognate *gráfico*. Read the title aloud with students. Ask: *Does the graph show the number of fires, the number of acres burned, or both?* (both) *Were more acres burned in 2010 or 2011?* (2011)	**Identify** Have students point to the graph on page 341 and read the title aloud. Ask: *What does this graph show? Why might more acres have burned in 2011 than in 2010?* Have partners describe what they see in the photographs on page 340 and discuss how the photographs and labels connect to the text.	**Discuss** Have students identify what the graph shows and explain why so many acres may have burned in 2011. Then have partners take turns asking and answering questions about the photographs, labels, and captions. Ask them to discuss why the author might have included these text features.

ON-LEVEL PRACTICE BOOK p. 226

Name _____

Moths and Changes in Weather

Scientists study moths to see how quickly they can adapt to climate change. Some moths adapt better than others. Some species of moths need cool weather and move north when the weather gets warmer. Moths already living in cool areas may not be able to find a cooler place to go. Warm weather affects the food caterpillars eat. Some caterpillars adapt to climate change and food supplies by hatching earlier or later than usual. It is hard to predict how climate change will affect moths over time.

Answer the questions about the text.

1. How do you know this is expository text?
   It gives information about how moths adapt to changing temperatures.

2. Is the heading a strong heading for the text? Why or why not?
   Possible response: It is a strong heading because it describes what information can be found in the text.

3. What text feature does this text include?
   a bar graph

4. What do you learn from the text feature and its title?
   The graph shows how far different moths have moved north to cooler places.

226 Practice • Grade 5 • Unit 5 • Week 3

| APPROACHING p. 226 | BEYOND p. 226 | ELL p. 226 |

→ Vocabulary Strategy

Reading/Writing
Workshop

MINILESSON
10 Mins

Context Clues

**Go
Digital**

1 Explain

Remind students that when they encounter an unfamiliar word while reading, they can use context clues to help them figure out its meaning.

→ Context clues that appear in the same sentence as the unfamiliar word are called sentence clues. Context clues that appear in other sentences within the paragraph are called paragraph clues.

→ Explain that some paragraph clues might help students identify a relationship between words. Students can then use this relationship to determine the meaning of an unfamiliar word.

**Present the
Lesson**

2 Model Close Reading: Text Evidence

Using the second paragraph of "Stability and Diversity" on page 340 of "Forests on Fire," model identifying paragraph clues that point to the meaning of the word *mature*.

3 Guided Practice of Close Reading

COLLABORATE

Have students work in pairs to figure out the meanings of *productive* and *regenerate* on page 339 and *diversity* on page 340. Encourage students to use paragraph clues to help them determine each word's meaning.

Use References Sources

Online Dictionary and Online Thesaurus Have students check an online dictionary, find the pronunciations of *productive, regenerate,* and *diversity,* and compare the meanings they find there with the meanings they came up with from using context clues.

Encourage students to look up the word *productive* in an online thesaurus. Discuss each part of the entry: the part of speech label, the meanings, and the lists of synonyms related to each meaning. Choose the meaning of *productive* that is closest to the meaning you found in the online dictionary and list the synonyms provided in the online thesaurus.

OBJECTIVES

CCSS Use context (e.g., cause/effect relationships and comparisons in text) as a clue to the meaning of a word or phrase. **L.5.4a**

CCSS Consult reference materials (e.g., dictionaries, glossaries, thesauruses), both print and digital, to find the pronunciation and determine or clarify the precise meaning of key words and phrases. **L.5.4c**

**ACADEMIC
LANGUAGE**
*context clues,
paragraph clues*

SKILLS TRACE

PARAGRAPH CLUES

Introduce U5W3

Review U5W3, U6W3

Assess U5, U6

Vocabulary Strategy

Context Clues

Sometimes you can figure out the meaning of unfamiliar or multiple meaning words by looking for **clues in the paragraph**. You may see a synonym, an antonym, or a comparison that can help you define a word that puzzles you.

 Find Text Evidence

When I read "Stability and Diversity" on page 340, the phrases new seedlings *and* small trees *refer to trees in early life. Since* mature trees *have been* untouched by fire for years, *the word* mature *must mean "fully grown or developed."*

> For example, a forest recently struck by fire will have new seedlings. Not far away, in a forest struck by fire twenty years earlier, there may be small trees. And nearby, there may be a forest of mature trees, untouched by fire for years.

Your Turn

Use context clues to figure out the meaning of the following words in "Forests on Fire":
productive, *page 339*
regenerate, *page 339*
diversity, *page 340*

345

READING/WRITING WORKSHOP, p. 345

A C T Access Complex Text

▶ Specific Vocabulary

The text contains some domain-specific words that students might not understand. Review strategies for finding their meanings.

→ *What context clues in the first paragraph on page 340 help you know that* nutrients *are natural elements in the soil that help plants grow?* (back into the soil, more fertile)

→ *What definition context clue helps you determine the meaning of* drought *in the fourth paragraph on page 339?* (when an area has experienced little rain)

Monitor and *Differentiate*

✓ Quick Check

Can students identify and use context clues to figure out the meanings of unfamiliar words such as *productive, regenerate,* and *diversity*?

⬇

Small Group Instruction

If No →	Approaching Level	Reteach p. T173
	ELL	Develop p. T189
If Yes →	On Level	Review p. T178
	Beyond Level	Extend p. T182

Develop Comprehension

Literature Anthology

Global Warming

Text Complexity Range

Lexile

740 ▲ 1010
980

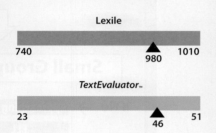

TextEvaluator™

23 ▲ 51
46

Options for Close Reading

→ Whole Class

→ Small Group

→ Independent

This selection is suggested for use as an Extended Complex Text. See pages T356–T361.

CCSS Genre · Expository Text

GLOBAL WARMING

by Seymour Simon

Essential Question
What changes in the environment affect living things?
Read about how a change in climate can affect living things.

Go Digital!

384

A C T Access Complex Text

What makes this text complex?

▶ **Organization**

▶ **Prior Knowledge**

▶ **Connection of Ideas**

▶ **Specific Vocabulary**

▶ **Purpose**

▶ Organization

Reread the last paragraph on page 385. Ask students what they notice about the forms of the sentences. (They are all questions.) Explain that when authors organize the introduction of an expository text with a series of questions, they will usually give information that answers the questions throughout the rest of the text. Ask:

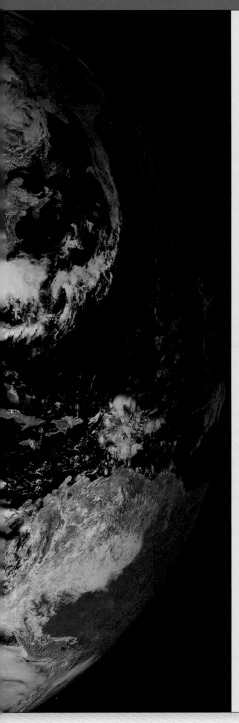

Thousands of years ago, large parts of the land mass on Earth were covered by ice. Since then, Earth has been getting warmer. In recent decades, the rise in average temperature has been particularly rapid. "Global warming" is the term that has been used to describe these changes. **1**

Weather and climate are different. Weather is what happens every day. Climate is the average weather over a period of years. For example, it's possible that the weather on any day might be cool but the average weather, the climate, is getting warmer.

Why is the climate changing? Could Earth be getting warmer by itself? Are people doing things that make the climate warmer? What will be the **impact** of global warming? Can we do anything about it?

385

NASA Goddard Space Flight Center Image by Reto Stöckli. TEXT: Global Warming Copyright © 2010 by Seymour Simon. Used with permission of HarperCollins Children's Books.

LITERATURE ANTHOLOGY, pp. 384–385

Predictive Writing

Have students read the title, preview the photos, and write their predictions about what this selection will be about.

ESSENTIAL QUESTION

Ask a student to read aloud the Essential Question. Have students discuss what information they expect to learn.

Note Taking: Use the Graphic Organizer *Analytical Writing*

As students read the selection, ask them to take notes by filling in the graphic organizer on **Your Turn Practice Book page 222** to record comparisons and contrasts in each section.

❶ Vocabulary: Context Clues

What does *global warming* mean? What paragraph clues helped you determine the meaning? (Global warming describes the rise in Earth's average temperature in recent decades. Clues: "Earth has been getting warmer"; "rise in average temperature"; "used to describe these changes")

→ *Based on the questions, what information do you expect the author to give about climate change?* (He will include why the climate might be changing, what impact climate change might have, and what can be done about it.)

Tell students that as they read, they should use the information they read to answer these questions.

Develop Comprehension

2 Skill: Compare and Contrast

How is Earth's atmosphere similar to a greenhouse? How is it different? (Like a greenhouse, Earth's atmosphere traps heat and keeps it from escaping. A greenhouse traps heat with glass. Earth's atmosphere traps heat with gases and water vapor.) Add this information to your organizer.

Greenhouse	Both	Earth's Atmosphere
traps heat with glass	trap heat	traps heat with gases and water vapor

3 Author's Craft: Word Choice

Authors of expository texts choose words precisely to help express their meaning. Reread the third paragraph on page 386. Why is *vast* a better word choice than *large*? (It is a more specific word that helps readers understand the enormous quantity of coal and oil that we burn.)

Global warming is happening because of the greenhouse effect. A greenhouse is a house made of glass. The glass lets in sunlight but keeps warm air from escaping. Earth is not a greenhouse, but certain gases in the **atmosphere** act like the glass in a greenhouse. Sunlight passes through Earth's atmosphere and warms the ground. Some of the heat bounces back into space, but much of it remains trapped near the ground by carbon dioxide, water vapor, and other greenhouse gases in the atmosphere.

The greenhouse effect helps make Earth warm enough for life to exist. But if greenhouse gases are released into the atmosphere in larger amounts much faster than before, then the warming will get much stronger and the climate will **noticeably** change.

In 2007, a report by 2,500 scientists from 130 countries concluded that humans are responsible for much of the current warming. No *one* person causes global warming. But there are billions of people on Earth. We cut down huge numbers of trees, drive hundreds of millions of cars and trucks, and burn vast amounts of coal and oil. All these activities contribute to a huge increase in greenhouse gases. Even if we decreased the amount of gases we now produce, it would not immediately stop the warming because greenhouse gases stay in the atmosphere for years.

The Earth's climate is very complex, and many factors play important roles in determining how the climate changes. Natural **variations** in Earth's orbit around the sun change the amount of sunlight we receive and thus the temperature. Earth has had much warmer and much colder climates in the distant past.

386

A C T Access Complex Text

▶ Prior Knowledge

Students may be unaware that there are usually multiple points of view in scientific discussions. As you discuss page 386, tell students that in 2007, the Intergovernmental Panel on Climate Change (IPCC) released a report citing humans as the primary cause of global warming. However, looking at many possibilities is an important part of science, and some scientists believe that more research is needed before it's certain that humans cause the problem. The scientists cite evidence that Earth has been both colder and warmer than it is today, during times that aren't linked to human activity. As a result, the debate is focusing less on what causes global warming and more on how to respond to it.

387

Mike Powell/LifeSize/Getty Images

LITERATURE ANTHOLOGY, pp. 386–387

4 Strategy: Ask and Answer Questions

Teacher Think Aloud As I read, I pause from time to time to **ask and answer questions** to check my understanding. One question I ask myself is why we can't stop global warming right away by cutting back on the amount of gas we produce. To find the answer, I can go back and reread. I will paraphrase the text to make sure I understand it: Decreasing the amount of gas we produce won't stop global warming right away because greenhouse gases remain in the atmosphere for a long time.

ELL Point out the cognates in the text on page 386: atmosphere/*atmósfera,* carbon dioxide/*dióxido de carbono,* vapor/*vapor,* climate/*clima.* As you read the first paragraph on page 386, use simple diagrams to clarify the greenhouse effect. Restate it more simply: "Earth's atmosphere has gases that trap heat." Ask:

→ *What gets trapped because of the greenhouse effect?* (heat)

→ *What traps the heat?* Have students point to the last sentence in the first paragraph. Read it aloud with them.

Develop Comprehension

⑤ Skill: Compare and Contrast

The atmosphere has greenhouse gases. Prior to today, what has the atmosphere been like for thousands of years? (The balance of greenhouse gases didn't change much.) What is the atmosphere like now? (There is 30 percent more carbon dioxide in the air now than there was 150 years ago.) Show these comparisons in your organizer.

Atmosphere for 1000s of Years	Both	Atmosphere Now
minimal changes in greenhouse gases	release green-house gases	30% more CO₂ in the air

STOP AND CHECK

Ask and Answer Questions Why has the atmosphere changed? (The atmosphere has changed because we burn large amounts of coal, oil, and natural gas, heavily use transportation, and cut down trees. These activities lead to more CO₂ in the air.)

388

J. Walter/Photo Researchers, Inc.

Most scientists agree that something different is happening now. While Earth's climate has always varied, it is now changing more rapidly than in any other time in recent centuries. Since we have been keeping weather records, nineteen of the twenty hottest years *ever* have happened since 1980.

For thousands of years, the balance of greenhouse gases in the atmosphere had not changed much. But now we burn huge amounts of coal, oil, and natural gas to generate energy. Every year, billions of tons of carbon dioxide pour out from the exhausts of cars, trains, trucks, airplanes, buses, and ships and from the chimneys of factories. There is 30 percent more carbon dioxide in the air than there was 150 years ago.

Trees, like other green plants, convert carbon dioxide into oxygen.

⑤ But trees and forests are cut down in huge numbers. When wood burns or **decays**, even more carbon dioxide is released. Carbon dioxide enters into the atmosphere much faster than the remaining forests and oceans can absorb it.

The release of other greenhouse gases adds to the speed at which the world's climate is changing. Methane is released by millions and millions of cattle and other farm animals. Nitrous oxide comes from chemicals used in soil fertilizers, as well as from automobiles.

STOP AND CHECK

Ask and Answer Questions According to the author, why has the atmosphere changed? Go back to the text to find the answer.

A C T Access Complex Text

▶ Connection of Ideas

Tell students that as they read, they should connect new information with what they have already read.

→ *Paraphrase what you learned on page 388 about the amount of carbon dioxide in the atmosphere now.* (There is a great deal more carbon dioxide in the atmosphere now than there was in earlier times.)

→ *Reread the first paragraph on page 386. What reason is given here to explain why the increase of carbon dioxide is harmful?* (Carbon dioxide traps heat near the ground.)

→ *How is global warming connected to what is happening in the Arctic?* (Arctic temperatures are rising because of trapped heat.)

The Arctic is already showing the effects of global warming. Average temperatures in the northern regions of Alaska, Canada, and Russia have risen twice as fast as in the rest of the world. The Ward Hunt Ice Shelf, the largest single sheet of ice in the Arctic, started to crack in 2000. By 2002, it had split. Now it is breaking into smaller pieces.

The Arctic Ocean is the great body of sea ice that covers the North Pole. Satellite photographs show that the ice pack has been shrinking and thinning in depth since the early 1990s. Scientists say that for the first time in human history, ice may disappear from the Arctic Ocean every summer.

Bernhard Edmaier/Photo Researchers, Inc.

389

LITERATURE ANTHOLOGY, pp. 388–389

6 Genre: Expository Text

Turn to a partner and discuss the features of expository text you notice on page 389. (The text gives facts and information about a real place. There are dates that tell when things happened. A photograph supports the text and helps readers visualize the information.)

ELL As you discuss global warming and its impact on the Arctic, use gestures to explain words like *risen, split, shrinking,* and *thinning*. As you demonstrate with gestures, ask students to guess the word you are demonstrating.

→ *Is the Arctic getting warmer or colder?* (warmer) Point to and read the second sentence on page 389, noting that temperatures have risen, so it has gotten warmer.

→ *What is happening to the ice?* Guide students to use the words *cracking, breaking, shrinking,* or *thinning* to describe the ice.

LITERATURE ANTHOLOGY **T153F**

Develop Comprehension

7 Skill: Compare and Contrast

How has Alaska changed in the past few decades? Add this info to your organizer.

Alaska Decades Ago
rivers of ice; glaciers not melting

Both
have snow and glaciers

Alaska Now
rock and soil exposed; glaciers receding

Authors often use more than one text structure. What clues tell you the author is using sequence? (*in the winter, as spring approaches, a few decades ago, now, in 1963, today, in the 1850s, by 1968, in 2008, each year*) What other structure does the author use on this page? How do these structures aid understanding? (cause and effect; By using cause and effect and sequence to aid understanding, the author is showing the changes that have occurred over time in Alaska and Montana—effect—and why those changes have occurred—cause.)

Global warming has also changed the feeding patterns and behaviors of polar bears, walruses, seals, and whales. It may even impact their survival.

Polar bears live only in the Arctic. They are completely dependent on the sea ice for all their life needs. In the winter, females give birth to cubs. The mother polar bear eats little or no food during the winter.

As spring approaches, the bear family makes a run onto the sea ice to feed on seals, their main source of food. If the ice melts, their food supply will be cut off and this will impact their survival.

Glaciers and mountain snow covers are rapidly melting. Almost every glacier in Alaska is **receding**. A few decades ago, huge rivers of ice stretched over the land. Now hundreds of feet or sometimes miles of bare rock and soil are exposed. In 1963, the Mendenhall Glacier Visitor Center in Juneau opened, very close to the glacier. Today, it is a mile or more away from the frozen edge of the retreating glacier.

In the 1850s, there were 150 glaciers in Montana. By 1968, there were 37. In 2008, there were fewer than 24. Glaciers that have lasted for thousands of years may be gone in two decades.

The icy coverings on tall mountain peaks are also disappearing. Each year, there is less snow remaining on the mountains during the summer. The snow melts earlier by a week or more in the spring, and snow falls later by a week or more in the autumn.

Dan Guravich/Corbis

390

A C T Access Complex Text

▶ Organization

Tell students that authors of expository text may organize their texts by explaining cause-and-effect relationships. Review that an *effect* is what happens and a *cause* is why something happens.

→ *What effect will ice melting have on polar bears?* (It will cut off their food supply and could impact their survival.)

Remind students that paying attention to dates helps them understand how things change over time.

→ *What do the dates given for the Montana glaciers help the reader understand about them?* (The dates help the reader understand how rapidly the glaciers are disappearing.)

Grinnell and Salamander Glaciers,
1957

Grinnell and Salamander Glaciers,
2004

391

8 Skill: Make Inferences

Based on the information about the glaciers in Montana, what inference can you make about the temperature change in Montana since 1850? (I can infer that the temperature has risen since 1850 because so many glaciers have disappeared. Glaciers are "huge rivers of ice," and warmer temperatures are melting the ice.)

9 Text Feature: Photographs

Turn to a partner and discuss the photographs on page 391. What differences do you notice? Why do you think the author included these photographs? (In the photograph on the right, more rock is exposed because so much ice has melted. The author included the photographs to help readers visualize the changes to the glacier that he describes in the text.)

 Guide students to use the photographs to help them better understand cause and effect in expository text. Point out the cognates: cause/*causa*, effect/*efecto*.

→ Point to the photograph of the glacier in 1957. *Is there snow and ice?* (yes) *Has the ice melted?* (no)

→ Point to the photograph of the glacier in 2004. *Is this the same glacier?* (yes) *What caused the ice to melt?* (a rise in temperatures)

Develop Comprehension

10 Strategy: Ask and Answer Questions

Teacher Think Aloud Page 392 discusses how rising temperatures affect the ocean. How can we be sure we understand this information?

Prompt students to apply the strategy in a Think Aloud by asking themselves a question. Then have them turn to a partner and paraphrase the text that answers it in order to confirm their understanding.

Student Think Aloud I ask myself what effect rising temperatures have on the ocean. Then I reread the first paragraph to make sure I understand. As temperatures rise, ocean levels will also rise.

11 Author's Craft: Word Choice

Reread the second paragraph on page 392. Why is *swamp* a better word choice than *flood*? (It is a stronger word that helps readers visualize that rising sea levels would overwhelm the Gulf Coast and East Coast with water.)

10 As temperatures rise, the level of the oceans will rise. A recent study found that if average temperatures rise by 3° Celsius (5.4° Fahrenheit), Greenland's enormous ice sheet will begin to melt and sea levels all over the world may rise by a half foot to 3 feet or more.

11 This may happen over years or decades or may take longer than a century. A 3-foot rise in sea level would swamp the Gulf Coast and every East Coast city from Boston to Miami. Rising water would cover low-lying areas such as the Nile Delta and countries such as Bangladesh. Millions of people would be forced to move.

The Antarctic ice cap holds about 90 percent of the world's ice and about 70 percent of its freshwater. It does not look as if the entire ice cap will melt anytime soon, but if it does happen, sea levels would rise 20 or more feet. Now, *that* would cause major flooding in coastal areas.

Yin enbiao · Imaginechina/AP Images

392

A C T Access Complex Text

▶ Specific Vocabulary

Tell students that when authors include specific vocabulary, such as weather terms, they will often provide context clues.

→ *What are some context clues that can help you figure out what* El Niño *is?* ("weather pattern," "warmed the seas")

→ *Based on context clues, what do you think a* drought *is?* (a period of little rain that causes the soil to dry up)

Point out that if there aren't sufficient context clues, students may need to use a dictionary. Have pairs use a dictionary to look up the meaning of the word *polyp.* (a small sea animal)

Atmospheric warming can cause a rise in ocean temperatures and place coral reefs in jeopardy. Coral reefs are huge branching structures made of the limestone skeletons of tiny animals called coral polyps. Coral reefs are found in warm, clear, shallow oceans. They are home to many kinds of fishes, jellyfish, anemones, crabs, turtles, sea snakes, clams, and octopuses and the algae that give the reefs their stunning colors.

Most coral reefs are highly sensitive. Even small changes in water temperature and in the amount of carbon dioxide in the water can kill algae in a reef. When the coral dies, it bleaches white. In 1998, a weather pattern called El Niño warmed the seas. In just one year, about one in every six of the world's reefs was lost. If coral reefs die, then much of the animal life they support will be wiped out as well.

Changing climate affects every ocean and every continent. Rising temperatures add heat energy and water vapor to the atmosphere. That can lead to heavier rainfalls and more powerful storms in some places, and long droughts in others. The changes will differ depending upon the location.

Many tropical areas may have greater rainfall. But in dry regions, even less rain may fall. Higher temperatures will cause the soil to dry up, and terrible droughts may ensue.

STOP AND CHECK

Ask and Answer Questions How might a warmer climate affect life in the oceans and on land? Look for details in the text to help you.

393

LITERATURE ANTHOLOGY, pp. 392–393

⑫ **Skill: Compare and Contrast**

Compare and contrast how the changing climate could affect tropical regions and dry regions. (With higher temperatures, tropical regions may get more rain, and dry regions may get even less rain than usual.) Tell students they can also use photos to compare and contrast information. Compare and contrast the corals on page 393. (Both corals have branching structures. The coral on the top is alive. It has marine animals surrounding it. The coral on the bottom is dead. It is bleached white and has no marine animals around it.)

STOP AND CHECK

Ask and Answer Questions How might a warmer climate affect life in the oceans and on land? (Rising temperatures might kill coral reefs, which would wipe out many aquatic animals. Rising temperatures might also cause more storms and heavy rain, or droughts on land.)

ELL Help students identify context clues for *branching structures* and *bleaches* by using the photos on page 393 to describe these words.

→ *Show me* branching structures *by using your fingers.*

→ *What color do coral reefs become when they get bleached?* (white)

Develop Comprehension

13 **Skill: Compare and Contrast**

How are climate changes and weather changes different? (Climate changes are more difficult to notice than weather changes.) What are some signs of climate change? (Spring-like weather comes earlier, the ice melts sooner, and there are fewer days with temperatures below freezing.)

14 **Vocabulary: Context Clues**

What does *migrating* mean? What paragraph clues help you determine the meaning? (*Migrating* means "moving from one place to another." The clues "adapted," "moved northward," "disappeared from its original home," and "adjusted to its new northern home" all help me determine the meaning.)

Wildfires may increase in forested areas as timberlands grow drier. The fires are likely to be bigger and more frequent and to burn longer. They would also release more carbon dioxide into the atmosphere and could lead to more warming.

Climate changes are not as easy to notice as changes in the weather. For example, a particular storm or a number of warm days during a winter is not really evidence of anything. We can all see day-to-day weather changes. But climate changes are noticeable as well. Plants and animals are already showing the effects of Earth's warming. Cold places, such as the North and South Poles and mountaintops, have been the first to feel the heat. Spring has come earlier, the ice has melted sooner, and there are fewer days where the temperatures are below freezing.

Many kinds of wildlife need the cold to survive. Some animals have adapted to the warmer weather by migrating to colder places. As the climate has warmed over the past century, the colorful checkerspot butterfly of the American West has moved northward or to higher elevations. The checkerspot butterfly has almost completely disappeared from its original home in Mexico and has adjusted to its new northern home in Canada. But not every animal can travel as easily. Scientists worry that crowding on mountaintops and colder places will cause some species to become extinct.

Robert Marien/Corbis

394

A C T Access Complex Text

▶ Purpose

Remind students that authors of expository text often explain or inform by including text features. These features, such as lists and photos, provide additional information or offer readers pictures of items discussed in the text.

→ *In addition to the photo, what helpful text feature can be found on page 395?* (a bulleted list)

→ *Why might it be better to put certain text into a bulleted list?* (A bulleted list is easy to read, and it makes important information stand out.)

→ *What information does this bulleted list include?* (It shows ways to deal with climate change.)

We can't do anything about some changes in our environment. Our planet may be going through a natural cycle of getting warmer. However, most scientists say that humans are at least partly responsible for climate change. That means it may be possible for people to slow down the change.

There is a debate about what we can do about our changing climate. Here's what people in some nations are trying to do:

- Improve fuel and energy economy so that people use less energy for vehicles, schools, offices, homes, and factories.
- Encourage the use of wind and solar power.
- Explore alternative ways of producing energies that do not directly release more greenhouse gases into the atmosphere.
- Protect and plant trees to increase forestlands.

(15)

395

LITERATURE ANTHOLOGY, pp. 394–395

→ *What does the list reveal about the author's purpose for writing the selection?* (The author not only presents information about the changing climate, he includes possible things that people can do to help.)

(15) Strategy: Ask and Answer Questions

Turn to a partner and tell him or her a question you asked yourself as you read this page. Paraphrase the text you used to answer it.

Student Think Aloud As I read, I asked myself the question, What are some people doing to help prevent climate change? To find the answer, I can read the bulleted list on page 395. This list says that people are looking for better ways to produce and use energy. They are also planting trees to increase forestlands.

SCIENCE

CONNECT TO CONTENT
IMPACT OF CLIMATE ON LIVING THINGS

Changes in climate affect living things. When the climate changes, the characteristics of some plants and animals allow them to survive and reproduce. Others die or must move to new locations to survive. For example, scientists believe the golden toad from Costa Rica is now extinct because of climate change. Additionally noted on page 394, students read about how the checkerspot butterfly has moved its home from Mexico northward to Canada in order to survive the warming climate.

STEM

Develop Comprehension

16 Skill: Compare and Contrast

On page 395, you read what some nations are trying to do to help with climate change. On page 396, you read about what individual people are doing. How are the efforts the same? How are they different? (Same: Everyone can choose to use less fuel and plant trees. Different: Nations are working to improve fuel and energy economy and produce new sources of energy. People are focusing on things they can do individually, such as walking instead of driving, reusing items, and taking shorter showers.) Add this information to your organizer.

Nations
improve fuel economy; produce new sources of energy

Both
use less fuel; plant trees

People
walk; reuse items; take shorter showers

Neil Massey/Reportage/Alamy

Nations and governments can do certain things to slow down dramatic climate changes. People can help, too. They can choose to use less energy to heat and cool their houses or use less fuel when getting around. Here are some things we might consider:

- Walking, biking, or using public transportation. One school bus can carry the same number of children as 30 or more cars.

- Using sturdy reusable bags for shopping and reusable cups and glasses is less wasteful than using disposable bags and cups.

- Taking short showers uses less energy than long showers.

 • Planting a single tree can make enough oxygen for the lifetimes of two people. If one million trees are planted, the trees would eventually absorb more than one million tons of carbon dioxide.

396

A C T Access Complex Text

▶ Connection of Ideas

Help students connect the ways people can help with what they have learned about global warming.

→ *What does burning fossil fuel release into the atmosphere?* (carbon dioxide) *Why would walking instead of using vehicles help?* (Walking doesn't put carbon dioxide into the atmosphere. Cars do.)

→ *What do plants and trees take from the air?* (carbon dioxide) *How might planting them be helpful?* (By absorbing the carbon dioxide, plants can help reduce greenhouse gases in the atmosphere.)

→ *Will any of these ideas produce an immediate result? Why or why not?* (No, greenhouse gases stay in the atmosphere for years [page 386].)

Here's what some families are doing to slow down rapid climate change:

- Using fans instead of air conditioners. They may set a house air conditioner slightly higher in the summer, and slightly lower their heaters. They may lower a water heater's thermostat from "hot" (about 135° F.) to "warm" (about 120° F.).

- Using energy-saving fluorescent lightbulbs instead of incandescent lightbulbs. Fluorescent lightbulbs are more energy efficient and save on electricity costs.

- Turning off electric appliances and lights when they are not being used.

- Installing double-paned windows, extra insulation, good weather stripping, and solar panels to houses also saves energy.

Global warming isn't just about the Arctic Ocean melting and distant deserts becoming drier and hotter. Climate change impacts all of us. It can affect the world's food supply and the economic **stability** of countries.

The people and governments of the world are developing the tools and the scientific know-how to meet these challenges. As Earth's climate continues to change, we all want to find ways to safeguard our own and future generations.

STOP AND CHECK

Summarize How are some people trying to slow climate change? The strategy Summarize may help you.

397

Bloomimage/Corbis

LITERATURE ANTHOLOGY, pp. 396–397

Return to Predictions

Review students' predictions and purposes for reading. Ask them to answer the Essential Question. (Climate changes, such as changes in temperature and in the weather, affect living things.)

STOP AND CHECK

Summarize How are some people trying to slow climate change? (People are trying to use less energy by walking, riding bikes, or using public transportation instead of driving cars. They are reusing bags and cups and saving energy in their homes.)

 Write *reusable* on the boad. Ask:

→ *What word parts do you see in the word* reusable? (prefix *re-*, base word *use,* suffix *-able*)

→ *What does the prefix* re- *mean?* (again)

→ *What does* reusable *mean?* (able to be used again)

Point out the cognates in the bulleted list on pages 396–397: transportation/*transporte*, thermostat/*termostato*. Use gestures, demonstrations, and restatements to clarify the bulleted ideas as needed.

About the Author

Meet the Author

Seymour Simon

Have students read the biography of the author and photographer. Ask:

→ How is Seymour Simon's interest in the natural world reflected in his books?

→ How might his interest in nature have inspired him to write about global warming?

Author's Purpose

To Inform

Review that when authors write to inform, they may use photographs to illustrate their ideas. The author includes two photographs of a coral reef: one of a live reef with other living things it supports around it, and the other of a lifeless, bleached reef. This supports the author's point that climate change jeopardizes coral reefs and other living things.

Author's Craft

Word Choice

Explain that authors of expository texts often use domain-specific words, or words that are used in a certain area of study such as science.

→ Authors use scientific words to express concepts precisely. For example, on page 393 the author uses *coral polyps* instead of "very tiny sea animals."

→ Have students find other examples of domain-specific words such as *methane* and *nitrous oxide* on page 388, and *water vapor* on page 393.

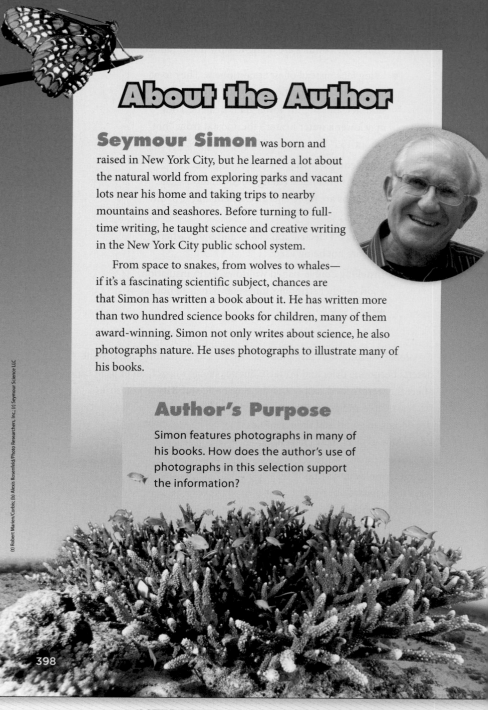

About the Author

Seymour Simon was born and raised in New York City, but he learned a lot about the natural world from exploring parks and vacant lots near his home and taking trips to nearby mountains and seashores. Before turning to full-time writing, he taught science and creative writing in the New York City public school system.

From space to snakes, from wolves to whales—if it's a fascinating scientific subject, chances are that Simon has written a book about it. He has written more than two hundred science books for children, many of them award-winning. Simon not only writes about science, he also photographs nature. He uses photographs to illustrate many of his books.

Author's Purpose

Simon features photographs in many of his books. How does the author's use of photographs in this selection support the information?

398

(t) Robert Marien/Corbis; (b) Alexis Rosenfeld/Photo Researchers, Inc.; (r) Seymour Science LLC

LITERATURE ANTHOLOGY, pp. 398–399

Respond to Reading

Summarize

Use the most important details from *Global Warming* to summarize what you learned about changes in the environment. Details from your Venn Diagram may help you.

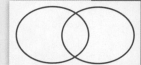

Text Evidence

1. How can you tell that this selection is expository text? Give an example of a text feature and explain how it helps you understand the information. **GENRE**

2. How is Earth's climate today different from that of the past? Identify signal words the author uses to make the comparison. **COMPARE AND CONTRAST**

3. What is the meaning of the word *coastal* on page 392? Give examples of context clues in the paragraph that helped you figure out the meaning. **PARAGRAPH CLUES**

4. Write to compare how a rise in temperature affects the Arctic Ocean and oceans with coral reefs. **WRITE ABOUT READING**

Make Connections

How has a change in climate affected wildlife in different locations? **ESSENTIAL QUESTION**

Give one example of what some nations are doing about climate change. How might this activity affect the environment? **TEXT TO WORLD**

399

(b) Bloomimage/Corbis

Make Connections • *Analytical Writing*

Essential Question Have partners work together to cite evidence from the text that explains how climate changes have affected ocean animals and animals in the Arctic region. Have partners share with the class.

Text to World Have students share one thing nations are doing about climate change and how it may impact the environment. Discuss which effort students think will be most effective and why.

Respond to Reading

Summarize

Review with students the information from their organizers. Model how to use the information to summarize *Global Warming*.

Analytical Writing **Write About Reading: Compare and Contrast** Have students compare and contrast information about climate change to use as evidence in a summary. Have them share their summaries with a partner.

Text Evidence

1. **Genre** <u>Answer</u> The selection gives facts about real events and includes photographs. <u>Evidence</u> The bulleted list on page 395 is an example of a text feature.

2. **Compare and Contrast** <u>Answer</u> Earth's climate today is changing more rapidly. The signal words are *different, while, more, but, now*. <u>Evidence</u> Most scientists agree that something different is happening now. Nineteen of the twenty hottest years *ever* have happened since 1980.

3. **Paragraph Clues** <u>Answer</u> It means "near or along the seashore." <u>Evidence</u> The previous paragraph states "a 3-foot rise in sea level would swamp the Gulf Coast."

4. *Analytical Writing* **Write About Reading: Compare and Contrast** As temperatures rise, ocean levels rise. The Arctic Ocean's ice pack shrinks, changing feeding patterns of animals that live there. A rise in ocean temperatures can threaten or kill coral reefs and the life that they support.

Develop Comprehension

Literature Anthology
Complex vocabulary places this selection above Lexile range. Content is grade-level appropriate.

"When Volcanoes Erupt"

Text Complexity Range

Lexile

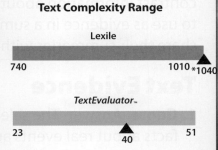

740   1010 *1040

TextEvaluator™

23   40   51

Options for Close Reading

→ Whole Class
→ Small Group
→ Independent

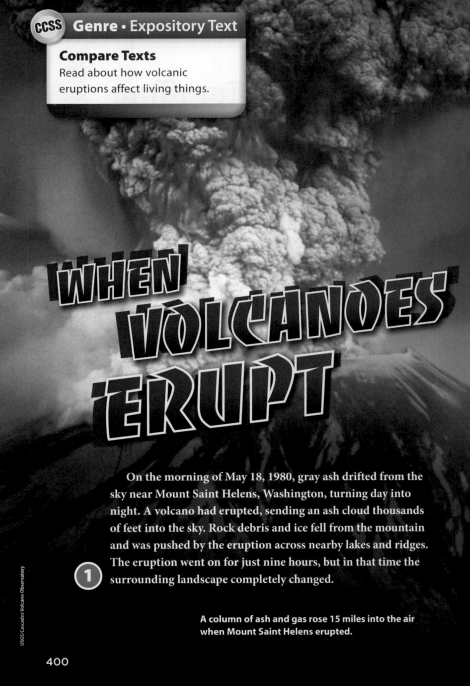

CCSS Genre • Expository Text

Compare Texts
Read about how volcanic eruptions affect living things.

WHEN VOLCANOES ERUPT

On the morning of May 18, 1980, gray ash drifted from the sky near Mount Saint Helens, Washington, turning day into night. A volcano had erupted, sending an ash cloud thousands of feet into the sky. Rock debris and ice fell from the mountain and was pushed by the eruption across nearby lakes and ridges. The eruption went on for just nine hours, but in that time the surrounding landscape completely changed.

A column of ash and gas rose 15 miles into the air when Mount Saint Helens erupted.

USGS Cascades Volcano Observatory

400

A C T Access Complex Text

What makes this text complex?
▶ **Specific Vocabulary**
▶ **Connection of Ideas**

▶ Specific Vocabulary

Remind students to use context clues to find the meaning of an unfamiliar word. Point out the word *debris* on page 400.

→ *What came out of Mount Saint Helens when it exploded?* (rock debris and ice)

→ *What is volcanic debris?* (Volcanic debris includes the rocks that come out of a volcano.)

VENTS IN THE EARTH

What causes a volcano like Mount Saint Helens to erupt? Beneath Earth's rocky crust, there is a layer that consists partly of hot, melted rock. This molten rock is called magma. A **gradual** buildup of pressure caused by gases within Earth can cause magma to burst or seep through vents, or openings, in Earth's surface.

Magma that has escaped to the surface is called lava. Depending on the type of volcano, lava can explode upward or flow slowly outward. As it hardens, lava forms into solid rock.

An active volcano is one that is currently erupting, has recently erupted, or is about to erupt. An eruption can last days, weeks, months, or years. A dormant volcano has been quiet for many years, yet is still capable of erupting. An extinct volcano hasn't erupted in perhaps thousands of years and is not expected to erupt again.

2

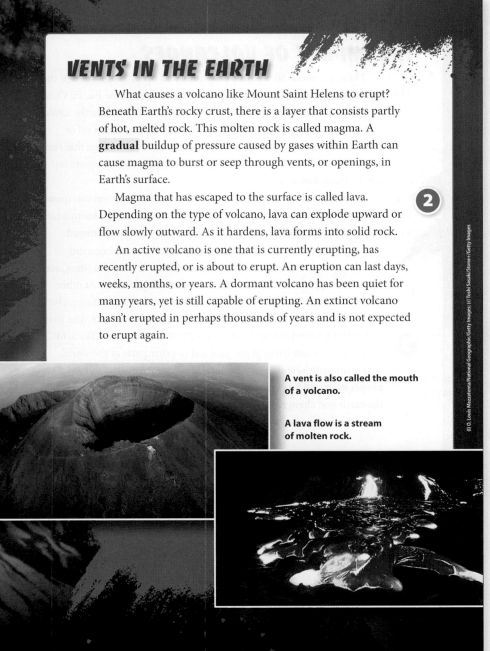

A vent is also called the mouth of a volcano.

A lava flow is a stream of molten rock.

(l) O. Louis Mazzatenta/National Geographic/National Geographic Image; (r) Toshi Sasaki/Stone+/Getty Images

401

LITERATURE ANTHOLOGY, pp. 400–401

Compare Texts

Students will read another informational text on changes that affect the environment. Ask students to do a close reading of the text to understand the content. Encourage students to use the **reread** strategy or other strategies they know that will help them. They will also take notes as they read. Students will then use the text evidence that they gathered to compare this text with *Global Warming*.

❶ Ask and Answer Questions

How did the eruption of Mount Saint Helens affect the surrounding area? Paraphrase the answer with a partner. (Ash was forced into the sky, and rock debris and ice were pushed to nearby lakes and ridges.)

❷ Ask and Answer Questions

How does a volcano erupt?

Write About Reading Explain the process that takes place when a volcano erupts. (Pressure from gases inside Earth causes magma to escape through vents in Earth's surface. Lava can explode upward or flow slowly outward. Lava hardens into rock.)

ELL Point out the cognate: volcano/*volcán*. Help ELLs understand why volcanoes produce rock debris.

→ *How do volcanic eruptions occur?* (Pressure from gases within Earth causes an eruption.)

→ Demonstrate for students how pressure works. Place a lightweight object on the edge of a surface so that a portion of it hangs over the edge. Very lightly apply pressure to the portion that is hanging over the edge.

→ *What happens when pressure is applied to something?* (The pressure moves the object.)

→ *How does this apply to volcanoes?* (Pressure forces rock debris out of the volcano.)

Develop Comprehension

③ Ask and Answer Questions

Turn to a partner and paraphrase the first paragraph. Then discuss the negative effects described in the third paragraph. What are the environmental effects of a volcanic eruption?

Analytical Writing **Write About Reading** Take notes on the global effects of a volcanic eruption. (Clouds of ash and gas can circle the globe. Gases and water vapor can combine to create acid rain. Haze from the volcanic cloud can block the sun and cool temperatures.)

④ Ask and Answer Questions

What are some of the positive and negative effects that occur in an area where a volcano erupts? (Volcanic ash helps make the soil fertile, promoting the growth of living things. Living things can be killed or harmed by debris and poisonous gases. Crops and property can be destroyed.)

THE IMPACT OF VOLCANOES

There are about 50 volcanic eruptions that occur somewhere in the world every year. Many are concentrated in an area of the Pacific Ocean known as the "Ring of Fire." The most frequent volcanoes in the United States occur in Hawaii and in the southwestern island chain off of Alaska. Volcanoes in the Cascade Range, the mountain range that runs from western Canada south through California, are less frequent but can be more dangerous.

Eruptions can devastate surrounding areas. An eruption can spew lava, ash, rocks, mud, and poisonous gases into the air and harm nearby plants, animals, and people. Crops and property can be destroyed.

Eruptions can even have a global **impact** on the environment. Winds can move clouds of ash and gas far from an eruption site. Gases from an eruption can absorb heat and warm temperatures. At other times a volcanic cloud can block sunlight and cool temperatures. Over time, these atmospheric changes can affect a region's climate. The gases ③ in a volcanic cloud can also combine with water vapor to make acid rain. This rain can harm plants and soil in other parts of the world.

Fortunately, scientific predictions of volcanic activity can help people escape the dangers of eruptions. Scientists monitor tremors in the earth and changes in gases emitted from a volcano. These signals of an impending eruption allow scientists to give advance warning.

The eruption of Mount Pinatubo in the Philippines in 1991 caused a haze that cooled temperatures worldwide. It also dusted the area with ash.

402

A C T Access Complex Text

▶ Connection of Ideas

Remind students that authors of expository text may include information in text features, such as photo captions. Readers need to connect the captions to other information they have read.

→ *How did the haze from the eruption of Mount Pinatubo cause worldwide temperatures to cool?* (The haze blocked the sunlight.)

→ *Why might the area of Mount Saint Helens be showing signs of recovery?* (The soil may be more fertile from the scattered ash.)

→ *How do the captions connect to the text on these pages?* (The author has explained volcanic eruptions, and these captions discuss specific examples.)

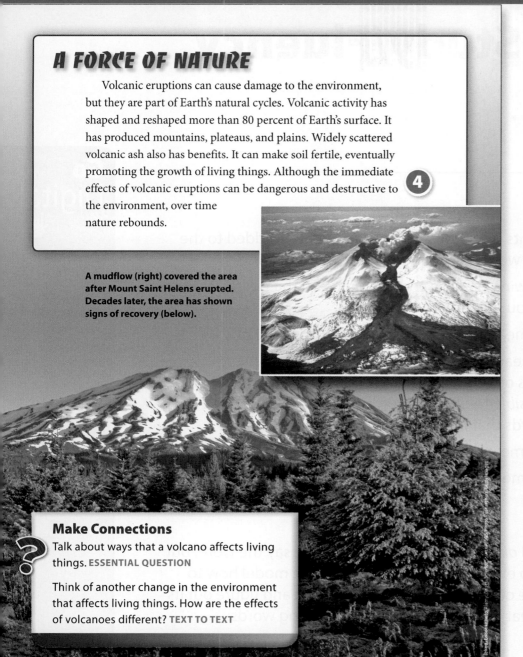

A FORCE OF NATURE

Volcanic eruptions can cause damage to the environment, but they are part of Earth's natural cycles. Volcanic activity has shaped and reshaped more than 80 percent of Earth's surface. It has produced mountains, plateaus, and plains. Widely scattered volcanic ash also has benefits. It can make soil fertile, eventually promoting the growth of living things. Although the immediate effects of volcanic eruptions can be dangerous and destructive to the environment, over time nature rebounds.

4

A mudflow (right) covered the area after Mount Saint Helens erupted. Decades later, the area has shown signs of recovery (below).

Make Connections

Talk about ways that a volcano affects living things. **ESSENTIAL QUESTION**

Think of another change in the environment that affects living things. How are the effects of volcanoes different? **TEXT TO TEXT**

403

LITERATURE ANTHOLOGY, pp. 402–403

Make Connections ◂ Analytical Writing

Essential Question Have students paraphrase and share information about what happens when a volcano erupts. Suggest that they reread headings and captions to identify how a volcanic eruption affects living things.

Text to Text Have groups of students compare their responses to the Ask and Answer Questions prompts with what they learned in *Global Warming*. Each group can report back to the whole class. First, have each group compare the effects of volcanic eruptions and global warming. (Both have harmful effects on humans, animals, and the environment. Both can cause changes to the land and temperature.) Next, have each group contrast the effects of volcanic eruptions and global warming. (The effects of a volcano are felt when it erupts, but the effects of global warming are slower. Human actions can be one cause of global warming, but a volcanic eruption is due to natural causes. Humans can help slow global warming, but they can't control volcanoes.)

 As you discuss the impact of volcanic eruptions, explain that the word *devastate* on page 402 means "to destroy."

→ *How can eruptions devastate an area?* (They can harm plants, animals, people, and land.)

Word Study/Fluency

MINILESSON 20 Mins — Prefixes

OBJECTIVES

CCSS Know and apply grade-level phonics and word analysis skills in decoding words. Use combined knowledge of all letter-sound correspondences, syllabication patterns, and morphology (e.g., roots and affixes) to read accurately unfamiliar multisyllabic words in context and out of context. **RF.5.3a**

CCSS Read on-level prose and poetry orally with accuracy, appropriate rate, and expression on successive readings. **RF.5.4b**

Rate: 129–149 WCPM

ACADEMIC LANGUAGE

• *rate*

• Cognate: *ritmo*

1 Explain

Remind students that a *prefix* is a group of letters added to the beginning of a word that changes the word's meaning.

Write the following prefixes and meanings on the board. Read each one aloud as you point to it.

→ *dis-*, often means "not," "absence of," or "opposite of"

→ *in-*, often means "not," or "opposite of"
   Other forms of *in-* are *im-* (before words that begin with *m* or *p*, as in *impossible*), *ir-* (before words that begin with *r*), and *il-* (before words that begin with *l*, as in *illogical*)

→ *mis-*, often means "wrong"

→ *pre-*, often means "before"

2 Model

Write the word *disappear* on the board. Do not say the word, but ask students to examine the word's parts. Then model how to use knowledge of prefixes to decode the word and figure out its meaning. Repeat the activity using the following words:

disagree	discontinue	inactive	immature
irregular	illegal	misbehave	preheat

3 Guided Practice

Write the following words on the board. Have students underline the prefix in each word, define the prefix, and then use its meaning to determine the meaning of the whole word.

distrust	disobey	disinterest	disarm
incorrect	immobile	irresponsible	illogical
miscount	misread	preset	precaution
disinterest	impolite	preview	mistreat

Read Multisyllabic Words

Transition to Longer Words Write the following on the board. Have students chorally read the prefixes in the first and third columns. Then have them underline the prefixes in the words in the second and fourth columns. Model how to read the words in the second column and how to determine their meaning based on the meaning of the prefixes. Then have students read and define the words in the fourth column.

dis-	disagreement	dis-	displacement
mis-	misunderstanding	mis-	misalignment
in-	inseparable	ir-	irreplaceable
im-	impersonal	il-	illegible
pre-	prefabricate	pre-	prejudgment

Monitor and *Differentiate*

 Quick Check

Can students decode multisyllabic words with prefixes? Can students read at an appropriate rate?

Small Group Instruction

If No →	**Approaching Level**	**Reteach** pp. T170, T174
	ELL	**Develop** pp. T187, T190
If Yes →	**On Level**	**Apply** pp. T176–T177
	Beyond Level	**Apply** pp. T180–T181

Rate

Explain/Model Remind students that *rate* refers to the speed with which they read. Explain that reading too quickly or too slowly might make a text difficult to understand. Turn to "Forests on Fire," **Reading/Writing Workshop** pages 338–341. Model reading page 340 first very quickly and then again at a more careful, measured rate. Ask students which rate made the text easier to understand.

Remind students that you will be listening for their use of appropriate rate as you monitor their reading during the week.

Practice/Apply Have partners take turns reading the passage, modeling the rate you used.

Daily Fluency Practice FLUENCY

Students can practice fluency using **Your Turn Practice Book** passages.

ON-LEVEL PRACTICE BOOK p. 228

Word Study: **Prefixes**

Name _____

dis- means "not," "absence of," or "opposite of"
in- means "not" or "opposite of"
mis- means "wrong" or "not"
pre- means "before"

Add a prefix from the box to complete the word in each sentence below. Use context clues to help you decide which prefix to use.

1. She will ___pre___ wash the fabric to make sure it will not shrink.
2. Please remember to ___dis___ connect from the Internet before you turn off the computer.
3. Their visitors will stay for an ___in___ definite amount of time.
4. He felt some ___dis___ comfort when he hurt his leg.
5. If you do not speak clearly, they will ___mis___ understand your directions.
6. She has little money, so she hopes to find an ___in___ expensive gift.
7. The teacher will ___pre___ view the video before showing it to the class.
8. A friendship can be harmed if there is ___mis or dis___ trust between two people.
9. Always ___pre___ heat the oven before you bake bread.
10. I ___dis___ approve of the way they are behaving.

228 Practice • Grade 5 • Unit 5 • Week 3

APPROACHING p.228	BEYOND p. 228	ELL p. 228

Wrap Up the Week
Integrate Ideas

Go Digital

www.connected.mcgraw-hill.com
RESOURCES
Research and Inquiry

RESEARCH AND INQUIRY

Our Changing Earth

OBJECTIVES

CCSS Conduct short research projects that use several sources to build knowledge through investigation of different aspects of a topic. **W.5.7**

CCSS Include multimedia components (e.g., graphics, sound) and visual displays in presentations when appropriate to enhance the development of main ideas or themes. **SL.5.5**

- Develop a research plan.
- Choose reliable sources.
- Use media to publish information.

ACADEMIC LANGUAGE

- *nature reserve, wildlife sanctuary, environment*
- Cognates: *reserva natural, santuario*

Create a Web Site Entry or a Podcast

COLLABORATE

Explain that students will work with a partner to research nature reserves or wildlife sanctuaries. They will focus on how these areas protect wildlife from human changes to the environment. Then they will summarize their findings by making an entry on a class Web site or by creating a podcast. Discuss the following steps:

1 Develop a Research Plan Have partners create a plan for their research. Have them list possible search terms to use in their research, and questions they want their research to answer. Ask students to post their search terms and questions on the Shared Research Board.

2 Find Resources Have partners search reliable print and digital sources for information about nature reserves and wildlife sanctuaries. Tell them to look for Web sites that describe ways the reserve or sanctuary protects wildlife. Ask students to choose one reserve or sanctuary to focus on as they answer their research questions. Suggest that students use Research Process Checklist 3.

3 Guided Practice Model for students how to create an entry on your class Web site or how to create a podcast. Include instruction on how to upload the completed presentation. You may want to write the steps involved on the board for students to refer to as they work.

4 Create a Web Site Entry or Podcast Have partners create either a written or oral presentation, depending on whether they plan to publish their work on a Web page entry or a podcast.

Present a Web Site Entry or Podcast

Have partners upload their Web page entries or their podcast. Then have students share their entries or podcasts with the class.

STEM

TEXT CONNECTIONS *Analytical Writing*

OBJECTIVES

CCSS Integrate information from several texts on the same topic in order to write or speak about the subject knowledgeably. **RI.5.9**

CCSS Review the key ideas expressed and draw conclusions in light of information and knowledge gained from the discussions. **SL.5.1d**

Text to Text

Cite Evidence Explain that students will work in groups to compare information about environmental changes from the week's readings. Model how to make comparisons using examples from the week's **Leveled Readers** and from "Forests on Fire," **Reading/Writing Workshop** pages 338–341.

Have groups use Shutter Foldable® to organize information from the week's texts. They should record at least three examples of environmental change and how the change affects living things.

Present Information Have groups meet to present the examples cited and their conclusions. Encourage them to discuss any differences in their conclusions.

Environmental Changes

Effects on Living Things

Dinah Zike's **FOLDABLES**

WRITE ABOUT READING *Analytical Writing*

OBJECTIVES

CCSS Explain the relationships or interactions between two or more individuals, events, ideas, or concepts in a historical, scientific, or technical text based on specific information in the text. **RI.5.3**

CCSS Draw evidence from literary or informational texts to support analysis, reflection, and research. **W.5.9**

Write an Analysis

Cite Evidence Explain that students will write about one of the texts they read this week. Using text evidence, students will analyze how the author compared and contrasted information to explain a topic.

Discuss how to analyze text structure by asking *how* and *why* questions.

→ How does the author show that two events or ideas are similar and different?

→ Why are comparisons in the text important to understanding the topic?

Use **Your Turn Practice Book** page 229 to read and discuss the student model. Then have students choose a text and review information that the author compared and contrasted. Have them write to show how the author's use of this text structure helps explain the topic. Remind students that good explanatory writers include precise language.

 Present Your Ideas Ask partners to share their paragraphs and discuss how the evidence they cited from the text supports their ideas.

→ # Readers to Writers

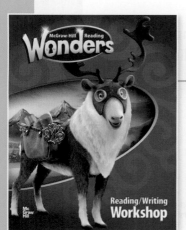

Reading/Writing Workshop

CCSS **OBJECTIVES**
Develop the topic with facts, definitions, concrete details, quotations, or other information and examples related to the topic. **W.5.2b**

CCSS Write routinely over extended time frames (time for research, reflection, and revision) and shorter time frames (a single sitting or a day or two) for a range of discipline-specific tasks, purposes, and audiences. **W.5.10**

Analyze models to understand how details develop a topic.

ACADEMIC LANGUAGE
• *develop, topic, concrete details*
• Cognate: *detalles*

Writing Traits: Ideas

Develop a Topic

Expert Model Explain that writers support and explain a central idea with details that relate to the topic. Writers use facts, definitions of unfamiliar words or ideas, examples that illustrate the topic, quotations from people that know about the topic, and concrete details. Concrete details are specific and precise details that support facts and make the meaning clear to readers. For example, "water and fertilize the plants once a week" is more concrete than "take care of the plants." While readers might interpret "take care of the plants" in different ways, the concrete instruction gives readers an exact message with a clear meaning.

 Read aloud the expert model "Forests on Fire." Ask students to listen and think about the examples, facts, and concrete details the writer uses to develop the topic: *the benefits of wildfires*. Point out that "fire resistant roots" is a concrete detail that supports the idea: *Often this new plant life will be better adapted to fire than what existed before.* Have students talk with partners to identify additional details that support, explain, or expand on the topic.

Expert Model

Student Model Remind students that adding details helps readers better understand the writer's topic. Read aloud the student model "Autumn Leaves." As students follow along, have them notice how details develop the topic.

 Invite partners to talk about the model and the details Marcus added. Ask them to suggest other places where Marcus could add more details to explain his topic more completely.

Student Model

 Genre Writing

Informational Text

For full writing process lessons and rubrics see:
→ Informational Article, pp. T344–T349
→ Research Report, pp. T350–T355

Writing Traits Ideas

Readers to ...

A writer **develops a topic**, or central idea, with details. To engage readers, writers often include facts, definitions, concrete details, quotations, and examples that develop and explain a topic. All the details in the text relate to the topic and expand on it.

Expert Model

Develop a Topic
Identify details the writer uses to develop the topic of wildfires' benefits.

Wildfires have happened throughout history, and they help to regenerate Earth and its species. When vegetation decays, wildfires clear it away so that new plant life can grow.

Fire also releases nutrients back into the soil making it more fertile. And by eliminating leafy canopies of mature trees, fire allows nourishing sunlight to reach a forest floor.

Often, this new plant life will be better adapted to fire than what existed before. Some species will have fire resistant roots, leaves, or bark. Other species will actually depend on fire to reproduce and thrive.

346

Writers

Marcus wrote an expository text about a change he has observed in nature. Read his revision of this section.

Student Model

Autumn Leaves

Why do the trees change color every fall? By the end of summer, the leaves look tired. they're dry from the
and
summer sun. They're a dull green. Then, one day, I'll notice a gold maple leaf in the middle of the green one's.
sp
Soon, all the trees are dressed up in brillient colors, as if covered in
patchwork
a red and gold quilt. Not only do
bold, new
we get great colors—the trees get a rest from all that growth!

347

READING/WRITING WORKSHOP, pp. 346–347

Editing Marks

∧ Add
⌃ Add a comma.
⌿ Take out.
sp Check spelling.
≡ Make a capital letter.

Grammar Handbook
Adjectives
See page 466.

Your Turn COLLABORATE

✓ How does Marcus use concrete details and examples to develop his topic?
✓ Look at the adjectives Marcus used.
✓ Tell how revisions improved Marcus's writing.

Go Digital!
Write online in Writer's Workspace

ELL ENGLISH LANGUAGE LEARNERS SCAFFOLD

Provide support to help English Language Learners understand the writing trait.

Beginning

Respond Orally Help students complete each sentence frame about the student model. *The topic is why trees change [size/color]. The summer sun makes the leaves turn [dull/bright] green. In the fall, the leaves turn [different colors/one color].*

Intermediate

Practice Ask students to complete the sentence frames. Encourage students to provide details. *The topic is ____. At the end of the summer, the leaves ____. In the fall, the leaves ____.*

Advanced/High

Understand Check for understanding. Ask: *What is the topic? How do leaves change in the summer and in the fall? What other details did Marcus include to explain the topic?*

Writing Every Day: Ideas

Writing Entry: Develop a Topic

Prewrite Provide students with the prompt below.

Write about a change you have seen in nature. Tell whether you think the change is positive or negative and why.

Have partners list changes they have seen in nature. Ask students to jot down details about the changes they might include in their drafts.

Draft Have students select one change in nature they would like to write about. Remind students to use details to develop their topic.

Focus on Developing a Topic

Use **Your Turn Practice Book** page 230 to model developing a topic.

Our region is experiencing a drought. It hasn't rained in a long time. Things aren't growing. Everything is brown.

Model adding details by revising the first sentence.

Our region is experiencing the most severe drought ever recorded.

Discuss how adding details develops the topic. Guide students to add more details to the rest of the model.

Writing Entry: Develop a Topic

Revise Have students revise their writing from Day 1 by adding two or three details that develop their topic.

Use the **Conferencing Routines**. Circulate among students and stop briefly to talk with individuals. Provide time for peer review.

Edit Have students use Grammar Handbook page 466 in the **Reading/Writing Workshop** to edit for errors in adjectives.

Conferencing Routines

Teacher Conferences

STEP 1

Talk about the strengths of the writing.

You have a strong opening—you introduce the topic clearly and state your main idea.

STEP 2

Focus on how the writer uses the target trait for the week.

You used some interesting facts that help me understand the topic. It would help if you added some concrete details that support those facts.

STEP 3

Make concrete suggestions for revisions. Have students work on a specific assignment, such as those to the right, and then meet with you to review progress.

DAY 3

Writing Entry: Develop a Topic

Prewrite Ask students to search their Writer's Notebooks for topics for a new draft. Or, provide a prompt such as the following:

Tell about an outdoor place you think others should visit.

Draft Once students have chosen their topics, ask them to create a word web with the topic in the center. Then have them think about facts, concrete details, examples, definitions, or quotations they might use to develop their topic. Students can use their word webs to begin their drafts.

DAY 4

Writing Entry: Develop a Topic

Revise Have students revise the draft writing from Day 3 by adding two or three details to develop the topic. As students revise, hold teacher conferences with individual students. You may also wish to have students work with partners to peer conference.

Edit Invite students to review the rules for adjectives on Grammar Handbook page 466 in the **Reading/Writing Workshop** and then check their drafts for errors.

DAY 5

Share and Reflect

Discuss with students what they learned about developing a topic. Invite volunteers to read and compare draft text with text that has been revised. Have students discuss the writing by focusing on the importance of using details to develop a topic. Allow time for individuals to reflect on their own writing progress and record observations in their Writer's Notebooks.

Suggested Revisions

Provide specific direction to help focus young writers.

Focus on a Sentence
Read the draft and target one sentence for revision. *Rewrite this sentence by adding concrete details that support the topic.*

Focus on a Section
Underline a section that needs to be revised. Provide specific suggestions. *This section could be developed with facts or examples that explain your point. Add details to help me understand better.*

Focus on a Revision Strategy
Underline a section. Have students use a specific revision strategy such as deleting. *Reread your draft and delete details that don't relate to your topic.*

Peer Conferences

Focus peer response groups on adding details to develop a topic. Provide this checklist to frame discussion.

- ☑ Does the writing include details that explain and support the topic?
- ☑ Are all the details related to the topic?
- ☑ Are any parts of the writing unclear?
- ☑ What details can be added to clarify the writing?

Grammar: Adjectives

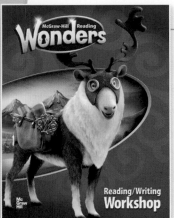

Reading/Writing Workshop

OBJECTIVES

 CCSS Demonstrate command of the conventions of standard English grammar and usage when writing or speaking. Order adjectives within sentences according to conventional patterns (e.g., *a small red* bag rather than *a red small bag*). **L4.1d**

 CCSS Use underlining, quotation marks, or italics to indicate titles of works. **L.5.2d**

Proofread sentences.

Go Digital

Adjectives

Grammar Activities

DAY 1

DAILY LANGUAGE ACTIVITY

Although I am hungry. I will wait for dinner. Your going to love my mothers lentil soup. (1: hungry, I; 2: You're; 3: mother's)

Introduce Adjectives

→ An **adjective** modifies a noun or a pronoun.

→ Adjectives tell what kind: *tall, shiny, round, slow.*

→ Adjectives tell how many or how much: *ten, some, few.*

→ **Demonstrative adjectives** tell which one: *this, that, these, those.*

→ **Proper adjectives** should be capitalized: <u>Cuban</u> food.

→ The **articles** *a, an,* and *the* are also adjectives.

Have partners discuss adjectives on page 466 of the Grammar Handbook in **Reading/Writing Workshop**.

DAY 2

DAILY LANGUAGE ACTIVITY

Kyle a star runner ran down elm road. His dad followd. (1: Kyle,; 2: runner,; 3: Elm Road; 4: followed)

Review Adjectives

Remind students that adjectives modify a noun or a pronoun. Proper adjectives should be capitalized.

Introduce Order of Adjectives

When more than one adjective is used to modify a noun, the adjectives must be listed in order.

→ Opinions come first: *a <u>good</u> used book.*

→ Size comes next: *a nice <u>long</u> scarf.*

→ Age comes next: *a pretty <u>new</u> rug; a thick <u>new</u> rug.*

→ Color comes next: *a pointy <u>green</u> hat; a long <u>red</u> scarf; an old <u>blue</u> pen.*

 # TALK ABOUT IT

COLLABORATE

USE ADJECTIVES

Ask partners to list adjectives that describe a change in nature. Then have them use four of the adjectives in sentences to tell their partner about what happened.

THESAURUS HUNT

Have partners write three sentences that use adjectives to describe an animal. Ask them to read their sentences aloud. Then have partners exchange papers and replace the adjectives with new ones. Suggest they use a thesaurus.

DAY 3

Mechanics and Usage: Capitalization and Punctuation

→ Acronyms are abbreviations that contain all capital letters and no periods: *TV, NASA, IRS.*

→ You underline titles from long pieces of work, such as books, and put quotation marks around smaller pieces of work, such as chapters. *I read the book Origami Yoda. "Flossy Returns" is the first chapter in my new book.*

As students write, refer them to Grammar Handbook pages 475 and 480.

DAY 4

Proofread

Have students correct errors in these sentences:

1. I ate at the spanish restaurant. (Spanish)
2. Use a green shiny bow for the presence. (1: shiny green; 2: presents)
3. I did not watch T.V. because I was reading the book "Winter Days." (1: TV; 2: Winter Days)
4. My blue new bike is great. (new blue)

Have students check their work using Grammar Handbook pages 466, 475, and 480.

DAY 5

Assess

Use the Daily Language Activity and Grammar Practice Reproducibles page 115 for assessment.

Reteach

Use Grammar Practice Reproducibles pages 111–114 and selected pages from the Grammar Handbook for additional reteaching. Remind students that it is important to use adjectives correctly as they speak and write.

Check students' writing for use of the skill and listen for it in their speaking. Assign Grammar Revision Assignments in their Writer's Notebooks as needed.

See Grammar Practice Reproducibles pp. 111–115.

WRITE CAPTIONS

Ask students to find a picture of a person or place and write a caption for it. Captions should include multiple adjectives, including one proper adjective. Have them show the pictures and read aloud their captions to the group.

TAKE A GUESS

Have students complete this sentence: *I'm thinking of something that is ____, ____, and ____.* Ask them to put their sentences in a pile. Students will take turns choosing a sentence, reading it aloud, and guessing what is described.

DESCRIBE NATURE

Have partners write sentences describing an area after a natural disaster. At least one sentence should include two adjectives that precede a noun. Ask pairs to exchange sentences and check the order of the adjectives.

Spelling: Prefixes

DAY 1

OBJECTIVES

 CCSS Spell grade-appropriate words correctly, consulting references as needed.
L.5.2e

Spelling Words

prewash	disconnect	disobey
disable	preview	dishonest
discolor	prejudge	injustice
mistaken	misjudge	disapprove
preheats	discomfort	inexpensive
mistrust	dismount	indefinite
incorrect	misunderstand	

Review presence, stationary, current
Challenge prehistoric, misbehave

Differentiated Spelling

Approaching Level

prewash	dislike	disobey
disable	preview	dishonest
discolor	pretest	instep
mistaken	mislead	disagree
preheats	discomfort	indirect
misplace	dismount	invisible
incorrect	misunderstand	

Beyond Level

preview	prerequisite	discontent
disable	disconnect	dishearten
dismantle	inaccurate	injustice
mistaken	misjudge	disapprove
dismount	predisposition	inexpensive
mistrust	discomfort	indefinite
prejudge	misunderstand	

Assess Prior Knowledge

Read the spelling words aloud, emphasizing the prefix in each word.

Point out the prefixes in *disobey*, *mistrust*, *incorrect*, and *preview*. Pronounce each word while drawing a line under the prefix. Explain that a prefix is a group of letters added to the beginning of a word. A prefix changes the meaning of the base word.

Demonstrate sorting spelling words by prefix. Sort a few words, pointing out the prefix as each word is sorted. Ask students to name other words with the same prefixes.

Use the Dictation Sentences from Day 5 to give the pretest. Say the underlined word, read the sentence, and repeat the word. Have students write the words. Then have students check their papers.

DAY 2

Spiral Review

Review the homophones *presence*, *stationary*, and *current*. Read each sentence below, repeat the review word, and have students write it.

1. His friend's <u>presence</u> was comforting.
2. Steven's bike is parked in the garage, <u>stationary</u> for the winter.
3. The <u>current</u> issue of the magazine shows the president on the cover.

Have students trade papers and check their spellings.

Challenge Words Review this week's prefixes. Read each sentence below, repeat the challenge word, and have students write the words.

1. Dinosaurs lived in <u>prehistoric</u> times.
2. If the puppies <u>misbehave</u>, do not give them any treats.

Have students check and correct their spellings and write the words in their word study notebooks.

 # WORD SORTS

COLLABORATE

OPEN SORT

Have students cut apart the **Spelling Word Cards** in the Online Resource Book and initial the back of each card. Have them read the words aloud with partners. Then have partners do an **open sort**. Have them record their sorts in their word study notebooks.

PATTERN SORT

Complete the **pattern sort** from Day 1 by using the Spelling Word Cards. Point out the different prefixes. Partners should compare and check their sorts. Have them record their sorts in their word study notebooks.

DAY 3

Word Meanings

Have students copy the three analogies below into their word study notebooks. Say the sentences aloud. Then ask students to fill in the blanks with a spelling word.

1. *Incorrect* is to *mistaken* as _____ is to *cheap*. (inexpensive)

2. *Disable* is to *enable* as _____ is to *right*. (incorrect)

3. *Prewash* is to *clothes* as _____ is to *food*. (preheats)

Challenge students to create analogies for their other spelling, review, or challenge words. Encourage them to use synonyms and antonyms. Have students share their analogies with a partner.

See Phonics/Spelling Reproducibles pp. 133–138.

SPEED SORT

Have partners do a **speed sort** to see who is fastest and then compare and discuss their sorts. Then have them do a word hunt in this week's readings to find words with prefixes. Ask them to record the words in their word study notebooks.

DAY 4

Proofread and Write

Write these sentences on the board. Have students circle and correct each misspelled word. Have them use a print or a digital dictionary to check and correct their spellings.

1. Don't misjuge the amount of detergent to use, or you could disscolor the clothes. (misjudge, discolor)

2. Neil told Jana to disconect the incorreckt cord. (disconnect, incorrect)

3. You will not be able to preewash the clothes if you disabel the machine. (prewash, disable)

4. Since she has never been dishonnest, you have no reason to misstrust her. (dishonest, mistrust)

Error Correction When spelling words with prefixes, students may pay special attention to the spelling of the prefix and misspell the base word. Remind students to pay attention to both parts of the word.

BLIND SORT

Have partners do a **blind sort**: one reads a Spelling Word Card; the other tells under which prefix it belongs. Then have partners use one set of word cards to play Concentration. Have them match words with the same prefix.

DAY 5

Assess

Use the Dictation Sentences for the posttest. Have students list the misspelled words in their word study notebooks. Look for students' use of these words in their writings.

Dictation Sentences

1. Soak it in water to <u>prewash</u> it.
2. We had to <u>disable</u> the machine.
3. The sun can <u>discolor</u> clothes.
4. She admitted she was <u>mistaken</u>.
5. Mom <u>preheats</u> the oven before baking.
6. People seem to <u>mistrust</u> him.
7. The answer was <u>incorrect</u>.
8. They can <u>disconnect</u> the wires.
9. I saw a <u>preview</u> of the movie.
10. It's unfair to <u>prejudge</u> people.
11. Don't <u>misjudge</u> her strength.
12. I cannot bear this <u>discomfort</u>.
13. Quickly <u>dismount</u> the horse.
14. They <u>misunderstand</u> her actions.
15. James will not <u>disobey</u> the rules.
16. He regretted being <u>dishonest</u>.
17. Segregation laws are an example of <u>injustice</u>.
18. They <u>disapprove</u> of video games.
19. The meal was <u>inexpensive</u>.
20. Our plans are still <u>indefinite</u>.

Have students self-correct their tests.

Build Vocabulary

OBJECTIVES

CCSS Use context (e.g., cause/effect relationships and comparisons in text) as a clue to the meaning of a word or phrase. **L.5.4a**

CCSS Use the relationship between particular words (e.g., synonyms, antonyms, homographs) to better understand each of the words. **L.5.5c**

Expand vocabulary by adding inflectional endings and suffixes.

Vocabulary Words

atmosphere	noticeably
decays	receding
gradual	stability
impact	variations

Go Digital

Vocabulary

Vocabulary Activities

DAY 1

Connect to Words

Practice this week's vocabulary.

1. Describe the **atmosphere**.
2. Which **decays** faster: fruit or a tree trunk? Why?
3. What **gradual** change has happened around you?
4. Who has had an **impact** on you? How?
5. When has your appearance changed **noticeably**?
6. When would floodwaters begin **receding**?
7. What are some ways you can add **stability** to your life?
8. Describe **variations** in land from season to season.

DAY 2

Expand Vocabulary

Help students generate different forms of this week's words by adding, changing, or removing inflectional endings.

→ Draw a four-column chart on the board. Write *receding* in the last column. Then write *recede*, *recedes*, and *receded* in the first three columns. Read aloud the words with students.

→ Have students share sentences using each form of *receding*.

→ Students should add to the chart for *decays*, then share sentences using the different forms of the words.

→ Have students copy the chart in their word study notebooks.

BUILD MORE VOCABULARY

COLLABORATE

ACADEMIC VOCABULARY

→ Display *consume, temporary*, and *occurring*.

→ Define the words and discuss their meanings with students.

→ Write *consumer* under *consume*. Have partners write other words with the same root and define them. Then have partners ask and answer questions using the words.

→ Repeat with *temporary* and *occurring*.

PREFIXES AND SUFFIXES *Review*

Remind students to look for prefixes and suffixes to help them figure out the meanings of unknown words.

→ Write *unexpectedly*. Explain that the base word is *expected*, and elicit how the prefix *un-* ("not") and the suffix *-ly* ("in a way") change the base word's meaning.

→ Have partners write a sentence with *unexpectedly*.

→ Have students write the word and their sentences in their word study notebooks.

DAY 3

Reinforce the Words

Review this week's vocabulary words. Have students orally complete each sentence stem.

1. Beyond Earth's <u>atmosphere</u> is _____.

2. Fruit <u>decays</u> after _____.

3. One thing <u>noticeably</u> different about me is _____.

4. The clouds began <u>receding</u> after _____.

5. I like <u>stability</u> in _____.

6. Cici observed <u>variations</u> in the _____.

Display the previous week's vocabulary: *assume, guarantee, nominate, obviously, sympathy, weakling*. Have partners ask and answer questions for each word.

DAY 4

Connect to Writing

→ Have students write sentences in their word study notebooks using this week's vocabulary.

→ Tell them to write sentences that provide word information they learned from this week's readings.

→ **ELL** Provide the Day 3 sentence stems 1–6 for students needing extra support.

Write About Vocabulary Have students write something they learned from this week's words in their word study notebooks. For example, they might write about the layers of the *atmosphere* or about the *impact* that different people can have on one's life.

DAY 5

Word Squares

Ask students to create Word Squares for each vocabulary word.

→ In the first square, students write the word (e.g., *atmosphere*).

→ In the second square, students write their own definition of the word and any related words, such as synonyms (e.g., *air, sky, heavens, gases*).

→ In the third square, students draw a simple illustration that will help them remember the word (e.g., drawing of Earth with air and clouds above it and outer space beyond).

→ In the fourth square, students write nonexamples, including antonyms for the word(e.g., *land, ocean, river*).

Have partners discuss their squares.

CONTEXT CLUES

Remind students to look for paragraph clues to help figure out the meanings of unfamiliar words.

→ Display **Your Turn Practice Book pages 223–224.** Model using paragraph clues to figure out the meaning of the word *invasive* in the first paragraph on page 224.

→ Have students complete page 227.

→ Partners can confirm meanings in a print or an online dictionary.

SHADES OF MEANING

Help students generate words related to *gradual*. Draw a synonym/antonym scale.

→ Have small groups use a thesaurus to find at least two synonyms and two antonyms for the word.

→ Ask groups to write the words on the scale in order from most to least. Have groups share their scales with the class and agree on the best scale.

→ Ask groups to copy the best scale in their word study notebooks.

MORPHOLOGY

Use *noticeably* as a springboard to learn more words. Draw a word web. Write *noticeably* in the center.

→ In the outer circles, elicit and write words that share the same root, such as *noticeable* and *notice*.

→ Review the meanings of the new words. Have students create a sentence for each one.

→ Have partners write the words and example sentences in their word study notebooks.

Approaching Level

Lexile 830
TextEvaluator™ 38

OBJECTIVES

CCSS Explain the relationships or interactions between two or more individuals, events, ideas, or concepts in a historical, scientific, or technical text based on specific information in the text. **RI.5.3**

CCSS Read on-level prose and poetry orally with accuracy, appropriate rate, and expression on successive readings. **RF.5.4b**

ACADEMIC LANGUAGE
- expository text, compare, contrast, ask and answer questions
- Cognates: *texto expositivo, comparar, contrastar*

Leveled Reader:
Ocean Threats

Before Reading

Preview and Predict

→ Read the Essential Question with students.

→ Have students preview the title, table of contents, and first page of *Ocean Threats*. Students should predict what they think the selection will be about. Encourage them to confirm or revise their predictions as they read.

Review Genre: Expository Text

Tell students that this selection is expository text. Expository text provides facts, details, examples, and explanations about a topic. The information is often organized into chapters with titles or sections with headings. Graphs, photographs, and captions may also be included. Have students identify features of expository text in *Ocean Threats*.

During Reading

Close Reading

Note Taking: Ask students to use their graphic organizer as they read.

Pages 2–3 *How are species of algae different?* (Different species vary in size. Many algae are harmless, but others are deadly.) *Why are scientists worried about algal blooms?* (They are larger, are happening more often, and are lasting longer.)

Pages 4–7 *How are algae different from plants?* (Algae don't have roots, stems, and leaves.) *Summarize the information in the text to answer the question in the chapter title on page 4: "What Are Algae?"* (Algae are organisms mostly found in water but also on land. They supply food for other organisms.) *How does the amount of algae differ with changes in the environment?* (When temperatures rise, algae increase.)

Pages 8–11 *Summarize information in the text in order to answer the question in the chapter title on page 8: "What Causes Algal Blooms?"* (a rise in CO_2 levels in the atmosphere from volcanic eruptions and the burning of fossil fuels, nutrient-rich ocean water, warm temperatures)

Go Digital

Leveled Readers

Use Graphic Organizer

What does gradual *mean? What clues help you figure out the meaning?* (*Gradual* means slowly. The word *rapidly* has the opposite meaning.)

Pages 12–15 *Contrast the different effects of algal blooms.* (Some blooms simply discolor water and are harmless. Others are harmful and cause health problems.) *What clue in the first paragraph on page 15 helps you figure out the meaning of* decay? (The word *dead* is a clue.)

Pages 16–17 *Turn to a partner and paraphrase the conclusion.* (While algal blooms are natural, changes in the environment have resulted in an increase that is harmful.) *Why might caring for the environment help?* (It might limit more harmful algal blooms.)

After Reading

Respond to Reading Revisit the Essential Question and ask students to complete the Text Evidence Questions on page 18.

✎ Analytical Writing | Write About Reading Check that students have written an accurate description of water before and during an algal bloom. Make sure they have included details from the text.

Fluency: Rate

Model Model reading page 5 with an appropriate rate. Next, read the passage aloud and have students read along with you.

Apply Have students practice reading with partners.

PAIRED READ

"Floating Trash"

Make Connections: Write About It ✎ Analytical Writing

Before reading, ask students to note that the genre of this text is also expository text. Then discuss the Essential Question. After reading, ask students to write connections between *Ocean Threats* and "Floating Trash."

Leveled Reader

🧪 FOCUS ON SCIENCE

Students can extend their knowledge of algal blooms by completing the research activity on page 24. **STEM**

Literature Circles

Ask students to conduct a literature circle using the Thinkmark questions to guide the discussion. You may wish to have a whole-class discussion, using information in both selections in the Leveled Reader, about how changes in the environment affect living things.

Level Up

Level-up lessons available online.

IF students read the **Approaching Level** fluently and answered the questions

THEN pair them with students who have proficiently read the **On Level** and have students

- echo-read the **On Level** main selection.
- identify three traits of expository text.

A C T Access Complex Text

The **On Level** challenges students by including more **domain-specific words** and **complex sentence structures**.

→ Approaching Level

Word Study/Decoding

TIER 2

REVIEW WORDS WITH PREFIXES

 OBJECTIVES

Know and apply grade-level phonics and word analysis skills in decoding words. Use combined knowledge of all letter-sound correspondences, syllabication patterns, and morphology (e.g., roots and affixes) to read accurately unfamiliar multisyllabic words in context and out of context. **RF.5.3a**

Decode words with prefixes.

 I Do Review with students that a prefix is a group of letters added to the beginning of a word that changes that word's meaning. Write the verbs *place* and *view* on the board and review their meanings. Then add the prefix *mis-* to *place* and the prefix *pre-* to *view* to create new words: *misplace, preview*. Explain how the meaning of each prefix ("wrong," "before") changes the meaning of the original word.

 We Do Write the words *miscount* and *precook* on the board. Read the words aloud and underline each prefix. Tell what each word means, emphasizing the meaning of the prefix. Then write these words on the board: *misuse, predate*. Guide students to identify each prefix and use its meaning to determine the meaning of each word.

 You Do Add the following examples to the board: *misbehave, prewash*. Have students identify each prefix, tell its meaning, and give the meaning of each word.

TIER 2

BUILD WORDS WITH PREFIXES

 OBJECTIVES

Know and apply grade-level phonics and word analysis skills in decoding words. Use combined knowledge of all letter-sound correspondences, syllabication patterns, and morphology (e.g., roots and affixes) to read accurately unfamiliar multisyllabic words in context and out of context. **RF.5.3a**

Build words with prefixes.

 I Do Display the **Word-Building Cards** *dis, pre, mis,* and *in* and write the words *active, lead, view,* and *like* on the board. Model reading each prefix and word aloud.

 We Do Have students chorally read each prefix and word. Work with students to combine the Word-Building Cards with words to form longer words. Have students chorally read the words *dislike, preview, mislead,* and *inactive*. Guide students to use the meanings of the prefixes to determine the meanings of the words.

 You Do Write other words on the board, such as *correct, plan, match,* and *appear*. Have partners add the Word-Building Card prefixes to these words to make longer words. Then have students share the words they built and identify their meanings.

PRACTICE WORDS WITH PREFIXES

OBJECTIVES

(CCSS) Know and apply grade-level phonics and word analysis skills in decoding words. Use combined knowledge of all letter-sound correspondences, syllabication patterns, and morphology (e.g., roots and affixes) to read accurately unfamiliar multisyllabic words in context and out of context. **RF.5.3a**

Practice words with prefixes.

 I Do Write the words *imbalance, disable,* and *incomplete* on the board. Read the words aloud, identify each prefix and its meaning, and give the meaning of each word.

 We Do Write the words *immature, disappoint,* and *insincere* on the board. Help students identify and define each prefix and then use this information to determine the meaning of each word.

 You Do To provide additional practice, write the following words on the board. Read aloud the first word, identify the prefix, and give the word's meaning.

disagree	inaction	misnumber
incapable	disapprove	preorder
prejudge	irregular	disconnect
preseason	impossible	misunderstand

Then have students read the remaining words aloud. Ask them to identify each prefix and give the meaning of each word.

Afterward, point to the words in the list in random order for students to read chorally.

ELL **ENGLISH LANGUAGE LEARNERS**

For the **ELLs** who need **phonics, decoding,** and **fluency** practice, use scaffolding methods as necessary to ensure students understand the meaning of the words. Refer to the **Language Transfers Handbook** for phonics elements that may not transfer in students' native languages.

Approaching Level
Vocabulary

REVIEW HIGH-FREQUENCY WORDS

TIER 2

OBJECTIVES

 Acquire and use accurately grade-appropriate general academic and domain-specific words and phrases, including those that signal contrast, addition, and other logical relationships (e.g., *however, although, nevertheless, similarly, moreover, in addition*). **L.5.6**

 I Do Use **High-Frequency Word Cards** 181–190. Display one word at a time, following the routine:

Display the word. Read the word. Then spell the word.

 We Do Ask students to state the word and spell the word with you. Model using the word in a sentence and have students repeat after you.

 You Do Display the word. Ask students to say the word then spell it. When completed, quickly flip through the word card set as students chorally read the words. Provide opportunities for students to use the words in speaking and writing. For example, provide sentence starters such as *I am ___ than ____*. Ask students to write each word in their Writer's Notebook.

REVIEW VOCABULARY WORDS

TIER 2

OBJECTIVES

Acquire and use accurately grade-appropriate general academic and domain-specific words and phrases, including those that signal contrast, addition, and other logical relationships (e.g., *however, although, nevertheless, similarly, moreover, in addition*). **L.5.6**

 I Do Display each **Visual Vocabulary Card** and state the word. Explain how the photograph illustrates the word. State the example sentence and repeat the word.

 We Do Point to the word on the card and read the word with students. Ask them to repeat the word. Engage students in structured partner talk about the image as prompted on the back of the vocabulary card.

 You Do Display each visual in random order, hiding the word. Have students match the definitions and context sentences of the words to the visuals displayed.

UNDERSTAND VOCABULARY WORDS

OBJECTIVES
CCSS Acquire and use accurately grade-appropriate general academic and domain-specific words and phrases, including those that signal contrast, addition, and other logical relationships (e.g., *however, although, nevertheless, similarly, moreover, in addition*).
L.5.6

I Do Display the *atmosphere* **Visual Vocabulary Card** and ask: *Is oxygen or soil part of the* atmosphere? Explain that oxygen is part of the atmosphere because the atmosphere is made up of gases.

We Do Ask these questions. Help students explain their answers.

→ Is something that *decays* rotting or thriving?

→ Which changes you more *noticeably*, getting a short haircut or wearing a new t-shirt?

→ Which is *receding*, the tide going out or the tide coming in?

You Do Have pairs respond to these questions and explain their answers.

→ Does a schedule or the weather have more *stability*?

→ Which has more *variations* in color, a door or the sky?

→ Is a sunrise or a clap of thunder more *gradual*?

→ What sort of *impact* do pets have on your life?

CONTEXT CLUES

OBJECTIVES
CCSS Determine or clarify the meaning of unknown and multiple-meaning words and phrases based on *grade 5 reading and content*, choosing flexibly from a range of strategies. Use context (e.g., cause/effect relationships and comparisons in text) as a clue to the meaning of a word or phrase.
L.5.4a

I Do Display the Comprehension and Fluency passage on **Approaching Reproducibles** pages 223–224. Read aloud the first paragraph on page 223. Point to the word *overrun*. Tell students that they can use context clues within the paragraph to determine its meaning.

Think Aloud In the sentence before, I see the word *floods*. This context clue helps me understand that *overrun* must mean something similar, such as "overflow."

We Do Ask students to point to the word *habitats* in the second paragraph on page 223. Discuss how the phrase *nowhere to live* in this paragraph points to the meaning of *habitats*: "places where plants or animals live and grow."

You Do Have students use context clues to determine the meanings of *detrimental* and *pesticides* (page 223, paragraph 3).

Approaching Level

Comprehension

FLUENCY

 TIER 2

 OBJECTIVES
Read on-level prose and poetry orally with accuracy, appropriate rate, and expression on successive readings. **RF.5.4b**

Read fluently, varying rate as necessary for comprehension.

 I Do Explain that good readers vary their reading rate, slowing down to read important or challenging information. Read the first two paragraphs of the Comprehension and Fluency passage on **Approaching Reproducibles** pages 223–224. Tell students to monitor the speed at which you read.

 We Do Read the rest of the page aloud. Have students repeat each sentence after you, matching your rate. Explain that you monitored your rate, slowing down when you read more difficult text to ensure that you also read accurately.

 You Do Have partners take turns reading sentences from the Comprehension and Fluency passage. Remind them to focus on their rate. Listen in and provide corrective feedback as needed by modeling proper fluency.

IDENTIFY DIFFERENCES

TIER 2

OBJECTIVES
Explain the relationships or interactions between two or more individuals, events, ideas, or concepts in a historical, scientific, or technical text based on specific information in the text. **RI.5.3**

 I Do Read the first three paragraphs of the Comprehension and Fluency passage on **Approaching Reproducibles** pages 223–224. Write *"The Mississippi River is made of fresh water."* Then write *"The Gulf is made of salt water."* Point out that these two sentences demonstrate a contrast. They show how the two bodies of water are different.

 We Do Read the third and fourth paragraphs of the Comprehension and Fluency passage. Ask: *How did the dangers faced by the fish in the Gulf of Mexico and the fish in the Mississippi River differ?* Guide students to understand that the difference between the dangers demonstrates another contrast that is explored in the text.

 You Do Have students read the rest of the passage. After each paragraph, they should write down any examples of when two things are contrasted.

REVIEW TEXT STRUCTURE: COMPARE AND CONTRAST

 I Do Remind students that an author may organize a text to show how two topics or ideas are similar or different. Tell them to look for words such as *however, on the other hand,* and *just as* to determine if a writer is using a compare-and-contrast structure.

 We Do Chorally read the first two paragraphs of the Comprehension and Fluency passage on **Approaching Reproducibles** pages 223–224. Model using the signal words *just as* to identify a comparison in the last sentence of the second paragraph: *floods can hurt fish just as they harm animals that live on land.* Then work with students to identify comparisons or contrasts in each paragraph in the passage.

 You Do Have students use the comparisons and contrasts in each paragraph to summarize the impact of floods on wildlife.

SELF-SELECTED READING

Read Independently

Have students choose an expository nonfiction book for sustained silent reading. Remind students that:

→ writers use the compare-and-contrast text structure to tell how things are alike and different.

→ asking and answering questions can help them better understand and remember what they have read.

Read Purposefully

Have students record comparisons and contrasts on Graphic Organizer 67 as they read independently. After they finish, students can conduct a Book Talk about what they read.

→ Students should share their organizers and the most interesting similarity or difference they identified.

→ They should also tell the group any questions they asked themselves and how they answered them.

→ On Level

Lexile 950
TextEvaluator™ 48

ACADEMIC LANGUAGE

• *expository text, compare, contrast, ask and answer questions*

• Cognates: *texto expositivo, comparar, contrastar*

Leveled Reader:
Ocean Threats

Go Digital

Leveled Readers

Before Reading

Preview and Predict

→ Read the Essential Question with students.

→ Have students preview the title, table of contents, and first page of *Ocean Threats*. Students should predict what they think the selection will be about. Encourage them to confirm or revise their predictions as they continue reading.

Review Genre: Expository Text

Tell students that this selection is expository text. Expository text provides facts, details, examples, and explanations about a topic. The information is often organized into chapters with titles or sections with headings. Graphs, photographs, and captions may also be included. Have students identify features of expository text in *Ocean Threats*.

During Reading

Close Reading

Note Taking: Ask students to use their graphic organizer as they read.

Pages 2–3 *How are all algae the same? How are they different?* (They are all plant-like organisms found throughout the planet. Some are harmless, while others can be deadly.) *What does* favorable *on page 3 mean? What clues help you figure out the meaning?* (*Favorable* means "positive." The next sentence contains the comparison phrase *too good*.)

Pages 4–7 *Turn to a partner and summarize information in the text to answer the question in the chapter title on page 4: "What Are Algae?"* (Algae are non-plant organisms mostly found in water but also found on land. They rely on photosynthesis to create their food.) *How are algae different during normal times and when there is instability in the environment?* (During normal times we don't notice them, but when there is instability they produce a noticeable algal bloom. Water becomes discolored.) *What does* vast *mean? What clues help you figure out the meaning?* (*Vast* means "huge." *Abnormally large* and *can be seen from satellites* are clues.)

Use Graphic Organizer

Pages 8–11 *Compare and contrast the effects of natural and human activity on algal blooms.* (Both can cause algal blooms to increase, but human activity may make them occur more frequently and severely.)

Pages 12–15 *Turn to a partner and form a question based on the chapter title: "Why Should We Be Concerned?"* (What is a health risk of algal blooms?) *Answer your question.* (Bacteria can cause diseases.) *How do algae cause a dead zone?* (Lots of algae consume large levels of oxygen, which causes low levels of oxygen in the water, which in turn causes fish to leave.)

Pages 16–17 *Contrast the ways that small and large changes affect an ecosystem.* (Small changes won't have much effect, but large changes create an imbalance in population numbers that has harmful effects.)

After Reading

Respond to Reading Revisit the Essential Question and ask students to complete the Text Evidence Questions on page 18.

Write About Reading *(Analytical Writing)* Check that students have correctly compared the water before and during an algal bloom using details.

Fluency: Rate

Model Model reading page 5 with an appropriate rate. Next, read the passage aloud and have students read along with you.

Apply Have students practice reading the passage with partners.

PAIRED READ

"Floating Trash"

Make Connections:
Write About It *(Analytical Writing)*

Before reading, ask students to note that the genre of this text is also expository text. Then discuss the Essential Question. After reading, ask students to write connections between *Ocean Threats* and "Floating Trash."

Leveled Reader

FOCUS ON SCIENCE

Students can extend their knowledge of algal blooms and their impact by completing the research activity on page 24. **STEM**

Literature Circles

Ask students to conduct a literature circle using the Thinkmark questions to guide the discussion. You may wish to have a whole-class discussion, using information in both selections in the Leveled Reader, about how changes in the environment affect living things.

Level Up

Level-up lessons available online.

IF students read the On Level fluently and answered the questions

THEN pair them with students who have proficiently read the Beyond Level and have students

• partner-read the Beyond Level main selection.

• identify three comparisons in the text.

A C T Access Complex Text

The Beyond Level challenges students by including more **domain-specific words** and **complex sentence structures**.

On Level

Vocabulary

REVIEW VOCABULARY WORDS

 OBJECTIVES
Demonstrate understanding of figurative language, word relationships, and nuances in word meanings. Use the relationship between particular words (e.g., synonyms, antonyms, homographs) to better understand each of the words. **L.5.5c**

 I Do Use the **Visual Vocabulary Cards** to review the key selection words *atmosphere, decays, noticeably, receding, stability,* and *variations*. Point to each word, read it aloud, and have students repeat it.

 We Do Read aloud the word set. Help students identify the word in each set that does not belong and tell why.

atmosphere, ground, gases

decays, rots, thrives

noticeably, barely, visibly

 You Do Have students work in pairs to identify the word in each set that does not belong and tell why.

receding, withdrawing, advancing

stability, steadiness, ability

variations, fluctuations, similarities

CONTEXT CLUES

 OBJECTIVES
Determine or clarify the meaning of unknown and multiple-meaning words and phrases based on *grade 5 reading and content*, choosing flexibly from a range of strategies. Use context (e.g., cause/effect relationships and comparisons in text) as a clue to the meaning of a word or phrase. **L.5.4a**

 I Do Remind students they can often figure out the meaning of an unknown or multiple-meaning word by looking for context clues. Use the Comprehension and Fluency passage on **Your Turn Practice Book** pages 223–224 to model.

Think Aloud I want to determine what the word *overrun* means in the first paragraph. When I read the second sentence, I see the word *floods*. I think that *floods* and *overrun* have similar meanings.

 We Do Have students read paragraph 2 on page 223. Help students find the meaning of *habitats* by pointing out context clues such as *nowhere to live*.

 You Do Have pairs use context clues to determine the meanings of *detrimental, pesticides* (page 223, paragraph 3), *invasive* (page 224, paragraph 1), and *spawn* (page 224, paragraph 4).

Comprehension

REVIEW TEXT STRUCTURE: COMPARE AND CONTRAST

OBJECTIVES

CCSS Explain the relationships or interactions between two or more individuals, events, ideas, or concepts in a historical, scientific, or technical text based on specific information in the text. **RI.5.3**

 I Do Remind students that writers may use a compare-and-contrast text structure to show how topics or ideas are alike and different. Signal words such as *however, on the other hand,* and *just as* can help them recognize this text structure.

 We Do Have a volunteer read the first paragraph of the Comprehension and Fluency passage on **Your Turn Practice Book** pages 223–224. Model using the signal words *just as* to identify a comparison in the last sentence: *"floods can hurt fish populations just as they harm many animals that live on land."*

 You Do Have partners identify comparisons and contrasts in each paragraph in the rest of the passage. Then have them summarize what the similarities and differences they identified show about the impact of floods on wildlife.

SELF-SELECTED READING

OBJECTIVES

CCSS Explain the relationships or interactions between two or more individuals, events, ideas, or concepts in a historical, scientific, or technical text based on specific information in the text. **RI.5.3**

Ask and answer questions to increase understanding of a text.

Read Independently

Have students choose an expository nonfiction book for sustained silent reading.

→ Before they read, have students preview the book, reading the title and viewing the front cover.

→ As students read, remind them to ask and answer questions to better understand and remember the text and identify its main ideas.

Read Purposefully

Encourage students to select books about a variety of topics.

→ As students read, have them complete Graphic Organizer 67 with similarities and differences they identify between ideas in the text.

→ They can use the organizer to help them summarize the text's overall message about the topic.

→ Ask students to share the most interesting fact they learned from the book.

→ # Beyond Level

Lexile 990
TextEvaluator™ 48

OBJECTIVES

CCSS Explain the relationships or interactions between two or more individuals, events, ideas, or concepts in a historical, scientific, or technical text based on specific information in the text. **RI.5.3**

CCSS Read on-level prose and poetry orally with accuracy, appropriate rate, and expression on successive readings. **RF.5.4b**

ACADEMIC LANGUAGE

• *expository text, compare, contrast, ask and answer questions*

• Cognates: *texto expositivo, comparar, contrastar*

Leveled Reader: *Ocean Threats*

Go Digital

Before Reading

Preview and Predict

→ Have students read the Essential Question.

→ Have students preview the title, table of contents, and first page of *Ocean Threats*. Then have them skim the text for text features and predict what they think the selection will be about. Encourage them to confirm or revise their predictions as they continue reading.

Review Genre: Expository Text

Tell students that this selection is expository text. Expository text provides facts, details, examples, and explanations about a topic. The information is often organized into chapters with titles or sections with headings. Graphs, photographs, and captions may also be included. Have students identify features of expository text in *Ocean Threats*.

Leveled Readers

During Reading

Close Reading

Note Taking: Ask students to use their graphic organizer as they read.

Pages 2–3 *What does* toxic *mean? What clues help you figure out the meaning?* ("poisonous;" *threaten animal and human health* and *nothing else can live*) *Summarize the problem identified in the introduction.* (Environmental changes cause bigger and more frequent algal blooms, which may have a serious impact on the ecology of our waterways.)

Pages 4–7 *Summarize the text to answer the question in the Chapter 1 title.* (Algae are simple, mostly aquatic organisms of different sizes. They are primary producers in the food web and use photosynthesis to make food.) *Contrast the difference in algal populations during stable and unstable times in an ecosystem.* (When the ecosystem is stable, we don't notice algae, but when the ecosystem is out of balance, the algae increase and create noticeable algal blooms that discolor the water.)

Pages 8–11 *What natural and human activities cause an increase in CO_2 in the environment, which in turns causes algal blooms?* (volcanic eruptions, burning fossil fuels, clearing forests)

Use Graphic Organizer

What are elements? *What clues on page 11 help you answer?* (Elements cause plants to grow. The text gives examples, such as nitrogen and phosphorous.)

Pages 12–15 *Turn to a partner and answer the question in the Chapter 3 title.* (We should be concerned about the health risks and the marine dead zones caused by algae.) *Describe how dust storms in the Moroccan desert can lead to cholera.* (Storms dump iron into the sea, which causes the growth of a dangerous bacteria, which in turn triggers the disease.)

Pages 16–17 *Contrast the ways that small and large changes affect an ecosystem.* (Small changes won't have much effect, but large changes create an imbalance that leads to explosions in populations, such as algal blooms, that can have harmful effects on the environment.)

After Reading

Respond to Reading Revisit the Essential Question and ask students to complete the Text Evidence Questions on page 18.

Analytical Writing Write About Reading Check that students have correctly described a lake or area of ocean before and after an algal bloom. Make sure they include details from the text.

Fluency: Rate

Model Model reading page 5 with an appropriate rate. Next, read the passage aloud and have students read along with you.

Apply Have students practice reading with partners.

PAIRED READ

Leveled Reader

"Floating Trash"

Make Connections:
Write About It Analytical Writing

Before reading, ask students to note that the genre of this text is also expository text. Then discuss the Essential Question. After reading, ask students to write connections between *Ocean Threats* and "Floating Trash."

 FOCUS ON SCIENCE

Students can extend their knowledge of algal blooms by completing the research activity on page 24. **STEM**

Literature Circles

Ask students to conduct a literature circle using the Thinkmark questions to guide the discussion. You may wish to have a whole-class discussion, using information from both selections in the Leveled Reader, about how changes in the environment affect living things.

Gifted and Talented

Synthesize Encourage students to investigate changes in the environment in their own area. For example, suggest that they focus on a body of water in their community. They can interview scientists, local authorities, or knowledgeable residents about changes in the environment that have had an effect on the plant and animal life in or near this body of water. Before the interview, have students write a series of questions they want to ask. Remind them to record the answers they obtain. Have them display their findings in a poster about environmental changes and their impact.

→ Beyond Level

Vocabulary

REVIEW DOMAIN-SPECIFIC WORDS

OBJECTIVES
 Acquire and use accurately grade-appropriate general academic and domain-specific words and phrases, including those that signal contrast, addition, and other logical relationships (e.g., *however, although, nevertheless, similarly, moreover, in addition*). **L.5.6**

 Model Use the **Visual Vocabulary Cards** to review the meaning of the words *gradual* and *impact*. Use each word in a science-related sentence.

Write the words *populations* and *pollutants* on the board and discuss the meanings with students. Then help students write sentences using these words.

 Apply Have students work in pairs to review the meanings of the words *endangered* and *toxic*. Then have partners write sentences using the words.

CONTEXT CLUES

OBJECTIVES
 Determine or clarify the meaning of unknown and multiple-meaning words and phrases based on *grade 5 reading and content*, choosing flexibly from a range of strategies. Use context (e.g., cause/effect relationships and comparisons in text) as a clue to the meaning of a word or phrase. **L.5.4a**

 Model Read aloud the first paragraph of the Comprehension and Fluency passage on **Beyond Reproducibles** pages 223–224.

Think Aloud When I read this paragraph, I want to know the meaning of *overrun*. I see the word *floods* in the fourth sentence of the same paragraph, which helps me determine that *overrun* has a similar meaning.

With students, read the second paragraph on page 223. Help them use the context clue *nowhere to live* to figure out the meaning of the word *habitats*.

 Apply Have pairs of students read the rest of the passage. Ask them to use context clues within the paragraphs to determine the meanings of the following words: *detrimental, pesticides* (page 223, paragraph 3), *invasive* (page 224, paragraph 1), and *spawn* (page 224, paragraph 4).

 Shades of Meaning Challenge students to use a thesaurus to find synonyms for *detrimental*. Have students list the synonyms they find and rank them from strongest to weakest shades of meaning. Ask them to explain why they ranked the words the way they did.

Comprehension

REVIEW TEXT STRUCTURE: COMPARE AND CONTRAST

OBJECTIVES

Explain the relationships or interactions between two or more individuals, events, ideas, or concepts in a historical, scientific, or technical text based on specific information in the text. **RI.5.3**

Model

Remind students that writers may use a compare-and-contrast text structure to show how topics or ideas are alike and different. Signal words such as *however, on the other hand,* and *just as* can help them recognize this text structure.

Have students read the second paragraph of the Comprehension and Fluency passage on **Beyond Reproducibles** pages 223–224. Ask questions to facilitate discussion, such as *How is the impact of a flood similar for fish and for animals on land?* Students should support their response with details from the selection.

Apply

Have students identify comparisons and contrasts in each paragraph in the rest of the passage as they independently fill in Graphic Organizer 67. Then have partners use their work to summarize the impact of floods on wildlife.

SELF-SELECTED READING

OBJECTIVES

Explain the relationships or interactions between two or more individuals, events, ideas, or concepts in a historical, scientific, or technical text based on specific information in the text. **RI.5.3**

Ask and answer questions to increase understanding of a text.

Read Independently

Have students choose an expository nonfiction book for sustained silent reading.

→ As students read, have them fill in Graphic Organizer 67 to compare and contrast information.

→ Remind them to ask and answer questions to confirm their understanding of the text and identify its main ideas.

Read Purposefully

Encourage students to keep a reading journal. Ask them to select books on a variety of different topics.

→ Students can write summaries of the books in their journals.

→ Ask students to share what they learned from the books with classmates.

Independent Study Challenge students to discuss how their books relate to the weekly theme of understanding our changing Earth. Have students use all of their reading materials to compare how changes in the environment affect living things.

→ English Language Learners

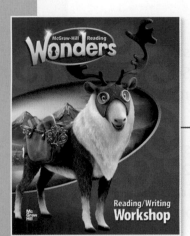

Reading/Writing Workshop

LANGUAGE OBJECTIVE

Compare and contrast text structure.

ACADEMIC LANGUAGE

• *compare, contrast, ask and answer questions, context clues*

• Cognates: *comparar, contrastar*

Shared Read
Forests on Fire

Go Digital

View "Forests on Fire"

Before Reading

Build Background

Read the Essential Question: *What changes in the environment affect living things?*

→ Explain the meaning of the Essential Question, including the vocabulary in the question: *The environment includes all of the natural things around you: the land, sea, and air.* Affect *means "to influence or act upon."*

→ **Model an answer:** *Changes in temperature, the amount of rain, and the amount of food available affect all living things.*

→ Ask students a question that ties the Essential Question to their own background knowledge: *Think of a change in the environment you have noticed. Think about how that change affected living things. Discuss your observations with a partner.* Call on several pairs.

During Reading

Interactive Question-Response

→ Ask questions that help students understand the meaning of the text after each paragraph.

→ Reinforce the meanings of key vocabulary.

→ Ask students questions that require them to use key vocabulary.

→ Reinforce strategies and skills of the week by modeling.

Page 339

Paragraph 1

Explain the term *endangered species* and have students repeat the words with you. *Is the red squirrel an endangered species?* (yes) *Why are the red squirrels in the zoo?* (The squirrels' home in the forest was destroyed by a big fire.)

Destructive and Productive

Paragraph 1

Explain and Model Compare and Contrast
Choral-read the paragraph. Point out that the word *like* signals a comparison, or similarity, between rainstorms and wildfires and *unlike* signals a contrast, or a difference.

Paragraph 2

Have students read the paragraph with a partner. Provide vocabulary support as needed. Have partners tell how wildfires and rainstorms are alike. (They are both destructive and terrifying, but also productive. They both allow new life to grow.)

Benefits of Naturally Occurring Wildfires

Explain and Model the Strategy *I can ask a question about this section. I know a benefit is something good. What benefits could a fire have? I will keep reading to answer my question.*

Paragraph 1

Is a naturally occurring wildfire caused by humans? (no) *A naturally occurring wildfire needs ____, ____, and ____.* (fuel, oxygen, a heat source)

Paragraph 2

Explain and Model Context Clues Model using the context clues "new plant life" and "grow" to help you figure out the meaning of the word *regenerate*.

Page 340

Have students share some benefits of forest fires with a partner. (Fire releases nutrients into the soil; Fire allows sunlight to reach the forest floor; New plant life will be better adapted to fire)

Stability and Diversity

Define *stability* and *diversity* and have students repeat the words with you.

Paragraph 1

Choral-read the paragraph. *How does fire promote stability?* (It destroys invasive species.)

Paragraph 2

How does fire promote diversity? (It ensures that there will be trees in different stages of development.)

Paragraph 3

In your own words, tell your partner how fire brings diverse animals to the forest. (Birds may find insects and seeds after a fire. Predators may follow the birds and other small animals.)

Page 341

The Human Factor

Paragraph 1

Did the government try to stop wildfires during the 20th century? (yes) *Was the impact of this policy positive or negative?* (negative) *Tell a partner what happened.* (A buildup of decayed plants provided more fuel to feed the fires.)

Paragraph 2

The government tries to manage wild fires in two ways. What are they? (Limit fires before they burn out of control. Set small fires to use up some of the natural fuel.)

Paragraph 3

Are fires caused by humans beneficial, or helpful? (no)

After Reading

Make Connections

→ Review the Essential Question.

→ Make text connections and have students complete **ELL Reproducibles** pages 223–225.

English Language Learners

Lexile 870
TextEvaluator 36

OBJECTIVES

Explain the relationships or interactions between two or more individuals, events, ideas, or concepts in a historical, scientific, or technical text based on specific information in the text. **RI.5.3**

Read on-level prose and poetry orally with accuracy, appropriate rate, and expression on successive readings. **RF.5.4b**

ACADEMIC LANGUAGE

- *expository text, compare, contrast, ask and answer questions*
- Cognates: *texto expositivo, comparar, contrastar*

Leveled Reader:
Ocean Threats

Before Reading

Preview and Predict

→ Read the Essential Question: *What changes in the environment affect living things?*

→ Refer to A Change in the Air: *What are some changes that take place in our environment?*

→ Preview *Ocean Threats* and "Floating Trash": *Our purpose for reading is to learn about how changes in the ocean can affect the environment.*

Vocabulary

Use the **Visual Vocabulary Cards** to pre-teach the ELL vocabulary: *availability, exposed, tainted, cope.* Use the routine found on the cards.

During Reading

Interactive Question-Response

Note Taking: Ask students to use the graphic organizer on **ELL Reproducibles** page 222. Use the questions below after each page is read with students. As you read, use the glossary definitions to define vocabulary in context and visuals to help students understand key vocabulary.

Pages 2–3 Use these frames to compare and contrast algae. *Some algae are tiny _____.* (plankton) *Some are huge _____.* (seaweeds) Point to the words *algal bloom* and have students repeat them after you. *A large population of algae is called _____.* (an algal bloom)

Pages 4–7 *Are we able to see algae in stable environments?* (no) *What happens when water environments become unstable?* (algae grows quickly) *What is a large algae bloom called?* (a super bloom)

Pages 8–11 *What three things does algae need to grow?* (nutrients, carbon dioxide, sunlight) *The title of this chapter is a question. With a partner, paraphrase the text to answer the question.* (Many changes in nature can cause algal blooms.)

Go Digital

Leveled Readers

Use Graphic Organizer

Pages 12–15 *How are people harmed by algal blooms?* (People can get sick if they eat seafood that has been exposed to an algal bloom.) *Algal blooms harm plants and animals, too. Explain how.* (They change the ecology of a body of water so other life dies out.)

Pages 16–17 Have students complete the sentence: *Algal blooms happen when there are too many ____, when there is too much ____, or when the temperature ____.* (nutrients, carbon dioxide, increases) *Is algae a natural part of the environment?* (yes)

After Reading

Respond to Reading Revisit the Essential Question and ask students to complete the Text Evidence Questions on page 18.

Write About Reading *Analytical Writing* Check that students have correctly compared the water before and during an algal bloom using details in the text.

Fluency: Rate

Model Model reading page 5 with appropriate rate. Next, read the passage aloud and have students read along with you.

Apply Have students practice reading with partners.

PAIRED READ

"Floating Trash"

Make Connections:
Write About It *Analytical Writing*

Before reading, point out that the genre of this text is also expository text and discuss the Essential Question. After reading, ask students to list connections between *Ocean Threats* and "Floating Trash."

Leveled Reader

FOCUS ON SCIENCE

Students can extend their knowledge of algal blooms by completing the research activity on page 24. **STEM**

Literature Circles

Ask students to conduct a literature circle using the Thinkmark questions to guide the discussion. You may wish to use both selections in the Leveled Reader to have a whole-class discussion about how changes in the environment affect living things.

Level Up

Level-up lessons available online.

IF students read the **ELL Level** fluently and answered the questions,

THEN pair them with students who have proficiently read **On Level** and have ELL students

• echo-read the **On Level** main selection.

• list words with which they have difficulty and discuss them with a partner.

A C T Access Complex Text

The **On Level** challenges students by including more **domain-specific words** and **complex sentence structures**.

English Language Learners
Vocabulary

PRETEACH VOCABULARY

 OBJECTIVES
Acquire and use accurately grade-appropriate general academic and domain-specific words and phrases, including those that signal contrast, addition, and other logical relationships. **L.5.6**

LANGUAGE OBJECTIVE
Use vocabulary words.

I Do Preteach vocabulary from "Forests on Fire," following the Vocabulary Routine found on the **Visual Vocabulary Cards** for the words *atmosphere, decays, gradual, impact, noticeably, receding, stability,* and *variations.*

We Do After completing the Vocabulary Routine for each word, point to the word on the Card and read the word with students. Ask them to repeat the word.

You Do Have students work in pairs to use two or more words in sentences. Then have each pair read the sentences aloud.

Beginning	Intermediate	Advanced/High
Help students write the sentences correctly and read them aloud.	Ask students to write longer sentences.	Challenge students to use more than one vocabulary word in each sentence.

REVIEW VOCABULARY

 OBJECTIVES
Acquire and use accurately grade-appropriate general academic and domain-specific words and phrases, including those that signal contrast, addition, and other logical relationships. **L.5.6**

LANGUAGE OBJECTIVE
Use vocabulary words.

I Do Review the previous week's vocabulary words over a few days. Read each word aloud, pointing to the word on the **Visual Vocabulary Card**. Have students repeat. Then follow the Vocabulary Routine on the back of each card.

We Do Choose a word and draw a picture of it. Have students suggest a caption for your picture that uses the vocabulary word.

You Do In pairs, have each student choose a word to illustrate. Have students switch illustrations and write a caption for the illustration they receive. Ask them to read the caption aloud.

Beginning	Intermediate	Advanced/High
Help students write the vocabulary word that describes the picture.	Have students write a short, complete sentence to describe the picture.	Challenge students to write a longer complete sentence to describe the picture.

CONTEXT CLUES

OBJECTIVES

Determine or clarify the meaning of unknown and multiple-meaning words and phrases based on grade 5 reading and content, choosing flexibly from a range of strategies. Use context (e.g., cause/effect relationships and comparisons in text) as a clue to the meaning of a word or phrase. **L.5.4a**

LANGUAGE OBJECTIVE

Use context clues.

I Do Read aloud the first paragraph of the Comprehension and Fluency passage on **ELL Reproducibles** pages 223–224, while students follow along. Summarize the paragraph. Point to the word *overrun*. Explain that context clues can help students figure out the meaning of the word.

Think Aloud I see a context clue that can help me figure out the meaning of *overrun*. It says that every few years, the river floods. When a river *overruns* its banks, it must mean about the same thing as *flood*.

We Do Have students point to the word *damage* in the second paragraph on page 223. Find the context clues for the word with students. Write the definition of the word on the board.

You Do In pairs, have students write a definition for *pesticides* in the third paragraph on page 223 using context clues.

Beginning	Intermediate	Advanced/High
Help students locate the words and context clues.	Ask students to locate and read aloud the context clues.	Have students explain how they used context clues to define the words.

ADDITIONAL VOCABULARY

OBJECTIVES

Acquire and use accurately grade-appropriate general academic and domain-specific words and phrases, including those that signal contrast, addition, and other logical relationships. **L.5.6**

LANGUAGE OBJECTIVE

Use academic vocabulary and high-frequency words.

I Do List some academic vocabulary and high-frequency words from "Forests on Fire": *destroyed, flames, force;* and *Ocean Threats*: *algae, environment, nutrients*. Define each word for students: Destroyed *means "ruined completely."*

We Do Model using the words for students in a sentence: *The bugs destroyed my garden. Wildfires destroyed the land.* Then provide sentence frames and complete them with students: *The land was destroyed by ____.*

You Do Have pairs make up their own sentences and share them with the class to complete them.

Beginning	Intermediate	Advanced/High
Provide sentence frames and help students correctly complete them.	Provide sentence starters, if necessary.	Have students define the words they used.

English Language Learners
Writing/Spelling

WRITING TRAIT: IDEAS

 OBJECTIVES
Write informative/explanatory texts to examine a topic and convey ideas and information clearly. Develop the topic with facts, definitions, concrete details, quotations, or other information and examples related to the topic. **W.5.2b**

LANGUAGE OBJECTIVE
Use details to support ideas.

 I Do Explain that good writers support their ideas with details. Details can include facts, quotations, and examples. Read the Expert Model aloud as students follow along and identify the details that support the topic—the benefits of wildfires.

 We Do Read aloud a passage from "Forests on Fire" as students follow along. Identify the topic. Then use a word web to generate details. Model sentences to describe the topic and details using the word web.

 You Do Have pairs write their own short paragraph, using the word web. They should include a topic sentence and a few sentences with supporting details that use adjectives. Edit each pair's writing. Then ask students to revise and check their details.

Beginning	Intermediate	Advanced/High
Have students copy the edited sentences.	Have students add more details to support the topic and edit for errors.	Have students expand on their topic and explain how the details support the main idea.

SPELL WORDS WITH PREFIXES

 OBJECTIVES
Spell grade-appropriate words correctly, consulting references as needed. **L.5.2e**

LANGUAGE OBJECTIVE
Spell words with prefixes.

 I Do Read aloud the Spelling Words on page T164, segmenting them into syllables and attaching a spelling to each sound. Point out the prefix in each word. Have students repeat the words.

 We Do Read the Dictation Sentences on page T165 aloud for students. With each sentence, read the underlined word slowly, segmenting it into syllables. Have students repeat after you and then write the word.

 You Do Display the words. Have students exchange their list with a partner to check the spelling and write the words correctly.

Beginning	Intermediate	Advanced/High
Help students copy the words with correct spelling and say them aloud.	After students have corrected their words, have pairs quiz each other.	Have students correct their words and discuss why some were challenging.

Grammar

ADJECTIVES

OBJECTIVES

CCSS Demonstrate command of the conventions of standard English grammar and usage when writing or speaking. **L.5.1**

LANGUAGE OBJECTIVE
Identify and use adjectives correctly.

Language Transfers Handbook

Speakers of Haitian Creole, Hmong, Spanish, Vietnamese, Cantonese, and Korean may place adjectives after nouns. Model correct placement of adjectives before nouns in additional examples, and have students repeat.

 I Do   Remind students that adjectives describe nouns and pronouns. They tell what kind, how many, or which one. Write: *The red ball bounced.* Underline the adjective that tells what kind. Write: *Ten balls bounced.* Underline the adjective that tells how many. Write: *That ball bounced.* Underline the adjective that tells which one.

We Do   Write the sentence frames below on the board. Have students suggest an adjective to complete each frame. Fill the sentence frames with students' responses. Identify whether the adjective tells what kind, how many, or which one. Then read the completed sentences aloud for students to repeat.

> _____ *coins are in my pocket.*
>
> *A* _____ *clown came to the party.*
>
> *A* _____ *bird was in the tree.*

 You Do   Brainstorm a list of adjectives with students. Have students work in pairs to write three sentences using adjectives. One sentence should use an adjective that tells what kind, one should use an adjective that tells how many, and one should use an adjective that tells which one.

Beginning	Intermediate	Advanced/High
Help students copy their sentences and underline the adjectives. Read the sentences aloud. Have students repeat.	Ask students to underline each adjective and indicate whether it tells what kind, how many, or which one.	Have students add an additional adjective to one or more of their sentences.

For extra support, have students complete the activities in the **Grammar Practice Reproducibles** during the week, using the routine below:

→ Explain the grammar skill.

→ Model the first activity in the Grammar Practice Reproducibles.

→ Have the whole group complete the next couple of activities, then do the rest with a partner.

→ Review the activities with correct answers.

PROGRESS MONITORING

Weekly Assessment

✔ **COMPREHENSION:**	✔ **VOCABULARY:**	✔ **WRITING:**
Text Structure: Compare and Contrast **RI.5.3**	Context Clues: Paragraph Clues **L.5.4a**	Writing About Text **RI.5.3, W.5.9b**

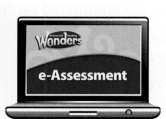

Assessment Includes

→ Performance Tasks

→ Approaching-Level Assessment online PDFs

Fluency Goal 129 to 149 words correct per minute (WCPM)

Accuracy Rate Goal 95% or higher

Administer oral reading fluency assessments using the following schedule:

→ **Weeks 1, 3, 5** Provide Approaching-Level students at least three oral reading fluency assessments during the unit.

→ **Weeks 2 and 4** Provide On-Level students at least two oral reading fluency assessments during the unit.

→ **Week 6** If necessary, provide Beyond-Level students an oral reading fluency assessment at this time.

Also Available: Selection Tests online PDFs

Go Digital! www.connected.mcgraw-hill.com

Using Assessment Results

✓ TESTED SKILLS	If ...	Then ...
COMPREHENSION	Students answer 0–6 multiple-choice items correctly ...	... assign Lessons 70–72 on Analyze Text Structure from the *Tier 2 Comprehension Intervention online PDFs.*
VOCABULARY	Students answer 0–6 multiple-choice items correctly ...	... assign Lesson 142 on Using Paragraph Context Clues from the *Tier 2 Vocabulary Intervention online PDFs.*
WRITING	Students score less than "3" on the constructed responses ...	... assign Lessons 70–72 on Analyze Text Structure and/or Write About Reading Lesson 200 from the *Tier 2 Comprehension Intervention online PDFs.*
	Students have a WCPM score of 120–128 ...	... assign a lesson from Section 1, 7, 8, 9, or 10 of the *Tier 2 Fluency Intervention online PDFs.*
	Students have a WCPM score of 0–119 ...	... assign a lesson from Section 2, 3, 4, 5, or 6 of the *Tier 2 Fluency Intervention online PDFs.*

Response to Intervention

Use the appropriate sections of the *Placement and Dignostic Assessment* as well as students' assessment results to designate students requiring:

TIER 2 **Intervention Online PDFs**

TIER 3 **WonderWorks Intervention Program**

Text Complexity Range for Grades 4–5

Lexile

740 _TextEvaluator_ 1010

23 51

TEACH AND MODEL

Reading/Writing Workshop

Wonders
McGraw-Hill Reading

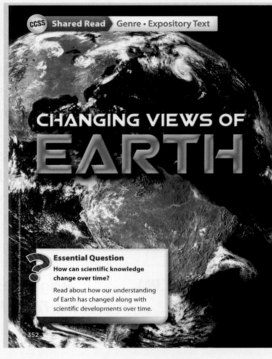

✔ Vocabulary

approximately

astronomical

calculation

criteria

diameter

evaluate

orbit

spheres

🔍 Close Reading of Complex Text

Shared Read "Changing Views of Earth," 352–359

Genre Expository Text

Lexile 910L

ETS _TextEvaluator_™ 56

Minilessons ✔ Tested Skills **CCSS**

✔ **Comprehension Strategy**	Ask and Answer Questions, T210–T211
✔ **Comprehension Skill**	Text Structure: Cause and Effect, T212–T213
✔ **Genre**	Expository Text, T214–T215
✔ **Vocabulary Strategy**	Greek Roots, T216–T217
✔ **Writing Traits**	Organization, T222–T223
Grammar Handbook	Adjectives That Compare, T226–T227

☞ **Go Digital**

www.connected.mcgraw-hill.com

APPLY WITH CLOSE READING

Complex Text

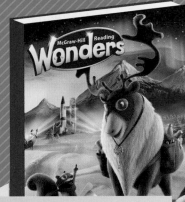

Literature Anthology

PAIRED READ

When Is a Planet Not a Planet?, 404–419
Genre Expository Text
Lexile 980L
ETS *TextEvaluator* 41

"New Moon," 422–423
Genre Science Fiction
Lexile 870L
ETS *TextEvaluator* 33

Differentiated Text

Leveled Readers   *Include Paired Reads*

APPROACHING
Lexile 700L
ETS *TextEvaluator* 26

ON LEVEL
Lexile 900L
ETS *TextEvaluator* 43

BEYOND
Lexile 970L
ETS *TextEvaluator* 46

ELL
Lexile 700L
ETS *TextEvaluator* 27

Extended Complex Text

Volcano: The Eruption and Healing of Mount St. Helens
Genre Expository Text
Lexile 830L
ETS *TextEvaluator* 31

Classroom Library

Arctic Lights, Arctic Nights
Genre Expository Text
Lexile 890L
ETS *TextEvaluator* 36

Classroom Library lessons available online.

TEACH AND MANAGE

How You Teach

INTRODUCE

Weekly Concept

Now We Know

Reading/Writing Workshop
348–349

TEACH

Close Reading
"Changing Views of Earth"

Minilessons

Ask and Answer Questions, Cause and Effect, Expository Text, Greek Roots, Writing Traits

Reading/Writing Workshop
352–361

APPLY

Close Reading

When Is a Planet Not a Planet?

"New Moon"

Literature Anthology
404–423

👉 **Go Digital**

| Interactive Whiteboard | Interactive Whiteboard | Mobile |

How Students Practice

WEEKLY CONTRACT

PDF Online

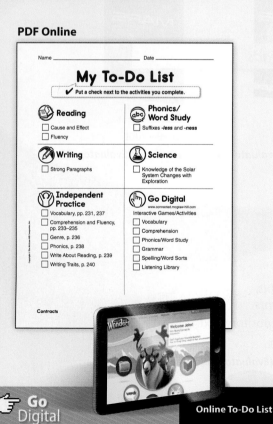

LEVELED PRACTICE AND ONLINE ACTIVITIES

Your Turn Practice Book
231–240

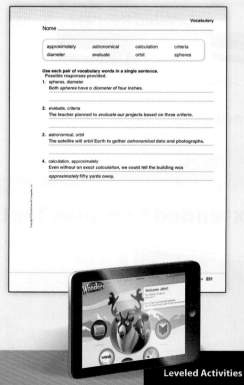

Leveled Readers

👉 **Go Digital**

| Online To-Do List | Leveled Activities | Writer's Workspace |

DIFFERENTIATE

SMALL GROUP INSTRUCTION

Leveled Readers

Mobile

INTEGRATE

Research and Inquiry
Summary, T220

Text Connections
Compare Changes, T221

Write About Reading
Analytical Writing Write an Analysis, T221

Online Research and Writing

ASSESS

Weekly Assessment
277–288

Online Assessment

LEVELED WORKSTATION CARDS

24

Seeing the Solar System

Knowledge about our solar system has changed over time. Sometimes, this scientific investigation has paralleled the scientific method, but at other times, it has not.

- Find one diagram of the solar system today. Find a second diagram showing how scientists thought the solar system

SCIENCE

8

Greek Roots

Knowing Greek roots can help you understand the meanings of English words that contain those roots.

- *Astro* is a Greek root meaning "star" and is the root of the word *astronomy*. Research other Greek roots and list five that you have learned about.

- Make a word web for each Greek root on your list. Include as many words as you can find.

- Combine your webs into a book of roots. Select one word each to illustrate. Label your drawing with the root, the word, and the definition.

Greek roots

You need
30 Minutes
> paper and pencil
> dictionary or Internet
> crayons or markers

PHONICS/WORD STUDY

Go Digital! www.connected.mcgraw-hill.com • Interactive Games and Activities • Grade 5
8

11

Organization: Strong Paragraphs

Read this paragraph from Isabel's narrative about one of her family's traditions.

A tradition in my family is to go to the park on the weekend. We ride our bikes to a park about a mile away. My younger brother's bike has training wheels. My brother and I play on the swings. We watch and laugh...

- Identify Isabel's topic sentence. State the main idea. Does each sentence support the main idea?

- Delete or revise any sentences that do not support Isabel's topic or the main idea.

WRITING

More Activities on back

11

Text Structure: Cause and Effect

A cause is an action or event that makes something happen. An effect happens as a result of the cause.

- Choose an informational text you have read this week.

- Identify causes and effects the author discusses. Use the graphic organizer to help you.

Cause	→	Effect

- Look for effects that in turn cause other events or problems to happen.

- Write a paragraph about the cause and effect process. How does this text structure help you understand information?

You need
30 Minutes
> informational text
> paper and pen or pencil

READING

Go Digital! www.connected.mcgraw-hill.com • Interactive Games and Activities • Grade 5
11

DEVELOPING READERS AND WRITERS

Write About Reading • Analytical Writing

Write to Sources and Research

Text Structure: Cause and Effect, T212–T213

Note Taking, T217B, T217S

Summarize, T217R

Cause and Effect, T217R

Make Connections: Essential Question, T217R, T217T, T221

Key Details, T217T

Research and Inquiry, T220

Analyze to Share an Opinion, T221

Comparing Texts, T233, T241, T245, T251

Predictive Writing, T217B

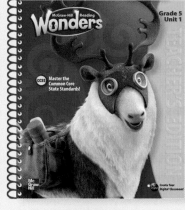
Teacher's Edition

Summarize, p. 421
Cause and Effect, p. 421
Literature Anthology

Leveled Readers
Comparing Texts
Cause and Effect

Cause and Effect, pp. 233–235
Genre, p. 236
Analyze to Share an Opinion, p. 239
Your Turn Practice Book

Go Digital
Interactive Whiteboard

Writing Process • Genre Writing

Informative Text
Research Report, T350–T355

Conferencing Routines
Teacher Conferences, T352
Peer Conferences, T353

Go Digital
Interactive Whiteboard

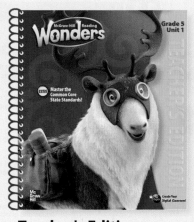
Teacher's Edition

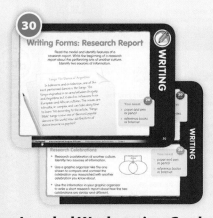
Leveled Workstation Card
Research Report, Card 30

Go Digital
Writer's Workspace
Informative Text:
Research Report
Writing Process
Multimedia Presentations

Writing Traits • **Write Every Day**

Writing Trait: Organization
Strong Paragraphs, T222–T223

Conferencing Routines
Teacher Conferences, T224
Peer Conferences, T225

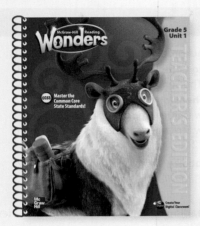

Teacher's Edition

Organization:
Strong Paragraphs,
pp. 360–361

Reading/Writing Workshop

Interactive Whiteboard

Leveled Workstation Card

Organization:
Strong
Paragraphs,
11

Your Turn Practice Book

Organization: Strong
Paragraphs, p. 240

Grammar and Spelling

Grammar
Adjectives That Compare,
T226–T227

Spelling
Suffixes -*less* and -*ness*,
T228–T229

Interactive Whiteboard

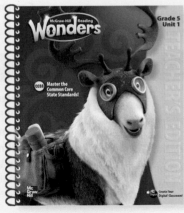

Teacher's Edition

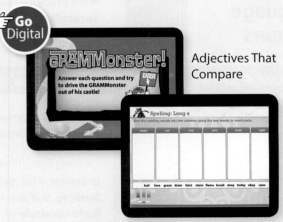

Adjectives That
Compare

Suffixes -*less*
and -*ness*
Word Sorts

Online Spelling and Grammar Games

SUGGESTED LESSON PLAN

✔ **TESTED SKILLS**

	DAY 1	DAY 2

READING

Whole Group

Teach, Model and Apply

Reading/Writing Workshop

Workshop

DAY 1

Build Background Now We Know, T202–T203
Listening Comprehension Interactive Read Aloud: "The Sun: Our Star," T204–T205
Comprehension
- Preview Genre: Expository Text, T214–T215
- Preview Strategy: Ask and Answer Questions, T210–T211

✔ **Vocabulary** Words in Context, T206–T207
Practice *Your Turn* 231

Close Reading of Complex Text "Changing Views of Earth," 352–355

DAY 2

✔ **Comprehension**
- Strategy: Ask and Answer Questions, T210–T211
- Skill: Cause and Effect, T212–T213
- Write About Reading ● *Analytical Writing*
- Genre: Expository Text, T214–T215

✔ **Vocabulary** Strategy: Greek Roots, T216–T217
Practice *Your Turn* 232–237

DIFFERENTIATED INSTRUCTION Choose across the week to meet your students' needs.

Small Group

Approaching Level

DAY 1
Leveled Reader *Mars,* T232–T233
Word Study/Decoding Review Suffixes, T234 **TIER 2**
Vocabulary
- Review High-Frequency Words, T236 **TIER 2**
- Understand Vocabulary Words, T237

DAY 2
Leveled Reader *Mars,* T232–T233
Vocabulary Review Vocabulary Words, T236 **TIER 2**
Comprehension
- Identify Causes, T238 **TIER 2**
- Review Cause and Effect, T239

On Level

DAY 1
Leveled Reader *Mars,* T240–T241
Vocabulary Review Vocabulary Words, T242

DAY 2
Leveled Reader *Mars,* T240–T241
Comprehension Review Cause and Effect, T243

Beyond Level

DAY 1
Leveled Reader *Mars,* T244–T245
Vocabulary Review Domain-Specific Words, T246

DAY 2
Leveled Reader *Mars,* T244–T245
Comprehension Review Cause and Effect, T247

English Language Learners

DAY 1
Shared Read "Changing Views of Earth," T248–T249
Word Study/Decoding Review Suffixes, T234
Vocabulary
- Preteach Vocabulary, T252
- Review High-Frequency Words, T236

DAY 2
Leveled Reader *Mars,* T250–T251
Vocabulary Review Vocabulary, T252
Writing Writing Trait: Organization, T254
Grammar Adjectives That Compare, T255

LANGUAGE ARTS Writing Process: Research Report T350–T355 Use with Weeks 4–6

Whole Group

Writing
Grammar
Spelling
Build Vocabulary

DAY 1

✔ **Readers to Writers**
- Writing Trait: Organization/Strong Paragraphs, T222–T223
- Writing Entry: Prewrite and Draft, T224

Grammar Adjectives That Compare, T226
Spelling Suffixes *-less* and *-ness*, T228
Build Vocabulary
- Connect to Words, T230
- Academic Vocabulary, T230

DAY 2

Readers to Writers
- Writing Entry: Revise, T224

Grammar Adjectives That Compare, T226
Spelling Suffixes *-less* and *-ness*, T228
Build Vocabulary
- Expand Vocabulary, T230
- Review Context Clues, T230

Because astronomers still believed this theory about how our planets formed, they had a problem with Pluto. When it was first discovered in 1930, astronomers assumed Pluto was made of ice and gas because of its great distance from the sun. However, by 1987, Pluto had moved into a position that only occurs twice in its 248-year orbit and scientific instruments had improved. Astronomers were able to study Pluto and the light that reflected off it. Their instruments told them that Pluto was dense and must have a rocky core. That new information raised questions. If the planets closest to the Sun were rocky and the planets farthest away from the Sun were mostly made of gas, why was Pluto—the most distant planet of all—made of rock?

6

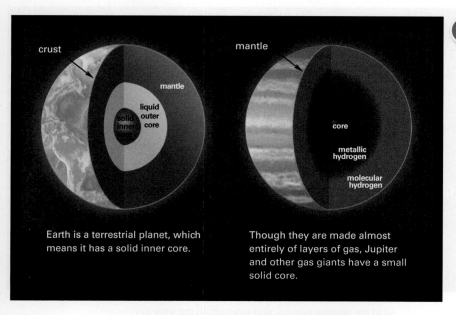

7

crust

mantle

mantle

solid inner

liquid outer core

core

metallic hydrogen

molecular hydrogen

Earth is a terrestrial planet, which means it has a solid inner core.

Though they are made almost entirely of layers of gas, Jupiter and other gas giants have a small solid core.

Michclit Cengaro Kalman

STOP AND CHECK

Ask and Answer Questions According to theory, why are some planets mostly made of gas and others mostly made of rock? Go back to the text to find the answer.

409

LITERATURE ANTHOLOGY, pp. 408–409

7 Text Features: Diagram

On page 409, what information do you learn about Earth and the gas giants from the diagram that is not contained in the text? (The diagram shows the names of the layers of planets, such as *crust* and *mantle*, and where they are located in relation to each other; the types of gases present in a gas giant; and that Earth has a liquid outer core surrounding the solid inner core.)

STOP AND CHECK

Ask and Answer Questions According to theory, why are some planets mostly made of gas and others mostly made of rock? (Planets close to the Sun are made of rock because heat from the Sun blasted away the gas. In the planets far away from the Sun, the gas didn't burn up because it was cooler.)

ELL Help ELLs understand why Pluto's dense core and its location raised questions about its being a planet. Use a rock and a cotton ball to illustrate planets that are dense and planets that are mostly gas.

→ *What are planets close to the sun like?* (the rock)

→ *Where is Pluto?* (far from the Sun) *What is Pluto like?* (the rock)

CONNECT TO CONTENT
INNER AND OUTER PLANETS

The four planets closest to the Sun—Mercury, Venus, Earth, and Mars—are known as the inner planets. The planets farthest away from the Sun—Jupiter, Saturn, Uranus, and Neptune—are known as the outer planets. On pages 408–409, the author compares and contrasts several properties of the inner and outer planets, including their surfaces, climates, and origins.

STEM

Develop Comprehension

8 Strategy: Ask and Answer Questions

Teacher Think Aloud There is a lot of information about orbits on this page. What questions can we ask to be sure we understand it?

Prompt students to apply the strategy in a Think Aloud by asking themselves questions about orbits and finding answers for their questions in the text. Have them turn to a partner and paraphrase what they read.

Student Think Aloud The text says that an orbit is like a lane on a racetrack. How are they similar? As I keep reading, I see that each planet has its own path around the Sun, just like runners each have their own lane on a track.

There were other questions as well. Pluto's orbit is different from the orbits of the planets. Think of an orbit as a lane on a racetrack. Just as runners have their own lanes on the track, each planet has its own orbit around the Sun. For the runners, all the lanes together make up the racetrack. For the planets, all their orbits, taken together, make up the "orbital plane." Just as runners don't run outside their individual lanes, planets don't travel around the Sun outside their individual orbits. Except for Pluto. Pluto crosses Neptune's orbit.

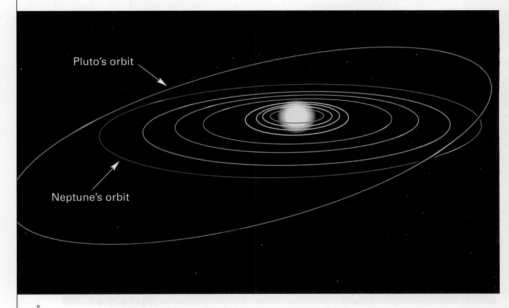

All of the planets, comets, and asteroids in the solar system are in orbit around the Sun. Their orbits line up with each other, creating an imaginary flat disk called the orbital plane. Pluto's orbit, which takes 248 Earth years to complete, brings it outside the orbital plane. For 20 years of each orbit, Pluto moves inside the orbit of Neptune, making Neptune farther from the sun than Pluto. Pluto was inside Neptune's orbit from 1979 to 1999.

410

A C T Access Complex Text

▶ Genre

Diagrams are often included in expository text to give information visually. Remind students to use the diagram on page 410 to help them understand text on page 411.

→ Read aloud the second and third sentences, calling attention to the words "oval-shaped" and "stretched-out oblong."

→ *How does the diagram help you understand these descriptions?* (The diagram shows the shapes of all the planets' orbits, making it obvious how the shape of Pluto's orbit is different.)

→ *What does* oblong *mean?* ("a long distorted circle")

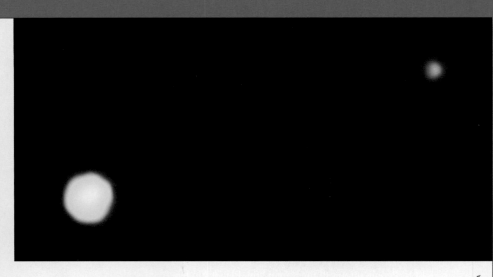

Pluto and its moon, Charon. Pluto was 2.6 billion miles from Earth when the Hubble Space Telescope took this photo.

Dr. R. Albrecht, ESA/ESO Space Telescope European Coordinating Facility; NASA

The shape of Pluto's orbit is different, too. The larger planets travel around the Sun in an oval-shaped orbit. Pluto's orbit is more of a stretched-out oblong. The other planets' orbits are level with the Sun. Pluto's is tilted. Comets' orbits are often tilted, so astronomers wondered, Could Pluto be a comet?

And of course there is Pluto's size. Astronomers knew Pluto was tiny when it was discovered in 1930. But because it was so far away, it was hard to see the planet clearly. Pluto appeared as a tiny dot of light in the night sky. Then telescopes improved. In 1976, American astronomer James Christy discovered that the tiny dot everyone thought was Pluto was really two objects: Pluto had a moon—Charon (CARE-en). Once astronomers discovered that Charon was separate from Pluto, they realized that Pluto was even smaller than they had originally thought. Pluto is only 1,440 miles in **diameter**. (Charon's diameter is 790 miles.) They began to ask, Is Pluto too small to be a planet? And since they had found Charon, they wondered, Were there more objects out there the size of Pluto? Were *they* planets, too?

411

LITERATURE ANTHOLOGY, pp. 410–411

⑨ Vocabulary: Greek Roots

The Greek root *tele* means "far," and the Greek root *scop* means "view." How does knowing these roots help you figure out the meaning of *telescope*? (Combining the roots produces the definition: "an instrument used to view far away objects.")

⑩ Skill: Cause and Effect

Why was Pluto hard to see? (It was very far away.) What happened as a result of telescopes improving? (James Christy discovered that Pluto had a moon.) What questions did this lead scientists to ask? (Was Pluto too small to be a planet? Were there more objects the size of Pluto?) Add the causes and effects to your organizer.

Cause	→	Effect
Pluto was very far away.	→	It was hard to see.
Telescopes improved.	→	James Christy discovered that the tiny dot scientists thought was Pluto was actually two objects.

CONNECT TO CONTENT
CHARACTERISTICS OF PLANETS

On page 410, students read that one of the major characteristics all planets have in common is staying within a fixed orbit around the Sun. One of the reasons that Pluto was demoted as a planet is that it does not share this characteristic; it travels outside of its orbital plane.

STEM

ELL ELLs may need support to understand the concept of orbits. Point out the cognate orbit/*órbita*.

→ An *orbit* is a path that goes around and around.

→ *Look at the diagram. Use your finger to trace Pluto's orbit.*

→ *Is Pluto's orbit the same or different than Neptune's orbit?* (different)

Develop Comprehension

⑪ Strategy: Ask and Answer Questions

Reread page 412. Ask yourself a question about the text. Then share your question with a partner and search together for the answer.

Student Think Aloud The fourth paragraph says that robots changed the way astronomers study the night sky. I wonder how things changed? As I continue reading, I find out that astronomers no longer have to stay up at night to watch the sky. Robots take photographs for them. The photos are sent to special computers.

FINDING PLANETS

In 1992, astronomers made an amazing discovery: 9.3 *billion* miles away from our sun is another region of space, shaped like a disk. Astronomers believe it contains **approximately** 70,000 icy objects, including Pluto.

This area of space was named the Kuiper Belt, after the Dutch-American astronomer Gerard Kuiper (KI-per) who lived from 1905 to 1973. In 1951, more than forty years before its discovery, Kuiper actually predicted that a region like this might exist.

Michael Brown, Chad Trujillo, and David Rabinowitz are planetary astronomers who study Kuiper Belt Objects, or KBOs. People often call these men "the Planet Finders." Together, they hunt for planets at the outer edges of our solar system using the Samuel Oschin Telescope at the Palomar Observatory in California. The Oschin telescope is a wide-field telescope, which means it views broad regions of the sky at once. When paired with a camera at the observatory, it can take pictures of these large areas.

In the past, astronomers had to spend their evenings peering through telescopes in order to study the night sky. Now things have changed. Robots control the Oschin telescope and its camera.

⑪ In the evenings, the cameras in the telescope at the Palomar Observatory are at work. They take three photographs over three hours of the part of the night sky the men want to study. Any object moving across the background of billions of stars and galaxies will be captured in pictures. The pictures are then sent from the telescope's cameras to a bank of ten computers at the California Institute of Technology. Next, the computers decide which objects appear to be moving and therefore might be a planet. Usually, the computers select about 100 objects; when the men arrive at work each morning, the pictures are ready for them to view.

412

A C T Access Complex Text

▶ Connection of Ideas

Tell students that on page 412, the author builds on previous ideas in each new paragraph.

→ *The first paragraph tells about the discovery of a special region of space.*

→ *What do we learn in the second paragraph that is related to the first paragraph?* (The region mentioned in paragraph one is named the Kuiper Belt; Gerard Kuiper predicted its existence more than 40 years earlier.)

Objects in the Kuiper Belt are so far away, it takes them hundreds of Earth years to orbit the Sun. **12**

Dan Durda, Fellow, International Association of Astronomical Artists

413

LITERATURE ANTHOLOGY, pp. 412–413

12 Genre: Expository Text

Expository text provides information and facts about a topic. Authors use text features to organize ideas and share information. Turn to a partner and discuss text features you find on page 412. (I see the subheading "Finding Planets" and a photograph and caption.) How do the photo and caption on page 413 add to the information on page 412? (They help the reader visualize the Kuiper Belt and understand how far away it is.)

→ *How does information about "the Planet Finders" in the third paragraph relate to the first two paragraphs?* (They are the people who look for planets in the Kuiper Belt.)

▶ Sentence Structure

Help students understand the first sentence in paragraph two by removing descriptive phrases.

→ *Restate the sentence using just the essential information.* (This area of space was named the Kuiper Belt after Gerard Kuiper.)

→ *What do the omitted details tell about?* (They give additional facts about Gerard Kuiper.)

Develop Comprehension

13 Author's Craft: Comparison

Authors of expository text may compare two things or ideas to help readers make connections. **What comparison does the author make between Pluto and Xena?** (Pluto is 3.6 billion miles away, but Xena is 10 billion miles away. Xena is 400 miles bigger in diameter than Pluto. Xena takes twice as long as Pluto to orbit Earth.) **How does this comparison help you understand why scientists asked whether or not Xena was a planet?** (Xena was much bigger than Pluto, so it could be a planet.)

They call David Rabinowitz (left), Chad Trujillo (upper left), and Mike Brown (center) "the Planet Finders." The team used the Oschin telescope (right) to discover Eris.

Mike Brown says most of the objects he looks at on his computer screen are not planets. Many are caused by some kind of flaw in the telescope's camera. But every once in a while, an astronomer will get very lucky and something new and exciting will appear. That's how Mike and his team discovered 2003UB313, or Xena (ZEE-nah), as it was nicknamed, on October 21, 2003. Mike says, "The very first time I saw Xena on my screen, I thought that there was something wrong. It was too big and too bright. Then I did a **calculation** of how big it was and how far away it was. Xena is the most distant object ever seen in orbit around the Sun."

13 Pluto is 3.6 billion miles away, but Xena is 10 billion miles away and is approximately 400 miles bigger in diameter than Pluto. It takes Xena more than twice as long as Pluto to orbit the Sun.

Xena was always a nickname. On September 13, 2006, the newly discovered celestial body officially became Eris (AIR-is), for the Greek goddess of strife and discord. It seems an appropriate name, since there was a lot of strife and discord surrounding Eris. Was it a planet, or not?

414

(l) Courtesy of Caltech, Palomar Observatory, (c) Courtesy of Chad Trujillo, (r) Courtesy of Caltech, Palomar Observatory

A C T Access Complex Text

▶ Specific Vocabulary

Point out the words *strife* and *discord* in the last paragraph on page 414.

→ *Identify context clues to figure out what* strife *and* discord *mean.* ("Was it a planet or not?" implies that scientists argued and disagreed about the discovery. On page 415 we find out they did argue about it. *Strife* and *discord* mean "a disagreement.")

→ Have partners confirm their definitions in a dictionary. Point out that the two words are synonyms.

Discuss why scientists disagreed about Eris.

→ *What was the problem with the dictionary definition of* planet? (It was too general. A "large body" wasn't specific enough.)

An artist's conception of the Milky Way, our home galaxy. A galaxy is a group of billions of stars and their solar systems. The Milky Way is a spiral galaxy that contains 200 billion stars.

WHAT IS A PLANET?

Because scientists always check and recheck their work, Mike Brown and his team of astronomers didn't announce their discovery of Eris until January 5, 2005, after they had had a chance to verify their information. When they revealed their discovery, many people thought the solar system had gained its tenth planet. But others disagreed. Soon an argument was raging among astronomers all over the world. And the argument came down to one question. What, exactly, is a planet?

It seems surprising, but until August 24, 2006, science had never had a definition for the word "planet." Dictionaries had definitions, of course, but most said something similar to "A large celestial body that circles around the Sun or another star." For a scientist, that definition had problems. For one thing, what is meant by "large body"? Jupiter, the largest planet in our solar system, is 88,700 miles in diameter, and it is a planet. Pluto is only 1,440 miles in diameter and—at the time—it was a planet, too. The question "What is a planet?" needed an answer, and the International Astronomical Union decided to create not one definition but three.

14

Mark Garlick (Space-art)

415

LITERATURE ANTHOLOGY, pp. 414–415

 Skill: Cause and Effect

Why didn't the astronomers announce their discovery right away? (They wanted to recheck their work.) Why did people all around the world begin arguing about whether or not Eris was a planet? (Scientists had never defined the word "planet.") Add the causes and effects to your organizer.

Cause	→	Effect
The astronomers checked and rechecked their work.	→	They didn't announce their discovery of Eris until 2005.
Science had never defined the word "planet."	→	Astronomers around the world argued whether or not Eris was a planet.

▶ **Connection of Ideas**

Remind students to connect pictures with the text.

→ *How is the photograph of the Oschin telescope on page 414 connected to the text on page 413?* (Page 413 tells how astronomers used the telescope to take large pictures of the sky.)

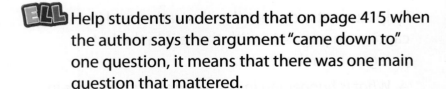**ELL** Help students understand that on page 415 when the author says the argument "came down to" one question, it means that there was one main question that mattered.

→ *What question did scientists argue about?* (What is a planet?)

Develop Comprehension

15 Skill: Main Idea and Key Details

What do the details in each paragraph on page 416 have in common? (They are all about the definition of a planet.) What is the main idea on this page? (The IAU made three rules used to decide whether a celestial body is a planet.)

The IAU came up with three classes of objects that orbit the Sun: planets, dwarf planets, and small solar-system bodies.

The IAU decided that a celestial body is a planet if it:

1. orbits the Sun
2. is round or nearly round, because its gravity has pulled it into that shape
3. is big enough and has enough gravity to "clear the neighborhood" around its orbit

The first two qualifications for planethood, orbiting the Sun and a round shape, are easy to understand. The concept of "clearing the neighborhood" is a little more difficult.

It might help to think of planets as the schoolyard bullies of the solar system. In order to clear the neighborhood, a planet has to be big enough, and have enough gravity, to get rid of any celestial objects in its way. A large planet might clear its orbit by using its gravity to pull other, smaller, objects toward it and destroy them, the way asteroids are destroyed when they hit Earth.

A cosmic collision. Planets often "clear their neighborhoods" in this manner.

416

NASA/JPL

A C T Access Complex Text

▶ Genre

Help students connect the illustration and its caption on page 416 with the text in the last paragraph on that page.

→ *What is happening in the picture?* (Two objects in space are colliding, and one is breaking apart.)

→ *What sentence in the text describes the action shown in the illustration?* (the last sentence)

▶ Connection of Ideas

Help students connect the term *celestial body* in paragraph two on page 416 to the existing definition of a planet on page 415.

→ *How did scientists define a planet before? How is the new definition different?* (A planet was defined as a large celestial body; the new definition distinguishes planets from other celestial bodies.)

Or a planet might clear its orbit by attracting smaller objects toward it, then turning them into moons that remain in orbit around the planet.

Sometimes a planet will simply push a smaller body into a completely different orbit and get rid of it that way. But no matter how it does the clearing, according to the IAU definition, a planet must travel in its orbit by itself.

The secondary category of planets, called "dwarf planets," have the following characteristics. They must:

1. orbit the Sun
2. be round
3. not be a moon or satellite of another planet

By this definition, Pluto is a dwarf planet. And although Charon, its former moon, is still locked in an orbit with Pluto, it is a dwarf planet, too. Now they are known as a double-planet system. Ceres is a dwarf planet, also, and Mike Brown's discovery, Eris, is one as well. They are dwarf planets because they orbit the Sun, they are round, and they are not moons of another planet—but they're too small to have enough gravity to clear their neighborhood. Pluto, Charon, Ceres, and Eris are all KBOs—orbiting far out in space with other objects in the Kuiper Belt.

STOP AND CHECK

Ask and Answer Questions How does the size and gravity of a planet affect other objects around it? Look for details in the text to find the answer.

417

NASA/JPL

LITERATURE ANTHOLOGY, pp. 416–417

16 Strategy: Ask and Answer Questions

Generate a question of your own about the definition of planets. For example, you might ask, "What is the difference between a planet and a dwarf planet?" Answer this question by paraphrasing the text. (A planet orbits the Sun, is round or nearly round, and is big enough to clear away objects in its path. A dwarf planet is also round and orbits the Sun, but it is not as big as a planet, so it doesn't have enough gravity to clear its path. A dwarf planet cannot be a moon or satellite of another planet.)

STOP AND CHECK

Ask and Answer Questions How does the size and gravity of a planet affect other objects around it? (A planet can attract objects to it and destroy them or turn them into moons, or it can push smaller bodies into another orbit.)

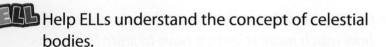

ELL Help ELLs understand the concept of celestial bodies.

→ *In this context, a* body *means "an object." Planets and dwarf planets are* celestial bodies, *meaning "objects in space."*

→ *Planets, dwarf planets, and smaller bodies all orbit the Sun.*

Discuss with students the new definition for planets asking them to demonstrate what "clearing the neighborhood" might look like.

→ *Show me a planet that clears its neighborhood by pulling smaller objects to it and destroying them.*

→ *Show me a planet that clears its neighborhood by turning a smaller object into a moon.*

Develop Comprehension

17 Skill: Make Inferences

Reread the final paragraph on page 418. What can you infer about the number of planets in the future? (As "new information is discovered," the number of planets changes, as shown by the past. So the number might change again as more new information is discovered.) **The author says, "And that is just in *our* solar system!" What is the author implying?** (By italicizing *our*, the author implies that other solar systems in space may also have planets.)

Everything else—asteroids, comets, meteors—are now members of the third class of objects that orbit the Sun and are called "small solar-system bodies."

Some astronomers think the definition of a planet will change again in the future. Others think the current definition is a good one and will last.

17 Science is exciting, because it continually changes as new information is discovered. A long time ago, we thought there were six planets. Then we thought there were eight. For a while, there were nine. Then it was back to eight. Then, with Pluto, the number jumped up to nine again. And now it's back to eight. And that is just in *our* solar system!

An artist's conception of the New Horizons spacecraft as it arrives at Pluto. Charon is visible in the distance.

418

A C T Access Complex Text

▶ Purpose

Point out that the author concludes the selection by explaining that scientists have a great deal more to learn about planets.

→ *On page 418, what changes does the author say might occur in the future?* (the definition of planet, the number of planets in our solar system)

→ *On page 419, how does the author show readers how much more scientists have to learn?* (She lists many questions that don't yet have answers.)

→ *What is the author's purpose for writing this selection?* (Readers can infer that the author may want to inspire future scientists.)

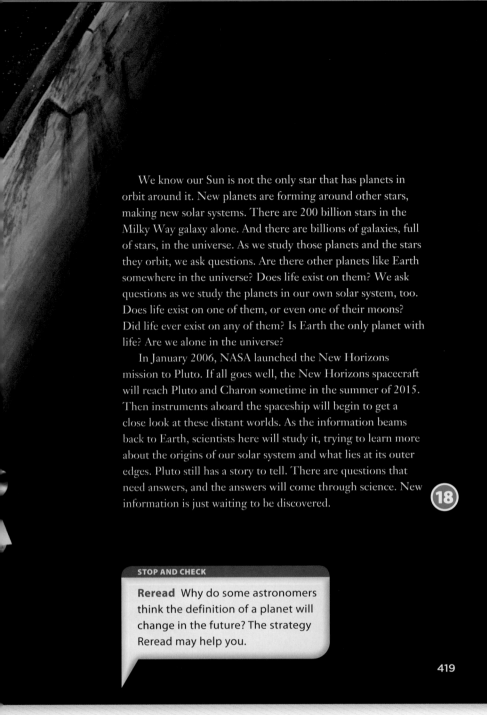

We know our Sun is not the only star that has planets in orbit around it. New planets are forming around other stars, making new solar systems. There are 200 billion stars in the Milky Way galaxy alone. And there are billions of galaxies, full of stars, in the universe. As we study those planets and the stars they orbit, we ask questions. Are there other planets like Earth somewhere in the universe? Does life exist on them? We ask questions as we study the planets in our own solar system, too. Does life exist on one of them, or even one of their moons? Did life ever exist on any of them? Is Earth the only planet with life? Are we alone in the universe?

In January 2006, NASA launched the New Horizons mission to Pluto. If all goes well, the New Horizons spacecraft will reach Pluto and Charon sometime in the summer of 2015. Then instruments aboard the spaceship will begin to get a close look at these distant worlds. As the information beams back to Earth, scientists here will study it, trying to learn more about the origins of our solar system and what lies at its outer edges. Pluto still has a story to tell. There are questions that need answers, and the answers will come through science. New information is just waiting to be discovered. **18**

STOP AND CHECK

Reread Why do some astronomers think the definition of a planet will change in the future? The strategy Reread may help you.

419

LITERATURE ANTHOLOGY, pp. 418–419

---

18 Skill: Cause and Effect

What will happen if the New Horizons spacecraft reaches Pluto and Charon? Paraphrase the text to explain the effect. (Instruments on the spacecraft will be able to get a close look at these distant worlds.) What will happen as scientists receive new data from the spacecraft? (They will learn more about how our solar system formed and what is at its outer edges.)

STOP AND CHECK

Reread Why do some astronomers think the definition of a planet will change in the future? (As we learn new information about space, definitions may change.)

Return to Predictions

Review students' predictions and purposes for reading. Ask them to answer the Essential Question. (Scientists discover new information that refutes old conclusions, such as the evidence that showed Pluto could no longer be considered a planet.)

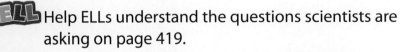 Help ELLs understand the questions scientists are asking on page 419.

→ Explain that in this context, *life* meanings living things, such as plants and animals. Point out the cognate exist/*existir*.

→ *Does life exist on Earth?* (yes)

→ *What do scientists want to know about other planets?* (Does life exist on other planets?)

About the Author

Meet the Author

Elaine Scott

Have students read the biography of the author. Ask:

→ Why did Elaine Scott decide to write for children instead of adults?

→ What sources did Elaine Scott use to write this story? Why did she use these sources?

Author's Purpose

To Inform

Remind students that the main purpose of most nonfiction is to give information. Students may say that Elaine Scott ends a paragraph with a question to get readers thinking about what the answer might be and to make them interested in reading on to find the answer.

Author's Craft

Text Features

Explain that text features include captions, diagrams, sidebars, photographs, and illustrations. Discuss what diagrams add to the text.

→ Some information is easier to show with images or charts than to explain with words. Example: The diagram on page 409 shows the layers of terrestrial planets and gas giants.

→ Have students locate another text feature that showed information, such as the diagram of the orbits on page 410.

About the Author

Elaine Scott's first published work was a poem she wrote in the sixth grade that made it into the local newspaper. Twenty-five years later, she returned to writing as a career. At first, she wrote for adults but soon got hooked on the fun of writing for children. Elaine knows that young people are perfectly capable of grasping difficult ideas as long as the subject is explained clearly. Sometimes she visits schools, where she talks with the students about how she researches and writes her books.

Elaine likes to get information for her books first hand. As she was writing *When Is a Planet Not a Planet?*, astronomers were still arguing over whether Pluto was or wasn't a planet. Elaine interviewed experts and checked their Web sites to stay tuned to the latest developments in scientific discovery.

Author's Purpose
In this selection, the author often ends a paragraph with a question. Identify one example. Why do you think she does this?

t and cl) NASA/JPL; (cr)Cynthia S. Qualline; (b)Johns Hopkins University Applied Physics Laboratory/Southwest Research Institute

420

LITERATURE ANTHOLOGY, pp. 420–421

 Comprehension Strategy

Ask and Answer Questions

Asking and answering questions as you read helps you stay focused. Try it with "Changing Views of Earth." Think about each question the author asks, and form your own questions, too. Then read on for the answers.

 Find Text Evidence

In the first paragraph on page 353, the author asks a question: *Where does all that information about the weather come from?* This may lead you to another question.

> **page 353**
>
> No matter where on Earth you go, people like to talk about the weather. This weekend's forecast may provide the main criteria for planning outdoor activities. Where does all that information about the weather come from?

I think about what I already know—that weather forecasters use scientific instruments. So I ask myself, "What kinds of instruments do scientists use to make forecasts?" I will read on to find the answer.

Your Turn

Reread "Out in Space, Looking Back Home" on page 355. Ask a question and then read to find the answer. Use the strategy Ask and Answer Questions as you read.

356

READING/WRITING WORKSHOP, p. 356

Monitor and *Differentiate*

✓ Quick Check

Do students ask a question about a specific section of text? Do they reread the section for details and evidence in order to answer?

⬇

Small Group Instruction

If No →	**Approaching Level**	Reteach p. T232
	ELL	Develop p. T249
If Yes →	**On Level**	Review p. T240
	Beyond Level	Extend p. T244

ENGLISH LANGUAGE LEARNERS SCAFFOLD

Beginning

Identify Reread the first paragraph. Point out difficult words or phrases: *forecast, droughts, centuries, scientific innovation.* Define them. Help students replace the words with words they know. Ask: *Does the author ask where weather information comes from?* (yes)

Intermediate

Distinguish Reread the first paragraph with students. Point out that it may be difficult to identify what the focus of the text will be. Ask: *Which sentence in the paragraph is a question asked by the author?* Help students understand that the text will focus on answering this question.

Advanced/High

Discuss Have students reread the first paragraph of the text and identify the question. Elicit from students why it may be confusing. Ask: *Why does the author pose a question here and then not answer it right away? Where can you find the answer? Turn to a partner and explain.*

ON-LEVEL PRACTICE BOOK pp. 233–234

Comprehension and Fluency

Name _____

Read the passage. Use the ask and answer questions strategy to check your understanding as you read.

Is There Life Out There?

"Is there life out there?" is a question scientists who study astrobiology are trying to answer. They look for life in space. In recent years, they have turned their attention to Europa, one of Jupiter's four largest moons.

Europa is a little smaller than Earth's moon and is covered by a sheet of ice. Its surface is too cold and exposed to too much radiation for anything to live there. Scientists want to know what lies beneath the ice, for that is where any life on Europa would most likely be.

The Necessities of Life

For years, scientists believed all life on Earth depended on energy from the sun. During a process called photosynthesis, plants use energy from sunlight to make food and to release oxygen into the atmosphere. Aerobic creatures rely on that oxygen to breathe. In addition to providing the fuel for photosynthesis, sunlight also provides the necessary warmth for life to survive. Scientists believed life could not survive in extreme temperatures.

Scientists also believed that all food chains led back to photosynthesis and the food produced by plants. Recent discoveries, however, have changed the way scientists think about life. They have discovered tube-shaped, worm-like creatures and other animals living around hydrothermal vents on the ocean floor. These newfound creatures do not rely on the sun or plants for food and energy.

Practice • Grade 5 • Unit 5 • Week 4 **233**

APPROACHING	BEYOND	ELL
pp. 233–234	pp. 233–234	pp. 233–234

→ Comprehension Skill

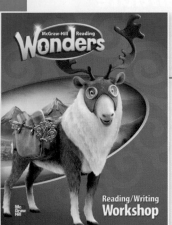

Reading/Writing Workshop

OBJECTIVES

CCSS Compare and contrast the overall structure (e.g., chronology, comparison, cause/effect, problem/solution) of events, ideas, concepts, or information in two or more texts. **RI.5.5**

ACADEMIC LANGUAGE
• *text structure, cause, effect*
• Cognates: *causa, efecto*

MINILESSON 15 Mins

Text Structure: Cause and Effect

1 Explain

Explain to students that a text's structure is the way ideas within it are organized. Remind students that they learned about compare and contrast text structure earlier in the unit. Tell them that **cause and effect** is a type of text structure in which an author explains what happens (effect) and why it happens (cause).

→ Readers can monitor their understanding of causes and effects by asking themselves, *What happened? Why did it happen?*

→ Point out that just as signal words identify compare-contrast relationships, such words can help students identify cause-and-effect relationships in a text. They include *because, so, due to,* and *as a result*.

→ Explain that sometimes causes and effects occur in a chain. An event causes an effect, which in turn causes something else to happen.

2 Model Close Reading: Text Evidence

Identify the causes and effects under the heading "On the Ground, Looking Around" on page 353. Then model using the information in the graphic organizer to determine the chain of causes and effects that led to our recognition that Earth orbits the sun.

 Write About Reading: Summarize Model how to use the details from the organizer to summarize why the invention of the telescope was so important to our understanding of Earth.

3 Guided Practice of Close Reading

 Have pairs complete a graphic organizer for the remainder of "Changing Views of Earth," identifying cause-and-effect connections between events described on pages 354 and 355. Discuss the organizer as students complete it for each page.

 Write About Reading: Compare and Contrast Text Structure
Ask pairs to write a summary that compares and contrasts the text structures of "Forests on Fire" and "Changing Views of Earth." Select students to share their summaries with the class.

Go Digital

Present the Lesson

SKILLS TRACE

TEXT STRUCTURE

Introduce U1W3

Review U1W4, U1W6, U2W1, U2W3, U4W6, U5W3, U5W4, U5W6, U6W3, U6W4

Assess U1, U2, U5, U6

Comprehension Skill CCSS

Cause and Effect

Science and history authors want you to know not just *what* happens but *why* it happens. They show that one event is the **cause** of another event, called the **effect**. Cause-and-effect relationships often form a chain, with the effect of one event becoming the cause of another event.

 Find Text Evidence

In the section "On the Ground, Looking Around" on page 353, I read that people once believed the sun orbits Earth. I learn the cause of this mistake: people had only their eyes for viewing the skies. The invention of the telescope had an important effect—the discovery that Earth actually orbits the sun.

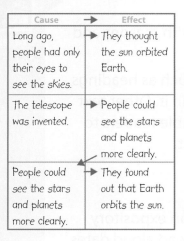

Cause	→	Effect
Long ago, people had only their eyes to see the skies.	→	They thought the sun orbited Earth.
The telescope was invented.	→	People could see the stars and planets more clearly.
People could see the stars and planets more clearly.	→	They found out that Earth orbits the sun.

Your Turn COLLABORATE

Reread the rest of "Changing Views of Earth." Show important connections between certain events by recording causes and effects in your own graphic organizer.

Go Digital!
Use the interactive graphic organizer

357

READING/WRITING WORKSHOP, p. 357

ELL ENGLISH LANGUAGE LEARNERS SCAFFOLD

Beginning

Recognize Read the last paragraph on page 353. Point out the Spanish cognate *telescopio*. Ask: *Did using a telescope help Galileo see into space more clearly?* (yes) Help students identify the cause and effect: *Using the telescope was the _____, and seeing into space more clearly was the _____.*

Intermediate

Respond Orally Reread the last paragraph on page 353 with students. Ask: *What happened as a result of Galileo's heightened vision from the telescope? Then what happened as a result of Galileo seeing more clearly into space?* Have partners identify causes and effects: *The cause was _____, and the effect was _____.*

Advanced/High

Identify Have students identify the chain of causes and effects in the section "On the Ground, Looking Around" on page 353. Then have them discuss with a partner how some effects eventually became causes.

Monitor and *Differentiate*

 Quick Check

Are students able to identify connections between important events by recording causes and effects in the graphic organizer?

↓

Small Group Instruction

If No →	**Approaching Level**	Reteach p. T239
	ELL	Develop p. T249
If Yes →	**On Level**	Review p. T243
	Beyond Level	Extend p. T247

ON-LEVEL PRACTICE BOOK pp. 233–235

Comprehension: Cause and Effect and Fluency

Name _____

A. Reread the passage and answer the questions. Possible responses provided.

1. What details from the first two paragraphs help explain why astrobiologists are interested in Europa, one of Jupiter's moons?
Astrobiologists look for life in space, and they think that there is a chance that life might exist beneath the ice sheets of Europa.

2. What discovery on Earth caused scientists to become more interested in Europa?
The discovery of chemosynthetic life on Earth led scientists to change their ideas about what is needed to sustain life in space. Because of this, they turned their attention to Europa, which might be able to support chemosynthetic life.

3. What is the scientists' main reason for studying Lake Vostok in Antarctica? What effect might their research have?
Because Lake Vostok is buried deep under ice, its environment is similar to Europa's. Finding life there would support theories about possible life on Europa.

B. Work with a partner. Read the passage aloud. Pay attention to accuracy. Stop after one minute. Fill out the chart.

	Words Read	–	Number of Errors	=	Words Correct Score
First Read		–		=	
Second Read		–		=	

Practice • Grade 5 • Unit 5 • Week 4 **235**

APPROACHING pp. 233–235	BEYOND pp. 233–235	ELL pp. 233–235

→ Genre: Informational Text

Reading/Writing Workshop

OBJECTIVES

CCSS Interpret information presented visually, orally, or quantitatively (e.g., in charts, graphs, diagrams, time lines, animations, or interactive elements on Web pages) and explain how the information contributes to an understanding of the text in which it appears. **RI.4.7**

Identify characteristics of expository text.

ACADEMIC LANGUAGE

• *expository text, headings, subheadings, photographs, diagrams*

• Cognates: *texto expositivo, fotografías, diagramas*

MINILESSON 20 Mins

Expository Text

1 Explain

Share with students these characteristics of **expository text:**

→ An expository text is a nonfiction text that presents factual information about a topic in a logical order.

→ Authors of expository text support their points with reasons and evidence.

→ An expository text often includes text features, such as headings and subheadings, that organize the information in it. Other text features, such as photographs and diagrams, enable readers to visualize ideas and information related to the text.

2 Model Close Reading: Text Evidence

Model how to identify "Changing Views of Earth" as an expository text in which facts are presented in a logical order. Read aloud dates in the text (such as i*n the early 1600s* and *in the mid-1700s*) to show students how the author discusses inventions in the order they occurred. Then model using the diagram on page 354.

Diagrams Remind students that a diagram is a drawing that shows the different parts of something and how they relate to each other. Read aloud the title and caption of the diagram on page 354 and explain that this diagram show layers of Earth's atmosphere and inventions that can reach each. Ask: *How does the diagram connect to information in the text?*

3 Guided Practice of Close Reading

Have partners identify three other examples of things that show the selection is expository text. Encourage students to consider factual statements from the text, the use of headings and other text features, evidence presented to support a point, and examples of logical order. Then have partners share their work with the class.

Go Digital

Present the Lesson

Genre Informational Text

Expository Text

The selection "Changing Views of Earth" is an expository text.

Expository text:
- Presents information and facts about a topic in a logical order
- Supports specific points with reasons and evidence
- May include text features, such as subheadings, photos, and diagrams

 Find Text Evidence

"Changing Views of Earth" is an expository text. The facts about inventions are given in a logical order. The author backs up her points with evidence, including a diagram.

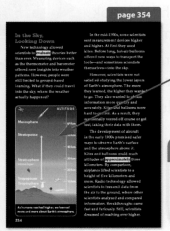

page 354

Diagrams A diagram is a drawing that shows the different parts of something and how they relate to each other. A title tells what the diagram illustrates, and labels identify each main part.

Your Turn

List three other examples of things in "Changing Views of Earth" that show that this is expository text.

358

READING/WRITING WORKSHOP, p. 358

A C T Access Complex Text

▶ **Connection of Ideas**

Students may have difficulty determining how the diagram connects to the text.

→ *According to the text, which inventions helped people measure weather from above the ground?* (kites, balloons, airplanes, rockets, satellites)

→ *What additional information about these inventions does the diagram provide?* (It provides more specific information about which levels in Earth's atmosphere some of these inventions were able to reach.)

Monitor and *Differentiate*

 Quick Check

Do students identify details, including text features, that show that "Changing Views of Earth" is expository text?

⬇

Small Group Instruction

If No → **Approaching Level** Reteach p. T233
ELL Develop p. T251

If Yes → **On Level** Review p. T241
Beyond Level Extend p. T245

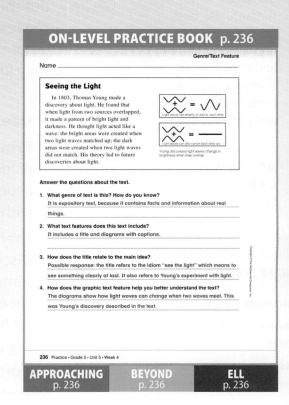

ON-LEVEL PRACTICE BOOK p. 236

Genre/Text Feature

Name _____

Seeing the Light

In 1803, Thomas Young made a discovery about light. He found that when light from two sources overlapped, it made a pattern of bright light and darkness. He thought light acted like a wave: the bright areas were created when two light waves matched up; the dark areas were created when two light waves did not match. His theory led to future discoveries about light.

Answer the questions about the text.

1. What genre of text is this? How do you know?
It is expository text, because it contains facts and information about real things.

2. What text features does this text include?
It includes a title and diagrams with captions.

3. How does the title relate to the main idea?
Possible response: the title refers to the idiom "see the light" which means to see something clearly at last. It also refers to Young's experiment with light.

4. How does the graphic text feature help you better understand the text?
The diagrams show how light waves can change when two waves meet. This was Young's discovery described in the text.

236 Practice • Grade 5 • Unit 5 • Week 4

| APPROACHING p. 236 | BEYOND p. 236 | ELL p. 236 |

→ Vocabulary Strategy

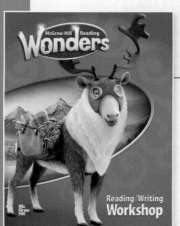

Reading/Writing Workshop

Greek Roots

MINILESSON **20** Mins

1 Explain

Remind students that a root is the basic part of a word that gives the word its meaning. Explain that many English words contain Greek roots.

→ When they encounter an unfamiliar word, students should look for a Greek root that might help them determine its meaning.

→ Point out that context clues might be helpful in determining the meaning of an unknown word that also contains a Greek root.

→ Remind students to confirm that the meaning they determine is correct by looking up the word in a dictionary.

2 Model Close Reading: Text Evidence

Model using the Greek roots *therm* ("heat") and *meter* ("measure") to determine the meaning of *thermometer* ("a device that records or measures temperature") in the first paragraph on page 354.

3 Guided Practice of Close Reading

COLLABORATE

Have students work in pairs to use the given Greek roots to figure out the meanings of *geocentric* and *heliocentric* on page 353 of the text. Encourage partners to use context clues to help them determine each word's meaning and to confirm that the meanings they identify are correct by using a dictionary.

Use Reference Sources

Print and Online Dictionaries Have students check a print dictionary and compare the meanings they find there for *geocentric* and *heliocentric* with the meanings they came up with from the Greek roots.

Then review an online dictionary entry for the word *geocentric*. Discuss each part of the entry: the meanings and example sentences; the syllabication and phonetic respelling; the part of speech label. Have students identify each element in the entry for *heliocentric*.

Ask students to describe how the online entries for these two words are both similar to and different from the print ones.

OBJECTIVES

CCSS Use common, grade-appropriate Greek and Latin affixes and roots as clues to the meaning of a word (e.g., *photograph*, *photosynthesis*). **L.5.4b**

CCSS Consult reference materials (e.g., dictionaries, glossaries, thesauruses), both print and digital, to find the pronunciation and determine or clarify the precise meaning of key words and phrases. **L.5.4c**

ACADEMIC LANGUAGE
Greek roots

SKILLS TRACE

GREEK ROOTS

Introduce U1W4

Review U1W4, U3W3, U5W4

Assess U1, U3, U5

Go Digital

Present the Lesson

Vocabulary Strategy CCSS

Greek Roots

Many English words contain Greek roots. For example, the Greek root *meter* means "measure," so any English word containing *meter* (*thermometer, barometer, kilometer*) usually has to do with measuring something.

 Find Text Evidence

On page 354 of "Changing Views of Earth," I come across the word thermometer. *The Greek root* therm *has to do with heat. Since I know that* meter *means "measure," I can figure out that a thermometer is something that records or measures temperature.*

Measuring devices such as the thermometer and barometer offered new insights into weather patterns.

Your Turn COLLABORATE

Use the Greek roots below to figure out the meanings of two words from "Changing Views of Earth":

Greek Roots: *geo* = earth   *helio* = sun   *centr* = center
geocentric, page 353
heliocentric, page 353

Brand X Pictures/PunchStock

359

READING/WRITING WORKSHOP, p. 359

Monitor and *Differentiate*

✓ Quick Check

Can students use Greek roots to determine the meanings of the words *geocentric* and *heliocentric*?

Small Group Instruction

If No →

| Approaching Level | Reteach p. T237 |
| ELL | Develop p. T253 |

If Yes →

| On Level | Review p. T242 |
| Beyond Level | Extend p. T246 |

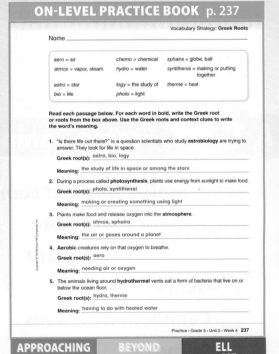

ON-LEVEL PRACTICE BOOK p. 237

ELL ENGLISH LANGUAGE LEARNERS SCAFFOLD

Beginning	**Intermediate**	**Advanced/High**
Understand Point out the words *geocentric* and *heliocentric* on page 353 and define them for students. Then write each word on the board and circle the Greek roots. Write the meaning below each root. Point to and say aloud each root and its meaning, as students repeat after you.	**Describe** Point out *geocentric* and *heliocentric* on page 353 and define them. Point out that each word has two Greek roots. Have partners identify the two Greek roots and their meanings in each word. Then have them combine the roots' meanings to determine the meaning of each word as a whole.	**Discuss** Point out the words *geocentric* and *heliocentric* on page 353 and ask students to define them. Have partners identify the Greek roots and any context clues that helped them figure out the meanings of the words.

Develop Comprehension

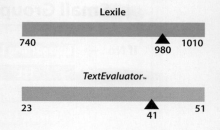

When is a Planet Not a Planet?

Literature Anthology

Text Complexity Range

Lexile

740 ▲ 1010
980

TextEvaluator™

23 ▲ 51
41

Options for Close Reading

→ Whole Class

→ Small Group

→ Independent

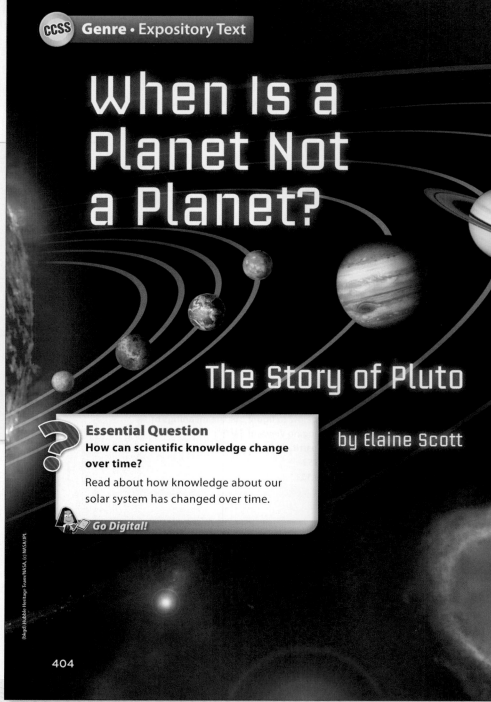

CCSS Genre · Expository Text

When Is a Planet Not a Planet?

The Story of Pluto

by Elaine Scott

? Essential Question

How can scientific knowledge change over time?

Read about how knowledge about our solar system has changed over time.

Go Digital!

(bkgd) Hubble Heritage Team/NASA, (c) NASA/JPL

404

A C T Access Complex Text

What makes this text complex?

▶ **Sentence Structure**

▶ **Specific Vocabulary**

▶ **Genre**

▶ **Connection of Ideas**

▶ **Purpose**

▶ **Sentence Structure**

Point out the second sentence on page 405. Explain that sometimes an author may write in a conversational style. As part of this style, the author may omit parts of a sentence, such as the subject, which can be confusing to the reader.

My very eager mother just served us nine pizzas.

A silly sentence, yet schoolchildren have memorized it for years, because it helps them remember the planets in our solar system. The first letter of every word stands for a planet, in the order of how close it is to the Sun. *My very eager mother just served us nine pizzas.* Mercury, Venus, Earth, Mars, Jupiter, Saturn, Uranus, Neptune, and Pluto. Mercury is the planet closest to the Sun, and tiny Pluto is the farthest away. That is, until recently.

Pluto is still there, of course. Along with the planets, asteroids, comets, meteors, and bits of space rock and ice, Pluto is part of our solar system. Pluto and all those other objects **orbit**, or travel around, the Sun.

①

My very eager mother just served us nine pizzas. This is a composite of photos taken on many different NASA missions. It illustrates our solar system. Our star, the Sun, is at the far left; Pluto is at the far right. The wispy tail of a comet is shown in the lower left, and the Southern Ring Nebula is near the lower right. The other faint objects in the image are artistic additions, created with a computer.

405

LITERATURE ANTHOLOGY, pp. 404–405

Predictive Writing

Have students read the title and preview the photos, illustrations, and captions. Have them write their predictions about what this selection will be about.

ESSENTIAL QUESTION

Ask a student to read aloud the Essential Question. Have students discuss what information they expect to learn.

Note Taking:
Use the Graphic Organizer ✏️ *Analytical Writing*

As students read, ask them to take notes by filling in the graphic organizer on **Your Turn Practice Book page 232** to record causes and effects in each section.

❶ Vocabulary: Greek Roots

Point out the word *asteroids* on page 405. Explain that it comes from the Greek root *aster-*, meaning "star," and the Greek suffix *-oid*, meaning "like." Have students look for words with the same root as they continue reading. (astronomical, astronomers)

→ *Are there words missing in this sentence? Where?* (Yes, at the beginning, before "A silly sentence.")

→ *What words could you add that would make a complete sentence?* (It is; It's)

→ *What words could you add to the last sentence in the paragraph to make a full sentence?* (That is, Pluto was the farthest, until recently.)

 Help students understand that "until recently" refers to the change in Pluto's definition as a planet.

Use the illustration on pages 404–405 to help ELLs understand the mnemonic device, "My very eager mother just served us nine pizzas." Point to each planet as you read and name the planets.

→ *Where is Pluto?* (farthest from the Sun)

Develop Comprehension

2 **Skill: Cause and Effect**

Why doesn't the old memory clue for planets— "My very eager mother just served us nine pizzas" —work anymore? (Pluto is no longer a planet, so the word *pizzas* must be eliminated from the sentence.)

However, on August 24, 2006, the International **Astronomical** Union (IAU), a group of individual astronomers and astronomical societies from around the world, made an announcement. They declared that Pluto was not a planet. Suddenly, "My very eager mother just served us nine pizzas" didn't work anymore, because now there are only eight major planets orbiting the Sun. Perhaps someone will create a new sentence to help us **2** remember their names and order.

Names are important, but they are not the only things to know about the planets. Learning how planets form, where they are located, and what they are like is the kind of activity that makes science exciting and fun.

NASA/JPL

406

A C T Access Complex Text

▸ **Sentence Structure**

Help students break down complex sentences to understand the subject and action. Guide them to identify the subject and verb in the first sentence on page 406.

→ *What is the verb, or action, in the sentence?* (made)

→ *What was made?* (an announcement)

→ *Who made the announcement?* (the International Astronomical Union) *This is the subject.*

If students erroneously identify the subject as *group, astronomers,* or *societies,* review how these words are part of an appositive phrase. This phrase gives a description of the subject, the International Astronomical Union.

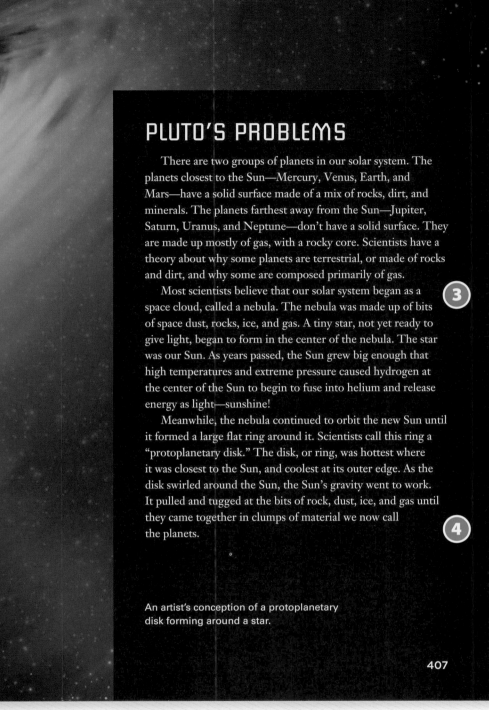

PLUTO'S PROBLEMS

There are two groups of planets in our solar system. The planets closest to the Sun—Mercury, Venus, Earth, and Mars—have a solid surface made of a mix of rocks, dirt, and minerals. The planets farthest away from the Sun—Jupiter, Saturn, Uranus, and Neptune—don't have a solid surface. They are made up mostly of gas, with a rocky core. Scientists have a theory about why some planets are terrestrial, or made of rocks and dirt, and why some are composed primarily of gas.

Most scientists believe that our solar system began as a space cloud, called a nebula. The nebula was made up of bits of space dust, rocks, ice, and gas. A tiny star, not yet ready to give light, began to form in the center of the nebula. The star was our Sun. As years passed, the Sun grew big enough that high temperatures and extreme pressure caused hydrogen at the center of the Sun to begin to fuse into helium and release energy as light—sunshine!

Meanwhile, the nebula continued to orbit the new Sun until it formed a large flat ring around it. Scientists call this ring a "protoplanetary disk." The disk, or ring, was hottest where it was closest to the Sun, and coolest at its outer edge. As the disk swirled around the Sun, the Sun's gravity went to work. It pulled and tugged at the bits of rock, dust, ice, and gas until they came together in clumps of material we now call the planets.

An artist's conception of a protoplanetary disk forming around a star.

407

LITERATURE ANTHOLOGY, pp. 406–407

③ Strategy: Ask and Answer Questions

Teacher Think Aloud As I read, I ask myself questions to make sure I understand the information in an expository text. When I read the word *nebula* in the second paragraph, I asked myself what it meant. I reread the first sentence, and I found out that a nebula is a space cloud.

④ Skill: Cause and Effect

What happened when the Sun grew bigger? (High temperatures and pressure turned hydrogen into helium, which released energy as light.) What effect did the Sun's gravity have? (It made rock, dust, ice, and gas come together to form the planets.) Add the causes and effects to your organizer.

Cause	→	Effect
The Sun grew bigger.	→	High temperatures and pressure made hydrogen join with helium to give off light.
The new Sun had gravity.	→	The gravity pulled and tugged at rock, dust, ice, and gas until they joined together to form the planets.

ELL Copy the first sentence on page 406. Underline the subject and predicate: *the International Astronomical Union . . . made an announcement.* Point out cognates: astronomical/*astronómico*, announcement/*anuncio*, individual/*individuo*, society/*sociedad*. Have students find the phrases that answer these questions:

→ *When was the announcement made?* (on August 24, 2006)

→ *What is the International Astronomical Union?* (a group of astronomers and societies)

Develop Comprehension

5 Author's Craft: Captions

Authors use text features such as captions to provide information about illustrations, photos, or diagrams. Turn to a partner and share what information you learn from the caption on page 408. How does this relate to the main text? (The caption tells that the photograph shows the Orion Nebula and explains that 153 stars with protoplanetary disks are forming new solar systems there. The caption relates to the information about the nebula that became a protoplanetary disk on page 407.)

6 Skill: Cause and Effect

What caused astronomers to have a problem with Pluto? Paraphrase the text. (It didn't fit into the theory about how planets far from the Sun are formed.) Add the cause and effect to your organizer.

NASA/JPL–Caltech/T. Megeath(University of Toledo) & M. Robberto(STScI)

A small portion of the Orion Nebula, 1,500 light years away from Earth. At least 153 stars in this region have protoplanetary disks swirling around them, forming new solar systems. Scientists believe our solar system formed in just this way. **5**

The planets that were closest to the Sun didn't keep much of their gas. The Sun's heat blasted it away, leaving behind solid **spheres** of matter, with only a little gas. Those spheres became the terrestrial planets—Mercury, Venus, Earth, and Mars. But on the outer edges of the disk, far away from the Sun's heat, it was much cooler. The clumps of rock and dirt there still had their thick layers of gas; they didn't burn away. The planets farthest from the Sun became the gas giants—Jupiter, Saturn, Uranus, and Neptune.

408

A C T Access Complex Text

▶ Sentence Structure

Point out that a dash sets off information that explains the part of the sentence before it. On page 408, the author uses dashes to explain terrestrial planets and gas giants.

→ *Which planets are terrestrial planets?* (Mercury, Venus, Earth, Mars) *Which planets are the gas giants?* (Jupiter, Saturn, Uranus, Neptune)

▶ Specific Vocabulary

Point out the word *dense* on page 409.

→ *Identify context clues to figure out what* dense *means.* (rocky core, made of rock, [not] made of gas) *What is another word for* dense? (thick, solid)

Have students use context clues to figure out the phrase *raised questions.* (made people ask questions)

Because astronomers still believed this theory about how our planets formed, they had a problem with Pluto. When it was first discovered in 1930, astronomers assumed Pluto was made of ice and gas because of its great distance from the sun. However, by 1987, Pluto had moved into a position that only occurs twice in its 248-year orbit and scientific instruments had improved. Astronomers were able to study Pluto and the light that reflected off it. Their instruments told them that Pluto was dense and must have a rocky core. That new information raised questions. If the planets closest to the Sun were rocky and the planets farthest away from the Sun were mostly made of gas, why was Pluto—the most distant planet of all—made of rock?

6

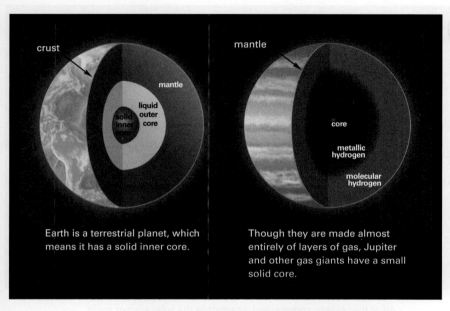

crust mantle mantle

liquid outer core solid inner core

core

metallic hydrogen

molecular hydrogen

Earth is a terrestrial planet, which means it has a solid inner core.

Though they are made almost entirely of layers of gas, Jupiter and other gas giants have a small solid core.

Michelle Gengaro-Kokmen

STOP AND CHECK

Ask and Answer Questions According to theory, why are some planets mostly made of gas and others mostly made of rock? Go back to the text to find the answer.

409

LITERATURE ANTHOLOGY, pp. 408–409

7 Text Features: Diagram

On page 409, what information do you learn about Earth and the gas giants from the diagram that is not contained in the text? (The diagram shows the names of the layers of planets, such as *crust* and *mantle*, and where they are located in relation to each other; the types of gases present in a gas giant; and that Earth has a liquid outer core surrounding the solid inner core.)

7

STOP AND CHECK

Ask and Answer Questions According to theory, why are some planets mostly made of gas and others mostly made of rock? (Planets close to the Sun are made of rock because heat from the Sun blasted away the gas. In the planets far away from the Sun, the gas didn't burn up because it was cooler.)

CONNECT TO CONTENT
INNER AND OUTER PLANETS

The four planets closest to the Sun—Mercury, Venus, Earth, and Mars—are known as the inner planets. The planets farthest away from the Sun—Jupiter, Saturn, Uranus, and Neptune—are known as the outer planets. On pages 408–409, the author compares and contrasts several properties of the inner and outer planets, including their surfaces, climates, and origins.

STEM

ELL Help ELLs understand why Pluto's dense core and its location raised questions about its being a planet. Use a rock and a cotton ball to illustrate planets that are dense and planets that are mostly gas.

→ *What are planets close to the sun like?* (the rock)

→ *Where is Pluto?* (far from the Sun) *What is Pluto like?* (the rock)

Develop Comprehension

⑧ **Strategy: Ask and Answer Questions**

Teacher Think Aloud There is a lot of information about orbits on this page. What questions can we ask to be sure we understand it?

Prompt students to apply the strategy in a Think Aloud by asking themselves questions about orbits and finding answers for their questions in the text. Have them turn to a partner and paraphrase what they read.

Student Think Aloud The text says that an orbit is like a lane on a racetrack. How are they similar? As I keep reading, I see that each planet has its own path around the Sun, just like runners each have their own lane on a track.

⑧ There were other questions as well. Pluto's orbit is different from the orbits of the planets. Think of an orbit as a lane on a racetrack. Just as runners have their own lanes on the track, each planet has its own orbit around the Sun. For the runners, all the lanes together make up the racetrack. For the planets, all their orbits, taken together, make up the "orbital plane." Just as runners don't run outside their individual lanes, planets don't travel around the Sun outside their individual orbits. Except for Pluto. Pluto crosses Neptune's orbit.

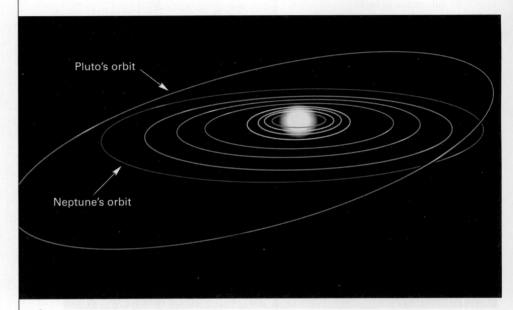

Pluto's orbit

Neptune's orbit

Michelle Gengaro-Kokmen

All of the planets, comets, and asteroids in the solar system are in orbit around the Sun. Their orbits line up with each other, creating an imaginary flat disk called the orbital plane. Pluto's orbit, which takes 248 Earth years to complete, brings it outside the orbital plane. For 20 years of each orbit, Pluto moves inside the orbit of Neptune, making Neptune farther from the sun than Pluto. Pluto was inside Neptune's orbit from 1979 to 1999.

410

A C T Access Complex Text

▶ **Genre**

Diagrams are often included in expository text to give information visually. Remind students to use the diagram on page 410 to help them understand text on page 411.

→ Read aloud the second and third sentences, calling attention to the words "oval-shaped" and "stretched-out oblong."

→ *How does the diagram help you understand these descriptions?* (The diagram shows the shapes of all the planets' orbits, making it obvious how the shape of Pluto's orbit is different.)

→ *What does* oblong *mean?* ("a long distorted circle")

Pluto and its moon, Charon. Pluto was 2.6 billion miles from Earth when the Hubble Space Telescope took this photo.

Dr. R. Albrecht, ESA/ESO Space Telescope European Coordinating Facility; NASA

The shape of Pluto's orbit is different, too. The larger planets travel around the Sun in an oval-shaped orbit. Pluto's orbit is more of a stretched-out oblong. The other planets' orbits are level with the Sun. Pluto's is tilted. Comets' orbits are often tilted, so astronomers wondered, Could Pluto be a comet?

And of course there is Pluto's size. Astronomers knew Pluto was tiny when it was discovered in 1930. But because it was so far away, it was hard to see the planet clearly. Pluto appeared as a tiny dot of light in the night sky. Then telescopes improved. In 1976, American **9** astronomer James Christy discovered that the tiny dot everyone thought was Pluto was really two objects: Pluto had a moon— Charon (CARE-en). Once astronomers discovered that Charon was separate from Pluto, they realized that Pluto was even smaller than they had originally thought. Pluto is only 1,440 miles in **diameter**. (Charon's diameter is 790 miles.) They began to ask, Is Pluto too small to be a planet? And since they had found Charon, they wondered, Were there more objects out there the size of Pluto? **10** Were *they* planets, too?

411

LITERATURE ANTHOLOGY, pp. 410–411

9 Vocabulary: Greek Roots

The Greek root *tele* means "far," and the Greek root *scop* means "view." How does knowing these roots help you figure out the meaning of *telescope*? (Combining the roots produces the definition: "an instrument used to view far away objects.")

10 Skill: Cause and Effect

Why was Pluto hard to see? (It was very far away.) What happened as a result of telescopes improving? (James Christy discovered that Pluto had a moon.) What questions did this lead scientists to ask? (Was Pluto too small to be a planet? Were there more objects the size of Pluto?) Add the causes and effects to your organizer.

Cause	→	Effect
Pluto was very far away.	→	It was hard to see.
Telescopes improved.	→	James Christy discovered that the tiny dot scientists thought was Pluto was actually two objects.

CONNECT TO CONTENT
CHARACTERISTICS OF PLANETS

On page 410, students read that one of the major characteristics all planets have in common is staying within a fixed orbit around the Sun. One of the reasons that Pluto was demoted as a planet is that it does not share this characteristic; it travels outside of its orbital plane.

STEM

ELLs may need support to understand the concept of orbits. Point out the cognate orbit/*órbita*.

→ An *orbit* is a path that goes around and around.

→ *Look at the diagram. Use your finger to trace Pluto's orbit.*

→ *Is Pluto's orbit the same or different than Neptune's orbit?* (different)

Develop Comprehension

⑪ Strategy: Ask and Answer Questions

Reread page 412. Ask yourself a question about the text. Then share your question with a partner and search together for the answer.

Student Think Aloud The fourth paragraph says that robots changed the way astronomers study the night sky. I wonder how things changed? As I continue reading, I find out that astronomers no longer have to stay up at night to watch the sky. Robots take photographs for them. The photos are sent to special computers.

FINDING PLANETS

In 1992, astronomers made an amazing discovery: 9.3 *billion* miles away from our sun is another region of space, shaped like a disk. Astronomers believe it contains approximately 70,000 icy objects, including Pluto.

This area of space was named the Kuiper Belt, after the Dutch-American astronomer Gerard Kuiper (KI-per) who lived from 1905 to 1973. In 1951, more than forty years before its discovery, Kuiper actually predicted that a region like this might exist.

Michael Brown, Chad Trujillo, and David Rabinowitz are planetary astronomers who study Kuiper Belt Objects, or KBOs. People often call these men "the Planet Finders." Together, they hunt for planets at the outer edges of our solar system using the Samuel Oschin Telescope at the Palomar Observatory in California. The Oschin telescope is a wide-field telescope, which means it views broad regions of the sky at once. When paired with a camera at the observatory, it can take pictures of these large areas.

In the past, astronomers had to spend their evenings peering through telescopes in order to study the night sky. Now things have changed. Robots control the Oschin telescope and its camera.

⑪ In the evenings, the cameras in the telescope at the Palomar Observatory are at work. They take three photographs over three hours of the part of the night sky the men want to study. Any object moving across the background of billions of stars and galaxies will be captured in pictures. The pictures are then sent from the telescope's cameras to a bank of ten computers at the California Institute of Technology. Next, the computers decide which objects appear to be moving and therefore might be a planet. Usually, the computers select about 100 objects; when the men arrive at work each morning, the pictures are ready for them to view.

412

A C T Access Complex Text

▶ Connection of Ideas

Tell students that on page 412, the author builds on previous ideas in each new paragraph.

→ *The first paragraph tells about the discovery of a special region of space.*

→ *What do we learn in the second paragraph that is related to the first paragraph?* (The region mentioned in paragraph one is named the Kuiper Belt; Gerard Kuiper predicted its existence more than 40 years earlier.)

Objects in the Kuiper Belt are so far away, it takes them hundreds of Earth years to orbit the Sun. **12**

Dan Durda, Fellow, International Association of Astronomical Artists

413

LITERATURE ANTHOLOGY, pp. 412–413

12 Genre: Expository Text

Expository text provides information and facts about a topic. Authors use text features to organize ideas and share information. Turn to a partner and discuss text features you find on page 412. (I see the subheading "Finding Planets" and a photograph and caption.) How do the photo and caption on page 413 add to the information on page 412? (They help the reader visualize the Kuiper Belt and understand how far away it is.)

→ How does information about "the Planet Finders" in the third paragraph relate to the first two paragraphs? (They are the people who look for planets in the Kuiper Belt.)

▶ Sentence Structure

Help students understand the first sentence in paragraph two by removing descriptive phrases.

→ *Restate the sentence using just the essential information.* (This area of space was named the Kuiper Belt after Gerard Kuiper.)

→ *What do the omitted details tell about?* (They give additional facts about Gerard Kuiper.)

Develop Comprehension

13 Author's Craft: Comparison

Authors of expository text may compare two things or ideas to help readers make connections. **What comparison does the author make between Pluto and Xena?** (Pluto is 3.6 billion miles away, but Xena is 10 billion miles away. Xena is 400 miles bigger in diameter than Pluto. Xena takes twice as long as Pluto to orbit Earth.) **How does this comparison help you understand why scientists asked whether or not Xena was a planet?** (Xena was much bigger than Pluto, so it could be a planet.)

They call David Rabinowitz (left), Chad Trujillo (upper left), and Mike Brown (center) "the Planet Finders." The team used the Oschin telescope (right) to discover Eris.

(l) Courtesy of Caltech, Palomar Observatory, (c) Courtesy of Chad Trujillo, (r) Courtesy of Caltech, Palomar Observatory

Mike Brown says most of the objects he looks at on his computer screen are not planets. Many are caused by some kind of flaw in the telescope's camera. But every once in a while, an astronomer will get very lucky and something new and exciting will appear. That's how Mike and his team discovered 2003UB313, or Xena (ZEE-nah), as it was nicknamed, on October 21, 2003. Mike says, "The very first time I saw Xena on my screen, I thought that there was something wrong. It was too big and too bright. Then I did a **calculation** of how big it was and how far away it was. Xena is the most distant object ever seen in orbit around the Sun."

13 Pluto is 3.6 billion miles away, but Xena is 10 billion miles away and is approximately 400 miles bigger in diameter than Pluto. It takes Xena more than twice as long as Pluto to orbit the Sun.

Xena was always a nickname. On September 13, 2006, the newly discovered celestial body officially became Eris (AIR-is), for the Greek goddess of strife and discord. It seems an appropriate name, since there was a lot of strife and discord surrounding Eris. Was it a planet, or not?

414

ACT Access Complex Text

▶ Specific Vocabulary

Point out the words *strife* and *discord* in the last paragraph on page 414.

→ *Identify context clues to figure out what* strife *and* discord *mean.* ("Was it a planet or not?" implies that scientists argued and disagreed about the discovery. On page 415 we find out they did argue about it. *Strife* and *discord* mean "a disagreement.")

→ Have partners confirm their definitions in a dictionary. Point out that the two words are synonyms.

Discuss why scientists disagreed about Eris.

→ *What was the problem with the dictionary definition of* planet? (It was too general. A "large body" wasn't specific enough.)

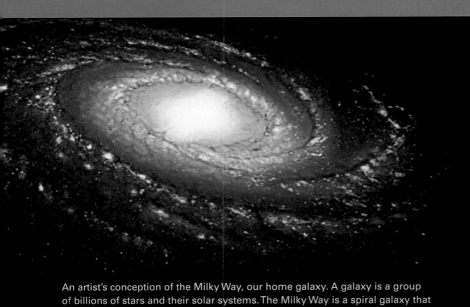

An artist's conception of the Milky Way, our home galaxy. A galaxy is a group of billions of stars and their solar systems. The Milky Way is a spiral galaxy that contains 200 billion stars.

WHAT IS A PLANET?

Because scientists always check and recheck their work, Mike Brown and his team of astronomers didn't announce their discovery of Eris until January 5, 2005, after they had had a chance to verify their information. When they revealed their discovery, many people thought the solar system had gained its tenth planet. But others disagreed. Soon an argument was raging among astronomers all over the world. And the argument came down to one question. What, exactly, is a planet?

It seems surprising, but until August 24, 2006, science had never had a definition for the word "planet." Dictionaries had definitions, of course, but most said something similar to "A large celestial body that circles around the Sun or another star." For a scientist, that definition had problems. For one thing, what is meant by "large body"? Jupiter, the largest planet in our solar system, is 88,700 miles in diameter, and it is a planet. Pluto is only 1,440 miles in diameter and—at the time—it was a planet, too. The question "What is a planet?" needed an answer, and the International Astronomical Union decided to create not one definition but three.

Mark Garlick (Space art)

415

LITERATURE ANTHOLOGY, pp. 414–415

Skill: Cause and Effect

Why didn't the astronomers announce their discovery right away? (They wanted to recheck their work.) **Why did people all around the world begin arguing about whether or not Eris was a planet?** (Scientists had never defined the word "planet.") **Add the causes and effects to your organizer.**

Cause	→	Effect
The astronomers checked and rechecked their work.	→	They didn't announce their discovery of Eris until 2005.
Science had never defined the word "planet."	→	Astronomers around the world argued whether or not Eris was a planet.

► **Connection of Ideas**

Remind students to connect pictures with the text.

→ *How is the photograph of the Oschin telescope on page 414 connected to the text on page 413?* (Page 413 tells how astronomers used the telescope to take large pictures of the sky.)

ELL Help students understand that on page 415 when the author says the argument "came down to" one question, it means that there was one main question that mattered.

→ *What question did scientists argue about?* (What is a planet?)

Develop Comprehension

15 **Skill: Main Idea and Key Details**

What do the details in each paragraph on page 416 have in common? (They are all about the definition of a planet.) What is the main idea on this page? (The IAU made three rules used to decide whether a celestial body is a planet.)

The IAU came up with three classes of objects that orbit the Sun: planets, dwarf planets, and small solar-system bodies.

The IAU decided that a celestial body is a planet if it:

1. orbits the Sun
2. is round or nearly round, because its gravity has pulled it into that shape
3. is big enough and has enough gravity to "clear the neighborhood" around its orbit

The first two qualifications for planethood, orbiting the Sun and a round shape, are easy to understand. The concept of "clearing the neighborhood" is a little more difficult.

It might help to think of planets as the schoolyard bullies of the solar system. In order to clear the neighborhood, a planet has to be big enough, and have enough gravity, to get rid of any celestial objects in its way. A large planet might clear its orbit by using its gravity to pull other, smaller, objects toward it and destroy them, the way asteroids are destroyed when they hit Earth.

A cosmic collision. Planets often "clear their neighborhoods" in this manner.

NASA/JPL

416

A C T Access Complex Text

▶ Genre

Help students connect the illustration and its caption on page 416 with the text in the last paragraph on that page.

→ *What is happening in the picture?* (Two objects in space are colliding, and one is breaking apart.)

→ *What sentence in the text describes the action shown in the illustration?* (the last sentence)

▶ Connection of Ideas

Help students connect the term *celestial body* in paragraph two on page 416 to the existing definition of a planet on page 415.

→ *How did scientists define a planet before? How is the new definition different?* (A planet was defined as a large celestial body; the new definition distinguishes planets from other celestial bodies.)

Or a planet might clear its orbit by attracting smaller objects toward it, then turning them into moons that remain in orbit around the planet.

Sometimes a planet will simply push a smaller body into a completely different orbit and get rid of it that way. But no matter how it does the clearing, according to the IAU definition, a planet must travel in its orbit by itself.

The secondary category of planets, called "dwarf planets," have the following characteristics. They must:

1. orbit the Sun
2. be round
3. not be a moon or satellite of another planet

By this definition, Pluto is a dwarf planet. And although Charon, its former moon, is still locked in an orbit with Pluto, it is a dwarf planet, too. Now they are known as a double-planet system. Ceres is a dwarf planet, also, and Mike Brown's discovery, Eris, is one as well. They are dwarf planets because they orbit the Sun, they are round, and they are not moons of another planet—but they're too small to have enough gravity to clear their neighborhood. Pluto, Charon, Ceres, and Eris are all KBOs—orbiting far out in space with other objects in the Kuiper Belt.

STOP AND CHECK

Ask and Answer Questions How does the size and gravity of a planet affect other objects around it? Look for details in the text to find the answer.

NASA/JPL

417

LITERATURE ANTHOLOGY, pp. 416–417

16 Strategy: Ask and Answer Questions

Generate a question of your own about the definition of planets. For example, you might ask, "What is the difference between a planet and a dwarf planet?" Answer this question by paraphrasing the text. (A planet orbits the Sun, is round or nearly round, and is big enough to clear away objects in its path. A dwarf planet is also round and orbits the Sun, but it is not as big as a planet, so it doesn't have enough gravity to clear its path. A dwarf planet cannot be a moon or satellite of another planet.)

STOP AND CHECK

Ask and Answer Questions How does the size and gravity of a planet affect other objects around it? (A planet can attract objects to it and destroy them or turn them into moons, or it can push smaller bodies into another orbit.)

ELL Help ELLs understand the concept of celestial bodies.

→ *In this context, a* body *means "an object." Planets and dwarf planets are* celestial bodies, *meaning "objects in space."*

→ *Planets, dwarf planets, and smaller bodies all orbit the Sun.*

Discuss with students the new definition for planets asking them to demonstrate what "clearing the neighborhood" might look like.

→ *Show me a planet that clears its neighborhood by pulling smaller objects to it and destroying them.*

→ *Show me a planet that clears its neighborhood by turning a smaller object into a moon.*

Develop Comprehension

17 Skill: Make Inferences

Reread the final paragraph on page 418. What can you infer about the number of planets in the future? (As "new information is discovered," the number of planets changes, as shown by the past. So the number might change again as more new information is discovered.) **The author says, "And that is just in *our* solar system!" What is the author implying?** (By italicizing *our*, the author implies that other solar systems in space may also have planets.)

Everything else—asteroids, comets, meteors—are now members of the third class of objects that orbit the Sun and are called "small solar-system bodies."

Some astronomers think the definition of a planet will change again in the future. Others think the current definition is a good one and will last.

Science is exciting, because it continually changes as new information is discovered. A long time ago, we thought there were six planets. Then we thought there were eight. For a while, there were nine. Then it was back to eight. Then, with Pluto, the number jumped up to nine again. And now it's back to eight. And that is just in *our* solar system!

An artist's conception of the New Horizons spacecraft as it arrives at Pluto. Charon is visible in the distance.

Johns Hopkins University Applied Physics Laboratory/Southwest Research Institute

418

A C T Access Complex Text

▶ Purpose

Point out that the author concludes the selection by explaining that scientists have a great deal more to learn about planets.

→ *On page 418, what changes does the author say might occur in the future?* (the definition of planet, the number of planets in our solar system)

→ *On page 419, how does the author show readers how much more scientists have to learn?* (She lists many questions that don't yet have answers.)

→ *What is the author's purpose for writing this selection?* (Readers can infer that the author may want to inspire future scientists.)

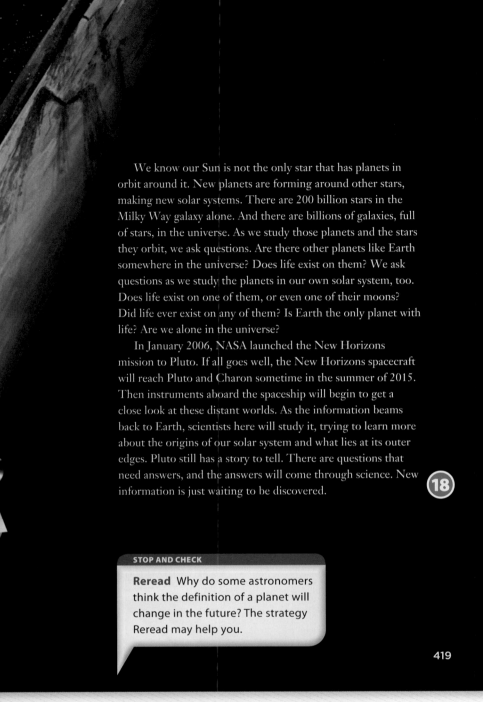

We know our Sun is not the only star that has planets in orbit around it. New planets are forming around other stars, making new solar systems. There are 200 billion stars in the Milky Way galaxy alone. And there are billions of galaxies, full of stars, in the universe. As we study those planets and the stars they orbit, we ask questions. Are there other planets like Earth somewhere in the universe? Does life exist on them? We ask questions as we study the planets in our own solar system, too. Does life exist on one of them, or even one of their moons? Did life ever exist on any of them? Is Earth the only planet with life? Are we alone in the universe?

In January 2006, NASA launched the New Horizons mission to Pluto. If all goes well, the New Horizons spacecraft will reach Pluto and Charon sometime in the summer of 2015. Then instruments aboard the spaceship will begin to get a close look at these distant worlds. As the information beams back to Earth, scientists here will study it, trying to learn more about the origins of our solar system and what lies at its outer edges. Pluto still has a story to tell. There are questions that need answers, and the answers will come through science. New information is just waiting to be discovered. **18**

STOP AND CHECK

Reread Why do some astronomers think the definition of a planet will change in the future? The strategy Reread may help you.

419

LITERATURE ANTHOLOGY, pp. 418–419

---

18 Skill: Cause and Effect

What will happen if the New Horizons spacecraft reaches Pluto and Charon? Paraphrase the text to explain the effect. (Instruments on the spacecraft will be able to get a close look at these distant worlds.) What will happen as scientists receive new data from the spacecraft? (They will learn more about how our solar system formed and what is at its outer edges.)

STOP AND CHECK

Reread Why do some astronomers think the definition of a planet will change in the future? (As we learn new information about space, definitions may change.)

Return to Predictions

Review students' predictions and purposes for reading. Ask them to answer the Essential Question. (Scientists discover new information that refutes old conclusions, such as the evidence that showed Pluto could no longer be considered a planet.)

ELL Help ELLs understand the questions scientists are asking on page 419.

→ Explain that in this context, *life* meanings living things, such as plants and animals. Point out the cognate exist/*existir*.

→ *Does life exist on Earth?* (yes)

→ *What do scientists want to know about other planets?* (Does life exist on other planets?)

About the Author

Meet the Author

Elaine Scott

Have students read the biography of the author. Ask:

→ Why did Elaine Scott decide to write for children instead of adults?

→ What sources did Elaine Scott use to write this story? Why did she use these sources?

Author's Purpose

To Inform

Remind students that the main purpose of most nonfiction is to give information. Students may say that Elaine Scott ends a paragraph with a question to get readers thinking about what the answer might be and to make them interested in reading on to find the answer.

Author's Craft

Text Features

Explain that text features include captions, diagrams, sidebars, photographs, and illustrations. Discuss what diagrams add to the text.

→ Some information is easier to show with images or charts than to explain with words. Example: The diagram on page 409 shows the layers of terrestrial planets and gas giants.

→ Have students locate another text feature that showed information, such as the diagram of the orbits on page 410.

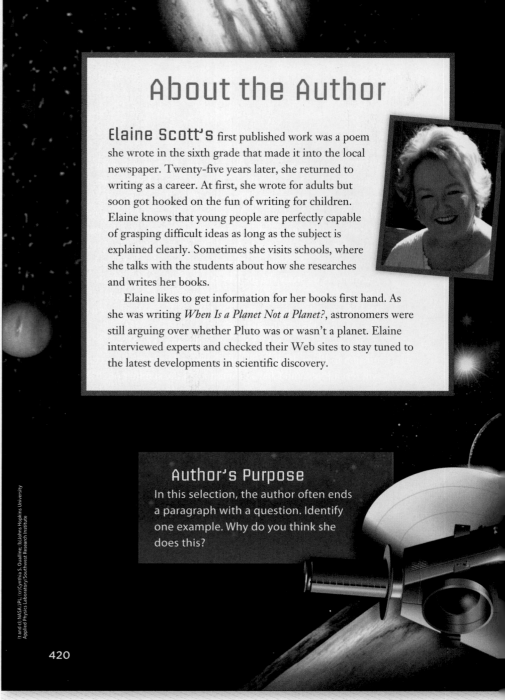

About the Author

Elaine Scott's first published work was a poem she wrote in the sixth grade that made it into the local newspaper. Twenty-five years later, she returned to writing as a career. At first, she wrote for adults but soon got hooked on the fun of writing for children. Elaine knows that young people are perfectly capable of grasping difficult ideas as long as the subject is explained clearly. Sometimes she visits schools, where she talks with the students about how she researches and writes her books.

Elaine likes to get information for her books first hand. As she was writing *When Is a Planet Not a Planet?*, astronomers were still arguing over whether Pluto was or wasn't a planet. Elaine interviewed experts and checked their Web sites to stay tuned to the latest developments in scientific discovery.

Author's Purpose
In this selection, the author often ends a paragraph with a question. Identify one example. Why do you think she does this?

420

LITERATURE ANTHOLOGY, pp. 420–421

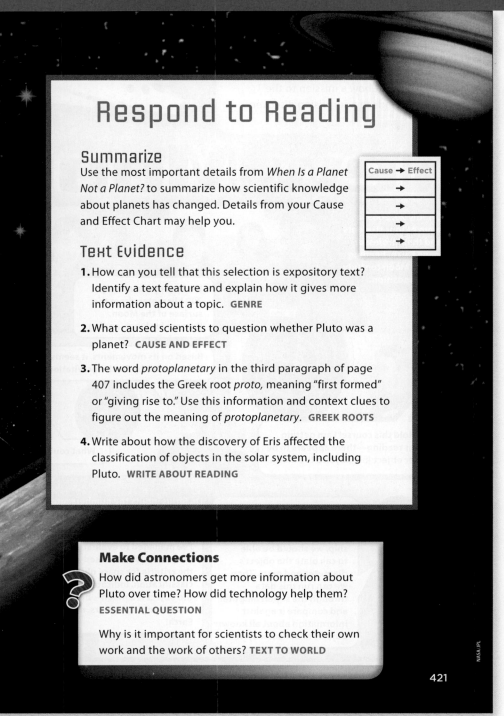

Respond to Reading

Summarize

Use the most important details from *When Is a Planet Not a Planet?* to summarize how scientific knowledge about planets has changed. Details from your Cause and Effect Chart may help you.

Cause → Effect
→
→
→
→

Text Evidence

1. How can you tell that this selection is expository text? Identify a text feature and explain how it gives more information about a topic. **GENRE**

2. What caused scientists to question whether Pluto was a planet? **CAUSE AND EFFECT**

3. The word *protoplanetary* in the third paragraph of page 407 includes the Greek root *proto,* meaning "first formed" or "giving rise to." Use this information and context clues to figure out the meaning of *protoplanetary*. **GREEK ROOTS**

4. Write about how the discovery of Eris affected the classification of objects in the solar system, including Pluto. **WRITE ABOUT READING**

Make Connections

How did astronomers get more information about Pluto over time? How did technology help them? **ESSENTIAL QUESTION**

Why is it important for scientists to check their own work and the work of others? **TEXT TO WORLD**

NASA.JPL

421

Make Connections · *Analytical Writing*

Essential Question Have partners work together to cite evidence from the text to tell how astronomers gathered information about Pluto and how technology helped them. Ask partners to discuss their findings with the class.

Text to World Have students discuss why it is important for scientists to recheck their work. Ask them to share ideas about what might happen if scientists are not careful.

Respond to Reading

Summarize

Review with students the information from their graphic organizers. Model how to use the information to summarize *When Is a Planet Not a Planet?*

Analytical Writing **Write About Reading: Summarize** Ask students to write a summary explaining the causes and effects relating to defining planets. Have them begin their summaries by giving the title and genre of the selection.

Text Evidence

1. **Genre** <u>Answer</u> It gives facts about a topic and it uses subheadings, photos, captions, illustrations, and diagrams. <u>Evidence</u> The diagram shows information about the layers of planets. Facts, such as there are 200 billion stars in our galaxy, tell about the topic.

2. **Cause and Effect** <u>Answer</u> Its size, its solid core, and its orbit caused scientists to question Pluto. <u>Evidence</u> Telescopes showed that Pluto was smaller than previously thought. It was dense, unlike the other distant planets, and it had a different orbit than the other planets.

3. **Greek Roots** <u>Answer</u> *Protoplanetary* means "relating to the formation of planets." <u>Evidence</u> The definition of the root *proto-*; the sentence "It pulled and tugged at the bits of rock, dust, ice, and gas until they came together in clumps of material we now call planets."

4. *Analytical Writing* **Write About Reading: Cause and Effect** Pages 415–417 explain that the discovery led to arguments about the definition of a planet. This caused the IAU to create definitions for planets, dwarf-planets, and

Develop Comprehension

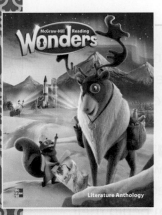

Literature Anthology

"New Moon"

Text Complexity Range

Lexile

740 — ▲ 870 — 1010

TextEvaluator™

23 — ▲ 33 — 51

Compare Texts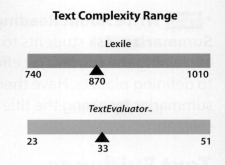

Students will do a close reading of this science-fiction graphic story, which appears as a comic strip. Have students **ask and answer questions** or use other strategies they know. As they reread they will note text evidence to compare this text with *When Is a Planet Not a Planet?*

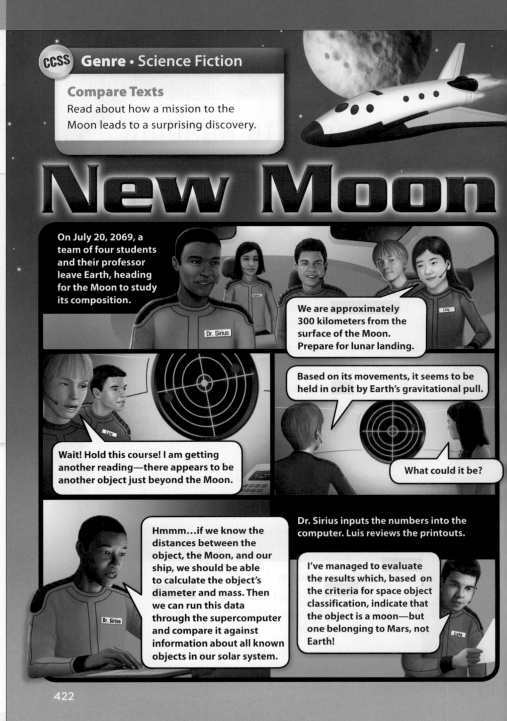

CCSS Genre · Science Fiction

Compare Texts
Read about how a mission to the Moon leads to a surprising discovery.

New Moon

On July 20, 2069, a team of four students and their professor leave Earth, heading for the Moon to study its composition.

We are approximately 300 kilometers from the surface of the Moon. Prepare for lunar landing.

Based on its movements, it seems to be held in orbit by Earth's gravitational pull.

Wait! Hold this course! I am getting another reading—there appears to be another object just beyond the Moon.

What could it be?

Hmmm…if we know the distances between the object, the Moon, and our ship, we should be able to calculate the object's diameter and mass. Then we can run this data through the supercomputer and compare it against information about all known objects in our solar system.

Dr. Sirius inputs the numbers into the computer. Luis reviews the printouts.

I've managed to evaluate the results which, based on the criteria for space object classification, indicate that the object is a moon—but one belonging to Mars, not Earth!

422

A C T Access Complex Text

What makes this text complex?
▶ **Prior Knowledge**

▶ Prior Knowledge

Explain that authors of science fiction often blend real scientific knowledge with a fictional situation. Point out the panels about tides on page 423.

→ Explain that the gravity of the Moon pulls on Earth's water, creating tides. *Tides* are changes in the water level of large bodies of water. The distance of the Moon determine the tides.

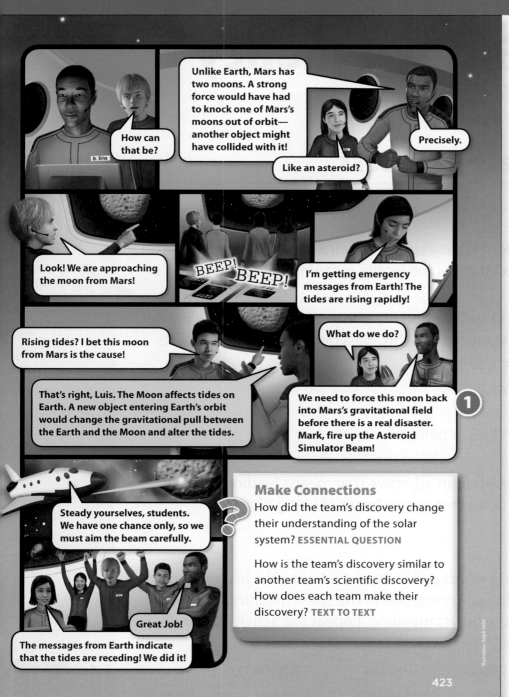

LITERATURE ANTHOLOGY, pp. 422–423

1 Ask and Answer Questions

How does the team solve the problem of the new moon?

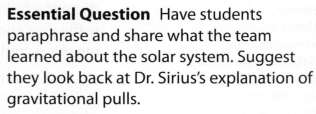 **Write About Reading** With a partner, paraphrase the text. (They use an Asteroid Simulator Beam to force the moon out of Earth's orbit and back into Mars's gravitational field.)

Make Connections

Essential Question Have students paraphrase and share what the team learned about the solar system. Suggest they look back at Dr. Sirius's explanation of gravitational pulls.

Text to Text Have partners use their response to the Ask and Answer Questions prompt to compare this text with *When Is a Planet Not a Planet?* (In both selections, both teams use scientific knowledge and technology to explore space and apply what they already know to new situations. However, the Planet Finders work from Earth, while this team works on a space shuttle. Also, the Planet Finders take time to verify their discoveries, whereas the team in this story must act quickly to prevent disaster.)

→ *Why does having a second moon in orbit cause tides on Earth to rise rapidly?* (Another moon adds to the gravitational pull on Earth's water, so the tides get higher.)

→ *What problems could especially high tides cause?* (They could cause flooding.)

ELL Help students understand the concept of tides. Point out the cognate: gravitational/*gravitacional*.

→ Using images of the Moon and the ocean, gesture to show how the Moon pulls on Earth's oceans.

→ *In the story, what new object enters Earth's orbit?* (another moon) *Now two moons are pulling the ocean. What disaster might happen?* (a flood)

Word Study/Fluency

MINILESSON
20 Mins

Suffixes *-less* and *-ness*

OBJECTIVES

CCSS Know and apply grade-level phonics and word analysis skills in decoding words. Use combined knowledge of all letter-sound correspondences, syllabication patterns, and morphology (e.g., roots and affixes) to read accurately unfamiliar multisyllabic words in context and out of context. **RF.5.3a**

CCSS Use context to confirm or self-correct word recognition and understanding, rereading as necessary. **RF.5.4c**

Rate: 129–149 WCPM

ACADEMIC LANGUAGE
accuracy

Refer to the sound transfers chart in the **Language Transfers Handbook** to identify sounds that do not transfer in Spanish, Cantonese, Vietnamese, Hmong, and Korean.

1 Explain

Review with students that a suffix is a word part added to the end of a word. A suffix changes the word's meaning as well as its part of speech.

Write the following suffixes and meanings on the board. Review the suffix *-less* and introduce the suffix *-ness* by reading each suffix, its meaning, and the sample word.

→ *-less*, means "without"
thankless

→ *-ness*, means "state of being"
kindness

Explain that *thankless* is an adjective that means "without thanks," and *kindness* is a noun that means "state of being kind."

2 Model

Write the following words on the board. Point to the first word, and model how to use knowledge of the suffix meaning to decode the word and figure out its meaning. Repeat the activity using the remaining words:

goodness	tireless	happiness
fearless	careless	ageless

3 Guided Practice

Write the following words on the board. Have students underline the suffix in each word, define the suffix, and then use its meaning to determine the meaning of the whole word.

darkness	hopeless	stainless	greatness
toothless	seamless	sweetness	gentleness
skinless	thoughtless	calmness	treeless
wingless	dryness	hairless	rightness
bitterness	clueless	brightness	colorless

Go Digital

Suffixes *-less* and *-ness*

Present the Lesson

View "Changing Views of Earth"

Read Multisyllabic Words

Transition to Longer Words Write on the board the following words with more than one suffix. Have students read a base word in the first column. Then model how to read the longer words in the second and third columns. To help students gain awareness of suffixes as common word parts, circle the suffix or suffixes added to each word.

help	helpless	helplessness
self	selfless	selflessness
worth	worthless	worthlessness
time	timeless	timelessness
use	useless	uselessness

To review prefixes and suffixes, guide students to decode the following words: *unhappiness, hopefulness, healthfulness, unkindness.*

 **FLUENCY**

Accuracy

Explain/Model Explain that reading with accuracy means reading each word as it appears on the page and pronouncing words correctly. Turn to "Changing Views of Earth," **Reading/Writing Workshop** pages 352–355. Model reading page 353 with accuracy.

Remind students that you will be listening for accuracy as you monitor their reading during the week.

Practice/Apply Have partners take turns reading page 353. As one student reads, have the other student follow along, checking for accuracy. Afterward, have students review any skipped or mispronounced words.

Daily Fluency Practice

Students can practice fluency using **Your Turn Practice Book** passages.

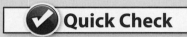 **Monitor and** *Differentiate*

 Quick Check

Can students read words with suffixes *-less* and *-ness*? Can students read with accuracy?

Small Group Instruction

If No →	Approaching Level	Reteach pp. T234, T238
	ELL	Develop pp. T251, 254
If Yes →	On Level	Apply pp. T240–T241
	Beyond Level	Apply pp. T244–T245

ON-LEVEL PRACTICE BOOK p. 238

Word Study: Suffixes -less and -ness

Name _____

A. Read each sentence. Write the word with the suffix -less or -ness on the line. Then circle the suffix.

1. The owls went hunting under the cover of darkness. ____ dark(ness)
2. The fearless police officers raced to the rescue. ____ fear(less)
3. "I will not tolerate this foolishness," our teacher said. ____ foolish(ness)
4. Were you filled with sadness when your team lost the game? ____ sad(ness)
5. The photographer captured the fullness of the moon. ____ full(ness)
6. The situation seemed hopeless, but we kept trying. ____ hope(less)

B. Add the suffix -less or -ness to the word in parentheses. Write the new sentence on the line.

7. Our boat drifted for hours on the (motion) sea.
   Our boat drifted for hours on the *motionless* sea.
8. Did you see the (fierce) in the tiger's eyes?
   Did you see the *fierceness* in the tiger's eyes?
9. The spider looked (harm), but I decided not to touch it.
   The spider looked *harmless*, but I decided not to touch it.
10. My parents and I have a (fond) for picnics in the woods.
    My parents and I have a *fondness* for picnics in the woods.

238 Practice • Grade 5 • Unit 5 • Week 4

| APPROACHING p. 238 | BEYOND p. 238 | ELL p. 238 |

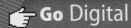

Go Digital

www.connected.mcgraw-hill.com
RESOURCES
Research and Inquiry

Wrap Up the Week

Integrate Ideas

RESEARCH AND INQUIRY

Now We Know

OBJECTIVES

CCSS Conduct short research projects that use several sources to build knowledge through investigation of different aspects of a topic. **W.5.7**

- Narrow a research topic.
- Summarize and paraphrase information.
- Take notes.
- Avoid plagiarism.

ACADEMIC LANGUAGE

- *summarize, verify, paraphrase, plagiarism*
- Cognates: *resumir, verificar, parafrasear*

Create a Summary

Explain that students will work in small groups to research historical changes in one area of medicine, such as surgery, pharmaceuticals, nursing, or nutrition. Then groups will summarize their findings in five to ten bullet points and post them on the Shared Research Board. Discuss the following steps:

1 Narrow a Research Topic Have groups narrow their research topic to one that is focused and able to be researched. For example, they might begin by researching surgery and then select a type of surgery, such as brain or heart.

2 Find Resources Ask groups to search reliable Web sites for information about their topic. Explain that it is a good practice to verify all facts with at least two sources. Have students take notes to use in their summaries. Remind them that their notes should paraphrase the information they find. Stress the importance of avoiding plagiarism, or copying someone else's words. Have students use online Research Process Checklist 3 to evaluate their research.

3 Guided Practice Review with students that a summary includes only the most important ideas about a topic. Check each group's work as they begin, and guide them to make any necessary changes to their summaries.

4 Create a Summary Have groups create a summary of their research, listing five to ten bullet points. Stress that all group members should participate in the activity.

Present the Summary

Have groups post their summaries on the Shared Research Board.

STEM

TEXT CONNECTIONS  *Analytical Writing*

OBJECTIVES

CCSS Integrate information from several texts on the same topic in order to write or speak about the subject knowledgeably. **RI.5.9**

CCSS Review the key ideas expressed and draw conclusions in light of information and knowledge gained from the discussions. **SL.5.1d**

Text to Text

COLLABORATE

Cite Evidence Tell students they will work in groups to compare the changes in scientific knowledge in all of this week's reading. Model how to make comparisons using examples from the week's **Leveled Readers** and "Changing Views of Earth," **Reading/Writing Workshop** pages 352–355. Have students review the week's reading and their notes and graphic organizers. Help them set up an Accordion Foldable® to organize their findings. From each selection, students should record examples of early scientific ideas and scientific ideas today. They should then use this information to draw conclusions about how scientific knowledge has changed over time.

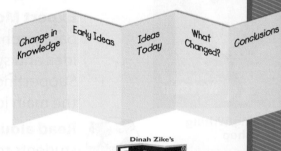

Present Information Have groups present their findings to the class. Encourage students to discuss any differences in their examples and conclusions.

WRITE ABOUT READING  *Analytical Writing*

OBJECTIVES

CCSS Draw evidence from literary or informational texts to support analysis, reflection, and research. **W.5.9**

Write an Analysis

Cite Evidence Using evidence from a selection they have read, students will analyze how an author clearly shows the cause-and-effect relationships between events and ideas.

Discuss how to analyze a text by asking *how* questions.

→ How does the author clearly show what causes an event to happen?

→ How does the author show that one event or idea affects another?

Discuss the student model on **Your Turn Practice Book** page 239. Then have students choose a selection and review their notes. Have them write an analysis that explains how the author clearly shows cause-and-effect relationships between events or ideas. Remind students that good explanatory writing includes transition words and uses adjectives and adverbs correctly.

COLLABORATE

Present Your Ideas Ask partners to share their paragraphs and discuss how the evidence they cited from the text supports their ideas.

→ Readers to Writers

MINILESSON
10 Mins

Writing Traits: Organization

Reading/Writing Workshop

OBJECTIVES

CCSS Introduce a topic clearly, provide a general observation and focus, and group related information logically; include formatting (e.g., headings), illustrations, and multimedia when useful to aiding comprehension. **W.5.2a**

CCSS Write routinely over extended time frames (time for research, reflection, and revision) and shorter time frames (a single sitting or a day or two) for a range of discipline-specific tasks, purposes, and audiences. **W.5.10**

ACADEMIC LANGUAGE
paragraph, topic, supporting sentences
Cognate: *párrafo*

Strong Paragraphs

Expert Model Explain that writers group related ideas together into paragraphs. Each paragraph has a topic sentence that states the main idea and supporting sentences that clearly relate to the main idea. Supporting sentences include facts, details, and examples that explain the main idea.

Read aloud the expert model from "Changing Views of Earth." Ask students to listen to how the writer grouped related ideas into paragraphs. Have students talk with partners to identify the topic sentence and supporting sentences in each paragraph.

Student Model Remind students that strong paragraphs have a topic sentence and supporting sentences. Read aloud the student model "Through a Magnifying Glass." As students follow along, have them focus on how the writer's changes create a strong paragraph.

Invite partners to talk about the topic sentence and supporting sentences Gillian used to write a strong paragraph. Ask them to suggest other changes Gillian could make to improve her paragraph.

 Genre Writing

> **Informational Text**
>
> For full writing process lessons and rubrics see:
> → Informational Article, pp. T344–T349
> → Research Report, pp. T350–T355

Go Digital

Expert Model

Student Model

CCSS Writing Traits — Organization

Readers to ...

Writers should not change the subject in the middle of a paragraph. In expository writing, a **strong paragraph** is one in which every sentence supports the *same* main idea. Writers may state the main idea in one of the sentences, called the topic sentence, and the other sentences support it. Read these strong paragraphs from "Changing Views of Earth."

Strong Paragraphs

Identify the topic sentence in each paragraph.

In what way does another sentence in each paragraph support its main idea?

Expert Model

In the mid-1700s, some scientists sent measurement devices higher and higher. At first, they used kites. Before long, hot-air balloons offered new ways to transport the tools—and sometimes scientists themselves—into the sky.

However, scientists were not satisfied studying the lower layers of Earth's atmosphere. The more they learned, the higher they wanted to go. They also wanted to obtain information more quickly and accurately. Kites and balloons were hard to control. As a result, they occasionally veered off course or got lost, taking their data with them.

Chris Lynn/Getty Images

360

Writers

Gillian wrote an expository paragraph about using a magnifying glass. Read her revision of this section.

Student Model

Through a Magnifying Glass

A magnifying glass is the ~~most~~ simplest ~~simple~~ way to open up a hidden world. Use it to look at your fingertips, and you'll see the ~~lines~~ swirls that leave fingerprints. ~~Footprints are also great clues for detectives.~~ Have you ever looked at salt close up? Salt grains are shaped like tiny cubes. Insects are great to see ~~magnafied~~ (sp) too. ~~But~~ They look like robots with lots of interesting parts ~~tarantulas are huge—no magnifying glass needed!~~ You'd be amazed at what you miss with your ~~bear~~ bare eyes.

Editing Marks

∧ Add

⌄ Add a comma.

⟍ Take out.

(SP) Check spelling.

≡ Make a capital letter.

Grammar Handbook

Adjectives that Compare
See page 467.

Your Turn

☑ Identify Gillian's topic sentence for her paragraph.

☑ Find adjectives that compare in Gillian's writing.

☑ Tell how her revisions improve her writing.

Go Digital!
Write online in Writer's Workspace

361

READING/WRITING WORKSHOP, pp. 360–361

ELL ENGLISH LANGUAGE LEARNERS SCAFFOLD

Provide support to help English Language Learners understand the writing trait.

Beginning	Intermediate	Advanced/High
Respond Orally Using the student model, help students complete the sentence frames. *The topic is [a magnifying glass/salt]. All the sentences tell about [the magnifying glass/insects]. All supporting sentences [are/are not] about the topic.*	**Practice** Ask students to complete the sentence frames. *This paragraph is about ____. The topic sentence is ____. One idea that supports the topic sentence is ____.*	**Understand** Check for understanding. Ask: *Which is the topic sentence? What is the main idea? How do the other sentences support it?*

Writing Every Day: Organization

DAY 1

Writing Entry: Strong Paragraphs

Prewrite Provide students with the prompt below.

What do you think is the best way to learn about space? Support your opinion with reasons.

Have partners list ways to learn about space. Ask them to jot down details about each method.

Draft Have students select what they think is the best way to learn about space. Remind students group related ideas into paragraphs.

DAY 2

Focus on Strong Paragraphs

Use **Your Turn Practice Book** page 240 to model developing a strong paragraph.

The best way to learn about space is with a telescope. You can see what the surface of Earth's moon looks like. The moon is not a planet.

Model adding related ideas and deleting the unrelated idea in the last sentence.

You can also see the moons around Mars.

Discuss how related ideas make a paragraph strong. Guide students to continue revising the model.

Writing Entry: Strong Paragraphs

Revise Have students revise their writing from Day 1 by checking that all sentences support a main idea in each paragraph.

Use the **Conferencing Routines**. Circulate among students and stop briefly to talk with individuals. Provide time for peer review.

Edit Have students use Grammar Handbook page 467 in the **Reading/Writing Workshop** to edit for errors in adjectives that compare.

Conferencing Routines

Teacher Conferences

STEP 1

Talk about the strengths of the writing.

You stated a clear opinion about the best way to study space. You also gave a reason for your opinion.

STEP 2

Focus on how the writer uses the target trait for the week.

You used supporting sentences that give information about the topic. One sentence, however, does not relate well to the topic.

STEP 3

Make concrete suggestions for revisions. Have students work on a specific assignment, such as those to the right, and then meet with you to review progress.

DAY 3

Writing Entry: Strong Paragraphs

Prewrite Ask students to search their Writer's Notebooks for topics for a new draft. Or, provide a prompt such as the following:

What scientific discovery is interesting to you? Support your opinion with reasons.

Draft Once students have chosen their topics, ask them to create a word web with the main idea in the center. Then have them think about related ideas that they might include in their writing. Students can use their word webs to begin their drafts.

DAY 4

Writing Entry: Strong Paragraphs

Revise Have students revise their drafts from Day 3 by checking that all sentences in a paragraph support the main idea. As students revise, hold teacher conferences with individual students. You may also wish to have students work with partners to peer conference.

Edit Invite students to review the rules for adjectives that compare on Grammar Handbook page 467 in the **Reading/Writing Workshop** and then check their drafts for errors.

DAY 5

Share and Reflect

Discuss with students what they learned about writing a strong paragraph. Invite volunteers to read and compare draft text with text that has been revised. Have students discuss the writing by focusing on the importance of using one paragraph to develop each main idea. Allow time for individuals to reflect on their own writing progress and record observations in their Writer's Notebooks.

Suggested Revisions

Provide specific direction to help focus young writers.

Focus on a Sentence
Read the draft and target one sentence for revision. *Rewrite this sentence so that it more clearly supports the main idea.*

Focus on a Section
Underline a section that needs to be revised. Provide specific suggestions. *Some sentences clearly support the main idea. Revise or remove those that do not.*

Focus on a Revision Strategy
Underline a section. Have students use a specific revision strategy, such as rearranging. *Check that each paragraph has only one main idea. Move ideas to a new paragraph if necessary.*

Peer Conferences

Focus peer response groups on writing strong paragraphs.

☑ Does the paragraph include a topic sentence with a main idea?

☑ Do all other sentences support the main idea?

☑ Does the paragraph need additional support to more clearly explain the main idea?

Grammar: Adjectives That Compare

Reading/Writing Workshop

OBJECTIVES

 Demonstrate command of the conventions of standard English grammar and usage when writing or speaking. Form and use comparative and superlative adjectives and adverbs, and choose between them depending on what is to be modified. **L.3.1g**

Proofread sentences.

Go Digital

Adjectives That Compare

Grammar Activities

DAY 1

DAILY LANGUAGE ACTIVITY

My dad and me hiked to the higher point on the mountain. Although I was scared. I kept going. (1: I; 2: highest; 3: scared,)

Adjectives That Compare

→ **Comparative adjectives** compare two nouns or pronouns. Add *-er* to most adjectives to compare two items.

→ **Superlative adjectives** compare more than two nouns or pronouns. Add *-est* to most adjectives to compare items.

→ Drop the *e* in adjectives such as *pale* before adding *-er* or *-est*. Change the *y* to *i* for adjectives such as *sunny*.

→ For one-syllable adjectives such as *red,* double the final consonant.

Refer to Grammar Handbook page 467 for adjectives that compare.

DAY 2

DAILY LANGUAGE ACTIVITY

When our dog barks we open the door. He has the louder bark of any dog I know. (1: barks, 2: loudest)

Review Adjectives That Compare

Remind students that comparative adjectives compare two items and usually end in *-er*. Superlative adjectives compare more than two items and usually end in *-est*.

Introduce More and Most

→ Use *more* in front of most long adjectives to compare two items. *This play is* <u>more exciting</u> *than the one we saw yesterday.*

→ Use *most* in front of most long adjectives to compare more than two items. *This play is the* <u>most exciting</u> *of all.*

TALK ABOUT IT

COLLABORATE

COMPARE WITH ADJECTIVES

Ask students to name one city, one athlete, and one movie. Have students share lists with a partner. Ask students to write sentences comparing the two cities, two athletes, and two movies.

LONGER ADJECTIVES

Provide partners with a list of longer adjectives such as *glamorous, magnificent,* and *mysterious.* Have partners use each adjective to compare two places and then compare more than two places.

DAY 3

DAILY LANGUAGE ACTIVITY

Franco saw a blue rusty bike outside. He raced inside and said "Is that mine bike?" (1: rusty blue; 2: said,; 3: my)

Mechanics and Usage: Using More and Most

→ Never add *-er* and *more* to the same adjective.
Incorrect: *Amy's skit was more funnier than mine.*
Correct: *Amy's skit was funnier than mine.*

→ Never add *-est* and *most* to the same adjective.
Incorrect: *Snowboarding is the most thrillingest sport in the Winter Olympics.*
Correct: *Snowboarding is the most thrilling sport in the Winter Olympics.*

As students write, refer them to Grammar Handbook page 467.

DAY 4

DAILY LANGUAGE ACTIVITY

Our family loves italian food. Mom makes the deliciousest ravioli, which is my favorite meal. (1: Italian; 2: most delicious)

Proofread

Have students correct errors in these sentences:

1. He is the most wisest man I know. (the wisest)

2. This stone is shiniest than that one, but the stone over there is the most shiniest of all. (1: shinier; 2: the shiniest)

3. Apple pie is more sweeter than pumpkin pie. (is sweeter)

4. This is the larger squash in the garden. (largest)

Have students check their work using Grammar Handbook page 467 on adjectives that compare.

DAY 5

DAILY LANGUAGE ACTIVITY

This is the dillon bridge. It is the most long bridge in the state. (1: Dillon Bridge; 2: longest)

Assess

Use the Daily Language Activity and Grammar Practice Reproducibles page 120 for assessment.

Reteach

Use Grammar Practice Reproducibles pages 116–119 and selected pages from the Grammar Handbook for additional reteaching. Remind students that it is important to use comparative adjectives correctly as they speak and write.

Check students' writing for use of the skill and listen for it in their speaking. Assign Grammar Revision Assignments in their Writer's Notebooks as needed.

See Grammar Practice Reproducibles pp. 116–120.

DEBATE

Have groups compare inventions from the early 1900s to modern inventions. Have groups debate the merits of the two inventions, using adjectives that compare.

PERSUADE ME

Have each student think of a favorite hobby. Then have groups compare their hobbies using adjectives that compare and write a persuasive paragraph about what the best hobby is and why.

MAKE A COMMERCIAL

Have groups think of a product that could be advertised on TV. Have them create a TV commercial for their product, using adjectives that compare. Ask groups to perform their commercial for the class.

Spelling: Suffixes *-less* and *-ness*

OBJECTIVES

 Spell grade-appropriate words correctly, consulting references as needed.

L.5.2e

Spelling Words

sadness	hopeless	meaningless
gladness	fearless	emptiness
needless	weakness	forgiveness
harmless	bottomless	motionless
darkness	foolishness	ceaseless
fullness	fondness	fierceness
stillness	effortless	

Review disobey, mistrust, preview
Challenge weightlessness, thoughtlessness

Differentiated Spelling

Approaching Level

sadness	hopeless	restless
gladness	fearless	happiness
needless	weakness	forgiveness
harmless	bottomless	motionless
darkness	foolishness	tireless
fullness	fondness	goodness
stillness	effortless	

Beyond Level

vastness	merciless	meaningless
eeriness	sleeveless	emptiness
breathless	weakness	forgiveness
harmless	bottomless	motionless
ceaseless	foolishness	peacefulness
numbness	fondness	fierceness
stillness	effortless	

DAY 1

Assess Prior Knowledge

Read the spelling words aloud, emphasizing the suffix in each word.

Point out the suffixes in *fearless* and *stillness*. Pronounce each word and draw a line under the suffix as you draw out its sound. Explain that a suffix changes the meaning, and sometimes the part of speech, of the base word.

Demonstrate sorting spelling words by the suffixes *-less* and *-ness*, using the key words *fearless* and *stillness*. Sort a few words, pointing out the suffix as each word is sorted. Ask students to name other words with the same suffixes.

Use the Dictation Sentences from Day 5 to give the pretest. Say the underlined word, read the sentence, and repeat the word. Have students write the words. Then have students check their papers.

DAY 2

Spiral Review

Review the prefixes in *disobey*, *mistrust*, and *preview*. Read each sentence below, repeat the review word, and have students write the words.

1. Terry would not <u>disobey</u> her coach.
2. People <u>mistrust</u> Brent because he sometimes tells lies.
3. I saw a movie <u>preview</u>.

Have students trade papers and check their spellings.

Challenge Words Review this week's *-less* and *-ness* spelling patterns. Read each sentence below, repeat the challenge word, and have students write the words.

1. The astronaut adapted to <u>weightlessness</u> in space.
2. Mira's <u>thoughtlessness</u> kept everyone waiting.

Have students check and correct their spellings and write the words in their word study notebooks.

 WORD SORTS

COLLABORATE

OPEN SORT

Have students cut apart the **Spelling Word Cards** in the Online Resource Book and initial the back of each card. Have them read the words aloud with partners. Then have partners do an **open sort**. Have them record their sorts in their word study notebooks.

PATTERN SORT

Complete the **pattern sort** from Day 1 by using the boldfaced key words in the Spelling Word Cards. Point out the suffixes *-less* and *-ness*. Partners should compare and check their sorts. Have them record their sorts in their word study notebooks.

DAY

Word Meanings

Have students copy the three cloze sentences below into their word study notebooks. Say the sentences aloud. Then ask students to fill in the blanks with a spelling word.

1. The family set up their tent before _____ began to fall. (darkness)

2. Although the spider was _____, Maribel was still afraid of it. (harmless)

3. The deer in the woods was _____ for a moment and then ran away. (motionless)

Challenge students to create cloze sentences using their other spelling, review, or challenge words. Have students post their statements on the board.

See Phonics/Spelling Reproducibles pp. 139–144.

SPEED SORT

Have partners do a **speed sort** to see who is fastest and then compare and discuss their sorts. Then have them brainstorm other words with *-less* and *-ness*. Have students record the words in their word study notebooks.

DAY

Proofread and Write

Write these sentences on the board. Have students circle and correct each misspelled word. Have students use a print or a digital dictionary to check and correct their spellings.

1. A botommless cup of coffee is my mom's greatest weekness. (bottomless, weakness)

2. The stilness of the room filled Mary with saddness. (stillness, sadness)

3. Neadless to say, the soldiers were feerless. (needless, fearless)

4. I asked foregiveness for my foolishnnness. (forgiveness, foolishness)

Error Correction Remind students that the suffixes *-less* and *-ness* are separate syllables in the spelling words. Students should segment the words syllable by syllable in order to spell them, maintaining the spelling of the suffix.

BLIND SORT

Have partners do a **blind sort:** one reads a Spelling Word Card; the other tells under which key word it belongs. Then have students use their word cards to play Concentration. Have them match words with the same suffix.

DAY 5

Assess

Use the Dictation Sentences for the posttest. Have students list the misspelled words in their word study notebooks. Look for students' use of these words in their writings.

Dictation Sentences

1. Grandpa cried tears of <u>sadness</u>.
2. Luther experienced <u>gladness</u> when his daughter was born.
3. Her worries were <u>needless</u>.
4. He flicked the <u>harmless</u> fly.
5. The wolf hunted in <u>darkness</u>.
6. I love the moon's <u>fullness</u>.
7. The <u>stillness</u> was calming.
8. The situation is not <u>hopeless</u>.
9. The skydivers were <u>fearless</u>.
10. The rope showed no <u>weakness</u>.
11. His stomach is a <u>bottomless</u> pit.
12. There's no time for <u>foolishness</u>.
13. She smiled with <u>fondness</u>.
14. Lena makes the dance look <u>effortless</u>.
15. His work was <u>meaningless</u>.
16. The room's <u>emptiness</u> is scary.
17. She asked for my <u>forgiveness</u>.
18. He stood <u>motionless</u> in fear.
19. The fighting was <u>ceaseless</u>.
20. The lion's <u>fierceness</u> is unmatched.

Have students self-correct their tests.

→ Build Vocabulary

OBJECTIVES

CCSS Use context (e.g., cause/effect relationships and comparisons in text) as a clue to the meaning of a word or phrase. **L.5.4a**

CCSS Use common, grade-appropriate Greek and Latin affixes and roots as clues to the meaning of a word (e.g., *photograph*, *photosynthesis*). **L.5.4b**

Expand vocabulary by adding inflectional endings and suffixes.

Vocabulary Words

approximately	diameter
astronomical	evaluate
calculation	orbit
criteria	spheres

DAY 1

Connect to Words

Practice this week's vocabulary.

1. **Approximately** how many people do you know?
2. Describe an **astronomical** object or phenomenon.
3. When might you make a **calculation**?
4. What **criteria** do you use when buying a gift?
5. Name three things that have a **diameter**.
6. **Evaluate** a recent meal.
7. Would you like to **orbit** Earth? Why or why not?
8. Describe two different types of **spheres**.

DAY 2

Expand Vocabulary

Help students generate different forms of this week's words by adding, changing, or removing inflectional endings.

→ Draw a four-column chart on the board. Write *orbit* in the first column. Then write *orbits*, *orbited,* and *orbiting* in the next three columns. Read aloud the words with students.

→ Have students share sentences using each form of *orbit*.

→ Students should add to the chart for *evaluate*, then share sentences using the different forms of the word.

→ Have students copy the chart in their word study notebooks.

Go Digital

Vocabulary

Vocabulary Activities

BUILD MORE VOCABULARY

COLLABORATE

ACADEMIC VOCABULARY

→ Display *innovation, centuries,* and *telescope.*

→ Define the words and discuss their meanings with students.

→ Write *innovate* under *innovation.* Have partners write other words with the same root and define them. Then have partners ask and answer questions using the words.

→ Repeat with *centuries* and *telescope.*

CONTEXT CLUES Review

Remind students to look for comparisons to help figure out the meanings of unfamiliar words.

→ Write: *Many newly discovered planets have a solid inner layer that is similar to Earth's core.*

→ Have partners discuss the meaning of *core* and then use other resources to confirm their ideas.

→ Have students write the meaning of *core* in their word study notebooks.

DAY

Reinforce the Words

Review this week's vocabulary words. Have students orally complete each sentence stem.

1. I am <u>approximately</u> _____.
2. The <u>astronomical</u> observatory is _____.
3. Her <u>calculation</u> was _____.
4. The <u>diameter</u> of a penny is about _____.
5. Planets <u>orbit</u> the _____.
6. Trina collects <u>spheres</u> made of _____.

Display the previous week's vocabulary: *atmosphere, decays, noticeably, receding, stability, variations.* Have partners ask and answer questions for each word.

DAY

Connect to Writing

→ Have students write sentences in their word study notebooks using this week's vocabulary.

→ Tell them to write sentences that provide word information they learned from this week's readings.

→ **ELL** Provide the Day 3 sentence stems 1–6 for students needing extra support.

Write About Vocabulary Have students write something they learned from this week's words in their word study notebooks. For example, they might write about how teachers *evaluate* their work.

DAY 5

Word Squares

Ask students to create Word Squares for each vocabulary word.

→ In the first square, students write the word (e.g., *spheres*).

→ In the second square, students write their own definition of the word and any related words, such as synonyms (e.g., *globes, orbs*).

→ In the third square, students draw a simple illustration that will help them remember the word (e.g., drawing of a basketball).

→ In the fourth square, students write nonexamples, including antonyms for the word (e.g., *oval, circle, ellipse, square, pyramid*).

Have partners discuss their squares.

GREEK ROOTS

Elicit from students what Greek roots are and how they can be helpful.

→ Display **Your Turn Practice Book pages 233–234.** Model using Greek roots to figure out the meaning of the word *photosynthesis* in the third paragraph on page 233.

→ Have students complete page 237.

→ Partners can confirm meanings in a print or an online dictionary.

SHADES OF MEANING

Help students generate words related to *approximately*. Draw a T-chart. Head the columns "Synonyms" and "Antonyms."

→ Have partners generate words to add to the T-chart. Ask students to use a thesaurus.

→ Add synonyms not included, such as *almost, around,* and *roughly.* Add antonyms, such as *exactly* and *precisely.*

→ Ask students to copy the words in their word study notebooks.

MORPHOLOGY

Use *evaluate* as a springboard for students to learn more words. Draw a T-chart. Write *evaluate* in the left column.

→ In the right column, write *-ion* and *-ive.* Discuss how the suffixes change the meaning and part of speech.

→ Have students add the suffixes to *evaluate.* Review the meanings of the new words.

→ Ask partners to do a search for other words with these suffixes.

→ Approaching Level

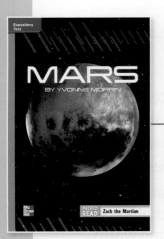

Lexile 700
TextEvaluator™ 26

OBJECTIVES

CCSS Explain the relationships or interactions between two or more individuals, events, ideas, or concepts in a historical, scientific, or technical text based on specific information in the text. **RI.5.3**

CCSS Use context to confirm or self-correct word recognition and understanding, rereading as necessary. **RF.5.4c**

ACADEMIC LANGUAGE

- *expository text, cause, effect, ask and answer questions, Greek roots*
- Cognates: *texto expositivo, causa, efecto*

Leveled Reader:
Mars

Before Reading

Preview and Predict

→ Read the Essential Question with students.

→ Have students preview the title, table of contents, and first page of *Mars*. Students should predict what they think the selection will be about. Encourage them to confirm or revise their predictions as they continue reading.

Review Genre: Expository Text

Tell students that this selection is expository text. Expository text provides factual information about a topic. Points are organized logically and supported by reasons and evidence. Features such as photographs, captions, and diagrams add information that might not be in the text. Have students identify features of expository text in *Mars*.

During Reading

Close Reading

Note Taking: Ask students to use their graphic organizer as they read.

Pages 2–3 *Which Greek root helps you figure out the meaning of* astronomers? (*Astro* means "star." *Astronomers* are people who study stars, or space.) *What questions have astronomers asked about Mars?* (What is it made of? How big is it? Is it hot or cold? Could it have life?)

Pages 4–6 *How are Mars and Earth alike? Work with a partner to answer using the table on page 4.* (The length of their days is only about an hour apart.) *How do the lengths of their years differ?* (A year on Mars has almost double the number of days of a year on Earth.) *Which Greek root helps you figure out the meaning of* orbit *on page 6?* (*Orb* means "circle" or "ring." An orbit is a circular path.)

Pages 7–9 *How did the use of a telescope help Herschel?* (He identified polar ice caps.) *What was the effect of the incorrect translation of* canali? (People thought Martians made canals.) *How do Mars' moons differ from Earth's?* (Mars has two moons. They are smaller than Earth's moon and are oddly shaped.)

Go Digital

Leveled Readers

Use Graphic Organizer

Pages 10–12 *Why are rovers and landers tested before they are used?* (They must land safely, carry out tests, communicate with Earth, and move over rough ground.)

Pages 13–16 *Turn to a partner and summarize the text to answer the question in the Chapter 3 title, "Life on Mars?"* (Mars may be able to support life. Future missions will explore this possibility.) *What is the Goldilocks zone? Why is it important?* (It is the zone where life can exist because it is not too hot or too cold. Mars may be in this zone.)

Page 17 *What kind of equipment might an astronaut on Mars need?* (spacecraft, protective spacesuit) *Why?* (Mars is very far away, is very cold, and has an atmosphere mostly made up of carbon dioxide.)

After Reading

Respond to Reading Revisit the Essential Question and ask students to complete the Text Evidence Questions on page 18.

Analytical Writing **Write About Reading** Check that students have correctly explained how studying Mars and improving technology have helped ideas about Mars to change over time. Make sure they include details.

Fluency: Accuracy

Model Model reading page 2 with accuracy. Next, read the passage aloud and have students read along with you.

Apply Have students practice reading the passage with partners.

PAIRED READ

"Zach the Martian"

Make Connections: Write About It *Analytical Writing*

Before reading, ask students to note that the genre of this text is science fiction. Then discuss the Essential Question. After reading, ask students to write connections between *Mars* and "Zach the Martian."

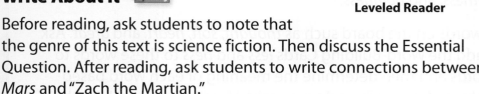

Leveled Reader

FOCUS ON SCIENCE

Students can extend their knowledge of Mars by completing the research and observation activity on page 24. **STEM**

Literature Circles

Ask students to conduct a literature circle using the Thinkmark questions to guide the discussion. You may wish to have a whole-class discussion, using information from both selections in the Leveled Reader, about how scientific knowledge can change over time.

Level Up

Level-up lessons available online.

IF students read the **Approaching Level** fluently and answered the questions

THEN pair them with students who have proficiently read the **On Level** and have students

• echo-read the **On Level** main selection.

• identify three traits of expository text.

A C T Access Complex Text

The **On Level** challenges students by including more **domain-specific words** and **complex sentence structures**.

Approaching Level

Word Study/Decoding

REVIEW SUFFIXES

 TIER 2

 OBJECTIVES
Know and apply grade-level phonics and word analysis skills in decoding words. Use combined knowledge of all letter-sound correspondences, syllabication patterns, and morphology (e.g., roots and affixes) to read accurately unfamiliar multisyllabic words in context and out of context. **RF.5.3a**

Decode words with suffixes -*less* and -*ness*.

 I Do Review with students that a suffix is a group of letters added to the end of a base word that changes that word's meaning. It can also change the word's part of speech. Remind students that -*less* is a common suffix that means "without" and -*ness* is a common suffix that means "state of being."

 We Do Write the words *careless* and *goodness* on the board. Read each word aloud and model using the meaning of the suffix to determine that *careless* means "without care" and *goodness* means "state of being good." Then write the words *clueless* and *happiness* on the board. Guide students to use the meaning of the suffix to define each word.

You Do Add the following examples to the board: *hopeless, kindness.* Have students identify the suffix, tell its meaning, and give the meaning of each word.

BUILD WORDS WITH SUFFIXES -*less* AND -*ness*

TIER 2

 OBJECTIVES
Know and apply grade-level phonics and word analysis skills in decoding words. Use combined knowledge of all letter-sound correspondences, syllabication patterns, and morphology (e.g., roots and affixes) to read accurately unfamiliar multisyllabic words in context and out of context. **RF.5.3a**

Build words with suffixes -*less* and -*ness*.

 I Do Display these **Word-Building Cards**: *less, ness, light, point.* Model reading each suffix and word aloud.

 We Do Work with students to combine the Word-Building Cards to form words with suffixes -*less* and -*ness*. Have students chorally read the words *lightless, lightness,* and *pointless.*

 You Do Write other words on the board such as *thought, soft, heart,* and *great.* Ask partners to add the Word-Building Cards *less* and *ness* to these words to form new words and then determine the meaning of each word based on the meanings of the suffix and base word. Have volunteers share their work with the class.

PRACTICE WORDS WITH SUFFIXES -less AND -ness

OBJECTIVES

Know and apply grade-level phonics and word analysis skills in decoding words. Use combined knowledge of all letter-sound correspondences, syllabication patterns, and morphology (e.g., roots and affixes) to read accurately unfamiliar multisyllabic words in context and out of context. **RF.5.3a**

Practice words with suffixes -less and -ness.

 I Do Write these words on the board: *darkness, harmless*. Read the words aloud, identify each suffix and its meaning, and give the meaning of each word.

 We Do Write the words *illness, forgiveness, powerless,* and *worthless* on the board. Model how to determine the meaning of the first word using the suffix. Then have students determine the meaning of each of the remaining words. As necessary, help students identify and define the suffix in each word.

You Do To provide additional practice, write the following words on the board. Read aloud the first word, identify the suffix, and give the word's meaning.

boldness	freshness	aimless	dizziness
cloudless	bossiness	cordless	odorless
closeness	keyless	likeness	sweetness

Then have students read aloud the remaining words. Ask them to identify each suffix and give the meaning of each word.

Afterward, point to the words in the list in random order for students to read chorally.

 ENGLISH LANGUAGE LEARNERS

For the **ELLs** who need **phonics, decoding,** and **fluency** practice, use scaffolding methods as necessary to ensure students understand the meaning of the words. Refer to the **Language Transfers Handbook** for phonics elements that may not transfer in students' native languages.

Approaching Level

Vocabulary

REVIEW HIGH-FREQUENCY WORDS

TIER 2

 OBJECTIVES
Acquire and use accurately grade-appropriate general academic and domain-specific words and phrases, including those that signal contrast, addition, and other logical relationships (e.g., *however, although, nevertheless, similarly, moreover, in addition*).
L.5.6

 Use **High-Frequency Word Cards** 191–200. Display one word at a time, following the routine:

Display the word. Read the word. Then spell the word.

 Ask students to state the word and spell the word with you. Model using the word in a sentence and have students repeat after you.

 Display the word. Ask students to say the word then spell it. When completed, quickly flip through the word card set as students chorally read the words. Provide opportunities for students to use the words in speaking and writing. For example, provide sentence starters such as *I think that _____.* Ask students to write each word in their Writer's Notebook.

REVIEW VOCABULARY WORDS

TIER 2

 OBJECTIVES
Acquire and use accurately grade-appropriate general academic and domain-specific words and phrases, including those that signal contrast, addition, and other logical relationships (e.g., *however, although, nevertheless, similarly, moreover, in addition*).
L.5.6

 Display each **Visual Vocabulary Card** and state the word. Explain how the photograph illustrates the word. State the example sentence and repeat the word.

 Point to the word on the card and read the word with students. Ask them to repeat the word. Engage students in structured partner talk about the image as prompted on the back of the vocabulary card.

 Display each visual in random order, hiding the word. Have students match the definitions and context sentences of the words to the visuals displayed.

UNDERSTAND VOCABULARY WORDS

OBJECTIVES

 CCSS Acquire and use accurately grade-appropriate general academic and domain-specific words and phrases, including those that signal contrast, addition, and other logical relationships (e.g., *however, although, nevertheless, similarly, moreover, in addition*).
L.5.6

I Do Display the *approximately* **Visual Vocabulary Card** and ask: *If you know* approximately *how many people were at a party, do you know about or exactly how many people were there?*

Explain that if you know approximately how many, you don't know the exact number.

We Do Ask these questions. Help students explain their answers.
→ Are people in an *astronomical* society interested in stars or animals?
→ Would you do a *calculation* while swimming or doing math homework?
→ Would you measure the *diameter* of a circle or a car?

You Do Have pairs respond to these questions and explain their answers.
→ What are three planets that *orbit* the sun?
→ Which are *spheres,* planets or boxes?
→ Which has *criteria,* a diary entry or a scored essay?
→ Who is qualified to *evaluate* a dance performance?

GREEK ROOTS

OBJECTIVES

CCSS Determine or clarify the meaning of unknown and multiple-meaning words and phrases based on *grade 5 reading and content,* choosing flexibly from a range of strategies. Use common, grade-appropriate Greek and Latin affixes and roots as clues to the meaning of a word (e.g., *photograph, photosynthesis*).
L.5.4b

I Do Display the Comprehension and Fluency passage on **Approaching Reproducibles** pages 233–234. Point to the word *astrobiology* in the first paragraph. Tell students that they can use their knowledge of Greek roots to determine its meaning.

Think Aloud The Greek prefix *astro-* means "star" and the Greek root *bio* means "life." The suffix *-logy* means "the study of." I also see a context clue: "life in space." *Astrobiology* must be the study of life in space.

We Do Ask students to point to the word *photosynthesis* in paragraph three on page 233. Provide the Greek root *syntithenai* ("put together") and the Greek prefix *photo-* ("light") and discuss how these can help students tell the word's meaning. Write the definition of the word.

You Do Have students determine the meaning of *hydrothermal* (page 233, paragraph 4) and *chemosynthesis* (page 234, paragraph 1) using Greek roots: *therm* ("heat"), *hydro* ("water"), *chemo* ("chemical"), and *syntithenai* ("put together").

Approaching Level

Comprehension

FLUENCY

TIER 2

 OBJECTIVES
CCSS Read with sufficient accuracy and fluency to support comprehension. Use context to confirm or self-correct word recognition and understanding, rereading as necessary. **RF.5.4c**

Read fluently with accuracy.

 I Do Remind students that pronouncing words accurately can help them better understand the meaning of each word and the overall meaning of a text. Read the first two paragraphs of the Comprehension and Fluency passage on **Approaching Reproducibles** pages 233–234. Tell students to monitor your accuracy.

 We Do Read the rest of the page aloud. Have students repeat each sentence after you, pronouncing each word correctly. Explain that you used your knowledge of letter/sound correspondences and context clues to pronounce each word correctly.

 You Do Have partners take turns reading sentences from the Comprehension and Fluency passage, focusing on their accuracy. Listen in and provide corrective feedback as needed by modeling proper fluency.

IDENTIFY CAUSES

TIER 2

 OBJECTIVES
CCSS Explain the relationships or interactions between two or more individuals, events, ideas, or concepts in a historical, scientific, or technical text based on specific information in the text. **RI.5.3**

 I Do Read aloud the second paragraph of the Comprehension and Fluency passage on **Approaching Reproducibles** page 233. Write *Europa has a cold surface and a lot of radiation*. Tell students that this sentence explains a cause. It tells the cause, or the reason why, nothing can live on Europa's surface.

 We Do Read page 233 of the Comprehension and Fluency passage in the **Approaching Reproducibles** selection. Ask questions such as *What process causes oxygen to be released into the atmosphere?* Then guide students to find answers by identifying causes in the text.

 You Do Have partners read the rest of the passage. After each paragraph, they should write down any causes that they find. Discuss the relationship between the causes students identify and their effects.

REVIEW TEXT STRUCTURE: CAUSE AND EFFECT

OBJECTIVES

Explain the relationships or interactions between two or more individuals, events, ideas, or concepts in a historical, scientific, or technical text based on specific information in the text. **RI.5.3**

 I Do

Remind students that science and history authors often show that one event is the cause of another event. A cause is why something happens. An effect is what happens. A cause may have more than one effect.

We Do

Choral-read the "What Life Needs" section of the Comprehension and Fluency passage on **Approaching Reproducibles** page 233. Model identifying the chain of causes and effects that enables the existence of life on Earth's surface. For example, photosynthesis causes oxygen to be released into the atmosphere, an effect which in turn causes aerobic creatures to be able to live and breathe. Then work with students to identify causes and effects in the rest of the passage. Discuss how a single cause can lead to more than one effect.

You Do

Have students use the causes and effects explored in the text to summarize how the discovery of chemosynthetic life changed the way astrobiologists think about life on Earth and in space.

SELF-SELECTED READING

OBJECTIVES

Explain the relationships or interactions between two or more individuals, events, ideas, or concepts in a historical, scientific, or technical text based on specific information in the text. **RI.5.3**

Ask and answer questions to increase understanding of a text.

Read Independently

Have students choose an expository nonfiction book for sustained silent reading. Remind students that:

→ a cause is why something happens; an effect is what happens as a result of a cause.

→ asking and answering questions can help them better understand and remember important information.

Read Purposefully

Have students record the causes and effects on Graphic Organizer 86 as they read independently. After students finish, they can conduct a Book Talk about what they read.

→ Students should share their organizers and describe the relationship between the causes and effects they identified in the text.

→ They should also tell the group any questions they asked themselves and how they answered them.

On Level

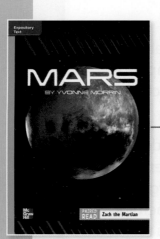

Lexile 900
TextEvaluator™ 43

OBJECTIVES

Explain the relationships or interactions between two or more individuals, events, ideas, or concepts in a historical, scientific, or technical text based on specific information in the text. **RI.5.3**

Use context to confirm or self-correct word recognition and understanding, rereading as necessary. **RF.5.4c**

ACADEMIC LANGUAGE

- *expository text, cause, effect, ask and answer questions, Greek roots*
- Cognates: *texto expositivo, causa, efecto*

Leveled Reader:
Mars

Before Reading

Preview and Predict

→ Read the Essential Question with students.

→ Have students preview the title, table of contents, and first page of *Mars*. Students should predict what they think the selection will be about. Encourage them to confirm or revise their predictions as they continue reading.

Review Genre: Expository Text

Tell students that this selection is expository text. Expository text provides factual information about a topic. Points are organized logically and supported by reasons and evidence. Features such as photographs, captions, and diagrams add information that might not be in the text. Have students identify features of expository text in *Mars*.

During Reading

Close Reading

Note Taking: Ask students to use their graphic organizer as they read.

Pages 2–3 *Which Greek root helps you figure out the meaning of* astronomers*?* (*Astro* means "star." *Astronomers* are people who study stars, or space.) *Why might the Romans have called the planet "Mars"?* (Mars is the Roman god of war, and the planet's red color might have reminded them of blood in battle.)

Pages 4–6 *How are Mars and Earth similar and different? Use the text and table on page 4 to help you answer.* (Similar: Mars has seasons and an atmosphere. Its day is almost the same length as Earth's; Different: Mars is farther from the sun, has a smaller diameter, is much colder, and has a much longer year.) *Which Greek root helps you figure out the meaning of* orbit *on page 6?* (*Orb* means "circle" or "ring." An orbit is a circular path.)

Pages 7–9 *What is one effect of the development of telescope technology?* (Astronomers observed features on the surface of Mars.) *What caused people to think Martians dug canals on Mars?* (The incorrect translation of the word *canali*.)

Go Digital

Leveled Readers

Use Graphic Organizer

What discoveries did Asaph Hall make about Mars' moons? (Mars has two moons. They are smaller than Earth's moon and are irregularly shaped.)

Pages 10–12 *Why must lander and rover designs be tested first?* (They must land safely; have reliable energy supplies, communication devices, and testing equipment; and move across rough terrain.)

Pages 13–16 *Turn to a partner and summarize the text to answer the question in the chapter title.* (Mars may have some of the conditions needed to support life. Future missions will explore the possibility.) *What discovery would be the best clue to finding life?* (water) *Why would humans need special transportation and protective suits to explore Mars?* (It's far away, it's cold, and its atmosphere is mostly carbon dioxide.)

After Reading

Respond to Reading Revisit the Essential Question and ask students to complete the Text Evidence Questions on page 18.

Analytical Writing **Write About Reading** Check that students have correctly explained how observation and improving technology caused ideas about Mars to change over time. Make sure they include details from the text.

Fluency: Accuracy

Model Model reading page 5 with accuracy. Next, read the passage aloud and have students read along with you.

Apply Have students practice reading the passage with partners.

PAIRED READ

Leveled Reader

"Zach the Martian"

Make Connections: Write About It *Analytical Writing*

Before reading, ask students to note that the genre of this text is science fiction. Then discuss the Essential Question. After reading, ask students to write connections between *Mars* and "Zach the Martian."

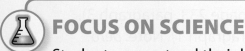 **FOCUS ON SCIENCE**

Students can extend their knowledge of Mars by completing the research and observation activity on page 24. **STEM**

 **Literature Circles**

Ask students to conduct a literature circle using the Thinkmark questions to guide the discussion. You may wish to have a whole-class discussion, using information from both selections in the Leveled Reader, about how scientific knowledge can change over time.

Level Up

Level-up lessons available online.

IF students read the **On Level** fluently and answered the questions,

THEN pair them with students who have proficiently read the **Beyond Level** and have students

• partner-read the **Beyond Level** main selection.

• identify three causes and effects.

A C T **A**ccess **C**omplex **T**ext

The **Beyond Level** challenges students by including more **domain-specific words** and **complex sentence structures**.

On Level

Vocabulary

REVIEW VOCABULARY WORDS

OBJECTIVES
Demonstrate understanding of figurative language, word relationships, and nuances in word meanings. Use the relationship between particular words (e.g., synonyms, antonyms, homographs) to better understand each of the words. **L.5.5c**

 I Do Use the **Visual Vocabulary Cards** to review the key selection words *approximately, calculation, criteria, evaluate, orbit,* and *spheres*. Point to each, read it aloud, and have students repeat.

 We Do Real aloud the word set. Help students identify the word in each set that has almost the same meaning as the first word.

approximately, absolutely, nearly

calculation, computation, explanation

criteria, standards, cafeteria

You Do Have students work in pairs to identify the word that has almost the same meaning as the first word.

evaluate, elevate, judge

orbit, circle, delete

spheres, cubes, globes

GREEK ROOTS

OBJECTIVES
Determine or clarify the meaning of unknown and multiple-meaning words and phrases based on *grade 5 reading and content,* choosing flexibly from a range of strategies. Use common, grade-appropriate Greek and Latin affixes and roots as clues to the meaning of a word (e.g., *photograph, photosynthesis*). **L.5.4b**

 I Do Remind students that they can use Greek roots to find the meaning of words. Point to *astrobiology* in the first paragraph of the Comprehension and Fluency passage on **Your Turn Practice Book** pages 233–234.

Think Aloud The Greek prefix *astro-* and the root *bio* mean "star" and "life." The Greek suffix *-logy* means "the study of." I also see a context clue: "life in space." These clues tell me that *astrobiology* means "the study of life in space."

 We Do Have students read paragraph 3 on page 233 and find *photosynthesis*. Help students find its meaning by pointing out the Greek root *syntithenai,* meaning "put together," and the Greek prefix *photo-,* meaning "light."

 You Do Have pairs determine the meanings of *Aerobic* (page 233, paragraph 3), *hydrothermal* and *chemosynthesis* (page 234, paragraph 1). Note: *aero* ("air"), *bio* ("life"), *therm* ("heat"), *hydro* ("water"), and *chemo* ("chemical").

Comprehension

REVIEW TEXT STRUCTURE: CAUSE AND EFFECT

OBJECTIVES

Explain the relationships or interactions between two or more individuals, events, ideas, or concepts in a historical, scientific, or technical text based on specific information in the text. **RI.5.3**

I Do
Remind students that authors of science and history texts may organize text by causes and effects to explain what happened and why.

We Do
Have a volunteer read the second paragraph of the Comprehension and Fluency passage on **Your Turn Practice Book** page 233. Guide students to identify a cause and effect about Europa: its surface is too cold (cause) for life to exist (effect).

You Do
Have partners identify causes and effects in the rest of the passage. Then have them explain how a single cause, the discovery of chemosynthetic life, affected how scientists began to view life on Earth and in space.

SELF-SELECTED READING

OBJECTIVES

Explain the relationships or interactions between two or more individuals, events, ideas, or concepts in a historical, scientific, or technical text based on specific information in the text. **RI.5.3**

Ask and answer questions to increase understanding of a text.

Read Independently

Have students choose an expository nonfiction book for sustained silent reading.

→ Before they read, have students preview the text, reading the title and viewing the front and back cover.

→ As students read, remind them to ask and answer questions in order to better understand and remember details in the text.

Read Purposefully

Encourage students to select books about topics that interest them.

→ As students read, have them record causes and effects on Graphic Organizer 86.

→ They can use the causes and effects they identify to summarize the main message in the text.

→ Ask students to share their reactions to the book with classmates.

→ Beyond Level

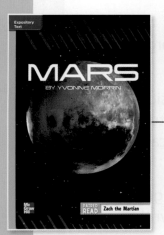

Lexile 970
TextEvaluator™ 46

OBJECTIVES

CCSS Explain the relationships or interactions between two or more individuals, events, ideas, or concepts in a historical, scientific, or technical text based on specific information in the text. **RI.5.3**

CCSS Use context to confirm or self-correct word recognition and understanding, rereading as necessary. **RF.5.4c**

ACADEMIC LANGUAGE

• *expository text, cause, effect, ask and answer questions, Greek roots*

• Cognates: *texto expositivo, causa, efecto*

Leveled Reader:
Mars

Go Digital

Before Reading

Preview and Predict

→ Have students read the Essential Question.

→ Have students preview the title, table of contents, and first page of *Mars*. Then have them predict what they think the selection will be about. Encourage them to confirm or revise their predictions as they continue reading.

Review Genre: Expository Text

Tell students that this selection is expository text. Expository text provides factual information about a topic. Points are organized logically and supported by reasons and evidence. Features such as photographs, captions, and diagrams add information that might not be in the text. Have students identify features of expository text in *Mars*.

Leveled Readers

During Reading

Close Reading

Note Taking: Ask students to use their graphic organizer as they read.

Pages 2–3 *Which Greek root helps you figure out the meaning of* astronomers? (*Astro* means "star;" *astronomers* are people who study space.) *Why might the Greeks and Romans have named the planet after the god of war?* (The planet is red, reminding them of blood in battle.)

Pages 4–6 *Identify a similarity and difference between Mars and Earth using the table on page 4.* (The days on Mars and Earth are a similar length; Mars is much colder than Earth.) *Look at the sidebar on page 5. How is the planet still associated with war?* (*Martial* comes from Mars, the Roman god of war.) *Which Greek root helps you figure out the meaning of* orbit *on page 6?* (*Orb* means "circle" or "ring." An orbit is a circular path.)

Pages 7–9 *Paraphrase the discoveries of some early Mars astronomers.* (Herschel found polar ice caps. Hall found and named the two moons.) *What was the effect of Kepler's use of mathematical calculations? Use the timeline to help you answer.* (Kepler figured out that all the planets move in elliptical orbits around the sun.)

Use Graphic Organizer

Pages 10–12 *Review the sidebar on page 11. How do natural features on Mars compare with those on Earth?* (Mars has taller mountains and longer canyons.) *How did we discover this?* (space program missions)

Pages 13–16 *Summarize the text to answer the question in the chapter title. Have a partner reread to verify your answer.* (Mars may be able to support life. Future missions will explore this.) *Why is discovering water so important?* (It could prove that there is life on Mars, since some living things can survive in extreme conditions without sunlight or oxygen.)

Page 17 *What conditions on Mars would cause human explorers to need special transportation and protective suits?* (Mars is very far away, is very cold, and has an atmosphere primarily made up of carbon dioxide.)

After Reading

Respond to Reading Revisit the Essential Question and ask students to complete the Text Evidence Questions on page 18.

Analytical Writing **Write About Reading** Check that students have correctly explained how observation and improving technology have caused ideas about Mars to change. Make sure they include text details.

Fluency: Accuracy

Model Model reading page 2 with accuracy. Next, read the passage aloud and have students read along with you.

Apply Have students practice reading the passage with partners.

PAIRED READ

"Zach the Martian"

Make Connections:
Write About It **Analytical Writing**

Leveled Reader

Before reading, ask students to note that the genre of this text is science fiction. Then discuss the Essential Question. After reading, ask students to write connections between *Mars* and "Zach the Martian."

FOCUS ON SCIENCE

Students can extend their knowledge of Mars by completing the research and observation activity on page 24. **STEM**

Literature Circles

Ask students to conduct a literature circle using the Thinkmark questions to guide the discussion. You may wish to have a whole-class discussion, on information learned from both selections in the Leveled Reader, about how scientific knowledge can change over time.

Gifted and Talented

Synthesize Have students choose one of the theories about Mars presented in the article and trace changes in the theory over time as a result of new discoveries. Students should write a short paper that describes the theory and explains the work scientists did to develop and change the theory. Tell them to include a graphic organizer such as a sequence chain or a timeline to show the changes in the theory over time as a result of further scientific study.

→ Beyond Level

Vocabulary

REVIEW DOMAIN-SPECIFIC WORDS

 OBJECTIVES
Acquire and use accurately grade-appropriate general academic and domain-specific words and phrases, including those that signal contrast, addition, and other logical relationships (e.g., *however, although, nevertheless, similarly, moreover, in addition*).
L.5.6

 Model Use the **Visual Vocabulary Cards** to review the meaning of the words *criteria* and *evaluate*. Use each word in a science-related sentence.

Write the words *environments* and *radiation* on the board and discuss the meanings with students. Then help students write sentences using these words.

 Apply Have students work in pairs to review the meanings of the words *chemicals* and *oxygen*. Then have partners write sentences using the words.

GREEK ROOTS

 OBJECTIVES
Determine or clarify the meaning of unknown and multiple-meaning words and phrases based on *grade 5 reading and content,* choosing flexibly from a range of strategies. Use common, grade-appropriate Greek and Latin affixes and roots as clues to the meaning of a word (e.g., *photograph, photosynthesis*).
L.5.4b

 Model Read aloud the first three paragraphs of the Comprehension and Fluency passage on **Beyond Reproducibles** pages 233–234.

Think Aloud I want to know the meaning of *atmosphere* in the third paragraph. I see the Greek roots *atmos*, which means "vapor" and *sphaira*, meaning "globe." So *atmosphere* must mean "vapors or gases around Earth."

With students, reread the third paragraph on page 233. Help them figure out the meaning of *photosynthesis* by pointing out the Greek root *syntithenai* ("put together") and the Greek prefix *photo-* ("light").

 Apply Have pairs of students read the rest of the passage. Ask them to use Greek roots to determine the meaning of the following words: *Aerobic* (page 233, paragraph 3), *hydrothermal* (page 233, paragraph 4), and *chemosynthesis* (page 234, paragraph 1). Note the following: *aero* ("air"), *bio* ("life"), *therm* ("heat"), *hydro* ("water"), and *chemo* ("chemical").

 Independent Study Challenge students to identify three other words explored this week that contain Greek roots and identify their meanings. Have them write sentences in which the words are used appropriately.

Comprehension

REVIEW TEXT STRUCTURE: CAUSE AND EFFECT

OBJECTIVES
Explain the relationships or interactions between two or more individuals, events, ideas, or concepts in a historical, scientific, or technical text based on specific information in the text. **RI.5.3**

 Model Review that authors of science and history texts may organize their texts by causes and effects to explain what happened and why.

Have students read the first two paragraphs of the Comprehension and Fluency passage on **Beyond Reproducibles** pages 233–234. Ask open-ended questions to facilitate discussion such as *What is a cause you notice? What effect does it have?* Students should support their responses with details from the selection.

 Apply Have students identify the causes and effects in the rest of the passage as they independently fill in Graphic Organizer 86. Then have partners use their work to explain how the causes and effects explored in the text connect to the search for life in space.

SELF-SELECTED READING

OBJECTIVES
Explain the relationships or interactions between two or more individuals, events, ideas, or concepts in a historical, scientific, or technical text based on specific information in the text. **RI.5.3**

Ask and answer questions to increase understanding of a text.

Read Independently

Have students choose an expository nonfiction book for sustained silent reading.

→ Have them identify causes and effects in the text on Graphic Organizer 86.

→ Remind them to ask and answer questions as they read to monitor their comprehension.

Read Purposefully

Encourage students to keep a reading journal. Suggest that they select books on topics that interest them.

→ Students can write summaries of the books in their journals.

→ Ask students to share with classmates an interesting fact they learned from the text.

Independent Study Challenge students to discuss how their books relate to the weekly theme of now we know. Have students use all of their reading materials to compare the different ways our scientific knowledge has changed over time.

English Language Learners

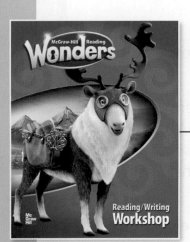

Reading/Writing Workshop

Shared Read
Changing Views of Earth

 **Go Digital**

 View "Changing Views of Earth"

Before Reading

Build Background

Read the Essential Question: *How can scientific knowledge change over time?*

→ Explain the meaning of the Essential Question, including the vocabulary in the question: *Scientific knowledge includes facts and information about nature and the physical world. When things change over time, they become different slowly, sometimes after many years.*

→ **Model an answer:** *Many years ago, it was difficult for scientists to explore the ocean. Now they have submersible vehicles that allow them to study parts of the ocean they could not get to before. This has led to increased knowledge about the ocean and its inhabitants.*

→ Ask students a question that ties the Essential Question to their own background knowledge: *Think of an example of scientific knowledge, such as medicines used to treat disease. Now consider how that knowledge might have changed over time. Discuss your thoughts with a partner.* Call on several pairs.

During Reading

Interactive Question-Response

→ Ask questions that help students understand the meaning of the text after each paragraph.

→ Reinforce the meanings of key vocabulary.

→ Ask students questions that require them to use key vocabulary.

→ Reinforce strategies and skills of the week by modeling.

Page 353

On the Ground, Looking Around

Paragraph 1

Explain and Model the Strategy *Asking questions can help you understand what you read.* Point to the question in the first paragraph and have students read it with you. *Let's look for the answer to this question as we read.*

Paragraph 2

People long ago believed that the Earth stayed in one place while the _____ rotated around it. (sun) *What is the scientific term for this idea?* (the geocentric model)

Paragraph 3

What was the name of the new tool Galileo used? (the telescope) *What was Galileo able to see with the telescope?* (He could see stars and planets more clearly.) Have students pantomime looking at the stars through a telescope.

Explain and Model Cause and Effect Point out the cause and effect relationship. *Because of his observations with the telescope, Galileo began to support a new model of the solar system. The cause is making observations with the telescope; the effect is supporting a new idea.*

Define *radical* for students. *What was radical about the model proposed by Copernicus?* (In this model, Earth moved around the sun.) *What is the scientific term for this model?* (the heliocentric model)

Help students understand the difference between the geocentric and heliocentric models by discussing the diagrams on page 353.

Page 354

In the Sky, Looking Down

Paragraph 1

Explain and Model Greek Roots Choral-read the paragraph. Point out that the word *thermometer* contains the Greek roots *therm*, which means "heat," and *meter*, which means "measure." *A thermometer measures heat.*

Point to the word *barometer* and identify the Greek roots. Have partners determine the meaning of *barometer.* (A barometer measures pressure.)

Paragraphs 2–3

What did scientists use to send measurement devices into the sky? (kites and balloons) *What problems did scientists have with the kites and balloons?* (They were hard to control and got lost.)

Paragraph 4

Define *atmosphere* and provide the Spanish cognate, *atmósfera. What new development helped scientists to observe Earth's surface and atmosphere?* (the airplane)

Point to the diagram on page 354. Discuss the different layers of the atmosphere.

Page 355

Out in Space, Looking Back Home

Paragraph 1

Point to the word *meteorologists* and have students say it with you. Ask for a volunteer to tell what a meteorologist does. *How did the introduction of satellites affect meteorologists' predictions?* (It made them more accurate.)

Paragraph 3

Explain that *inspire awe* means "to create a powerful feeling of wonder." Share an experience that might inspire awe, such as viewing the Grand Canyon. Ask students to share a time when they felt awe-inspired. *Why might viewing Earth from space inspire awe?*

After Reading

Make Connections

→ Review the Essential Question: *How can scientific knowledge change over time?*

→ Make text connections.

→ Have students complete **ELL Reproducibles** pages 233–235.

→ English Language Learners

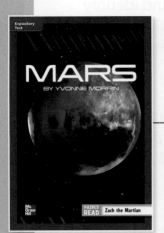

Lexile 700
TextEvaluator™ 27

 OBJECTIVES

CCSS Explain the relationships or interactions between two or more individuals, events, ideas, or concepts in a historical, scientific, or technical text based on specific information in the text. **RI.5.3**

CCSS Use context to confirm or self-correct word recognition and understanding, rereading as necessary. **RF.5.4c**

ACADEMIC LANGUAGE

• ask and answer questions, cause, effect, expository text, Greek roots

• Cognates: *causa, efecto, texto expositivo*

Leveled Reader:
Mars

Go Digital

Leveled Readers

Before Reading

Preview and Predict

→ Read the Essential Question: *How can scientific knowledge change over time?*

→ Refer to Going Deeper: *How have new technologies contributed to changes in our scientific knowledge about the ocean?*

→ Preview *Mars* and "Zach the Martian": *Our purpose for reading is to find out how science can help us learn more about the mysteries of Mars.*

Vocabulary

Use the **Visual Vocabulary Cards** to pre-teach the ELL vocabulary: *develop, conducted.* Use the routine found on the cards.

During Reading

Interactive Question-Response

Note Taking: Ask students to use the graphic organizer on **ELL Reproducibles** page 232. Use the questions below after each page is read with students. As you read, use the glossary definitions to define vocabulary in context and visuals to help students understand key vocabulary.

Pages 2–3 Point to the word *telescope. The Greek root* tele- *means "far".* Pantomime using a telescope. *If we use a telescope, are we looking at something close to us or far away from us?* (far away) *Look at the questions on page 2. Tell a partner one question you would like to have answered as you read the text.* (Is there life on Mars?)

Pages 4–5 Reread the first paragraph on page 4 and discuss the information in the table. *Do the Earth and Mars have any similarities?* (Yes, the both have seasons and an atmosphere. The length of a day is almost the same.) *Have astronomers always been correct in their conclusions about Mars?* (no)

Pages 6–7 Use the diagram to discuss how the planets orbit the sun. *Who discovered that the plants orbit in an elliptical shape?* (Kepler)

Use Graphic Organizer

Pages 8–9 *Are there canals on Mars?* (no) *How many moons does Mars have?* (two) *Describe them.* (They are irregularly shaped and smaller than the Earth's moon.)

Pages 10–12 *We can now explore Mars using _____, _____, and _____.* (probes, landers, rovers)

Pages 13–17 Say the word *extremophiles* and have students repeat it. *Where do extremophiles get energy?* (from chemicals or heat in the Earth's core) *Is it possible that there are extremophiles on Mars?* (yes)

After Reading

Respond to Reading Revisit the Essential Question and ask students to complete the Text Evidence Questions on page 18.

📝 *Analytical Writing* **Write About Reading** Check that students have correctly explained how observation and improving technology caused ideas about Mars to change over time. Make sure they include details from the text.

Fluency: Accuracy

Model Model reading page 5 with accuracy and expression. Next, read the passage aloud and have students read along with you.

Apply Have students practice reading with partners.

PAIRED READ

"Zach the Martian"

Make Connections:
Write About It 📝 *Analytical Writing*

Before reading, ask students to note that the genre of this text is science fiction. Then discuss the Essential Question. After reading, ask students to list connections between *Mars* and "Zach the Martian."

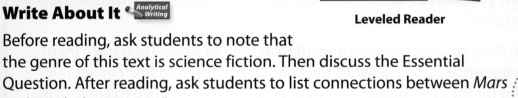

Leveled Reader

 FOCUS ON SCIENCE

Students can extend their knowledge of Mars by completing the research and observation activity on page 24. **STEM**

Literature Circles

Ask students to conduct a literature circle using the Thinkmark questions to guide the discussion. You may wish to have a whole-class discussion, on information learned from both selections in the Leveled Reader, about the topic of how scientific knowledge can change over time.

Level Up

Level-up lessons available online.

IF students read the **ELL Level** fluently and answered the questions,

THEN pair them with students who have proficiently read **On Level** and have ELL students

• echo-read the **On Level** main selection.

• list words with which they have difficulty and discuss them with a partner.

A C T Access Complex Text

The **On Level** challenges students by including more **domain-specific words** and **complex sentence structures**.

English Language Learners
Vocabulary

PRETEACH VOCABULARY

OBJECTIVES
(CCSS) Acquire and use accurately grade-appropriate general academic and domain-specific words and phrases, including those that signal contrast, addition, and other logical relationships. **L.5.6**

LANGUAGE OBJECTIVE
Use vocabulary words.

 Preteach vocabulary from "Changing Views of Earth" following the Vocabulary Routine found on the **Visual Vocabulary Cards** for the words *approximately, astronomical, calculation, criteria, diameter, evaluate, orbit,* and *spheres.*

 After completing the Vocabulary Routine for each word, point to the word on the card and read the word with students. Ask them to repeat the word.

 Have students work in pairs to use two words in questions and answer the questions. Then have them share their work.

Beginning	Intermediate	Advanced/High
Help students write and answer questions.	Ask students to write the answers to the questions.	Challenge students to write a question for each word.

REVIEW VOCABULARY

OBJECTIVES
(CCSS) Acquire and use accurately grade-appropriate general academic and domain-specific words and phrases, including those that signal contrast, addition, and other logical relationships. **L.5.6**

LANGUAGE OBJECTIVE
Use vocabulary words.

 Review the previous week's vocabulary words over a few days. Read each word aloud, pointing to the word on the **Visual Vocabulary Card**. Have students repeat after you. Then follow the Vocabulary Routine on the back of each card.

 Choose a word that you can draw or demonstrate. Have students name the word you drew or acted out. Then have them define the word or use it in a sentence.

 In pairs, have students choose a word to act out or draw. Then have them write a sentence using the word they chose. Ask them to draw or act out the word for the class to guess. They can read their sentence to confirm a correct guess.

Beginning	Intermediate	Advanced/High
Help students choose a word to draw or act out and write a sentence to go with it.	Have students use the word in a sentence that shows its meaning.	Challenge students to draw or act out and write sentences for additional words.

GREEK ROOTS

CCSS **OBJECTIVES**
Determine or clarify the meaning of unknown and multiple-meaning words and phrases based on grade 5 reading and content, choosing flexibly from a range of strategies. Use common, grade-appropriate Greek and Latin affixes and roots as clues to the meaning of a word (e.g., *photograph, photosynthesis*). **L.5.4b**

LANGUAGE OBJECTIVE
Identify and use Greek roots.

I Do Read aloud the first paragraph of the Comprehension and Fluency passage on **ELL Reproducibles** pages 233–234. Summarize the paragraph. Point to the word *astrobiology*. Tell students that Greek roots can help them figure out the meaning of the word.

Think Aloud Look at the word *astrobiology*. The Greek prefix *astro-* means "star" and the Greek root *bio-* means "life." The suffix *-logy* means "the study of." I can also use context clues such as "life in space." *Astrobiology* must mean "the study of life in space."

We Do Have students point to the word *photosynthesis* in the third paragraph on page 233. Find the Greek root in the word with students. Write the definition of the word on the board.

You Do In pairs, have students write a definition for *hydrothermal* (page 233, paragraph 4) and *chemosynthesis* (page 234, paragraph 1) using Greek roots.

Beginning	Intermediate	Advanced/High
Help students locate the words and Greek roots.	Ask students to identify and define the Greek roots.	Have students explain how they used Greek roots.

ADDITIONAL VOCABULARY

CCSS **OBJECTIVES**
Acquire and use accurately grade-appropriate general academic and domain-specific words and phrases, including those that signal contrast, addition, and other logical relationships. **L.5.6**

LANGUAGE OBJECTIVE
Use academic vocabulary and high-frequency words.

I Do List some academic vocabulary and high-frequency words from "Changing Views of Earth": *device, telescope, theory;* and *Mars: ancient, questions, astronomer*. Define each word for students: *A device is a tool made for a certain purpose.*

We Do Model using the words for students in a sentence: *A calculator is a device I use in math class. Scientists use measuring devices to learn about the weather.* Then provide sentence frames and complete them with students: *A device we use often at home is ____.*

You Do Have pairs make up their own sentence frames and share them with the class to complete them.

Beginning	Intermediate	Advanced/High
Help students copy the sentence frames correctly and complete them.	Have students read the completed sentences aloud.	Have students define the words they used.

→ English Language Learners
Writing/Spelling

WRITING TRAIT: ORGANIZATION

OBJECTIVES
Introduce a topic clearly, provide a general observation and focus, and group related information logically; include formatting (e.g. headings), illustrations, and multimedia when useful to aiding comprehension.
W.5.2a

LANGUAGE OBJECTIVE
Support main ideas in writing.

 Explain that in a well-written paragraph, every sentence supports the same main idea. Read the Expert Model aloud as students follow along. Identify the main idea in each paragraph and the details that support it.

 Read aloud one paragraph from "Changing Views of Earth" as students follow along. Identify the main idea. Then use a word web to list the details. Model sentences to describe the main idea and details using the word web. Point out that every detail should support the same main idea.

 Have pairs write their own short paragraph, using the word web. They should include a main idea sentence and details that support only that main idea. Edit each pair's writing. Then ask students to revise.

Beginning	Intermediate	Advanced/High
Have students copy the edited sentences.	Have students revise, deleting or editing sentences that are off topic.	Have students revise, making their details more specific and deleting or revising unrelated details.

SPELL WORDS WITH SUFFIXES -less AND -ness

OBJECTIVES
Spell grade-appropriate words correctly, consulting references as needed.
L.5.2e

LANGUAGE OBJECTIVE
Spell words with suffixes -less and -ness.

 Read aloud the Spelling Words on page T228, segmenting them into syllables and attaching a spelling to each sound. Point out the suffix in each word and draw out its sound as you pronounce it. Have students repeat.

 Read the Dictation Sentences on page T229 aloud for students. With each sentence, read the underlined word slowly, segmenting it into syllables. Have students repeat after you and write the word.

 Display the words. Have students exchange their list with a partner to check the spelling and write the words correctly.

Beginning	Intermediate	Advanced/High
Help students copy the words with correct spelling and say them aloud.	After students have corrected their words, have pairs quiz each other.	After students corrected their words, have them identify and practice writing difficult words.

Grammar

ADJECTIVES THAT COMPARE

OBJECTIVES

CCSS Demonstrate command of the conventions of standard English grammar and usage when writing or speaking. Form and use comparative and superlative adjectives and adverbs, and choose between them depending on what is to be modified. **L.3.1g**

LANGUAGE OBJECTIVE

Identify and use comparative adjectives.

Language Transfers Handbook

In Hmong, Korean, and Spanish, comparative adjectives do not change form. Students who speak these languages are more likely to use *more* and *most* with all adjectives instead of using *-er* and *-est* forms. Give students additional support in forming comparative adjectives with the *-er* and *-est* endings.

I Do Review that comparative adjectives compare people, places, and things. Adjectives that end in *-er* compare two things and adjectives that end in *-est* compare three or more things. Write these sentences: *I am older than my brother. My sister is the oldest.* Underline the adjectives and double underline the *-er* and *-est* endings.

We Do Write the sentence frames below on the board. Have students fill in the correct comparative adjective for each sentence. Then read the completed sentences aloud for students to repeat.

> Today is _____ than yesterday.
>
> Mr. Lopez grew the _____ pumpkin I've ever seen.
>
> Susan ran _____ than Lee.

You Do Brainstorm a list of adjectives that can be used to compare things. Have students work in pairs to write two sentences, one that compares two things and one that compares three or more things. Remind students to use the correct endings.

Beginning	**Intermediate**	**Advanced/High**
Help students copy their sentences and use comparative adjectives correctly. Read the sentences aloud. Have students repeat.	Ask students to underline the endings they added to their comparative adjectives and check that they are correct.	Challenge students to write an additional pair of sentences using comparative adjectives formed with *more* or *most*.

For extra support, have students complete the activities in the **Grammar Practice Reproducibles** during the week, using the routine below:

→ Explain the grammar skill.

→ Model the first activity in the Grammar Practice Reproducibles.

→ Have the whole group complete the next couple of activities, then do the rest with a partner.

→ Review the activities with correct answers.

Weekly Assessment

✓ TESTED SKILLS

✓ **COMPREHENSION:**	✓ **VOCABULARY:**	✓ **WRITING:**
Text Structure: Cause and Effect **RI.5.5**	Greek Roots **L.5.4b**	Writing About Text **RI.5.5, W.5.9b**

Assessment Includes
→ Performance Tasks
→ Approaching-Level Assessment online PDFs

Fluency Goal 129 to 149 words correct per minute (WCPM)

Accuracy Rate Goal 95% or higher

Administer oral reading fluency assessments using the following schedule:

→ **Weeks 1, 3, 5** Provide Approaching-Level students at least three oral reading fluency assessments during the unit.

→ **Weeks 2 and 4** Provide On-Level students at least two oral reading fluency assessments during the unit.

→ **Week 6** If necessary, provide Beyond-Level students an oral reading fluency assessment at this time.

Also Available: Selection Tests online PDFs

Go Digital! www.connected.mcgraw-hill.com

Using Assessment Results

✓ TESTED SKILLS	If ...	Then ...
COMPREHENSION	Students answer 0–6 multiple-choice items correctly ...	... assign Lessons 76–78 on Cause and Effect from the *Tier 2 Comprehension Intervention online PDFs.*
VOCABULARY	Students answer 0–6 multiple-choice items correctly ...	... assign Lesson 157 on Greek, Latin, and Other Roots from the *Tier 2 Vocabulary Intervention online PDFs.*
WRITING	Students score less than "3" on the constructed responses ...	... assign Lessons 76–78 on Cause and Effect and/or Write About Reading Lesson 200 from the *Tier 2 Comprehension Intervention online PDFs.*
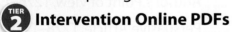	Students have a WCPM score of 120–128 ...	... assign a lesson from Section 1, 7, 8, 9, or 10 of the *Tier 2 Fluency Intervention online PDFs.*
	Students have a WCPM score of 0–119 ...	... assign a lesson from Section 2, 3, 4, 5, or 6 of the *Tier 2 Fluency Intervention online PDFs.*

Response to Intervention

Use the appropriate sections of the *Placement and Dignostic Assessment* as well as students' assessment results to designate students requiring:

TIER 2 Intervention Online PDFs

TIER 3 WonderWorks Intervention Program

Text Complexity Range for Grades 4–5

Lexile	
740	1010

TextEvaluator™	
23	51

Reading/Writing Workshop

TEACH AND MODEL

CCSS Shared Read TIME

Should Plants and Animals from Other Places Live Here?

New Arrivals Welcome

Nonnative species are good for the economy—and they taste good, too!

Some of America's most important immigrants are plants and animals. Called *nonnative species*, these creatures arrive here from other regions or countries. Nonnative species are known as *invasive* when they harm the environment, our health, or the economy. Invasive species often take over a **widespread** area and overwhelm native wildlife. The population of some native species has **declined** because of a few newcomers, but the news is not all bad. We would be a lot worse off without some of them.

In Florida, for example, about 2,000 species of familiar plants and animals are nonnative. These include oranges, chickens, and sugarcane. In fact, 90 percent of farm sales can be traced directly to nonnative species.

Nonnative species help to control insects and other pests that harm crops. Some scientists **identify** a pest's natural enemy and bring in nonnative enemy species, such as insects, to kill the pests. Killing the pests is a good thing, and an even better result is that pesticide use is reduced. Vedalia beetles were transported here from Australia to eat insects that killed citrus fruit. The beetles completed their mission without any side effects. They also help keep citrus farmers in business!

Not all new arrivals benefit humans. However, many nonnative species are just what the doctor ordered. Many of the dogs and cats we love so much originated in other parts of the world. Would you want to ban Labrador retrievers and Siamese cats? Creatures like these surely make our lives and our nation better!

Essential Question
How do natural events and human activities affect the environment?
Read two different views on the arrival of new species into the United States.

It's hard to imagine life without oranges and chickens, which are examples of nonnative species.

366

367

✔ Vocabulary

agricultural

declined

disorder

identify

probable

thrive

unexpected

widespread

🔍 Close Reading of Complex Text

Shared Read "Should Plants and Animals from Other Places Live Here?," 366–373

Genre Persuasive Article

Lexile 930L

 TextEvaluator™ 57

Minilessons ✔ Tested Skills CCSS

 Go Digital

www.connected.mcgraw-hill.com

SCIENTIFIC VIEWPOINTS

Essential Question

How do natural events and human activities affect the environment?

WEEK 5 →

APPLY WITH CLOSE READING

Complex Text

Literature Anthology

PAIRED READ

The Case of the Missing Bees, 424–427
Genre Persuasive Article
Lexile 950L
ETS *TextEvaluator™* 59

"Busy, Beneficial Bees," 428–429
Genre Expository Text
Lexile 980L
ETS *TextEvaluator™* 45

Differentiated Text

Leveled Readers *Include Paired Reads*

APPROACHING
Lexile 760L
ETS *TextEvaluator™* 34

ON LEVEL
Lexile 910L
ETS *TextEvaluator™* 43

BEYOND
Lexile 1020L
ETS *TextEvaluator™* 48

ELL
Lexile 830L
ETS *TextEvaluator™* 37

Extended Complex Text

Volcano: The Eruption and Healing of Mount St. Helens
Genre Expository Text
Lexile 830L
ETS *TextEvaluator™* 3

Classroom Library

Arctic Lights, Arctic Nights
Genre Expository Text
Lexile 890L
ETS *TextEvaluator™* 36

Classroom Library lessons available online.

TEACH AND MANAGE

How You Teach

INTRODUCE

Weekly Concept

Scientific Viewpoints

Reading/Writing Workshop
362–363

TEACH

Close Reading

"Should Plants and Animals from Other Places Live Here?"

Minilessons

Ask and Answer Questions, Author's Point of View, Persuasive Article, Root Words, Writing Traits

Reading/Writing Workshop
366–375

APPLY

Close Reading

The Case of the Missing Bees

"Busy, Beneficial Bees"

Literature Anthology
424–429

 **Go Digital** Interactive Whiteboard   Interactive Whiteboard   Mobile

---

How Students Practice

WEEKLY CONTRACT

PDF Online

Name _____ Date _____

My To-Do List

✔ Put a check next to the activities you complete.

📖 **Reading**
- ☐ Author's Point of View
- ☐ Fluency

🔤 **Phonics/ Word Study**
- ☐ -ion

✏️ **Writing**
- ☐ Strong Conclusions

🔬 **Science**
- ☐ Natural Events and Humans Affect Environment

👐 **Independent Practice**
- ☐ Vocabulary, pp. 241, 247
- ☐ Comprehension and Fluency, pp. 243–245
- ☐ Genre, p. 246
- ☐ Phonics, p. 248
- ☐ Write About Reading, p. 249
- ☐ Writing Traits, p. 250

🖑 **Go Digital**
www.connected.mcgraw-hill.com
Interactive Games/Activities
- ☐ Vocabulary
- ☐ Comprehension
- ☐ Phonics/Word Study
- ☐ Grammar
- ☐ Spelling/Word Sorts
- ☐ Listening Library

26 Unit 5 • Week 5 • Scie...

LEVELED PRACTICE AND ONLINE ACTIVITIES

Your Turn Practice Book
241–250

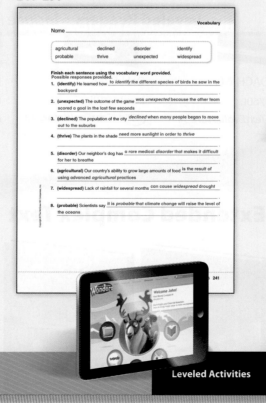

Leveled Readers

 **Go Digital**   Online To-Do List   Leveled Activities   Writer's Workspace

---

Go Digital! www.connected.mcgraw-hill.com

DIFFERENTIATE

SMALL GROUP INSTRUCTION

Leveled Readers

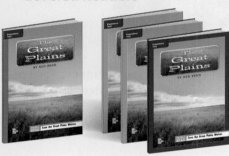

Mobile

INTEGRATE

Research and Inquiry
Bibliography, T284

Text Connections
Compare Information on the Environment, T285

Write About Reading
Analytical Writing Write an Analysis, T285

Online Research and Writing

ASSESS

Grade 5

Wonders

Weekly Assessment

Assessing the Common Core State Standards

Weekly Assessment
289–300

Online Assessment

LEVELED WORKSTATION CARDS

More Activities on back

25
Humans and the Environment

Scientists study ways that human beings affect the environment. A control group without human activity helps scientists compare.

- Discuss one way that humans can change the environment. For example, building dams will affect the wildlife of the river that is dammed.

SCIENCE

9
Organization: Strong Conclusions

Read Cameron's conclusion to a letter to the editor of his school newspaper.

Finally, it is important for students to recycle. We need to put recycling bins in every classroom. There should be bins for glass, paper, plastic. Spread the

- What does the conclusion tell you about Cameron's opinion? What key points does his conclusion mention?

WRITING

7
Root Words

You can add prefixes, suffixes, and endings to root words to make new words.

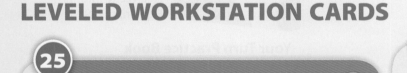

- List five vocabulary words you have learned that contain root words.

- Draw a Venn diagram. Label the circle on the left "Vocabulary Word." Label the intersection "Root Word." Label the circle on the right "New Word."

| Vocabulary Word | Root Word expect | New Word |

interesting
completion
complicated
interruption

- Write a vocabulary word in the left circle. Write its root word in the intersection. Write the new word with the same root in the right circle. Do the same for the other four words.

You need
15
› paper
› pencil or pen
› dictionary

PHONICS/WORD STUDY

23
Author's Point of View

- With a partner, choose a section of an informational text to read. Each of you will read the same section of text independently.

- As you read, look for details that help you determine the author's point of view. Record each detail in the outer circle of a web.

- Decide what all the details have in common. Use this to identify the author's point of view. Write it in the middle circle of the web.

well-respected

- Share your web with your partner. Talk about the clues you chose. Did you come up with the same point of view? Why or why not?

You need
20
› informational text
› paper and pen or pencil

READING

DEVELOPING READERS AND WRITERS

Write to Sources and Research

Author's Point of View, T276–T277

Note Taking, T281B, T281E

Make Connections: Essential Question, T281F, T285

Key Details, T281F

Research and Inquiry, T284

Analyze to Inform/Explain, T285

Comparing Texts, T297, T305, T309, T315

Predictive Writing, T281A

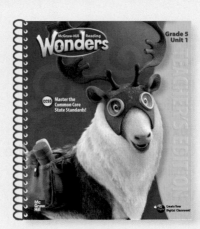

Teacher's Edition

Author's Point of View, p. 427

Literature Anthology

Interactive Whiteboard

Leveled Readers
Comparing Texts
Author's Point of View

Author's Point of View, pp. 243–245
Genre, p. 246
Analyze to Inform/Explain, p. 249

Your Turn Practice Book

Informative Text
Research Report, T350–T355

Conferencing Routines
Teacher Conferences, T352
Peer Conferences, T353

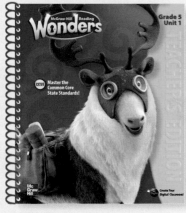

Interactive Whiteboard

Teacher's Edition

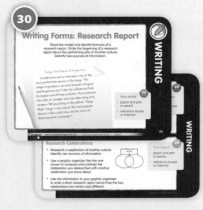

Leveled Workstation Card
Research Report, Card 30

Writer's Workspace
Informative Text:
Research Report
Writing Process
Multimedia Presentations

Writing Traits • Write Every Day

Writing Trait: Organization
Strong Conclusions, T286–T287

Conferencing Routines
Teacher Conferences, T288
Peer Conferences, T289

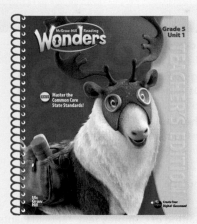

Teacher's Edition

Organization:
Strong Conclusions,
pp. 374–375

Reading/Writing Workshop

Go Digital

Interactive Whiteboard

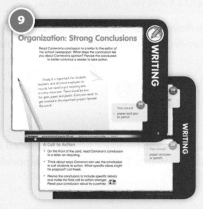

Leveled Workstation Card

Organization:
Strong
Conclusions, 9

Your Turn Practice Book

Organization: Strong
Conclusions, p. 250

Grammar and Spelling

Grammar
Comparing with *Good* and *Bad*, T290–T291

Spelling
Suffix *-ion*, T292–T293

Go Digital

Interactive Whiteboard

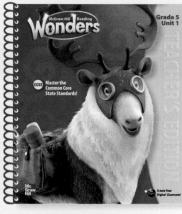

Teacher's Edition

Go Digital

Comparing with
Good and *Bad*

Suffix *-ion*
Word Sorts

Online Spelling and Grammar Games

SUGGESTED LESSON PLAN

✔ TESTED SKILLS 	DAY 1	DAY 2

READING

Whole Group

Teach, Model and Apply

Reading/Writing Workshop

DAY 1

Build Background Scientific Viewpoints, T266–T267

Listening Comprehension Interactive Read Aloud: "Dams: Harnessing the Power of Water," T268–T269

Comprehension
• Preview Genre: Persuasive Article, T278–T279
• Preview Strategy: Ask and Answer Questions, T274–T275

✔ **Vocabulary** Words in Context, T270–T271
Practice *Your Turn* 241

Close Reading of Complex Text "Should Plants and Animals from Other Places Live Here?," 366–369

DAY 2

✔ **Comprehension**
• Strategy: Ask and Answer Questions, T274–T275
• Skill: Author's Point of View, T276–T277
• Write About Reading  *Analytical Writing*
• Genre: Persuasive Article, T278–T279

✔ **Vocabulary** Strategy: Root Words, T280–T281
Practice *Your Turn* 242–247

DIFFERENTIATED INSTRUCTION Choose across the week to meet your students' needs.

Small Group

Approaching Level

DAY 1
Leveled Reader *The Great Plains*, T296–T297
Word Study/Decoding Review Words with Suffix *-ion*, T298
Vocabulary
• Review High-Frequency Words, T300 TIER 2
• Understand Vocabulary Words, T301

DAY 2
Leveled Reader *The Great Plains*, T296–T297
Vocabulary Review Vocabulary Words, T300 TIER 2
Comprehension
• Identify Important Details, T302 TIER 2
• Review Author's Point of View, T303

On Level

DAY 1
Leveled Reader *The Great Plains*, T304–T305
Vocabulary Review Vocabulary Words, T306

DAY 2
Leveled Reader *The Great Plains*, T304–T305
Comprehension Review Author's Point of View, T307

Beyond Level

DAY 1
Leveled Reader *The Great Plains*, T308–T309
Vocabulary Review Domain-Specific Words, T310

DAY 2
Leveled Reader *The Great Plains*, T308–T309
Comprehension Review Author's Point of View, T311

English Language Learners

DAY 1
Shared Read "Should Plants and Animals from Other Places Live Here?," T312–T313
Word Study/Decoding Review Words with Suffix *-ion*, T298
Vocabulary
• Preteach Vocabulary, T316
• Review High-Frequency Words, T300

DAY 2
Leveled Reader *The Great Plains*, T314–T315
Vocabulary Review Vocabulary, T316
Writing Writing Trait: Organization, T318
Grammar Comparing with *Good* and *Bad*, T319

LANGUAGE ARTS Writing Process: Research Report T350–T355

Use with Weeks 4–6

Whole Group

Writing
Grammar
Spelling
Build Vocabulary

DAY 1

✔ **Readers to Writers**
• Writing Trait: Organization/Strong Conclusions, T286–T287
• Writing Entry: Prewrite and Draft, T288

Grammar Comparing with *Good* and *Bad*, T290
Spelling Suffix *-ion*, T292
Build Vocabulary
• Connect to Words, T294
• Academic Vocabulary, T294

DAY 2

Readers to Writers
• Writing Entry: Revise, T288

Grammar Comparing with *Good* and *Bad*, T290
Spelling Suffix *-ion*, T292
Build Vocabulary
• Expand Vocabulary, T294
• Review Context Clues, T294

Go Digital

CUSTOMIZE YOUR OWN LESSON PLANS

www.connected.mcgraw-hill.com

WEEK 5 →

DAY 3	DAY 4	DAY 5 Review and Assess

READING

Word Study/Decoding Words with *-ion*, T282–T283

Practice *Your Turn* 248

Close Reading *The Case of the Missing Bees*, 424–427 *Analytical Writing*

Literature Anthology

Fluency Expression and Phrasing, T283

Integrate Ideas *Analytical Writing*
• Research and Inquiry, T284

Practice *Your Turn* 243–245

Close Reading "Busy, Beneficial Bees," 428–429 *Analytical Writing*

Integrate Ideas *Analytical Writing*
• Research and Inquiry, T284
• Text Connections, T285
• Write About Reading, T285

Practice *Your Turn* 249

DIFFERENTIATED INSTRUCTION

Leveled Reader *The Great Plains*, T296–T297
Word Study/Decoding Build Words with Suffix *-ion*, T298
Fluency Expression and Phrasing, T302 **TIER 2**
Vocabulary Root Words, T301

Leveled Reader Paired Read: "Save the Great Plains Wolves," T297 *Analytical Writing*
Word Study/Decoding Practice Words with Suffix *-ion*, T299

Leveled Reader Literature Circle, T297
Comprehension Self-Selected Reading, T303

Leveled Reader *The Great Plains*, T304–T305
Vocabulary Root Words, T306

Leveled Reader Paired Read: "Save the Great Plains Wolves," T305 *Analytical Writing*

Leveled Reader Literature Circle, T305
Comprehension Self-Selected Reading, T307

Leveled Reader *The Great Plains*, T308–T309
Vocabulary
• Root Words, T310
• Independent Study, T310

Gifted and Talented

Leveled Reader Paired Read: "Save the Great Plains Wolves," T309 *Analytical Writing*

Leveled Reader Literature Circle, T309
Comprehension
• Self-Selected Reading, T311
• Independent Study: The Environment, T311

Gifted and Talented

Leveled Reader *The Great Plains*, T314–T315
Word Study/Decoding Build Words with Suffix *-ion*, T298
Vocabulary Root Words, T317
Spelling Words with Suffix *-ion*, T318

Leveled Reader Paired Read: "Save the Great Plains Wolves," T315 *Analytical Writing*
Vocabulary Additional Vocabulary, T317
Word Study/Decoding Practice Words with Suffix *-ion*, T299

Leveled Reader Literature Circle, T315

LANGUAGE ARTS

Readers to Writers
• Writing Entry: Prewrite and Draft, T289

Grammar Mechanics and Usage, T291

Spelling Suffix *-ion*, T293

Build Vocabulary
• Reinforce the Words, T295
• Root Words, T295

Readers to Writers
• Writing Entry: Revise, T289

Grammar Comparing with *Good* and *Bad*, T291

Spelling Suffix *-ion*, T293

Build Vocabulary
• Connect to Writing, T295
• Shades of Meaning, T295

Readers to Writers
• Writing Entry: Share and Reflect, T289

Grammar Comparing with *Good* and *Bad*, T291

Spelling Suffix *-ion*, T293

Build Vocabulary
• Word Squares, T295
• Morphology, T295

DIFFERENTIATE TO ACCELERATE

 Scaffold to **A**ccess **C**omplex **T**ext

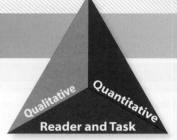

IF ▶ the text complexity of a particular selection is too difficult for students

THEN ▶ see the references noted in the chart below for scaffolded instruction to help students Access Complex Text.

Qualitative · Quantitative
Reader and Task
TEXT COMPLEXITY

	Reading/Writing Workshop	**Literature Anthology**	**Leveled Readers**	**Classroom Library**

Quantitative	"Should Plants and Animals from Other Places Live Here?" **Lexile** 930 *TextEvaluator* 57	*The Case of the Missing Bees* **Lexile** 950 *TextEvaluator* 59 "Busy, Beneficial Bees" **Lexile** 980 *TextEvaluator* 45	**Approaching Level** **Lexile** 760 *TextEvaluator* 34 **Beyond Level** **Lexile** 1020 *TextEvaluator* 48 · **On Level** **Lexile** 910 *TextEvaluator* 43 **ELL** **Lexile** 830 *TextEvaluator* 37	*Volcano: The Eruption and Healing of Mount St. Helens* **Lexile** 830 *TextEvaluator* 31 *Arctic Lights, Arctic Nights* **Lexile** 890 *TextEvaluator* 36
Qualitative	What Makes the Text Complex? • **Connection of Ideas** Author's Point of View T273; Chart T279 **ⒶⒸⓉ** *See Scaffolded Instruction in Teacher's Edition T273 and T279.*	What Makes the Text Complex? • **Organization** Cause and Effect T281A • **Sentence Structure** T281C • **Purpose** Inform T281E **ⒶⒸⓉ** *See Scaffolded Instruction in Teacher's Edition T281A–T281F.*	What Makes the Text Complex? • **Specific Vocabulary** • **Prior Knowledge** • **Sentence Structure** • **Connection of Ideas** • **Genre** **ⒶⒸⓉ** *See Level Up lessons online for Leveled Readers.*	What Makes the Text Complex? • **Genre** • **Specific Vocabulary** • **Prior Knowledge** • **Sentence Structure** • **Organization** • **Purpose** • **Connection of Ideas** **ⒶⒸⓉ** *See Scaffolded Instruction in Teacher's Edition T360-T361.*
Reader and Task	The Introduce the Concept lesson on pages T266–T267 will help determine the reader's knowledge and engagement in the weekly concept. See pages T272–T281 and T284–T285 for questions and tasks for this text.	The Introduce the Concept lesson on pages T266–T267 will help determine the reader's knowledge and engagement in the weekly concept. See pages T281A–T281F and T284–T285 for questions and tasks for this text.	The Introduce the Concept lesson on pages T266–T267 will help determine the reader's knowledge and engagement in the weekly concept. See pages T296–T297, T304–T305, T308–T309, T314–T315, and T284–T285 for questions and tasks for this text.	The Introduce the Concept lesson on pages T266–T267 will help determine the reader's knowledge and engagement in the weekly concept. See pages T360-T361 for questions and tasks for this text.

Monitor and *Differentiate*

IF you need to differentiate instruction

THEN use the Quick Checks to assess students' needs and select the appropriate small group instruction focus.

 Quick Check

Comprehension Strategy Ask and Answer Questions T275

Comprehension Skill Author's Point of View T277

Genre Persuasive Article T279

Vocabulary Strategy Root Words T281

Word Study/Fluency Words with *-ion*, Expression and Phrasing T283

If No →	**Approaching Level**	Reteach T296–T303
	ELL	Develop T312–T319
If Yes →	**On Level**	Review T304–T307
	Beyond Level	Extend T308–T311

Level Up with Leveled Readers

IF students can read their leveled text fluently and answer comprehension questions

THEN work with the next level up to accelerate students' reading with more complex text.

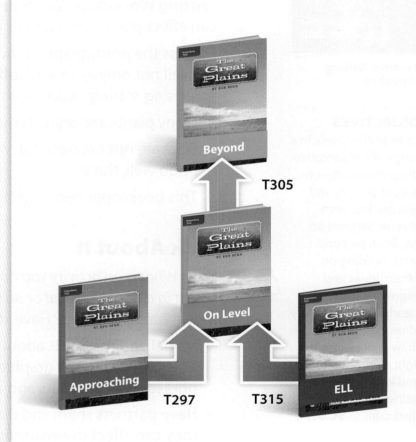

ENGLISH LANGUAGE LEARNERS
SCAFFOLD

IF ELL students need additional support **THEN** scaffold instruction using the small group suggestions.

Reading/Writing Workshop "Should Plants and Animals from Other Places Live Here?" T312–T313	Leveled Reader *The Great Plains* T314–T315 "Save the Great Plains Wolves" T315	Additional Vocabulary T317 climate native droughts species familiar	Root Words T317	Writing Trait: Organization T318	Spelling Suffix *-ion* T318	Grammar Comparing with *Good* and *Bad* T319

Note: Include ELL Students in all small groups based on their needs.

→ Introduce the Concept

Wonders

Reading/Writing
Workshop

**Reading/Writing
Workshop**

OBJECTIVES

CCSS Engage effectively in a range of collaborative discussions (one-on-one, in groups, and teacher-led) with diverse partners on *grade 5 topics and texts,* building on others' ideas and expressing their own clearly. Review the key ideas expressed and draw conclusions in light of information and knowledge gained from the discussions. **SL.5.1d**

Build background knowledge on scientific viewpoints.

ACADEMIC LANGUAGE
• *agricultural, thrive*
• Cognate: *agrícola*

MINILESSON
10 Mins

Build Background

ESSENTIAL QUESTION
How do natural events and human activities affect the environment?

Have students read the Essential Question on page 362 of the **Reading/ Writing Workshop**. Tell them that natural events and human actions can affect plants and animals in positive and negative ways.

Discuss the photograph of the beekeeper. Talk about how bees can do well not only in an **agricultural** setting, such as a farm, but also in surprising settings, such as an urban environment.

→ Many plants and animals that live around us are not native to the area.

→ Bees are not native to busy cities, but they can live and even **thrive**, or do well, there.

→ This beekeeper keeps his bees in the city and enjoys their honey.

Talk About It

COLLABORATE

Ask: *What is an activity you have done that affected the environment? Was it in an **agricultural** or an urban environment? How did your actions help something **thrive**?* Have students discuss in pairs or groups.

→ Model adding words about positively and negatively affecting the environment to the graphic organizer. Then generate words and phrases with students and add their ideas.

→ Have partners share and discuss what they have learned about how they can affect the environment. Tell them to add the ideas they shared to the organizer.

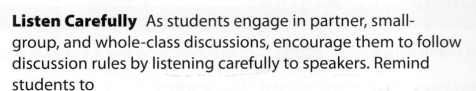

Collaborative Conversations

Listen Carefully As students engage in partner, small-group, and whole-class discussions, encourage them to follow discussion rules by listening carefully to speakers. Remind students to

→ always look at the person who is speaking.

→ respect others by not interrupting them.

→ repeat peers' ideas to check understanding.

Go Digital

Dicuss the Concept

Watch Video

Use Graphic Organizer

ENGLISH LANGUAGE LEARNERS SCAFFOLD

Beginning	Intermediate	Advanced/High
Use Visuals Point to the bees in the photograph. Say: *The bees thrive. They are strong and healthy.* Have students repeat. Elicit simple examples of things we need to thrive, such as good food, water, and shelter. Ask: *Are this man's bees thriving? What parts of the photograph show that they are thriving? Point to them.* Elaborate on students' responses.	**Describe** Have students describe the bees in the photograph. Ask: *How would you describe these bees?* Provide sentence frames such as: *The bees have what they need to be healthy and _____ in this _____ environment.* (thrive, city/urban) Ask: *What other environment could bees thrive in?* (agricultural) Elicit details.	**Discuss** Have students use the words *thrive* and *agricultural* to discuss the bees in the photograph. Ask questions to help them elaborate. Ask: *Where can bees live? How does the beekeeper help the bees thrive?* Correct students' grammar and pronunciation as needed.

GRAPHIC ORGANIZER 61

→ Listening Comprehension

⏱ **10 Mins** MINILESSON

Interactive Read Aloud

Go Digital

View Photos

OBJECTIVES

CCSS Analyze multiple accounts of the same event or topic, noting important similarities and differences in the point of view they represent. **RI.5.6**

CCSS Summarize a written text read aloud or information presented in diverse media and formats, including visually, quantitatively, and orally. **SL.5.2**

- Listen for a purpose.
- Identify characteristics of persuasive articles.

ACADEMIC LANGUAGE

- *persuasive article, ask and answer questions*
- Cognate: *artículo persuasivo*

Connect to Concept: Scientific Viewpoints

Remind students that scientists do not always agree on the best way to solve a problem. Point out that scientists on different sides of a controversial topic or issue will defend their viewpoint on the basis of evidence. Tell students that the selection you will read aloud presents two opposing views on the benefits and costs of building dams.

Preview Genre: Persuasive Article

Explain that the text you will read aloud is a persuasive article. Discuss features of persuasive articles:

→ present factual details and well-supported opinions

→ attempt to persuade

→ may include text features such as headers, captions, and labels

Preview Comprehension Strategy: Ask and Answer Questions

Tell students that active reading is an ongoing process in which readers ask and answer questions before, during, and after they read. For nonfiction text, readers might ask themselves the following questions as they read: What do I understand from what I just read? What is the main idea? Are there sections of text I can reread in order to improve my comprehension? When rereading a persuasive article, readers can decide whether or not information from the text supports their answers.

Use the Think Alouds on page T269 to model the strategy.

Respond to Reading

Think Aloud Clouds Display Think Aloud Master 1: *I wonder . . .* to reinforce how you used the ask and answer questions strategy to understand content.

Model Think Alouds

Genre Features With students, discuss the elements of the Read Aloud that let them know it is a persuasive article. Ask them to think about other texts that you have read or they have read independently that were persuasive articles.

Genre Chart

Summarize Have students restate in their own words the most important information from "Dams: Harnessing the Power of Water." Have them take turns with a partner to summarize key details.

Dams: Harnessing the Power of Water

Point: *The world depends on dams.* **1**

Dams have long provided people with a way to control the flow and supply of water. They also give us an efficient way to produce electricity.

Dams Produce Hydroelectric Power

Dams provide power plants with moving water to make electricity. Since the water is free, hydropower produces electricity inexpensively. Hydroelectric plants release few greenhouse gases, as they do not burn fossil fuels.

Dams Supply Water and Control Flooding

When a river is dammed, it creates an artificial lake called a reservoir. The water in a reservoir can be used to irrigate crops and for activities such as drinking and cooking.

Flood-control dams store a river's overflow in the reservoir. This keeps the excess water from flooding homes and destroying farm animals and crops.

Dams are indispensable to modern life. Thanks to dams, we have a reliable source of water. **2**

Counterpoint: *The destructive impact of dams on the environment outweighs their benefits.*

Despite the benefits provided by dams, they are not the answer to the world's need for cheap, renewable energy.

Dams Can Harm Wildlife

Damming a river and creating a reservoir floods the land, drowning some wildlife and destroying habitats. Building a dam requires constructing roads and power lines, which also causes the destruction of natural habitats.

When a river is dammed, its water flow changes. This keeps some fish from swimming upstream to breed.

Reservoirs Emit Greenhouse Gases

Scientific studies show that some reservoirs from dams release large amounts of methane and carbon dioxide. These gases contribute to climate change.

Without a better understanding of how dams impact the environment, dams will continue to create more problems than they solve. **3**

1 Think Aloud When I read the title of this article, I wonder: "Why does the world depend on dams?" I'll keep reading to find out.

2 Think Aloud Now that I've finished this section, I can ask and answer a question: "What is the main idea of this article?" The main idea is that dams are necessary for modern life.

3 Think Aloud After reading both the point and counterpoint, I can ask a question: "What are the benefits and drawbacks of dams?" To answer my question, I will reread the main points of each article.

Andersen Ross/Blend Images/Getty Images

→ Vocabulary

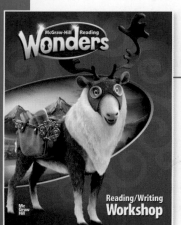

Reading/Writing Workshop

MINILESSON
10 Mins

Words in Context

Model the Routine

Introduce each vocabulary word using the Vocabulary Routine found on the **Visual Vocabulary Cards**.

Visual Vocabulary Cards

Vocabu

Define:
Example:
Ask:

Vocabulary Routine

Define: Something that is **agricultural** has to do with farms or farming.

Example: Sam and Gina gathered apples and other agricultural products for the market.

Ask: How do agricultural products make a difference in your life?

Definitions

→ **declined** If something **declined**, it grew weaker or smaller in number.

→ **disorder** A **disorder** is a sickness or ailment.

→ **identify** If you can **identify** something, you can tell exactly what it is.
  Cognate: *identificar*

→ **probable** Something that is **probable** is likely to happen or be true.
  Cognate: *probable*

→ **thrive** If crops **thrive**, they are successful and strong.

→ **unexpected** Something **unexpected** is not planned for or predicted.

→ **widespread** If something is **widespread**, it is happening over a large area or affecting many people. *or things*

Talk About It

Have students work with a partner and look at each photograph. Ask them to discuss the definition of each word. Then ask students to choose three words and write questions for their partner to answer.

OBJECTIVES
Acquire and use accurately grade-appropriate general academic and domain-specific words and phrases, including those that signal contrast, addition, and other logical relationships (e.g., *however, although, nevertheless, similarly, moreover, in addition*).
L.5.6

ACADEMIC LANGUAGE
• *agricultural, thrive*
• Cognate: *agrícola*

Go Digital

agricultural

Use Visual Glossary

CCSS Words to Know

Vocabulary

Use the picture and the sentences to talk with a partner about each word.

agricultural
Sam and Gina gathered apples and other **agricultural** products for the market.

How do agricultural products make a difference in your life?

declined
Because many businesses closed, the town had clearly **declined** over the years.

What actions can a restaurant take when its profits have declined?

disorder
The veterinarian examined the cow for a stomach **disorder**.

What kind of medical disorder might keep you home from school?

identify
People are able to **identify** my dog not only by his dog tag, but by his smile.

How would you identify your best friend in a crowd?

probable
The **probable** cause of the shattered window was Jake and his soccer ball.

What type of weather is most probable in the winter where you live?

thrive
Some plants manage to grow and **thrive** even in snow.

What would you do to help a pet thrive?

unexpected
As the wildebeests drank at the river, the crocodile's arrival was **unexpected**.

How might an unexpected event change your plans?

widespread
Starlings, introduced from England, are now a **widespread** bird species.

What is a good example of a widespread fad?

 COLLABORATE

Your Turn

Pick three words. Write three questions for your partner to answer.

Go Digital! Use the online visual glossary

364

365

READING/WRITING WORKSHOP, pp. 364–365

ELL ENGLISH LANGUAGE LEARNERS SCAFFOLD

Beginning

Use Visuals Point to the photograph and say *agricultural*. Have students repeat. Say: *The girls have agricultural products like apples and lettuce.* Elicit that another way to say *agricultural* is *from a farm*. Help students name or draw agricultural products, such as food crops, farm animals, wool, eggs, and milk. Point out the cognate *agrícola*.

Intermediate

Describe Have students describe the photograph for *agricultural*. Review the word's meaning and pronunciation. Ask: *What are some other agricultural products?* Have partners discuss, and prompt them for details. Elaborate on correct answers, modeling how to answer in complete sentences using the word *agricultural*.

Advanced/High

Discuss Ask students to discuss with a partner what the girls in the photograph for *agricultural* are doing. Then have partners discuss what agricultural products they might find at a supermarket. Elicit details to support students' responses.

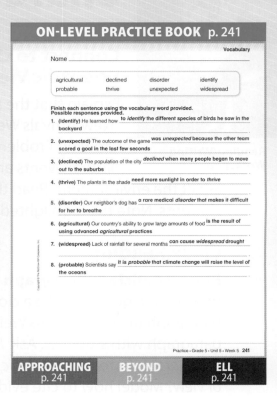

ON-LEVEL PRACTICE BOOK p. 241

Name _____

| agricultural | declined | disorder | identify |
| probable | thrive | unexpected | widespread |

Finish each sentence using the vocabulary word provided. Possible responses provided.

1. (identify) He learned how *to identify the different species of birds he saw in the backyard*

2. (unexpected) The outcome of the game *was unexpected because the other team scored a goal in the last few seconds*

3. (declined) The population of the city *declined when many people began to move out to the suburbs*

4. (thrive) The plants in the shade *need more sunlight in order to thrive*

5. (disorder) Our neighbor's dog has *a rare medical disorder that makes it difficult for her to breathe*

6. (agricultural) Our country's ability to grow large amounts of food *is the result of using advanced agricultural practices*

7. (widespread) Lack of rainfall for several months *can cause widespread drought*

8. (probable) Scientists say *it is probable that climate change will raise the level of the oceans*

Practice • Grade 5 • Unit 5 • Week 5 **241**

| APPROACHING p. 241 | BEYOND p. 241 | ELL p. 241 |

CCSS **Shared Read** TIME FOR KIDS®

Essential Question

How do natural events and human activities affect the environment?

Read two different views on the arrival of new species into the United States.

It's hard to imagine life without oranges and chickens, which are examples of nonnative species.

366

Should Plants and Animals from Other Places Live Here?

POINT COUNTERPOINT

New Arrivals Welcome

Nonnative species are good for the economy—and they taste good, too!

Some of America's most important immigrants are plants and animals. Called *nonnative species,* these creatures arrive here from other regions or countries. Nonnative species are known as *invasive* when they harm the environment, our health, or the economy. Invasive species often take over a **widespread** area and overwhelm native wildlife. The population of some native species has **declined** because of a few newcomers, but the news is not all bad. We would be a lot worse off without some of them.

In Florida, for example, about 2,000 species of familiar plants and animals are nonnative. These include oranges, chickens, and sugarcane. In fact, 90 percent of farm sales can be traced directly to nonnative species.

Nonnative species help to control insects and other pests that harm crops. Some scientists **identify** a pest's natural enemy and bring in nonnative enemy species, such as insects, to kill the pests. Killing the pests is a good thing, and an even better result is that pesticide use is reduced. Vedalia beetles were transported here from Australia to eat insects that killed citrus fruit. The beetles completed their mission without any side effects. They also help keep citrus farmers in business!

Not all new arrivals benefit humans. However, many nonnative species are just what the doctor ordered. Many of the dogs and cats we love so much originated in other parts of the world. Would you want to ban Labrador retrievers and Siamese cats? Creatures like these surely make our lives and our nation better!

367

Reading/Writing Workshop

Shared Read

READING/WRITING WORKSHOP, pp. 366–367

Lexile 930   *TextEvaluator* ™ 57

Connect to Concept: Scientific Viewpoints

Explain that the persuasive articles "New Arrivals Welcome" and "A Growing Problem" will show how natural events and human activities affect the environment. Read the articles with students. Note the highlighted vocabulary words.

Close Reading

Reread Article 1, Paragraph 1: Tell students that you are going to take a closer look at the first paragraph of "New Arrivals Welcome." Reread the paragraph with students. Ask: *How does the author of the article introduce the topic and his or her point of view?* Model how to cite evidence to answer.

The author defines nonnative species and then explains that some of these species become invasive when they overwhelm native species and harm the environment. The paragraph ends with the claim that despite these problems, we would be worse off without nonnative species. This is the position that the author will try to support.

Reread Article 2, Paragraph 1: Model how to use details in the text to make inferences about this author's point of view.

The author of this article begins with an example of how a nonnative species can cause problems: pythons have become a widespread menace in the Florida Everglades. This example shows that the author has an opposing point of view about nonnative species and thinks they are dangerous.

A Growing Problem

Thousands of foreign plant and animal species threaten our country.

Visitors to the Florida Everglades expect to see alligators, not pythons. These huge snakes are native to Southeast Asia. But about 150,000 of the reptiles are crawling through the Everglades. The **probable** reason they got there is that pet owners dumped the snakes in the wild. Now the nonnative pythons have become a **widespread** menace, threatening to reduce the population of endangered native species.

Some nonnative species may be useful, but others are harmful to the nation. It costs the U.S. $137 billion each year to repair the damage these species cause to the environment. The trouble occurs when nonnative species become invasive. Invasive species are a nuisance just about everywhere in the nation. For example, the

Asian carp, which was introduced unintentionally to the U.S., has been able to **thrive** in the Mississippi River and now threatens the Great Lakes ecosystem. Because of its large appetite, the population of native fish has gone down.

Some germs are also invasive species, and they are especially harmful to humans. One, the avian influenza virus, came to the U.S. carried by birds. This microbe can cause a serious lung **disorder** in infected people.

Some **agricultural** experts have introduced nonnative species on purpose to improve the environment. However, this can sometimes create **unexpected** problems. A hundred years ago, melaleuca trees were brought to Florida from Australia to stabilize swampy areas. Now millions of the trees blanket the land, crowding out native plants and harming endangered plants and animals.

The facts about this alien invasion lead to one conclusion: We must remove invasive species and keep new ones from our shores.

This community is trying to control the invasive melaleuca plant that has taken over this marsh.

368

Nonnative Species: Benefits and Costs

Over the years, about 50,000 nonnative species have entered the U.S. These four examples show the positive and negative impacts they can have.

SPECIES	NATIVE LAND	WHEN AND HOW INTRODUCED TO U.S.	POSITIVE IMPACT	NEGATIVE IMPACT
Horse	Europe	Early 1500s, on purpose	Used for work, transportation, and recreation	Made large-scale wars possible
Kudzu	Asia	Early 1800s, on purpose	Stops soil erosion	Crowds out native plants
Olives	Middle East and Europe	Early 1700s, on purpose, cultivation began in 1800s	Major food and cooking oil source, important industry in California	Most olives must be imported because they do not grow everywhere.
Mediterranean Fruit Fly	Sub-Saharan Africa	1929 (first recorded), accidentally	May be a food source for creatures such as spiders	Destroys 400 species of plants, including citrus and vegetable crops

(t to b) Ingram Publishing; Matt Meadows/Peter Arnold/Getty Images; Emilio Simion/Photodisc/Getty Images; Jack Dykinga/USDA

Make Connections

Talk about the uses and harmful effects of species introduced into the United States. **ESSENTIAL QUESTION**

Would you give up eating or using a species if you discovered it was nonnative? Explain your reasons. **TEXT TO SELF**

369

CAUTION
MELALEUCA CONTROL PROJECT
IN MARSH AREAS

READING/WRITING WORKSHOP, pp. 368–369

Make Connections

ESSENTIAL QUESTION

Encourage students to reread the text for evidence as they discuss the uses and harmful effects of nonnative species. Ask students to explain, using the text, how natural events and human activities affect the environment.

Continue Close Reading

Use the following lessons for focused rereadings.

→ Ask and Answer Questions, pp. T274–T275

→ Author's Point of View, pp. T276–T277

→ Persuasive Article, pp. T278–T279

→ Root Words, pp. T280–T281

A C T Access Complex Text

▶ Connection of Ideas

Understanding connected ideas in the first two paragraphs of "A Growing Problem" can help students see the author's viewpoint.

→ *What two nonnative species are mentioned in these paragraphs?* (pythons, Asian carp)

→ *What problem are both animals causing in local ecosystems?* (They kill native animals.)

→ *How does this damage affect the country?* (It costs billions of dollars to repair.)

→ *Is the author's viewpoint about nonnative species positive or negative?* (negative)

→ Comprehension Strategy

Reading/Writing Workshop

OBJECTIVES

CCSS Determine two or more main ideas of a text and explain how they are supported by key details; summarize the text. **RI.5.2**

ACADEMIC LANGUAGE

ask and answer questions, persuasive article

MINILESSON
10 Mins

Ask and Answer Questions

1 Explain

Explain to students that they can check their understanding of a persuasive text by asking and answering questions about it.

→ Remind students to pause now and then to ask themselves questions about what they just read.

→ If students are confused about a paragraph or section, they should go back and reread. They may need to reread the section or paragraph more than once before they discover the answers to their questions.

Point out that students should ask questions before they read as a way of setting a purpose for reading. They should then ask and answer questions about each section while they read and about the entire article after they finish reading.

2 Model Close Reading: Text Evidence

Model how to ask and answer questions using the article "New Arrivals Welcome." For example, after completing the text, you might ask yourself, *What is the main idea of this article?* When you reread the second paragraph on page 367, you understand that the main idea is that many species in the United States are nonnative but are very useful. Details about nonnative species such as chickens and oranges support this main idea.

3 Guided Practice of Close Reading

COLLABORATE

Have pairs ask and answer a question about "A Growing Problem" on page 368. For example, suggest that students ask themselves, *What is the main idea of this article?* Remind them to reread and identify key details that help them answer. To ensure their understanding of the text, suggest that partners take turns asking each other questions and rereading for answers.

Go Digital

Present the Lesson

Comprehension Strategy

Ask and Answer Questions

To check your understanding of a persuasive article, pause at different points and ask yourself questions about what you have read so far. Then look for answers. You can also ask questions about the whole text when you have finished.

 Find Text Evidence

After you read the article "New Arrivals Welcome" on page 367, you might ask yourself, *What is the main idea of this article?*

> **page 367**
>
> In Florida, for example, about 2,000 species of familiar plants and animals are nonnative. These include oranges, chickens, and sugarcane. In fact, 90 percent of farm sales can be traced directly to nonnative species.

When I reread, I learn the answer to my question. The main idea is that many species in the United States are nonnative, but can be very useful to us. Examples such as oranges and sugarcane support this.

Your Turn COLLABORATE

Ask and answer a question about "A Growing Problem" on page 368. As you read, use the strategy Ask and Answer Questions.

370

READING/WRITING WORKSHOP, p. 370

ENGLISH LANGUAGE LEARNERS SCAFFOLD

Beginning

Listen Reread the first paragraph of "New Arrivals Welcome" on page 367. Point out difficult words such as *immigrants, nonnative, invasive,* and *overwhelm.* Define them for students. Help students replace the words with words and phrases they know. Ask: *Are nonnative species from the area where they are found?* (no)

Intermediate

Identify Help students reread the first two paragraphs of "New Arrivals Welcome." Ask: *What are nonnative species?* (species that come from other places) *Are there nonnative species that are not harmful?* (yes) *What some examples?* (oranges, chickens, sugarcane) Have students complete the frame: *The main idea is ____.*

Advanced/High

Explain Have students reread the first two paragraphs of "New Arrivals Welcome." Elicit why this text might be confusing. Ask: *What is a nonnative species? How can nonnative species be both harmful and helpful? What is the main idea about these species that the author wants to share? Ask and answer other questions with a partner.*

 Monitor and *Differentiate*

✓ **Quick Check**

Do students ask relevant questions about the article? Do they reread the text to find the answers to their questions?

⬇

Small Group Instruction

If No → | **Approaching Level** | Reteach p. T296 |
| **ELL** | Develop p. T313 |

If Yes → | **On Level** | Review p. T304 |
| **Beyond Level** | Extend p. T308 |

 **ON-LEVEL PRACTICE BOOK pp. 243–244**

Comprehension and Fluency

Name _____

Read the two passages. Use the ask and answer questions strategy to check your understanding as you read.

WHAT IS THE FUTURE OF THE RAIN FORESTS?

Rain Forests Support People

People must make economic use of the rain forests.

The removal of rain forest trees has some negative consequences, but it is necessary for the survival of people and national economies. Therefore, it is not practical or desirable to try to stop the cutting of all rain forest trees. A better plan is to make economic use of rain forests.

Farming in the Rain Forests

In most cases, when part of a rain forest is cut down, subsistence agriculture takes its place. Subsistence agriculture is farming or ranching that produces only enough for a family to meet its everyday needs. The families need these farms or ranches in order to survive.

Commercial Use of Rain Forests

Commercial activities also play a role in the use of rain forest land. Lumber from rain forest trees is used to make furniture, flooring, and paper. Many countries buy beef that comes from cattle ranches on former rain forest land. Other rain forest land is converted to farms that grow coffee, soybeans, and palm trees. Oil from those palm trees can be used to make biofuels. Companies build roads through the rain forests to transport goods to and from the farms. These businesses often play necessary roles in their countries. Without them, their countries' economies would suffer.

Rain Forest Loss Can Be Controlled

The loss of rain forest trees does threaten wildlife habitats and the quality of the soil. But a complete halt to rain forest cutting would create other serious problems. A more sensible goal is to manage the use of rain forest land so that the negative outcomes are limited.

Practice • Grade 5 • Unit 5 • Week 5 **243**

| **APPROACHING** pp. 243–244 | **BEYOND** pp. 243–244 | **ELL** pp. 243–244 |

→ Comprehension Skill

Reading/Writing Workshop

OBJECTIVES

 CCSS Determine an author's point of view or purpose in a text and explain how it is conveyed in the text. **RI.6.6**

CCSS Explain how an author uses reasons and evidence to support particular points in a text, identifying which reasons and evidence support which point(s). **RI.5.8**

ACADEMIC LANGUAGE
• *point of view, author, reasons, evidence*
• Cognates: *punto de vista, autor(a), razones*

SKILLS TRACE

AUTHOR'S POINT OF VIEW

Introduce U1W5

Review U3W5, U3W6, U4W3, U4W4, U5W5, U6W6

Assess U1, U3, U4, U5

Author's Point of View

MINILESSON 10 Mins

1 Explain

Explain to students that the author of a persuasive text gives his or her **point of view** about, or position on, a topic.

→ As support for this point of view, the author of a persuasive text provides reasons and evidence.

→ Word choice can help readers understand an author's point of view. Some words, such as *toxic* and *dangerous*, express negative feelings, whereas other words, such as *benefits* and *cuddly*, express positive feelings.

→ Point out that examining reasons, evidence, and word choice in persuasive writing can help students identify the author's point of view and determine whether or not they agree with it.

2 Model Close Reading: Text Evidence

Identify word choices in the title, in the heading following the title, and in the text of "A Growing Problem" on page 368 that reveal the author's point of view. Then use the details listed on the graphic organizer to determine the author's negative point of view toward nonnative species.

 Write About Reading: Summary Model how to use the notes from the graphic organizer to write a brief summary of the author's argument that introducing nonnative species into the United States causes big problems.

3 Guided Practice of Close Reading

 Have pairs identify important details in "New Arrivals Welcome" on page 367 and record them in their graphic organizers. Ask partners to use these details to determine the author's point of view about nonnative species.

 Write About Reading: Summary Ask each pair to work together to summarize the reasons and evidence the author of "New Arrivals Welcome" provides to support his or her point of view about nonnative species. Then ask partners to tell which article's reasons and evidence they found most convincing and why. Have them share their views in a class discussion.

Go Digital

Present the Lesson

Comprehension Skill CCSS

Author's Point of View

In a persuasive article, the author's **point of view** is the author's position on a topic. To identify an author's point of view, look for the author's word choices, reasons, and factual evidence used to explain the argument for or against an idea.

Find Text Evidence

I see from the title "A Growing Problem" on page 368 that the author might have a negative point of view toward nonnative species. The word threaten *expresses a negative emotion, and the facts about pythons support a negative viewpoint.*

Details	Author's Point of View
"A Growing Problem"	The author opposes nonnative species because many become invasive, or hurt native species.
"threaten our country"	
150,000 pythons a "menace"	
Asian carp eat native fish	
"crowding out native plants"	

Your Turn

Identify important details in "New Arrivals Welcome" and write them in your graphic organizer. Then identify the author's point of view.

Go Digital!
Use the interactive graphic organizer

371

READING/WRITING WORKSHOP, p. 371

Monitor and *Differentiate*

✓ Quick Check

As students complete the graphic organizer, do they identify details that help them determine the author's point of view?

Small Group Instruction

If No →	**Approaching Level**	Reteach p. T303
	ELL	Develop p. T313
If Yes →	**On Level**	Review p. T307
	Beyond Level	Extend p. T311

 ENGLISH LANGUAGE LEARNERS SCAFFOLD

Beginning	Intermediate	Advanced/High
Respond Orally Reread the title and heading of "A Growing Problem." Ask: *Does the word* problem *create positive or negative feelings?* (negative) *Does the phrase* threaten our country *create a negative feeling?* (yes) Have students complete the frame: *The author has a ____ point of view about nonnative species.*	**Describe** Reread the title and heading on page 368. Ask: *What words in the title and heading express strong feelings?* (problem, threaten) *What problem are pythons causing in Florida?* (They are killing native wildlife.) Have partners complete the frame: *The author's point of view about nonnative species is ____ because ____.*	**Explain** Have students reread the title, heading, and first paragraph on page 368. Ask them to determine the author's point of view by considering reasons, evidence, and word choice. Have students explain to partners how they determined the author's point of view, using appropriate academic language.

ON-LEVEL PRACTICE BOOK pp. 243–245

Comprehension: Author's Point of View and Fluency

Name _____

A. Reread the passages and answer the questions. Possible responses provided.

1. **What is the first author's point of view about rain forests?**
The author thinks that it is necessary to cut down some rain forest trees.

2. **What facts from the text support this point of view?**
Cutting down part of a rain forest makes farming and commercial activities possible. These activities are necessary for the survival of families and the success of countries' economies.

3. **What is the second author's point of view about rain forests?**
The author thinks that people need to preserve rain forests for the benefit of the world.

4. **What facts from the text support this point of view?**
Destroying rain forests causes loss of biodiversity, which threatens the long-term survival of life on our planet; it changes global rainfall patterns, and it contributes to climate change.

B. Work with a partner. Read the passage aloud. Pay attention to expression and phrasing. Stop after one minute. Fill out the chart.

	Words Read	–	Number of Errors	=	Words Correct Score
First Read		–		=	
Second Read		–		=	

Practice • Grade 5 • Unit 5 • Week 5   245

APPROACHING pp. 243–245	**BEYOND** pp. 243–245	**ELL** pp. 243–245

→ Genre: Informational Text

Reading/Writing Workshop

OBJECTIVES

 CCSS Analyze multiple accounts of the same event or topic, noting important similarities and differences in the point of view they represent. **RI.5.6**

CCSS Interpret information presented visually, orally, or quantitatively (e.g., in charts, graphs, diagrams, time lines, animations, or interactive elements on Web pages) and explain how the information contributes to an understanding of the text in which it appears. **RI.4.7**

ACADEMIC LANGUAGE

- *informational text, persuasive article, facts, details, chart, heading*
- Cognates: *texto informativo, detalles*

MINILESSON 10 Mins

Persuasive Article

1 Explain

Share with students the following key characteristics of **persuasive articles**.

→ Persuasive articles try to convince readers to support an idea or position.

→ Authors of persuasive articles usually state their points of view clearly and then support those positions with facts and details.

Persuasive articles typically include text features such as headings and charts.

2 Model Close Reading: Text Evidence

Identify text evidence and text features that indicate that "New Arrivals Welcome" and "A Growing Problem" are persuasive articles. Point out that the titles and headings in the articles reveal the authors' points of view about nonnative species. The text of the articles contains facts as support for these positions. Then direct students' attention to the chart on page 369.

Chart Explain that the chart on page 369 organizes data so that it can be easily analyzed and compared. With students, read the title of the chart, "Nonnative Species: Benefits and Costs", and identify the heading of each row and column. Ask: *How does this chart help you analyze the authors' different points of view about nonnative species?*

Headings Point out that the last two column headings in the chart—"Positive Impact" and "Negative Impact"—make it easy to compare the positive and negative effects of each nonnative species.

3 Guided Practice of Close Reading

Have students work with partners to review the chart on page 369 and identify one species that has a mostly positive impact and one that has a mostly negative impact. Have partners discuss how they came to their conclusions. Then have students share and compare their findings with the class.

Go Digital

Present the Lesson

Genre **Informational Text**

Persuasive Article

"New Arrivals Welcome" and "A Growing Problem" are persuasive articles.

Persuasive articles:
- Persuade a reader to support an idea or viewpoint
- Include facts and evidence that support opinions
- May include text features, such as charts and headings

 Find Text Evidence

"New Arrivals Welcome" and "A Growing Problem" are persuasive articles. The titles reveal the authors' opinions about nonnative species. Facts and evidence support their opinions. A chart has headings and information for comparing the two points of view.

page 369

Chart A chart organizes data so that information can be easily analyzed and compared.

Headings Headings identify the main categories of information.

Your Turn
COLLABORATE

Analyze the information in the chart on page 369. Identify a species that has a mostly positive impact and one that has a mostly negative impact. Explain your conclusions.

372

READING/WRITING WORKSHOP, p. 372

A C T **Access Complex Text**

▶ **Connection of Ideas**

Connect the chart and the two texts.

→ *What kinds of animals and plants are listed in the first column?* (nonnative species)

→ *Are these examples mentioned in either of the two persuasive articles?* (no)

→ *What view of nonnative species does the chart provide support for —positive, negative, or both?* (both)

→ *Why is the chart a helpful feature?* (Readers can evaluate benefits and costs of nonnative species more objectively.)

Monitor and *Differentiate*

✓ **Quick Check**

Are students able to use the chart to identify a species that has a mostly positive impact and one that has a mostly negative impact? Can students explain how they reached their conclusions?

⬇

Small Group Instruction

If No → | Approaching Level | Reteach p. T297
| ELL | Develop p. T315

If Yes → | On Level | Review p. T305
| Beyond Level | Extend p. T309

ON-LEVEL PRACTICE BOOK p. 246

Genre/Text Feature

Name _____

Expand Our Urban Forests

Trees play a very important role in the landscape of cities. Noise levels and summer temperatures are higher in cities than in outlying areas. Trees absorb noise and heat and keep cities quieter and cooler. Trees help keep the air clean and save energy. Trees soak up pollutants from the air and give off oxygen. Being around green, wooded areas helps keep people healthy. All cities should plant more trees and expand their forests.

Answer the questions about the text.

1. What genre of text is this? How do you know?
   It is informational persuasive text. It gives facts about the topic of urban forests and it expresses the author's opinion, or viewpoint.

2. What opinion does the author express in the text?
   The author expresses the opinion that all cities should plant more trees.

3. What text feature does this text include?
   It includes a chart that gives information about how urban trees benefit people.

4. How does the text feature help you better understand the author's viewpoint?
   The chart gives details about specific ways trees benefit people and communities.

246 Practice • Grade 5 • Unit 5 • Week 5

| APPROACHING p. 246 | BEYOND p. 246 | ELL p. 246 |

→ Vocabulary Strategy

MINILESSON
20 Mins

Root Words

Reading/Writing Workshop

OBJECTIVES

CCSS Determine or clarify the meaning of unknown and multiple-meaning words and phrases based on grade 5 reading and content, choosing flexibly from a range of strategies. Use common, grade-appropriate Greek and Latin affixes and roots as clues to the meaning of a word (e.g., *photograph, photosynthesis*).
L.5.4b

ACADEMIC LANGUAGE
root word

1 Explain

Explain to students that a **root word** is the basic word part that gives the word its main meaning.

→ A root word, or root, often comes from a Latin or Greek word.

→ Knowing the meaning of a word's root can help readers understand the meaning of that word. It can also help clarify the meanings of other words that contain the same root.

2 Model Close Reading: Text Evidence

Model how to determine the meaning of the word *invasive* in the first paragraph of "New Arrivals Welcome" on page 367. Point out that *invasive* has the same root as *invade: vas* and *vad* both come from a Latin word meaning "to go." Therefore, something that is *invasive* goes into areas beyond its boundaries.

3 Guided Practice of Close Reading

COLLABORATE

Have partners use the meanings of the roots *nativus, spec,* and *avis* to determine the meanings of the words *nonnative* and *species* on page 367 and *avian* on page 368. Encourage partners to locate the words in the text and see if the meanings they determine from the roots make sense in context. Then have partners list other words they know that contain the same roots. As necessary, encourage students to use a dictionary to locate words with the same roots.

Go Digital

Present the Lesson

SKILLS TRACE

ROOT WORDS	
Introduce	U5W5
Review	U5W5, U6W1
Assess	U5

Vocabulary Strategy

Root Words

A **root word** is the basic word part that gives a word its main meaning. Knowing the meaning of a root is a key to recognizing and understanding many words that share that root.

 Find Text Evidence

In the first paragraph of "New Arrivals Welcome" on page 367, I read the word invasive. *It has the same root as* invade: vas *and* vad *both come from a Latin word meaning "to go." Something* invasive *goes into areas beyond its boundaries.*

page 367

Nonnative species are known as *invasive* when they harm the environment, our health, or the economy.

Matt Meadows/Peter Arnold/Getty Images

Your Turn

COLLABORATE

Use the roots below to figure out the meanings of words from "New Arrivals Welcome" and "A Growing Problem." List other words you know that contain those roots.

Roots: *nativus* = to be born   *spec* = appearance, kind
   avis = bird

nonnative, *page 367*   **avian,** *page 368*
species, *page 367*

373

READING/WRITING WORKSHOP, p. 373

Monitor and *Differentiate*

 Quick Check

Do students use the given roots to determine the meanings of words? Can they list other words they know that contain the same roots?

⬇

Small Group Instruction

If No → | **Approaching Level** | Reteach p. T301
         | **ELL** | Develop p. T317
If Yes → | **On Level** | Review p. T306
         | **Beyond Level** | Extend p. T310

 ENGLISH LANGUAGE LEARNERS SCAFFOLD

Beginning	**Intermediate**	**Advanced/High**
Respond Orally Write the words *nonnative, species,* and *avian* on the board, read them aloud, and define the words for students. Help students replace the words with words they know. Point out that *species* and *especie* are cognates. Help students brainstorm examples of each word, such as *crows* and *robins* for *avian*.	**Recognize** Write the words *nonnative, species,* and *avian* on the board and the roots *nativus, spec,* and *avis* below. Define each. Help students recognize the correct root in each word and use the root's meaning to determine the word's meaning. Point out that *species* and *especie* are cognates.	**Explain** Have students identify the roots in the words *nonnative, species,* and *avian* and use the meanings of the roots to determine the meanings of the words. Ask students to identify any cognates. Then have partners use a dictionary to identify other words with the same roots.

ON-LEVEL PRACTICE BOOK p. 247

Name _____

Vocabulary Strategy: **Root Words**

Latin root	**Meaning**	**Examples**
vivere	to live	surviv<u>al</u>, sur<u>vive</u>
cultura	cultivation	<u>agriculture</u>
merc/merx	merchandise	commerce, commercial
portare	to carry	transport
sedere	to sit	reside
sorbere	to suck in/suck up	absorb, absorbing
specere	to look at	perspective

Read each passage below. Use the root words in the box and sentence clues to you figure out the meaning of each word in bold. Write the word's meaning on the line. Then write your own sentence that uses the word in the same way. Possible responses provided.

1. In most cases, when part of a rain forest is cut down, subsistence **agriculture** takes its place. Subsistence agriculture is farming or ranching that produces only enough for a family to meet its everyday needs.

   farming; Many states rely on agriculture to provide food and jobs for people.

2. The families need these farms or ranches in order to **survive**.

   live; People need air, food, and water to survive.

3. **Commercial** activities also play a role in the use of rain forest land. Lumber from rain forest trees is used to make furniture, flooring, and paper. Many countries buy beef that comes from cattle ranches on former rain forest land. Other rain forest land is converted to farms that grow coffee, soybeans, and palm trees. Oil from those palm trees can be used to make biofuels.

   buying and selling; The teens developed their Web site into a commercial venture.

Practice • Grade 5 • Unit 5 • Week 5 **247**

| APPROACHING p. 247 | BEYOND p. 247 | ELL p. 247 |

Develop Comprehension

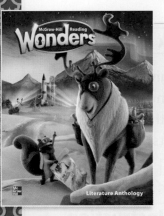

"The Case of the Missing Bees"

Literature Anthology
Complex organization and sentence structure place this selection above TextEvaluator range. Content is grade-level appropriate.

Text Complexity Range

Lexile

740   950   1010

TextEvaluator™

23   51   *59

Predictive Writing

Have students preview the article titles, point and counterpoint sentences, and headings. Ask them to write their predictions about what the articles will be about.

CCSS **Genre · Persuasive Article**   TIME FOR KIDS®

The Case of the MISSING BEES

Essential Question

How do natural events and human activities affect the environment?

Read two views about how natural events and human activities have affected honeybee colonies.

Go Digital!

Jane/Johner Images/Corbis

424

A C T Access Complex Text

What makes this text complex?

> **Organization**

> **Sentence Structure**

▸ Organization

In "A Germ of an Idea," a cause-and-effect relationship is discussed in relation to the problem of the decreasing honeybee population.

→ *What are some possible causes of this problem?* (a fungus, a virus, pesticides, and parasites) *What additional effect could this problem have?* (Crops could suffer without bees to pollinate them.)

A Germ of an Idea

An infection seems to have caused the decline of honeybee populations.

Where have all the honeybees gone? Over the past few years, billions of honeybees have disappeared. They fly away from their colonies and seem to never return. This **widespread** problem is called Colony Collapse **Disorder** (CCD). It's the main reason the honeybee population in the U.S. today has **declined** to half of what it was 50 years ago. Because one-third of crops in the U.S. require honeybees to help pollinate them, some experts predict CCD could create an **agricultural** catastrophe.

What's responsible for the **unexpected** disappearance? There are several suspects, including stress on bees from overcrowded hives, lack of pollen, parasites, and pesticides. Scientists have yet to identify any one of these as the definite cause of CCD. But recently, researchers have found two **probable** causes: a fungus and a virus. A fungus is an organism that breaks down matter; some fungi can cause infection. A virus is a microbe, or germ.

A Deadly Combination

Bees infected with either the fungus or the virus separately could become sick, but they probably would survive. Bees infected with the fungus and the virus at the same time would most certainly die. That is what scientists who did research in Montana concluded. They tested samples of empty hives against hives that **thrive**, a control group that was unaffected by CCD. They compared their findings and discovered the virus and fungus in every empty hive they tested.

Though the fungus and virus combination is the most probable cause so far, investigations into CCD continue. Other scientists are investigating whether CCD could have been caused by a combination of many factors: pesticides, parasites, fungus, and virus. Each of these can weaken a bee's immune system and make it sick. A combination could be deadly.

Only when scientists find the cause of CCD can they find the cure to saving the bees.

(1)

STOP AND CHECK

Ask and Answer Questions
According to the author, why are honeybees disappearing? Find the answer in the text.

(2)

425

Don Farrall/Digital Vision/Getty Images

ELL To help ELLs understand the decline in bee populations, define key terms: *virus, fungus, pesticide, parasite.* Explain that *fungi* is the plural of *fungus.*

→ *A virus is a germ. Germs can make bees _____.* (sick) *_____ can also make bees sick.* (Fungi)

→ Point out the cognates: colony/*colonia*, pollination/*polinización*, pesticide/*pesticida*.

ESSENTIAL QUESTION

Ask students to discuss how the two essays could help to answer the Essential Question.

Note Taking: Graphic Organizer Analytical Writing

As students read, have them fill in the graphic organizer on **Your Turn Practice Book page 242** to record each author's point of view.

❶ Genre: Persuasive Article

Which feature of a persuasive article can you find on page 425? (claims supported by facts and studies) How does this information affect your understanding of the text? (It explains the idea that a combination of a virus and fungus likely causes CCD.)

❷ STOP AND CHECK

Strategy: Ask and Answer Questions

Teacher Think Aloud The author explains the reasons on page 425.

Have students scan to find the answer.

Student Think Aloud I see that the likely cause is a fungus and a virus, but it may be caused by pesticides or parasites as well.

CONNECT TO CONTENT
SURVIVING CHANGE

When the environment changes, some plants and animals adapt and survive while others die or move to new locations. On pages 424–427, students read about environmental changes that may be causing Colony Collapse Disorder, resulting in the death of honeybees. Scientists have noted that native bee species that do not live in colonies are not affected by CCD. Differences among the species allow some to survive when others cannot.

Develop Comprehension

3 Vocabulary: Root Words

Explain that *pesticide* has the same root as *germicide: cide* comes from a Latin word meaning "kill" or "cut down" *Germicide* is a substance used to kill germs. Have students work with a partner to write the meaning of *pesticide* and to check the meaning in a dictionary. (A *pesticide* is a substance used to kill pests.)

4 Skill: Author's Point of View

According to the author of this article, what may cause CCD? (pesticides) Add the information to your organizer.

Details	Point of View
Researchers found one pesticide that is harmful to bees.	Pesticides should be cut back because they may cause CCD.
Even small amounts can affect bee behavior.	
Sick bees might get lost and never return to the colony.	
Scientists found 50 different chemicals in hives hit by CCD.	

Farmers use pesticides to keep away insects that will damage crops. Some pesticides can harm beneficial insects, like honeybees.

COUNTERPOINT POINT

Pointing to Pesticides

Lately, honeybees have not been very busy. Are pesticides to blame?

It's a honey of a mystery. In recent years, beekeepers in many countries have lost thousands of colonies and billions of bees. The insects would suddenly disappear and not return to their hives. This condition, called Colony Collapse Disorder (CCD), has caused 20 to 40 percent of U.S. honeybee colonies to die out. Unfortunately, the reduction in the bee population could affect the country's food production. That's because honeybees pollinate crops of flowering plants. Without these insects, the production of fruits and vegetables would be threatened.

David R. Frazier/Photolibrary, Inc./Alamy

426

The Unusual Suspects

Most scientists believe the probable cause of CCD is a fungus or a virus, working alone or in combination. But some experts have reached a different conclusion. Their main suspect is pesticides. Pesticides are chemicals sprayed on crops to keep away pests. Researchers in France managed to **identify** one pesticide as harmful to bees. This has led other scientists to investigate how other pesticides affect bees.

Pesticides can be absorbed by pollen that the bees consume or that drifts into the hive. Some studies have shown that even small amounts of certain pesticides can affect bee behavior, such as how they search for flower nectar. Sick bees may not be able to figure out where they're going, get lost, and never return to their colonies. This would explain the decline in honeybee populations.

LITERATURE ANTHOLOGY, pp. 426–427

A C T Access Complex Text

▶ Sentence Structure

Help students break down complex sentence structures in the article, such as the second and third sentences in paragraph two of "The Unusual Suspects."

→ *What is an important bee behavior noted in the second sentence?* (how bees search for flower nectar)

→ *What happens when bees "get lost?"* (They are unable to return to their colonies) *Why does this matter?* (Fewer bees means less pollination.)

TIME FOR KIDS®

Are Pesticides to Blame?

A study of hives hit by CCD in Florida and California found 50 different human-made chemicals in the samples. The study could not confirm that the pesticides had directly caused CCD, but other scientists are still investigating whether pesticides are at least partly to blame. At the least, the chemicals may weaken bees enough to allow infection by a virus or a fungus. Until scientists know the exact cause of the honeybee disappearance, the use of these harsh poisons should be cut back.

Beekeepers examine hives to make sure the honeybee colonies are healthy.

427

(t) Don Farrall/Digital Vision/Getty Images; (b) Eco Images/Universal Images Group/Getty Images

Respond to Reading

1. How can you tell that "A Germ of an Idea" and "Pointing to Pesticides" are persuasive articles? Give examples from the texts. **GENRE**

2. What do the two authors agree on? How are the two views different? Identify reasons and evidence that the authors use to support their points. **AUTHOR'S POINT OF VIEW**

3. The word *unfortunately* on page 426 includes the root *fortunate* meaning "lucky." Use the root word and word parts to tell the meaning of *unfortunately*. **ROOT WORDS**

4. What do you think caused the bees to disappear? Support your answer with reasons. How could people help honeybees? **TEXT TO WORLD**

CONNECT TO CONTENT
SCIENTIFIC USE OF CONTROL GROUPS

Students read about researchers who found one pesticide harmful to bees. Scientists often run experiments using a control group—a separate group to serve as a point of comparison. Have students discuss why, during research, scientists might compare one group of bees that is exposed to a certain pesticide with another group that is not.

STEM

Respond to Reading

Return to Predictions

Review students' predictions and purposes for reading. Ask them to answer the Essential Question. (Naturally occurring fungi and viruses might cause honeybee colonies to die, which would greatly affect the agricultural industry. Human activities, such as spraying pesticides, might have the same effect.)

Text Evidence

1. **Genre** <u>Answer</u> Each article gives facts as evidence to support a particular opinion. <u>Evidence</u> "A Germ of an Idea" cites a study of hives that found evidence of a fungus and a virus causing CCD. "Pointing to Pesticides" cites a study of hives that found evidence that human-made chemicals may cause CCD.

2. **Author's Point of View** <u>Answer</u> Both agree that CCD is a big problem for bees and humans, but they disagree about the causes. <u>Evidence</u> The author of "A Germ of an Idea" discusses the effects of a fungus and a virus on bee health and evidence that both have been found in infected hives. The author of "Pointing to Pesticides" discusses the effects of pesticides on bee behavior and studies of bee samples.

3. **Root Words** <u>Answer</u> The word *unfortunately* means "in a way that is not lucky." <u>Evidence</u> The root word *fortune* means "luck"; the prefix *un-* means "not;" the suffix *-ly* means "in a way."

4. **Write About Reading: Text to World** Possible response: I think a combination of pesticides, a fungus, and a virus cause CCD, since all have been found in infected hives. People can help honeybees by starting new colonies and not using pesticides.

Analytical Writing

Develop Comprehension

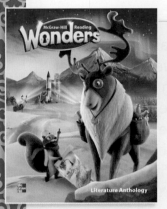

Literature Anthology

"Busy, Beneficial Bees"

Lexile

740 ▲ 1010
980

TextEvaluator™

23 ▲ 51
45

Compare Texts

Students will do a close reading of an expository text about honeybees. While they read, have them **ask and answer questions** and use other strategies they know. Then ask them to reread and take notes. They will use the text evidence they gathered to compare this text with "The Case of the Missing Bees."

CCSS **Genre · Expository Text** TIME FOR KIDS

Compare Texts
Read how honeybees affect humans and the environment.

Busy, Beneficial BEES

Billions of honeybees are disappearing from a **widespread** mysterious condition called Colony Collapse **Disorder**. The disappearance of honeybees is bad news for two big reasons. Obviously, without honeybees, there would be no honey. Worse, many important foods wouldn't make it to our supermarkets or tables.

Honeybees are responsible for about one-third of the food in the human diet, including vegetables, fruits, seeds, and nuts. Honeybees help many crop plants **thrive**. They pollinate flowering plants, which allows the plants to produce the foods we eat and the seeds that will grow into new plants.

①

Robert Postma/First Light/Getty Images

428

A C T Access Complex Text

What makes this text complex?

▶ **Purpose**

▶ Purpose

Clarify that the purpose of the text is to inform.

→ *How is this text different from the previous articles on honeybees?* (It's not persuasive. Its purpose is to give facts about honeybees and human diet.)

→ *How do the photograph and diagram support this purpose?* (The photo shows pollination in action. The chart gives details about how bees help crops.)

Crops Depend on Honeybees

Many crops depend on insects to pollinate them. For some crops, honeybees make up a large percentage of those pollinators.

Numbers based on estimates in 2000. Source: Compiled by CRS using values reported in R. A. Morse, and N.W. Calderone, *The Value of Honey Bees as Pollinators of U.S. Crops in 2000*, March 2000, Cornell University.

Crop	Dependence on Insect Pollination	Proportion That Are Honeybees
Alfalfa, hay & seed	100%	60%
Apples	100%	90%
Almonds	100%	100%
Citrus	20–80%	10–90%
Cotton	20%	90%
Soybeans	10%	50%
Broccoli	100%	90%
Carrots	100%	90%
Cantaloupe	80%	90%

Honeybees use nectar from flowers to make honey, their winter food source. When the bees visit flowers to get nectar, tiny grains of pollen cling to their bodies. The bees carry the pollen from flower to flower and plant to plant. This process of pollination makes flowers turn into fruits. For farmers, this means a harvest!

Honeybees were brought to the U.S. from Europe about 400 years ago for **agricultural** purposes. Beekeepers today still maintain hives. Some sell honey. Others may rent hives to farmers to pollinate crops. In addition to honeybees, there are about 4,000 species of native "wild" bees in North America which also pollinate flowering plants. Most of these bees do not live in colonies and have not been affected by CCD.

In the U.S., honeybees pollinate about $15 billion worth of crops a year. That's on top of the $150 million worth of honey they produce annually. Although some crops can be pollinated by other nectar-feeding insects, many crops depend specifically on honeybees for pollination. Without honeybees, our crops and our economy would really feel the sting!

Make Connections

How do honeybees affect the environment? **ESSENTIAL QUESTION**

Think of an agricultural activity you've read about that affects the environment. How are the effects of beekeeping different? **TEXT TO TEXT**

429

LITERATURE ANTHOLOGY, pp. 428–429

❶ Ask and Answer Questions

How are honeybees able to help agriculture?

Analytical Writing **Write About Reading** With a partner, summarize the answer. (As honeybees go from plant to plant in search of nectar, pollen sticks to their bodies. The bees carry the pollen to the next plant. This pollination makes the plants able to produce fruit and seeds.)

Make Connections

Essential Question Have students paraphrase and share information about how beekeeping affects the environment. Suggest that they scan the text and look at the chart to identify benefits of beekeeping.

Text to Text Have groups of students compare beekeeping to another agricultural activity they have read about and discuss how the activities are similar and different. (Another activity is using pesticides on crops. Pesticides keep away insects that damage crops, which helps crops grow. However, pesticides can harm the environment by hurting bees and other beneficial insects. Beekeeping is not harmful because it is a natural process.)

 Point out the chart on page 429. Have ELLs work with a partner to answer the following questions.

→ *What is the title of the chart?* (Crops Depend on Honeybees)

→ *What does the chart show?* (It shows crops that depend on honeybees for pollination.)

→ *Which crop in the chart depends on honeybees the most?* (almonds) *Which crop in the chart depends on honeybees the least?* (soybeans)

Word Study/Fluency

MINILESSON 20 Mins

Suffix -ion

OBJECTIVES

CCSS Know and apply grade-level phonics and word analysis skills in decoding words. Use combined knowledge of all letter-sound correspondences, syllabication patterns, and morphology (e.g., roots and affixes) to read accurately unfamiliar multisyllabic words in context and out of context. **RF.5.3a**

CCSS Read on-level prose and poetry orally with accuracy, appropriate rate, and expression on successive readings. **RF.5.4b**

Rate: 100–120 WCPM

ACADEMIC LANGUAGE

• *expression, phrasing*
• Cognates: *expresión, fraseo*

ELL

Refer to the sound transfers chart in the **Language Transfers Handbook** to identify sounds that do not transfer in Spanish, Cantonese, Vietnamese, Hmong, and Korean.

1 Explain

Review with students that a suffix is a word part that is added to the end of a base word or root. One common suffix, *-ion*, is added to certain words to change them from verbs to nouns. Write the following example on the board:

narrate (verb)   **narration** (noun)

2 Model

Write the following words on the board, and model pronouncing each one:

correction   imitation   donation

Discuss that each word is a noun made up of a base word and the suffix *-ion*. Identify the base words as the verbs *correct*, *imitate*, and *donate*. Model determining the meaning of *correction* by connecting it with the verb *correct*. Repeat the process with *imitation* and *donation*. Point out that when the base word ends in an *e*, as in *imitate* and *donate*, the *e* is dropped before the suffix *-ion* is added.

Next, write the words *mission, notion,* and *fusion* on the board. Read each word aloud, emphasizing the /sh/ and /zh/ sounds. Explain that when the letter *s* is followed by *y, i,* or *u* in the middle of words, it may be pronounced /zh/ or /sh/ as in *measure* and *fission*. When the letter *i* follows *c, s, ss, sc,* or *t* in the last part of a word, it is usually silent and the consonants represent the /sh/ sound as in *nation, delicious,* and *conscious*.

3 Guided Practice

Write the following words with the suffix *-ion* on the board. Have students underline the suffix in each word and identify its beginning sound as /sh/ or /zh/. Then have them chorally read the words.

action	production	confusion	revision
devotion	pollution	emotion	rotation
eviction	restriction	medication	creation

Have pairs of students determine the meaning of the words in the list. Remind them to connect the meaning of the verb to the related noun with the *-ion* suffix.

Read Multisyllabic Words

Transition to Longer Words To help students transition to longer words with the suffix *-ion*, write the following four- and five-syllable words on the board. Have students use their knowledge of word parts to decode these longer words.

generation	appreciation	concentration
recollection	aggravation	remediation
disintegration	proposition	replication
population	interrogation	duplication

Model how to determine the meaning of the first word by covering the suffix with your finger and displaying only the base word. Define the base word, and then uncover the suffix. Connect the meaning of the verb to the longer word to determine its meaning. Then have students use these steps to define the remaining words.

Expression and Phrasing

Explain/Model Review with students that using expression when they read can help bring the writing to life. Remind them that paying attention to punctuation helps them group words into meaningful phrases. Model reading page 367 of "Should Plants and Animals from Other Places Live Here?"

Reading/Writing Workshop pages 366–369. Use expression as you read to enliven the text, and emphasize grouping words in phrases as indicated by punctuation marks.

Remind students that you will be listening for their use of expression and phrasing as you monitor their reading during the week.

Practice/Apply Have partners take turns reading the paragraphs on page 367, modeling the expression and phrasing you used.

Daily Fluency Practice

Students can practice fluency using **Your Turn Practice Book** passages.

Monitor and *Differentiate*

 Quick Check

Do students decode multisyllabic words with the suffix -ion? Can students read with appropriate expression and phrasing?

Small Group Instruction

If No →	**Approaching Level**	**Reteach** pp. T298, T302
	ELL	**Develop** pp. T315, T318
If Yes →	**On Level**	**Apply** pp. T304–T305
	Beyond Level	**Apply** pp. T308–T309

ON-LEVEL PRACTICE BOOK p. 248

Word Study: Suffix -ion

Name _____

Add the suffix *-ion* to the verb in parentheses to complete each sentence. Remember that when a base word ends in the letter e, the e is dropped before the suffix *-ion* is added.

1. The class held a lively **(discuss)** ___discussion___ about water conservation.

2. He only needs to make one **(correct)** ___correction___ to complete his work.

3. We purchased a new **(decorate)** ___decoration___ that will hang on the bedroom wall.

4. The wind changed **(direct)** ___direction___ before it started to rain.

5. It is smart to study the candidates and the issues before voting in an **(elect)** ___election___

6. Our family trip to the national park made a lasting **(impress)** ___impression___

7. Try to maintain your **(concentrate)** ___concentration___ when taking a test.

8. If everyone talks at the same time, it will lead to **(confuse)** ___confusion___

9. In my **(estimate)** ___estimation___ that is not a valuable painting.

10. After hiking all day, the campers were overcome with **(exhaust)** ___exhaustion___

248 Practice • Grade 5 • Unit 5 • Week 5

APPROACHING p. 248	BEYOND p. 248	ELL p. 248

☞ **Go** Digital

www.connected.mcgraw-hill.com
RESOURCES
Research and Inquiry

→ **Wrap Up the Week**
Integrate Ideas

RESEARCH AND INQUIRY

Scientific Viewpoints

OBJECTIVES

CCSS Engage effectively in a range of collaborative discussions (one-on-one, in groups, and teacher-led) with diverse partners on grade 5 topics and texts, building on others' ideas and expressing their own clearly. **SL.5.1**

Create a bibliography.

ACADEMIC LANGUAGE

• *bibliography, invasive species*

• Cognates: *bibliografía, especies invasores*

COLLABORATE

Create a Bibliography

Explain that students will work with a partner to select and research an invasive species of plant or animal in their area. They will create a bibliography of reliable resources to use in their research. Discuss the following steps:

1 Select an Invasive Species Help partners research and identify invasive species in your area and select one to research. You may wish to provide suggestions such as Asian carp, purple loosestrife, or zebra mussels.

2 Identify Research Sources Have partners identify a variety of reliable sources, such as reference books and reputable Web sites, that will aid them in their research. Suggest that students use online Research Process Checklist 3 when gathering sources and post their findings to the Shared Research Board.

3 Guided Practice Remind students that a bibliography is a list of sources presented in alphabetical order. Provide example citations in your school's preferred style for a variety of print and digital sources.

4 Create the Project: Bibliography Have partners work together to organize their sources in alphabetical order and then list them on a bibliography page.

Critique a Bibliography

Have partners exchange bibliographies with another pair of students. Ask them to review the bibliography and provide constructive feedback on the reliability of sources listed and the accuracy of style used in listing the sources. Guide a discussion about the importance of identifying and using

STEM

TEXT CONNECTIONS

OBJECTIVES

Integrate information from several texts on the same topic in order to write or speak about the subject knowledgeably. **RI.5.9**

Review the key ideas expressed and draw conclusions in light of information and knowledge gained from the discussions. **SL.5.1d**

Text-to-Text

Cite Evidence Tell students they will work in groups to compare what they have learned this week about things that impact the environment and then draw some conclusions about the Essential Question: *How do natural events and human activities affect the environment?* Model how to make comparisons using examples from "Should Plants and Animals from Other Places Live Here?" **Reading/Writing Workshop** pages 366–369, and the week's **Leveled Readers**. Help students set up an Accordion Foldable® to organize their notes. Students should record what they learned about factors that affect the environment, including animals and plants, before drawing conclusions about the week's Essential Question.

Present Information Have groups meet to present their findings to the class. Encourage discussion, asking students to comment on different natural events and human activities they recorded and how they are similar and different.

Factors that Affect the Environment | Human Activities | Natural Events | Conclusions

Dinah Zike's **FOLDABLES**®

WRITE ABOUT READING

OBJECTIVES

Draw evidence from literary or informational texts to support analysis, reflection, and research. **W.5.9**

Explain how an author uses reasons and evidence to support particular points in a text, identifying which reasons and evidence support which point(s). **RI.5.8**

Write an Analysis

Cite Evidence Using evidence from a text they have read, students will show how an author uses reasons and evidence to support a position on a topic. Discuss how to analyze a text by asking *how*, what, and why questions.

→ How does the author support his or her position? What reasons, facts, and details does the author include?

→ Why is the author's position convincing?

Use **Your Turn Practice Book** page 249 to read and discuss the student model. Then have students choose one text that argues for or against an issue and review what they recorded about the author's position. Have them write to show how the author used reasons and evidence to support his or her position. Remind them to develop their topic with concrete details and use any comparative adjectives correctly.

Present Your Ideas Ask partners to share their paragraphs and discuss how the evidence they cited from the text supports their ideas.

→ Readers to Writers

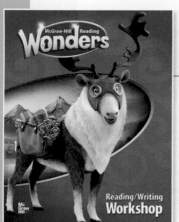

Reading/Writing Workshop

Writing Traits: Organization

Strong Conclusions

Expert Model Explain that writers craft a strong conclusion, or ending, to bring closure to a piece of writing. A strong conclusion often restates the main idea or sums up the most important points of the text. In opinion writing, a conclusion may be used to make a final point or request that the reader take some kind of action.

Read aloud the expert models from "New Arrivals Welcome" and "A Growing Problem." Ask students to pay close attention to how the authors conclude each piece. Have partners discuss similarities and differences between the two endings. Also have them describe the impression each one made on them.

Student Model Remind students that writers use strong conclusions to summarize important points, to restate main ideas, and to give the reader a sense of closure. Read aloud the student draft "Keep Birds Safe!" As students follow along, remind them to focus on the conclusion.

Invite partners to talk about the draft and how Abby revises the conclusion to make it stronger. Ask them to suggest other ways that Abby might have ended her essay.

Go Digital

Expert Model

Student Model

OBJECTIVES

CCSS Provide a concluding statement or section related to the opinion presented. **W.5.1d**

CCSS Write routinely over extended time frames (time for research, reflection, and revision) and shorter time frames (a single sitting or a day or two) for a range of discipline-specific tasks, purposes, and audiences. **W.5.10**

- Analyze models to understand how strong conclusions influence readers.
- Write to share an opinion.
- Add strong conclusions to revise writing.

ACADEMIC LANGUAGE
- *conclusions, restates*
- Cognate: *conclusiones*

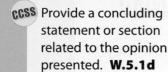 **Genre Writing**

Informational Text

For full writing process lessons and rubrics, see:

→ Informational Article, pp. T344–T349

→ Research Report, pp. T350–T355

CCSS Writing Traits Organization

Readers to...

Writers

Editing Marks

∧ Add
⌄ Add a comma.
⌿ Take out.
SP Check spelling.
≡ Make a capital letter.

Grammar Handbook

Comparing with Good and Bad
See page 467.

Writers close their texts with a **strong conclusion**. A persuasive article supports a view, and the job of the conclusion is to make the final point with a strong, effective statement. The author often restates the main idea in the conclusion. Reread the conclusions of "New Arrivals Welcome" and "A Growing Problem."

Abby wrote a persuasive text arguing to protect neighborhood birds. Read Abby's revision of her conclusion.

Strong Conclusions

Identify the main idea restated in each conclusion.

How do the authors use specific language to create strong conclusions?

Expert Model

New Arrivals Welcome

Many of the dogs and cats we love so much originated in other parts of the world. Would you want to ban Labrador retrievers and Siamese cats? Creatures like these surely make our lives and our nation better!

A Growing Problem

The facts about this alien invasion lead to one conclusion: We must remove invasive species and keep new ones from our shores.

Student Model

Keep Birds Safe!

It's great to have birds nesting in your area. However, Living around people can be dangerous for them. Every year, hundreds of birds die from flying into windows. even worse, cats roaming outdoors kill birds, as well. How can we can help? Taping shapes on clear glass can prevent birds from flying at their reflections ~~themselves.~~ Also, keep cats indoors. Doing our part to keep ~~Keeping~~ birds safe is a small price to pay for the beauty they bring us!

Your Turn

- ☑ Identify Abby's conclusion and what makes it strong.
- ☑ Identify comparisons Abby used with *good* and *bad*.
- ☑ Tell how Abby's revisions improved her writing.

Go Digital!
Write online in Writer's Workspace

374 | 375

READING/WRITING WORKSHOP, pp. 374–375

ELL ENGLISH LANGUAGE LEARNERS SCAFFOLD

Provide support to help English Language Learners understand the writing trait.

Beginning

Respond Orally Help students complete the sentence frames about "New Arrivals Welcome." *The author describes dogs and cats as ____.* (cuddly) *The author thinks that "cuddly creatures" can make our lives ____.* (better) *The author wants readers to (like/dislike) cats and dogs.* (like)

Intermediate

Practice Ask students to complete the sentence frames. *The author says that people ____ cats and dogs.* (love) *The author asks a question to ____.* (make the reader think of specific lovable animals) *This is a strong conclusion because ____.* (Possible response: it leaves readers with a final thought.)

Advanced/High

Understand Check for understanding. Ask: *How does the author describe cats and dogs?* (well-loved, cuddly) *What benefit do people get from cats and dogs?* (they "make our lives better") *Do you think the conclusion is effective? Why?* (Possible response: Yes, it leaves the reader feeling good about cats and dogs.)

Writing Every Day: Organization

DAY 1

Writing Entry: Strong Conclusions

Prewrite Provide students with the prompt below.

Write an editorial convincing others to take action that would help solve a critical problem.

Have students work with partners to brainstorm a list of possible problems and reasons it should be resolved. Have each student choose one topic to write about.

Draft Students may use their lists of ideas as they begin to draft their editorial. Remind students to focus on strong conclusions as they work on their drafts.

DAY 2

Focus on Strong Conclusions

Use **Your Turn Practice Book** page 250 to model strong conclusions.

So that's why I think volunteering is important. Volunteering is a good thing to do. Learning new skills is good too, but try volunteering. You'll like it.

Model making the conclusion stronger by restating main ideas the writer may have included.

Volunteering helps others and makes the volunteer feel good too.

Discuss how the revision improves the conclusion.

Writing Entry: Strong Conclusions

Revise Have students revise their writing from Day 1 by checking for a strong conclusion. Have them focus on restating the main idea or most important points of the writing.

Use the **Conferencing Routines**. Circulate among students and stop briefly to talk with individuals. Provide time for peer review.

Edit Have students use Grammar Handbook page 467 in the **Reading/Writing Workshop** to check for errors in comparisons with *good* and *bad*.

Conferencing Routines

Teacher Conferences

STEP 1

Talk about the strengths of the writing.

You state your opinion clearly and include several good supporting reasons. You also use a voice that is appealing to the reader.

STEP 2

Focus on how the writer uses the target trait for the week.

Your conclusion could be stronger. What idea could you share to leave a lasting impression on the reader?

STEP 3

Make concrete suggestions for other revisions. Have students work on specific assignments, such as those to the right. Then have students meet with you to review progress.

DAY 3

Writing Entry: Strong Conclusions

Prewrite Ask students to search their Writer's Notebooks for topics for a new draft. Or provide a prompt, such as the following:

Which single daily action has the greatest impact on our environment? Why?

Draft Have students complete word webs by listing activities or events in the center circles. In the radiating circles, have students add supporting reasons and details. Students may use these webs as they draft. Remind them to add a strong conclusion.

DAY 4

Writing Entry: Strong Conclusions

Revise Have students revise their drafts from Day 3 by checking to make sure they have written a strong conclusion. As students revise, hold teacher conferences with individual students. You may also wish to have students work with partners to conduct peer conferences.

Edit Invite students to review the rules for comparing with *good* and *bad* on Grammar Handbook page 467 in the **Reading/ Writing Workshop** and then check their drafts for errors.

DAY 5

Share and Reflect

Discuss with the class what they learned about writing strong conclusions. Invite volunteers to read and compare draft text with text that has been revised. Have students discuss the writing by focusing on each conclusion. Allow time for individuals to reflect on their own writing progress and record observations in their Writer's Notebooks.

Suggested Revisions

Provide specific direction to help focus young writers.

Focus on a Sentence
Read the draft and target one sentence for revision. *Rewrite the final sentence by restating why the topic is important to the reader.*

Focus on a Section
Underline a section that needs to be revised. Provide specific suggestions. You conclude by retelling the main idea. *Can you add a final thought that will make a lasting impression on the reader?*

Focus on a Revision Strategy
Underline a section. Have students use a specific revision strategy, such as substituting words. *Your introduction and conclusion are worded very similarly. Try using different wording.*

Peer Conferences

Focus peer response groups on strong conclusions.

☑ Does the conclusion give a sense of closure?

☑ Is the main idea and/or are key points restated?

☑ Does the conclusion leave readers with something to think about?

Grammar: Comparing with *Good* and *Bad*

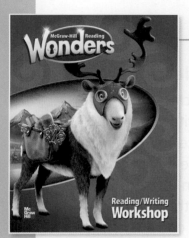

Reading/Writing Workshop

OBJECTIVES

CCSS Form and use comparative and superlative adjectives and adverbs, and choose between them depending on what is to be modified. **L.3.1g**

CCSS Demonstrate command of the conventions of standard English grammar and usage when writing or speaking. **L.5.1**

Proofread sentences.

Go Digital

Comparing with *Good* and *Bad*

Grammar Activities

DAY 1

DAILY LANGUAGE ACTIVITY

Evan is the most nice person in class. But Rita is the funnier.
(1: nicest; 2: class, but; 3: funniest)

Introduce Irregular Comparative and Superlative Forms; Comparing with *Good*

Present the following:

→ **Comparatives** and **superlatives** are special forms of adjectives used to compare two or more things. They are usually formed by adding -er (comparatives) and -est (superlatives) to an adjective.

→ *Good* has an irregular comparative and superlative form. Use *better* to compare two people, places, or things. Use *best* to compare more than two.

Have partners discuss comparatives and superlatives using pages 467–468 of the Grammar Handbook in **Reading/Writing Workshop**.

DAY 2

DAILY LANGUAGE ACTIVITY

Tia studied more hard and got a gooder grade on todays test.
(1: harder; 2: better; 3: today's)

Review Comparing with *Good*

Review that the word *better* should be used to compare two people, places, or things. *Best* should be used to compare more than two people, places, or things

Introduce Comparing with *Bad*

Present the following:

→ Use *worse* to compare two people, places, or things. *The weather is worse today than it was yesterday.*

→ Use *worst* to compare more than two people, places, or things. *It was the worst storm we've had in years.*

TALK ABOUT IT

COLLABORATE

GOOD, BETTER, BEST

Have partners take turns telling about three related ideas about the environment. Have them describe them as *good, better,* and *best*. For example, students might compare three kinds of conservation efforts.

BAD, WORSE, WORST

Have partners discuss three or more natural events that they would describe as *bad, worse,* and *worst*. For example, students might compare three weather patterns or three natural disasters. Ask volunteers to share their ideas.

DAY **3**

DAY **4**

DAY 5

anna climbed the tree so that she could see the most beautifulist view on the sea. (1: Anna; 2: most beautiful; 3: of)

It was the worse day ever! Much of the clouds are gone. (1: worst; 2: most)

Fall is more good than summer. It is the better season of all! (1: better; 2: best)

Mechanics and Usage: Irregular Comparative Forms

Present the following:

→ In comparisons, *better* and *best* are the irregular forms of the adjective *good*; *worse* and *worst* are the forms of the adjective *bad*.

→ The comparative form of *many* is *more*; the superlative form is *most*. The comparative form of *much* is *more*; the superlative form is *most*.

→ Never add *-er*, *-est*, *more*, or *most* to an irregular form.

As students write, refer them to Grammar Handbook pages 467–468.

See Grammar Practice Reproducibles pp. 121–125.

Proofread

Have students correct errors in these sentences:

1. That was the worse movie I've ever seen! (worst)
2. Jake's essay was gooder, but Mark's was the better in the class. (1: good; 2: best)
3. Ben's headache was badder, and it got more worst as the day went on. (1: bad; 2: much worse)
4. Which do you like best, math or science? (better)

Have students check their work using Grammar Handbook pages 467–468 on adjectives that compare, and the irregular comparatives and superlatives *more, most, good,* and *bad*.

Assess

Use the Daily Language Activity and Grammar Practice Reproducibles page 125 for assessment.

Reteach

Use Grammar Practice Reproducibles pages 121–124 and selected pages from the Grammar Handbook for additional reteaching. Remind students that it is important to use irregular comparatives and superlatives correctly as they speak and write.

Check students' writing for use of the skill and listen for it in their speaking. Assign Grammar Revision Assignments in their Writer's Notebooks as needed.

MANY, MORE, MOST, MUCH

Have partners imagine they are environmentalists. Ask them to describe their work using *many, more, most,* and *much*. For example: *Many plants and animals are in danger. We need more people to help protect them.*

PROS AND CONS

Ask partners to discuss how humans impact nature. Have them tell how human interaction is both good and bad for the environment. Encourage them to use *best, worst,* and other comparative adjectives as they speak.

RANK THE EVENTS

Display a list of five natural events, both good and bad. Ask students to rank them from 1 to 5, with 1 being the *best* to experience in their opinion. Have partners discuss their lists, using this week's comparatives and superlatives.

Spelling: Suffix *-ion*

OBJECTIVES
Spell grade-appropriate words correctly, consulting references as needed. **L.5.2e**

Spelling Words

impress	confusion	estimate
impression	correct	estimation
elect	correction	decorate
election	discuss	decoration
locate	discussion	exhaust
location	concentrate	exhaustion
confuse	concentration	

Review hopeless, fearless, forgiveness
Challenge conclude, conclusion

Differentiated Spelling

Approaching Level

impress	confusion	estimate
impression	correct	estimation
elect	correction	relate
election	discuss	relation
locate	discussion	direct
location	decorate	direction
confuse	decoration	

Beyond Level

impress	estimation	appreciate
impression	inflect	appreciation
predict	inflection	concentrate
prediction	exhaust	concentration
discuss	exhaustion	confuse
discussion	motivate	confusion
estimate	motivation	

DAY 1

Assess Prior Knowledge

Read the spelling words aloud. Segment the words syllable by syllable.

Point out the *-ion* suffix in *impress<u>ion</u>*. Draw a line under the spelling pattern. Point out that students should consider the suffix *-ion* and the base word in spelling the entire word. When dealing with words that end in *e*, they must first remove the *e* before adding *-ion*.

Demonstrate sorting the spelling words by part of speech. Discuss any words that have unexpected pronunciations.

Use the Dictation Sentences from Day 5 to give the pretest. Say the underlined word, read the sentence, and repeat the word. Have students write the words and then check their papers.

DAY 2

Spiral Review

Review the *-less* and *-ness* suffixes in *hopeless, fearless,* and *forgiveness*. Read each sentence below, repeat the review word, and have students write the word.

1. The situation was <u>hopeless</u>.
2. Alex is a <u>fearless</u> adventurer.
3. Joaquin asked Millie for <u>forgiveness</u>.

Have partners trade papers and check their spellings.

Challenge Words Review this week's *-ion* suffix. Read each sentence below, repeat the challenge word, and have students write the word.

1. The show will <u>conclude</u> at 8:00.
2. The book's <u>conclusion</u> was shocking!

Have students check and correct their spellings and write the words in their word study notebooks.

WORD SORTS

COLLABORATE

OPEN SORT

Have students cut apart the **Spelling Word Cards** in the Online Resource Book and initial the back of each card. Have them read the words aloud with partners. Then have partners do an **open sort**. Have them record their sorts in their word study notebooks.

PATTERN SORT

Complete the **pattern sort** from Day 1 by using the Spelling Word Cards. Point out the different parts of speech. Partners should compare and check their sorts. Have them record their sorts in their word study notebooks.

DAY 3

Word Meanings

Have students copy the four definitions below into their word study notebooks. Say the definitions aloud. Then ask students to write the spelling word that each one refers to.

1. to focus or think intensely (concentrate)
2. to fix errors (correct)
3. conversation; a talk (discussion)
4. tiredness; fatigue (exhaustion)

Challenge students to write definitions for their other spelling, review, or challenge words. Have them write the definitions in their word study notebooks.

DAY 4

Proofread and Write

Write these sentences on the board. Have students circle and correct each misspelled word. Have students use a print or a digital dictionary to make corrections.

1. Nina decided to deccorate her house to make a good impresion on her visitors. (decorate, impression)
2. There was much confussion during the elektion. (confusion, election)
3. I couldn't conncentrate during our discusion. (concentrate, discussion)
4. The city planners met to disscus the locattion of the new park. (discuss, location)

Error Correction Remind students that when dealing with words that end in *e*, they must first remove the *e* before adding *-ion*.

See Phonics/Spelling Reproducibles pp. 145–150.

DAY 5

Assess

Use the Dictation Sentences for the posttest. Have students list the misspelled words in their word study notebooks. Look for students' use of these words in their writings.

Dictation Sentences

1. She wants to <u>impress</u> the teacher.
2. He made a good first <u>impression</u>.
3. We will <u>elect</u> new officers.
4. Everyone voted in the <u>election</u>.
5. Try to <u>locate</u> Canada on the map.
6. We know the whale's <u>location</u>.
7. People always <u>confuse</u> the twins.
8. The noise added to the <u>confusion</u>.
9. Please <u>correct</u> the mistakes.
10. She made the <u>correction</u> in red.
11. Let's <u>discuss</u> the problem.
12. Jake led a book <u>discussion</u>.
13. <u>Concentrate</u> during the test.
14. Chess requires <u>concentration</u>.
15. Our <u>estimate</u> was not even close.
16. Their <u>estimation</u> was too high.
17. I want to <u>decorate</u> the classroom.
18. The wreath is a nice <u>decoration</u>.
19. Running uphill will <u>exhaust</u> us.
20. I felt <u>exhaustion</u> after the race.

Have students self-correct their tests.

SPEED SORT

Have partners compete in a **speed sort** to see who is fastest, then compare and discuss their sorts. Then have them do a word hunt in this week's readings to find words with the *-ion* suffix. Have them record the words in their word study notebooks.

BLIND SORT

Have partners do a **blind sort**: one reads a Spelling Word Card; the other tells under which part of speech it belongs. Have students compare sorts. Then have partners use two sets of cards to play Concentration, matching words with the same part of speech.

Build Vocabulary

DAY 1

DAY 2

OBJECTIVES

CCSS Determine or clarify the meaning of unknown and multiple-meaning words and phrases based on *grade 5 reading and content,* choosing flexibly from a range of strategies. Use context (e.g., cause/ effect relationships and comparisons in text) as a clue to the meaning of a word or phrase. **L.5.4a**

CCSS Use common, grade-appropriate Greek and Latin affixes and roots as clues to the meaning of a word (e.g., *photograph, photosynthesis*). **L.5.4b**

Vocabulary Words

agricultural	probable
declined	thrive
disorder	unexpected
identify	widespread

Go Digital

Vocabulary

Vocabulary Activities

Connect to Words

Practice this week's vocabulary.

1. What are some **agricultural** products?

2. If your health **declined**, what would you do?

3. Describe a common medical **disorder**.

4. What are some things that scientists **identify**?

5. Is it **probable** that the sun will rise tomorrow? Why or why not?

6. What do plants need to **thrive**?

7. Has anything **unexpected** happened to you lately?

8. How might a song become **widespread**?

Expand Vocabulary

Help students generate different forms of this week's words by adding, changing, or removing inflectional endings.

→ Draw a four-column chart on the board. Write *thrive* in the first column. Then write *thrives, thrived,* and *thriving* in the next three columns. Read aloud the words with students.

→ Have students share sentences using each form of *thrive*.

→ Students should add to the chart for *declined* and *identify*, then share sentences using different forms of the words.

→ Have students copy the chart in their word study notebooks.

 BUILD MORE VOCABULARY

COLLABORATE

ACADEMIC VOCABULARY

→ Display *investigate, conclusion,* and *population*.

→ Define the words and discuss their meanings with students.

→ Write *investigated* under *investigate*. Have partners write other words with the same root and define them. Then have partners ask and answer questions using the words.

→ Repeat with *conclusion* and *population*.

CONTEXT CLUES

→ Remind students that context clues are words or phrases that help a reader figure out unknown words. Some context clues show cause and effect.

→ Display this sentence: *Liam was so insistent about my joining the team that I couldn't say no.*

→ Have partners discuss the meaning of *insistent*. Have students write the meaning in their word study notebooks.

DAY 3

Reinforce the Words

Review this week's vocabulary words. Have students orally complete each sentence stem.

1. There was <u>widespread</u> panic when ____.

2. If you have a sleeping <u>disorder</u>, you might ____.

3. Maria got an <u>unexpected</u> call from ____.

4. The town's economy <u>declined</u> after the ____ closed.

5. It is <u>probable</u> that I will ____.

6. Kevin had to <u>identify</u> his lost ___ in order to pick it up.

Display last week's vocabulary: *approximately, astronomical, calculation, diameter, orbit, spheres.* Have partners ask and answer questions using each of the words.

DAY 4

Connect to Writing

→ Have students write sentences in their word study notebooks using this week's vocabulary.

→ Tell them to write sentences that provide word information they learned from this week's readings.

→ Provide the Day 3 sentence stems 1–6 for students needing extra support.

Write About Vocabulary Have students write something they learned from this week's words in their word study notebooks. For example, they might write about an *unexpected* gift they received or something that is *probable* to happen in the near future.

DAY 5

Word Squares

Ask students to create Word Squares for each vocabulary word.

→ In the first square, students write the word (e.g., *agricultural*).

→ In the second square, students write a definition and any related words, such as synonyms (e.g., *rural, farming*).

→ In the third square, students draw a simple sketch that will help them remember the word (e.g., a farm with crops and a barn).

→ In the fourth square, students write nonexamples, including antonyms for the word (e.g., *urban, metropolitan*).

Have partners discuss their squares.

ROOT WORDS

Remind students that root words can help them find the meaning of unknown words as they read.

→ Display **Your Turn Practice Book page 243–244.** Model using root words to figure out the meaning of *economies*.

→ Have students complete page 247. Partners can confirm meanings in a print or an online dictionary.

SHADES OF MEANING

Help students generate words related to *disorder,* meaning "illness." Draw a word web and write *disorder* in the center.

→ Have partners generate related words, such as synonyms, to add to the outer circles. Ask students to use a thesaurus.

→ Add words not included, such as *syndrome, malady, ailment,* and *condition.*

→ Ask students to copy the words in their word study notebooks.

MORPHOLOGY

Use *probable* as a springboard for students to learn more words. Draw a T-chart. Write *probable* in the left column. In the right column, write *suffixes.*

→ Discuss how the suffixes *-y* and *-ity* change the meaning or part of speech of *probable.*

→ Have students write *probably* and *probability.* Discuss the meanings of the words.

→ Ask partners to do a search for other words with these suffixes.

Approaching Level

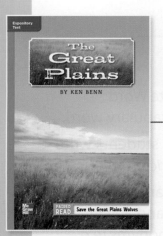

Lexile 760
TextEvaluator 34

OBJECTIVES

CCSS Explain how an author uses reasons and evidence to support particular points in a text, identifying which reasons and evidence support which point(s). **RI.5.8**

ACADEMIC LANGUAGE

- *point of view, author, ask and answer questions, persuasive article*
- Cognates: *punto de vista, autor(a)*

Leveled Reader:
The Great Plains

Go Digital

Before Reading

Preview and Predict

→ Read the Essential Question with students.

→ Have students preview the title, table of contents, and first page of *The Great Plains*. Students should use information in the text and images to predict what they think the selection will be about.

Review Genre: Persuasive Text

Tell students that this selection is a persuasive article. It tries to convince readers to support an idea or position. The author of a persuasive article states his or her points clearly and supports these points with reasons and evidence. Persuasive articles often contain text features such as diagrams, maps, charts, and photographs. Have students identify features of persuasive text in *The Great Plains*.

Leveled Readers

During Reading

Close Reading

Note Taking: Ask students to use their graphic organizer as they read.

Pages 2–3 Point out the word *ecosystems* on page 2. *The root word* eco *comes from a Latin word* meaning "house." Systems *means "a group of things that work together." Use the meanings of* eco *and* systems *to define* ecosystems. ("a group of living things in one habitat") *What effect did settlers have on the environment of the Great Plains?* (They converted large areas of land for agriculture; they hunted some species of animals until almost none were left.)

Pages 4–5 *What forces have shaped the land in the Great Plains?* (Streams carried rocks and soil from the Rockies and built up mounds of earth; water heading to the ocean dug out canyons and wore down hills.) Point out *biodiversity. The root word* bio *means "life." Diversity means a "variety." What does* biodiversity *mean?* ("a variety of life")

Pages 6–7 *What question might you ask after reading page 6?* (Which animals adapted to live in the grasslands, and which did not?) *What answer do you determine after rereading?* (bison; mammoth)

Use Graphic Organizer

Pages 8–11 *Did Native Americans greatly impact the environment?* (no) *How did fur traders affect the environment?* (Numbers of some animals, such as beavers, declined.) *What activity created disorder in the ecology of the grasslands?* (plowing up large areas to plant crops)

Pages 12–13 *What evidence supports the author's point that crossbred crops are better for the Great Plains?* (Crossbred crops don't need chemicals to grow well.) *How have viewpoints about prairie fires changed?* (Now people think they help the ecology of the area.)

Pages 14–17 *What is the first step to restore an animal population?* (make sure there is enough food) *What does the author think should be done to restore the ecology of the Great Plains?* (do more research)

After Reading

Respond to Reading Revisit the Essential Question and ask students to complete the Text Evidence questions on page 18.

Analytical Writing **Write About Reading** Check that students have correctly identified the author's point of view and identified details that support it.

Fluency: Expression and Phrasing

Model Model reading page 13 with proper expression and phrasing. Next reread the page aloud and have students read along with you.

Apply Have students practice reading with a partner.

PAIRED READ

"Save the Great Plains Wolves"

Leveled Reader

Make Connections: Write About It **Analytical Writing**

Before reading, ask students to note that the genre of this text is a persuasive article. Then discuss the Essential Question. After reading, ask students to write connections between the points of view conveyed in *The Great Plains* and "Save the Great Plains Wolves."

 FOCUS ON SCIENCE

Students can extend their knowledge of life science by completing the activity on page 24. **STEM**

 **Literature Circles**

Ask students to conduct a literature circle using the Thinkmark questions to guide the discussion. You may wish to have a whole-class discussion, using both selections in the Leveled Reader, about how natural events and human activities affect the environment.

Level Up

Level-up lessons available online.

IF students read the **Approaching Level** fluently and answered the questions,

THEN pair them with students who have proficiently read the **On Level** and have students

• echo-read the **On Level** main selection.

• use self-stick notes to mark details that identify the author's point of view.

A C T **Access Complex Text**

The **On Level** challenges students by including more **domain-specific words** and **complex sentence structures**.

Approaching Level
Word Study/Decoding

REVIEW SUFFIX -*ion*

TIER 2

OBJECTIVES

CCSS Know and apply grade-level phonics and word analysis skills in decoding words. Use combined knowledge of all letter-sound correspondences, syllabication patterns, and morphology (e.g., roots and affixes) to read accurately unfamiliar multisyllabic words in context and out of context. **RF.5.3a**

Decode words with -*ion*.

I Do Review with students that -*ion* is a common suffix that, when added to certain verbs, changes them to nouns. Write the word pair *act, action* on the board. Explain that the verb *act* changes to the noun *action* when the suffix –*ion* is added. Review that -*tion* is usually pronounced *shun* (as in *action*).

We Do Write the word pair *create, creation* on the board and read it aloud, stressing the /sh/ sound as you pronounce *creation*. Point out that when the verb ends in an *e*, as in *create*, the *e* is dropped before the suffix -*ion* is added. Guide students to determine the meaning of the noun *creation*.

You Do Write the words *donation* and *permission* on the board. Have students pronounce each word correctly and underline the suffix. Remind them that -*tion* and -*ssion* are usually pronounced *shun*. Ask students to determine the meanings of *donation* and *permission* by connecting them to the verbs *donate* and *permit*.

BUILD WORDS WITH SUFFIX -*ion*

TIER 2

OBJECTIVES

CCSS Know and apply grade-level phonics and word analysis skills in decoding words. Use combined knowledge of all letter-sound correspondences, syllabication patterns, and morphology (e.g., roots and affixes) to read accurately unfamiliar multisyllabic words in context and out of context. **RF.5.3a**

Build words with -*ion*.

I Do Explain that students will build new words by combining verbs with the suffix -*ion*. On the board, write the suffix -*ion* and the following verbs: *construct, subtract, confuse, correct*.

We Do Work with students to combine the verbs and the suffix to build nouns. Have them chorally read the words *construction, subtraction, confusion,* and *correction*. Remind students that -*sion* is usually pronounced *zhun*, as in *confusion*, but -*tion* is usually pronounced *shun*, as in *construction, subtraction,* and *correction*. Point out that the *e* in *confuse* was dropped when -*ion* was added. Then guide students to use the meanings of the verbs to determine the meanings of the nouns.

You Do Write the verbs *concentrate, decorate,* and *revise* on the board. Have partners build nouns by adding the suffix -*ion* to each. Ask them to write each new word and then pronounce it.

PRACTICE WORDS WITH SUFFIX *-ion*

OBJECTIVES

CCSS Know and apply grade-level phonics and word analysis skills in decoding words. Use combined knowledge of all letter-sound correspondences, syllabication patterns, and morphology (e.g., roots and affixes) to read accurately unfamiliar multisyllabic words in context and out of context. **RF.5.3a**

Practice words with *-ion*.

 I Do Write these words on the board: *appreciation* and *television*. Read the words aloud, underlining the *-ion* suffixes with your finger as you read. Emphasize the difference between the /sh/ and /zh/ pronunciations in the words.

 We Do Write the words *division* and *discussion* on the board. Model how to pronounce the word *division*, underlining the *-ion* with your finger. Have students repeat the word. Then have students pronounce the word *discussion*. Lead students to identify the difference between the /zh/ and /sh/ pronunciations in the two words.

 You Do To provide additional practice, write these words on the board. Read aloud the first word and underline *-ion*.

omission	conclusion	decision
donation	education	equation
session	explosion	confusion
imitation	action	infection

Then have students read aloud the remaining words. Ask them to point out the *-ion* in each word and to tell whether the sound preceding it is /sh/ or /zh/. Have partners determine the meaning of each noun by connecting it to the meaning of the related verb.

Afterward, point to the words in the list in random order for students to read chorally.

 ENGLISH LANGUAGE LEARNERS

For the **ELLs** who need **phonics, decoding,** and **fluency** practice, use scaffolding methods as necessary to ensure students understand the meaning of the words. Refer to the **Language Transfers Handbook** for phonics elements that may not transfer in students' native languages.

Approaching Level

Vocabulary

REVIEW HIGH-FREQUENCY WORDS

TIER 2

 OBJECTIVES
Acquire and use accurately grade-appropriate general academic and domain-specific words and phrases, including those that signal contrast, addition, and other logical relationships (e.g., *however, although, nevertheless, similarly, moreover, in addition*).
L.5.6

 I Do Choose review words from **High-Frequency Word Cards** 161–200. Display one word at a time, following the routine:

Display the word. Read the word. Then spell the word.

 We Do Ask students to state the word and spell the word with you. Model using the word in a sentence and have students repeat after you.

 You Do Display the word. Ask students to say the word and then spell it. When completed, quickly flip through the word card set as students chorally read the words. Provide opportunities for students to use the words in speaking and writing. For example, provide sentence starters such as *I think that ____*. Ask students to write each word in their Writer's Notebook.

REVIEW VOCABULARY WORDS

TIER 2

 OBJECTIVES
Acquire and use accurately grade-appropriate general academic and domain-specific words and phrases, including those that signal contrast, addition, and other logical relationships (e.g., *however, although, nevertheless, similarly, moreover, in addition*).
L.5.6

 I Do Display each **Visual Vocabulary Card** and state the word. Explain how the photograph illustrates the word. State the example sentence and repeat the word.

 We Do Point to the word on the card and read the word with students. Ask them to repeat the word. Engage students in structured partner talk about the image as prompted on the back of the vocabulary card.

 You Do Display each visual in random order, hiding the word. Have students match the definitions and context sentences of the words to the visuals displayed.

UNDERSTAND VOCABULARY WORDS

OBJECTIVES

CCSS Acquire and use accurately grade-appropriate general academic and domain-specific words and phrases, including those that signal contrast, addition, and other logical relationships (e.g., *however, although, nevertheless, similarly, moreover, in addition*).
L.5.6

 I Do Display the *agricultural* **Visual Vocabulary Card** and ask: *Which would you describe as an* agricultural *tool, a wrench or a hoe?* Explain that a hoe would be an agricultural tool because it is used for farming.

 We Do Ask these questions. Help students explain their answers.

→ If sales *declined*, would a store make more or less money?

→ If a person has a *disorder*, is that person sick or healthy?

→ If you *identify* a plant, do you guess what it is or tell exactly what it is?

 You Do Have students work in pairs to respond to these questions and explain their answers.

→ Which is *probable*, finding a penny or buried treasure?

→ If plants *thrive*, are they healthy or sick?

→ Which is *unexpected*, winning a raffle or doing homework?

→ Which is more *widespread*, a sickness at home or at school?

ROOT WORDS

OBJECTIVES

CCSS Determine or clarify the meaning of unknown and multiple-meaning words and phrases based on *grade 5 reading and content,* choosing flexibly from a range of strategies. Use common, grade-appropriate Greek and Latin affixes and roots as clues to the meaning of a word (e.g., *photograph, photosynthesis*).
L.5.4b

 I Do Display the Comprehension and Fluency passage on **Approaching Reproducibles** pages 243–244. Read aloud the first paragraph. Point to the word *survival*. Tell students that they can use their knowledge of word roots to help them figure out the meaning of the word.

Think Aloud I know that the Latin root *vivere* means "live." Words with *viv* and *vivi* usually have something to do with life. I think *survival* means "to stay alive." When I use this meaning in the sentence, it makes sense.

 We Do Ask students to point to the word *agriculture* in the second paragraph on page 243. With students, discuss how to use the Latin roots *agri*, meaning "field," and *cultura*, meaning "cultivation," to figure out the meaning of the word. Write the definition of the word.

 You Do Have students determine the meanings of *Commercial, transport* (page 243, paragraph 3), and *reside* (page 244, paragraph 2) by using context clues and word roots (*merc*: "merchandise"; *portare*: "to carry"; *sedere*: "to sit").

Approaching Level

Comprehension

FLUENCY

TIER **2**

 OBJECTIVES
Read on-level prose and poetry orally with accuracy, appropriate rate, and expression on successive readings. **RF.5.4b**

Read fluently with good expression and phrasing.

 I Do
Explain that good readers group words into meaningful phrases. They also change their volume, tone, and emphasis to convey the meaning of the text. Read the first two paragraphs of the Comprehension and Fluency passage on **Approaching Reproducibles** pages 243–244. Tell students to listen for your phrasing and the way you change your expression to match the text.

 We Do
Read the rest of the page aloud and have students repeat each sentence after you, matching your phrasing and expression. Point out that you change your volume, tone, and emphasis to read expressively.

 You Do
Have partners take turns reading sentences from the Comprehension and Fluency passage. Remind them to focus on their phrasing and expression. Provide corrective feedback as needed by modeling proper fluency.

IDENTIFY IMPORTANT DETAILS

TIER **2**

 OBJECTIVES
Explain how an author uses reasons and evidence to support particular points in a text, identifying which reasons and evidence support which point(s). **RI.5.8**

Identify important details and opinions.

 I Do
Review that the author of a persuasive text includes reasons and evidence as support for his or her point of view, or position, on a topic. Facts, opinions, details, and word choices in the text provide clues about the author's point of view.

 We Do
Display the Comprehension and Fluency passage on **Approaching Reproducibles** pages 243–244. Read the first paragraph of "Rain Forests Support People" on page 243. Point out that each sentence expresses an opinion. Explain that the author's powerful or practical word choices, such as *necessary for the survival of people, not realistic,* and *better plan*, reveal the author's position that it is necessary to cut down some rain forest trees.

 You Do
Have students read the rest of the passage. After each paragraph, they should list details and word choices that help convey the author's position.

REVIEW AUTHOR'S POINT OF VIEW

OBJECTIVES

CCSS Determine an author's point of view or purpose in a text and explain how it is conveyed in the text. **RI.6.6**

CCSS Explain how an author uses reasons and evidence to support particular points in a text, identifying which reasons and evidence support which point(s). **RI.5.8**

I Do Review that the author of a persuasive text gives his or her point of view, or position, on a topic. Examining facts, opinions, details, and word choices in the text can help readers determine the author's point of view.

We Do Display the Comprehension and Fluency passage on **Approaching Reproducibles** pages 243–244. Read the first section of "Rain Forests Support People" on page 243. Refer to the list of word choices and details the students have already compiled. Model how to use them to determine the author's point of view. Work with students to determine the author's point of view in the second section of the passage.

You Do Have pairs read "The World Needs Rain Forests" on page 244. After each section, have them identify facts, opinions, details, and word choices and then use these to determine the author's point of view in the text as a whole.

SELF-SELECTED READING

OBJECTIVES

CCSS Determine an author's point of view or purpose in a text and explain how it is conveyed in the text. **RI.6.6**

CCSS Explain how an author uses reasons and evidence to support particular points in a text, identifying which reasons and evidence support which point(s). **RI.5.8**

Ask and answer questions to increase understanding.

Read Independently

Have students choose a persuasive text for sustained silent reading. Remind students that:

→ the author's point of view is his or her position on the topic.

→ asking and answering questions about the reasons and evidence the author provides in the text can help them better identify and understand his or her point of view.

Read Purposefully

As they read independently, students should use Graphic Organizer 145 to record details that help them determine the author's point of view. After they finish, they can conduct a Book Talk about what they read.

→ Students should share their organizers and answer this question: *What is the author's point of view about the topic?*

→ They should also share a question they asked and answered as they read.

On Level

Lexile 910
TextEvaluator™ 43

OBJECTIVES

CCSS Explain how an author uses reasons and evidence to support particular points in a text, identifying which reasons and evidence support which point(s). **RI.5.8**

ACADEMIC LANGUAGE

• *point of view, author, ask and answer questions, persuasive article*

• Cognates: *punto de vista, autor(a)*

Leveled Reader:
The Great Plains

Go
Digital

Leveled Readers

Before Reading

Preview and Predict

→ Read the Essential Question with students.

→ Have students preview the title, table of contents, and first page of *The Great Plains*. Students should use information in the text and images to predict what they think the selection will be about.

Review Genre: Persuasive Text

Tell students that this selection is a persuasive article. It tries to convince readers to support an idea or position. The author of a persuasive article states his or her points clearly and supports these points with reasons and evidence. Persuasive articles often contain text features such as diagrams, maps, charts, and photographs. Have students identify features of persuasive text in *The Great Plains*.

During Reading

Close Reading

Note Taking: Ask students to use their graphic organizer as they read.

Use Graphic Organizer

Pages 2–3 *The root word* eco *comes from a Latin word meaning "house." What does* ecosystems *mean?* ("a group of living things in one habitat") *What question might you ask after reading this section?* (How did settlers affect the environment of the Great Plains?) *What answer might you determine after rereading?* (They converted large areas for agriculture; they hunted some species of animals until there were almost none left.)

Pages 4–7 *How did streams and rivers affect the land on their way to the ocean?* (Water cut into rock, dug out canyons, and wore down hills.) *The root word* bio *means "life." Diversity means "a variety." What does* biodiversity *mean?* ("a variety of life") *How would a drought likely affect wildlife near streams in the Great Plains?* (Frogs and crustaceans could die; birds, beavers, and raccoons could be forced to leave the area.)

Pages 8–10 *How did the arrival of Spanish explorers and, later, European fur traders affect wildlife populations?* (More bison were killed; numbers of some animal species, such as beavers, declined drastically.)

Pages 11–12 *What question might you ask as you read page 11?* (What effects did chemicals in fertilizers and pesticides have?) *How might you answer it?* (They killed beneficial as well as harmful insects.)

Pages 13–15 *What evidence supports the author's point that crops crossbred with grasses are better for the Great Plains ecosystems?* (They don't need a lot of fertilizers and pesticides.) *How have people's views about prairie fires changed?* (People now see them as helpful.)

Pages 16–17 *Paraphrase the author's point of view about restoring the ecology of the Great Plains.* (It is a complicated task. Because all the ecosystems are closely linked, it can be difficult to tell which plant or animal species should be restored first. More research is needed.)

After Reading

Respond to Reading Revisit the Essential Question and ask students to complete the Text Evidence questions on page 18.

Write About Reading Check that students have correctly identified the author's point of view and identified details that support it.

Fluency: Expression and Phrasing

Model Model reading page 11 with proper expression and phrasing. Next reread the page aloud and have students read along with you.

Apply Have students practice reading with partners.

PAIRED READ

Leveled Reader

"Save the Great Plains Wolves"

Make Connections: Write About It

Before reading, ask students to note that the genre of this text is a persuasive article. Then discuss the Essential Question. After reading, ask students to write connections between the points of view conveyed in *The Great Plains* and "Save the Great Plains Wolves."

FOCUS ON SCIENCE

Students can extend their knowledge of life science by completing the activity on page 24. **STEM**

Literature Circles

Ask students to conduct a literature circle using the Thinkmark questions to guide the discussion. You may wish to have a whole-class discussion, using the Leveled-Reader selections, about how natural events and human activities affect the environment.

Level Up

Level-up lessons available online.

IF students read the On Level fluently and answered the questions,

THEN pair them with students who have proficiently read the Beyond Level and have students

• partner-read the Beyond Level main selection.

• make a list of details that help them identify the author's point of view.

• make a list of questions while reading the selection and then reread for answers.

A C T Access Complex Text

The Beyond Level challenges students by including more **domain-specific words** and **complex sentence structures**.

→ On Level

Vocabulary

REVIEW VOCABULARY WORDS

 OBJECTIVES
Acquire and use accurately grade-appropriate general academic and domain-specific words and phrases, including those that signal contrast, addition, and other logical relationships (e.g., *however, although, nevertheless, similarly, moreover, in addition*).
L.5.6

 I Do Use the **Visual Vocabulary Cards** to review key selection words *declined, disorder, identify, probable, unexpected,* and *widespread.* Point to each word, read it aloud, and have students chorally repeat it.

 We Do Ask these questions. Help students explain their answers.

→ What might a store owner do if his or her profits *declined*?

→ What is a *disorder* you would like to find a cure for?

→ What are some characteristics you use to *identify* people?

 You Do Have students work in pairs to respond and explain their answers.

→ What is a *probable* question someone might ask you tonight?

→ How would you feel if your teacher gave an *unexpected* quiz?

→ What is a *widespread* problem you have heard about?

ROOT WORDS

 OBJECTIVES
Determine or clarify the meaning of unknown and multiple-meaning words and phrases based on *grade 5 reading and content,* choosing flexibly from a range of strategies. Use common, grade-appropriate Greek and Latin affixes and roots as clues to the meaning of a word (e.g., *photograph, photosynthesis*).
L.5.4b

 I Do Remind students they can often figure out the meaning of a word by using their knowledge of word roots. Use the Comprehension and Fluency passage on **Your Turn Practice Book** pages 243–244 to model.

Think Aloud The word *survival* in the first paragraph contains the Latin root *vivere,* which means "live." I think *survival* means "to stay alive." This meaning makes sense in the sentence.

 We Do Have students read the second paragraph on page 243 where they encounter *agriculture.* Help students figure out the definition by pointing out the Latin root *agri,* meaning "field," and *cultura,* meaning "cultivation."

 You Do Have pairs determine the meanings of *Commercial, transport* (page 243, paragraph 3), *reside* (page 244, paragraph 2), and *perspective* (page 244, paragraph 5) by using context clues and word roots (*merc:* "merchandise"; *portare:* "to carry"; *sedere:* "to sit"; *specere:* "to look at").

Comprehension

REVIEW AUTHOR'S POINT OF VIEW

OBJECTIVES

 Determine an author's point of view or purpose in a text and explain how it is conveyed in the text. **RI.6.6**

 Explain how an author uses reasons and evidence to support particular points in a text, identifying which reasons and evidence support which point(s). **RI.5.8**

 I Do

Review that the author of a persuasive text gives his or her point of view, or position, on a topic. Examining facts, opinions, details, and word choices in the text can help readers determine the author's point of view.

 We Do

Display the Comprehension and Fluency passage on **Your Turn Practice Book** pages 243–244. Have a volunteer read the first section of "Rain Forests Support People" on page 243. Have students record the most important facts, opinions, details, and word choices. Model using these to determine the author's point of view about rain forests.

You Do

Have pairs read "The World Needs Rain Forests" on page 244 . Tell them to stop after each section and identify key facts, opinions, details, and word choices. They should use them to determine the author's point of view in each section and in the text as a whole.

SELF-SELECTED READING

OBJECTIVES

 Determine an author's point of view or purpose in a text and explain how it is conveyed in the text. **RI.6.6**

Explain how an author uses reasons and evidence to support particular points in a text, identifying which reasons and evidence support which point(s). **RI.5.8**

Ask and answer questions to increase understanding.

Read Independently

Have students choose a persuasive text for sustained silent reading.

→ Before they read, have students preview the text, reading the title and headings and viewing any images that accompany it.

→ As students read, remind them to ask and answer questions to determine the author's point of view and improve comprehension of complex text.

Read Purposefully

Encourage students to read different texts about the same topic or event to enhance their understanding of multiple perspectives.

→ As students read, have them record facts, opinions, details, and word choices on Graphic Organizer 145.

→ They can use the organizer to summarize the text and explain how the author uses this evidence to convey his or her point of view.

→ Ask students to share their reactions to the text.

Beyond Level

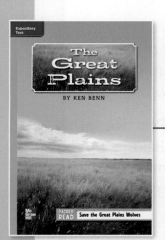

Lexile 1020
TextEvaluator™ 48

OBJECTIVES
Explain how an author uses reasons and evidence to support particular points in a text, identifying which reasons and evidence support which point(s). **RI.5.8**

ACADEMIC LANGUAGE
• *point of view, author, ask and answer questions, persuasive article*
• Cognates: *punto de vista, autor(a)*

Leveled Reader:
The Great Plains

Go Digital

Leveled Readers

Before Reading

Preview and Predict

→ Read the Essential Question with students.

→ Have students preview the title, table of contents, and first page of *The Great Plains*. Students should use information in the text and images to predict what they think the selection will be about.

Review Genre: Persuasive Text

Tell students that this selection is a persuasive article. It tries to convince readers to support an idea or position. The author of a persuasive article states his or her points clearly and supports these points with reasons and evidence. Persuasive articles often contain text features such as diagrams, maps, charts, and photographs. Have students identify features of persuasive text in *The Great Plains*.

During Reading

Close Reading

Note Taking: Ask students to use their graphic organizer as they read.

Use Graphic Organizer

Pages 2–7 *Identify a word with the root* eco, *which comes from a Latin word meaning "house," and identify the meaning of the word.* (ecosystems: "a group of living things in one habitat") *What natural events have affected the Great Plains?* (droughts, blizzards, wildfires) *What human activities have affected them?* (converting large areas for agriculture, hunting some species to near extinction) *What does* biodiversity *mean? Use the root word* bio, *meaning "life," to answer.* ("variety of life") *How do droughts affect wildlife near streams?* (Frogs and crustaceans may die; beavers and raccoons may be forced to leave the area.)

Pages 8–11 *What question did you ask on page 9?* (What effect did fur trappers have on wildlife?) *What answer did you identify?* (They reduced numbers of some species, such as beavers.) *Why are roots and grasses important to the ecology of the Great Plains?* (They hold soil in place and reduce erosion.) *What caused the Dust Bowl in the 1930s?* (Crops, which replaced grasslands, died in droughts, leading to a dust storm.)

Pages 12–13 *What evidence supports the author's point of view that crops crossbred with prairie grasses are better for the natural ecosystems of the Great Plains?* (They don't need a lot of fertilizers and pesticides; they regrow when harvested; their deep roots prevent soil erosion.)

Pages 13–17 *Paraphrase the change in people's point of view about prairie fires.* (At one time, people tried to put out prairie fires. Now, people believe fires are beneficial to the land.) *What question did you have while reading this section?* (Why don't farmers like prairie dogs?) *What answer did you determine?* (Livestock can trip in their burrows and become injured.) *What is the author's point of view about restoring the ecology of the Great Plains?* (It is complicated, because all the ecosystems are closely linked. More research needs to be conducted.)

After Reading

Respond to Reading Revisit the Essential Question and ask students to complete the Text Evidence questions on page 18.

Analytical Writing **Write About Reading** Check that students have correctly identified the author's point of view and identified details that support it.

Fluency: Expression and Phrasing

Model Model reading page 9 with proper expression and phrasing. Next reread the page aloud and have students read along with you.

Apply Have students practice reading with partners.

PAIRED READ

"Save the Great Plains Wolves"

Leveled Reader

Make Connections: Write About It **Analytical Writing**

Before reading, ask students to note that the genre of this text is a persuasive article. Then discuss the Essential Question. After reading, ask students to make connections between the points of view conveyed in *The Great Plains* and "Save the Great Plains Wolves."

 FOCUS ON SCIENCE

Students can extend their knowledge of life science by completing the activity on page 24. **STEM**

Literature Circles

Ask students to conduct a literature circle using the Thinkmark questions to guide the discussion. You may wish to have a whole-class discussion, using information from both selections in the Leveled Reader, about how natural events and human activities affect the environment.

Gifted and Talented

Synthesize Have students conduct research, using both print and Internet sources, to identify other examples of species that conservationists seek to protect or increase in the Great Plains. Have partners choose a species, explain why it is endangered or why its population needs to be restored, and describe what strategies scientists think can help the species survive. Have students present their research in the format of a brochure, including both text and images as support.

→ Beyond Level

Vocabulary

REVIEW DOMAIN-SPECIFIC WORDS

OBJECTIVES

 Acquire and use accurately grade-appropriate general academic and domain-specific words and phrases, including those that signal contrast, addition, and other logical relationships. **L.5.6**

 Model Use the **Visual Vocabulary Cards** to review the meaning of the words *agricultural* and *thrive*. Use each word in a context sentence.

Write the words *endangers* and *biodiversity* on the board and discuss the meanings with students. Then help students write sentences using these words.

 Apply Have students work in pairs to review the meanings of the words *biofuels, converted,* and *vital*. Then have partners write sentences using the words.

ROOT WORDS

OBJECTIVES

 Determine or clarify the meaning of unknown and multiple-meaning words and phrases based on *grade 5 reading and content,* choosing flexibly from a range of strategies. Use common, grade-appropriate Greek and Latin affixes and roots as clues to the meaning of a word (e.g., *photograph, photosynthesis*). **L.5.4b**

 Model Read aloud the second paragraph of the Comprehension and Fluency passage on **Beyond Reproducibles** pages 243–244.

Think Aloud I am uncertain about the meaning of *agriculture*. I see two Latin roots—*agri*, which means "field," and *cultura*, which means "cultivation." Based on word roots and context clues, I think that *agriculture* means "the science of cultivating the soil."

With students, read the first paragraph on page 243. Help them figure out the meaning of *survival* by using the Latin root *vivere,* which means "live."

 Apply Have pairs use word roots and context clues to determine the meanings of *Commercial* and *transport* (page 243, paragraph 3), *reside* (page 244, paragraph 2), *absorbing* (page 244, paragraph 4), and *perspective* (page 244, paragraph 5).

 Independent Study Challenge students to identify other words with the root *vivere* or *sedere*. Have them list as many words as they can find and then choose three to use in sentences that contain context clues. Have partners trade papers and determine the meanings of the words.

Comprehension

REVIEW AUTHOR'S POINT OF VIEW

OBJECTIVES

 Determine an author's point of view or purpose in a text and explain how it is conveyed in the text. **RI.6.6**

 Explain how an author uses reasons and evidence to support particular points in a text, identifying which reasons and evidence support which point(s). **RI.5.8**

Model Review that the author of a persuasive text gives his or her point of view, or position, on a topic. Examining facts, opinions, details, and word choices in the text can help readers determine the author's point of view.

Display the Comprehension and Fluency passage on **Beyond Reproducibles** pages 243–244. Have students read the first section of "Rain Forests Support People." Ask open-ended discussion questions, such as *What does the author think about rain forests? What words or phrases give you clues?* Students should support their responses with text evidence.

Apply Have students read "The World Needs Rain Forests" on page 244 and identify key facts, opinions, details, and word choices as they independently fill in Graphic Organizer 145. Have partners discuss how the author's point of view in "The World Needs Rain Forests" differs from that in "Rain Forests Support People" and which they found most convincing.

SELF-SELECTED READING

OBJECTIVES

 Determine an author's point of view or purpose in a text and explain how it is conveyed in the text. **RI.6.6**

 Explain how an author uses reasons and evidence to support particular points in a text, identifying which reasons and evidence support which point(s). **RI.5.8**

Ask and answer questions to increase understanding.

Read Independently

Have students choose a persuasive text for sustained silent reading.

→ Have them to fill in Graphic Organizer 145 with facts, opinions, details, and word choices to determine the author's point of view.

→ Tell them to monitor understanding of complex text and identify evidence the author provides by asking and answering questions as they read.

Read Purposefully

Encourage students to keep a reading journal. Ask them to select texts about topics that interest them and to explore a variety of perspectives.

→ Students can write summaries of the text in their journals.

→ Ask them to share with classmates the most interesting fact they learned.

 Independent Study Challenge students to discuss how their books relate to the weekly theme of scientific viewpoints. Have students use their class and independent texts to compare the different ways that natural events and human activities affect the environment.

→ English Language Learners

Shared Read

Should Plants and Animals from Other Places Live Here?

Reading/Writing Workshop

OBJECTIVES

CCSS Analyze multiple accounts of the same event or topic, noting important similarities and differences in the point of view they represent. **RI.5.6**

CCSS Explain how an author uses reasons and evidence to support particular points in a text, identifying which reasons and evidence support which point(s). **RI.5.8**

LANGUAGE OBJECTIVE

Identify the author's point of view.

ACADEMIC LANGUAGE

• author, point of view, ask and answer questions

• Cognates: *autor(a), punto de vista*

Go Digital

View "Should Plants and Animals from Other Places Live Here?"

Before Reading

Build Background

Read the Essential Question: *How do natural events and human activities affect the environment?*

→ Explain the meaning of the Essential Question, including the vocabulary in the question: *Natural events are things such as storms, earthquakes, and floods. Human activities are things people do, such as cutting down trees. The environment includes everything around you: air, water, land, and buildings.*

→ **Model an answer:** *Cutting down trees in the rain forest is a human activity. It has many effects on the environment. It makes the rain forest smaller, and it leaves many animals without homes.*

→ Ask students a question that ties the Essential Question to their own background knowledge: *Turn to a partner and think of a natural event that affects the environment. Discuss the event and how it affects the environment.* Call on several pairs to share with the class.

During Reading

Interactive Question-Response

→ Ask questions that help students understand the meaning of the text after each paragraph.

→ Reinforce the meanings of key vocabulary.

→ Ask students questions that require them to use key vocabulary.

→ Reinforce strategies and skills of the week by modeling.

Page 367

New Arrivals Welcome

Paragraph 1

Remember that the prefix non- means "not." What are nonnative species? (plants or animals that are not native or come from other places)

Paragraph 2

Explain and Model Author's Point of View

Choral-read the last sentence. *The author gives facts about how nonnative species help people in Florida make money. Does the author think that nonnative species can be helpful?* (yes)

Paragraph 3

Turn to a partner. Discuss how nonnative species can control insects that harm crops. (Nonnative insects can be brought to farms to kill pests.)

Paragraph 4

Choral-read the paragraph. *Does the author say that nonnative species can be a good thing?* (yes) *What example does the author give in this paragraph to support this position?* (Many of our pets are from other parts of the world.)

Page 368

A Growing Problem

Paragraph 1

What nonnative species is in the Florida Everglades? (pythons) *How does the author describe this species?* (The author says they are a menace.)

Paragraph 2

What fact does the author give to support the idea that nonnative species are harmful? (They cause $137 billion in damage every year.)

Explain that *nuisance* means "problem." Have students repeat the word. *Why are Asian carp a nuisance?* (They eat all of the food, and native fish are dying.)

Paragraph 3

How did the avian influenza virus come to the U.S.? (it was carried by birds)

Paragraph 4

Sometimes people introduce nonnative species on purpose. Why were melaleuca trees brought to Florida? (to stabilize swampy areas) *What was the unintended consequence?* (the trees are crowding out native species)

Paragraph 5

Turn to a partner and explain the author's position on nonnative species. (Nonnative species are harmful and should not be allowed to spread.)

Page 369

Nonnative Species: Benefits and Costs

What information does the chart give? (It lists positive and negative effects of nonnative species.)

After Reading

Make Connections

→ Review the Essential Question: *How do natural events and human activities affect the environment?*

→ Make text connections.

→ Have students complete **ELL Reproducibles** pages 243–245.

English Language Learners

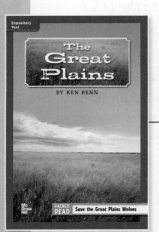

Lexile 830
TextEvaluator 37

OBJECTIVES

CCSS Explain how an author uses reasons and evidence to support particular points in a text, identifying which reasons and evidence support which point(s). **RI.5.8**

ACADEMIC LANGUAGE

• *point of view, author, ask and answer questions, persuasive article*

• Cognates: *punto de vista, autor(a)*

Leveled Reader:
The Great Plains

Leveled Readers

Before Reading

Preview

→ Read the Essential Question: *How do natural events and human activities affect the environment?*

→ Refer to Friend or Foe?: *Do you know of any nonnative plants or animals in your area?*

→ Preview *The Great Plains* and "Save the Great Plains Wolves": *Our purpose for reading is to learn how people and nature can change the world around us.*

Vocabulary

Use the **Visual Vocabulary Cards** to pre-teach the ELL vocabulary: *depleted, forces, native, restore.* Use the routine found on the cards.

During Reading

Interactive Question-Response

Note Taking: Ask students to use the graphic organizer on **ELL Reproducibles** page 242. Use the questions below after each page is read with students. As you read, use the glossary definitions to define vocabulary in context and use visuals to help students understand key vocabulary.

Use Graphic Organizer

Pages 2–3 *Eco is a root word that means "house." Systems means "a group of things that work together." Ecosystems means a group of things living and working together.* Have students retell the definition.

Pages 4–5 *What is one force that changed the land?* (streams) *Megafauna is a word that means "large animals." What are some large animals that lived on the Great Plains?* (mammoth, camel, bears)

Pages 6–7 *Has the climate of the Great Plains changed over time or stayed the same?* (It has changed.) *What happens to animals that cannot adapt to climate changes?* (They die out.)

Pages 8–9 *Turn to a partner and tell how the arrival of humans affected the bison and beaver populations.* (They declined because of hunting and trapping.)

Go Digital

Pages 10–11 Make a simple drawing that shows grass roots holding soil. *What did grass roots do?* (held the soil in place)

Pages 12–13 *The text says that fertilizers and pesticides cause problems. What type of crop is better for the ecosystem?* (crossbred)

Pages 14–15 *The first sentence on page 15 tells us something about the author's point of view. What is it?* (The author thinks bison are important to the ecosystem.)

Pages 16–17 *Choral read the last paragraph on page 17. What does the author think we need to do to restore the Great Plains?* (understand the biodiversity of the Great Plains)

After Reading

Respond to Reading Revisit the Essential Question and ask students to complete the Text Evidence questions on page 18.

Analytical Writing **Write About Reading** Check that students have correctly identified the author's point of view and identified details that support it.

Fluency: Expression and Phrasing

Model Model reading page 11 with proper expression and phrasing. Then reread the page aloud and have students read along with you.

Apply Have students practice reading with partners.

PAIRED READ

"Save the Great Plains Wolves"

Make Connections: Write About It **Analytical Writing**

Before reading, ask students to note that the genre of this text is a persuasive article. Then discuss the Essential Question. After reading, ask students to list connections between what they learned from *The Great Plains* and "Save the Great Plains Wolves."

Leveled Reader

FOCUS ON SCIENCE

Students can extend their knowledge of life science by completing the activity on page 24. **STEM**

Literature Circles

Ask students to conduct a literature circle using the Thinkmark questions to guide the discussion. You may wish to have a whole-class discussion about natural events and human activities using information from both selections in the Leveled Reader.

Level Up

Level-up lessons available online.

IF students read the **ELL Level** fluently and answered the questions,

THEN pair them with students who have proficiently read **On Level** and have ELL students

• echo-read the **On Level** main selection.

• list words with which they have difficulty and discuss them with a partner.

A C T **Access Complex Text**

The **On Level** challenges students by including more **domain-specific words** and **complex sentence structures**.

English Language Learners
Vocabulary

PRETEACH VOCABULARY

 OBJECTIVES
CCSS Acquire and use accurately grade-appropriate general academic and domain-specific words and phrases, including those that signal contrast, addition, and other logical relationships. **L.5.6**

LANGUAGE OBJECTIVE
Use vocabulary words.

 I Do Preteach vocabulary from "New Arrivals Welcome" and "A Growing Problem," following the Vocabulary Routine found on the **Visual Vocabulary Cards** for the words *agricultural, declined, disorder, identify, probable, thrive, unexpected,* and *widespread.*

 We Do After completing the Vocabulary Routine for each word, point to the word on the Visual Vocabulary Card and read the word with students. Ask students to repeat the word.

You Do Have students work with a partner to use two or more words in sentences or questions. Then have each pair read the sentences aloud.

Beginning	Intermediate	Advanced/High
Help students write the sentences or questions correctly and read them aloud.	Ask students to write one sentence and one question.	Challenge students to write one sentence and one question for each word.

REVIEW VOCABULARY

 OBJECTIVES
CCSS Acquire and use accurately grade-appropriate general academic and domain-specific words and phrases, including those that signal contrast, addition, and other logical relationships. **L.5.6**

LANGUAGE OBJECTIVE
Use vocabulary words.

 I Do Review the previous week's vocabulary words over a few days. Read each word aloud, pointing to the word on the **Visual Vocabulary Card**. Have students repeat. Then follow the Vocabulary Routine on the back of each card.

 We Do Review the words quickly again. Then model saying a sentence, omitting the vocabulary word for students to guess.

 You Do Have student pairs write sentences for all of the words, omitting the vocabulary word in each sentence. Ask them to read the sentences aloud for the class to guess the missing word.

Beginning	Intermediate	Advanced/High
Help students read aloud the sentences and determine the missing words.	Ask students to include a context clue in each sentence.	Have students use two or more vocabulary words in each sentence.

ROOT WORDS

OBJECTIVES

 Determine or clarify the meaning of unknown and multiple-meaning words and phrases based on grade 5 reading and content, choosing flexibly from a range of strategies. Use common, grade-appropriate Greek and Latin affixes and roots as clues to the meaning of a word (e.g., *photograph, photosynthesis*). **L.5.4b**

LANGUAGE OBJECTIVE

Identify and use root words.

I Do Read aloud the first paragraph of the Comprehension and Fluency passage on **ELL Reproducibles** pages 243–244. Point to the word *survival*. Explain that using word parts such as roots can help them figure out the meaning of the word.

Think Aloud When I read the word *survival*, I see the Latin root *vivere*, which means "live." I know that words with *viv* and *vivi* in them have meanings related to "live." This helps me understand that *survival* means "to stay alive."

We Do Have students point to the word *agriculture* in second paragraph on page 243. Help students use the root *agri*, meaning "field," to figure out its meaning. Write the meaning on the board.

You Do In pairs, have students write the meanings of *commercial* and *transport* (page 243, paragraph 3), and *reside* (page 244, paragraph 2) using root words as well as context clues.

Beginning	Intermediate	Advanced/High
Help students locate the words and roots.	Ask students to identify and define the root words.	Have students explain how they used the root to define the word.

ADDITIONAL VOCABULARY

OBJECTIVES

 Acquire and use appropriate general academic and domain-specific words and phrases, including those that signal contrast, addition, and other logical relationships. **L.5.6**

LANGUAGE OBJECTIVE

Use academic vocabulary and high-frequency words.

I Do List academic and high-frequency words from "New Arrivals Welcome" and "A Growing Problem": *native, species, familiar;* and from *The Great Plains: climate, droughts.* Define each word for students: Familiar *means "often seen or experienced."*

We Do Model using the words for students in a sentence: *I see many familiar faces at the grocery store.* Then provide sentence frames and complete them with students: *Being in a familiar place makes me feel _____.*

You Do Have pairs create their own sentences to share with the class.

Beginning	Intermediate	Advanced/High
Help students copy the sentence frames correctly.	Provide sentence starters, if necessary.	Have students define the words they used.

English Language Learners
Writing/Spelling

WRITING TRAIT: ORGANIZATION

OBJECTIVES
Write opinion pieces on topics or texts, supporting a point of view with reasons and information. **W.5.1**

LANGUAGE OBJECTIVE
Write strong conclusions.

 I Do Explain that writers end their texts with a strong conclusion. Often the conclusion restates the main idea. Read the Expert Model passage aloud as students follow along and identify the main idea restated in each conclusion.

 We Do Reread the conclusions for "New Arrivals Welcome" and "A Growing Problem." Identify the main idea that is restated in each. Use a word web to record the main ideas and how they are restated. Model another way that one main idea could be restated.

 You Do Have pairs write a new concluding paragraph, using one of the restatements in the word web.

Beginning	Intermediate	Advanced/High
Have students copy the model you provided and read it aloud.	Have students revise what they have written, making sure the main idea is clearly restated and editing for errors.	Have students revise to make their final sentence more thought-provoking.

SPELL WORDS WITH SUFFIX *-ion*

OBJECTIVES
Spell grade-appropriate words correctly, consulting references as needed. **L.5.2e**

LANGUAGE OBJECTIVE
Spell words with *-ion*.

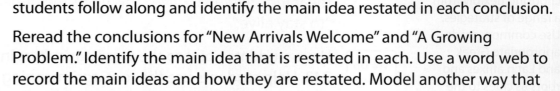 **I Do** Read aloud the Spelling Words on page T292, segmenting them into syllables and attaching a spelling to each sound. Point out the *-ion* ending and model its pronunciation in each word. Have students repeat the words.

 We Do Read the Dictation Sentences on page T293 aloud for students. With each sentence, read the underlined word slowly, segmenting it into syllables. Have students repeat after you and write the word.

 You Do Display the words. Have students exchange their list with a partner to check the spelling and write the words correctly.

Beginning	Intermediate	Advanced/High
Help students copy the words with correct spelling and say the words aloud.	After students have corrected their words, have pairs quiz each other.	After students have corrected their words, have them practice writing words that were hard for them.

Grammar

COMPARING WITH *GOOD* AND *BAD*

OBJECTIVES
Demonstrate command of the conventions of standard English grammar and usage when writing or speaking **L.5.1**

LANGUAGE OBJECTIVE
Use the comparative forms of good and bad.

Language Transfers Handbook

In Haitian Creole, Hmong, Spanish, and Vietnamese, nouns often precede adjectives. Speakers of these languages may need additional support in the correct placement of adjectives.

 Review that the adjectives *good* and *bad* have special forms that we use to compare. Write these sentences: *Jordan is a good soccer player. Darius is a better player. Lionel is the best player on the team.* Read the sentences aloud. Underline the adjective in each sentence. Point out that the second sentence compares two players and the third sentence compares all the players. Repeat for *bad, worse,* and *worst.*

 Write the sentence frames below on the board. Have students fill in the correct form of the adjective for each sentence. Have them read the sentences aloud.

> Today was _____ than yesterday. (good)
>
> That is the _____ pizza I've ever had. (good)
>
> I feel _____ today than yesterday. (bad)

 Write *bad/worse/worst* and *good/better/best.* Have students work in pairs to choose a set of adjectives and write three sentences, one for each comparative form. Have students read their sentences aloud.

Beginning	Intermediate	Advanced/High
Help students write their sentences and use the comparative forms of good or bad. Read the sentences aloud. Have students repeat.	Ask students to underline the comparative form they used in each sentence and check that they've used it correctly.	Challenge students to write sentences for both sets of comparatives.

For extra support, have students complete the activities in the **Grammar Practice Reproducibles** during the week, using the routine below:

→ Explain the grammar skill.

→ Model the first activity in the Grammar Practice Reproducibles.

→ Have the whole group complete the next couple of activities, then review the rest with a partner.

→ Review the activities with correct answers.

PROGRESS MONITORING

Weekly Assessment

CCSS TESTED SKILLS

✔ COMPREHENSION:	✔ VOCABULARY:	✔ WRITING:
Author's Point of View **RI.6.6, RI.5.8**	Root Words **L.5.4b**	Writing About Text **RI.6.6, RI.5.8, W.5.9b**

Assessment Includes

→ Performance Tasks

→ Approaching-Level Assessment online PDFs

Fluency Goal 129 to 149 words correct per minute (WCPM)

Accuracy Rate Goal 95% or higher

Administer oral reading fluency assessments using the following schedule:

→ **Weeks 1, 3, 5** Provide Approaching-Level students at least three oral reading fluency assessments during the unit.

→ **Weeks 2 and 4** Provide On-Level students at least two oral reading fluency assessments during the unit.

→ **Week 6** If necessary, provide Beyond-Level students an oral reading fluency assessment at this time.

Also Available: Selection Tests online PDFs

Go Digital! www.connected.mcgraw-hill.com

Using Assessment Results

TESTED SKILLS	If ...	Then ...
COMPREHENSION	Students answer 0–6 multiple-choice items correctly ...	... assign Lessons 61–63 on Author's Point of View from the *Tier 2 Comprehension Intervention online PDFs.*
VOCABULARY	Students answer 0–6 multiple-choice items correctly ...	... assign Lesson 157 on Greek, Latin, and Other Roots from the *Tier 2 Vocabulary Intervention online PDFs.*
WRITING	Students score less than "3" on the constructed responses ...	... assign Lessons 61–63 on Author's Point of View and/or Write About Reading Lesson 200 from the *Tier 2 Comprehension Intervention online PDFs.*
	Students have a WCPM score of 120–128 ...	... assign a lesson from Section 1, 7, 8, 9, or 10 of the *Tier 2 Fluency Intervention online PDFs.*
	Students have a WCPM score of 0–119 ...	... assign a lesson from Section 2, 3, 4, 5, or 6 of the *Tier 2 Fluency Intervention online PDFs.*

Response to Intervention

Use the appropriate sections of the *Placement and Dignostic Assessment* as well as students' assessment results to designate students requiring:

TIER 2 **Intervention Online PDFs**

TIER 3 **WonderWorks Intervention Program**

WEEKLY OVERVIEW

The Big Idea: *In what ways can things change?*

REVIEW AND EXTEND

Reader's Theater

Jane Addams and Hull House

Genre Play

Fluency Accuracy, Rate, and Prosody

Reading Digitally

TIME. "Is Anybody Out There?"

Comprehension Close Reading

Study Skills Using Online Sources

Research Navigate Links to Information

Go Digital!

Level Up Accelerating Progress

From **APPROACHING** To **ON LEVEL**	From **ON LEVEL** To **BEYOND LEVEL**	From **ENGLISH LANGUAGE LEARNERS** To **ON LEVEL**	From **BEYOND LEVEL** To **SELF-SELECTED TRADE BOOK**

Advanced Level **Trade Book**

ASSESS

Presentations

Research and Inquiry
Project Presentations
Project Rubric

Writing
Informative Writing Presentations
Writing Rubric

Digital Vision/Getty Images

Unit Assessments

McGraw-Hill Reading
Wonders

Grade 5

Unit Assessment

CCSS Assessing the Common Core State Standards

UNIT 5 TEST

McGraw-Hill Reading
Wonders

Grades 1-6

Fluency Assessment

CCSS Assessing the Common Core State Standards

FLUENCY

Evaluate Student Progress

Use the McGraw-Hill Reading Wonders eAssessment reports to evaluate student progress and help you make decisions about small group instruction and assignments.

→ Student and Class Assessment Report

→ Student and Class Standards Proficiency Report

→ Student Profile Summary Report

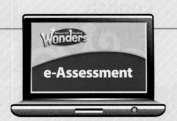

Wonders
e-Assessment

Digital Vision/Getty Images

SUGGESTED LESSON PLAN

		DAY 1	DAY 2

READING

Whole Group

Reader's Theater "Jane Addams and Hull House"

"Is Anybody Out There?"

DAY 1

Reader's Theater, T326

"Jane Addams and Hull House"

Assign Roles

Model Fluency: Accuracy, Rate, and Prosody

DAY 2

Reader's Theater, T326

"Jane Addams and Hull House"

Model Fluency: Accuracy, Rate, and Prosody

Reading Digitally, T328

TIME FOR KIDS "Is Anybody Out There?"

Research and Inquiry, T330–T331

Interviewing

Research and Inquiry Projects

DIFFERENTIATED INSTRUCTION Level Up to Accelerate

Small Group

Approaching Level

Level Up to On Level

Ocean Threats, T336

🌀 **Spiral Review** Comprehension Skills Unit 5 Revised PDFs Online ✏ *Analytical Writing*

Level Up to On Level

Ocean Threats, T336

🌀 **Spiral Review** Comprehension Skills Unit 5 Revised PDFs Online ✏ *Analytical Writing*

On Level

Level Up to Beyond Level

Ocean Threats, T337

Level Up to Beyond Level

Ocean Threats, T337

Beyond Level

Level Up to Self-Selected Trade Book, T339

Level Up to Self-Selected Trade Book, T339

English Language Learners

Level Up to On Level

Ocean Threats, T338

Level Up to On Level

Ocean Threats, T338

LANGUAGE ARTS

Writing Process

Whole Group

Writing

Share Your Writing, T334

Informative Writing

Prepare to Present Your Writing

Share Your Writing, T334

Informative Writing

Discuss Peer Feedback

DAY 3	DAY 4	DAY 5
Reading Digitally, T328 TIME "Is Anybody Out There?" *Analytical Writing*	**Reader's Theater,** T326 Performance	**Research and Inquiry,** T332–T333 Presentations ✓ **Unit Assessment,** T340–T341
Research and Inquiry Projects	**Research and Inquiry Projects** *Analytical Writing*	

Level Up to On Level *Ocean Threats,* T336 ◎ **Spiral Review** Comprehension Skills Unit 5 Revised PDFs Online *Analytical Writing*	**Level Up to On Level** "Floating Trash," T336	**Level Up to On Level** Literature Circle, T336
Level Up to Beyond Level *Ocean Threats,* T337	**Level Up to Beyond Level** "Floating Trash," T337	**Level Up to Beyond Level** Literature Circle, T337
Level Up to Self-Selected Trade Book, T339	**Level Up to Self-Selected Trade Book,** T339	**Level Up to Self-Selected Trade Book,** T339
Level Up to On Level *Ocean Threats,* T338	**Level Up to On Level** "Floating Trash," T338	**Level Up to On Level** Literature Circle, T338

Share Your Writing, T334 Informative Writing Rehearse Your Presentation	**Share Your Writing,** T334 Present Your Informational Writing Evaluate Your Presentation	**Share Your Writing,** T335 Informative Writing Portfolio Choice

Reader's Theater

JANE ADDAMS AND HULL HOUSE
by Navidad O'Neill, 1996

CAST OF CHARACTERS:
Narrator
Jane Addams
Ellen Gates Starr, her friend
George, John, Charles,
Alice, Mary and Julia,
all Hull House volunteers
Marie and Helen,
German immigrants
John and Joseph,
Italian immigrants

Jane Addams and Hull House

Go Digital!

Teacher's Resource Online PDF,
pp. 2–3, 57–64

OBJECTIVES

CCSS Read on-level text with purpose and understanding. **RF.5.4a**

CCSS Read on-level prose and poetry orally with accuracy, appropriate rate, and expression on successive readings. **RF.5.4b**

CCSS Use context to confirm or self-correct word recognition and understanding, rereading as necessary. **RF.5.4c**

Jane Addams and Hull House

Introduce the Play

Explain that *Jane Addams and Hull House* is an appropriate title for the play students will soon read. It is about how Jane Addams and her friend Ellen Starr opened Hull House, the first settlement house in the United States. Distribute the Elements of Drama handout and scripts from the **Teacher's Resource Online PDF,** pages 2–3, 57–64.

→ Review the features of a play.

→ Review the cast of characters and the background information about why Jane Addams opened Hull House. Highlight aspects of life as an immigrant in the early 1900s, including cramped living quarters, low wages, and long work hours.

→ Point out the stage directions.

Shared Reading

Model reading the play as students follow along in their scripts.

Focus on Vocabulary Stop and discuss any vocabulary words that students may not know. You may wish to teach:

→ settlement
→ ponders
→ slums
→ ought
→ embroidered

Model Fluency As you read each part, state the name of the character and read the part, emphasizing the appropriate phrasing and expression.

Discuss Each Role

→ After reading the part of the narrator, ask students to identify what information the narrator provides.

→ After reading each character part, ask partners to note the character's traits. Model how to find text evidence that tells them about the characters.

Assign Roles

Depending on the number of students, you may wish to split the class into two groups. If you need additional roles, you can assign the parts of the narrator, Jane, or Ellen to more than one student.

Practice the Play

Each day, allow students time to practice their parts in the play. Pair fluent readers with less fluent readers. Pairs can echo read or chorally read their parts. As needed, work with less fluent readers to mark pauses in their scripts using one slash for a short pause and two slashes for longer pauses.

Throughout the week, have students work on **Reader's Theater Workstation Activity Card 29.**

Once students have practiced reading their parts several times, allow students time to practice performing the script.

Perform the Reader's Theater

→ Remind students to focus on their scripts as the play is being performed and follow along, even when they are not in the scene.

→ Lead a class discussion on ways that students could make their performances more enjoyable for the audience.

ACTIVITIES

SPOTLIGHT ON SETTLEMENTS

Settlement houses were founded in many major U.S. cities in the early 1900s. These houses improved neighborhoods by providing a safe place for people to learn and play. Many of them also worked for reform.

In *Jane Addams and Hull House*, the characters focus on making improvements in their city. Discuss these questions with students:

1. What services did Hull House provide?

2. What was the purpose of the Labor Museum?

3. What other goals for the neighborhood did Jane Addams and Hull House volunteers work toward?

4. What social reforms did they hope to make?

RECORD IT!

Have students use an audio recorder to record the performance. Listen to the performance and discuss as a class how the play sounds. Ask:

1. What did you like about the performance?

2. What would you do differently next time?

3. If you could perform the play again, would you add sound effects or music? At what points in the play might you include them?

ELL ENGLISH LANGUAGE LEARNERS

→ Review the definitions of difficult words and phrases, including *inspiring*, *desperate*, *sick of*, *appreciate*, *situation*, and *admiring*.

→ Team an ELL student with a fluent reader who is also reading the part of the narrator or Jane. Have each reader take turns reading the lines. Determine which reader will read which lines at the performance.

→ Ask ELLs to read their lines to you. Give students corrective feedback and model proper fluency.

Reading Digitally

Is Anybody Out There?

Before Reading

Preview Scroll through the online article "Is Anybody Out There?" at www.connected.mcgraw-hill.com and have students identify text features. Clarify how to navigate through the article. Point out the interactive features, such as **hyperlinks**, **slide shows**, and **pop-ups**. Explain that you will read the article first and then access these features.

Close Reading Online

Take Notes Scroll back to the top. As you read the article aloud, ask questions to focus students on how the solar bodies described in the text are similar and different. Have students take notes on the similarities and differences using Graphic Organizer 67. After each section, have partners paraphrase the main ideas, giving text evidence. Review idioms, such as "easier said than done" and "is in the cards."

Access Interactive Features Help students access the interactive features by clicking or rolling over each feature. Discuss what information these elements add to the text.

Tell students they will reread parts of the article to help them answer a specific question: *How are some planets in distant galaxies similar to and different from Earth?*

Have students skim to find text detailing how Earth is alike and different from planets in other galaxies. Have partners share what they find.

Navigate Links to Information Remind students that online texts may include **hyperlinks**, colored or underlined text on a Web page that connects to another Web page with related information.

Do an online search about looking for life on other planets. Model using a hyperlink to jump to another Web page. Discuss any information on the new Web page related to the question *How do scientists search for life on other planets?* Examine the information on the Web page with students and make a list of relevant facts and evidence. Point out that students should compare information from multiple sources in order to understand the topic deeply and to develop a well-informed opinion.

WRITE ABOUT READING *Analytical Writing*

Summarize Review students' graphic organizers. Model using the information to summarize "Is Anybody Out There?"

Ask students to write a summary of the article, stating the ways that different solar bodies are similar and different. Partners should discuss their summaries.

Make Connections Have students compare what they learned about the way our understanding of space has changed with what they have learned about how things change in texts they have read in this unit.

CONNECT TO CONTENT

Astronomy

Point out that our knowledge of outer space is continually growing. Technology has helped us move beyond our own galaxy to look for other planets and, possibly, other forms of life.

Help students identify information in this article about new discoveries people have made.

→ In 1995, astronomers found the first planet orbiting a star other than the sun.

→ The HARPS device found 50 new planets in our own galaxy, the Milky Way. At least 19 of them are super-Earths!

RESEARCH ONLINE

Search Results Model conducting an Internet search using key words related to outer space. Then discuss the results page. Point out that the most relevant results are usually listed first. Demonstrate clicking on the hyperlink at the top of a result to jump to that page and then using the Back button to return to the results.

Tracking and Citing Sources Encourage students to keep a list of sites they visit while conducting research. Have them include details such as the URL, date, and information gleaned from the site. Set up a format for them to follow.

INDEPENDENT STUDY

Investigate

Choose a Topic Students should brainstorm questions related to the article. For example, they might ask: *What conditions are necessary for life on another planet?* Then have students choose a question to research. Help them narrow it.

Conduct Internet Research Review how to recognize relevant results for an Internet search. Have students keep a list of research sites and help them eliminate irrelevant ones.

Present Have groups present a round-table discussion on the topic of life on other planets.

RESEARCH AND INQUIRY

The Big Idea: *In what ways can things change?*

Assign the Projects Break students into five groups. Assign each group one of the five projects that follow or let groups self-select their project. Before students begin researching, present these minilessons.

Research Skill: Interviewing

OBJECTIVES

CCSS With some guidance and support from adults, use technology, including the Internet, to produce and publish writing as well as to interact and collaborate with others; demonstrate sufficient command of keyboarding skills to type a minimum of two pages in a single sitting. **W.5.6**

CCSS Conduct short research projects that use several sources to build knowledge through investigation of different aspects of a topic. **W.5.7**

CCSS Include multimedia components (e.g., graphics, sound) and visual displays in presentations when appropriate to enhance the development of main ideas or themes. **SL.5.5**

Conducting an Interview

→ Explain that conducting an interview requires four basic steps: scheduling the interview, preparing for the interview, interviewing the subject, and following up with the subject after the interview is over.

→ First, interviewers contact the person they plan to interview to establish the date, time, and place of the interview. They determine whether the interview will be conducted in person, over the phone, or online. An adult should help arrange the interview.

→ To prepare for the interview, have students write a set of questions. Students might list what they need to know and then write a question for each item. Students may also use the Interview Form Online PDF.

→ During the interview, remind students to take thorough notes but also engage with the subject of the interview by listening carefully and recording answers accurately. After the interview, have students follow up by thanking the subject in person as well as via letter or e-mail.

Organizing Information

Once students have gathered information, they will need to organize it. An outline is a useful strategy for organizing information and identifying places where more information is needed.

→ Have students review their notes and categorize related ideas. These categories will form the basis for the different sections of an outline.

→ Have students write a topic sentence or heading for each category.

→ Once students have categorized their notes, they can begin drafting their outlines. Outlines should begin with the introduction and end with the conclusion. The body is formed by the categories of information students previously identified.

→ Point out that the topics and subtopics in an outline do not need to be complete sentences. Model creating a brief outline for a familiar topic.

Go Digital

COLLABORATE
Post student questions and monitor student online discussions. Create a Shared Research Board.

Choose a Project!

A Multimedia Presentation

1

ESSENTIAL QUESTION
What experiences can change the way you see yourself and the world around you?

Goal
Research teams will create a multimedia presentation about how changes in photography that helped people see the world in a different way.

A Formal Presentation

2

ESSENTIAL QUESTION
How do shared experiences help people adapt to change?

Goal
Research teams will create an expanded, formal presentation that describes how musicians and other entertainers helped lift people's spirits during the Great Depression.

A Slide Show

3

ESSENTIAL QUESTION
What changes in the environment can affect living things?

Goal
Research teams will create a slide show using visuals that describes how a specific nature preserve or wildlife sanctuary protects wildlife.

STEM

A Mock Interview

4

ESSENTIAL QUESTION
How can scientific knowledge change over time?

Goal
Research teams will gather information about a scientist or doctor associated with an important medical innovation and conduct a mock interview with that person.

STEM

A Persuasive Speech

5

ESSENTIAL QUESTION
How do natural events and human activities affect the environment?

Goal
Research teams will research an invasive species that has had a negative impact and present a persuasive speech arguing for or against one strategy of managing its spread.

STEM

RESEARCH AND INQUIRY

Distribute the Research Roadmap Online PDF. Have students use the roadmap to complete the project.

Conducting the Research

STEP 1 ▸ Set Research Goals

Discuss with students the Essential Question and the research project. As appropriate, have them look at the Shared Research Board for information they have already gathered. Each group should

→ make sure they are clear on their research focus and end product.

→ evaluate library resources they are familiar with and brainstorm new resources they would like to learn more about.

STEP 2 ▸ Identify Sources

Have the group brainstorm where they can find the information they need. Sources might include

→ art museum Web sites, art and image databases, or nonfiction books about art history.

→ photographs, journals, letters, or newspaper articles.

→ social studies or science textbooks and reliable Web sites.

If students plan to conduct an online search, remind them to use key words to narrow their search results.

STEP 3 ▸ Find and Record Information

Have students review the note-taking strategies presented on page T330. Then have them do research. If students are quoting from a primary source, remind them to record the quotation accurately.

STEP 4 ▸ Organize

After team members have completed their research, they can classify and categorize their information in an outline to determine the most important ideas and clearest structure for their presentation.

STEP 5 ▸ Synthesize and Present

Have team members synthesize their research and decide on their final message.

→ Remind students to link their opinions and reasons with words, phrases, and clauses, such as *therefore* or *consequently* to make the connections between their ideas clear.

→ Students should check that their key ideas are included and their findings relate to the Big Idea.

Audience Participation

→ Encourage the audience to pose questions and elaborate on the comments of others.

→ Ask students to draw a conclusion in light of the information presented.

Review and Evaluate

Distribute the Student Checklist and Project Rubric Online PDFs. Use the Project Rubric and the Teacher Checklist below to evaluate students' research and presentations.

Student Checklist

Research Process
☑ Did you narrow your focus for your research?

☑ Did you use several sources?

☑ Did you give credit to all your sources?

Presenting
☑ Did you practice your presentation?

☑ Did you speak clearly and loud enough for others to hear?

☑ Did you make eye contact with your audience?

☑ Did you answer the Essential Question and Big Idea?

☑ Did you use appropriate visuals and technology?

Teacher Checklist

Assess the Research Process
☑ Selected a focus.

☑ Used multiple sources to gather information.

☑ Cited sources for information.

☑ Used time effectively and collaborated well.

Assess the Presentation
☑ Spoke clearly and at an appropriate pace and volume.

☑ Used appropriate gestures.

☑ Maintained eye contact.

☑ Established a main message that answered the Essential Question and Big Idea.

☑ Used appropriate visuals and technology.

☑ Shared responsibility and tasks among all group members.

Assess the Listener
☑ Listened quietly and politely.

☑ Made appropriate comments and asked clarifying questions.

☑ Responded with an open mind to different ideas.

Research and Inquiry Rubric

4 Excellent	3 Good	2 Fair	1 Unsatisfactory
The student	**The student**	**The student**	**The student**
→ presents the information clearly.	→ presents the information adequately.	→ attempts to present information.	→ may show little grasp of the task.
→ includes many details.	→ provides adequate details.	→ may offer few or vague details.	→ may present irrelevant information.
→ may include sophisticated observations.	→ includes relevant observations.	→ may include few or irrelevant personal observations.	→ may reflect extreme difficulty with research or presentation.

Celebrate Share Your Writing

Presentations

Giving Presentations

Now is the time for students to share one of the pieces of expository writing that they have worked on through the unit.

You may wish to invite parents or students from other classes to the Publishing Celebrations.

Preparing for Presentations

Tell students that they will need to prepare in order to best present their writing.

Allow students time to rehearse their presentations. Encourage them to reread their writing a few times. This will help them become more familiar with their pieces so that they won't have to read word by word as they present.

Students should consider any visuals or digital elements that they may want to use to present their informational articles and research reports. Discuss a few possible options with students.

→ Do they have photos, charts, maps, or diagrams that would support their topic?

→ Is there a video that connects to the focus of their informational writing?

→ Is there a Web site or multimedia presentation that they could use to offer additional information on their topic?

Students can practice presenting to a partner in the classroom. They can also practice with family members at home, or in front of a mirror. Share the following checklist with students to help them focus on important parts of their presentation as they rehearse. Discuss each point on the checklist.

Speaking Checklist

Review the Speaking Checklist with students as they practice.

- ☑ Have all of your notes and visuals ready.
- ☑ Take a few deep breaths.
- ☑ Stand up straight.
- ☑ Look at the audience.
- ☑ Speak clearly and slowly, particularly when communicating complex information.
- ☑ Speak loud enough so everyone can hear.
- ☑ Emphasize important points.
- ☑ Use appropriate gestures.
- ☑ Hold your visual aids so everyone can see them.
- ☑ Point to relevant features of your visual aids as you speak.

Listening to Presentations

Remind students that they will be part of the audience for other students' presentations. A listener serves an important role. Review with students the following Listening Checklist.

Listening Checklist

During the presentation

☑ Pay attention to how the speaker uses visuals to enhance his or her main ideas.

☑ Notice how the speaker uses facts and details to help develop his or her topic.

☑ Take notes on one or two things you like about the presentation.

☑ Write one question or comment you have about the information.

☑ Do not talk during the presentation.

After the presentation

☑ Tell why you liked the presentation.

☑ Ask a question or make a comment based on the information presented.

☑ Only comment on the presentation when it is your turn.

☑ If someone else makes the same comment first, elaborate on that person's comment.

Portfolio Choice

Ask students to select one finished piece of writing, as well as two revisions, to include in their writing portfolio. As students consider their choices, have them use the questions below.

Published Writing

Does your writing

→ organize information about a topic logically?

→ have a strong conclusion?

→ have few or no spelling and grammatical errors?

→ demonstrate neatness when published?

Writing Entry Revisions

Do your revisions show

→ more facts, definitions, and concrete details that develop the topic?

→ stronger openings?

→ additional time-order words, phrases, and clauses?

 Go Digital

PORTFOLIO
Students can submit their writing to be considered for inclusion in their digital Portfolio. Students' portfolios can be shared with parents.

Level Up Accelerating Progress

Leveled Reader

Approaching Level to On Level

Ocean Threats

Level Up Lessons also available online

Before Reading

Preview Discuss what students remember about algae and algal blooms. Tell them they will be reading a more challenging version of *Ocean Threats*.

Vocabulary Use the Visual Vocabulary Cards and routine to review.

A C T During Reading

▶ **Specific Vocabulary** Review with students the following content-area words that are new to this title. Model how to use word parts, context clues or the glossary to determine the meaning of *aquatic* and *fertilized*.

▶ **Connection of Ideas** Students may need help connecting and synthesizing information in longer or more complex paragraphs. For example, model paraphrasing paragraph 3 on page 8. Then have students reread the paragraph. Ask them to turn to a partner and paraphrase. Follow this procedure for other longer or more complex paragraphs, such as paragraph 1 on page 11.

▶ **Sentence Structure** Students may need help understanding the purpose of bulleted lists. Chorally read paragraph 2 on page 10. Point out that bulleted lists call attention to important points. Bullet points are not sentences. They are key points to which the author wants to call attention. Ask: *What are the three main reasons people burn fossil fuels?* (motorized transportation, factories and industry, power plants for generating electricity)

After Reading

Ask students to complete the Respond to Reading on page 18. Have students complete the Paired Read and hold Literature Circles.

On Level
to Beyond Level

Ocean Threats

Level Up Lessons also available online

Leveled Reader

OBJECTIVES

By the end of the year, read and comprehend informational texts, including history/ social studies, science, and technical texts, at the high end of the grades 4–5 complexity band independently and proficiently.
RI.5.10

Before Reading

Preview Discuss what students remember about the algae and algal blooms. Tell them they will be reading a more challenging version of *Ocean Threats*.

Vocabulary Use the Visual Vocabulary Cards and routine to review.

A C T During Reading

▶ **Specific Vocabulary** Review content-area words that are new. Model using context clues or word parts to find the meaning of *classify, consumption, macroalgae,* and *microalgae.*

▶ **Connection of Ideas** Students may need help connecting and synthesizing information from section to section. After completing Chapter 1, model stating the main ideas in a sentence or two. Then explain how the information connects to Chapter 2. Say: *In Chapter 1, we learned what algae is and what an algal bloom is. Now we're going to learn more about what causes algal blooms, including natural causes and human causes.* Have partners repeat this procedure to connect subsequent chapters.

▶ **Sentence Structure** Students may need help with more complex sentences. Read aloud the following sentence on page 8: *The ocean soaks and stores gases like a sponge, so if there is an excess of CO_2 in the atmosphere, much of it will be absorbed by the ocean.* Break it down into two sentences that show the relationship between ideas: *If there is an excess of CO_2 in the atmosphere, much of it will end up in the ocean. That's because the ocean stores gases like a sponge.* Have students read the sentence aloud.

After Reading

Ask students to complete the Respond to Reading on page 18. Have students complete the Paired Read and hold Literature Circles.

Level Up Accelerating Progress

Leveled Reader

OBJECTIVES

By the end of the year, read and comprehend informational texts, including history/ social studies, science, and technical texts, at the high end of the grades 4–5 complexity band independently and proficiently. **RI.5.10**

English Language Learners to On Level

Ocean Threats

Level Up Lessons also available online

Before Reading

Preview Remind students that informational text gives facts about a topic. Discuss with them what they remember reading about algae and algal blooms.

Vocabulary Use the Visual Vocabulary Cards and routine to review. Present cognates: *atmósfera, variaciones, estabilidad, gradual, impacto.*

(A)(C)(T) During Reading

▶ **Specific Vocabulary** Review with students figurative language that may be unfamiliar. Read aloud the first sentence in paragraph 3 on page 8: *Carbon dioxide (CO_2) is plentiful in the ocean because the ocean serves as a big "sponge" for the atmosphere.* Explain that a sponge soaks things up. Tell students that the ocean is like a sponge because it soaks up extra carbon dioxide.

▶ **Connection of Ideas** Students may need help connecting ideas from page to page and chapter to chapter. Model pointing out the key details and main ideas you identified. Then use this information to help students summarize the chapter. Have students turn to a partner and summarize each chapter in their own words.

▶ **Sentence Structure** Students may need help understanding the purpose of bulleted lists. Chorally read paragraph 2 on page 10. Explain that bullet points are key points the author wants to call attention to. Ask: *What are the three main reasons people burn fossil fuels?* (motorized transportation, factories and industry, power plants for generating electricity)

After Reading

Ask students to complete the Respond to Reading on page 19. Have students complete the Paired Read and hold Literature Circles.

Beyond Level
to Self-Selected Trade Book

Advanced Level Trade Book

Leveled Reader

OBJECTIVES

By the end of the year, read and comprehend literature, including stories, dramas, and poetry, at the high end of the grades 4–5 text complexity band independently and proficiently. **RL.5.10**

By the end of the year, read and comprehend informational texts, including history/social studies, science, and technical texts, at the high end of the grades 4–5 text complexity band independently and proficiently. **RI.5.10**

Independent Reading

Level Up Lessons also available online

Before Reading

Together with students identify the particular focus of their reading based on the text they choose. Students who have chosen the same title will work in groups to closely read the selection.

Close Reading

Taking Notes Assign a graphic organizer for students to use to take notes as they read. Reinforce a specific comprehension focus from the unit by choosing one of the graphic organizers that best fits the book.

Examples:

Fiction	**Informational Text**
Character, Setting, Plot: Compare and Contrast	Text Structure: Cause and Effect
Graphic Organizer 66	Graphic Organizer 86

Ask and Answer Questions Remind students to ask questions as they read and record them on a piece of chart paper. As students meet, have them discuss the section that they have read. They can discuss the questions they noted and work together to find text evidence to support their answers. Have them write their responses.

After Reading

Write About Reading

Have students work together to respond to the text using text evidence to support their writing.

Examples:

Fiction	**Informational Text**
How are the settings and characters alike? How are they different?	How is the text structure in this text similar to or different from the text structure in another expository text you have read?

SUMMATIVE ASSESSMENT

Unit Assessment

TESTED SKILLS

✔ **COMPREHENSION:**	✔ **VOCABULARY:**	✔ **ENGLISH LANGUAGE CONVENTIONS:**	✔ **WRITING:**
• Character, Setting, Plot: Compare and Contrast Settings **RL.5.1, RL.5.3**	• Context Clues: Comparison **L.5.4a**	• Independent and Dependent Clauses **L.3.1i, L.5.1a**	• Writing About Text **W.5.9a–b**
• Character, Setting, Plot: Compare and Contrast Characters **RL.5.3, RL.5.1**	• Idioms **L.5.5b**	• Complex Sentences **L.3.1i, L.5.1a**	• Writing Prompt: Informative **W.5.2a–e**
• Text Structure: Compare and Contrast **RI.5.3**	• Context Clues: Paragraph Clues **L.5.4a**	• Adjectives **L.4.1d, L.5.2d**	
• Text Structure: Cause and Effect **RI.5.5**	• Greek Roots **L.5.4b**	• Adjectives That Compare **L.3.1g**	
• Author's Point of View **RI.6.6, RI.5.8**	• Root Words **L.5.4b**	• Comparing with *Good* and *Bad* **L.3.1g, L.5.1**	

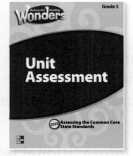

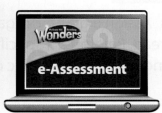

Assessment Includes
→ Performance Tasks
→ Writing Prompt

Additional Assessment Options

Conduct assessments individually using the differentiated passages in *Fluency Assessment*. Students' expected fluency goal for this Unit is **129–149 WCPM** with an accuracy rate of 95% or higher.

Running Records

Use the instructional reading level determined by the Running Record calculations for regrouping decisions. Students at Level 50 or below should be provided reteaching on specific Comprehension skills.

Using Assessment Results

✓ TESTED SKILLS	If ...	Then ...
COMPREHENSION	Students answer 0–9 multiple-choice items correctly ...	... reteach the necessary skills using Lessons 43–45, 61–63, 70–72, and 76–78 from the ***Tier 2 Comprehension Intervention online PDFs.***
VOCABULARY	Students answer 0–7 multiple-choice items correctly ...	... reteach the necessary skills using Lessons 141, 142, 157, and 166 from the ***Tier 2 Vocabulary Intervention online PDFs.***
ENGLISH LANGUAGE CONVENTIONS	Students answer 0–7 multiple-choice items correctly ...	... reteach the necessary skills using Lessons 33–35, 49, and 51 from the ***Tier 2 Writing and Grammar Intervention online PDFs.***
WRITING	Students score less than "2" on short-response items and "3" on extended constructed response items ...	... reteach tested skills using appropriate lessons from the Strategies and Skills and/or Write About Reading sections in the ***Tier 2 Comprehension Intervention online PDFs.***
	Students score less than "3" on the writing prompt ...	... reteach the necessary skills using the ***Tier 2 Writing and Grammar Intervention online PDFs.***
FLUENCY	Students have a WCPM score of 0–128 ...	... reteach tested skills using the ***Tier 2 Fluency Intervention online PDFs.***

Response to Intervention

Use the appropriate sections of the ***Placement and Dignostic Assessment*** as well as students' assessment results to designate students requiring:

 Intervention Online PDFs

 WonderWorks Intervention Program

Reevaluate Student Grouping

View the ***McGraw-Hill Reading Wonders eAssessment Class Unit Assessment*** reports available for this Unit Assessment. Note students who are below the overall proficiency level for the assessment, and use the reports to assign small group instruction for students with similar needs.

Genre Writing

 # Reading Extended Complex Text

Program Information

For Additional Resources

Review Comprehension Lessons

Unit Bibliography

Word Lists

Literature and Informational Text Charts

Web Sites

Resources

www.connected.mcgraw-hill.com

INFORMATIVE TEXT Informational Article

EXPERT MODEL

Read Like a Writer

Point out that people read articles in newspapers and magazines to learn information about a current topic. An informational article is a type of explanatory writing that provides facts about a topic. Discuss articles students have read recently, including the topic and the source of the article. Explain that some informational articles explain a topic using a comparison and contrast structure.

Provide copies of Expert Model Online PDF 81 and Features of an Informational Article Online PDF 82 in Writer's Workspace.

Go Digital

Writer's Workspace

Features of an Informational Article

→ It shares information about a current topic, such as a scientific advancement or a new law.

→ It has a lead that grabs readers' attention.

→ It includes facts, definitions, quotations, and details to support and develop ideas.

→ It groups related facts, definitions, and details into paragraphs.

→ It uses linking words to connect ideas.

→ It has a conclusion that gives readers something to think about.

Discuss the Expert Model

Use the questions below to prompt discussion of the features of an informational article.

→ What is the topic of this informational article? (It informs readers about the progress that has been made in communication in America.)

→ How does the lead grab readers' attention? (The writer asks an engaging question that readers can relate to.)

→ How does the writer organize the information? (Each paragraph adds another improvement made to communication and gives facts, details, and other information about the improvement.)

→ Give examples of linking words used to connect ideas. (*for example; however; but*)

→ What does the writer leave readers to think about? (The possibilities of what is to come in the field of communications are endless. The only thing we know for sure is it will continue to change.)

EXPERT MODEL

OBJECTIVES

CCSS Write informative/explanatory texts to examine a topic and convey ideas and information clearly. Introduce a topic clearly, provide a general observation and focus, and group related information logically; include formatting (e.g., headings), illustrations, and multimedia when useful to aiding comprehension. **W.5.2a**

ACADEMIC LANGUAGE

• *informational article, prewrite, purpose, audience, logical order*

• Cognate: *orden lógico*

PREWRITE

Discuss and Plan

Purpose Discuss the purpose for writing an informational article: to share information about a topic that may be new to readers. Explain that students will write an article that compares and contrasts two people, places, items, events, or ideas.

Audience Encourage students to think about who will read their articles: members, community, or classmates. Ask: *What do you want your readers to know?*

Teach the Minilesson

Logical Order Discuss with students that informational articles group related information into paragraphs. There are many ways to organize a compare-and-contrast article. Writers may use a paragraph or two to explain similarities, and another paragraph or two to show differences. Writers may use each paragraph to discuss the similarities and differences about one particular aspect of their topic. When comparing the past with the present, writers may use paragraphs to compare and contrast key changes over time.

In any chosen organizational structure, an informational article always begins with a lead, or introduction, that states the topic in a clear and interesting way. It always ends with a conclusion, which wraps up ideas and leaves readers with a final thought.

Distribute copies of the Model Graphic Organizer Online PDF 83 in Writer's Workspace. Point out that the writer lists similarities and differences between communication in the past and the present.

ENGLISH LANGUAGE LEARNERS

Beginning

Demonstrate Comprehension Have students draw what they will compare and contrast. Give sentence frames to help them explain the pictures.

Intermediate

Explain Guide students to list words related to *comparison* (*same, alike, common*) and *contrast* (*different, difference, unlike*).

Advanced/High

Expand Show a postal letter and an e-mail. Have students describe how the two are alike and different.

MODEL GRAPHIC ORGANIZER

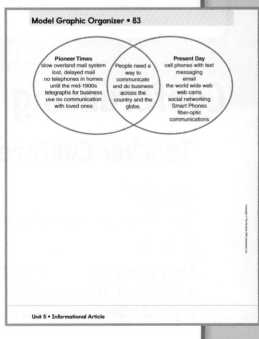

Model Graphic Organizer • 83

Pioneer Times slow overland mail system lost, delayed mail no telephones in homes until the mid-1900s telegraphs for business use no communication with loved ones

People need a way to communicate and do business across the country and the globe.

Present Day cell phones with text messaging email the world wide web web cams social networking Smart Phones fiber-optic communications

Unit 5 • Informational Article

Your Turn

Choose Your Topic Have students work with partners or in small groups to brainstorm topics for their informational articles. Remind them to consider what similarities and differences make their topic interesting. Have students record their topics in their Writer's Notebooks.

→ What current topic would you like to compare and contrast?

→ What are the similarities? What are the differences?

→ How will you organize your facts and details?

Plan Provide students with copies of the blank Graphic Organizer Online PDF 84 in the Writer's Workspace. Ask students to use it to organize the information they use to write their compare and contrast articles.

INFORMATIVE TEXT Informational Article

DRAFT

OBJECTIVES

CCSS Develop the topic with facts, definitions, concrete details, quotations, or other information and examples related to the topic. **W.5.2b**

CCSS Link ideas within and across categories of information using words, phrases, and clauses (e.g., *in contrast, especially*). **W.5.2c**

ACADEMIC LANGUAGE

• *draft, develop, topic, revise, transitions*

• Cognates: *revisar, transiciones*

Discuss the Student Draft Model

Provide copies of the Student Draft Model Online PDF 85 in Writer's Workspace. Read the draft and have students identify the features of an informational article.

Teach the Minilesson

Develop the Topic Explain that writers use paragraphs to develop their topics. Each paragraph has a main idea, stated in the form of a topic sentence. Supporting sentences explain the main idea with facts, concrete details, examples, and quotations from reliable sources, such as books or experts.

Writers also use precise language and specific vocabulary related to their topic. They may include definitions of specific terms that may be unfamiliar to readers.

Point out paragraph two in the Student Model. Ask students to find a specific word that the writer defined for readers. Explain that the writer included the word *fluency* to help readers understand the common goal of both French and Spanish classes.

Your Turn

Write a Draft Have students review the graphic organizer they prepared in Prewrite. Remind them to develop their topics as they draft.

Conferencing Routines

Teacher Conferences

STEP 1

Talk about the strengths of the writing.

Every paragraph has a topic sentence, so your article's organization is easy to follow.

STEP 2

Focus on how the writer uses a writing trait.

Your use of transitional words and phrases helps to show the compare/contrast relationship between ideas.

STEP 3

Make concrete suggestions for revision.

Your lead could do a bit more to grab readers' attention. Consider posing a thought-provoking question.

REVISE

Discuss the Revised Student Model

Distribute copies of the Revised Student Model Online PDF 86 in Writer's Workspace. Read the model aloud. Show how the writer expanded, combined, and rearranged sentences to make the writing clearer.

Teach the Minilesson

Transitions Writers use transitional words, phrases, and clauses to help readers understand how ideas are related. Some transitions signal a comparison, such as *similarly*, *also*, or *in the same way*. Other transitions signal a contrast, such as *however*, *in contrast*, *instead*, *on the other hand*, *rather*, *yet*, and *but*. Other transitions signal an example that explains an idea (*for example*, *especially*).

Have students identify a transition the writer added to the Revised Student Model. Discuss how this revision helps make the relationship between the two ideas clearer.

Your Turn

COLLABORATE

Revise Have students use the peer review routine and questions to review their partner's drafts. Then have students select suggestions from the peer review to incorporate into their revisions. Provide the Revise and Edit Checklist Online PDF 88 in Writer's Workspace to guide them. Have them look for opportunities to add transitions that clarify their ideas. Circulate as students work and conference as needed.

REVISED STUDENT MODEL

Revised Student Model • Informational Article • 86

A New Language
by Keiko S.

Learning a second language has become more important than ever before. Speaking a foreign language lets us comunicate with people we may not otherwise be able to. It helps us learn about other cultures and people from other countries. It might even help us get into college or get a job later in life. In our school, sixth graders must choose to attend either French class or Spanish class. While the two are different, there are also similarities.

No matter which language students choose, they attend foreign language classes three times a week. In both French class and Spanish class, a teacher helps them learn new vocabulary and the grammar rules for that language. The hope is that by the time they graduate high school students will be able to speak the language with some fluency, which means smoothly without stumbling too much. In both classes, students practice reading, writing, listening to, and speaking the language. Teachers agree that speaking is the most difficult of these is speaking? The brain must be able to process language pretty quickly when speaking.

While the classes are similar, the languages are different. French is the language of France. It is also an official language in Belgium, Canada, Haiti, Luxembourg, Switzerland, and many African countries. It is even the official language of the United nations. French is so widely spoken that it and English are the only two global languages.

Unit 5 • Informational Article

Peer Conferences

Review with students the routine for peer review of writing. They should listen carefully as the writer reads his or her work aloud. Begin by telling what they liked about the writing. Then ask a question that will help the writer think more about the writing. Finally, make a suggestion that will make the writing stronger.

Use these questions for peer review:

☑ Does the article examine a topic and explain ideas and information clearly?

☑ Does every paragraph have a topic sentence?

☑ Are transitions used to connect ideas?

☑ Is there a concluding statement related to the information presented?

INFORMATIVE TEXT Informational Article

PROOFREAD/EDIT AND PUBLISH

OBJECTIVES

CCSS Produce clear and coherent writing in which the development and organization are appropriate to task, purpose, and audience. **W.5.4**

CCSS With guidance and support from peers and adults, develop and strengthen writing as needed by planning, revising, editing, rewriting, or trying a new approach. **W.5.5**

ACADEMIC LANGUAGE

- *proofread, edit, publish, present, rubric*
- Cognates: *publicar, presentar*

EDITED STUDENT MODEL

Edited Student Model • Informational Article • 87

A New Language
by Keiko S.

Learning a second language has become more important than ever before. **communicate**
Speaking a foreign language lets us communicate with people we may not otherwise be able to. It helps us learn about other cultures and people from other countries. It might even help us get into college or get a job later in life. In our school, sixth graders must choose to attend either French class or Spanish class. While the two are different, there are also similarities.

No matter which language students choose, they attend foreign language classes three times a week. In both French class and Spanish class, a teacher helps them learn new vocabulary and the grammar rules for that language. The hope is that by the time they graduate high school, students will be able to speak the language with some fluency, which means smoothly without stumbling too much. In both classes, students practice reading, writing, listening to, and speaking the language. Teachers agree that speaking is the most difficult of these is speaking? The brain must be able to process language pretty quickly when speaking.

While the classes are similar, the languages are different. French is the language of France. It is also an official language in Belgium, Canada, Haiti, Luxembourg, Switzerland, and many African countries. It is even the official language of the United nations. French is so widely spoken that it and English are the only two global languages.

Unit 5 • Informational Article

Discuss the Edited Student Model

Provide copies of the Edited Student Model Online PDF 87 in Writer's Workspace. Read the model aloud and have students note the edits that Keiko made. Use the specific changes to show how editing for grammar, spelling, punctuation, and capitalization improve the informational article.

Your Turn

Edit Have students use the questions from the Revise and Edit Checklist Online PDF 88 in Writer's Workspace to guide them as they review and edit their drafts independently. Remind them to read for one type of error at a time.

Publish

For the final presentation of their informational articles, have students choose a format for publishing. Students may want to consider:

Print Publishing	Digital Publishing
Class Bulletin Board Display	Writer's Workspace
School Newspaper Article	Class Blog
Collaborative Class Magazine	Class Wiki

Remind students to format their final drafts using standard margins and formatting so their readers can follow their article easily. They may wish to include headings to divide their article into sections, or add illustrations, videos, or audio to help explain a key point. Encourage students to practice their keyboarding skills by typing their final draft in a single sitting.

Go Digital

Writer's Workspace

EVALUATE

Discuss Rubrics

Guide students as they use the Informational Article Rubric Online PDF 89 in Writer's Workspace. Explain that students can improve their writing by using rubrics to identify areas that might need further work. Review the bulleted points on the rubric with the class.

→ **Focus and Coherence** Does the article share information about a topic? Is the writing clear and interesting?

→ **Organization** Are ideas organized in a way that makes sense to readers? Does it have a clear lead and strong conclusion?

→ **Ideas and Support** Is the topic developed with related information, such as facts, details, examples, and definitions?

→ **Word Choice** Does the writer use precise language and vocabulary that relates to the topic? Do transitions connect ideas?

→ **Voice/Sentence Fluency** Does the writer show awareness of readers and a sense of purpose throughout? Does the article include sentences in which ideas flow smoothly?

→ **Conventions** Is the article free or almost free of errors?

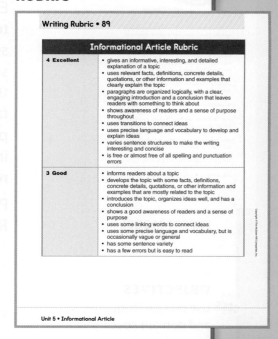

INFORMATIONAL ARTICLE RUBRIC

Your Turn

Reflect and Set Goals After students have evaluated their informational article, tell them to reflect on their progress as writers. Encourage them to consider areas where they have shown improvement, and to identify what areas need further improvement. Have them set writing goals to prepare for their conference with the teacher.

Conference with Students

Use the Informational Article Rubric Online PDF 89 and the Anchor Papers Online PDF 90 in Writer's Workspace as you evaluate student writing. The anchor papers provide samples of papers that score from 1 to 4. These papers reflect the criteria described in the rubric. Anchor papers offer a standard against which to judge writing.

Review with individual students the writing goals they have set. Discuss ways to achieve these goals and suggest any further areas of improvement students may need to target.

INFORMATIVE TEXT Research Report

EXPERT MODEL

The Kepler Mission
by Ramón S.

Scientists have theorized for years that there are other Earth-like planets orbiting stars like the sun in other solar systems of our galaxy. Until recently, the have not had a way to test these theories. Then, in May 2009, the Kepler telescope began making observations. NASA's Kepler Mission is beginning to unearth some answers. The Kepler Mission is expected to last 3½ years, but it could go on longer if necessary. It is named for Johannes Kepler, the German astronomer who discovered the laws of planetary motion. Kepler is a project under NASA's Discovery Program.

Kepler is a space-based telescope that is specifically designed to search for other Earth-like planets. Kepler's main goal is to find small, rocky planets that orbit a sun's habitable zone. The habitable zone is the place where liquid water can exist. Many scientists believe that water is essential for life.

Kepler observes many stars simultaneously to check for small changes in brightness that may indicate a passing planet. This is called a transit. During a transit, the planet blocks the star's light from reaching Earth. Kepler is searching for transits that occur at regular intervals, such as every few days, or every few years. To increase the likelihood of finding planets, Kepler continuously observes nearly 100,000 stars.

Unit 5 • Research Report

EXPERT MODEL

OBJECTIVES

CCSS Use precise language and domain-specific vocabulary to inform about or explain the topic. **W.5.2d**

CCSS Recall relevant information from experiences or gather relevant information from print and digital sources; summarize or paraphrase information in notes and finished work, and provide a list of sources. **W.5.8**

ACADEMIC LANGUAGE

- *research report, prewrite, purpose, audience, relevant information*
- Cognate: *información*

Read Like a Writer

Explain that research reports share information about a topic. Writers gather the information from reliable sources, such as encyclopedias, Web sites and other electronic sources, interviews, books, and periodicals. The writer then summarizes the information and groups related facts, definitions, quotations, and details into supporting paragraphs. Discuss with students that research reports often include content words that may have special meanings in relation to the topic.

Provide copies of the Expert Model and the Features of a Research Report Online PDFs 91–92 in Writer's Workspace.

Features of a Research Report

→ It provides information focused on a central topic.

→ It has an introduction that presents the main ideas of that topic.

→ It groups related facts, definitions, quotations, details, and other information into supporting paragraphs.

→ It uses content words and has a formal tone.

→ It uses linking words to connect ideas.

→ It provides a conclusion that relates to the topic.

Discuss the Expert Model

Use the questions below to prompt discussion of the features of a research report.

→ What central topic is the focus of the research report? (NASA's Kepler Mission)

→ What does the introduction tell the reader? (The Kepler Mission has begun to uncover answers about other Earth-like planets.)

→ What sources does the writer use in the research report? (NASA and an online encyclopedia)

→ Give examples of content words the writer uses. (*solar system, galaxy, telescope, habitable zone, astronomer, planetary motion, NASA, transit, Jupiter, orbit, structure, diversity*)

→ How does the conclusion relate to the topic? (It discusses the impact the mission will have on understanding planetary systems.)

Writer's Workspace

PREWRITE

Discuss and Plan

Purpose Explain that the students' purpose in writing a research report is to inform readers about a particular topic. This requires research. It is a good idea to consider a topic that will be interesting and engaging.

Audience Encourage students to think about who will read their reports: teachers, classmates, or family members. Have them consider what their audience may already know and what they may want to learn about the topic. Ask: *What information do you want your readers to have?*

Teach the Minilesson

Relevant Information In a research report, the writer develops the topic with relevant information, facts, and details. This information should come from at least three reputable print and digital sources, including interviews and electronic resources. Explain that writers may often take more notes than they ultimately use in their reports. They should always look for the most relevant, or related, information they can find. If writers choose to use the exact words from a source, they must use quotation marks in their report. If they summarize information, they must be careful to use their own words. All sources referenced in the report must be cited in a bibliography at the end of the report.

Distribute copies of the Model Graphic Organizer Online PDF 93 in Writer's Workspace. Point out that the middle circle contains the report's topic, while the four remaining circles each contain relevant information in the form of a supporting fact or detail.

Your Turn

Choose Your Topic Have students work with partners or in small groups to brainstorm topics for their research reports.

→ What topic interests you? What question would you like to answer about this topic?

→ Where can you find relevant information on this topic?

Have students record their topics in their Writer's Notebooks.

Plan Provide students with copies of the blank Graphic Organizer Online PDF 94 in Writer's Workspace. Ask students to use the organizer to plan their report and organize their notes.

ENGLISH LANGUAGE LEARNERS

Beginning

Demonstrate Comprehension Ask students to create a list of 3 topics that interest them. Have them finish this stem: *I like this topic because ___.*

Intermediate

Explain Have students ask questions to narrow topic choices. For example: *Which topic would have the most information available?*

Advanced/High

Expand Suggest that students skim one or two sources for each possible topic and select a topic with the most support.

MODEL GRAPHIC ORGANIZER

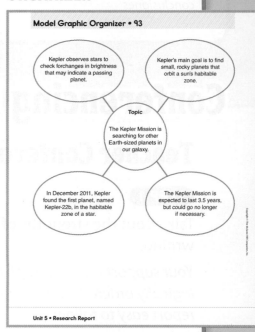

Model Graphic Organizer • 93

Kepler observes stars to check for changes in brightness that may indicate a passing planet.

Kepler's main goal is to find small, rocky planets that orbit a sun's habitable zone.

Topic

The Kepler Mission is searching for other Earth-sized planets in our galaxy.

In December 2011, Kepler found the first planet, named Kepler-22b, in the habitable zone of a star.

The Kepler Mission is expected to last 3.5 years, but could go no longer if necessary.

Unit 5 • Research Report

INFORMATIVE TEXT Research Report

DRAFT

Discuss the Student Draft Model

Review the features of a research report. Provide copies of the Student Draft Model Online PDF 95 in Writer's Workspace. Read the draft and have students identify the features of a research report.

Teach the Minilesson

Logical Order Explain that a successful research report has a clear structure. It begins with an introduction that states the topic and the purpose of the report. Body paragraphs provide information about the topic. Each body paragraph focuses on one main idea that is explained with facts and details. Writers will either summarize these facts and details in their own words, or use a quotation to show that the exact words have come from the source. Writers may include headings to help organize their report into logical sections. Sometimes writers find that using a chart, map, table, or graph is the most logical way to present certain facts and make the topic easier for readers to understand.

Your Turn

Write a Draft Have students review the graphic organizer they prepared in Prewrite. Remind them to group related facts, details, examples, or quotations into paragraphs that support the topic.

Go Digital

Writer's Workspace

Conferencing Routines

Teacher Conferences

STEP 1

Talk about the strengths of the writing.

Your supporting paragraphs are logically ordered, making your report easy to follow.

STEP 2

Focus on how the writer uses a writing trait.

Your conclusion does a good job of summarizing the main points of your report.

STEP 3

Make concrete suggestions for revision.

When using formal tone, try to avoid using contractions.

REVISE

Discuss the Revised Student Model

Distribute copies of the Revised Student Model Online PDF 96 in Writer's Workspace. Read the model aloud and have students note the revisions that Annie made. Use the specific revisions to show how she checked her draft for relevant information and logical order.

Teach the Minilesson

Strong Conclusions Explain that a research report must have a strong concluding section or statement that is related to the information presented. A conclusion usually restates the main idea and summarizes the writer's key points. Writers often provide a sense of closure by leaving readers with something to think about after they have finished reading.

Have students look at the conclusion in the Revised Student Model. Discuss how the writer improved the conclusion by restating the main idea in the concluding sentence.

Your Turn

Revise Have students use the peer review routine and questions to review their partner's drafts. Have students select suggestions from the peer review to incorporate into their revisions. Provide the Revise and Edit Checklist Online PDF 98 in Writer's Workspace to guide them. Have them look carefully for a strong conclusion. Circulate and conference as needed.

REVISED STUDENT MODEL

Revised Student Model • Research Report • 96

To the Moon
by Annie R.

NASA's Apollo program ran from 1968 to 1972. It's goal was to land humans on the moon and return them safely to Earth. There were 13 Apollo missions in all. Six of them— Apollos 11, 12, 14, 15, 16, and 17—landed astronauts on the moon. The Apollo astronauts tested new spacecraft and traveled to unexplored territories.

U.S. President John F. Kennedy was happy *enthusiastic* about space exploration. Kennedy once said, "We choose to go to the moon in this decade and do other things, not because they are easy, but because they are hard." The first space flights to carry human beings occurred while he was in office.

All thirteen Apollo missions returned with gooder information about the moon than could be expected. Astronauts studied soil, meteoroids, heat flow, solar wind, and other aspects of life in outer space. They took pictures, collected rock samples, and did *performed* experiments on the moons surface.

Apollo 11 was the first mission to land a human being on the moon. On July 16, 1969 astronauts Michael Collins, Edwin (Buzz) Aldrin, Jr. and Neil Armstrong blasted off into space. *Four days later on July 20,* Armstrong and Aldrin successfully landed on the moon, in a large flat area called the Sea of Tranquility. It was there that Neil Armstrong uttered his famous phrase, "That's one small

Unit 5 • Research Report

Peer Conferences

Review with students the routine for peer review of writing. They should listen carefully as the writer reads his or her work aloud. Begin by telling what they liked about the writing. Then ask a question that will help the writer think more about the writing. Finally, make a suggestion that will make the writing stronger.

Use these questions for peer review:

- ☑ Does the introduction clearly state the topic and main idea?
- ☑ Does the writer develop the topic with relevant information?
- ☑ Is the information ordered logically?
- ☑ Is there a strong conclusion?

INFORMATIVE TEXT Research Report

PROOFREAD/EDIT AND PUBLISH

EDITED STUDENT MODEL

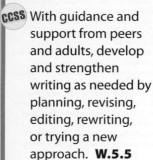

Discuss the Edited Student Model

Provide copies of the Edited Student Model Online PDF 97 in Writer's Workspace. Read the model aloud and have students note the changes that Annie made. Use the specific edits to show how editing for spelling, verb tenses, and punctuation improves the research report.

Your Turn

Edit Have students use the questions from the Revise and Edit Checklist to guide them as they review and edit their drafts independently. Remind them to read for one type of error at a time.

Publish

Before publishing, each student should create a one-page bibliography for his or her research report. Explain that a bibliography is a list of sources the author has used to research and write a report. Have students look at the Edited Student Model to see how to format a bibliography, and share the formats for commonly used sources below:

→ Books: Author (last name, first name). <u>Title</u>. Publisher, date.

→ Articles: Author (last name, first name). "Article title." Newspaper or magazine title and date: issue.

→ Online articles: Author (last name, first name). "Article title." Web site name. Date. <URL>.

For the final presentations of their research reports, have students choose a format for publishing. Students may want to consider:

Print Publishing	Digital Publishing
Personal Book	Writer's Workspace
School-Wide Information Fair	Class Blog
Collaborative Class Encyclopedia	Podcast

Remind students to format their final drafts using standard margins and formatting so their readers can follow their reports easily.

Go Digital

Writer's Workspace

EVALUATE

Discuss Rubrics

Distribute copies of the Research Report Rubric Online PDF 99 in Writer's Workspace. Explain that students can improve their writing by using rubrics to identify areas that might need further work. Work with the class to review the bulleted points on the rubric.

→ **Focus and Coherence** Does the research report provide information focused on a central topic?

→ **Organization** Is it well structured, with a strong introduction and a conclusion that sums up ideas?

→ **Ideas and Support** Does the research report use reliable sources and have interesting, relevant facts?

→ **Word Choice** Does the writer use linking words and vivid vocabulary?

→ **Voice/Sentence Fluency** Does the research report include sentences that flow and hold the reader's interest?

→ **Conventions** Is the report free or almost free of errors?

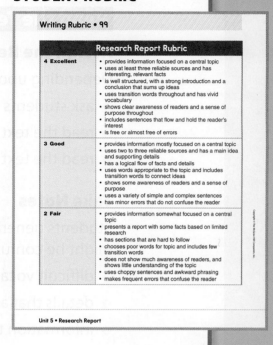

Your Turn

Reflect and Set Goals After students have evaluated their research reports, tell them to reflect on their progress as writers. Encourage them to consider areas where they feel they have shown improvement, and to identify what areas need further improvement. Have them set writing goals to prepare for their conference with the teacher.

Conference with Students

Use the Research Report Rubric and the Anchor Papers Online PDFs 99–100 in Writer's Workspace as you evaluate student writing. The anchor papers provide samples of papers that score from 1 to 4. These papers reflect the criteria described in the rubric. Anchor papers offer a standard against which to judge writing.

Review with individual students the writing goals they have set. Discuss ways to achieve these goals and suggest any further areas of improvement students may need to target.

Read the Text *What does the author tell us?*

Assign the Reading

Depending upon the needs of your students, you can

→ ask students to read the text silently.

→ read the text together with students.

→ read the text aloud.

Take Notes

Students generate questions and take notes about aspects of the text that might be confusing for them. Encourage students to note

→ difficult vocabulary words or phrases.

→ details that are not clear.

→ information that they do not understand.

Students complete a graphic organizer to take notes on important information from the text.

Reread the Text *What does the text mean?*

Ask Text Dependent Questions/Generate Questions

Students reread and discuss and take notes on important shorter passages from the text. Students should

→ generate questions about the text.

→ work with partners or small groups to answer questions using text evidence.

Write About the Text *Think about what the author wrote.*

Students write a response to the text, using evidence from the text to support their ideas or arguments.

Use the Literature Anthology

Getting Ready

Close Reading of *Global Warming*, pages 384–397

Suggested Pacing

Days 1–3	Read
	pp. 384–388
	pp. 389–393
	pp. 394–397
Days 4–8	**Reread**
	pp. 384–387
	pp. 388–389
	pp. 390–393
	pp. 394–395
	pp. 396–397
Days 9–10	**Write About Text**

Use the suggestions in the chart to assign reading of the text and to chunk the text into shorter passages for rereading.

ESSENTIAL QUESTION *What changes in the environment affect living things?*

Ask students to discuss what changes in the environment affect living things.

COLLABORATE

Read the Text *What does the author tell us?*

Assign the Reading

Ask students to read the text independently. You may want to read together with students pages 386–389 due to difficult vocabulary used in the text.

Take Notes

As students read, ask them to generate questions and other notes on features they find difficult to understand. For this selection, students may note:

→ the author's use of text features, such as questions

→ details and information they do not understand

→ words they do not know

Model for students how to take notes.

Think Aloud The last paragraph on page 385 is a series of questions. I wonder why the author did that. Will the author answer those questions, or am I supposed to answer them?

p. 385
Why is the last paragraph a series of questions?

READING Extended Complex Text

Use the Literature Anthology

Assign **Graphic Organizer 67** to help students take notes on how the author compares and contrasts information.

 As students share their questions and notes, use the Access Complex Text suggestions on pages T153A–T153N to help address features about the text that students found difficult.

Reread the Text   *How does the author tell us?*

Ask Text Dependent Questions/Generate Questions

Ask students to reread the shorter passages from the text, focusing on how the author provides information about global warming. Ask questions about

→ **Text Structure, pages 384–387, 390–393, 395–397**

→ How does the author organize information?

→ **Word Choice, pages 384–387, 390–393**

→ How does the author's word choice affect the meaning of the text?

→ **Text Features, pages 390–393**

→ How is information provided in the photographs?

→ How do the photographs support the text?

→ **Compare and Contrast, pages 388–394**

→ What things does the author compare and contrast?

→ How does the compare and contrast organization help you understand our changing climate?

Use the prompts on Teacher Edition pages T153A–T153N for suggested text dependent questions. Remind students that they are to look back into the text to cite evidence to support their answers.

Model citing text evidence as needed.

Alaska has glaciers and its mountains are covered in snow. How have these things changed in the past few decades?

Think Aloud On page 390, the text says almost all of the glaciers in Alaska are receding. I'm not sure what this means. When I read further, the text tells me that rivers of ice covered the land a few decades ago. Now much of the rock and soil are exposed. This evidence tells me that the snow and ice in Alaska have melted in the past few decades and the glaciers are disappearing.

As they reread each section, students should continue to generate their own questions about the text. As each student shares a question, ask all students to go back into the text to find text evidence to answer the question. Encourage students to

→ point out the exact place within the text they found the evidence.

→ reread and paraphrase the section of the text that they think supports their answer.

→ discuss how strong the evidence cited is in answering the question.

→ identify when an answer to a question cannot be found in the text.

Write About the Text   *Think about what the author wrote.*

Essential Question

Have students respond in writing to the Essential Question using evidence from the text.

What changes in the environment affect living things?

Students should use their notes and graphic organizers to cite evidence from the text to support their answer.

Model how to use notes to respond to the Essential Question:

Think Aloud I read through all the notes I took while reading to find text evidence that can help me answer the question. My notes from page 393 say rising temperatures might kill coral reefs, which would wipe out many aquatic animals. This is an example of a change in the environment that affects living things. I can use that information to support my answer. Then I will read through the rest of my notes to find additional text evidence that I can use.

Students can work with a partner and use their notes and graphic organizer to locate evidence that can be used to answer the question. Encourage students to discuss the strength of the evidence cited and give arguments about what may be strong or weak about a particular citation.

Use Your Own Text

Classroom Library

Classroom Library lessons available online.

or Choose from your own **Trade Books**

The Penderwicks: A Summer Tale of Four Sisters, Two Rabbits, and a Very Interesting Boy
Genre Fantasy

Lexile 800
TextEvaluator™ 42

Volcano: The Eruption and Healing of Mount St. Helens
Genre Expository Text

Lexile 830
TextEvaluator™ 31

Ida B...and her Plans to Maximize Fun, Avoid Disaster, and (Possibly) Save the World
Genre Historical Fiction

Lexile 970
TextEvaluator™ 49

Arctic Lights, Arctic Nights
Genre Expository Text

Lexile 890
TextEvaluator™ 36

→ Use this model with a text of your choice. Go online for title specific classroom library book lessons.

→ Assign reading of the text. You may wish to do this by section or chapters.

→ Chunk the text into shorter important passages for rereading.

→ Present an Essential Question. You may want to use the Unit Big Idea.

Read the Text *What does the author tell us?*

Assign the Reading

Ask students to read the assigned sections of the text independently. For sections that are more difficult for students, you may wish to read the text aloud or ask students to read with a partner.

Take Notes

As students read, ask them to take notes on difficult parts of the text. Model how to take notes on

→ identifying details or parts that are unclear.

→ words they do not know.

→ information they feel is important.

→ ways in which information or events are connected.

→ the genre of the text.

You may wish to have students complete a graphic organizer, chosen from within the unit, to take notes on important information as they read. The graphic organizer can help them summarize the text.

Help students access the complex text features of the text. Scaffold instruction on the following features as necessary:

- → Purpose
- → Genre
- → Specific Vocabulary
- → Sentence Structure
- → Connection of Ideas
- → Organization
- → Prior Knowledge

Reread the Text   *How does the author tell us?*

Ask Text Dependent Questions/Generate Questions

 Ask students to reread the shorter passages from the text, focusing on how the author provides information or develops the characters, setting, and plot. Focus questions on the following:

Literature Selections	**Informational Text**
Character, Setting, and Plot Development	Main Idea and Supporting Key Details
Word Choice	Word Choice
Genre	Text Structure
Point of View	Text Features
	Genre
	Author's Point of View

Have students discuss questions they generated. As each student shares a question, ask all students to go back into the text to find text evidence to answer the question. Encourage students to

- → point out the exact place within the text they found the evidence.
- → reread and paraphrase the section of the text that they think supports their answer.
- → discuss how strong the evidence cited is in answering the question.
- → identify when an answer to a question cannot be found in the text.

Write About the Text   *Think about what the author wrote.*

Essential Question

Have students respond in writing to the Essential Question, considering the complete text. Students can work with a partner and use their notes and graphic organizer to locate evidence that can be used to answer the question.

 SCOPE & SEQUENCE

	K	1	2	3	4	5	6
READING PROCESS							
Concepts About Print/Print Awareness							
Recognize own name							
Understand directionality (top to bottom; tracking print from left to right; return sweep, page by page)	✔						
Locate printed word on page	✔						
Develop print awareness (concept of letter, word, sentence)	✔						
Identify separate sounds in a spoken sentence	✔						
Understand that written words are represented in written language by a specific sequence of letters	✔						
Distinguish between letters, words, and sentences	✔						
Identify and distinguish paragraphs							
Match print to speech (one-to-one correspondence)	✔						
Name uppercase and lowercase letters	✔						
Understand book handling (holding a book right-side-up, turning its pages)	✔						
Identify parts of a book (front cover, back cover, title page, table of contents); recognize that parts of a book contain information	✔						
Phonological Awareness							
Recognize and understand alliteration							
Segment sentences into correct number of words							
Identify, blend, segment syllables in words		✔					
Recognize and generate rhyming words	✔	✔					
Identify, blend, segment onset and rime	✔	✔					
Phonemic Awareness							
Count phonemes	✔	✔					
Isolate initial, medial, and final sounds	✔	✔					
Blend spoken phonemes to form words	✔	✔					
Segment spoken words into phonemes	✔	✔					
Distinguish between long- and short-vowel sounds	✔	✔					
Manipulate phonemes (addition, deletion, substitution)	✔	✔					
Phonics and Decoding /Word Recognition							
Understand the alphabetic principle	✔	✔					
Sound/letter correspondence	✔	✔	✔	✔			
Blend sounds into words, including VC, CVC, CVCe, CVVC words	✔	✔	✔	✔			
Blend common word families	✔	✔	✔	✔			

KEY	✔ = Assessed Skill
	Tinted panels show skills, strategies, and other teaching opportunities.

	K	1	2	3	4	5	6
Initial consonant blends		✔	✔	✔			
Final consonant blends		✔	✔	✔			
Initial and medial short vowels	✔	✔	✔	✔	✔	✔	✔
Decode one-syllable words in isolation and in context	✔	✔	✔	✔			
Decode multisyllabic words in isolation and in context using common syllabication patterns		✔	✔	✔	✔	✔	✔
Distinguish between similarly spelled words	✔	✔	✔	✔	✔	✔	✔
Monitor accuracy of decoding							
Identify and read common high-frequency words, irregularly spelled words	✔	✔	✔	✔			
Identify and read compound words, contractions		✔	✔	✔	✔	✔	✔
Use knowledge of spelling patterns to identify syllables		✔	✔	✔	✔	✔	✔
Regular and irregular plurals	✔	✔	✔	✔	✔	✔	✔
Long vowels (silent e, vowel teams)	✔	✔	✔	✔	✔	✔	✔
Vowel digraphs (variant vowels)		✔	✔	✔	✔	✔	✔
r-Controlled vowels		✔	✔	✔	✔	✔	✔
Hard/soft consonants		✔	✔	✔	✔	✔	✔
Initial consonant digraphs		✔	✔	✔	✔	✔	
Medial and final consonant digraphs		✔	✔	✔	✔	✔	
Vowel diphthongs		✔	✔	✔	✔	✔	✔
Identify and distinguish letter-sounds (initial, medial, final)	✔	✔	✔				
Silent letters		✔	✔	✔	✔	✔	✔
Schwa words			✔	✔	✔	✔	
Inflectional endings		✔	✔	✔	✔	✔	✔
Triple-consonant clusters		✔	✔	✔	✔	✔	
Unfamiliar and complex word families					✔	✔	✔	✔

Structural Analysis/Word Analysis

	K	1	2	3	4	5	6
Common spelling patterns (word families)		✔	✔	✔	✔	✔	✔
Common syllable patterns		✔	✔	✔	✔	✔	✔
Inflectional endings		✔	✔	✔	✔	✔	✔
Contractions		✔	✔	✔	✔	✔	✔
Compound words		✔	✔	✔	✔	✔	✔
Prefixes and suffixes		✔	✔	✔	✔	✔	✔
Root or base words			✔	✔	✔	✔	✔
Comparatives and superlatives			✔	✔	✔	✔	✔
Greek and Latin roots			✔	✔	✔	✔	✔

Fluency

	K	1	2	3	4	5	6
Apply letter/sound knowledge to decode phonetically regular words accurately	✔	✔	✔	✔	✔	✔	✔
Recognize high-frequency and familiar words	✔	✔	✔	✔	✔	✔	✔
Read regularly on independent and instructional levels							
Read orally with fluency from familiar texts (choral, echo, partner, Reader's Theater)							
Use appropriate rate, expression, intonation, and phrasing		✔	✔	✔	✔	✔	✔
Read with automaticity (accurately and effortlessly)		✔	✔	✔	✔	✔	✔

	K	1	2	3	4	5	6
Use punctuation cues in reading		✔	✔	✔	✔	✔	✔
Adjust reading rate to purpose, text difficulty, form, and style							
Repeated readings							
Timed readings		✔	✔	✔	✔	✔	✔
Read with purpose and understanding		✔	✔	✔	✔	✔	✔
Read orally with accuracy		✔	✔	✔	✔	✔	✔
Use context to confirm or self-correct word recognition		✔	✔	✔	✔	✔	✔

READING LITERATURE

Comprehension Strategies and Skills

	K	1	2	3	4	5	6
Read literature from a broad range of genres, cultures, and periods		✔	✔	✔	✔	✔	✔
Access complex text		✔	✔	✔	✔	✔	✔
Build background							
Preview and predict							
Establish and adjust purpose for reading							
Evaluate citing evidence from the text							
Ask and answer questions	✔	✔	✔	✔	✔	✔	✔
Inferences and conclusions, citing evidence from the text	✔	✔	✔	✔	✔	✔	✔
Monitor/adjust comprehension including reread, reading rate, paraphrase							
Recount/Retell	✔	✔					
Summarize			✔	✔	✔	✔	✔
Story structure (beginning, middle, end)	✔	✔	✔	✔	✔	✔	✔
Visualize							
Make connections between and across texts		✔	✔	✔	✔	✔	✔
Point of view		✔	✔	✔	✔	✔	✔
Author's purpose							
Cause and effect	✔	✔	✔	✔	✔	✔	✔
Compare and contrast (including character, setting, plot, topics)	✔	✔	✔	✔	✔	✔	✔
Classify and categorize		✔	✔				
Literature vs informational text	✔	✔	✔				
Illustrations, using	✔	✔	✔	✔			
Theme, central message, moral, lesson		✔	✔	✔	✔	✔	✔
Predictions, making/confirming	✔	✔	✔				
Problem and solution (problem/resolution)		✔	✔	✔	✔	✔	✔
Sequence of events	✔	✔	✔	✔	✔	✔	✔

Literary Elements

	K	1	2	3	4	5	6
Character	✔	✔	✔	✔	✔	✔	✔
Plot development/Events	✔	✔	✔	✔	✔	✔	✔
Setting	✔	✔	✔	✔	✔	✔	✔
Stanza				✔	✔	✔	✔
Alliteration						✔	✔
Assonance						✔	✔
Dialogue							

KEY ✔ = Assessed Skill
Tinted panels show skills, strategies, and other teaching opportunities.

	K	1	2	3	4	5	6
Foreshadowing						✔	✔
Flashback						✔	✔
Descriptive and figurative language		✔	✔	✔	✔	✔	✔
Imagery					✔	✔	✔
Meter					✔	✔	✔
Onomatopoeia							
Repetition		✔	✔	✔	✔	✔	✔
Rhyme/rhyme schemes		✔	✔	✔	✔	✔	✔
Rhythm		✔	✔				
Sensory language							
Symbolism							
Write About Reading/Literary Response Discussions							
Reflect and respond to text citing text evidence		✔	✔	✔	✔	✔	✔
Connect and compare text characters, events, ideas to self, to other texts, to world							
Connect literary texts to other curriculum areas							
Identify cultural and historical elements of text							
Evaluate author's techniques, craft							
Analytical writing							
Interpret text ideas through writing, discussion, media, research							
Book report or review							
Locate, use, explain information from text features		✔	✔	✔	✔	✔	✔
Organize information to show understanding of main idea through charts, mapping							
Cite text evidence	✔	✔	✔	✔	✔	✔	✔
Author's purpose/ Illustrator's purpose							

READING INFORMATIONAL TEXT

Comprehension Strategies and Skills

	K	1	2	3	4	5	6
Read informational text from a broad range of topics and cultures	✔	✔	✔	✔	✔	✔	✔
Access complex text		✔	✔	✔	✔	✔	✔
Build background							
Preview and predict	✔	✔	✔				
Establish and adjust purpose for reading							
Evaluate citing evidence from the text							
Ask and answer questions	✔	✔	✔	✔	✔	✔	✔
Inferences and conclusions, citing evidence from the text	✔	✔	✔	✔	✔	✔	✔
Monitor and adjust comprehension including reread, adjust reading rate, paraphrase							
Recount/Retell	✔	✔					
Summarize			✔	✔	✔	✔	✔
Text structure	✔	✔	✔	✔	✔	✔	✔
Identify text features		✔	✔	✔	✔	✔	✔
Make connections between and across texts	✔	✔	✔	✔	✔	✔	✔

	K	1	2	3	4	5	6
Author's point of view				✔	✔	✔	✔
Author's purpose		✔	✔				
Cause and effect	✔	✔	✔	✔	✔	✔	✔
Compare and contrast	✔	✔	✔	✔	✔	✔	✔
Classify and categorize		✔	✔				
Illustrations and photographs, using	✔	✔	✔	✔			
Instructions/directions (written and oral)		✔	✔	✔	✔	✔	✔
Main idea and key details	✔	✔	✔	✔	✔	✔	✔
Persuasion, reasons and evidence to support points/persuasive techniques						✔	✔
Predictions, making/confirming	✔	✔					
Problem and solution		✔	✔	✔	✔	✔	✔
Sequence, chronological order of events, time order, steps in a process	✔	✔	✔	✔	✔	✔	✔

Writing About Reading/Expository Critique Discussions

	K	1	2	3	4	5	6
Reflect and respond to text citing text evidence		✔	✔	✔	✔	✔	✔
Connect and compare text characters, events, ideas to self, to other texts, to world							
Connect texts to other curriculum areas							
Identify cultural and historical elements of text							
Evaluate author's techniques, craft							
Analytical writing							
Read to understand and perform tasks and activities							
Interpret text ideas through writing, discussion, media, research							
Locate, use, explain information from text features		✔	✔	✔	✔	✔	✔
Organize information to show understanding of main idea through charts, mapping							
Cite text evidence		✔	✔	✔	✔	✔	✔
Author's purpose/Illustrator's purpose							

Text Features

	K	1	2	3	4	5	6
Recognize and identify text and organizational features of nonfiction texts		✔	✔	✔	✔	✔	✔
Captions and labels, headings, subheadings, endnotes, key words, bold print	✔	✔	✔	✔	✔	✔	✔
Graphics, including photographs, illustrations, maps, charts, diagrams, graphs, time lines	✔	✔	✔	✔	✔	✔	✔

Self-Selected Reading/Independent Reading

	K	1	2	3	4	5	6
Use personal criteria to choose own reading including favorite authors, genres, recommendations from others; set up a reading log							
Read a range of literature and informational text for tasks as well as for enjoyment; participate in literature circles							
Produce evidence of reading by retelling, summarizing, or paraphrasing							

Media Literacy

	K	1	2	3	4	5	6
Summarize the message or content from media message, citing text evidence							
Use graphics, illustrations to analyze and interpret information	✔	✔	✔	✔	✔	✔	✔
Identify structural features of popular media and use the features to obtain information, including digital sources				✔	✔	✔	✔
Identify reasons and evidence in visuals and media message							
Analyze media source: recognize effects of media in one's mood and emotion							

KEY ✔ = Assessed Skill
Tinted panels show skills, strategies, and other teaching opportunities.

	K	1	2	3	4	5	6
Make informed judgments about print and digital media							
Critique persuasive techniques							

WRITING

Writing Process

	K	1	2	3	4	5	6
Plan/prewrite							
Draft							
Revise							
Edit/proofread							
Publish and present including using technology							
Teacher and peer feedback							

Writing Traits

	K	1	2	3	4	5	6
Conventions		✔	✔	✔	✔	✔	✔
Ideas		✔	✔	✔	✔	✔	✔
Organization		✔	✔	✔	✔	✔	✔
Sentence fluency		✔	✔	✔	✔	✔	✔
Voice		✔	✔	✔	✔	✔	✔
Word choice		✔	✔	✔	✔	✔	✔

Writer's Craft

	K	1	2	3	4	5	6
Good topic, focus on and develop topic, topic sentence			✔	✔	✔	✔	✔
Paragraph(s); sentence structure			✔	✔	✔	✔	✔
Main idea and supporting key details			✔	✔	✔	✔	✔
Unimportant details							
Relevant supporting evidence			✔	✔	✔	✔	✔
Strong opening, strong conclusion			✔	✔	✔	✔	✔
Beginning, middle, end; sequence		✔	✔	✔	✔	✔	✔
Precise words, strong words, vary words			✔	✔	✔	✔	✔
Figurative and sensory language, descriptive details							
Informal/formal language							
Mood/style/tone							
Dialogue					✔	✔	✔	✔
Transition words, transitions to multiple paragraphs				✔	✔	✔	✔
Select focus and organization			✔	✔	✔	✔	✔
Points and counterpoints/Opposing claims and counterarguments							
Use reference materials (online and print dictionary, thesaurus, encyclopedia)							

Writing Applications

	K	1	2	3	4	5	6
Writing about text	✔	✔	✔	✔	✔	✔	✔
Personal and fictional narrative (also biographical and autobiographical)	✔	✔	✔	✔	✔	✔	✔
Variety of expressive forms including poetry	✔	✔	✔	✔	✔	✔	✔
Informative/explanatory texts	✔	✔	✔	✔	✔	✔	✔
Description	✔	✔	✔	✔			
Procedural texts		✔	✔	✔	✔	✔	✔
Opinion pieces or arguments	✔	✔	✔	✔	✔	✔	✔
Communications including technical documents		✔	✔	✔	✔	✔	✔

	K	1	2	3	4	5	6
Research report	✔	✔	✔	✔	✔	✔	✔
Responses to literature/reflection				✔	✔	✔	✔
Analytical writing							
Letters		✔	✔	✔	✔	✔	✔
Write daily and over short and extended time frames; set up writer's notebooks							

Penmanship/Handwriting

	K	1	2	3	4	5	6
Write legibly in manuscript using correct formation, directionality, and spacing							
Write legibly in cursive using correct formation, directionality, and spacing							

SPEAKING AND LISTENING

Speaking

	K	1	2	3	4	5	6
Use repetition, rhyme, and rhythm in oral texts							
Participate in classroom activities and discussions							
Collaborative conversation with peers and adults in small and large groups using formal English when appropriate							
Differentiate between formal and informal English							
Follow agreed upon rules for discussion							
Build on others' talk in conversation, adding new ideas							
Come to discussion prepared							
Describe familiar people, places, and things and add drawings as desired							
Paraphrase portions of text read alone or information presented							
Apply comprehension strategies and skills in speaking activities							
Use literal and nonliteral meanings							
Ask and answer questions about text read aloud and about media							
Stay on topic when speaking							
Use language appropriate to situation, purpose, and audience							
Use nonverbal communications such as eye contact, gestures, and props							
Use verbal communication in effective ways and improve expression in conventional language							
Retell a story, presentation, or spoken message by summarizing							
Oral presentations: focus, organizational structure, audience, purpose							
Give and follow directions							
Consider audience when speaking or preparing a presentation							
Recite poems, rhymes, songs							
Use complete, coherent sentences							
Organize presentations							
Deliver presentations (narrative, summaries, research, persuasive); add visuals							
Speak audibly (accuracy, expression, volume, pitch, rate, phrasing, modulation, enunciation)							
Create audio recordings of poems, stories, presentations							

Listening

	K	1	2	3	4	5	6
Identify musical elements in language							
Determine the purpose for listening							
Understand, follow, restate, and give oral directions							
Develop oral language and concepts							

KEY	✔ = Assessed Skill Tinted panels show skills, strategies, and other teaching opportunities.

	K	1	2	3	4	5	6
Listen openly, responsively, attentively, and critically							
Listen to identify the points a speaker makes							
Listen responsively to oral presentations (determine main idea and key details)							
Ask and answer relevant questions (for clarification to follow-up on ideas)							
Identify reasons and evidence presented by speaker							
Recall and interpret speakers' verbal/nonverbal messages, purposes, perspectives							

LANGUAGE

Vocabulary Acquisition and Use

	K	1	2	3	4	5	6
Develop oral vocabulary and choose words for effect							
Use academic language		✔	✔	✔	✔	✔	✔
Identify persons, places, things, actions		✔	✔	✔			
Classify, sort, and categorize words	✔	✔	✔	✔	✔	✔	✔
Determine or clarify the meaning of unknown words; use word walls		✔	✔	✔	✔	✔	✔
Synonyms, antonyms, and opposites		✔	✔	✔	✔	✔	✔
Use context clues such as word, sentence, paragraph, definition, example, restatement, description, comparison, cause and effect		✔	✔	✔	✔	✔	✔
Use word identification strategies		✔	✔	✔	✔	✔	✔
Unfamiliar words		✔	✔	✔	✔	✔	✔
Multiple-meaning words		✔	✔	✔	✔	✔	✔
Use print and online dictionary to locate meanings, pronunciation, derivatives, parts of speech		✔	✔	✔	✔	✔	✔
Compound words		✔	✔	✔	✔	✔	✔
Words ending in -er and -est		✔	✔	✔	✔	✔	
Root words (base words)		✔	✔	✔	✔	✔	✔
Prefixes and suffixes		✔	✔	✔	✔	✔	✔
Greek and Latin affixes and roots			✔	✔	✔	✔	✔
Denotation and connotation					✔	✔	✔
Word families		✔	✔	✔	✔	✔	✔
Inflectional endings		✔	✔	✔	✔	✔	✔
Use a print and online thesaurus			✔	✔	✔	✔	✔
Use print and online reference sources for word meaning (dictionary, glossaries)	✔	✔	✔	✔	✔	✔	✔
Homographs				✔	✔	✔	✔
Homophones			✔	✔	✔	✔	✔
Contractions		✔	✔	✔			
Figurative language such as metaphors, similes, personification			✔	✔	✔	✔	✔
Idioms, adages, proverbs, literal and nonliteral language			✔	✔	✔	✔	✔
Analogies							
Listen to, read, discuss familiar and unfamiliar challenging text							
Identify real-life connections between words and their use							
Use acquired words and phrases to convey precise ideas							
Use vocabulary to express spatial and temporal relationships							
Identify shades of meaning in related words	✔	✔	✔	✔	✔	✔	✔
Word origins				✔	✔	✔	✔

BM7

	K	1	2	3	4	5	6
Morphology				✔	✔	✔	✔

Knowledge of Language

	K	1	2	3	4	5	6
Choose words, phrases, and sentences for effect							
Choose punctuation effectively							
Formal and informal language for style and tone including dialects							

Conventions of Standard English/Grammar, Mechanics, and Usage

	K	1	2	3	4	5	6
Sentence concepts: statements, questions, exclamations, commands		✔	✔	✔	✔	✔	✔
Complete and incomplete sentences; sentence fragments; word order		✔	✔	✔	✔	✔	✔
Compound sentences, complex sentences				✔	✔	✔	✔
Combining sentences		✔	✔	✔	✔	✔	✔
Nouns including common, proper, singular, plural, irregular plurals, possessives, abstract, concrete, collective		✔	✔	✔	✔	✔	✔
Verbs including action, helping, linking, irregular		✔	✔	✔	✔	✔	✔
Verb tenses including past, present, future, perfect, and progressive		✔	✔	✔	✔	✔	✔
Pronouns including possessive, subject and object, pronoun-verb agreement, indefinite, intensive, reciprocal; correct unclear pronouns		✔	✔	✔	✔	✔	✔
Adjectives including articles, demonstrative, proper, adjectives that compare		✔	✔	✔	✔	✔	✔
Adverbs including telling how, when, where, comparative, superlative, irregular		✔	✔	✔	✔	✔	✔
Subject, predicate; subject-verb agreement		✔	✔	✔	✔	✔	✔
Contractions		✔	✔	✔	✔	✔	✔
Conjunctions				✔	✔	✔	✔
Commas			✔	✔	✔	✔	✔
Colons, semicolons, dashes, hyphens						✔	✔
Question words							
Quotation marks			✔	✔	✔	✔	✔
Prepositions and prepositional phrases, appositives		✔	✔	✔	✔	✔	✔
Independent and dependent clauses						✔	✔
Italics/underlining for emphasis and titles							
Negatives, correcting double negatives					✔	✔	✔
Abbreviations			✔	✔	✔	✔	✔
Use correct capitalization in sentences, proper nouns, titles, abbreviations		✔	✔	✔	✔	✔	✔
Use correct punctuation		✔	✔	✔	✔	✔	✔
Antecedents				✔	✔	✔	✔
Homophones and words often confused			✔	✔	✔	✔	✔
Apostrophes				✔	✔	✔	✔

Spelling

	K	1	2	3	4	5	6
Write irregular, high-frequency words	✔	✔	✔				
ABC order	✔	✔					
Write letters	✔	✔					
Words with short vowels	✔	✔	✔	✔	✔	✔	✔
Words with long vowels	✔	✔	✔	✔	✔	✔	✔
Words with digraphs, blends, consonant clusters, double consonants		✔	✔	✔	✔	✔	✔
Words with vowel digraphs and ambiguous vowels		✔	✔	✔	✔	✔	✔

KEY ✔ = Assessed Skill
Tinted panels show skills, strategies, and other teaching opportunities.

	K	1	2	3	4	5	6
Words with diphthongs		✔	✔	✔	✔	✔	✔
Words with r-controlled vowels		✔	✔	✔	✔	✔	✔
Use conventional spelling		✔	✔	✔	✔	✔	✔
Schwa words				✔	✔	✔	✔
Words with silent letters			✔	✔	✔	✔	✔
Words with hard and soft letters			✔	✔	✔	✔	✔
Inflectional endings including plural, past tense, drop final e and double consonant when adding -ed and -ing, changing y to i		✔	✔	✔	✔	✔	✔
Compound words		✔	✔	✔	✔	✔	✔
Homonyms/homophones			✔	✔	✔	✔	✔
Prefixes and suffixes		✔	✔	✔	✔	✔	✔
Root and base words (also spell derivatives)				✔	✔	✔	✔
Syllables: patterns, rules, accented, stressed, closed, open				✔	✔	✔	✔
Words with Greek and Latin roots						✔	✔
Words from mythology						✔	✔
Words with spelling patterns, word families		✔	✔	✔	✔	✔	✔

RESEARCH AND INQUIRY

Study Skills

	K	1	2	3	4	5	6
Directions: read, write, give, follow (includes technical directions)			✔	✔	✔	✔	✔
Evaluate directions for sequence and completeness				✔	✔	✔	✔
Use library/media center							
Use parts of a book to locate information							
Interpret information from graphic aids		✔	✔	✔	✔	✔	✔
Use graphic organizers to organize information and comprehend text	✔	✔	✔	✔	✔	✔	✔
Use functional, everyday documents				✔	✔	✔	✔
Apply study strategies: skimming and scanning, note-taking, outlining							

Research Process

	K	1	2	3	4	5	6
Generate and revise topics and questions for research					✔	✔	✔
Narrow focus of research, set research goals					✔	✔	✔
Find and locate information using print and digital resources		✔	✔	✔	✔	✔	✔
Record information systematically (note-taking, outlining, using technology)					✔	✔	✔
Develop a systematic research plan					✔	✔	✔
Evaluate reliability, credibility, usefulness of sources and information						✔	✔
Use primary sources to obtain information					✔	✔	✔
Organize, synthesize, evaluate, and draw conclusions from information							
Cite and list sources of information (record basic bibliographic data)					✔	✔	✔
Demonstrate basic keyboarding skills							
Participate in and present shared research							

Technology

	K	1	2	3	4	5	6
Use computer, Internet, and other technology resources to access information							
Use text and organizational features of electronic resources such as search engines, keywords, e-mail, hyperlinks, URLs, Web pages, databases, graphics							
Use digital tools to present and publish in a variety of media formats							

INDEX

A

Academic language, 1: S5–S6, S7–S8, S9–S10, S11–S12, S13–S14, S17–S18, S19–S20, S21–S22, S23–S24, S25–S26, S27–S28, S29–S30, S31, S33–S34, S35, **Units 1–6:** T10–T11, T12–T13, T14–T15, T18–T19, T20–T21, T22–T23, T24–T25, T26–T27, T28–T29, T30–T31, T38, T40–T41, T48–T49, T52–T53, T56–T57, T58–T59, T61, T74–T75, T76–T77, T78–T79, T82–T83, T84–T85, T86–T87, T88–T89, T90–T91, T92–T93, T94–T95, T102, T104–T105, T112–T113, T116–T117, T120–T121, T122–T123, T125, T138–T139, T140–T141, T142–T143, T146–T147, T148–T149, T150–T151, T152–T153, T154–T155, T158–T159, T166, T168–T169, T176–T177, T180–T181, T184–T185, T186–T187, T189, T202–T203, T204–T205, T206–T207, T210–T211, T212–T213, T214–T215, T216–T217, T218–T219, T220–T221, T222–T223, T230, T232–T233, T240–T241, T244–T245, T248–T249, T250–T251, T253, T266–T267, T268–T269, T270–T271, T274–T275, T276–T277, T278–T279, T280–T281, T282–T283, T284–T285, T286–T287, T294, T296–T297, T304–T305, T308–T309, T312–T313, T314–T315, T317, T328, T344–T345, T346–T347, T348–T349, T350–T351, T352–T353, T354–T355

See also **Language; Reading Informational Text: academic language; Vocabulary: academic vocabulary.**

Access complex text

connection of ideas, 1: S10, T17, S22, T25I–T25J, T25M, T85, T89C–T89D, T89G–T89H, T89I–T89J, T89O–T89P, T147, T153U–T153V, T217A–T217B, T217I–T217J, T217L, T217O, T217S–T217T, T217U–T217V, T281C, **2:** T25U–T25V, T89E–T89F, T89S–T89T, T153I–T153J, T153O–T153P, T217D, T217I–T217J, T217K–T217L, T217S–T217T, 273, **3:** T21, T25E–T25F, T25K–T25L, T89G, T89Q–T89R, T145, T153E, T153M–T153N, T153S–T153T, T217G–T217H, T281C, **4:** T25H, T81, T89I–T89J, T89M–T89N, T89O–T89P, T153E–T153F, T153K–T153L, T217E–T217F, T217I–T217J, T217O–T217P, T217S–T217T, **5:** T17, T21, T25E–T25F, T25Q–T25R, T83, T89C–T89D, T89E–T89F, T89G–T89H, T153E–T153F, T153M–T153N, T153S–T153T, T215, T217I–T217J, T217L, T217M–T217N, T273, T279, **6:** T25G, T25M, T81, T89D, T89E, T147, T153O, T217G–T217H, T277

genre, 1: S9, S10, S22, T23, T89C, T281E–T281F, **2:** T25I–T25J, T81, T89L, T153C–T153D, T153G–T153H, T153Q–T153R, T215, T217A–T217B, T217E–T217F, T217G–T217H, T217N, T281A–T281B, T281C, **3:** T25O–T25P, T89A–T89B, T89M–T89N, T151, T153C–T153D, T153K–T153L, T281E–T281F, **4:** T17, T25A–T25B, T25E–T25F, T25I–T25J, T25M–T25N, T25S–T25T, T89A–T89B, T151, T273, T281C, **5:** T89M–T89N, T217G–T217H, T217M, **6:** T153E–T153F, T153U–T153V, T217A–T217B, T217K–T217L, T281A–T281B

organization, 1: S10, S21, T25E–T25F, T25K, T25N, T25S, T81, T273, T277, **2:** T17, T25S–T25T, T85, T89A–T89B, T89G, T89K, T89M, T151, T209, T281E–T281F, **3:** T81, T153G–T153H, T217A–T217B, T217E–T217F, T217K–T217L, T273, **4:** T25G, T25K–T25L, T83, T89E–T89F, T89G–T89H, T153M–T153N, T213, **5:** T25A–T25B, T25G–T25H, T25I–T25J, T145, T153A–T153B, T153G–T153H, T281A–T281B, **6:** T23, T25Q–T25R, T89F, T89I–T89J, T153M–T153N, T153S–T153T, T153U, T209

prior knowledge, 1: S10, S22, T25A–T25B, T25Q–T25R, T89G, T153A–T153B, T209, **2:** T25A–T25B, T25C–T25D, T25O–T25P, T217Q–T217R, **3:** T25A–T25B, T89K–T89L, T153Q–T153R, T209, T217S–T217T, T275, T281A–T281B, **4:** T25C, T145, T153C–T153D, T153G–T153H, T153U–T153V, T281E, **5:** T25K, T81, T89A–T89B, T153C–T153D, T209, T217S–T217T, **6:** T17, T25D, T25K–T25L, T153I–T153J, T153O–T153P, T217E–T217F, T217I–T217J, T217O–T217P

purpose, 1: S9, S10, S22, T145, T153I–T153J, T153M–T153N, T217C–T217D, T217M–T217N, T281A–T281B, **2:** T89C–T89D, T153A–T153B, T153K, **3:** T17, T25G–T25H, T89C–T89D, T217C–T217D, T217M–T217N, **4:** T25Q–T25R, T217A–T217B, T217G–T217H, T217K–T217L, T217M–T217N, **5:** T153K, T217O–T217P, T281E–T281F, T89O–T89P, T281E–T281F, **6:** T89O–T89P, T281E–T281F

sentence structure, 1: S10, S21, T25G–T25H, T89E–T89F, T153E–T153F, T153O–T153P, T217, T217G, T217P, **2:** T25G–T25H, T89H, T89I–T89J, T89M–T89N, T217C, **3:** T83, **4:** T89C–T89D, T217I, **5:** T25D, T25K–T25L, T217A–T217B, T217C–T217D, T217E, T217J, T281C, **6:** T25A–T25B, T25H, T25K, T217C–T217D, T273, T281C

specific vocabulary, 1: S10, S22, T25C–T25D, T25L, T89A–T89B, T89M–T89N, T153C–T153D, T153G–T153H, T153K–

T153L, T153S–T153T, T217E–T217F, T217H, T217K, **2:** T25, T25E–T25F, T25K–T25L, T25M–T25N, T89Q–T89R, T145, T153E–T153F, T217E, T217M, T275, **3:** T25C–T25D, T25I–T25J, T89E–T89F, T89H, T89I–T89J, T153A–T153B, T153F, T153I–T153J, T217, T217I–T217J, T217Q–T217R, **4:** T25, T25D, T153A–T153B, T153I–T153J, T153O–T153P, T153S–T153T, T209, T217C–T217D, T217M, T281, T281A–T281B, T281F, **5:** T25O–T25P, T89I–T89J, T89K–T89L, T89Q–T89R, T89S–T89T, T153, T153I–T153J, T153Q–T153R, T217E–T217F, T217K, **6:** T25C, T25E–T25F, T25I–T25J, T25S–T25T, T85, T89A–T89B, T89C, T89G–T89H, T89K–T89L, T89Q–T89R, T145, T153A–T153B, T153C–T153D, T153G–T153H, T153K–T153L, T217

Adjectives. *See* **Grammar: adjectives.**
Adverbs. *See* **Grammar: adverbs.**
Affixes, 1: S17–S18, S28, S34, T27, T38–T39, T91, T102, T155, T219, T230–T231, T234, T242, T246, T280–T281, T281B, T281D, T283, T294–T295, T296, T298, T301, T304, T306, T308, T310, T313, T317, T328, **2:** T27, T38–T39, T90, T102–T103, T106, T107, T152–T153, T153F, T153G, T153N, T154–T155, T164, T166–T167, T168–T169, T170, T171, T173, T176–T177, T178, T180–T181, T182, T185, T189, T190, T228, T230–T231, T293, T294, T328, **3:** T27, T38–T39, T91, T102–T103, T106, T153D, T153P, T155, T166–T167, T216, T230–T231, T249, T283, T294–T295, **4:** T27, T38–T39, T90–T91, T100–T101, T102, T106, T107, T126, T152–T153, T153I, T153K, T153O, T153R, T164, T166–T167, T168, T173, T176, T178, T180, T182, T185, T186, T189, T209, T230–T231, T282–T283, T292–T293, T294–T295, T298–T299, T318, **5:** T26–T27, T36–T37, T38, T42, T43, T62, T89B, T100, T102–T103, T153N, T154–T155, T164–T165, T166, T170, T171, T190, T217B, T218–T219, T228–T229, T230–T231, T234, T235, T237, T242, T246, T253, T281D, T282–T283, T292–T293, T294–T295, T298, T299, T313, **6:** T25I, T27, T36, T38–T39, T89G, T89K, T91, T102, T106, T166, T170, T217, T217P, T218–T219, T228–T229, T230–T231, T234, T235, T254, T282–T283, T292–T293, T294–T295, T298, T299

See also **Vocabulary: prefixes, suffixes.**
Alliteration, 4: T270, T274–T275, T281D, T297, T305, T309, T315, T350

See also **Literary elements.**
Analogies. *See* **Spelling: analogies; Vocabulary: analogies.**
Analytical Writing. *See* **Write About Reading.**
Antonyms. *See* **Vocabulary: antonyms.**

T202, T209, T217B, T217P, T217R, T217T, T221, T232–T233, T240–T241, T244–T245, T248–T249, T250–T251, T259, T266, T273, T281B, T281D, T281F, T285, T296–T297, T304–T305, T308–T309, T312–T313, T314–T315, T332, T357, T358–T359, **6:** T3, T10, T17, T25B, T25N, T25P, T25T, T29, T40–T41, T48–T49, T52–T53, T56–T57, T58–T59, T67, T74, T81, T89B, T89L, T89N, T89R, T93, T104–T105, T112–T113, T116–T117, T120–T121, T122–T123, T131, T138, T153B, T153P, T153R, T153V, T157, T168–T169, T176–T177, T180–T181, T184–T185, T186–T187, T195, T202, T209, T217B, T217L, T217N, T217P, T221, T232–T233, T240–T241, T244–T245, T248–T249, T250–T251, T259, T266, T273, T281B, T281F, T285, T296–T297, T304–T305, T308–T309, T312–T313, T314–T315, T332, T357, T358–T359

Expository text. *See* Genre: Informational text.

Extended complex text, Units 1–6: T356–T361

Extra Support. *See* Access complex text *and* English Language Learners.

F

Fantasy, 3: T76, T86–T87, T89A, T89H
Figurative language. *See* Literary elements; Writer's Craft.
First-person point of view, 1: T344–T345, T350–T351, **2:** T304, **4:** T20–T21, T47, T51, T55, **5:** T22, **6:** T89M
Fluency
   accuracy, **1:** S37, **2:** T27, T91, **3:** T155, T219, **4:** T91, T219, **5:** T219, **6:** T155
   Approaching Level Options for. *See* Approaching Level Options: fluency.
   assessment, **1:** S37–S38, **Units 1–6:** T320–T321, T340–T341
   choral reading, **1:** T27, T155, T219, **2:** T27, T91, T155
   Daily Fluency Practice, **Units 1–6:** T27, T91, T155, T219, T283
   ELL. *See* English Language Learners: fluency.
   explain/practice, **Units 1–6:** T27, T91, T155, T219, T283
   expression/intonation, **1:** T27, T91, T155, T219, **2:** T91, T155, T283, **3:** T27, T91, T283, **4:** T27, T219, T283, **5:** T27, T91, T283, **6:** T27, T91, T219, T283
   modeling, **Units 1–6:** T27, T91, T155, T219, T283
   partner reading, **1:** T91, T283, **2:** T219, T283, **3:** T27, T91, T155, T219, T283, **4:** T27, T91, T155, T219, T283, **5:** T27, T91, T155, T219, T283, **6:** T27, T91, T155, T219, T283
   pausing, **1:** T155, T219, **2:** T155, **4:** T155
   phrasing, **1:** T155, T219, T283, **2:** T155, T283, **3:** T91, T283, **4:** T155, T283, **5:** T91, T283, **6:** T27, T219, T283

punctuation, 1: T155, T219, T283, **2:** T155, T283, **3:** T91, T283, **4:** T155, **5:** T91, T283, **6:** T27, T219
   rate, **1:** S37, **2:** T27, T219, **3:** T155, T219, **4:** T91, **5:** T155, **6:** T155
   Reader's Theater, **Units 1–6:** T326–T327
   speaking checklist, **Units 1–6:** T334
   syllable fluency, **Units 1–6:** T27, T91, T155, T219, T283
   writing fluency. *See* Writing Traits: sentence fluency.
Folktale, 1: S9, **2:** T204, T214–T215, T217A, T217L, **6:** T153S–T153T
Foreshadowing, 1: S10, **2:** T214, T217E, T244, **3:** T81, **4:** T105, T113, T117, T123
Foundational skills
   irregularly spelled words, **2:** T98–T99, T127, T162–T163, T191, T219, **3:** T162–T163
   Latin and Greek suffixes, **2:** T152–T153, T153F, T153G, T153N, T167, T173, T178, T182, T185, T189, **4:** T38
   letter-sound correspondences, **1:** T26–T27, T90–T91, T154–T155, T218–T219, T282–T283, **2:** T26–T27, T90–T91, T218–T219, T282–T283, **3:** T26–T27, T90–T91, T154–T155, T218–T219, T282–T283, **4:** T26–T27
   morphology, **1:** S28, **Units 1–6:** T39, T103, T167, T231, T295
   multisyllabic words, **1:** S17–S18, **Units 1–6:** T27, T91, T155, T219, T283
   phonics and decoding, **1:** S30, T26–T27, T42–T43, T90–T91, T106–T107, T154–T155, T170–T171, T218–T219, T234–T235, T282–T283, T298–T299, **2:** T26–T27, T42–T43, T90–T91, T106–T107, T218–T219, T234–T235, T282–T283, T298–T299, **3:** T26–T27, T42–T43, T90–T91, T106–T107, T154–T155, T170–T171, T218–T219, T234–T235, T282–T283, T298–T299, **4:** T26–T27, T42–T43
   prefixes, **1:** S28, **3:** T103, T167, T231, **4:** T90–T91, T100–T101, T106–T107, T126, T152–T153, T153K, T153R, T164, T167, T173, T178, T182, T185, T189, **5:** T89B, T154–T155, T164–T165, T166, T170–T171, T190, T228, **6:** T217, T218–T219, T228–T229, T234–T235, T254, T292, T293
   suffixes, **1:** S28, T231, T295, **2:** T39, T103, **3:** T39, T103, T167, T231, T295, **4:** T152–T153, T153I, T167, T173, T178, T182, T189, T231, T292, T295, **5:** T26–T27, T36–T37, T42–T43, T62, T103, T166, T218–T219, T228–T229, T231, T234–T235, T254, T282–T283, T292–T293, T295, T298–T299, T318, **6:** T36, T39, T231, T295
   syllabication patterns, **1:** S29, **2:** T282–T283, T292–T293, T318, **3:** T26–T27, T36, T90–T91, **4:** T26–T27, T36–T37, T62, T100, T218–T219, T228–T229, T234–T235, T254, T292
Frequently confused words. *See* Grammar: frequently confused words.

G

Genre,
   See also **Access Complex Text; Informational Text; Poetry.**
   discuss, **1:** S9, S11–S12, S21–S22, S23–S24, T12, T22–T23, T76, T86–T87, T150–T151, T153N, T214–T215, T217H, T274–T275, T281C, **2:** T12, T22–T23, T76, T86–T87, T89I, T140, T150–T151, T153B, T204, T214–T215, T217L, T268, T274–T275, **3:** T12, T22–T23, T76, T86–T87, T89H, T140, T150–T151, T153E, T204, T214–T215, T217E, T268, T274–T275, T281C, **4:** T12, T22–T23, T25B, T76, T86–T87, T89F, T140, T150–T151, T153E, T204, T214–T215, T217E, T268, T274–T275, **5:** T12, T22–T23, T25C, T76, T86–T87, T89D, T140, T150–T151, T153F, T204, T214–T215, T217J, T268, T274–T275, T281B, **6:** T12, T22–T23, T25D, T76, T86–T87, T140, T150–T151, T153F, T204, T214–T215, T217D, T268, T274–T275, T281C
   drama/play, **4:** T76, T86–T87, T89A, T89F
   features of, **1:** S9, S11, T22, T76, T86, T140, T153N, T204, T217H, T268, T281C, **2:** T12, T25L, T76, T89I, T140, T153B, T204, T217L, T268, **3:** T12, T76, T89H, T140, T153E, T204, T217E, T268, T281C, **4:** T12, T25B, T76, T89F, T140, T153E, T204, T217E, T268, **5:** T12, T25C, T76, T89D, T140, T153F, T204, T217J, T268, T281B, **6:** T12, T25D, T76, T140, T153F, T204, T217D, T268, T281C
   fiction
      adventure, **1:** T89A, T89M, **5:** T217S
      fairy tale, **2:** T76, T86–T87, T89A, T89I, T89P
      fantasy, **3:** T76, T86–T87, T89A, T89H
      folklore/folktale, **1:** S9, **2:** T204, T214–T215, T217A, T217L, **6:** T153S
      graphic story, **5:** T217S
      historical fiction, **5:** T76, T86–T87, T89A, T89D, **6:** T12, T22–T23, T25A, T25D
      legend, **4:** T25Q
      mystery, **4:** T76, T86–T87, T89F
      myth, **2:** T153P
      realistic fiction, **1:** T12, T22–T23, T25A, T25L, T76, T86–T87, T89A, T89D, T89M, **3:** T12, T22–T23, T25A, **4:** T89M, **5:** T12, T22–T23, T25A, T25C, T25O, **6:** T76, T86–T87, T89A
      science fiction, **5:** T217S
      tall tale, **4:** T12, T22–T23, T25A, T25B
   informational text
      autobiography, **1:** T153S
      biography, **1:** T204, T214–T215, T217A, T217H, **2:** T140, T150–T151, T153A, T153B, **4:** T140, T150–T151, T153A, T153E, **6:** T204, T214–T215, T217A, T217D
      essay, persuasive, **3:** T281A, T281C
      expository text, **1:** T25Q, **2:** T12, T22–T23, T25B, T25L, T25S, T217R,

H

Higher-level thinking. *See* Comprehension skills; Comprehension strategies; Text connections.

I

restatement, **2:** T24–T25, T39, T166, **4:** T216–T217
    sensory, **4:** T286–T289
    temporal, **1:** T222–T225, **2:** T222–T225, **6:** T30–T33, T94–T97
    synonyms, **4:** T24–T25, T39, T102, **5:** T38, **6:** T216–T217, T231
Language arts, Units 1–6: T34–T35, T36–T37, T38–T39, T98–T99, T100–T101, T102–T103, T162–T163, T164–T165, T166–T167, T226–T227, T228–T229, T230–T231, T290–T291, T292–T293, T294–T295
Latin roots. *See* **Vocabulary: Latin roots.**
Legend, 4: T25Q
Lesson plans, suggested weekly, Units 1–6: T6–T7, T70–T71, T134–T135, T198–T199, T262–T263, T324–T325
Lesson, present the, Units 1–6: T18–T19, T20–T21, T22–T23, T24–T25, T26–T27, T82–T83, T84–T85, T86–T87, T88–T89, T90–T91, T146–T147, T148–T149, T150–T151, T152–T153, T154–T155, T210–T211, T212–T213, T214–T215, T216–T217, T218–T219, T274–T275, T276–T277, T278–T279, T280–T281, T282–T283
Level of Complexity. *See* **Access complex text.**
Level Up, Units 1–6: T41, T49, T59, T105, T113, T123, T169, T177, T187, T233, T241, T251, T297, T305, T315, T336–T337, T338–T339
Leveled Reader Lessons. *See* **Approaching Level Options; Beyond Level Options; English Language Learners; On Level Options.**
Library or media center, using. *See* **Research and inquiry: using the library or media center.**
Listening
    audience participation, Units 1–6: T332
    comprehension, Units 1–6: T12–T13, T76–T77, T140–T141, T204–T205, T268–T269
    develop skills in speaking/listening, checklists, Units 1–6: T333, T334, T335,
    English Language Learner, listen, 1: T87, **4:** T279, **5:** T275, **6:** T89, T279
    for a purpose, Units 1–6: T12–T13, T76–T77, T140–T141, T204–T205, T268–T269, T335
    skit, 5: T99
    strategies,
        listen carefully/closely, 1: S6, T138 **2:** T266 **3:** T74, 220 **4:** T266 **5:** T266
    teamwork, Units 1–6: T330–T333
    to presentations, Units 1–6: T335
Literacy workstation activity cards, Units 1–6: T5, T69, T133, T197, T261
Literary Analysis. *See* **Comprehension skills; Comprehension strategies; Genre: fiction.**
Literary elements
    alliteration, 3: xii **4:** T297, T305, T309, T315
    assonance, 6: T270, T278–T279, T281A, T281B, T281C

character, 1: S11–S12, T20–T21, T25D, T25G, T25I, T40, T47, T48, T51, T52, T84, T89C, T89H, T89I, T110, T112, **2:** T89B, T89N, T89S, T217O, T238, T304, **3:** T46, T80, T89C, T110, **4:** T25I, T57, T89B, T89O, T296, T304, T314, **5:** T17, T110, **6:** T25D, T25G, T25J, T25L, T25M, T46, T51, T55, T57, T58, T81, T89E, T89F, T89J, T104, T112, T113, T122, T296, T297, T304, T305, T308, T314, T315
conflict and resolution, 3: T80
consonance, 6: T270, T278–T279
descriptive details, 6: T86, T87, T89H, T104
dialect, 4: T25D, **5:** T86, T89C, T89I
dialogue. *See* **Dialogue.**
figurative language, 2: T25O, T89O, **4:** T25O, T153B, T153Q, **5:** T25M, T41, T49, T53, T59, T89H, T89J, **6:** T25B, T25F, T25O, T89M, T217B, T217C, T217M, T281D
    imagery, 2: T214, **3:** T89O, **5:** xii, **6:** T270, T281C, T297, T305, T309, T315
    metaphor, 1: T153K, **2:** T25O, T88–T89, T89H, T89K, T89P, T103, T109, T114, T118, T121, T125, T230, T294, **3:** T89O, **4:** T153Q, T280–T281, T281C, T281F, T295, T301, T306, T309, T310, T317, **5:** T22, T102, **6:** T217B, T232
    personification, 2: T216–T217, T217B, T217P, T231, T237, T242, T246, T249, T253, **3:** xii, T86, T87, T102, **4:** T25D, **5:** T25J, T25M, **6:** T89A, T217L, T270, T280–T281, T295, T296, T301, T305, T306, T308, T310, T313, T317
    simile, 1: T41, T49, T53, T59, **2:** T88–T89, T89H, T89K, T89O, T89P, T103, T105, T109, T112, T114, T116, T118, T121, T125, T153D, T230, T294, **4:** T25O, T153B, T280–T281, T281C, T281D, T296, T301, T305, T306, T308, T309, T310, T315, T317, **5:** T25E, T25F, T102, **6:** T25O, T217C, T315
first-person, 2: T89K, **4:** xii, T20, T47, T51, T55, T84–T85, T115, **6:** T276, T281B
flashback, 1: S10, **2:** T89K, **5:** T25I, **6:** T12, T22–T23, T25E, T40, T41, T48, T49, T52, T53, T57, T59
foreshadowing, 1: S10, **2:** T214, T217E, T244, **3:** T81, **4:** T105, T113, T117, T123
hero, 4: T22, T23, T25R, T40
humor, 3: T25M, **5:** T89L
hyperbole/exaggeration, 4: T22, T23, T25A, T25H, T25P, T40, T48, T57, **5:** T22, **6:** T89M, T217E
meter, 4: T270, T274, T278–T279, T281C, **6:** T274–T275
mood, 1: T153Q, **2:** T153M, **6:** T105, T113, T117, T123, T281A, T281B
narrator, 2: T89K, T204, **4:** xii, T16, T17, T20, T21, T25C, T25E, T25J, T25M, T25P, T40–T41, T46, T48, T51, T52, T55, T84–T85, T89O, T110, **5:** T22, T23, T25E, T83, **6:** T89B, T89C, T89I, T296, T304, T327

pacing, 6: T86, T89G
personification, 2: T216–T217, T217B, T217P, T231, T237, T242, T246, T249, T253, **3:** xii, T86, T87, T102, **4:** T25D, **5:** T25J, T25M, **6:** T89A, T217L, T270, T280–T281, T295, T296, T301, T305, T306, T308, T310, T313, T317
point of view, 1: S13–S14, **2:** T89K, T204, **4:** xii, T20–T21, T25C, T25E, T25J, T25M, T25P, T40–T41, T47, T48, T51, T52, T55, T57, T84–T85, T89C, T89E, T89I, T89L, T104, T111, T112, T115, T116, T119, T121, **5:** T22, T23, **6:** T276, T281B, T281D, T281F, T296, T302, T303, T304, T305, T307, T308, T309, T311, T313, T314, T315
repetition, 2: T217G, T217L, T232, T278–T279, T281C, T281D, T297, T305, T309, T315, **4:** T153G, **6:** xii
rhyme, 2: T274, T278–T279, T297, T305, T309, T315
rhyme scheme, 1: xii
rhythm, 6: T281A, T281B
sensory language, 3: T86, T87, T89O, **4:** T25K, **5:** xii, T89O, **6:** T153Q
speaker, 4: T84, T110, **6:** T276, T277, T281B, T281C, T281F, T302, T303, T307, T311, T313
stanza, 1: xii, **4:** T278, **6:** T277, T281C
suspense, 1: T86, T87, T89I, T113, T116, **3:** T81, **4:** T89H
theme, 1: xii, S9, S13–S14, T25M, **2:** xii, T208, T212–T213, T217C, T217F, T217G, T217J, T217M, T217P, T239, T241, T243, T245, T247, T249, T276–T277, T281B, T281D, T303, T304, T305, T307, T311, T313, T315, **3:** xii, T20–T21, T25C, T25F, T25H, T25I, T25L, T25N, T46, T47, T51, T52, T55, T57, T59, T80, T84–T85, T89C, T89F, T89L, T89N, T89P, T105, T111, T113, T115, T117, T119, T121, T123, **4:** xii, T276–T277, T281B, T281D, T303, T307, T311, T313, **5:** xii, T17, **6:** xii, T20–T21, T25D, T25G, T25J, T25L, T25P, T40, T47, T51, T52–T53, T55, T57, T59, T84–T85, T89C, T89F, T89J, T89K, T89N, T104–T105, T111, T112, T113, T115, T119, T121, T217H, T272
Literary response,
See also **Text connections.**
    personal, 1: T25P, T41, T49, T53, T59, T89L, T105, T113, T117, T123, T153R, T169, T177, T181, T187, T217R, T233, T241, T245, T251, T281D, T297, T305, T309, T315, T336, T338, **2:** T25R, T41, T49, T53, T59, T89P, T105, T113, T117, T123, T153N, T169, T177, T181, T187, T217P, T233, T241, T245, T251, T281D, T297, T305, T309, T315, T336, T338, **3:** T25N, T41, T49, T53, T59, T89P, T105, T113, T117, T123, T153P, T169, T177, T181, T187, T217P, T233, T241, T245, T251, T281D, T297, T305, T309, T315, T336, T338, **4:** T25P, T41, T49, T53, T59, T89L, T105, T113, T117, T123, T153R, T169, T177, T181, T187, T217R, T233, T241, T245, T251, T281D, T297, T305, T309, T315, T336, T338, **5:** T25N, T41, T49,

KEY **3** = Unit 3

S

Scaffolding. *See* Access complex text; English Language Learners: scaffold.

Science, 1: T92, T197, T217J, T220, T233, T241, T245, T251, T261, T281B, T284, T297, T305, T309, T315, T329, T331, **2:** T69, T133, T153L, T156, T169, T177, T181, T187, T197, T217T, T233, T241, T245, T251, T261, T331, **3:** T69, T89R, T92, T133, T153H, T156, T169, T177, T181, T187, T197, T217L, T233, T241, T245, T249, T251, T331, **4:** T92, T197, T217F, T220, T233, T241, T245, T249, T251, T261, T329, T331, **5:** T5, T133, T153L, T156, T169, T177, T181, T187, T197, T217F, T217H, T220, T233, T241, T245, T251, T261, T281B, T281D, T284, T297, T305, T309, T315, T329, T331, **6:** T133, T153J, T156, T169, T177, T181, T187, T197, T217L, T220, T233, T241, T245, T251, T261, T329, T331

See also **Literacy workstation activity cards.**

Science fiction. *See under* Genre: fiction.

Scoring rubrics

research and inquiry projects, **Units 1–6:** T333

writing, **Units 1–6:** T30, T94, T158, T222, T286, T349, T355

Self-correction strategies. *See* Monitor and Clarify.

Self-monitoring strategies. *See* Monitor and Clarify.

Self-selected reading, Units 1–6: T47, T51, T55, T111, T115, T119, T175, T179, T183, T239, T243, T247, T303, T307, T311

Sentences. *See* Grammar: sentences; Writer's Craft: strong sentences; Writing traits: sentence fluency.

Sequence of events. *See* Comprehension skills: sequence; Writing traits: organization.

Setting. *See* Comprehension skills: setting.

Setting purposes for reading, 1: T58, T186, T250, T314, **2:** T58, T186, T250, T314, **3:** T58, T186, T250, T314, **4:** T58, T186, T250, T314, **5:** T58, T186, T250, T314, **6:** T58, T186, T250, T314

Shared Read, Units 1–6: T16–T17, T56–T57, T80–T81, T120–T121, T144–T145, T184–T185, T208–T209, T248–T249, T272–T273, T312–T313, T326

Sharing circles. *See* Literature Circle.

Signal words, 1: T148–T149, T153L, T212–T213, T222, T224–T225, **2:** T20, T148–T149, T174–T175, **3:** T89J, T153G, T217G, **4:** T158, T190, **5:** T148, T153P, T175, T179, T183, T212, **6:** T23, T149, T150, T153F, T153T, T175, T179, T183, T335

Similes, 1: T41, T49, T53, T59, **2:** T88–T89, T89H, T89K, T89P, T103, T109, T114, T118, T121, T125, T230, T294, **4:** T217N, T280–T281, T281C, T295, T301, T306, T310, T317, T352, **5:** T22, T25E–T254, T89H, T89J, T102, **6:** T25B, T25O, T217C

Small Group Options. *See* Approaching Level Options; Beyond Level Options; English Language Learners; On Level Options.

Social studies, 1: T5, T28, T69, T133, T153T, T156, T169, T177, T181, T187, T197, **2:** T5, T25P, T28, T41, T49, T53, T59, T331, **3:** T5, T261, T281B, T284, T297, T309, T315, T331, **4:** T5, T41, T49, T53, T59, T69, T133, T153N, T156, T169, T177, T181, T187, T329, T331, **5:** T53, T69, T92, T331, **6:** T5, T69, T331

See also **Literacy workstation activity cards.**

Speaking skills and strategies

See also Fluency: speaking checklist; Listening; Literature Circle.

act it out, **1:** T121, **2:** T185, **3:** T57, T252, **4:** T99, T123, **5:** T252, **6:** T185, T314

add new ideas, **1:** S6, T202, **5:** T202, **6:** T10

ask and answer questions, **1:** S20, T74, **2:** T74, **3:** T202, **4:** T10, T202, **5:** T10

audio presentation, **1:** T354, **2:** T331

be open to all ideas, **1:** S20, **2:** T138, **3:** T10, **6:** T74, T202

checklist, **Units 1–6:** T333, T334

debate, **1:** T331, **3:** T331, **5:** T227

dramatic presentation, **2:** T331

English Language Learner,

demonstrate, **1:** T275, **2:** T277, T281, **3:** T351, **4:** T275, T277, T279, **6:** T87, T275

explain, **1:** T19, T21, T25, T83, T89, T149, T151, T213, T215, T279, T281, **2:** T19, T21, T83, T87, T89, T149, T223, T277, T279, **3:** T25, T85, T87, T149, T153, T211, T215, T277, T279, T281, **4:** T21, T23, T87, T89, T149, T153, T211, T215, T277, **5:** T275, T281, **6:** T21, T83, T149, T151, T213, T275, T279

express, **2:** T217, **3:** T23, T25, **4:** T153

respond orally, **1:** T31, T95, T159, T223, T287, **2:** T153, T213, T223, T277, T287, **3:** T147, T211, T277, T287, **4:** T87, T95, T159, T223, T275, T277, T287, **5:** T31, T95, T159, T213, T223, T277, T287, **6:** T31, T95, T159, T223, T275, T287

formal presentation, **4:** T331, **5:** T331

mock interview, **5:** T331, **6:** T331

multimedia presentation, **5:** T331

oral presentations, **1:** S35, T28, T29, T92, T93, T156, T157, T220, T221, T284, T285, T331, T334, **2:** T28, T29, T92, T93, T156, T157, T220, T221, T284, T285, T331, **3:** T29, T92, T93, T156, T157, T220, T221, T284, T285, **4:** T28, T29, T92, T93, T157, T220, T221, T285, **5:** T28, T29, T92, T93, T156, T157, T221, T285, **6:** T29, T92, T93, T156, T157, T220, T221, T285, T331

perform commercial, **5:** T227

persuasive presentation, **1:** T331, **2:** T284, **5:** T331

poster, **3:** T331

present advertisement, **6:** T310

present ideas, **4:** T285

retell, **1:** T119, T148, T187, **3:** T217P, **4:** T28, T168, T187

role-play, **2:** T11, **6:** T89D, T89P

Reader's Theater, **1:** T326–T327, **2:** T326–T327, **3:** T326–T327, **4:** T326–T327, **5:** T326–T327, **6:** T326–T327

speak slowly and clearly, **1:** S35, **2:** T156, T220, **4:** T220

speech, **1:** T284, **5:** T331

summarize/summaries, **1:** T12, T76, T140, T204, T268, **2:** T12, T76, T140, T204, T268, **3:** T76, T140, T204, T268, **4:** T12, T76, T92, T140, T204, T220, T268, **5:** T12, T29, T76, T140, T204, T268, **6:** T12, T29, T76, T140, T204, T221, T268

take on discussion roles, **1:** S20, T10, **2:** T202, **3:** T138, **4:** T138, **5:** T74, T138

take turns talking, **1:** S6, T266, **2:** T10, **3:** T266, **4:** T74, **6:** T138

visual and digital elements, **1:** T92, 334, **2:** T334, **3:** T334, **4:** T334, **5:** T92, T334, **6:** T334

web site/podcast, **5:** T156

Speech, 1: T284, **4:** T84–T85, T185, T284, **5:** T156, **6:** T92, T334

Speed Sort, Units 1–6: T37, T101, T165, T229, T293

Spelling, Units 1–6: T36–T37, T100–T101, T164–T165, T228–T229, T292–T293

See also English Language Learners: writing/spelling; Phonics/Word Study.

analogies, **1:** T37, **2:** T37, T293, **4:** T101, **5:** T165, **6:** T165

antonyms, **1:** T37, **2:** T37, **3:** T37, **5:** T165

assess, **Units 1–6:** T37, T101, T165, T229, T293

assess prior knowledge, **Units 1–6:** T36, T100, T164, T228, T292

challenge words, **Units 1–6:** T36, T100, T164, T228, T292

closed syllables, **1:** S29, **2:** T292–T293, T318, **3:** T36

cloze sentences, **1:** T293, **3:** T101, **5:** T229, **6:** T101, T229

consonant + *le* syllables, **1:** S29, **3:** T228–T229, T254, T292

contractions, **2:** T228–T229, T254, T292

definitions, **3:** T165, **4:** T165, **5:** T37, T293

dictation sentences, **Units 1–6:** T37, T101, T165, T229, T293

differentiated spelling, **Units 1–6:** T36, T100, T164, T228, T292

diphthongs, **2:** T62

error correction, **Units 1–6:** T37, T101, T165, T229, T293

homographs, **4:** T154–T155, T164–T165, T170–T171, T190, T228

homophones, **5:** T90–T91, T100–T101, T106–T107, T126, T164

inflectional endings, **2:** T154–T155, T164–T165, T170–T171, T190, T228

link to spelling, **1:** S30

long vowels, **1:** T126, T164

number prefixes *uni-, bi-, tri-, cent-*, **6:** T218–T219, T228–T229, T234–T235, T254, T292

T

W

Common Core State Standards Correlations
English Language Arts

College and Career Readiness Anchor Standards for READING

The K-5 standards on the following pages define what students should understand and be able to do by the end of each grade. They correspond to the College and Career Readiness (CCR) anchor standards below by number. The CCR and grade-specific standards are necessary complements—the former providing broad standards, the latter providing additional specificity—that together define the skills and understandings that all students must demonstrate.

Key Ideas and Details

1. Read closely to determine what the text says explicitly and to make logical inferences from it; cite specific textual evidence when writing or speaking to support conclusions drawn from the text.

2. Determine central ideas or themes of a text and analyze their development; summarize the key supporting details and ideas.

3. Analyze how and why individuals, events, and ideas develop and interact over the course of a text.

Craft and Structure

4. Interpret words and phrases as they are used in a text, including determining technical, connotative, and figurative meanings, and analyze how specific word choices shape meaning or tone.

5. Analyze the structure of texts, including how specific sentences, paragraphs, and larger portions of the text (e.g., a section, chapter, scene, or stanza) relate to each other and the whole.

6. Assess how point of view or purpose shapes the content and style of a text.

Integration of Knowledge and Ideas

7. Integrate and evaluate content presented in diverse media and formats, including visually and quantitatively, as well as in words.

8. Delineate and evaluate the argument and specific claims in a text, including the validity of the reasoning as well as the relevance and sufficiency of the evidence.

9. Analyze how two or more texts address similar themes or topics in order to build knowledge or to compare the approaches the authors take.

Range of Reading and Level of Text Complexity

10. Read and comprehend complex literary and informational texts independently and proficiently.

CCSS Common Core State Standards
English Language Arts

Grade 5

Each standard is coded in the following manner:

Strand	Grade Level	Standard
RL	5	1

Reading Standards for Literature

Key Ideas and Details		*McGraw-Hill Reading Wonders*
RL.5.1	Quote accurately from a text when explaining what the text says explicitly and when drawing inferences from the text.	**READING/WRITING WORKSHOP:** Unit 1: 26, 40, 41 Unit 2: 113, 142 Unit 3: 170, 171, 212 Unit 4: 242, 243, 256, 257 Unit 5: 315, 329 Unit 6: 386, 387, 401, 402 **LITERATURE ANTHOLOGY:** Unit 1: 14, 18, 20, 25, 33, 35, 39, 41, 89 Unit 2: 129, 133, 137, 155, 169, 171, 179, 181 Unit 3: 185, 190, 192, 195, 202, 207, 213 Unit 4: 275, 277, 291, 293, 297, 343 Unit 5: 359, 377, 379 Unit 6: 434, 437, 443, 445, 454, 457, 461, 463, 509, 511 **LEVELED READERS:** Unit 1, Week 1: *Parker's Plan* (A), *Can-do Canines* (O), *Cleaning Up the Competition* (B) **Unit 1, Week 2:** *Dog Gone* (A), *Shhh! It's a Surprise!* (O), *Lost and Found* (B) **Unit 2, Week 4:** *The Lion's Whiskers* (A), *The Riddle of the Drum: A Tale from Mexico* (O), *Clever Manka* (B) **Unit 3, Week 2:** *Over the Top* (A), *In Drama Valley* (O), *Welcome to the Wilds* (B) **Unit 4, Week 2:** *The Mysterious Teacher* (A), *The Unusually Clever Dog* (O), *The Surprise Party* (B) **Unit 5, Week 2:** *The Picture Palace* (A), *Hard Times* (O), *Woodpecker Warriors* (B) **Unit 6, Week 2:** *Winning Friends* (A), *Enemy or Ally?* (O), *Jamayla to the Rescue* (B) **YOUR TURN PRACTICE BOOK:** 3–5, 13–15, 63–65, 83–85, 103–105, 113–115, 163–165, 203–205, 213–215, 223–225, 263–265 **READING WORKSTATION ACTIVITY CARDS:** 22 **TEACHER'S EDITION:** Unit 1: T25P, T29, T89I, T89L, T93 Unit 2: T89P, T93, T217G, T217P, T221 Unit 3: T25N, T89E, T89G, T89P, T93 Unit 4: T25P, T29, T89E, T89L, T93 Unit 5: T25G, T25N, T89H, T89J, T89P, T93 Unit 6: T25H, T25M, T25P, T89H, T89K
RL.5.2	Determine a theme of a story, drama, or poem from details in the text, including how characters in a story or drama respond to challenges or how the speaker in a poem reflects upon a topic; summarize the text.	**READING/WRITING WORKSHOP:** Unit 2: 141, 155 Unit 3: 170, 171, 184, 185 Unit 4: 299 Unit 6: 387, 400, 401 **LITERATURE ANTHOLOGY:** Unit 1: 25, 41 Unit 2: 133, 171, 179 Unit 3: 185, 190, 195, 207, 213 Unit 4: 275, 277, 293, 343 Unit 5: 359, 377, 379 Unit 6: 434, 437, 445, 454, 457, 463, 509, 511 **LEVELED READERS:** Unit 2, Week 4: *The Lion's Whiskers* (A), *The Riddle of the Drum: A Tale from Mexico* (O, ELL), *Clever Manka* (B) **Unit 2, Week 5:** *Clearing the Jungle* (A), *I Want to Ride!* (O, ELL), *Changing Goals* (B) **Unit 3, Week 1:** *All the Way from Europe* (A), *Dancing the Flamenco* (O, ELL), *A Vacation in Minnesota* (B) **Unit 3, Week 2:** *Over the Top* (A), *In Drama Valley* (O, ELL), *Welcome to the Wilds* (B) **Unit 4, Week 5:** *Tell Me the Old, Old Stories* (A), *From Me to You* (O, ELL), *Every Picture Tells a Story* (B) **Unit 6, Week 1:** *Mrs. Gleeson's Records* (A), *Norberto's Hat* (O, ELL), *The Victory Garden* (B) **Unit 6, Week 2:** *Winning Friends* (A), *Enemy or Ally?* (O, ELL), *Jamayla to the Rescue* (B) **YOUR TURN PRACTICE BOOK:** 83–85, 93–94, 103–105, 113–115, 193–194, 199, 253–255, 259, 263–265 **READING WORKSTATION STUDY CARDS:** 6 **TEACHER'S EDITION:** Unit 2: T212, T217P, T239, T243, T247, T249, T276, T281D, T303, T307, T311, T313 Unit 3: T20, T25N, T47, T51, T55, T57, T84, T89C, T89F, T89P Unit 4: T276, T281B, T285, T303, T307, T311, T313 Unit 6: T20, T25L, T25P, T29, T84, T111, T115, T119, T121

Reading Standards for Literature

Key Ideas and Details		McGraw-Hill Reading Wonders
RL.5.3	Compare and contrast two or more characters, settings, or events in a story or drama, drawing on specific details in the text (e.g., how characters interact).	**READING/WRITING WORKSHOP: Unit 2:** 113 **Unit 5:** 315, 329 **LITERATURE ANTHOLOGY: Unit 2:** 133 **Unit 4:** 293 **Unit 5:** 359, 379 **Unit 6:** 463 **LEVELED READERS: Unit 2, Week 2:** *The Bird of Truth* (A), *The Talking Eggs* (O, ELL), *Three Golden Oranges* (B) **Unit 5, Week 1:** *King of the Board* (A), *Snap Happy* (O, ELL), *No Place Like Home* (B) **Unit 5, Week 2:** *The Picture Palace* (A), *Hard Times* (O, ELL), *Woodpecker Warriors* (B) **YOUR TURN PRACTICE BOOK:** 62–65, 202–205, 212–215 **READING WORKSTATION ACTIVITY CARDS:** 3, 4, 5 **TEACHER'S EDITION: Unit 2:** T84, T89C, T89G, T89J, T89K, T89N, T89P **Unit 5:** T20, T25B, T25F, T25I, T25K, T25N, T84, T89E, T89I, T89K, T89M, T89P

Craft and Structure		McGraw-Hill Reading Wonders
RL.5.4	Determine the meaning of words and phrases as they are used in a text, including figurative language such as metaphors and similes.	**READING/WRITING WORKSHOP: Unit 1:** 43 **Unit 2:** 115 **Unit 3:** 173 **Unit 4:** 301 **Unit 5:** 331 **Unit 6:** 389 **LITERATURE ANTHOLOGY: Unit 1:** 41 **Unit 2:** 133 **Unit 3:** 195 **Unit 4:** 343 **Unit 5:** 379 **Unit 6:** 445 **YOUR TURN PRACTICE BOOK:** 17, 67, 107, 197, 217 **TEACHER'S EDITION: Unit 1:** T88, T89B, T89L, T89M, T109, T114, T118, T125 **Unit 2:** T88, T109, T114, T118, T125 **Unit 3:** T24, T25C, T25I, T25K, T25N **Unit 4:** T280, T281, T281A, T281C, T281D, T281F, T301, T306, T310, T317 **Unit 5:** T88, T89E, T89G, T109, T114, T118, T125 **Unit 6:** T24, T25C, T25E, T25H, T25I, T25P
RL.5.5	Explain how a series of chapters, scenes, or stanzas fits together to provide the overall structure of a particular story, drama, or poem.	**READING/WRITING WORKSHOP: Unit 4:** 300 **LITERATURE ANTHOLOGY: Unit 2:** 132 **Unit 4:** 343 **LEVELED READERS: Unit 4, Week 2:** *The Mysterious Teacher* (A), *The Unusually Clever Dog* (O, ELL), *The Surprise Party* (B) **YOUR TURN PRACTICE BOOK:** 99, 166, 196 **READING WORKSTATION ACTIVITY CARDS:** 26, 27 **TEACHER'S EDITION: Unit 2:** T81, T89G, T285 **Unit 4:** T86, T89E, T89F, T89G, T89K, T104, T105, T112, T113, T116, T117, T121–T123, T278, T350 **Unit 5:** T25I
RL.5.6	Describe how a narrator's or speaker's point of view influences how events are described.	**READING/WRITING WORKSHOP: Unit 4:** 243, 257 **Unit 5:** 316 **Unit 6:** 443 **LITERATURE ANTHOLOGY: Unit 4:** 277, 293 **Unit 5:** 358 **Unit 6:** 462 **LEVELED READERS: Unit 4, Week 1:** *Paul Bunyan* (A), *Pecos Bill* (O, ELL), *An Extraordinary Girl* (B) **Unit 4, Week 2:** *The Mysterious Teacher* (A), *The Unusually Clever Dog* (O, ELL), *The Surprise Party* (B) **Unit 6, Week 5:** *Your World, My World* (A), *Flying Home* (O, ELL), *Helping Out* (B) **YOUR TURN PRACTICE BOOK:** 153–155, 159, 163–165 **READING WORKSTATION ACTIVITY CARDS:** 7 **TEACHER'S EDITION: Unit 4:** T20, T25C, T25E, T25J, T25M, T25P, T29, T47, T51, T55, T57, T84, T89C, T89E, T89I, T89L, T111, T115, T119, T121, T274 **Unit 5:** T22, T25E **Unit 6:** T276, T281B, T281D, T303, T307, T311, T313

Integration of Knowledge and Ideas		McGraw-Hill Reading Wonders
RL.5.7	Analyze how visual and multimedia elements contribute to the meaning, tone, or beauty of a text (e.g., graphic novel, multimedia presentation of fiction, folktale, myth, poem).	**READING/WRITING WORKSHOP: Unit 2:** 114 **YOUR TURN PRACTICE BOOK:** 6, 9, 66 **READING WORKSTATION ACTIVITY CARDS:** 8 **TEACHER'S EDITION: Unit 1:** T22, T23, T25F, T25J, T29, T89K **Unit 2:** T86, T89E, T89O, T217I, T217N, T284 **Unit 3:** T25B, T89B, T93 **Unit 4:** T25E, T28 **www.connected.mcgraw-hill.com: RESOURCES:** **READING/WRITING WORKSHOP: Unit 2:** 108–115, 136–143 **Unit 6:** 438–445 **LITERATURE ANTHOLOGY: Unit 2:** 118–133, 156–171 **Unit 3:** 198–213 **STUDENT PRACTICE: Approaching Reproducibles:** 6, 9, 66 **Beyond Reproducibles:** 6, 9, 66 **ELL Reproducibles:** 6, 9, 66 **MEDIA:** Video, Images
RL.5.8	(Not applicable to Literature)	

Reading Standards for Literature

Integration of Knowledge and Ideas		*McGraw-Hill Reading Wonders*
RL.5.9	Compare and contrast stories in the same genre (e.g., mysteries and adventure stories) on their approaches to similar themes and topics.	**LITERATURE ANTHOLOGY:** Unit 1: 45 Unit 2: 137, 155 Unit 4: 281, 297 Unit 5: 363 Unit 6: 489 **LEVELED READERS:** Unit 1, Week 2: *Dog Gone* (A), *Shhh! It's a Surprise!* (O, ELL), *Lost and Found* (B) **READING WORKSTATION ACTIVITY CARDS:** 9 **TEACHER'S EDITION:** Unit 1: T29, T93, T105, T113, T117, T123 Unit 2: T89R, T89T, T93, T105, T113, T117, T123, T221 Unit 3: T29, T93 Unit 4: T25R, T25T, T89N, T89P, T93 Unit 5: T25P, T25R

Range of Reading and Level of Text Complexity		*McGraw-Hill Reading Wonders*
RL.5.10	By the end of the year, read and comprehend literature, including stories, dramas, and poetry, at the high end of the grades 4–5 text complexity band independently and proficiently.	**READING/WRITING WORKSHOP:** These Units reflect the range of text complexity found throughout the book. **Unit 1, Week 1:** "A Fresh Idea," 22; **Unit 2, Week 2:** "A Modern Cinderella," 108; **Unit 2, Week 4:** "The Magical Lost Brocade," 136; **Unit 3, Week 1:** "A Reluctant Traveler," 166; **Unit 3, Week 2:** "Survivaland," 180; **Unit 4, Week 1:** "How Mighty Kate Stopped the Train," 238; **Unit 4, Week 2:** "Where's Brownie?," 252; **Unit 5, Week 1:** "Miguel in the Middle," 310; **Unit 5, Week 2:** "The Day the Rollets Got Their Moxie Back," 324; **Unit 6, Week 2:** "The Bully," 396; **Unit 6, Week 5:** "To Travel!," 438 **LITERATURE ANTHOLOGY:** These Units reflect the range of text complexity found throughout the book. **Unit 1, Week 1:** *One Hen,* 10; **Unit 2, Week 2:** *Where the Mountain Meets the Moon,* 118; **Unit 2, Week 4:** *Blancaflor,* 156; **Unit 2, Week 5:** *Stage Fright,* 176; **Unit 3, Week 2:** *Weslandia,* 198; **Unit 4, Week 1:** *Davy Crockett Saves the World,* 262; **Unit 4, Week 2:** *A Window Into History,* 282; **Unit 5, Week 2:** *Bud, Not Buddy,* 364; **Unit 6, Week 1:** *The Unbreakable Code,* 430; **Unit 6, Week 2:** *The Friend Who Changed My Life,* 450; **Unit 6, Week 5:** *You Are My Music,* 506 **LEVELED READERS:** Unit 1, Week 1: *Parker's Plan* (A), *Can-do Canines* (O, ELL), *Cleaning Up the Competition* (B) **Unit 2, Week 2:** *The Bird of Truth* (A), *The Talking Eggs* (O, ELL), *Three Golden Oranges* (B) **Unit 2, Week 4:** *The Lion's Whiskers* (A), *The Riddle of the Drum: A Tale from Mexico* (O, ELL), *Clever Manka* (B) **Unit 3, Week 1:** *All the Way from Europe* (A), *Dancing the Flamenco* (O, ELL), *A Vacation in Minnesota* (B) **Unit 3, Week 2:** *Over the Top* (A), *In Drama Valley* (O, ELL), *Welcome to the Wilds* (B) **Unit 4, Week 1:** *Paul Bunyan* (A), *Pecos Bill* (O, ELL), *An Extraordinary Girl* (B) **Unit 4, Week 2:** *The Mysterious Teacher* (A), *The Unusually Clever Dog* (O, ELL), *The Surprise Party* (B) **Unit 4, Week 5:** *Tell Me the Old, Old Stories* (A), *From Me to You* (O, ELL), *Every Picture Tells a Story* (B) **Unit 5, Week 2:** *The Picture Palace* (A), *Hard Times* (O, ELL), *Woodpecker Warriors* (B) **Unit 6, Week 1:** *Mrs. Gleeson's Records* (A), *Norberto's Hat* (O, ELL), *The Victory Garden* (B) **Unit 6, Week 5:** *Your World, My World* (A), *Flying Home* (O, ELL), *Helping Out* (B) **YOUR TURN PRACTICE BOOK:** 16, 86, 106, 116, 266 **READING WORKSTATION ACTIVITY CARDS:** 24, 26, 27, 30 **TEACHER'S EDITION:** Unit 1: T22, T25A–T25P Unit 2: T86, T89A–T89T, T214, 217A–T217P, T274, T281A–T281F Unit 3: T22, T25A–T25N, T86, T89A–T89P Unit 4: T22, T25A–T25T, T86, T89A–T89L, T104–T105, T112–T113, T116–T117, T274, T281A–T281F Unit 5: T22, T25A–T25R, T86, T89A–T89P Unit 6: T86, T89A–T89R, T274, T281A–T281F

Reading Standards for Informational Text

Key Ideas and Details		*McGraw-Hill Reading Wonders*
RI.5.1	Quote accurately from a text when explaining what the text says explicitly and when drawing inferences from the text.	**READING/WRITING WORKSHOP:** Unit 1: 54, 55, 68 Unit 2: 98, 99, 126, 128 Unit 3: 198, 199, 212, 213 Unit 4: 271 Unit 5: 342, 356 Unit 6: 414, 428 **LITERATURE ANTHOLOGY:** Unit 1: 49, 54, 61, 63, 72, 78, 81, 85 Unit 2: 100, 103, 109, 113, 141, 145, 147, 151 Unit 3: 220, 223, 227, 231, 241, 246, 249, 251 Unit 4: 303, 307, 311, 315, 319, 324, 328, 332, 337 Unit 5: 388, 393, 397, 399, 409, 417, 419, 421 Unit 6: 473, 478, 485, 495, 497, 501, 503, 505 **LEVELED READERS:** Unit 1, Week 3: *Save This Space!* (A, O, B) Unit 2, Week 1: *The Bill of Rights* (A, O, B) Unit 3, Week 4: *The Power of a Team* (A, O, B) Unit 4, Week 3: *Jane Addams: A Woman of Action* (A, O, B) Unit 5, Week 4: *Mars* (A, O, B) Unit 6, Week 3: *Cave Creatures* (A, O, B) **YOUR TURN PRACTICE BOOK:** 23–25, 33–35, 53–55, 73–75, 123–125, 133–135, 173–175, 183–185, 223–225, 233–235, 273–275, 283–285 **READING WORKSTATION ACTIVITY CARDS:** 22 **TEACHER'S EDITION:** Unit 1: T153R, T217K, T217R, T221, T281D Unit 2: T25H, T25R, T153F, T153N, T157 Unit 3: T153N, T153P, T217L, T217P, T221 Unit 4: T153C, T153I, T153R, T157, T217R Unit 5: T153H, T153P, T217R, T221, T285 Unit 6: T153K, T153R, T217J, T217N, T221
RI.5.2	Determine two or more main ideas of a text and explain how they are supported by key details; summarize the text.	**READING/WRITING WORKSHOP:** Unit 3: 199, 213, 226 Unit 4: 270, 284 **LITERATURE ANTHOLOGY:** Unit 3: 231, 251 Unit 4: 315, 337 **LEVELED READERS:** Unit 3, Week 3: *Weather Patterns* (A, O, B, ELL) Unit 3, Week 4: *The Power of a Team* (A, O, B, ELL) Unit 4, Week 3: *Jane Addams: A Woman of Action* (A, O, B, ELL) Unit 4, Week 4: *The Delta* (A, O, B, ELL) **YOUR TURN PRACTICE BOOK:** 123–125, 133–135 **READING WORKSTATION ACTIVITY CARDS:** 10 **TEACHER'S EDITION:** Unit 3: T148, T153C, T153F, T153H, T153J, T153K, T153M, T153P, T175, T179, T183, T185, T212, T217C, T217H, T217M, T217P, T239, T243, T247, T249, T274 Unit 4: T146, T153G, T153L, T153R, T210, T217K, T217M, T217R Unit 5: T274
RI.5.3	Explain the relationships or interactions between two or more individuals, events, ideas, or concepts in a historical, scientific, or technical text based on specific information in the text.	**READING/WRITING WORKSHOP:** Unit 1: 55 Unit 5: 357 Unit 6: 415 **LITERATURE ANTHOLOGY:** Unit 1: 63 Unit 5: 388, 399, 403, 409, 417, 421, 427 Unit 6: 473, 483, 485 **LEVELED READERS:** Unit 1, Week 3: *Save This Space!* (A, O, B, ELL) Unit 5, Week 4: *Mars* (A, O, B, ELL) Unit 6, Week 3: *Cave Creatures* (A, O, B, ELL) **YOUR TURN PRACTICE BOOK:** 23–25, 233–235, 273–275 **READING WORKSTATION ACTIVITY CARDS:** 11 **TEACHER'S EDITION:** Unit 1: T153D, T153F, T153H, T153I, T153K, T153M, T153O Unit 5: T217D, T217E, T217H, T217L, T217P Unit 6: T153C, T153E, T153G, T153I, T153L, T212

Reading Standards for Informational Text

Craft and Structure		McGraw-Hill Reading Wonders
RI.5.4	Determine the meaning of general academic and domain-specific words and phrases in a text relevant to a *grade 5 topic or subject area*.	**LITERATURE ANTHOLOGY:** Unit 1: 63, 85, 93 **Unit 2:** 113, 151 **Unit 3:** 231, 251, 259 **Unit 4:** 315, 337 **Unit 5:** 399, 427 **Unit 6:** 485, 503 **YOUR TURN PRACTICE BOOK:** 37, 57, 77, 127, 137, 147, 187, 227, 237, 247, 277 **TEACHER'S EDITION:** Unit 1: T153J, T153R, T216, T217C, T217R **Unit 2:** T24, T25I, T25R, T153G, T153N **Unit 3:** T153D, T153P, T216, T217J, T217P **Unit 4:** T153K, T153R, T216, T217E, T217R **Unit 5:** T152, T153B, T153P, T217B, T217R **Unit 6:** T153D, T153R, T173, T178, T182, T185
RI.5.5	Compare and contrast the overall structure (e.g., chronology, comparison, cause/effect, problem/solution) of events, ideas, concepts, or information in two or more texts.	**LITERATURE ANTHOLOGY:** Unit 1: 95 **YOUR TURN PRACTICE BOOK:** 289 **READING WORKSTATION ACTIVITY CARDS:** 15 **TEACHER'S EDITION:** Unit 1: T212 **Unit 2:** T148 **Unit 5:** T212 **Unit 6:** T212, T221
RI.5.6	Analyze multiple accounts of the same event or topic, noting important similarities and differences in the point of view they represent.	**READING/WRITING WORKSHOP:** Unit 1: 56, 82 **Unit 3:** 226 **Unit 5:** 372 **LITERATURE ANTHOLOGY:** Unit 1: 93 **Unit 3:** 259 **Unit 5:** 427 **LEVELED READERS:** Unit 1, Week 5: *What About Robots?* (A, O, B, ELL) **YOUR TURN PRACTICE BOOK:** 43–45, 143–145, 243–245, 249 **READING WORKSTATION ACTIVITY CARDS:** 16 **TEACHER'S EDITION:** Unit 1: T150, T274, T276, T281C, T281D, T296–T297, T304–T305, T308–T309, T314–T315 **Unit 3:** T274, T276, T281C, T281D, T281F **Unit 5:** T278, T279, T281D, T285

Integration of Knowledge and Ideas		McGraw-Hill Reading Wonders
RI.5.7	Draw on information from multiple print or digital sources, demonstrating the ability to locate an answer to a question quickly or to solve a problem efficiently.	**READING WORKSTATION ACTIVITY CARDS:** 19 **TEACHER'S EDITION:** Unit 1: T157, T285, T328, T329 **Unit 2:** T29, T157, T328, T329 **Unit 3:** T157, T285, T328, T329 **Unit 4:** T92, T156, T157, T221, T328, T329 **Unit 5:** T156, T221, T285, T328, T329 **Unit 6:** T29, T93, T328, T329 www.connected.mcgraw-hill.com: **RESOURCES:** READING/WRITING WORKSHOP: Unit 4: 272 RESEARCH & INQUIRY: Weekly Lessons: Units 1–6 **Research Roadmaps:** Units 1–6 CARDS: Reading Workstation Activity Cards: 19
RI.5.8	Explain how an author uses reasons and evidence to support particular points in a text, identifying which reasons and evidence support which point(s).	**READING/WRITING WORKSHOP:** Unit 1: 83, 84 **Unit 3:** 227, 228 **Unit 4:** 271, 285 **Unit 5:** 371 **LITERATURE ANTHOLOGY:** Unit 1: 62, 93 **Unit 3:** 259 **Unit 4:** 337 **Unit 5:** 427 **LEVELED READERS:** Unit 3, Week 5: *The Anasazi* (A, O, B, ELL), **Unit 5, Week 5:** *The Great Plains* (A, O, B, ELL) **YOUR TURN PRACTICE BOOK:** 43–45, 46, 143–145, 146, 149, 173–175, 183–185, 189, 243–245 **READING WORKSTATION ACTIVITY CARDS:** 20 **TEACHER'S EDITION:** Unit 1: T274, T276, T281C, T281D **Unit 3:** T276, T278, T281C, T281D, T303, T307, T311, T313 **Unit 4:** T148, T153F, T153R, T212, T217H, T221 **Unit 5:** T276, T281D, T303, T307, T311, T313
RI.5.9	Integrate information from several texts on the same topic in order to write or speak about the subject knowledgeably.	**LITERATURE ANTHOLOGY:** Unit 1: 95 **READING WORKSTATION ACTIVITY CARDS:** 21 **TEACHER'S EDITION:** Unit 1: T157, T220, T221 **Unit 2:** T28, T29, T156, T157, T329 **Unit 3:** T156, T157, T220, T221, T329 **Unit 4:** T92, T157, T220, T221, T329 **Unit 5:** T156, T157, T220, T329 **Unit 6:** T29, T156, T157, T221, T329

Reading Standards for Informational Text

Range of Reading and Level of Text Complexity	McGraw-Hill Reading Wonders
RI.5.10 By the end of the year, read and comprehend informational texts, including history/social studies, science, and technical texts, at the high end of the grades 4–5 text complexity band independently and proficiently.	**READING/WRITING WORKSHOP:** These Units reflect the range of text complexity found throughout the book. **Unit 1, Week 3:** "A Life in the Woods," 50; **Unit 1, Week 4:** "Fantasy Becomes Fact," 64 **Unit 2, Week 1:** "Creating a Nation," 94; **Unit 2, Week 3:** "Growing in Place: The Story of E. Lucy Braun," 122; **Unit 3, Week 3:** "Patterns of Change," 194; **Unit 4, Week 3:** "Frederick Douglass: Freedom's Voice," 266; **Unit 4, Week 4:** "Power from Nature," 280; **Unit 5, Week 4:** "Changing Views of Earth," 352; **Unit 5, Week 5:** "Should Plants and Animals from Other Places Live Here?," 366; **Unit 6, Week 3:** "Mysterious Oceans," 410; **Unit 6, Week 4:** "Words to Save the World: The Work of Rachel Carson," 424 **LITERATURE ANTHOLOGY:** These Units reflect the range of text complexity found throughout the book. **Unit 1, Week 3:** *Camping with the President*, 46; **Unit 1, Week 4:** *The Boy Who Invented TV*, 68; **Unit 2, Week 1:** *Who Wrote the U.S. Constitution?*, 96; **Unit 2, Week 3:** *The Boy Who Drew Birds*, 138; **Unit 3, Week 3:** *The Story of Snow*, 216; **Unit 3, Week 5:** *Machu Picchu: Ancient City*, 256; **Unit 4, Week 3:** *Rosa*, 298; **Unit 4, Week 4:** *One Well*, 320; **Unit 5, Week 4:** *When Is a Planet Not a Planet?*, 404; **Unit 6, Week 3:** *Survival at 40 Below*, 468; **Unit 6, Week 4:** *Planting the Trees of Kenya*, 490 **LEVELED READERS: Unit 1, Week 4:** *Snapshot! The Story of George Eastman* (A, O, B, ELL) **Unit 2, Week 1:** *The Bill of Rights* (A, O, B, ELL) **Unit 2, Week 3:** *Norman Borlaug and the Green Revolution* (A, O, B, ELL) **Unit 3, Week 3:** *Weather Patterns* (A, O, B, ELL) **Unit 3, Week 4:** *The Power of a Team* (A, O, B, ELL) **Unit 4, Week 3:** *Jane Addams: A Woman of Action* (A, O, B, ELL) **Unit 4, Week 4:** *The Delta* (A, O, B, ELL) **Unit 5, Week 3:** *Ocean Threats* (A, O, B, ELL) **Unit 5, Week 4:** *Mars* (A, O, B, ELL) **Unit 6, Week 3:** *Cave Creatures* (A, O, B, ELL) **YOUR TURN PRACTICE BOOK:** 26, 36, 76, 125, 136, 176, 226, 276, 286 **READING WORKSTATION ACTIVITY CARDS:** 25, 30 **TEACHER'S EDITION: Unit 1:** T150, T153A–T153V, T214, T217A–T217R, T281E–T281F **Unit 2:** T22, T25A–T25V, T150, T153A–T153N **Unit 3:** T150, T153A–T153T, T278, T281A–T281F **Unit 4:** T150, T153A–T153V, T214, T217A–T217T **Unit 5:** T214, T217A–T217R, T278, T281A–T281F **Unit 6:** T150, T153A–T153R, T214, T217A–T217P

Reading Standards: Foundational Skills

Phonics and Word Recognition		McGraw-Hill Reading Wonders
RF.5.3	Know and apply grade-level phonics and word analysis skills in decoding words.	
RF.5.3a	Use combined knowledge of all letter-sound correspondences, syllabication patterns, and morphology (e.g., roots and affixes) to read accurately unfamiliar multisyllabic words in context and out of context.	**LITERATURE ANTHOLOGY:** Unit 1: 85, 93 Unit 2: 151 Unit 3: 231, 251 Unit 4: 315 Unit 5: 421, 427 **WORD STUDY WORKSTATION ACTIVITY CARDS:** 16–30 **YOUR TURN PRACTICE BOOK:** 8, 18, 28, 38, 48, 58, 68, 78, 88, 98, 108, 118, 128, 138, 148, 158, 168, 178, 188, 198, 208, 218, 228, 238, 248, 258, 268, 278, 288, 298 **TEACHER'S EDITION:** Unit 1: T26–T27, T40–T41, T48–T49, T52–T53, T90–T91, T154–T155, T218–T219, T282–T283 Unit 2: T26–T27, T90–T91, T104–T105, T112–T113, T116–T117, T154–T155, T218–T219, T282–T283 Unit 3: T26–T27, T90–T91, T154–T155, T168–T169, T176–T177, T180–T181, T218–T219, T282–T283 Unit 4: T26–T27, T90–T91, T154–T155, T218–T219, T232–T233, T240–T241, T244–T245, T282–T283 Unit 5: T26–T27, T154–T155, T218–T219, T282–T283, T296–T297, T304–T305, T308–T309 Unit 6: T26–T27, T40–T41, T48–49, T52–T53, T90–T91, T154–T155, T218–T219, T282–T283

Fluency		McGraw-Hill Reading Wonders
RF.5.4	Read with sufficient accuracy and fluency to support comprehension.	
RF.5.4a	Read on-level text with purpose and understanding.	**LEVELED READERS:** Unit 1, Week 2: *Dog Gone* (A), *Shhh! It's a Surprise!* (O, ELL), *Lost and Found* (B); **Unit 2, Week 3:** *Norman Borlaug and the Green Revolution* (A, O, B, ELL); **Unit 3, Week 1:** *All the Way from Europe* (A), *Dancing the Flamenco* (O, ELL), *A Vacation in Minnesota* (B); **Unit 4, Week 5:** *Tell Me the Old, Old Stories* (A), *From Me to You* (O, ELL), *Every Picture Tells a Story* (B); **Unit 5, Week 3:** *Ocean Threats* (A, O, B, ELL); **Unit 6, Week 2:** *Winning Friends* (A), *Enemy or Ally?* (O, ELL), *Jamayla to the Rescue* (B) **READING WORKSTATION ACTIVITY CARDS:** 29 **WORD STUDY WORKSTATION ACTIVITY CARDS:** 25, 26 **TEACHER'S EDITION:** Unit 1: T27, T91, T155, T219, T283 Unit 2: T27, T91, T155, T219, T283 Unit 3: T27, T91, T155, T219, T283 Unit 4: T27, T91, T155, T219, T283 Unit 5: T27, T91, T155, T219, T283 Unit 6: T27, T91, T155, T219, T283
RF.5.4b	Read on-level prose and poetry orally with accuracy, appropriate rate, and expression on successive readings.	**LEVELED READERS:** Unit 1, Week 2: *Dog Gone* (A), *Shhh! It's a Surprise!* (O, ELL), *Lost and Found* (B); **Unit 2, Week 3:** *Norman Borlaug and the Green Revolution* (A, O, B, ELL); **Unit 3, Week 1:** *All the Way from Europe* (A), *Dancing the Flamenco* (O, ELL), *A Vacation in Minnesota* (B); **Unit 4, Week 5:** *Tell Me the Old, Old Stories* (A), *From Me to You* (O, ELL), *Every Picture Tells a Story* (B); **Unit 5, Week 3:** *Ocean Threats* (A, O, B, ELL); **Unit 6, Week 2:** *Winning Friends* (A), *Enemy or Ally?* (O, ELL), *Jamayla to the Rescue* (B) **READING WORKSTATION ACTIVITY CARDS:** 28 **YOUR TURN PRACTICE BOOK:** 5, 15, 25, 35, 45, 55, 65, 75, 85, 95, 105, 115, 125, 135, 145, 155, 165, 175, 185, 195, 205, 215, 225, 235, 245, 255, 265, 275, 285, 294 **TEACHER'S EDITION:** Unit 1: T27, T155, T219 Unit 2: T27, T91, T155, T169, T177, T181, T219, T283 Unit 3: T91, T155, T219, T233, T241, T245, T283 Unit 4: T27, T91, T219, T283, T297, T305, T309 Unit 5: T27, T91, T155, T219, T283 Unit 6: T27, T155, T219, T283
RF.5.4c	Use context to confirm or self-correct word recognition and understanding, rereading as necessary.	**LEVELED READERS:** Unit 1, Week 2: *Dog Gone* (A), *Shhh! It's a Surprise!* (O, ELL), *Lost and Found* (B); **Unit 2, Week 3:** *Norman Borlaug and the Green Revolution* (A, O, B, ELL); **Unit 3, Week 1:** *All the Way from Europe* (A), *Dancing the Flamenco* (O, ELL), *A Vacation in Minnesota* (B); **Unit 4, Week 5:** *Tell Me the Old, Old Stories* (A), *From Me to You* (O, ELL), *Every Picture Tells a Story* (B); **Unit 5, Week 3:** *Ocean Threats* (A, O, B, ELL); **Unit 6, Week 2:** *Winning Friends* (A), *Enemy or Ally?* (O, ELL), *Jamayla to the Rescue* (B) **TEACHER'S EDITION:** Unit 1: T27, T41, T49, T53, T59 Unit 2: T27, T41, T49, T53, T91 Unit 3: T155, T169, T177, T181, T187 Unit 4: T91, T105, T219, T241, T245 Unit 5: T219, T233, T241, T245, T251 Unit 6: T155, T169, T177, T181, T187

College and Career Readiness Anchor Standards for WRITING

The K-5 standards on the following pages define what students should understand and be able to do by the end of each grade. They correspond to the College and Career Readiness (CCR) anchor standards below by number. The CCR and grade-specific standards are necessary complements—the former providing broad standards, the latter providing additional specificity—that together define the skills and understandings that all students must demonstrate.

Text Types and Purposes

1. Write arguments to support claims in an analysis of substantive topics or texts, using valid reasoning and relevant and sufficient evidence.

2. Write informative/explanatory texts to examine and convey complex ideas and information clearly and accurately through the effective selection, organization, and analysis of content.

3. Write narratives to develop real or imagined experiences or events using effective technique, well-chosen details, and well-structured event sequences.

Production and Distribution of Writing

4. Produce clear and coherent writing in which the development, organization, and style are appropriate to task, purpose, and audience.

5. Develop and strengthen writing as needed by planning, revising, editing, rewriting, or trying a new approach.

6. Use technology, including the Internet, to produce and publish writing and to interact and collaborate with others.

Research to Build and Present Knowledge

7. Conduct short as well as more sustained research projects based on focused questions, demonstrating understanding of the subject under investigation.

8. Gather relevant information from multiple print and digital sources, assess the credibility and accuracy of each source, and integrate the information while avoiding plagiarism.

9. Draw evidence from literary or informational texts to support analysis, reflection, and research.

Range of Writing

10. Write routinely over extended time frames (time for research, reflection, and revision) and shorter time frames (a single sitting or a day or two) for a range of tasks, purposes, and audiences.

CCSS Common Core State Standards
English Language Arts

Grade 5

Each standard is coded in the following manner:

Strand	Grade Level	Standard
W	5	1

Writing Standards

Text Types and Purposes	*McGraw-Hill Reading Wonders*
W.5.1	Write opinion pieces on topics or texts, supporting a point of view with reasons and information.
W.5.1a	Introduce a topic or text clearly, state an opinion, and create an organizational structure in which ideas are logically grouped to support the writer's purpose.	**WRITING WORKSTATION ACTIVITY CARDS:** 26, 27 **TEACHER'S EDITION:** Unit 1: T93 Unit 3: T345, T347, T351 Unit 4: T160, T161 Unit 5: T224, T225 Unit 6: T224, T225, T329, T345, T346, T347, T351
W.5.1b	Provide logically ordered reasons that are supported by facts and details.	**TEACHER'S EDITION:** Unit 3: T288, T289, T345, T346, T351, T353 Unit 4: T160, T161 Unit 5: T224, T225 Unit 6: T329, T345, T351
W.5.1c	Link opinion and reasons using words, phrases, and clauses (e.g., *consequently*, *specifically*).	**YOUR TURN PRACTICE BOOK:** 150 **TEACHER'S EDITION:** Unit 3: T29, T288, T289, T349, T352 Unit 4: T224, T225 Unit 5: T221 Unit 6: T352, T353, T355
W.5.1d	Provide a concluding statement or section related to the opinion presented.	**YOUR TURN PRACTICE BOOK:** 250 **WRITING WORKSTATION ACTIVITY CARDS:** 9 **TEACHER'S EDITION:** Unit 3: T347, T353 Unit 5: T288, T289, T318 Unit 6: T285, T329, T346, T347, T353
W.5.2	Write informative/explanatory texts to examine a topic and convey ideas and information clearly.
W.5.2a	Introduce a topic clearly, provide a general observation and focus, and group related information logically; include formatting (e.g., headings), illustrations, and multimedia when useful to aiding comprehension.	**WRITING WORKSTATION ACTIVITY CARDS:** 2, 8, 10, 11 **TEACHER'S EDITION:** Unit 2: T224, T225, T345, T346, T348, T351, T352, T354 Unit 3: T92, T329 Unit 4: T285 Unit 5: T32, T33, T254, T345, T346, T348, T351, T352, T354, T355 Unit 6: T28, T32, T33 www.connected.mcgraw-hill.com: **RESOURCES:** RESEARCH & INQUIRY: Research Roadmaps: Units 1–6 Note-taking Tools: Units 1–6 WRITER'S WORKSPACE: Unit 2, Unit 5 CARDS: Writing Workstation Activity Cards: 2, 8, 10, 11
W.5.2b	Develop the topic with facts, definitions, concrete details, quotations, or other information and examples related to the topic.	**LITERATURE ANTHOLOGY:** Unit 4: 337 **YOUR TURN PRACTICE BOOK:** 60, 80, 130 **WRITING WORKSTATION ACTIVITY CARDS:** 3, 6, 30 **TEACHER'S EDITION:** Unit 2: T32, T33, T62, T160, T161, T190, T329, T346, T351–T353, T355 Unit 3: T92, T160, T161, T329 Unit 4: T220 Unit 5: T190, T254, T285, T346, T349, T351, T353

Writing Standards

Text Types and Purposes | McGraw-Hill Reading Wonders

	Text Types and Purposes	McGraw-Hill Reading Wonders
W.5.2c	Link ideas within and across categories of information using words, phrases, and clauses (e.g., *in contrast*, *especially*).	**YOUR TURN PRACTICE BOOK:** 220 **WRITING WORKSTATION ACTIVITY CARDS:** 13, 17, 19 **TEACHER'S EDITION:** Unit 4: T157 Unit 5: T96, T97, T347 Unit 6: T29
W.5.2d	Use precise language and domain-specific vocabulary to inform about or explain the topic.	**WRITING WORKSTATION ACTIVITY CARDS:** 15 **TEACHER'S EDITION:** Unit 1: T190 Unit 2: T347, T355 Unit 5: T346, T349
W.5.2e	Provide a concluding statement or section related to the information or explanation presented.	**YOUR TURN PRACTICE BOOK:** 140 **TEACHER'S EDITION:** Unit 2: T346, T353 Unit 3: T92, T224, T225, T254, T329 Unit 5: T347, T352 Unit 6: T29, T221
W.5.3	Write narratives to develop real or imagined experiences or events using effective technique, descriptive details, and clear event sequences.	
W.5.3a	Orient the reader by establishing a situation and introducing a narrator and/or characters; organize an event sequence that unfolds naturally.	**YOUR TURN PRACTICE BOOK:** 70 **WRITING WORKSTATION ACTIVITY CARDS:** 5, 7, 22 **TEACHER'S EDITION:** Unit 1: T224, T225, T254, T345, T351 Unit 2: T96, T97, T126, T254 Unit 4: T96, T97, T345, T347 Unit 6: T96, T97
W.5.3b	Use narrative techniques, such as dialogue, description, and pacing, to develop experiences and events or show the responses of characters to situations.	**YOUR TURN PRACTICE BOOK:** 20, 109, 170 **WRITING WORKSTATION ACTIVITY CARDS:** 1, 5, 22, 28 **TEACHER'S EDITION:** Unit 1: T32, T33, T96, T97, T345, T347, T351 Unit 4: T96, T97, T126, T346
W.5.3c	Use a variety of transitional words, phrases, and clauses to manage the sequence of events.	**YOUR TURN PRACTICE BOOK:** 40, 270 **WRITING WORKSTATION ACTIVITY CARDS:** 7, 17, 19 **TEACHER'S EDITION:** Unit 1: T224, T225, T347, T351 Unit 4: T345 Unit 5: T126 Unit 6: T96, T97, T126
W.5.3d	Use concrete words and phrases and sensory details to convey experiences and events precisely.	**YOUR TURN PRACTICE BOOK:** 10, 30 **WRITING WORKSTATION ACTIVITY CARDS:** 1, 14, 18 **TEACHER'S EDITION:** Unit 1: T32, T33, T62, T160, T161, T346, T352 Unit 2: T288, T289, T318 Unit 4: T288, T289, T318, T351, T353 Unit 6: T288, T289, T318
W.5.3e	Provide a conclusion that follows from the narrated experiences or events.	**WRITING WORKSTATION ACTIVITY CARDS:** 23 **TEACHER'S EDITION:** Unit 1: T225, T351, T353 Unit 4: T345, T347

Production and Distribution of Writing | McGraw-Hill Reading Wonders

	Production and Distribution of Writing	McGraw-Hill Reading Wonders
W.5.4	Produce clear and coherent writing in which the development and organization are appropriate to task, purpose, and audience. (Grade-specific expectations for writing types are defined in standards 1–3 above.)	**WRITING WORKSTATION ACTIVITY CARDS:** 12, 24 **TEACHER'S EDITION:** Unit 1: T33, T97, T161, T225, T345, T347, T348 Unit 2: T32, T126, T160, T225, T348 Unit 3: T33, T97, T161, T225, T345, T347, T348 Unit 4: T33, T97, T161, T225, T345, T347, T348 Unit 5: T33, T97, T161, T225, T345, T347, T348 Unit 6: T33, T97, T161, T225, T345, T347, T348
W.5.5	With guidance and support from peers and adults, develop and strengthen writing as needed by planning, revising, editing, rewriting, or trying a new approach. (Editing for conventions should demonstrate command of Language standards 1–3 up to and including grade 5.)	**TEACHER'S EDITION:** Unit 1: T32, T96, T160, T224, T345, T346, T347, T348 Unit 2: T96, T160, T224, T351, T352, T353, T354 Unit 3: T32, T96, T160, T225, T351, T352, T353, T354 Unit 4: T32, T96, T126, T345, T346, T347, T348 Unit 5: T32, T96, T160, T224, T345, T346, T347, T348 Unit 6: T32, T96, T160, T224, T345, T346, T347, T348

Writing Standards

Production and Distribution of Writing	McGraw-Hill Reading Wonders
W.5.6	With some guidance and support from adults, use technology, including the Internet, to produce and publish writing as well as to interact and collaborate with others; demonstrate sufficient command of keyboarding skills to type a minimum of two pages in a single sitting.	**TEACHER'S EDITION: Unit 1:** T330–T332, T348, T354 **Unit 2:** T156, T330–T332, T348, T354 **Unit 3:** T330–T332, T348, T354 **Unit 4:** T330–T332, T333, T348, T354 **Unit 5:** T156, T330–T332, T348, T354 **Unit 6:** T330–T332, T348, T354 **www.connected.mcgraw-hill.com: RESOURCES:** **RESEARCH & INQUIRY: Weekly Lessons:** Units 1–6 **WRITER'S WORKSPACE:** Units 1–6 **TEACHER RESOURCES:** Writer's Checklists/Proofreading Marks

Research to Build and Present Knowledge	McGraw-Hill Reading Wonders
W.5.7	Conduct short research projects that use several sources to build knowledge through investigation of different aspects of a topic.	**WRITING WORKSTATION ACTIVITY CARDS:** 30 **TEACHER'S EDITION: Unit 1:** T28, T92, T156, T220, T330, T331, T332 **Unit 2:** T28, T92, T156, T330, T331, T332 **Unit 3:** T28, T92, T156, T220, T330, T331, T332 **Unit 4:** T28, T92, T156, T220, T330, T331, T332 **Unit 5:** T92, T156, T220, T284, T351, T352, T353, T354 **Unit 6:** T28, T156, T220, T330, T331, T332
W.5.8	Recall relevant information from experiences or gather relevant information from print and digital sources; summarize or paraphrase information in notes and finished work, and provide a list of sources.	**WRITING WORKSTATION ACTIVITY CARDS:** 30 **TEACHER'S EDITION: Unit 1:** S35, S36, T220, T329, T330, T331, T332 **Unit 2:** T92, T156, T284 **Unit 3:** T28, T92, T156, T220, T284 **Unit 4:** T28, T92, T156, T220, T284, T330, T331, T332 **Unit 5:** T28, T92, T156, T220, T351, T354 **Unit 6:** T28, T92, T156, T330, T331, T332 **www.connected.mcgraw-hill.com: RESOURCES:** **RESEARCH & INQUIRY: Note-taking Tools:** Units 1–6 **WRITER'S WORKSPACE:** Units 1–6 **TIME FOR KIDS ONLINE ARTICLES:** Units 1–6 **CARDS:** Writing Workstation Activity Cards: 29, 30
W.5.9	Draw evidence from literary or informational texts to support analysis, reflection, and research.	
W.5.9a	Apply *grade 5 Reading standards* to literature (e.g., "Compare and contrast two or more characters, settings, or events in a story or a drama, drawing on specific details in the text [e.g., how characters interact]").	**LITERATURE ANTHOLOGY: Unit 1:** 25, 41 **Unit 2** 133, 171 **Unit 3:** 213, 277 **Unit 4:** 293 **Unit 5:** 359, 379 **Unit 6:** 445, 463 **YOUR TURN PRACTICE BOOK:** 9, 19, 69, 79, 109, 119, 159, 169, 209, 219, 259, 269 **TEACHER'S EDITION: Unit 1:** T25P, T29, T89L, T93 **Unit 2:** T89P, T93, T217P, T221 **Unit 3:** T25N, T29, T89P, T93 **Unit 4:** T25P, T29, T89L, T93 **Unit 5:** T25N, T29, T89P, T93 **Unit 6:** T25P, T29, T89N, T93
W.5.9b	Apply *grade 5 Reading standards* to informational texts (e.g., "Explain how an author uses reasons and evidence to support particular points in a text, identifying which reasons and evidence support which point[s]").	**LITERATURE ANTHOLOGY: Unit 1:** 63, 85 **Unit 2:** 113, 151 **Unit 3:** 231, 251 **Unit 4:** 315, 337 **Unit 5:** 399, 421 **Unit 6:** 485, 503 **YOUR TURN PRACTICE BOOK:** 29, 39, 59, 89, 129, 139, 149, 279, 289 **TEACHER'S EDITION: Unit 1:** T153R, T157, T217R, T221, T285 **Unit 2:** T25R, T29, T153N, T157 **Unit 3:** T153P, T157, T221, T285 **Unit 4:** T153R, T157, T217R, T221 **Unit 5:** T153P, T157, T217R, T221, T285 **Unit 6:** T153R, T157, T217N, T221

Range of Writing	McGraw-Hill Reading Wonders
W.5.10	Write routinely over extended time frames (time for research, reflection, and revision) and shorter time frames (a single sitting or a day or two) for a range of discipline-specific tasks, purposes, and audiences.	**LITERATURE ANTHOLOGY: Unit 1:** 25, 41, 63, 85 **Unit 2:** 113, 133, 151, 171, 179 **Unit 3:** 195, 213, 231, 251, 277 **Unit 4:** 293, 315, 337, 343 **Unit 5:** 353, 379, 399, 429 **Unit 6:** 445, 463, 485, 503, 509 **YOUR TURN PRACTICE BOOK:** 9, 19, 29, 39, 49, 59, 69, 79, 89, 99, 109, 119, 129, 139, 149, 159, 169, 179, 189, 199, 209, 219, 229, 239, 249, 259, 269, 279, 289, 299 **TEACHER'S EDITION: Unit 1:** T32, T33, T96, T103, T160 **Unit 2:** T29, T32, T33, T96, T97 **Unit 3:** T93, T97, T160, T161, T345, T346, T347, T348 **Unit 4:** T221, T224, T351, T352, T353, T354 **Unit 5:** T285, T288, T289, T344, T347, T349 **Unit 6:** T345, T346, T347, T351, T352

College and Career Readiness Anchor Standards for
SPEAKING AND LISTENING

The K-5 standards on the following pages define what students should understand and be able to do by the end of each grade. They correspond to the College and Career Readiness (CCR) anchor standards below by number. The CCR and grade-specific standards are necessary complements—the former providing broad standards, the latter providing additional specificity—that together define the skills and understandings that all students must demonstrate.

Comprehension and Collaboration

1. Prepare for and participate effectively in a range of conversations and collaborations with diverse partners, building on others' ideas and expressing their own clearly and persuasively.

2. Integrate and evaluate information presented in diverse media and formats, including visually, quantitatively, and orally.

3. Evaluate a speaker's point of view, reasoning, and use of evidence and rhetoric.

Presentation of Knowledge and Ideas

4. Present information, findings, and supporting evidence such that listeners can follow the line of reasoning and the organization, development, and style are appropriate to task, purpose, and audience.

5. Make strategic use of digital media and visual displays of data to express information and enhance understanding of presentations.

6. Adapt speech to a variety of contexts and communicative tasks, demonstrating command of formal English when indicated or appropriate.

CCSS Common Core State Standards
English Language Arts

Grade 5

Each standard is coded in the following manner:

Strand	Grade Level	Standard
SL	5	1

Speaking and Listening Standards

Comprehension and Collaboration	McGraw-Hill Reading Wonders
SL.5.1	Engage effectively in a range of collaborative discussions (one-on-one, in groups, and teacher-led) with diverse partners on *grade 5 topics and texts*, building on others' ideas and expressing their own clearly.	
SL.5.1a	Come to discussions prepared, having read or studied required material; explicitly draw on that preparation and other information known about the topic to explore ideas under discussion.	**LITERATURE ANTHOLOGY: Unit 1:** 25, 29, 41, 63, 67, 85, 89 **Unit 2:** 113, 117, 133, 137, 151, 171 **Unit 3:** 195, 213, 231, 251 **Unit 4:** 277, 293, 315, 337 **Unit 5:** 359, 379, 403 **Unit 6:** 445, 463, 485, 503 **TEACHER'S EDITION: Unit 1:** S5, S19, T25P, T25T, T89L **Unit 2:** T29, T93, T157, T221, T285 **Unit 3:** T25N, T29, T89P, T93, T153P **Unit 4:** T25P, T29, T89L, T93, T157 **Unit 5:** T89P, T89T, T93, T157, T221 **Unit 6:** T25P, T89N, T93, T157, T221
SL.5.1b	Follow agreed-upon rules for discussions and carry out assigned roles.	**TEACHER'S EDITION: Unit 1:** S6, T10, T92, T138, T202, T266 **Unit 2:** T10, T138, T202, T266 **Unit 3:** T74, T138, T220, T266 **Unit 4:** T74, T138, T266 **Unit 5:** T74, T138, T266 **Unit 6:** T156, T266
SL.5.1c	Pose and respond to specific questions by making comments that contribute to the discussion and elaborate on the remarks of others.	**READING/WRITING WORKSHOP: Unit 1:** 19, 33, 47, 61, 75 **Unit 2:** 91, 105, 119, 133, 147 **Unit 3:** 163, 177, 191, 205, 219 **Unit 4:** 235, 249, 263, 277, 291 **Unit 5:** 307, 321, 335, 349, 363 **Unit 6:** 379, 393, 407, 421, 435 **LITERATURE ANTHOLOGY: Unit 1:** 25, 29, 41, 63, 67, 85, 89 **Unit 2:** 113, 117, 133, 137, 151, 171 **Unit 3:** 195, 213, 231, 251 **Unit 4:** 277, 293, 315, 337 **Unit 5:** 359, 379, 403 **Unit 6:** 445, 463, 485, 503 **TEACHER'S EDITION: Unit 1:** S5, T10, T25R, T74, T266 **Unit 2:** T10, T74, T138, T153P **Unit 3:** T10, T146, T202, T266 **Unit 4:** T10, T89G, T890, T153T, T202 **Unit 5:** T10, T74, T138, T202, T210 **Unit 6:** T10, T138, T146, T210, T266
SL.5.1d	Review the key ideas expressed and draw conclusions in light of information and knowledge gained from the discussions.	**TEACHER'S EDITION: Unit 1:** S6, S19, S35, T138, T285 **Unit 2:** T29, T93, T157, T221, T285 **Unit 3:** T29, T93, T157, T221, T285 **Unit 4:** T29, T93, T157, T221, T285 **Unit 5:** T29, T93, T157, T221, T266, T285 **Unit 6:** T29, T93, T157, T221, T285
SL.5.2	Summarize a written text read aloud or information presented in diverse media and formats, including visually, quantitatively, and orally.	**TEACHER'S EDITION: Unit 1:** T12, T76, T140, T204, T268, T281E, T296–T297, T304–T305, T308–T309, T326 **Unit 2:** T12, T17, T76, T89E, T140, T153D, T204, T268, T326 **Unit 3:** T12, T76, T140, T153C, T153I, T204, T217D, T268, T326 **Unit 4:** T12, T76, T140, T204, T268, T326 **Unit 5:** T12, T76, T140, T204, T268, T326 **Unit 6:** T12, T76, T140, T204, T268, T326
SL.5.3	Summarize the points a speaker makes and explain how each claim is supported by reasons and evidence.	**TEACHER'S EDITION: Unit 1:** T268, T335 **Unit 2:** T335 **Unit 3:** T268, T335 **Unit 4:** T335 **Unit 5:** T268, T335 **Unit 6:** T335

Speaking and Listening Standards

	Presentation of Knowledge and Ideas	McGraw-Hill Reading Wonders
SL.5.4	Report on a topic or text or present an opinion, sequencing ideas logically and using appropriate facts and relevant, descriptive details to support main ideas or themes; speak clearly at an understandable pace.	**TEACHER'S EDITION:** Unit 1: T92, T156, T284, T333, T334 Unit 2: T220, T333, T334 Unit 3: T284, T333, T334 Unit 4: T220, T333, T334 Unit 5: T285, T333, T334 Unit 6: T92, T156, T333, T334
SL.5.5	Include multimedia components (e.g., graphics, sound) and visual displays in presentations when appropriate to enhance the development of main ideas or themes.	**TEACHER'S EDITION:** Unit 1: T92, T156, T220, T354 Unit 2: T354 Unit 3: T220, T348, T354 Unit 4: T329, T348, T354 Unit 5: T92, T156 Unit 6: T28, T156, T220, T284, T348
SL.5.6	Adapt speech to a variety of contexts and tasks, using formal English when appropriate to task and situation. (See grade 5 Language standards 1 and 3 for specific expectations.)	**TEACHER'S EDITION:** Unit 1: S35, T333, T334 Unit 2: T333, T334 Unit 3: T220, T333, T334 Unit 4: T333, T334 Unit 5: T333, T334 Unit 6: T333, T334

College and Career Readiness Anchor Standards for LANGUAGE

The K-5 standards on the following pages define what students should understand and be able to do by the end of each grade. They correspond to the College and Career Readiness (CCR) anchor standards below by number. The CCR and grade-specific standards are necessary complements—the former providing broad standards, the latter providing additional specificity—that together define the skills and understandings that all students must demonstrate.

Conventions of Standard English

1. Demonstrate command of the conventions of standard English grammar and usage when writing or speaking.

2. Demonstrate command of the conventions of standard English capitalization, punctuation, and spelling when writing.

Knowledge of Language

3. Apply knowledge of language to understand how language functions in different contexts, to make effective choices for meaning or style, and to comprehend more fully when reading or listening.

Vocabulary Acquisition and Use

4. Determine or clarify the meaning of unknown and multiple-meaning words and phrases by using context clues, analyzing meaningful word parts, and consulting general and specialized reference materials, as appropriate.

5. Demonstrate understanding of figurative language, word relationships, and nuances in word meanings.

6. Acquire and use accurately a range of general academic and domain-specific words and phrases sufficient for reading, writing, speaking, and listening at the college and career readiness level; demonstrate independence in gathering vocabulary knowledge when encountering an unknown term important to comprehension or expression.

(CCSS) Common Core State Standards
English Language Arts

Grade 5

Each standard is coded in the following manner:

Strand	Grade Level	Standard
L	5	1

Language Standards

Conventions of Standard English		*McGraw-Hill Reading Wonders*
L.5.1	Demonstrate command of the conventions of standard English grammar and usage when writing or speaking.	
L.5.1a	Explain the function of conjunctions, prepositions, and interjections in general and their function in particular sentences.	**READING/WRITING WORKSHOP:** Unit 6: 433, 446, 447 **Grammar Handbook:** 452, 453, 457, 471, 472 **TEACHER'S EDITION: Unit 1:** T35, T98, T99, T162, T163, T191, T221, T226, T227, T255, T286, T319 **Unit 2:** T290, T291, T319 **Unit 3:** T286 **Unit 4:** T336 **Unit 5:** T34, T35, T98, T127 **Unit 6:** T224–T226, T255, T285, T286, T288–T291, T318, T319
L.5.1b	Form and use the perfect (e.g., *I had walked*; *I have walked*; *I will have walked*) verb tenses.	**READING/WRITING WORKSHOP: Grammar Handbook:** 461 **TEACHER'S EDITION: Unit 3:** T162, T290, T291
L.5.1c	Use verb tense to convey various times, sequences, states, and conditions.	**READING/WRITING WORKSHOP: Grammar Handbook:** 458, 461 **TEACHER'S EDITION: Unit 1:** T348, T354 **Unit 2:** T153J, T154, T155, T170, T171, T348, T354 **Unit 3:** T34, T35, T63, T93, T98, T99, T127, T157, T162, T163, T191, T290, T291, T319, T348, T354 **Unit 4:** T348 **Unit 5:** T354 **Unit 6:** 354
L.5.1d	Recognize and correct inappropriate shifts in verb tense.	**READING/WRITING WORKSHOP: Unit 3:** 189 **Grammar Handbook:** 459 **TEACHER'S EDITION: Unit 1:** T348, T354 **Unit 2:** T348, T354 **Unit 3:** T93, T96–T99, T127, T290, T291, T319, T348, T354 **Unit 4:** T348 **Unit 5:** T354 **Unit 6:** 354
L.5.1e	Use correlative conjunctions (e.g., *either/or, neither/nor*).	**TEACHER'S EDITION: Unit 1:** T98 **Unit 3:** T286 **Unit 6:** T226
L.5.2	Demonstrate command of the conventions of standard English capitalization, punctuation, and spelling when writing.	
L.5.2a	Use punctuation to separate items in a series.	**TEACHER'S EDITION: Unit 1:** T99 **Unit 4:** T291 **Unit 6:** T227
L.5.2b	Use a comma to separate an introductory element from the rest of the sentence.	**TEACHER'S EDITION: Unit 1:** T99, T226, T227, T286 **Unit 5:** T34, T98, T99, T127
L.5.2c	Use a comma to set off the words *yes* and *no* (e.g., *Yes, thank you*), to set off a tag question from the rest of the sentence (e.g., *It's true, isn't it?*), and to indicate direct address (e.g., *Is that you, Steve?*).	**READING/WRITING WORKSHOP: Grammar Handbook:** 479 **TEACHER'S EDITION: Unit 1:** T35, T99, T286

Language Standards

Conventions of Standard English		McGraw-Hill Reading Wonders
L.5.2d	Use underlining, quotation marks, or italics to indicate titles of works.	**READING/WRITING WORKSHOP:** Grammar Handbook: 480 **TEACHER'S EDITION:** Unit 2: T291 Unit 3: T227 Unit 5: T163
L.5.2e	Spell grade-appropriate words correctly, consulting references as needed.	**TEACHER'S EDITION:** Unit 1: T36–37, T100–101, T164–T165, T228–229, T292–293 **Unit 2:** T36–T37, T100–101, T164–165, T228–229, T292–T293 **Unit 3:** T36–37, T100–101, T164–165, T228–229, T292–T293 **Unit 4:** T36–37, T100–101, T164–T165, T228–229, T292–T293 **Unit 5:** T36–37, T100–101, T164–T165, T228–229, T292–T293 **Unit 6:** T36–37, T100–T101, T164–T165, T228–229, T292–T293

Knowledge of Language		McGraw-Hill Reading Wonders
L.5.3	Use knowledge of language and its conventions when writing, speaking, reading, or listening.	
L.5.3a	Expand, combine, and reduce sentences for meaning, reading/listener interest, and style.	**READING/WRITING WORKSHOP:** Unit 6: 418 Grammar Handbook: 452, 453, 468 **TEACHER'S EDITION:** Unit 1: T33, T290, T291, T319, T347, T353 Unit 2: T347, T353 Unit 3: T347, T353 Unit 4: T347, T353 Unit 5: T35, T99, T347, T353 Unit 6: T158, T160, T161, T226, T227, T347, T353
L.5.3b	Compare and contrast the varieties of English (e.g., dialects, registers) used in stories, dramas, or poems.	**READING/WRITING WORKSHOP:** Unit 5: 330 **TEACHER'S EDITION:** Unit 5: T86, T89C, T89I, T89M

Vocabulary Acquisition and Use		McGraw-Hill Reading Wonders
L.5.4	Determine or clarify the meaning of unknown and multiple-meaning words and phrases based on *grade 5 reading and content,* choosing flexibly from a range of strategies.	
L.5.4a	Use context (e.g., cause/effect relationships and comparisons in text) as a clue to the meaning of a word or phrase.	**READING/WRITING WORKSHOP:** Unit 1: 29 Unit 2: 101 Unit 3: 173, 187, 229 Unit 4: 287 Unit 5: 317, 345 Unit 6: 389, 417 **LITERATURE ANTHOLOGY:** Unit 1: 25, 63 Unit 2: 113, 179 Unit 3: 195, 213, 259 Unit 5: 359, 399 Unit 6: 445, 485 **YOUR TURN PRACTICE BOOK:** 7, 57, 107, 147, 187, 207, 227, 277 **WORD STUDY WORKSTATION ACTIVITY CARDS:** 1–3 **TEACHER'S EDITION:** Unit 1: T25C, T25D, T25H, T25L, T25P, T153C, T153J, T153K, T153R, T217E, T217H, T217K, T217R Unit 2: T24, T25E, T25G, T25I, T39, T153E, T166 Unit 3: T24, T25K, T25N, T39, T88, T89D, T89E, T89H, T89I, T89P, T153B, T153I, T166, T217I, T230, T280, Unit 4: T25, T88, T152, T153A, T153I, T153O, T166, T216, T217C, T217E, T217M, T217R, T231 Unit 5: T24, T25D, T25N, T39, T152, T153B, T167, T217E, T217K Unit 6: T24, T25H, T89A, T89C, T89K, T152, T153C, T153D, T153G, T153K, T153R
L.5.4b	Use common, grade-appropriate Greek and Latin affixes and roots as clues to the meaning of a word (e.g., *photograph, photosynthesis*).	**READING/WRITING WORKSHOP:** Unit 1: 71, 85 Unit 2: 129 Unit 3: 201, 215 Unit 5: 359, 373 **LITERATURE ANTHOLOGY:** Unit 1: 85, 93 Unit 2: 151 Unit 3: 231, 251 Unit 5: 421 **YOUR TURN PRACTICE BOOK:** 37, 47, 77, 127, 137, 237, 247 **WORD STUDY WORKSTATION ACTIVITY CARDS:** 7–11 **TEACHER'S EDITION:** Unit 1: T216, T217C, T217R, T231, T280, T281B, T295 Unit 2: T38, T152, T153F, T153G, T153N, T167 Unit 3: T152, T153D, T153P, T167, T216, T217J, T217P, T231 Unit 4: T38, T230 Unit 5: T216, T217B, T217H, T217R, T231, T280, T281C, T295 Unit 6: T25I, T38, T89K
L.5.4c	Consult reference materials (e.g., dictionaries, glossaries, thesauruses), both print and digital, to find the pronunciation and determine or clarify the precise meaning of key words and phrases.	**WORK STUDY WORKSTATION ACTIVITY CARDS:** 5 **TEACHER'S EDITION:** Unit 1: T24, T39, 133 (Reading Workstation Activity Cards), T167, T216, T217E, T217K, T231, T280, T284, T295; Unit 2: T24, T39, T25E, T152, T167, T261 (Reading Workstation Activity Cards), T295; Unit 3: T25C, T89E, T152; Unit 4: T24, T170, T171; Unit 5: T152, T153I; Unit 6: T88, T89Q, T153C

Language Standards

Vocabulary Acquisition and Use	McGraw-Hill Reading Wonders
L.5.5 Demonstrate understanding of figurative language, word relationships, and nuances in word meanings.	
L.5.5a Interpret figurative language, including similes and metaphors, in context.	**READING/WRITING WORKSHOP:** Unit 2: 115, 143 Unit 4: 301, 303 Unit 5: 316 Unit 6: 445 **LITERATURE ANTHOLOGY:** Unit 2: 133, 171 Unit 4: 343, 345 Unit 6: 509 **YOUR TURN PRACTICE BOOK:** 67, 87, 197, 297 **WORD STUDY WORKSTATION ACTIVITY CARDS:** 13, 14 **TEACHER'S EDITION:** Unit 1: T89A, T89B, T89L, 153K, T217F, T217M Unit 2: T88, T89H, T89K, T89P, T103, T216, T217B, T217P, T230, T231, T294 Unit 4: T280, T281C, T281D, T281F, T352 Unit 5: T102 Unit 6: T280, T281D, T295
L.5.5b Recognize and explain the meaning of common idioms, adages, and proverbs.	**READING/WRITING WORKSHOP:** Unit 1: 43 Unit 4: 259 Unit 5: 331 **LITERATURE ANTHOLOGY:** Unit 1: 41 Unit 4: 293 Unit 5: 379 **YOUR TURN PRACTICE BOOK:** 17, 167, 217 **WORD STUDY WORKSTATION ACTIVITY CARDS:** 12 **TEACHER'S EDITION:** Unit 1: T89A, T89B, T89L, T230 Unit 3: T38 Unit 4: T88, T89D, T89L, T103 Unit 5: T88, T89C, T89E, T89G, T89P, T103 Unit 6: T102
L.5.5c Use the relationship between particular words (e.g., synonyms, antonyms, homographs) to better understand each of the words.	**READING/WRITING WORKSHOP:** Unit 1: 57 Unit 2: 157 Unit 4: 245 Unit 6: 389, 431 **LITERATURE ANTHOLOGY:** Unit 1: 63 Unit 2: 179 Unit 4: 277 Unit 6: 503 **YOUR TURN PRACTICE BOOK:** 27, 97, 157, 287 **WORD STUDY WORKSTATION ACTIVITY CARDS:** 4–6 **TEACHER'S EDITION:** Unit 1: T153J, T153R, T294, T295 Unit 2: T103, T195, T231, T280, T281C, T281D, T295 Unit 4: T24, T25L, T25P, T39, T102, T167, T295 Unit 5: T38, T167, T231 Unit 6: T216, T217G, T217I, T217N
L.5.6 Acquire and use accurately grade-appropriate general academic and domain-specific words and phrases, including those that signal contrast, addition, and other logical relationships (e.g., *however, although, nevertheless, similarly, moreover, in addition*).	**READING/WRITING WORKSHOP:** Unit 1: 55, 69, 72 Unit 2: 99 Unit 3: 230, 231 Unit 4: 288, 289 **YOUR TURN PRACTICE BOOK:** 1, 11, 21, 31, 41, 51, 81, 91, 101, 111, 121, 131, 141, 171, 191, 241, 251, 261, 271, 281, 291 **TEACHER'S EDITION:** Unit 1: T14, T38, T78, T102, T142, T148, T153L, T166, T206, T212, T222–T225, T230, T270, T273, T294, T344, T346–T348, T350–T352, T354 Unit 2: T14, T20, T38, T78, T102, T142, T166, T206, T230, T270, T294, T344, T346, T348, T350, T352, T354 Unit 3: T14, T38, T78, T89J, T102, T142, T153J, T166, T206, T230, T270, T286–T289, T294, T344, T346, T348, T350, T352, T354 Unit 4: T14, T38, T78, T102, T142, T166, T206, T222–T225, T230, T270, T294, T344, T346, T348, T350, T352, T354 Unit 5: T14, T38, T78, T94–97, T102, T142, T166, T206, T230, T270, T294, T332, T344, T346–T348, T350, T352, T354 Unit 6: T14, T34, T38, T78, T94, T102, T142, T166, T206, T230, T270, T294, T344, T346, T348, T350, T352, T354

CCSS Language Progressive Skills

Below are the grades 3 and 4 Language standards indicated by CCSS to be particularly likely to require continued attention in grade 5 as they are applied to increasingly sophisticated writing and speaking.

Language Standards

Standard		McGraw-Hill Reading Wonders
L.3.1f	Ensure subject-verb and pronoun-antecedent agreement.	**TEACHER'S EDITION:** Unit 1: T348 Unit 2: T348 Unit 3: T34, T35, T63, T255, T348 Unit 4: T34, T35, T63, T98, T99, T157, T162, T163, T227, T348 Unit 5: T98, T99, T348 Unit 6: T348
L.3.3a	Choose words and phrases for effect.	**READING/WRITING WORKSHOP:** Unit 1: 44 Unit 2: 143 Unit 3: 174, 188 Unit 4: 302 Unit 5: 403, 445 **YOUR TURN PRACTICE BOOK:** 10, 20, 30, 100, 120, 200 **WRITING WORKSTATION ACTIVITY CARDS:** 14, 16, 18, 21 **TEACHER'S EDITION:** Unit 1: T30, T32, T33, T94, T96, T158, T160, T161, T345, T346, T350, T352 Unit 2: T286, T288, T289 Unit 3: T94, T96, T97, T126 Unit 4: T286, T288, T289, T318, T350, T351, T352 Unit 6: T286, T288, T289, T318, T350, T352
L.4.1f	Produce complete sentences, recognizing and correcting inappropriate fragments and run-ons.	**TEACHER'S EDITION:** Unit 1: T34, T35, T63, T162, T163, T290, T291, T319, T348, T354 Unit 2: T63, T252, T348, T354 Unit 3: T348, T354 Unit 4: T348, T354 Unit 5: T348, T354 Unit 6: T348, T354
L.4.1g	Correctly use frequently confused words (e.g., to, too, two; there, their).	**READING/WRITING WORKSHOP:** Unit 6: 389 **WORD STUDY WORKSTATION ACTIVITY CARDS:** 6 **TEACHER'S EDITION:** Unit 1: T25L Unit 2: T228 Unit 4: T285, T290, T291, T319 Unit 5: T90, T91, T100, T101, T106, T107, T126 Unit 6: T24, T25, T39, T45, T50, T54, T61, T230
L.4.3a	Choose words and phrases to convey ideas precisely.	**READING/WRITING WORKSHOP:** Unit 1: 58 Unit 2: 158 Unit 6: 446 **YOUR TURN PRACTICE BOOK:** 30, 80, 100, 300 **WORKSTATION ACTIVITY CARDS:** 15 **TEACHER'S EDITION:** Unit 1: T158, T160, T161, T190, T349, T353 Unit 2: T97, T157, T158, T160, T161, T286, T288, T289, T318, T344, T347, T350, T352 Unit 3: T285 Unit 4: T286, T353 Unit 5: T158, T161, T285, T346 Unit 6: T318
L.4.3b	Choose punctuation for effect.	**TEACHER'S EDITION:** Unit 1: T25G, T34, T35, T153G, T217G Unit 2: T25G, T89I, T217C Unit 4: T291 Unit 5: T217E Unit 6: T217C, T227